SILVIA GALAVIZ

Who Am I
in the Lives of Children?

Who Am I in the Lives of Children?

An Introduction to Teaching

Young Children

Stephanie Feeney
University of Hawaii at Manoa

Doris Christensen
Honolulu Community College

Eva Moravcik
Honolulu Community College

Merrill,
An Imprint of Prentice Hall
Englewood Cliffs, New Jersey   *Columbus,* Ohio

Library of Congress Cataloging-in-Publication Data
Feeney, Stephanie.
    Who am I in the lives of children? : an
introduction to teaching young children/
Stephanie Feeney, Doris Christensen, Eva
Moravcik : featuring photographs by Hella
Hammid and Jeffrey Reese.—5th ed.
        p.   cm.
    Includes bibliographical references and
    indexes.
    ISBN 0-02-336631-1
    1. Education, Preschool—United States.
2. Preschool teaching—United States. 3. Child
development—United States. 4. Early childhood
education—United States. I. Christensen, Doris.
II. Moravcik, Eva. III. Title
LB1140.23.F44 1995
372.21'0973—dc20   95-19953
                                             CIP

Cover photo: Jeff Reese
Editor: Ann Castel Davis
Developmental Editor: Carol Sykes
Production Editor: Mary Irvin
Design Coordinator: Jill E. Bonar
Text Designer: Rebecca M. Bobb
Cover Designer: Proof Positive/Farrowlyne
Associates
Production Manager: Laura Messerly
Illustrations: Romark Illustrations

This book was set in Garamond by Clarinda
Company and was printed and bound by
Quebecor. The cover was printed by Phoenix Color
Corp.

 © 1996 by Prentice-Hall, Inc.
A Simon & Schuster Company
Englewood Cliffs, New Jersey 07632

Earlier edition © 1991 by Macmillan Publishing
Company. Earlier editions 1987, 1983, 1979 by
Merrill Publishing Company.

Photo credits: Hella Hammid and Jeff Reese

Printed in the United States of America

10 9 8 7 6 5 4

ISBN: 0-02-336631-1

Prentice-Hall International (UK) Limited, *London*
Prentice-Hall of Australia Pty. Limited, *Sydney*
Prentice-Hall of Canada, Inc., *Toronto*
Prentice-Hall Hispanoamericana, S. A., *Mexico*
Prentice-Hall of India Private Limited, *New Delhi*
Prentice-Hall of Japan, Inc., *Tokyo*
Simon & Schuster Asia Pte. Ltd., *Singapore*
Editora Prentice-Hall do Brasil, Ltda., *Rio de Janeiro*

A Letter to Readers

Dear Reader:

Welcome to *Who Am I in the Lives of Children?*, an introduction to the field of early childhood education. Our purpose in writing this book is to support you in becoming a professional who can enhance the development of young children in many different settings.

When we read a book, we like to know about the authors–who they are and why they wrote the book. We want to share that kind of personal information with you. Among us we have been: preschool teacher, social worker, kindergarten teacher, center director, consultant, parent educator, CDA trainer, Head Start regional training officer, and college instructor. We have worked in parent cooperatives, child-care centers, preschools, infant-toddler programs, Head Start programs, public schools, resource and referral agencies, government agencies, and college settings. We have been child advocates and board members of our local

and national early childhood organizations. Today the three of us are all college instructors in early childhood education. Stephanie teaches at the University of Hawaii at Mānoa and Doris and Eva teach at Honolulu Community College. Eva oversees a small child development center as part of her responsibilities.

This book grows out of our experiences as children, as adults, as learners, and as educators. Our early educational experiences included not only child-oriented nursery schools much like those we describe in this book, but also large, dreary, anonymous public schools; a small multinational school; and a one-room country school. Although our childhood experiences were different, our values are very similar, and we have many of the same feelings and ideas about education and a strong commitment to programs for children that are nurturing and humane and support all aspects of their development.

In 1979, the first edition of *Who Am I in the Lives of Children?* was published when Stephanie was a new college instructor and

Doris and Eva were teaching assistants working with her. We began writing because we wanted an introductory text that was consistent with our belief that the personal and professional development of early childhood educators are inextricably linked, and that emphasized the importance of reflection on values and educational choices. Because we wanted to speak to our readers in as direct a way as possible, we wrote in an informal and personal voice. In this edition we continue to use an informal style and continue to focus on your development, values, and choices.

The cornerstone of this book and our work with children is what we refer to as the *developmental* approach to early childhood education. This approach has its roots in a long tradition of humanistic education and the unique history and philosophy of early childhood education. Our ideas have been profoundly shaped by the educators, psychologists, and philosophers whose work has influenced the developmental approach and educational practice: Friedrich Froebel, Maria Montessori, John Dewey, Arnold Gessell, Erik Erikson, Lev Vygotsky, Jean Piaget, Margaret Mahler, Abraham Maslow, Carl Rogers, Sylvia Ashton-Warner, Bruno Bettelheim, George Dennison, John Holt, Herb Kohl, A. S. Neill, Vivian Paley, Alice Miller, Barbara Biber, and Daniel Jordan.

Programs that evolve from the developmental tradition are dedicated to the development of the whole child—physical, social, emotional, and intellectual. They are characterized by a deep respect for the individual and the recognition that individual differences need to be responded to in educational settings. They reflect the understanding that children learn best from direct experience and spontaneous play. Educators in these programs begin with children as they are and try to understand and help them grow in ways that are right for the individual rather than according to a predetermined plan. They look at children in terms of potential to be actual-ized and in the context of their culture and family.

ABOUT THIS REVISION

Since the first edition in 1979 and through three subsequent revisions, we have used *Who Am I in the Lives of Children?* to teach in a variety of programs and places. We have worked with colleagues who have used the book across the United States and in other countries, including Canada, Australia, Japan, and Hong Kong. Each edition has reflected developments in our field, the feedback of our students and other instructors, and our own growth as teachers. This fifth edition, like the previous four, reflects a process of reading, reflection, and integration of new information and experiences.

Each time we rewrite, we revisit our basic values and philosophy. As we have written this revision we have strongly reaffirmed our values and commitment to a respectful and child-centered approach. In this edition we have tried to make the values and guiding principles of early education and care more visible and to make our the reasons for our commitment to these values clearer and stronger.

Revisions are needed to reflect new awareness, emphasis, and developments in the field. The societal changes and the needs of families that make early childhood education and care so important, diverse, and complex are reflected in this new edition. As one of tomorrow's early childhood educators, you need, in addition to a commitment to high quality education, knowledge of broader societal issues and the ability to advocate for the rights and needs of young children.

There are many approaches to helping others learn to work with young children. We have tried to give you guidance to discover who you are and what you value for children rather than teaching you content and skills in isolation.

Like creating a clay figure in which each part is drawn out of a central core, we strive to help your work to be an integral part of who you are. Without this base in values, you may not know how to respond when faced with a group of real children, and like a poorly constructed clay figurine formed by sticking head, arms, and legs onto a ball, you may "fall to pieces" when exposed to the heat of the fire.

It is not our intention for everyone to come to the same conclusions or to work with children in the same way. We feel strongly that you must develop your own style and philosophy and reflect on your values and actions so that you will continue to grow as a person and as a professional. It would be impossible to include everything you might need to know in this book. Rather, we have tried to provide you with a lens through which to view the many choices *you* have to make in designing meaningful and appropriate learning programs for young children.

You will play an important part in the lives of the children and families you will work with. We hope that *Who Am I in the Lives of Children?* will help you to become a competent, nurturing, and reflective early childhood educator.

S.F., D.C, and E.M.
Honolulu, Hawaii

Acknowledgments

We have been involved in writing and revising *Who Am I in the Lives of Children?* since 1977, and during that period of time have been influenced and supported by many colleagues, friends, and students. Our list of individuals to acknowledge continues to grow, as does our gratitude.

We would like to offer our thanks to some of the educators who have contributed to our personal and professional development over the last twenty years: Barbara Bowman, Elizabeth Brady, Richard Cohen, Harriet Cuffaro, Carol Darcy, Richard Feldman, Marjorie Fields, Elizabeth Gilkeson, Randy Hitz, James L. Hymes, Lilian Katz, Elizabeth Jones, Robert Peters, Rebecca Severeide, and Docia Zavitkovsky. Special thanks to Jean Fargo and Anita Trubitt for their continued contributions to our thinking, our lives, and this book.

This edition was enhanced by the work of colleagues who shared their expertise: Linda McCormick of the University of Hawaii, who gave us input on the chapter on special-needs children; Robert Peters of Hanahauoli School, Elizabeth Jones of Pacific Oaks College, and Marjorie Fields of the University of Alaska, who contributed greatly to our thinking about the topic of curriculum; Sherry Nolte and Barbara Essman of Honolulu Community College and Georgia Acevedo of the University of Hawaii at Manoa Children's Center, who sensitized us to the special needs of infants and toddlers and the people who work with them; and Robyn Chun of the University of Hawaii at Manoa Children's Center whose master's thesis on playgrounds for young children proved a valuable resource.

We are grateful to people who have provided consultation and assistance in writing previous editions: Christine Jackson, Linda Buck, Kathleen Reinhardt, Robyn Chun, Diana Ginsburg, Lynda Stone, and Kenneth Kipnis. They have contributed to our growth and understanding of philosophy, of working with children, and of teaching college.

Our students in the Early Childhood/Elementary education program at the University of

Hawaii at Manoa and the Early Childhood Program at Honolulu Community College have given us insight, asked thought-provoking questions, and helped us to create this book. Teaching them continues to be a learning process for us. Without them, our thinking and this text would lose the viewpoint of the future educator.

We would also like to thank the reviewers of this edition for their insights and comments: Kathleen Amershek, University of Maryland; R. Eleanor Duff, University of South Carolina-Columbia; Berta Harris, San Diego City College; Colleen Randel, The University of Texas at Tyler; Wayne Reinhardt, Edmonds Community College; and M. Francine Stuckey, Eastern New Mexico University.

Like you, we have learned by doing. Our attitudes, values, knowledge, and skills have been developed as we have worked with the children, families, and staff at the University of Hawai'i at Manoa Children's Center, The Early School in Honolulu, the Children's Centers of Honolulu Community College, St. Timothy's Children's Center in Aiea, and the Parent and Child Center of Hawaii.

The photographs that bring this book to life are the work of two talented photographers. We were deeply saddened by the passing of Hella Hammid, whose sensitive photographs we featured in the last three editions of this book. We continue to use many of her pictures. We are pleased to add new photographs taken for this edition by Jeffrey Reese, another talented photographer of young children. Photos for this and previous editions were taken at Pacific Oaks Children's School, the Harold E. Jones Child Study Center, Maggie Haves School, John Adams Child Development Center, Beverly Hills Montessori School, the Clay Street Center, St. Thomas Parish Preschool, and Hill 'n Dale Family Learning Center in California, St. Timothy's Children's Center, the Early School, the University of Hawaii at Mānoa Children's Center, Hanahauoli School, Pearl Harbor Sub Base Child Development Center, Promise Children's Center, and Castle Medical Center Child Development Center in Hawaii. We appreciate cooperation from the children, staff, and parents of these schools.

No book is written without affecting the lives of the friends and families of the authors. We thank and appreciate those closest to us who have supported our efforts with patience and good humor, especially Don Mickey, Diana Buckley, Gregory Field, and Jeffrey Reese.

Using this Book

Who Am I in the Lives of Children? is organized into five parts so that each lays the foundation for those that follow. The first four parts provide the basic information and skills needed for working effectively with groups of young children. The final part deals with additional skills needed by early childhood educators for working with children with special needs and with families.

Part I: Foundations of Early Childhood Education and Care introduces some of the distinctive traditions and features of the field of early childhood education. Chapter One, Becoming an Early Childhood Educator, explores the nature of the educator of young children as a person and a professional. Chapter Two, The Historical Roots of Current Practice, describes the origins of early childhood education, and Chapter Three, The Field of Early Childhood Education and Care, presents an overview of the programs and practices that you may encounter as you begin your career. Together

they provide the context for working with young children in group settings.

Part II: Understanding Children includes chapters designed to help you understand children's development and the significance of their play. Because understanding children is of central importance in early childhood education, these chapters form an essential foundation of practice. Chapter Four, Child Development: Theory into Practice, provides a basis for understanding young children. Chapter Five, Play, introduces a critical medium for children's development and discusses how you can support productive play. Chapter Six, Assessing Children, acquaints you with basic skills that you will use to appraise individuals and groups of children and to assess how to support their growth and development.

Part III: Living and Learning with Children focuses on the knowledge and expertise that you must have to create a nurturing and stimulating daily program for young children. These chapters address essential aspects of the program for children. They are based on the foundation laid down in the previous chapters and are necessary preconditions for curriculum as it is described in the chapters that follow. Chapter Seven, A Good Place for Children, explores the importance of meeting children's basic physical and psychological needs. Chapter Eight, The Learning Environment, looks at how you can structure the use of space and provide the equipment and material necessary to support children's development. Chapter Nine, Relationships and Guidance, deals with how you can develop positive relationships with children and help them learn to work and play in a group setting.

Part IV: The Curriculum addresses aspects of the curriculum in early childhood programs. Chapter Ten, Planning Curriculum, gives a framework for thinking about and designing meaningful and appropriate learning experiences for young children. Chapters Eleven through Fourteen deal with four broad areas of development: physical, creative, communication, and inquiry. In each chapter we provide you with a lens through which to view curriculum and an introduction to working with children in each area.

Part V: Special Relationships acquaints you with essential skills you will need to work with young children. Chapter Fifteen, Working with Children with Special Needs, will help you to identify and work with children who require special knowledge and attention, and Chapter Sixteen, Working with Families, provides an overview of your responsibilities to families and the importance of developing good relationships with them.

The relationship of the parts of the book can be graphically represented as a triangle (see Figure 1). A firm foundation is essential for strength and durability. Chapters in Parts I and II lay the foundation: Becoming an Early Childhood Educator, The Historical Roots of Current Practice, The Field of Early Childhood Education and Care, Child Development, and Play form a base of awareness and knowledge that underlie all of our work with children. Chapter Six, Assessing Children, introduces some basic and extremely valuable tools for your work. You will use these skills to learn about children, relationships, the learning environment, curriculum choices, and yourself. It intersects all of the levels of the triangle.

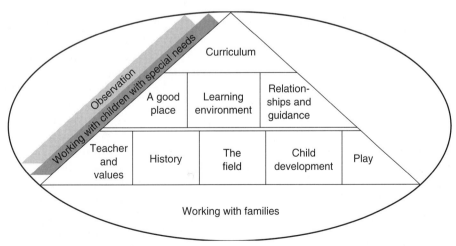

FIGURE 1
Graphic representation of parts of this book.

Chapter Seven, A Good Place for Children, Chapter Eight, The Learning Environment, and Chapter Nine, Relationships and Guidance, rest on the foundation because they provide the structural support for a viable program. These basics for living and learning with children need to be established before you can turn your attention to curriculum. The chapters on curriculum are placed at the apex of the triangle, supported by all of the rest. Chapter Fifteen, Working with Children with Special Needs, describes the awareness, knowledge, and skill needed to work effectively with diverse children. It cuts across all of the areas of the triangle. Finally, Chapter Sixteen, Working with Families, is portrayed graphically in Figure 1 as surrounding the triangle to suggest that the family provides the context for all that we do in early childhood programs.

Each chapter in this book is constructed to help you to gain awareness, acquire essential knowledge, and develop needed skills in an area of early childhood education. Throughout each chapter there are questions to stimulate reflection. We hope that you will take time to think and write about them as part of your learning process. At the end of each chapter are a bibliography and suggestions for projects to help you to learn more about the chapter's content. The bibliography at the end of each chapter includes the books we have used and referred to in the chapter. They may be helpful if you want to read more about a specific topic. We hope you will have the opportunity to read some of them as you prepare to work with children and to deepen your understanding and grow as an early childhood educator.

CONTENTS

Foundations of Early Childhood Education and Care

This section introduces some of the distinctive traditions and features of the field of early childhood education and care. Chapter One, Becoming an Early Childhood Educator, explores the nature of the early childhood educator as a person and a professional. Chapter Two, The Historical Roots of Current Practice, describes the origins of early childhood education and care. Chapter Three, The Field of Early Childhood Education and Care, presents an overview of the programs and practices that you may encounter as you begin your career. Together these three chapters provide the context for working with young children and their families.

CHAPTER ONE

Becoming an Early Childhood Educator

We teach who we are.   John Gardner

In this chapter we explore the nature of the early childhood educator as a person and as a professional. We discuss the effect of personality on young children and characteristics of effective early childhood educators. We examine the roles of early childhood educators and look at career and training opportunities in the field of early childhood education and care. We also consider personal and professional values and ethics.

Welcome to the field of early childhood education and care! You are embarking on an important career of educating and caring for young children. You may plan to be a teacher, hope to start a program, or wish to increase your understanding of the programs and people who work with young children. The kind of relationships, environment, and program that you will provide will make a lasting impact on children, families, and society. The purpose of this book is to help you become an early childhood educator who nourishes the growth of children and supports families. Your personality, attitudes, values, skills, and sense of professional identity will all play an important role in the kind of person you will be in children's lives. In the process of learning about early childhood education and care, you will create yourself as an early childhood educator.

WHAT ARE EARLY CHILDHOOD EDUCATORS AND WHAT DO THEY DO?

What is "early childhood"? What are "early childhood programs"? What is an early childhood "educator"? Answers are not universally agreed on. Child development theorists and most practitioners today consider early childhood to be the span from birth through age eight. Early childhood education and care refers to all programs providing education and care to children from birth through age eight in schools, centers, and homes. These programs are also called *early childhood programs, early child education, child development programs, early childhood care and education, preschools, kindergartens, schools, children's centers,* or *child care centers.* Young children cannot be separated from the context of their families, so early childhood programs we also refer to programs and services for families of young children.

There are many words that describe the people who work with and for young children and their families. In the field today the terms *early childhood educator, early childhood professional,* and *practitioner* are used to describe all who are involved in the care and education of young children. *Teacher* usually refers to a person who has completed a course of specialized early childhood training and who works with children between the ages of two and eight in a center-based program (a school, child development center, etc.). *Caregiver* and *provider* are terms that are often used to denote those who work with infants and toddlers or who work in home settings. We will use all of these terms but will use *early childhood educator, professional,* and *practitioner* interchangeably.

In previous editions of *Who Am I in the Lives of Children?* we called this chapter *The Teacher* and referred to those who worked with young children as *teachers.* Our change in this fifth edition reflects the changes that are emerging as the early childhood profession de-

fines itself. Names or nomenclature are important because words create an image of who we are and what we do. The more diverse words reflect a field that is increasing in diversity.

What Do Early Childhood Educators Do?

Programs, regardless of what they are called or where they are housed, provide care and education. People who work with young children, regardless of their job title or the age of the children, *nurture* and *teach*. They ensure children's well-being and help them to learn. This duality distinguishes early childhood programs and educators from other educators and schools. The term *early childhood education and care* emphasizes the dual focus on learning and care.

Many Tasks and Many People

You will have many tasks as an early childhood educator, both in your day-to-day interactions with children and as you perform related responsibilities. We have found this to be one of the most enjoyable aspects of working with young children. There are diverse tasks, many challenges, and much to learn while providing good programs.

Working with young children is no small undertaking, in part because you are involved in all aspects of the child's development (social, emotional, intellectual, and physical). This focus on the "whole child" is important because young children are vulnerable and dependent on adults for care as well as education. There is wide agreement that the responsibilities of the early childhood practitioner are to help children develop and learn and to provide physical care and psychological support.

If you embarked on a career in early childhood education because you prefer relating to young children, you may be surprised to find the extent to which early childhood professionals work with adults. You will interact with families and work with other staff members daily. You will also communicate with agencies concerned with children and work with other professionals as you further your own continuing professional development and advocate for children.

Early childhood programs resemble one another in the breadth of their responsibilities to children, in the organization of environments, and in curriculum. Because of this, every early childhood practitioner has some similar tasks.

Setting the Stage. Your work with young children will begin before the first child arrives, and it will continue each day after the last child has gone home. It starts when you create an environment for children, as you plan the daily schedule, design curriculum, and collect resources. This "stage setting" (Jones and Reynolds 1992) is an essential part of working with young children. It involves ensuring that the environment is safe, healthy, and stimulating. You will arrange learning centers, select picture books, mix paint, and choose toys for young children with the same care and attention that a college instructor gives to the selection of textbooks and media and preparation of classes. The learning environment is the primary teaching tool of an early childhood educator.

Working with Children. Each day you work with young children you will provide them with a sense of psychological comfort and security. The younger the children with whom you work, the more you will need to provide the same kind of nurturing usually provided by families. You will also observe and support children as they play, mediate relationships between children, and model the way you want people to treat one another. In a single day you may function as a teacher, friend, scribe, parent, colleague, nurse, janitor, counselor, entertainer, and diplomat.

Working with Families. Since early childhood programs provide the first transition from home to the larger world, you play an important role in helping families and children learn to be apart from each other for a period of time each day. In fact, you may be the second professional outside the home (the first is the pediatrician) who has a relationship with the family and the child. The role of the early childhood educator therefore involves working with families as well as children and includes sharing information with them that will help them to understand and relate to their child in positive ways.

Though there are important similarities between parents and early childhood professionals, we have found it helpful to consider some important distinctions made by Lilian Katz. Katz points out that family members and professionals need to be quite different in their attachment to a child. Professionals needs to appreciate children realistically, and they need to keep enough distance to observe children objectively, balance the requirements of the individual with the welfare of the group, and have goals and plans. Parents need to love and care about their children as an extension of themselves. They are their children's most passionate advocates and fans. Parents and educators each have important roles that complement one another in helping the child grow and learn (Katz 1980). Parents care about their children for an infinite amount of time while educators care about children for the time they help them to learn and grow.

Being Part of a Team. An important aspect of the role of the early childhood professional is working collaboratively with other adults. Being a part of a team can be rewarding. Early childhood practitioners have consistently reported that participating in a team gave them

support, stimulation, and a sense of belonging. Team support can reduce stress, contribute to a pleasant work environment, minimize conflict, and increase motivation (Rodd 1994). Teamwork involves many challenges. All team members need to work together on behalf of shared goals, support and respect one another, clearly understand their roles and responsibilities, include all team members, and resolve conflicts, which inevitably occur when people work together. The ability to work productively on a team is one of your most important professional skills, and the lack of this skill is a serious liability to you, to children, and to your prospective employer. Rodd summarizes this well.

> Being a part of a team is more than just turning up for work each day. It involves a special conceptualization of the roles and responsibilities of both the leader and each team member. For leaders, teamwork means acting more as a facilitator than a superior. For staff members, it means taking an active role in the work situation rather than being a passive follower of instructions and directions. (Rodd 1994, 91)

Working as part of a team may involve collaborating with co-workers, supervising staff and volunteers, interacting with program administrators, and working with a host of others from custodians to counselors. Each of these relationships requires communication. It is important with adults, as with children, to be a careful listener, to clearly communicate your goals and expectations, and to deal constructively with differing ideas about what is best. As a new early childhood educator, you are likely to work with people who have been working with children longer than you have and who have established practices and ideas. You will have to learn to work in harmony while not giving up your own values and ideals. You may find skills in active listening and peaceful conflict resolution (described in Chapter Nine, Relationships and Guidance) to be useful in relating to the other adults in the program.

THE EARLY CHILDHOOD EDUCATOR AS A PERSON

Who you are is the foundation for the professional you will become. Your personal characteristics have a powerful effect on how you relate to children and adults. Your values will influence the professional decisions you will make. Both your personal characteristics and values have an important impact on how you will evolve into an early childhood educator.

Personal Qualities

Personality is part of what makes you who you are, what makes you distinctive. It is the ways you think, act, and feel. It comes from the complex interaction of your inherited temperamental characteristics and your life experiences. Personality, in this sense, is neither good nor bad; it is simply part of you.

Awareness of your characteristic reactions and individual style can help you understand yourself. It is not necessary to have a particular kind of personality to be an early childhood educator, but it is important to be aware of your personal qualities and of your effect on children, families, and colleagues. Although many kinds of people can successfully work with young children, research suggests that certain attributes and characteristics correlate with skillful early childhood educators. These attributes include: a positive outlook, energy, physical strength, a sense of humor, flexibility, self-understanding, emotional stability, emotional warmth, and sensitivity (Feeney and Chun 1985).

As a prospective early childhood educator, it is important that you become aware of your characteristics and how they affect others and how they fit or do not fit with the styles of the adults and children with whom you work. Such awareness will help you to make conscious choices about your behavior and your career and can help you be a more sensitive educator.

We have found the research by pediatricians Alexander Thomas and Stella Chess on the temperament of infants, and applied to adults by therapists Jayne Burks and Melvin Rubenstein (Burks and Rubenstein 1979), to be helpful to our students in understanding their personality. Thomas and Chess refer to temperament as the observable manifestations; the "how" of behavior that explains a great deal about individual differences in style. They studied the temperament of infants and found that newborns show definite differences in certain traits that persist over time. Though often modified in adulthood through life experiences, the nine dimensions of temperament are helpful in explaining personality differences and can be used as a tool for personal reflection. For example, when a teacher we know who has a very low activity level reviewed the nine dimensions, she realized that a highly active child in her class was not misbehaving or deviant but was simply temperamentally different from her.

Each attribute can be thought of on a continuum from a high to low incidence with many possible in-between points. Figure 1.1 gives a brief description of the nine traits as they apply to adults and a continuum showing each. To heighten your awareness of your own temperament you may wish to plot yourself and one or two other people you know well on the continua.

If you are interested in learning more, there are other instruments available to help you to learn about your interests and abilities and other aspects of your personality. These are often administered in college counseling centers. As you develop greater self-awareness, you can begin to observe your preferences regarding kinds of activities and work settings. Awareness of your temperament and preferences will help you choose a professional setting that allows you to function most effectively.

1. ACTIVITY LEVEL—Level of physical and mental activity.
very active _____ very inactive/quiet
2. REGULARITY (Rhythmicity)—Preference for predictable routines or spontaneity.
highly regular/predictable _____ highly irregular/unpredictable
3. DISTRACTIBILITY—Degree to which extraneous stimuli affects behavior; readiness to leave one activity for another.
easily distracted _____ very focused despite distractions
4. APPROACH-WITHDRAWAL—Ways of responding to new situations.
enjoys new experiences _____ avoids new experiences
5. ADAPTABILITY—Ease of adjustment to new ideas or situations (after initial response).
adapts very easily to change _____ has difficulty adapting
6. PHYSICAL SENSITIVITY (Threshold of Responsiveness)—Sensitivity to changes in the environment including noise, taste, smell, and temperature.
very aware of changes _____ not too attuned to changes
7. INTENSITY OF REACTION—Energy level typical of response, both positive and negative.
very high intensity _____ very low intensity
8. PERSISTENCE/ATTENTION SPAN—The amount of time devoted to an activity, even when it is difficult, and the ability to continue working when distracted.
not easily distracted _____ very easily distracted
9. QUALITY OF MOOD—General optimism or pessimism; tendency to enjoy things uncritically or to be more selective about situations enjoyed.
generally happy or optimistic _____ generally sad or pessimistic

FIGURE 1.1
Thomas and Chess's Nine Dimensions of Temperament

Self-Knowledge and Self-Acceptance

Even though personality and temperament may vary greatly, there are some personal characteristics that appear to be essential for working with young children. To support children's development, an early childhood educator must have the capacity for caring, compassion, and nurturing. To become a person who possesses these qualities, you must know and accept yourself. Self-knowledge depends to a great extent on developing the ability to observe yourself in the same honest and nonjudgmental way that you observe children and to realistically appraise areas in which change may be needed. The capacity for self-knowledge and acceptance is the cornerstone for the quality of compassion that is so important in a person who works with young children and their families. Arthur Jersild describes it like this:

To be compassionate, one must be able to accept the impact of any emotion, love or hate, joy, fear, or grief—tolerate it and harbor it long enough and with sufficient absorption to accept its meaning and to enter into a fellowship of feeling with the one who is moved by the emotion. This is the heroic feature of compas-

Reflect and write about . . .

what you are like

Think about your temperament and personality:

Do you tend to be exuberant or calm?

Do you prefer vigorous activity or more sedentary pursuits?

Do you like novelty and change or predictability and order?

Do you choose large groups of people or intimate gatherings?

Do you crave quiet solitude or the excitement of a crowd?

Do you seek puzzling challenges or prefer tasks that are more easily mastered?

How has your temperament and personal style led you to your choice of early childhood education and care as a career? What do they suggest about the type of work settings you might enjoy the most?

sion in its fullest development: to be able to face the ravage of rage, the shattering impact of terror, the tenderest prompting of love, and then to embrace these in a larger context, which involves an acceptance of these feelings and an appreciation of what they mean to the one who experiences them. (Jersild 1955, 125–6)

It is important to be open to new experiences, to acknowledge and deal with feelings. It is also helpful to understand that although everyone experiences strong and unpleasant emotions like anger and fear at times, you can learn to be aware of your effect on others and choose to respond to these feelings in ways that are constructive.

Skills in gaining trust and developing relationships are acquired as you come to know yourself better, accept yourself, and then learn more about children and how to work successfully with them. Part of this process of development (and the major theme in this book) is to ask yourself frequently: "Who am I in the lives of children? Who do I want to be?" No one is completely self-aware, mature, wise, compassionate, and insightful all of the time. Everyone has tendencies to be defensive. It is important, however, to learn to accept feedback from others as valuable information instead of something to defend against or to use to berate or belittle yourself.

Sensitivity to others and a positive sense of self are essential requirements for becoming a person who can support the development of children. Your own early experiences are very important in the formation of the way that you feel about yourself and others. If you had your basic needs met in childhood, you are likely to see the world as a good and nurturing place and will more easily develop the ability to support the growth and development of children. If you did not have your needs met in consistent ways in your early life, you may find it more difficult.

This is not to say that if you had an unhappy childhood you can't become an early childhood educator. All of us have some happy and unhappy memories of our early lives. Our

---

Reflect and write about . . .

who you are and who you want to be

What experiences in your childhood influenced who you are today? What kind of person do you want to be? What are your strengths and what is challenging for you? Who do you want to be in the lives of children?

---

field would be depopulated if only those with a perfectly happy childhood could become early childhood practitioners. In fact, many good early childhood educators have overcome painful experiences and dedicated themselves to giving children some of what they missed. It is critical, however, if your motivation for working with children stems from an unhappy childhood that you come to terms with your experiences so you can better nurture children and families.

Bias and Prejudice

Everyone has personal preferences, matters of taste. You may prefer jazz to classical music and chocolate to pistachio ice cream. People also have expectations based on what they have experienced in the past, what they have heard from others, and what they hope for or fear. You have come to expect that you will enjoy yourself if you go to a jazz concert or order chocolate ice cream.

Just as we all have preferences and expectations for things like music and food, we all have preferences and expectations regarding individuals and groups of people. The inclination to favor or reject certain individuals or groups of people *(biases)* may be based simply on the human tendency to feel comfortable with people who are similar to us. Unlike preferences for food or music, these have the potential for negative impact on others. Judgments based on preconceptions rather than on

direct experience of an individual or group of people are called *prejudices.*

Prejudice creates distance. It can result in strong feelings about a child or family based on unfounded assumptions. If you can recall the experience of having been rejected or negatively judged because of your family, culture, gender, religion, language, ethnicity, appearance, ability, or status, you will be aware of the powerful effect of prejudice.

Most of us are unaware of our biases and prejudices, but we all have some. Experiences, family beliefs, personality, and personal values contribute to the biases that we hold. They influence our relationships with children, families, and colleagues. As an early childhood educator your awareness of your own biases will help you to know when you may be having negative effects on children or their families.

It is common to think of prejudice as negative feelings about a person or group. It can also be harmful to be prejudiced in favor of one group of children or families. When less favored individuals observe your preferences, they may perceive themselves as less worthy.

When you discover your own biases, simple awareness may be enough to help you to be more accepting of diversity or to correct a tendency to overreact to a child or family. Indeed, many fine teachers actively work to dispel these feelings when they occur by carefully identifying the things they like about the child

Reflect and write about . . .

bias and prejudice

In what ways and in what circumstances have you experienced prejudice in your own life? Have you ever been rejected or prejudged because of your family, culture, gender, religion, language, ethnicity, appearance, ability, or status? How did it influence your view of yourself and other people?

Who are the children you like best? What are they like? What makes a child attractive to you? Are there children you immediately dislike or with whom you feel uncomfortable? What are the characteristics of these children? How do you respond to children who swear, are loud, or are aggressive? How do you respond to children who are passive or whiny? Do you tend to prefer children of one sex? Do you feel comfortable or uncomfortable with children who are precocious, developmentally delayed, or disabled?

How do you feel about families whose lifestyles are very different from your own or who raise their children in ways that are very different from the way you or your family raises children? Do you feel less comfortable with people from any particular economic backgrounds, races, or cultures?

When you consider working with diverse children and families, what opportunities interest you? What challenges worry you?

or family member who triggers a negative reaction. The child or adult who began as one you disliked may become one for whom you have special affection.

If you become aware that you have strong prejudices that you cannot overcome, you should ask yourself if there are particular children or groups of children with whom you should not work. You may even need to consider seriously whether you should become an early childhood educator.

We live in an increasingly diverse world. As an early childhood educator you are almost certain to have close contact with people who have different racial, economic, cultural, and linguistic backgrounds and different lifestyles. This diversity offers challenges and opportunities. Although you may have moments of discomfort and self-doubt, you also have the possibility of gaining new appreciation and

insights. Each bias and prejudice that you overcome brings you a step closer to helping all children to reach their potential.

To learn something about your biases, you can begin by asking yourself questions such as those in the box on this page and answering them as honestly as you can.

THE EARLY CHILDHOOD EDUCATOR AS A PROFESSIONAL

You are on the threshold of entering a profession. You will join a group of individuals who share a mission, a set of values, and similar training. Although people have cared for and educated young children since the beginning of time, early childhood education and care is a relatively new field.

As early childhood practitioners strive to achieve greater recognition as professionals, they are becoming better at articulating philosophy, at basing work with children on sound child development theories, and at making choices based on their knowledge. They are taking greater pride in their work, because they know that they serve children and their families at a critical period in the life cycle.

The role of the early childhood educator has expanded as people have become more aware of the impact of early childhood education and as there has been increasing realization that care and education are inextricably linked. The expectations accompanying the role are many, varied, and sometimes contra-

dictory. It is not insignificant that the field has yet to find a job title that "fits." Teacher, caregiver, and practitioner—each describes only part of the multifaceted roles of early childhood educators.

Many Possibilities, Many Paths

Working with young children is varied and challenging; it demands knowledge, skill, sensitivity, creativity, and hard work. If these challenges excite you, you are probably in the right field. Early childhood education and care is especially rewarding for those who enjoy the spontaneous teaching and learning opportunities that abound in daily life with young children. It can be frustrating for people who think that teaching is a matter of dispensing subject matter to children or those who like things to be tidy and predictable. Sometimes college students who begin their careers with visions of shaping young minds become discouraged when they discover how much of their time is spent mixing paint, changing pants, mopping floors, and wiping noses. But while working with young children is demanding, difficult, and tiring, it can also be invigorating and gratifying.

Specialized training in early childhood education and care is essential to becoming a competent practitioner who can provide positive experiences for young children. Research has shown that professional training is one of the elements critical in program quality (Whitebook, Howes, and Phillips 1989). Teaching experience alone or a degree in another field (even a related field like elementary education) cannot provide you with the necessary knowledge and skill.

Not everyone enters early childhood education and care with this training. People come to the field in a variety of ways. It is estimated that only 25 percent of early childhood educators began their careers in the "traditional" manner by majoring in early childhood education before they began work in the field. Some were introduced to the field as parents, observing the benefits of a good program for their young child, then going to school to get the training they needed to join the field (about 25 percent). Others (about 50 percent) have come by a serendipitous route, discovering the field as a happy accident, often after receiving a degree in another field and later obtaining the necessary education to become an early childhood professional (Bredekamp 1992a). We reflect two of these typical paths. Stephanie and Doris "worked their way up" to early childhood education after training in anthropology and secondary education; Eva always knew she wanted to become a preschool or kindergarten

teacher and entered college with that goal in mind.

It is a good idea to experience a variety of different kinds of early childhood programs before you choose a specific training or career path. Some people who wish to work with young children get their initial experience by volunteering or taking a position as a classroom aide in a preschool or kindergarten. Many enroll in a high school or college course in child development or early childhood education to see if they might enjoy the field. Others go directly into an early childhood teacher education program in a two- or four-year college.

Early childhood education and care programs tend to have different professional requirements, compensation, and expectations. This division is important for you to understand as you plan for your career and your future. There is agreement in the field that all early childhood professionals need specialized knowledge and skills. Training requirements in programs for children under the age of five are usually quite different from programs for children from ages five through age eight.

Working with Children from Birth Through Age Five

If you want to work with children birth through age five, the training and experience that are required will be determined by program licensing, which is usually administered by state social service departments. Professional requirements vary from state to state and are often quite minimal—in some states only good health and a high school diploma are required. Most states require that teachers or caregivers in center-based programs be qualified for their jobs through training, either by having a college degree (in some places it must be in education, early childhood education, or child development) or a CDA credential. The nationally awarded Child Development Associate (CDA) credential involves some training, a standard exam, and demonstrated competency in working with young children. Training required for the CDA credential is available through a variety of agencies including community colleges and private agencies and through technologies such as interactive television or "distance learning." Positions that involve supervision of staff or curriculum development may require a master's degree in early childhood education or child development. The National Association for the Education of Young Children (NAEYC) has suggested five levels for professional categories and qualifications (NAEYC 1994).

Programs for children under the age of five vary widely in sponsorship and regulation, including center and home-based programs. There are many different job titles and many different requirements. These include:

Aides or teacher assistants help implement program activities in an early childhood classroom. Aides work with children under the supervision of a qualified early childhood educator. They usually need not have a recognized credential but generally receive orientation and on-the-job training.

Assistant Teachers or Caregivers are responsible for implementing program activities as part of a teaching team. They work with a supervising teacher or caregiver in providing care and education to a group of young children. Generally assistants help plan and implement activities, participate in assessing the needs of children, work with families, and may have responsibility for a small group within a larger class. They usually have some training to prepare them to work with young children.

Teachers or Caregivers are responsible for the care and education of a group of young children. They may also be part of a teaching team and function as a team leader with assistants or aides. Teachers or caregivers plan and implement the curriculum with the participation of other members of a team. They usually have completed specialized training to prepare them to work with young children and have an associate's or a bachelor's degree in early childhood education, or they may have a degree in another field with additional course work in early childhood education.

Master Teachers, Head Teachers, or Directors have overall responsibility for one or more groups of young children, perform administrative duties, and may serve as mentors and trainers to other teachers. They may also function as a team leader. They usually have completed specialized training to prepare them to work with young children and have a bachelor's or master's degree in early childhood education.

Family Child Care Providers and Nannies provide care and education for young children in a home setting. In most states no formal training is required to provide a home-based program. Family child care providers can receive a specific CDA credential or accreditation by the National Association for Family Day Care. A few colleges and many private agencies have nanny training programs. These are modeled on the British nursery nurse training that consists of a two-year program followed by a national examination. American counterparts are generally less rigorous and may vary from six weeks to a year in length.

Working with Children in Kindergarten Through Third Grade

There are two main types of programs for children between the ages of five and eight. These are elementary or primary school programs (public and private) and before and after school programs (private or public). To teach kindergarten and primary children, four-year-olds, or children with special needs in public schools, a bachelor's degree is usually required. Professional requirements for teaching in early childhood programs with children ages five through eight usually include elementary teacher certification, which varies from state to state and is usually given through state departments of education. Four-year college and university programs are designed to meet elementary certification requirements. Some states give a preschool-primary teaching credential, which covers preschool through the third grade; some offer an early childhood or kindergarten endorsement in addition to standard elementary certification; and some give a kindergarten through sixth grade certificate with no provision for early childhood training.

Programs for children from ages five through eight have fewer and more consistent job titles. They include:

Educational Assistants supervise children, implement activities, and tutor children. They might not have a recognized credential and work under the supervision of a qualified teacher. They rarely work with families. Educational assistants may participate in inservice training.

Teachers are responsible for the education and care of a class of young children. They plan and implement the daily program and work with parents. Teachers have completed specialized training to prepare them to teach and have a bachelor's or master's degree in education that may include specialized training in early childhood.

Resource Teachers or Specialists are responsible for supplementing the education of groups of young children in a school. They may provide special instruction to children and serve as trainers to other teachers. They usually have completed

training to prepare them to work in a subject area and may have a master's degree in their subject area in addition to a bachelor's degree in education.

Principals or Headmasters are responsible for a school. They perform administrative duties and serve as leaders for a staff of teachers. They usually have completed specialized training to prepare them to work with children and have a graduate degree in education with course work in administration.

School-age Caregivers, Supervisors, or Group Leaders work in before and after school care programs to provide supervision and activities for elementary children when school is not in session. In most states formal training is not required. After-school caregivers are often high school or college students who receive orientation and on-the-job training. They supervise a class of children under the direction of a qualified teacher, implement activities, and assist individual children with homework. They are responsible for the safety and management of the children and rarely work with families.

Other Roles

People concerned with the education and welfare of young children and trained in early childhood education can do many different jobs. Each person has to find the career that best reflects his or her interests, talents, and style.

In addition to working directly with young children, your training in early childhood education and care may help prepare you for positions that involve program support and administration (center directors, curriculum specialists, education directors); support services for families (parent education specialists, child psychologists, pediatricians and nurses, dieti-

Reflect and write about . . .

your future job

Imagine your perfect job in early childhood education and care. What is it like? Why does it appeal to you? What training would you need for this job?

tians, social workers, child-care licensing workers, resource and referral workers who help families in finding care and assist centers in improving program quality); support for teachers and programs (teacher training, consulting, research, curriculum design, support services); and as an advocate for children's rights (in private or governmental agencies).

Career decisions are not set in concrete and don't have to last forever. As you grow and change, so do your needs for professional fulfillment. The more experience you can have in working with children of different ages in a variety of early childhood settings, the sooner it will become clear whether working with young children is the right choice for you and what kinds of positions will suit you best. There are many kinds of work where you can act upon your commitment to children. What is most important is that you learn about yourself and make a good personal decision. Judith Seaver's book, *Careers with Young Children: Making Your Decision* (1979), provides an excellent resource for exploring alternatives and clarifying individual interests and concerns.

Stages of Professional Development

You are at the beginning of your career as an early childhood educator and have many joys and challenges ahead of you. Just like the children with whom you will work, you will pass through developmental stages. And just like the children, you need appropriate stimulation and nurturing to reach your full potential at each stage. Knowing the stages may help you understand what you are experiencing at different times in your career and what kinds of experiences will nurture you and enhance your professional growth.

Katz's Stages

Lilian Katz has described four stages of development of teachers of young children (Katz 1972).

Stage 1: Survival.   The first year of working with young children is a time when you will need to apply the knowledge you have gained in college. You are likely to find the task of working with young children challenging—Katz calls this *survival.* The first year is often hard and stressful because everything is new and also because you may have unrealistically high expectations of yourself. As a beginning practitioner you are likely to want advice and lots of practical suggestions. You will want to feel that you are appreciated and connected to other professionals.

Stage 2: Consolidation.   When you have become adept at basic "survival" in the classroom, you may want to bring together what you know to create a more personal approach to working with children. During this time you may find on-site assistance, consultants, and the advice of colleagues helpful.

Stage 3: Renewal.   When you have been working with children for three to five years, you may find yourself feeling somewhat bored

or dissatisfied. At this stage you may enjoy going to conferences, workshops, and films and joining professional associations. Visits to other schools may renew your enthusiasm and give you ideas as well as a greater sense of belonging and professionalism.

Stage 4: Maturity.   After five or more years of working with children, many early childhood professionals find themselves less interested in practical details (which they have mastered) and more interested in consideration of the values, theories, issues, and philosophy that underlie their work. When you reach this stage, seminars, work on advanced degrees, and professional reading may renew your sense of excitement and provide new areas of interest and involvement.

VanderVen's Stages

Karen VanderVen has suggested that there are three stages of career development for the early childhood practitioner (VanderVen 1991). These are similar to Katz's but reflect a professional path more typical of early childhood practitioners who work in settings for children under the age of five. VanderVen's stages reflect the movement from direct work with young children to more indirect roles.

Stage 1: Direct Care.   Practitioners who work in an early childhood program, have not yet received much professional training, and provide direct care of young children under supervision are in VanderVen's stage 1. This stage is characterized by the relatively immature orientation of a young or inexperienced individual.

Stage 2: Direct Care Advanced.   Practitioners who have completed professional training, made a commitment to working with young children and have experience, and work directly with young children are in VanderVen's stage 2 (similar to Katz's stage 3). Practitioners in this stage are characterized by more logical and rational behavior and choices than practitioners in stage 1. They are able to make choices and predict the outcomes of their behavior.

Stage 3: Indirect Care.   Practitioners who have moved beyond working directly with young children are in VanderVen's stage 3 (similar to Katz's stage 4). Practitioners in this stage take on leadership roles and responsibilities. They are characterized by deeper understanding and expertise in the field.

VALUES AND THE EARLY CHILDHOOD EDUCATOR

Your decisions about what you want to accomplish with children are, to a great extent, based on your values. It is important for early childhood educators to be aware of their personal values, their professional values, and values of the field. Your values, both personal and professional, will influence the goals that you set and the actions that grow from these goals. If you are not clear about your values or the values of your profession, you may find yourself moving from one practice to another without knowing whether your actions are consistent or if they really represent what you want for children.

Values are things you believe to be worthwhile, that are prized and desirable in themselves. Truth, beauty, love, honesty, wisdom, individuality, success, and loyalty are examples of values. In countless ways values underlie major and minor life decisions, both personal and professional. The things you do each day, the foods you eat, the places you live, and the work and play you choose are all influenced by your values. Your professional values will grow out of these personal values.

The development of values is a complex process that grows out of family background, culture, and life experiences. You acquired many values early in life without realizing it. Now, when you reflect, you can identify your values and recognize how they are similar to and different from those held by others. It is sometimes surprising to discover that other people do not share values that you believed were universal—one of the reasons the first year in a new community or a new intimate relationship and the first year of working in an early childhood program can be difficult. Awareness can help you to realize how many expectations reflect value differences.

As you begin your preparation for becoming an early childhood educator it is worthwhile to consider what values have brought you to this decision and how your values will influence the decisions you make about working with and for young children.

You have chosen the field of early childhood education in part because you value children. You may enjoy them and want a work environment in which you can have daily contact with children. You may have empathy for them and wish to make their world a better and more caring place. If you cherish and hold dear education, perhaps you hope to help young children realize their learning potential. You may value a playful work environment and see early childhood education as a field that shares your values. You may have religious values you want to actualize by caring for others. A commitment to world peace can lead you to the early childhood field if you believe peace begins with children. You may wish to give children the opportunity to express their individuality. If you value fairness, justice, aesthetics, diversity, or respect for nature, you may wish to share these values with children.

Professional Values

What goes on in your classroom will be a reflection of your personal values, the philosophy of the particular program in which you

Reflect and write about . . .

what you value

Make a list of things you value. Think about where each came from. Consider whether family, friends, culture, society, or some combination of these helped you to acquire your values.

What do you value about children and childhood? What personal values led you to your choice of careers in early childhood education and care? What values do you hope to reflect in your work with children and families?

work, the values of the community, and the values of the field of early childhood education and care. Your values evolve and change slowly as you gain new information and experience. Professional values are acquired as you combine your individual values with the commitments and responsibilities of your profession. Willingness to examine values, the capacity for self-awareness, and a commitment to lifelong learning are the hallmarks of an early

childhood professional. When you examine your own values and those of the field, you can weigh your decisions carefully and choose alternatives with clarity and wisdom.

It is important to work towards making your actions consistent with your values and those of the field. Sometimes early childhood practitioners are not aware of the ways in which their behavior may contradict their values. For example, we worked with teachers in a program where the values of independence and child-directed learning were clearly articulated but children were not allowed to choose their own materials from the open shelves. To avoid such discrepancies between your beliefs and actions you can examine your choices and consider how they relate to your goals for children. Thoughtful reflection combined with knowledge of child development can help you to make decisions that are based on the best interests of children.

Core Values in Early Childhood Care and Education

Every profession has values held consciously and knowingly that represent a commitment to contribute to society's well-being. Early childhood education has a long history of emphasizing those practices that recognize and respect

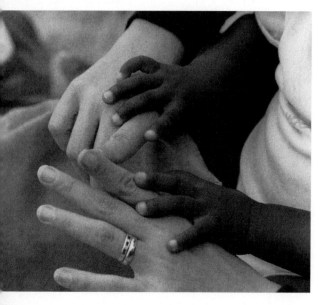

Standards of ethical behavior in early childhood education are based on commitment to core values that are deeply rooted in the history of our field. We have committed ourselves to:

- Appreciating childhood as a unique and valuable stage of the human life cycle;
- Basing our work with children on knowledge of child development;
- Appreciating and supporting the close ties between the child and family;
- Recognizing that children are best understood in the context of family, culture and society;
- Respecting the dignity, worth and uniqueness of each individual (child, family member and colleague);
- Helping children and adults achieve their full potential in the context of relationships that are based on trust, respect and positive regard.

Source: S. Feeney and K. Kipnis, "Code of Ethical Conduct and Statement of Commitment," *Young Children* (1989), 45(1):25.

FIGURE 1.2
Core values in early childhood education

the humanity and dignity of people and that support the development of children's potential while enhancing their sense of self-esteem.

In the 1980s early childhood educators across the United States worked together under the auspices of NAEYC to identify core values for the field (Feeney and Kipnis 1985). The list of core values represents consensus of American early childhood educators regarding the commitments that characterize the early childhood field. Clarity regarding these values enables professionals to formally recognize their commitments to children, families, society, and themselves. The core values imply an educational process in which individuality and social responsibilities are both considered important.

People who choose early childhood education and care as a career often find themselves in agreement with the spirit of the core values. Now, as you enter the field, is a good time to read through the core values and think about how they fit with your personal values (Figure 1.2). As you merge your personal values with the professional values of the field, you will join other early childhood practitioners in making a commitment to working with children and families in ways that are humane and respectful.

Values Conflicts

Dealing with values in everyday life in an early childhood classroom is, unfortunately, more complex than becoming clear about your own values and those of the field. You may find that in practice you have to make some hard choices. Trying to understand and reconcile value differences within yourself and with others is a recurring part of being an early childhood educator.

Value choices are not always clear-cut. They involve conflicting demands that call for a weighing and balancing of positive and negative. Conflicts may occur within yourself. For example, you may value freedom of expression (such as allowing children to role play whatever is important to them) versus the value of peace (forbidding war play since it brings the cruelty of war into the classroom). You may face value conflicts regarding the needs and demands of your professional and personal lives (such as when an important staff meeting is scheduled on your child's birthday). Or you may face the dilemma of having to choose between work that pays well and work you love. In these situations it will be helpful to analyze the nature of your value conflict and try to establish which value is most important for you.

You may also find yourself facing values conflicts with others. When these occur it is helpful to recognize that differences in values are a natural and healthy part of life in a diverse society. It is important to address values conflicts thoughtfully, though it may not be possible to resolve them neatly. For example, it is not uncommon for an administrator's values and actions (such as minimizing the risk of allegations of sexual abuse by forbidding staff to hug children) to be in direct conflict with yours (giving young children affectionate physical contact to build secure relationships). You may come into conflict with colleagues whose values lead them to different goals such as: whether to teach academic skills rather than encourage child choice and play; whether the curriculum should be planned in advance or deal with concerns and issues raised by the children; the protection of the innocence of childhood versus the education of children about social issues like homelessness, child abuse, and AIDS; and the relative emphasis to be placed on various topics like the arts, moral development, academics, peace education, feelings, and anti-bias issues. You may sometimes find yourself caught in a difficult dilemma between your beliefs and pressures from families who want you to teach and treat children in ways that violate these beliefs (for example, parents who are anxious about their children's success in school and who want them to master academic content for which they are developmentally unready).

Working with young children would be easier if your colleagues, administrators, and families of the children in your care were in complete agreement with you on early childhood issues. This doesn't often happen in a world characterized by diversity. As people from different backgrounds and with different values work together, different viewpoints inevitably arise. There are many different and contradictory points of view regarding what is best for children and how they should be educated. These differences need to be acknowledged and discussed. We have found that values conflicts among colleagues can be handled best when people take time to reflect on and clarify their goals and values. You may use the core values for guidance while recognizing that compromise may be reached, or the individuals may have to agree to disagree.

When a values conflict with families occurs it is essential to hear and carefully weigh family concerns and to communicate that you accept and respect their values. It is also important to remember that you and your colleagues have training and expertise in child development and cannot compromise what you know to be essential for children.

When competing views are based on strongly held values differences, there may be no easy solution. Occasionally differences may be so serious that you will find you cannot continue to work in the program. Coming to this conclusion can be painful but it may be your only alternative if the issue cannot be resolved. You may find that you are happier teaching in a setting that more closely reflects your values; for example, a former student of ours decided to leave a program because it did not adequately address her belief in the importance of creative development.

You may also choose to leave a program when you have serious concerns that program practice does not agree with the core values or if you believe the well-being of children is compromised. The Code of Ethical Conduct (see Appendix One) can be helpful to you when these kinds of values conflicts occur.

Ethics

Some values issues in early childhood education are not individual issues but are faced by all professionals who work with young children and their families. Ethics involve the

Reflect and write about . . .

values conflicts

Think about a time when you had to make a decision between two things that you valued. What did you do to resolve your value conflict?

Think about a time when you and another person had a disagreement based on values. What values did you each of you hold? How were your values or the relationship changed by the conflict?

Think about a time when you disagreed with another person about the treatment or education and care of young children. What values did each of you hold? How do these relate to the core values in early childhood education?

members of the profession's shared process of critical, systematic reflection on what is right and what is wrong. The following statement describes this process of consideration.

> First, it concerns what is the *right* thing to do, not just the most expedient or least trouble-making, the *fair* or *just* thing. Moral issues are usually characterized by certain kinds of language. Words such as *right, ought, just* and *fair* are common. Moral issues concern our duties and obligations to one another, what constitutes just or fair treatment of one another and what rights we each have. (Strike, Haller, and Soltis 1988, 3)

Professional ethics in early childhood education and care reflect the field's responsibilities to children, families, colleagues, and society. The core values guide practitioners as they deliberate on ethical dilemmas by helping them to ask themselves, "What should responsible early childhood educators try to do and what should they refuse to do?" (Feeney and Kipnis 1985, 24). Professional ethics help us to resolve moral dilemmas that cannot be settled by facts. These dilemmas often involve conflicting values for which there may be no obvious or easy solution. They require a special kind of reasoning characterized by exploring the elements of the dilemma and applying principles such as jus-

tice, fairness, and respect for the dignity and worth of individuals.

For example, if the aggressive behavior of an individual child leads some families to request that the aggressive child be expelled, you are caught in a conflict between obligations to an individual child and family and your obligations to the other children in your group and their families. Your primary responsibility is to the well-being of children; therefore, the first thing to be considered when facing a dilemma is the extent to which each alternative might cause harm or benefit. Practitioners can ask themselves the following questions to help guide them in decision making:

• Might this decision cause children any harm now or in the future?
• Which choice is most worth embracing in terms of the core values of the field of early childhood education?

A code of ethics provides guidance to practitioners who face moral dilemmas. Lilian Katz and Evangeline Ward's book, *Ethical Behavior in Early Childhood Education* (1993), describes the function of ethical codes in defining and unifying a profession by moving decision making from an individual enterprise to a process based on consensus. A code of ethics provides the basis for an argument or an action. It makes it easier to behave ethically because a practitioner is acting not as an individual but as a professional governed by the principles and requirements of the field. A code of ethics, when followed by members of the profession, can assure the public that practice in a profession is based on sound and agreed-upon standards that are in the best interests of society.

Ethical guidelines help us to do what we believe is right and good and not what is easiest, will bring us the most personal benefit, or will make others like us the most. Ethics are of particular concern in early childhood education and care because young children are very vulnerable and they have very little control over their lives or power to defend themselves. It is therefore extremely important that those who

work in early childhood programs behave fairly and responsibly on behalf of children.

The National Association for the Education of Young Children approved its Code of Ethical Conduct and Statement of Commitment (Feeney and Kipnis 1989) to guide its members in responsible professional practice. The code provides direction for thinking through and acting on some of the recurring ethical dilemmas that early childhood educators encounter in their daily work with children and families.

NAEYC's code is organized into four sections describing professional responsibilities to children, families, colleagues, and community and society. The items in the code offer ideals and principles designed to help practitioners make responsible ethical decisions. Ideals describe exemplary practice, and principles de-

scribe practices that are required, prohibited, and permitted. The code includes items that pertain to all professions, such as the importance of keeping personal information confidential, and some that are unique to early childhood education, such as how to balance the needs of the individual child with the needs of the group. (A copy of the code is found in Appendix 1.)

The idea of ethical dilemmas may seem abstract to you at first. You can be certain, however, that real ethical dilemmas will occur on a regular basis in your work in early childhood care and education. It is an important part of your professional role to identify and deal appropriately with ethical dilemmas when they do occur. NAEYC's ethical code is designed to help you do just that. When you find yourself torn between two possible actions and are uncertain what to do, you may be encountering an ethical dilemma. By consulting the code you may gain guidance in making a choice that is in the best interests of children.

FINAL THOUGHTS

We hope this book will help you to reflect on yourself as an early childhood professional. As a new practitioner it is important that you set realistic goals for yourself, that you find your strengths and build from them, and that you acknowledge your mistakes and learn from them. It is important to remember that you, like the children you will care for, are a person in the process of development.

Observing and understanding children is the first and usually most lasting challenge for early childhood professionals. In addition to fascination with children, you need a work environment that is stimulating, challenging, and responsive. Like children, you need resources, time, and encouragement to explore, experiment productively, and learn.

"Who am I?" and "Who am I in the lives of children?" are questions that you will need to ask yourself many times in your career. The questions will help you reflect on what you do and why you do it. The answers will become clearer, deeper, and more meaningful as you gain awareness and understanding through your experience with children and families.

You will be caring for the future by caring for the children—the most important job in the world. Tomorrow's adults, in their most vulnerable stage of life, will be in your hands. Today's children need to be protected so tomorrow's adults will be healthy and strong. They need nurturing so tomorrow's adults will be sensitive and care about those who are like themselves and those who are different. They need encouragement so tomorrow's adults will be creative thinkers, discoverers, and problem solvers. They will have many problems to solve. They need guidance so tomorrow's adults will appreciate the fragile world in which we live. Today's children need to learn to cooperate so tomorrow's adults will be peacemakers at home and in the world.

You will be caring for the future by caring for yourself. There is no book, toy, video, or computer program that can substitute for a human being who knows about, cares for, and is sensitive to young children. *You* are the vital ingredient. All you have to give is yourself—your caring, your energy, and your commitment. To accomplish this demanding task you need good physical and emotional health. Take care of your body by paying attention to nutrition, exercise, and relaxation. Nurture your mind so you stay excited and motivated as a learner. Stay connected to others so that you feel appreciated, meaningfully involved, and intellectually stimulated. Nurture your spirit by taking time for quiet reflection, for enjoying beauty, for spending time with literature and art. Elizabeth Jones suggests that educators can regard their intellectual interests and concerns as a form of play (Jones and Reynolds 1992). You can pursue topics that are interesting and fun and make decisions about what *you* want to learn and do.

You are caring for the future by caring for your profession. Remember that your job is worth doing. This is an exciting time to become an early childhood educator. It is the threshold of a new era. When you join a professional group, make a commitment to the field of early childhood education, speak to a friend or legislator on behalf of children, or take a stand based on the code of ethics, you are caring for the profession and the future of us all.

You have many choices to make as you join the field. They are personal choices, value choices, and career choices. They are professional choices. As your colleagues in this field, we welcome you.

PROJECTS

Remember a Teacher: Describe a teacher you remember clearly from your own childhood. Describe:

- His or her personal qualities.
- What you think your teacher valued and why.
- His or her effect on children.
- His or her effect in your life.
- How you would like to be similar to or different from this teacher and why.

Interview a Professional: Visit and interview an early childhood educator who has been working in the field for at least five years. Ask how he or she came to be in this present role. Find out about the person's job title, responsibilities, training, professional accomplishments, philosophy, and values. On the basis of your interview write an article that could be published in a student or community newspaper.

Compare Two Programs: Observe two early childhood programs. Describe the programs briefly and list what seems to be the primary values of each program. Explore the specific things you saw that led to your conclusions. Consider which program seems most consistent with your values for education.

Consider an Ethical Dilemma: Choose an ethical dilemma you have encountered, that an experienced professional has shared, or one from the list of ethical cases in Appendix Two. Describe possible ways that an early childhood educator could respond. Use the code of ethics and core values to evaluate the possible responses. Describe which response to the dilemma is best and why it is best in terms of ethical behavior.

Trace Your Path: Review the experiences and relationships in your life at home and in the world that led you to choose early childhood education and care as a career. Reflect on how these events helped to form your values. What do you see as you look ahead to becoming an early childhood professional?

Consider Your Values: List five of the most important values in your life. For each, discuss the influences and experiences that contributed to its development. Consider how these values influenced your decision to enter the field of early childhood education. Describe the ways they influence your values for the education of young children.

BIBLIOGRAPHY

Ade, W. 1982. Professionalism and Its Implications for the Field of Early Childhood Education. *Young Children* 37(3):25–32.

Almy, M. 1975. *The Early Childhood Educator At Work*. New York: McGraw-Hill.

Ashton-Warner, S. 1980. *Teacher*. London: Virago Press.

Ayers, W. 1989. *The Good Preschool Teacher: Six Teachers Reflect on Their Lives*. New York: Teachers College Press.

Biber, B. 1969. *Challenges Ahead for Early Childhood Education*. Washington, DC: National Association for the Education of Young Children.

Bredekamp, S. 1992a. Composing a Profession. *Young Children* 47(2):52–54.

Bredekamp, S. 1992b. The Early Childhood Profession Coming Together. *Young Children* 47(6):36–38.

Burks, J., and M. Rubenstein. 1979. *Temperament Styles in Adult Interaction*. New York: Brunner/Mazel.

Callahan, J. C. 1988. *Ethical Issues in Professional Life*. New York: Oxford University Press.

Costley, J. 1991. *Career Development Systems in Early Care and Education: A Planning Approach*. Boston: Wheelock College.

Dennison, G. 1969. *The Lives of Children*. New York: Vintage Books.

Feeney, S. 1992. *Early Childhood Education in Asia and the Pacific*. New York: Garland.

Feeney, S., and R. Chun. 1985. Effective Teachers of Young Children. *Young Children* 41(1):47–52.

Feeney, S., and K. Kipnis. 1985. Professional Ethics in Early Childhood Education. *Young Children* 45(1):24–29.

Feeney, S., and K. Kipnis. 1989. Code of Ethical Conduct and Statement of Commitment. *Young Children* 45(1):24–29.

Feeney, S., C. Phelps, and D. Stanfield. 1976. Values Examination: A Crucial Issue in Early Childhood Education. In J.D. Andrews, ed., *Early Childhood Education: It's An Art? It's A Science?* Washington DC: National Association for the Education of Young Children.

Fleet, A., and M. Clyde. 1993. *What's in a Day? Working in Early Childhood*. Wentworth Falls, NSW, Australia: Social Science Press.

Gonzalez-Mena, J. 1993. *The Child in the Family and the Community*. Englewood Cliffs, NJ: Merrill/Prentice Hall.

Hendrick, J. 1987. *Why Teach?* Washington, DC: National Association for the Education of Young Children.

Jersild, A. 1955. *When Teachers Face Themselves*. New York: Teachers College Press.

Johnson, J., and J. B. McCracken, Ed. 1994. *The Early Childhood Career Lattice: Perspectives on Professional Development*. Washington, DC: National Association for the Education of Young Children.

Jones, E., and G. Reynolds. 1992. *The Play's The Thing: Teacher's Roles in Children's Play*. New York: Teachers College Press.

Jorde-Bloom, P. 1988. *A Great Place to Work: Improving Conditions for Staff in Young Children's Programs*. Washington DC: National Association for the Education of Young Children.

Katz, L. 1972. Developmental Stages of Preschool Teachers. *The Elementary School Journal* 23(1):50–54.

Katz, L. 1980. Mothering and Teaching—Some Significant Distinctions. In L. Katz, ed., *Current Topics in Early Childhood Education*. Norwood, NJ: Ablex.

Katz, L., and E. Ward. 1993. *Ethical Behavior in Early Childhood Education*. Washington, DC: National Association for the Education of Young Children.

Keirsey, D., and M. Bates. 1978. *Please Understand Me: Character and Temperament Types*. Del Mar, CA: Prometheus Memesis Books.

Kipnis, K. 1987. How to Discuss Professional Ethics. *Young Children* 42(4): 26–33.

Kohl, H. 1984. *Growing Minds: On Becoming a Teacher*. New York: Harper & Row.

Maslow, A. 1968. *Towards a Psychology of Being*. New York: Van Nostrand Reinhold.

Moustakas, C. 1982. *The Authentic Teacher*. New York: Irvington.

Myers, I. B. 1980. *Gifts Differing*. Palo Alto, CA: Consulting Psychologists Press.

National Association for the Education of Young Children. 1991. Early Childhood Teacher Certification: A Position Statement of the Association of Teacher Educators and the National Association for the Education of Young Children. Adopted July/August 1991. *Young Children* 47(1):16–21.

National Association for the Education of Young Children. 1994. 1994 NAEYC Position Statement: A Conceptual Framework for Early Childhood Professional Development. *Young Children* 49(3):68–77.

Noddings, N. 1984. *Caring: A Feminine Approach to Ethics and Moral Education*. Berkeley, CA: University of California Press.

Riley, S. S. 1984. *How to Generate Values in Young Children*. Washington, DC: National Association for the Education of Young Children.

Rodd, J. 1994. *Leadership in Early Childhood: The Pathway to Professionalism*. New York: Teachers College Press.

Rogers, C. 1969. *Freedom to Learn*. Columbus, OH: Merrill.

Rosen, J. L. 1968. Personality and First Year Teacher's Relationships with Children. *The School Review* 76(3):294–311.

Seaver, J. 1979. *Careers with Young Children: Making Your Decision*. Washington, DC: National Association for the Education of Young Children.

Spodek, B., and O. Saracho, ed. 1990. *Early Childhood Teacher Preparation: Yearbook in Early Childhood Education*. New York: Teachers College Press.

Spodek, B., O. Saracho, and D. L. Peters 1988. *Professionalism and the Early Childhood Practitioner*. New York: Teachers College Press.

Strickland, J., and M. Levbarg. 1990. Teacher Aides and Other Dangerous Instruments—Lessons in Legal Self-Defense. *Child Care Information Exchange* (67):37–42.

Strike, K. A., E. Haller, and J. F. Soltis. 1988. *The Ethics of School Administration*. New York: Teachers College Press.

Thomas, A., and S. Chess. 1977. *Temperament and Development*. New York: Brunner/Mazel.

VanderVen, K. 1991. The Relationship Between Notions of Care Giving Held by Early Childhood Practitioners and Stages of Career Development. In B. Po-King Chan, ed., *Early Childhood Towards the 21st Century: A Worldwide Perspective* (pp. 245–56). Hong Kong: Yew Chung Educational Publishing.

Whitebook, M. 1980. *Who's Minding the Child Care Workers? A Look at Staff Burnout*. Berkeley, CA: Child Care Staff Education Project.

Whitebook, M., C. Howes, and D. Phillips. 1989. *Who Cares? Child Care Teachers and the Quality of Care in America*. Oakland, CA: Child Care Employee Project.

Yonemura, M. V. 1986. *A Teacher at Work: Professional Development and the Early Childhood Educator*. New York: Teachers College Press.

CHAPTER TWO

The Historical Roots of Current Practice

What is past is prologue. William Shakespeare

This chapter describes the historical roots of early childhood education and care and how persons and events in the past have influenced current programs and practices. It is written to provide you with a perspective on the origins of present philosophies and practices.

Knowledge of the history of early childhood education provides us with a vantage point for understanding where we are and where we are going as a field. A historical perspective can give an early childhood educator a sense of our roots in the past and an idea of how current approaches to working with children and families have grown out of past thought and practice. Knowing about the history of the field can help you to realize that much of what is called "innovation" in current practice has been thought about, written about, and experimented with before. And similarly, it becomes apparent that current philosophical debates are not new—they mirror conflicting views that have a long history. This knowledge can give you a sense of connection to the past and can help you to make sense out of many of the things you will do in your work with young children.

Early childhood education is a fairly new field, although it has old roots and emerges from a long historical tradition. In this chapter

we discuss some notable people who applied themselves to understanding children and to making the world a better place for them to grow and learn. We will also explore some of the important ideas generated by these people that continue to influence the field. It is not our intention to write a comprehensive history of childhood or of early education—that would require at least a whole book. Rather, we will focus on the evolution of some of the important ideas that have shaped the field of early education and care as it is practiced today.

Early childhood education as a specialized field is generally thought to have begun in Europe in the early nineteenth century. However, many of the values and practices found in today's programs grow from beliefs about children and child-rearing that have been passed down from generation to generation and from the ideas of religious leaders, philosophers, scholars, social reformers, and educators of the past.

Many of today's programs have their roots in what has been referred to as the *humanistic tradition* in education—a tradition that reflects concern for the values and potential of human beings. The people who contributed to this stream of thought were concerned with such issues as respect for human dignity, the role of education in contributing to all aspects of children's development, the connection between mind and body, the importance of play in development, the value of observing children, and the support of individual freedom. Many of them believed in universal education rather than educational opportunity only for males and for the elite. Those who contributed to this tradition tended to see childhood as a valuable time in its own right, not just as a preparation for adulthood.

The humanistic tradition was slow to be accepted, particularly during the lifetimes of the people we discuss here. Although their ideas were sometimes influential, they were often regarded as radical and treated with suspicion and hostility. Although there have been few times and places in history where the majority of practice in teaching young children was based on the ideas we discuss here, we can look back today and see that their influence has been immense in the United States and in many other parts of the world.

In order to put our historical discussion into perspective, it helps to realize that today's concept of childhood is relatively new. Until recently children had little status and virtually no rights. In ancient Greece, infanticide was accepted. Child selling was a common practice throughout the Roman empire. The Christian church condemned infanticide on the basis that every child possesses a soul, but its concept of original sin led to the interpretation of normal childhood playfulness as the work of the devil. During the Middle Ages, high mortality rates contributed to an indifferent attitude toward young children. Once children were past infancy and no longer needed constant care, they were expected to work and behave like adults. This is evident in the portrayal of children as miniature adults in the art of this period (Aries 1962).

A specialized field of early childhood education could not arise until the concept of childhood as a unique period of development emerged in the sixteenth and seventeenth centuries. Aries (1962) describes two views of childhood that date from this period. The first is that the child under seven was a source of amusement, to be fussed over and coddled. The second view, that children are vulnerable and in need of protection and education, is the link with the early education field today. By the eighteenth century, the idea was advanced that the obligations between children and parents did not rest solely on the children—parents had duties to their children as well. We know, however, that parental cruelty and child labor continued to occur.

Reflect and write about . . .

why history is important

Can you think of any ways that the history of early childhood education and care influenced your family or your life? Reflect on why it might be helpful for you to know about the history of early childhood education and policies affecting young children and their families.

BEGINNINGS OF THE FIELD OF EARLY CHILDHOOD EDUCATION AND CARE

Some notable people in history have significantly shaped the ideas that have guided the evolution of the field of early childhood education and care. The philosophers, religious leaders, scholars, and educators we discuss in this section had an influence on the field, though a number of them addressed education in general, rather than the education of young children in particular.

Ancient Greece and Rome

Our Western tradition of education can be traced back to ancient Greece where education was extolled as the means by which an "ideal state" could be realized. The education of young children was considered important to the achievement of that goal. Later in Rome,

the state subsidized an educational system, establishing secondary schools throughout the empire.

Many educational historians trace the humanistic tradition in education back to ancient Greece and to the ideas of Plato (428–348 B.C.) and Aristotle (384–322 B.C.). Plato was concerned with creating a society in which good people followed good laws and with the development of an ethical and reasonable ruling class. Plato advocated the use of games and structured play, was against the use of corporal punishment, and believed that boys and girls should receive the same training. For Aristotle the aims of education were to instill character and to make virtuous people. He believed that virtue would develop when children had the habits of virtue instilled in them. Both Plato and Aristotle recognized the importance of beginning education with young children, saw human beings as essentially good, emphasized the development of mind and body, and valued children's play.

In both Greece and Rome, play was considered a worthwhile activity. Structured physical play in the form of games and gymnastics began in childhood and continued to be important as recreation for adult men. The free play of young children was viewed as necessary and a way of learning. Plato recommended that adults observe children's play and games to gain better understanding of them; he also suggested gathering together all of the village children between the ages of three and six for group play under adult supervision. In Rome a similar view was held by Quintilian (A.D. 35–95), who believed that teachers could use play to help children develop intellectually (Caplan and Caplan 1974). After the fall of the Roman Empire, play seems to have been regarded as somehow sinful. Not until after the Renaissance was it again recognized and valued.

The Medieval Era, the Renaissance, and the Reformation

What formal education there was in the early medieval era (A.D. 500 to approximately A.D. 1500) was under the control of the Catholic church and generally restricted to boys and young men who aspired to the religious life. The children of the aristocracy learned courtly behaviors while children of peasants and artisans were educated through the apprenticeship system.

During the Renaissance period in Europe (which began in Italy in the 1400s and moved westward until the early 1600s) cities began to grow and to become powerful centers for trade and for the arts. Attention turned from the church to the individual and the arts, and there was a revival of interest in classical learning (Gutek 1972).

In fifteenth- and sixteenth-century Europe, religious reform was tied to new ideas about education. Martin Luther (1483–1546), the religious leader of the Renaissance whose work led to the Reformation, was a strong advocate of universal education. He believed that for people to take responsibility for their own salvation, they needed to read and understand the Bible for themselves. Luther believed that schools should develop the intellectual, religious, physical, emotional, and social qualities of children. An extensive school system was developed in Germany in response to Luther's views, but his goals of universal education did not become reality until nineteenth-century America.

Born and raised in what is now the Czech Republic, John Amos Comenius (1592–1670) was a bishop in the Protestant Moravian Church. Comenius wrote about education, developed teaching methods that anticipated elements of modern early childhood education, and produced some of the earliest materials for teaching children. His work was well received in Europe, where he consulted with governments and his books were widely translated. Like Luther, he believed in universal education. He saw all people as being equal before God and believed, therefore, that all individuals, rich or poor, common or noble, male or female, were entitled to the same education. Comenius believed that after the age of six children should attend schools taught in their native languages, not in Latin. These schools prepared them for life and for further education.

Long before the development of modern theories of child development, Comenius wrote about young children and how they learned. He believed that language was the foundation for later learning and designed programs for language and concept acquisition that were intended to begin in infancy and carry on through later childhood (Gutek 1972). Schooling for the youngest began in the maternal school, the "school of the mother's knee." The mother attended to her child's physical needs and encouraged play. She might show the child a book designed by Comenius that had woodcuts illustrating words and concepts (considered to be the first picture book). Comenius is regarded as the first advocate of children's play during that period. He encouraged classroom use of puzzles and other concrete objects as learning tools. Contemporary evolution of these practices can be seen in the ideas that children learn best when knowledge is personally relevant and that concrete experiences must precede abstract tasks. These are important in what we refer to today as *developmentally appropriate practice.*

After the Reformation, schooling was gradually substituted for apprenticeship as the primary vehicle for educating the young. Schools established under civil or church auspices enabled primary-aged children to learn to read and write in Latin. Charity schools for five-through eleven-year-old children were founded by churches to teach reading, writing, and arithmetic in local languages.

The Enlightenment

The Enlightenment refers to the spirit of the times in the late seventeenth and eighteenth centuries in Europe and North America. This period was characterized by a movement away from the influence of the church to a more humanistic view of life. Striving toward perfection through acquisition of knowledge became a major theme of the period. There was a renewal of interest in the writings and ideals of ancient Greece and Rome, which appeared in the courses of study for children of the upper classes (Williams 1993).

John Locke (1632–1704), academic, doctor, philosopher, and political theorist, was an influential thinker during the Enlightenment. He put forth the theory, based on his medical knowledge, experience, and emerging philosophy of human understanding, that the child comes into the world with a mind like a blank slate *(tabula rasa);* all knowledge is received through the senses and is converted to understanding by the application of reason. This view was in direct contradiction to the opinion, generally held during his time, that people entered the world with some aspects of their character already formed. Locke's belief in the importance of "nurture" over "nature" in determining the direction of human development led him to emphasize the influence of early training and education and to advocate for changes in parental care and education of children. He believed that infants should not be restricted by the common practice of swaddling them in tight strips of cloth, that young children should not be restrained from physical exploration, and that gentle forms of discipline rather than corporal punishment should be used from the time a child is young. Locke believed that respectful, loving relationships are the best way for parents and teachers to inspire the child to imitate their examples and that learning should never become a task imposed on the child. Locke's ideas anticipated the modern notion of the role of education in shaping human possibilities as well as the development of behaviorist psychology (Cleverley and Phillips 1986; Weber 1984).

Jean Jacques Rousseau (1712–1778), French philosopher, writer, and social theorist, eloquently challenged the prevalent view of his time that children came into the world with original sin and needed to establish habits of obedience, even if this required harsh treatment. Rousseau did not believe that people were born evil, but rather that their inherent good was spoiled by civilization. In his famous novel *Emile,* Rousseau presented his view that innate goodness will flower when people are raised out of contact with corrupt society. Rousseau developed a stage theory of development and believed that education should begin at birth and continue into adulthood. He advocated basing educational practice on knowledge of the nature of the child, whose ways of learning are different from those of adults. Educational practice, according to Rousseau, should be based on the knowledge that children learn best from direct experience and exploration of the environment. He envisioned children learning through their own natural, undirected play, free of adult interference and guidance. He encouraged parents and educators to express their confidence in the natural growth process by allowing for the interests and spontaneous activities of children. Rousseau's ideas—viewed as radical in his time, as well as by many in ours—had tremendous impact on the educators who followed and anticipated later research on developmental stages.

The Nineteenth Century

During the nineteenth century, national school systems were evolving in Europe, and the beginnings of public education were underway in the United States. New theories of education had widespread impact. Educational theorists and reformers Johann Pestalozzi and Robert Owen were directly involved in the education of young children, and both have had a strong influence on contemporary educational practice. These men were idealists, deeply humanitarian in their viewpoint, and concerned with social reform as it affected the poor.

Early childhood education as a distinct discipline had its beginning with Johann Pestalozzi (1746–1827), a Swiss educator who had been influenced by the views of Rousseau. His ideas laid the foundation for the reform of nineteenth-century education and had a strong impact on development of progressive education in the United States and Europe. Like Luther and Comenius before him, Pestalozzi believed that all children had the right to an education and the capacity to profit from it. He devoted his life to education, particularly for the orphaned and poor, and established several schools in which his ideas could be implemented. He believed that education could help to awake the potential of each child and could thereby lead to social reform. He wrote that the first year of life was the most important in the child's development. He suggested that instruction be adapted to each child's interests, abilities, and stage of development. He rejected the practice of memorization and advocated sensory exploration and observation as the basis of learning. The learning experiences he designed were sequenced from concrete to abstract. He believed that children learned through self-discovery and could pace their own learning. Pestalozzi was also concerned with teaching human relationships. He wrote, "My one aim was to . . . awaken a feeling of brotherhood . . . make them affectionate, just and considerate" (Braun and Edwards 1972, 52).

Welsh industrialist and social reformer Robert Owen (1771–1858) was a disciple of Pestalozzi. Owen became concerned with the condition of families who worked in the cotton mills during the Industrial Revolution. He abolished child labor in his textile factory and

worked for reforms in labor practices and the establishment of schools to improve the lives of children who labored in the mills for long hours from the age of six.

Owen believed that education, starting with the very young and combined with an environment that allowed people to live by the principal of mutual consideration, could transform the nature of people and society. His infant school, the first in England for children three to ten years of age, offered a nurturing and emotionally secure setting. Owen did not believe in pressuring children to learn or in punishing them; rather, he felt that the natural consequences of their actions would teach children right from wrong. Sensory learning, stories, singing, dance, nature study, and physical exercise were included in the school program.

Owen's ideas were considered extreme in his time, and his schools did not have lasting success in England. However, many of the practices originating in them can still be found in today's early childhood programs. These include periods of time during which children choose their activities, emphasis on a caring and nonpunitive teacher, and the use of spontaneous play as a vehicle for learning.

Table 2.1 summarizes the important ideas presented by these important theorists.

MAJOR INFLUENCES ON TODAY'S PROGRAMS

Some of the major innovations in education that occurred around the turn of the century have had a major impact on the nature of the field of early childhood education and care today. These approaches originated in different places and in response to different societal and educational concerns. They share, however, the caring and respectful attitude toward children that characterized the reformers we have just described. These approaches include the kindergarten created in Germany by Friedrich Froebel, progressive education in the United States represented by the ideas of educator/philosopher John Dewey, the nursery school founded by the McMillan sisters in England, and the Montessori method developed by Italian physician Maria Montessori.

The Kindergarten

Friedrich Wilhelm Froebel (1783–1852) established the first kindergarten program in Germany in 1837. Before becoming interested in education he studied mathematics, philosophy, and sciences and was trained as an architect. After working in a number of different settings, he discovered that he had a talent for teaching and chose to develop his skills by studying with Pestalozzi and working in one of his schools. After further study in sciences and linguistics, Froebel devoted his life to education. He founded several innovative schools and directed an orphanage. Over the years he developed a philosophy of education and a program for four- to six-year-olds that he envisioned as a transition between home and school and between infancy and childhood. Because it was intended to be a place where children were nurtured and protected from outside influences, as plants might be in a garden, he called his school *kinder* (child) *garten* (garden). We

TABLE 2.1

Some historical ideas influencing early education and care

Time Period	Key Figures	Influential Ideas and Practices
Ancient Greece and Rome	Plato Aristotle	• Education should begin with young children. • Human beings are essentially good. • Both boys and girls should be educated. • Development of mind and body are both important. • Play is a valuable tool for learning.
Reformation	Martin Luther	• Education should be for all children. • Individual literacy is important. • All aspects of development are important.
	John Amos Comenius	• Education should be universal. • Language development is important. • Education should begin in infancy. • Children learn through play. • The use of concrete objects should precede abstract tasks. • Schooling should be conducted in the child's native language. • The mother has a role in educating the young child. • Knowledge should be personally relevant.
Age of Enlightenment	John Locke	• Children learn through their senses. • "Nurture" is more important than "nature." • Respectful relationships are important in learning. • Children should be allowed freedom of movement. • Learning should not be imposed on children.
	Jean Jacques Rousseau	• People are inherently good. • Children go through developmental stages. • Learning should begin at birth and continue throughout life. • Children's thinking is different than that of adults. • Education should be based on knowledge of the nature of the child. • Children learn best from direct experience. • Education should allow for play and the child's spontaneous interests.
The Nineteenth Century	Johann Pestalozzi	• Education should be universal. • Education can awaken child's potential. • Education can lead to social reform. • The first year of life is the most important in children's development. • Instruction should be adapted to children's interests, abilities, and stage of development. • Sensory exploration and observation are the basis for learning. • Learning experiences should be designed sequentially so that they increase in level of complexity. • Children can pace their own learning. • Social relationships are important in children's learning.
	Robert Owen	• Children should have choice in their educational experiences. • Teachers should be caring and non-punitive. • Spontaneous play is an important vehicle for learning.

still use his term to describe programs for five-year-olds in the United States.

Like Comenius, Rousseau, and Pestalozzi, Froebel believed that children were social beings, that activity was the basis for knowing, and that play was an essential part of the educational process. Froebel, a deeply religious man, was particularly concerned with the education of children three through six and with the mother's relationship to the infant and the very young child. He believed that the education of young children should differ in content and teaching methods from that of older children, and he wanted children to have the opportunity to develop those positive impulses that came from within.

Children's play was channeled by the teacher, who carefully presented special materials and activities designed by Froebel to enhance their sensory and spiritual development. The materials, called *gifts,* included yarn balls, blocks, wooden tablets, geometric shapes, and natural objects. Among the gifts were the first wooden blocks used as tools for children's learning. These were intended to encourage discovery and manipulation and to lead children to an appreciation for people's unity with God. Handwork activities, called *occupations,* included molding, cutting, folding, bead stringing, and embroidery, which were intended to foster discovery, inventiveness, and skill. Songs and fingerplays (many written by Froebel himself), stories, and games were selected to encourage learning the spiritual values underlying the program. Froebel held that education must begin with the concrete and move to greater abstraction and that perceptual development precedes thinking skills.

Having conceived of the kindergarten as a nurturing place for the cultivation of children's natural goodness and an extension of the home, Froebel proposed training young women as kindergarten teachers. Educators from Europe and the United States studied his methods and returned to their homes to begin

kindergartens. Graduates of his teacher training institute who brought the ideals and practices of the Froebelian kindergarten to the United States included Elizabeth Peabody and Susan Blow.

The early American kindergartens (the first founded in 1855) were private ventures, often established in homes and taught in German by teachers who had studied with Froebel. Elizabeth Peabody founded the first English-speaking kindergarten in Boston in 1860. Later, after studying with Froebel's disciples in Germany, she founded the first kindergarten teacher training program in the United States. She was very influential in winning public support for kindergartens in the United States. The first publicly supported kindergarten was opened in St. Louis in 1873 and was followed by rapid expansion of the kindergarten movement between 1880 and 1900.

Two aspects of the society of that time appear to have contributed to the rapid growth of the kindergarten. The first was the belief that because children were inherently good, they required a nurturing and benevolent environment in their early years. The second, concern for the social problems created by the large influx of poor immigrants, gave rise to the field of philanthropic social work. Mission kindergartens for underprivileged children were established by social workers with the expectation that if children were taught the appropriate values and behaviors, they and their families would be more successful in assimilating into American society.

These early kindergartens, based on Froebel's approach, emphasized the importance of cleanliness and courtesy, the development of manual skills, physical activity, and preparation for later schooling. Kindergarten children were not made to sit still, memorize, and recite as older children were. The teacher's role was not that of taskmaster, but of affectionate leader.

Froebel was clearly the father of the modern kindergarten. His ideas dominated the kindergarten movement in the United States until they were challenged by progressive education at the beginning of the century. The program that he created represented a radical departure from the schools of his day. Although it allowed children to learn through play, it was far more structured than the individualized, free-play kindergarten advocated by the progressives, and it little resembled what we consider to be developmentally appropriate practice today. It could, however, be considered as the beginning of early childhood education as it is practiced today in much of the world, and it had a profound influence (Weber 1969; Williams 1993).

The Evolution of the Kindergarten

A period of ferment caused by conflicting philosophies began in the kindergarten movement in the 1890s and lasted for more than twenty years. The supporters of Froebelian principles and practices were challenged by the progressive educators who wanted to redesign the kindergarten to reflect their beliefs about education. By 1920, the conservative camp had yielded. The reformed kindergarten curriculum reflected many of Froebel's original ideas but added a new emphasis on free play, social interaction, art, music, nature study, and excursions. New unstructured materials, including large blocks and doll houses, encouraged children's inventive play. Books and songs reflected children's interests, rather than teaching a message, and activities were inspired by important here-and-now events in the children's daily lives.

As kindergartens gradually moved into public schools, they met with grudging acceptance. The rigid atmosphere of the traditional primary schools, with their emphasis on drill and skill development, was sharply contrasted to the more child-centered approach of kindergartens that valued the development of the whole child. However, the gap gradually narrowed. Many kindergarten activities found their way into the primary grades even as primary activities filtered down into the kindergarten.

Beginning in the 1920s, kindergarten teachers in public schools were urged to prepare children for reading. The emphasis on "readiness," matching the child's developmental stage with the school's demands, has been found in kindergartens since that time and has led to two very different educational approaches, which can still be seen in today's kindergartens.

The first viewpoint focuses on the developmental needs of the children. Educators who hold this view believe that literacy will emerge as children have many meaningful experiences with reading and writing. These programs provide an environment that is rich in print, opportunities for oral language throughout the day, and experiences with good children's literature. They also offer many opportunities for children to learn through play in a prepared learning environment.

The opposing viewpoint is that the role of the kindergarten is to prepare five-year-olds for the expectations of the next grades and for successful performance on standardized tests. These programs tend to use teaching techniques that are more appropriate for older children. They set aside time each day for formal instruction in the "basics." They tend to include drill on skills, phonics, and basal readers and the use of worksheets.

The kindergarten curriculum continues to be an arena of educational ferment, caught between the conflicting demands of elementary educators and administrators for teaching skills and accountability and of early childhood specialists for an approach based on knowledge of how children learn.

The first professional associations concerned with promoting early childhood education in the United States grew out of the kindergarten movement. These included the American

Froebel Union, established by Elizabeth Peabody in 1878; the International Kindergarten Union (IKU), begun in 1892 and merged with the National Council of Primary Education in 1930 to become the Association for Childhood Education (ACED), still an active organization today; and the National Kindergarten Association (NKA), founded in 1909 and active in working for universal acceptance of the kindergarten until it was phased out in 1976 (Williams 1993).

Progressive Education

Progressive education was part of the Progressive movement, begun in the nineteenth century to seek social and political reforms for political corruption, poverty, and other problems that resulted from industrialization. Progressives sought to use science and reason to better mankind. Progressive education evolved from a combination of the ideas of Rousseau and Pestalozzi and from nineteenth-century social reform movements (Williams 1993). The movement was based on its creators' desire for a "progressive" society where people could develop their full potential. Their goal was to improve society through fundamental changes in the schools. They attempted to transform dreary educational environments that offered a predetermined curriculum and skills learned by drill and recitation.

John Dewey (1859–1952), though not the founder of the movement, became its most influential spokesperson. Dewey taught high school before studying for a doctorate in philosophy. He then taught at the University of Chicago where he was instrumental in setting up a laboratory school where innovative educational ideas could be tried. Later he moved to Columbia University in New York where he continued to write about education and philosophy for the rest of his career.

Dewey believed that education should be viewed as the life of the child in the present and not only as preparation for the future. He stressed the importance of cooperation and problem solving. In Dewey's view, the school community offered children an opportunity to practice democratic ideals in a group situation and to learn through activities that were interesting and meaningful. Although early childhood programs at the University of Chicago laboratory school included some of the Froebelian kindergarten materials, they were used in very different ways. Dewey's approach emphasized greater freedom and spontaneity in play and involvement in the social life of the classroom instead of prestructured activities.

Progressive ideas about educational practice stressed the importance of: (1) learning through doing—through experiencing and experimenting in self-directed activities; (2) "teaching the whole child" (addressing physical, social, and emotional as well as intellectual development); (3) planning curriculum that is based on observation of children's interests and needs; and (4) the role of the teacher as guide and observer, not instructor and disciplinarian.

The ideas of progressive education combined with vigorous research interest in child development to trigger educational experimentation. In New York in 1916, Harriet Johnson, Caroline Pratt, and Lucy Sprague Mitchell organized the Bureau of Educational Experiments (known today as the Bank Street College of Education) as an agency for research on child development. Mitchell, a friend of Dewey and strong advocate of progressive education, directed Bank Street School and was influential in its evolution into a teacher training institution. She was deeply committed to the importance of children learning about their world through direct experience. Her book *Young Geographers* introduced the study of geography to young children through direct experiences in the community. This community study still character-izes the curriculum of Bank Street School. Caroline Pratt was responsible for the design of the wooden unit blocks, which are standard equipment in early childhood programs today.

Eventually progressive education came under fire from those who felt that students were not gaining sufficient mastery of basic school subjects. The movement had become associated with permissiveness, rather than with its guiding principles that curriculum must challenge children intellectually and help them to develop self-direction and responsibility. The progressive influence on American education waned after 1950 as teacher-directed, skill-based education again gained prevalence.

While progressive education as a dominant influence was phased out of most American schools, its impact is still felt. It has had a strong influence on today's kindergartens and nursery schools, which have remained more closely allied ideologically with Dewey than with more traditional academically oriented schools. Also, a number of highly respected private schools continue to reflect the philosophy of progressive education, including the Bank Street Children's School and College and the City and Country School in New York City, which evolved from the Bureau of Educational Experiments.

These programs continue to base practice on the progressive beliefs that curriculum should be integrated instead of based on distinct subject areas, that children should be active learners who have many opportunities to pursue their own interests as they gain understanding of their world, and that classrooms are places where children can live and learn democracy.

Many of the ideas of the progressive movement had a rebirth and reincarnation in England in the mid-1960s in state-supported schools for five- to eight-year-olds. These programs, called *infant schools,* combined Dewey's philosophy with the newly influential views regarding child development of Swiss Psychologist Jean Piaget.

In British infant schools young children learned from active involvement in tasks or projects. Interestingly enough, American educators who heard about these "innovative" programs began to visit England in the late 1960s and 1970s to observe and write about this new approach. Soon its influence began to be felt in some American schools, which returned to a more informal and child-centered curriculum. Hence Dewey's ideas had come back to their point of origin. It appears that they are revisited each time people become concerned about placing the child at the center of the educational process. In the 1970s and early 1980s a wave of concern with the "basics" led to the return of traditional academic instruction. But the late 1980s and the first part of the 1990s have seen efforts by early childhood educators to combine progressive ideas about children and learning with current knowledge of growth and development into what is now called *developmentally appropriate practice*. John Dewey's legacy continues to be felt in American education.

The Nursery School

Margaret McMillan (1860–1931) and her sister Rachel were raised in the United States and Scotland and later moved to England. They were social reformers who spent their lives trying to address the problems of poverty brought about by the Industrial Revolution. The McMillan sisters established the first open-air, play-oriented nursery school in England in 1911 as their response to health problems they witnessed in children of poor communities. They called their new program a *nursery school* to show that they were concerned with care and nurture *and* learning. They recognized that many poor children in England needed education and care in their first few years to give them a good foundation for later life. The nursery school was designed to identify and prevent health problems and to enhance children's physical and mental development, before they entered formal schooling. More than eighty

years later, programs like Head Start exemplify this same purpose.

The McMillans were concerned with basing education on the child's "sense of wonder" and believed that teachers must know what attracts and engages children (Williams 1993). In providing for children's physical needs they strongly emphasized the value of active outdoor work and play. Health and nutrition, perceptual-motor skills, and the development of imagination were stressed. The teacher's role was both to nurture and to informally teach children, using a planned learning environment (McMillan 1919). The nursery school included materials for sensory development, creative expression, gardening, nature study, and sand-box play. The work of the McMillans, particularly that of Margaret who lived the longest, exerted great influence on British, and later on American, early childhood education.

At the same time that kindergartens were gaining hold in the United States, the nursery school movement began to appear as another effort to meet the needs of young children. American nursery schools were not only directly influenced by the English nursery school, but also by Sigmund Freud's ideas about human development and Dewey's and other progressive educators' ideas about education.

One of the first nursery schools in the United States was the City and Country School, established in New York City in 1913 by Caroline Pratt. In 1916, the Bureau of Educational Experiments opened its laboratory nursery school, under the direction of Harriet Johnson. In the 1920s, a number of other laboratory nursery schools were established in the United States, including one organized by Patty Smith Hill at Columbia University Teachers College in New York City and the Ruggles Street Nursery School (1922) and Training Center (1924) in Roxbury, Massachusetts, which were directed by Abigail Eliot, who had studied with Margaret McMillan in England. Unlike most laboratory nursery schools, which served middle-class children, the Ruggles St. School followed the example of the McMillans' school by providing a full-day program for children and parents in a low-income neighborhood.

Cooperative nursery schools, formed by educated middle-class parents, first began in 1915 and spread rapidly. Also founded during this period were prominent child-study institutions with laboratory schools: Yale University's Clinic of Child Development in 1911, the Iowa Child Welfare Research Station in 1917, and the Merrill-Palmer Institute in Detroit in 1922. During the 1920s and 1930s, nursery schools were established in many college home economics departments to train future homemakers and to serve as centers for child development research.

Nursery schools were multidisciplinary in orientation, because the early pioneers came from a number of fields, including nursing, social work, medicine, psychology, and education—hence the whole-child orientation described in this book. The earliest nursery schools emphasized children's social, emotional, and physical development. The intellect received less attention, because of the common belief that significant cognitive development did not occur until children entered school at the age of six. In the early nursery schools the emphasis was on social and emotional development. Children played freely indoors and outdoors in an environment that was especially designed for them.

The early nursery schools and today's early childhood education and care programs are guided by similar views of children and learning and are characterized by similar educational practices. In both, children are seen as always growing, changing, experiencing, and learning through interactions with people and with the environment. The role of the school is to keep the paths of exploration open, so that children can develop in their own ways. The daily schedule is characterized by large time blocks in which children are free to choose activities and engage in them for long periods of time. The classroom is divided into activity areas,

typically those for block construction, dramatic play, art, water play, sand play, science, math, and reading. The role of the teacher is to create an environment that facilitates learning. Teachers also support social and emotional development by encouraging children to verbalize their feelings. Child management is carried out whenever possible by problem solving and by modifying the environment, rather than by imposing adult power.

In response to new information about human intellectual development and the needs of low income children, the traditional nursery school has continued to evolve, especially in recognition of the important cognitive development that occurs in early childhood. What remains constant is the insistence that the child is a person whose development can benefit by play in a carefully designed learning environment under the guidance of a caring and sensitive teacher. Today the terms *nursery school, preschool,* and *child development center* are generally used in the United States to describe programs that evolved from the legacy of the McMillan nursery school.

Concern with implementation and expansion of nursery school education led to the development of a professional organization for nursery educators. The emphasis was on programs that supported development of the "whole child." Patty Smith Hill, at Columbia University's Teachers College, founded the National Association for Nursery Education (NANE) in 1926. This organization has evolved into a very influential organization, the National Association for the Education of Young Children (NAEYC). See Chapter Three for information about its current status and projects.

The Montessori Method

Maria Montessori (1870–1952) overcame the opposition of her family and her society to become, in 1896, the first woman in Italy to receive a medical degree. Early in her medical career she devised successful approaches for working with retarded children previously regarded as incapable of learning. In 1907 she founded the *Casa Dei Bambini* (Children's House) in Rome, where she explored the applicability of her educational methods to normal children. The program she designed was based on her observation of young children and how they learned. She reached the conclusion that intelligence was not fixed and could be stimulated or stifled by the child's experiences. Further, she believed that children learn best through their own direct sensory experience of the world. Montessori was undoubtedly influenced by the work of Pestalozzi, Froebel, and Freud, but the foundation for her interest in education was her study of the writings of French physicians Seguin and Itard on their humane methods for educating retarded children. Although Montessori's training was in medicine, the contributions she made to education have been her lasting legacy.

Montessori was interested in the first years of life and believed that children went through *sensitive periods* during which they had interest and capacity for the development of particular knowledge and/or skills. She believed that children had an inherent desire to explore and understand the world in which they lived. She saw these young explorers as self-motivated and able to seek out the kinds of experiences and knowledge most appropriate for their stage of development. Concerned with preserving the dignity of the child, she valued the development of independence and productivity.

The classroom learning environment designed by Montessori was attractive and equipped with child-sized, movable furniture. Montessori stressed the importance of an orderly environment that helps children to focus on their learning and develop the ability to concentrate. The classrooms were equipped with *didactic materials* created by Montessori to help children develop their senses and learn concepts. These carefully crafted materials are still the basis of the curriculum in a Montessori school. They are treated with care and respect and are displayed on open shelves so children can use them independently. The materials are graded in difficulty, sequenced from known to unknown and from concrete to abstract. Each concept to be taught is isolated from other concepts that might be confusing or distracting. For example, if the child is learning the concept of shape, the materials will be of uniform size and color so that the attribute of shape can be seen readily. Materials are also designed to have immediate, self-correcting feedback, so children know if they have successfully completed a task.

In a Montessori classroom, children learn from firsthand experience—by observing and by doing. Practical life experiences such as buttoning, zipping, cutting, and gardening enable children to care for themselves and the environment while building skills that will be useful throughout their lives. All learning in a Montessori classroom is cumulative. Each activity paves the way to future, more complex activities. Activities are organized primarily for individual work, rather than group interaction. Children move freely about the classroom and choose their own activities. The focus of the Montessori is on the development of senses and concepts.

Montessori went beyond philosophy and guidance in the development of her method. She carefully prescribed the teaching techniques and materials for her schools. The role of the teacher was to observe and direct children's learning rather than to instruct; hence, the term used by Montessori was *directress*.

Montessori's schools were successful in Italy and the Netherlands (where she had her headquarters for many years), and they eventually spread throughout the world. Although there have been private Montessori schools in the United States since 1915, the approach was not originally embraced with the same enthusiasm as it was in other countries. Today there are many private Montessori schools in the United States, and the approach is also found in some public schools.

Montessori education has been quite controversial in the United States, possibly because it differed from the mainstream of nursery education in the individualized nature of instruction. Most Montessori programs do not allow for a great deal of social interaction or language development, because classrooms have had little or no provision for children's self-expression or for the development of creativity and in the arts or in the use of materials. Montessori schools are similar to the nursery schools in that children are viewed as inquisitive, self-motivated learners, capable of selecting activities appropriate for their current needs and developmental stage. Montessori was an important educational innovator, and a number of her ideas—such as the provision of a child-size environment and the use of sensory materials—have found their way into most contemporary early childhood programs.

There are two major professional associations concerned with implementing Montessori programs, training teachers, and accrediting schools and teachers. One is the original organization, Association Montessori Internationale (AMI), with headquarters in the Netherlands; the other is the American Montessori Society (AMS), founded in 1956 to adapt Montessori methods to an American style of working with children.

Table 2.2 summarizes the ideas of these important theorists.

Origins of Child Care in the United States

Another historical strand that helps us to understand the nature of today's early childhood education and care programs relates to the provision of care for the children of working parents. The day nursery movement of the nineteenth century served the most desperately needy of the great waves of immigration. By providing care for immigrant children, these privately run programs enabled parents employed in urban factories to keep their families

together. Personnel in the day nurseries were largely untrained, worked long hours with very high child-adult ratios, and provided minimal care for children. In the eyes of society, the great virtue of the day nursery was that the children served were given a reprieve from even more harmful environments. These programs were primarily concerned with the health of children, the daily bath being a major event, and not with more lofty educational goals. Many day nurseries provided quite comprehensive services with long hours of operation, infant care, family education and training programs, and even counseling.

The social climate of the early twentieth century in the United States was not supportive of publicly funded child-care programs. The prevalent view was that mothers should be at home caring for their children. Child-care services were permissible only as a temporary response to families in need of aid or during times of national political or economic crisis. Child care was not viewed as a basic social welfare service that government should help provide.

TABLE 2.2

Four programs that have significantly influenced current practice

Approach	Key Figures	Goals	Significant Ideas	Program/Curriculum
The Kindergarten	Friedrich Froebel (Germany)	• Appreciation of unity with God.	• Activity is the basis for knowing. • Play is an essential part of the educational process. • The role of the teacher is to support the development of positive impulses in children. • Teaching of young children should differ in content and process from teaching older children. • The teacher is an affectionate leader.	• The kindergarten. • Teaching materials called *gifts* and *occupations* for sensory and spiritual development. • Kindergarten teacher preparation program.
Progressive Education	John Dewey and early childhood educators Lucy Sprague Mitchell, Harriet Johnson, Caroline Pratt (United States)	• Improve society through schooling. • Help people to develop their full potential. • Prepare citizens to live in a democratic society.	• Education is the life of the child in the present, not just preparation for the future. • Cooperation and problem solving are important aspects of the curriculum. • Children learn through doing. • Education should concern itself with social, emotional, intellectual, and physical development. • The role of the teacher is to be a guide.	• Involvement in the social life of the classroom. • Curriculum based on interests and needs of the children. • Projects, active exploration at the core of the curriculum. • Unit blocks • The Community as a source of curriculum.
The Nursery School	Margaret and Rachel McMillan (England)	• To identify and prevent health problems. • To prepare low income children to enter formal schooling.	• It is important to stimulate the child's sense of wonder and imagination. • The teacher's role is to nurture and teach informally. • Outdoor work and play are important.	• Play in a planned learning environment. • Nutrition, gardening, creative expression, sand box.
The Montessori Method	Dr. Maria Montessori (Italy)	• Development of independence and-productivity. • Preserving dignity of child.	• Intelligence can be stimulated by experience. • Children learn best through sensory exploration. • There are sensitive periods for the development of skills. • Children are self-motivated. • Children seek out appropriate learning experiences. • The role of the teacher is to observe and direct learning. • Learning is sequential.	• Child-oriented learning environment. • Children choose activities. • Self-correcting, sequenced didactic materials. • Materials teach practical life activities and academic subjects. • Emphasis on individual work.

During the Depression in the 1930s, federal child-care centers, called Emergency Nursery Schools, were established to provide relief work for teachers, custodians, cooks, nurses, and others who needed employment. These programs were phased out as the Depression ended. Again, during World War II, the United States government became reinvolved in the business of sponsoring child care. This time, the purpose was to meet the needs of the large numbers of women employed in defense plants. Under the Lanham Act (1942–1946), federally funded child-care centers served approximately 600,000 children in forty-one states.

Employer-sponsored child care, which was common in Europe, also emerged in response to the demand for women as workers during World War II. Most notable were the two centers run by Kaiser shipyards in Portland, Oregon. The Kaiser Centers were outstanding for their comprehensive, high quality services made available to employees with children ages eighteen months to six years old.

Child-care services under government and industry sponsorship were contingent on a state of emergency and were soon phased out. They had been a temporary measure, intended only to support the war effort. Peace heralded a return to the image of the "traditional family," with mothers in the home, tending to their children. Of course, many mothers did not dutifully return home, but continued their employment.

As child-care facilities either closed or were reduced to prewar levels, these employed mothers had limited options for child care. A patchwork of private arrangements was the common solution. The California Children's Centers were among the few survivors of the Lanham Act programs. With state funding, they continue today to serve the children of employed parents and low income, full-time students.

The postwar attitude toward women's appropriate role as homemaker, combined with the belief that children of employed mothers suffered from a lack of maternal care, gave strength to the contention that child care was at best unnecessary and at worst harmful to children. Between 1950 and 1965, the need for child care received little attention or support. Meanwhile, family life in America started to undergo major changes. The extended family system began to disintegrate as family mobility increased and the divorce rate soared. More and more women entered the workforce out of financial necessity or because of a desire to find meaningful work outside the home. Single parents, if employed, could no longer assume complete responsibility for their young children, but had to share this responsibility with other caregivers, usually non-relatives.

Today's early childhood education and care programs grow out of the two historical developments we have just described—the nursery school, which addressed the developmental needs of young children, and the day

---

Reflect and write about . . .

your experience of the historical influences

How did the programs that you attended as a child, observed, or taught in seem to reflect the historical influences described in this chapter? To which of the programs were they similar? How were they different from the programs described?

nursery, which provided care for children while their parents were working.

PUBLIC POLICY AND CHILD CARE

The preceding review of historical antecedents of early childhood education and care gives us some insights into the origins and content of today's programs. But if we are to understand the challenges that face the field today, we need to address the question of who is responsible for meeting the needs of young children and their families. In the United States, as in many other places in the world, this issue has been, and continues to be, the subject of great debate. Public policy is government action that reflects values and concerns of the citizens. Countries differ tremendously in their policies regarding which needs of children and their families should be met by government resources and which by private means. Some have overall policy regarding programs and services, and others let them develop in patchwork fashion based on emerging needs.

In the United States it has been assumed historically that, barring disaster, families will care for their own children. Government involvement has generally been limited to the very neediest: care for orphans, protection for abused children, and food for the children of the poor. Churches, voluntary associations, and philanthropic organizations have also provided support and assistance.

Federal involvement in promoting the health, education, and welfare of children began with the creation of the Children's Bureau in 1912. Its charge was to investigate child health and labor, and its role was mainly to make investigations and report their findings. Since that time, the federal government established a Department of Health, Education, and Welfare in 1959 (now the Department of Health and Human Services). The Office of Child Development (now called the Administration for Children, Youth, and Families) was begun in 1969 as an agency of the Department of Health, Education, and Welfare. These agencies have been involved in providing welfare to families unable to care for their own children, health and nutrition programs, child abuse prevention, and educational programs for low income children. Sometimes they have supported care for children whose parents needed to work outside the home.

The 1960s and early 1970s were a period of national concern with social reform. During this period there was a swell of interest in early education as a public-policy issue. New research in child development, combined with a desire to counteract the effects of poverty on young children, led to the creation of a federally funded education program called Project Head Start. It was the first federally funded program to focus on the development of the child, rather than on providing a service for employed parents. During the rest of the 1970s, attempts to pass federal child-care legislation

---

Reflect and write about . . .

whose responsibility is early education and care?

Who do you think should be responsible for child care? Is it a family responsibility? A societal responsibility? Why? Would your family and friends agree with your view? What would be the view of most people in your community?

failed repeatedly because they were perceived as threatening the stability of the family. Direct federal support for early childhood programs was limited to Head Start.

In the 1980s, federal funding of early childhood programs mostly took the form of tax credits, an approach that was most beneficial to middle-class families. In the second half of the 1980s, the clamor for federal support of child-care programs resulted in numerous early childhood education and child-care bills being introduced into Congress, but none passed. In 1990 federal legislation supporting child care was finally passed; the specific bills will be described in Chapter Three.

Societal changes and major political events have a powerful influence on our views of the family and our attitudes toward children. There is a tendency for social and political trends to create pendulum swings of reaction and counterreaction in educational policies. The debate regarding government's role in services to children has centered around the question of whether intervention should occur only when the family is unable to meet children's basic needs, or whether there is a greater responsibility to see that the developmental needs of all children in society are met.

PUBLIC POLICY FOR SPECIAL POPULATIONS OF CHILDREN

Public policy and responsibility comes up again in relation to the provision of early childhood programs and services for children whose families have limited income and those who have physical, mental, or educational disabilities. Who is responsible for the education and care of these children? Over the last several decades government has taken an increasing responsibility for providing legislation and funding to assist in the education of these children.

Programs for Low Income Children

In the beginning of the twentieth century, educational programs for children in low socioeconomic groups existed in many American cities. These philanthropic kindergartens were intended to help children overcome the disadvantage of growing up in the slums by teaching them skills and middle-class values. When kindergartens became integrated into the free public school system, special attention to the educational needs of disadvantaged children was postponed until the 1960s.

During the 1960s, research by Jean Piaget, J. McVicker Hunt, and others began to dispel the widely accepted idea that intelligence was fixed and static and pointed to the importance of early experiences on later intellectual development. Researchers and educators suggested that planned intervention in the early years might enhance children's development, help them succeed in later schooling, and perhaps enable them to be more successful in their adult lives. Hence the idea that early childhood programs could help to ameliorate the effects of poverty became influential once again.

Given the surge of concern about the quality of American education in the 1950s and 1960s, the publicity given to this new child-development research meshed with the political climate in paving the way for a whole new era in early childhood education. President Johnson's concern with the plight of the underprivileged in America extended to an interest in the lost potential of those children disadvantaged by living in poverty. The Office of Economic Opportunity was formed, and the "War Against Poverty" was launched.

Head Start

Under the auspices of the Office of Economic Opportunity, an interdisciplinary panel representing the fields of pediatrics, education, child development, and social services was formed

Reflect and write about . . .

the early childhood programs you attended

What early childhood programs did you attend: nursery school/preschool, parent co-op, child-care center, Head Start, Montessori school, kindergarten, first grade? How did your family find that program for you? What do you remember doing? What historical influences do you think influenced your early childhood program?

and directed to develop a program to counter the effects of poverty on children. It was hoped that such a program would increase achievement and opportunities and give poor children a "head start." Project Head Start was unique in its focus on the total development of the child, its emphasis on strengthening the family, involvement of the community, and its provision of comprehensive services.

Head Start was begun in the summer of 1965 as a six-week demonstration project serving only children who would be starting school in the fall. It soon became clear that six weeks was not enough time to achieve the program's goals. In 1969 responsibility for Head Start's administration was transferred from the Office of Economic Opportunity to the Office of Child Development. Head Start today is a full-year program serving three- through six-year-old children.

Prior to Head Start, federal support for children's programs had been accomplished only when tied to a national emergency. The Head Start program represented a new view of child development as a valuable end in itself and an unprecedented mobilization of resources on behalf of children.

Although the results of early research studies on the effects of Head Start were mixed, later studies of children who participated demonstrate that the program has had a significant and lasting impact on cognitive develop-

ment, social behavior, and health of its participants and has benefited their families as well. Moreover, it has been demonstrated that the cost is more than compensated for in savings on later remedial education programs and correctional institutions (Lazar and Darlington 1983; McKey 1985; Schweinhardt and Weikart 1980).

The vision of changing children's achievement and attitudes has been realized for over ten million children who have been able to attend. Unfortunately, only a small percentage of the eligible children have been served, and the greater goal of diminishing the effects of poverty has yet to be achieved. In spite of these limitations, Head Start has caused educators and policy makers to recognize the value of comprehensive services for at-risk children and their families, has provided the impetus for a number of other valuable programs, and continues to be the beneficiary of public support and increased federal funding.

Follow Through

In 1968, the Office of Child Development of the Department of Health, Education, and Welfare authorized a study called Planned Variation to explore the impact of a variety of educational approaches in Head Start programs. A companion program, Follow Through, was introduced in 1969 by the United States Office of Education

to provide continuity in programs for children who had been enrolled in Head Start Planned Variation programs when they entered elementary school. Follow Through was designed to address the finding that test scores raised by children's Head Start experience dropped again after they entered the public schools. The research component was designed to study the effects of continuity in programming from preschool through third grade and to explore the effects of different program models on children's development.

Educational models representing a spectrum of approaches to early childhood education were developed by program sponsors from universities and educational research centers and implemented in selected communities. Models differed greatly in the learning

theories they drew from, their values, the role of the learning environment, the role of the teacher, and strategies for classroom management. Some programs, such as the Distar model developed by Carl Bereiter and Sigfried Englemann, featured high teacher direction and used behavior-modification techniques. Others, such as the Bank Street Model sponsored by Bank Street College and the Cognitively Oriented Curriculum developed by David Weikart and his colleagues in the High Scope Program in Michigan, stressed the role of the teacher in guiding children's interactions in a planned learning environment.

The Head Start portion of the study was phased out in 1973. And although funding for Follow Through was reduced over the years, it has continued into the 1990s in many of the original communities under the Division of Compensatory Education of the Office of Education. Although it was incorporated into the Chapter 1 Program in 1994 and the name Follow Through will no longer be used, there are many important lessons that have been learned over the years that will continue to impact on educational programs for low income children and their families.

Follow Through has demonstrated the effectiveness of comprehensive, well-designed educational approaches that include provision for systematic teacher education, involvement of families, and provision of health and social services. It has led to extensive curriculum development that has been widely disseminated and that has been adopted in school settings well beyond the original communities. We have also learned from the experiences of the Follow Through sponsors that translating theory into practice is not simple or automatic and that it is essential to build good working relationships with school systems, communities, and families. And Follow Through has led to expansion in our thinking about assessment from a focus on cognitive outcomes to a concern with measuring more divergent outcomes

53

and with documenting what is actually happening in classrooms.[1]

Programs for Children with Disabilities

Since the 1960s there has been growing recognition of the needs and rights of children with disabilities. Legislation and funding that support programs for these children has increased dramatically over the last two decades. The care and education of children with special needs is a field with its own history and traditions. The development of special education programs has been affected by the same social and political influences that have affected other early childhood programs. Today's emphasis on bringing children with special needs into the mainstream of society through placement in regular education classrooms has resulted in the gradual merging of two distinct approaches to education, special education and early childhood education, into a new field of early childhood special education (ECSE).

The challenge of providing education for all children, including those with disabilities, was first confronted in the early 1900s when compulsory school attendance laws were enacted. Public and private residential schools were established at that time for the severely handicapped. And special classes were set up in regular public schools when behavior problems arose as a result of educating children with special needs in regular classrooms.

From the 1920s to the 1960s, most children with disabilities were placed in special schools or segregated into classrooms in separate school buildings, far from classrooms and other activity centers. Usually only those children with mild disabilities who were considered "ready" for education were included in regular public school classes. Children with more severe and multiple handicaps were confined to institutions or residential schools.

The civil rights legislation of the early 1950s is often credited with providing the impetus for efforts to secure the rights of the handicapped in the United States. When the Supreme Court ruled that separate education for racial minorities could not be considered "equal," in the *Brown v. the Board of Education* decision in 1954, the groundwork was laid for the position that segregated schooling for any purpose was questionable.

In the mid-1960s, special education classes in the public schools became an issue of controversy. Some saw them as dumping grounds for problem children, including those who were culturally different, in which no real attempts were made to meet their social and educational needs. At this time, too, some educators began to question whether special education classes were the best approach. They suggested that children with disabilities of all kinds could learn better if they had daily contact with children in regular classroom settings. Adding to this ferment, parents who had banded together to lobby for special education legislation took their concerns to court. A number of significant court cases since the late 1960s affirmed the right of all children with disabilities, regardless of severity, to a public education (Noonan and McCormick 1993).

Preschool-aged children with disabilities were first served in demonstration programs in 1968 when Congress passed Public Law (P.L.) 90–538, the Handicapped Children's Early Education Assistance Act. Then in 1972, Head Start was mandated by P.L. 92–424 to reserve 10 percent of its enrollment for children with disabilities as a prerequisite for continued federal funding.

In 1975, the passage of P.L. 94–142, the Education for All Handicapped Children Act, required that all children with disabilities be provided with free, appropriate public education.

---

[1]We would like to thank Dr. Richard Feldman, Director of the Bank Street Follow Through Program, for sharing his views about the legacy of Follow Through.

In most states this legislation did not lead to the provision of free public programs for preschool-aged children with disabilities, even though small incentive grants were available for the development of these programs. Subsequent amendments to P.L. 94–142 have redefined the population to be served, specifically referring to children from birth through age eight. P.L. 98–199 (1983) and P.L. 99–457 (1986) offer financial assistance and technical assistance to school systems for programs for infants and toddlers with disabilities. These laws also emphasize the role of parents and families in making early intervention efforts work.

In the 1990s, early childhood special education has been implemented largely under the provisions of P.L. 101–476, the Individuals with Disabilities Education Act, which has replaced the 1975 Education for the Handicapped Act.

Increased attention and funding for early intervention over the last decade are a reflection of a considerable body of research, an improved level of public awareness, and advocacy efforts by many parents and professionals.

FINAL THOUGHTS

You are entering a field with a long history and a tradition of concern with the needs of children and their families. The pioneers in the field were often ahead of their time in their recognition that education had to address the "whole child," not just the intellect, and in their treatment of children in ways that were respectful and developmentally appropriate. These in- novators were aware of the role of play in learning. They advocated for universal educa- tion and recognized that the education of young children was a valuable strategy for min- imizing the effects of an impoverished back- ground. They were concerned with improving society and saw that the creation of a world that was caring and humane must begin with the children. These values of respect for chil- dren and development and the vision of a bet- ter, more humane world have been at the cen- ter of early childhood education and care since its beginning and have shaped the nature of the field today.

The philosophers and educators we have introduced in this chapter have influenced to- day's programs and policies effecting young children and their families. There has been slow progress over the years resulting in more humane and egalitarian treatment of young children and concern for their needs and those of their families. But much still needs to be done to educate the public and policy makers about the importance of the early years and the value of early childhood programs and ser- vices.

The philosophies and beliefs that have his- torically guided the field and many issues and questions which have arisen in the past con- tinue to be important today. The chapter which follows, The Field of Early Childhood Educa- tion and Care, will pick up some of the strands we have introduced here and will bring you up to date on the current status of the field and how it will impact on you as an early childhood professional.

PROJECTS

Write a Paper: Research one of the educators mentioned in the chapter. Write a paper explaining who the person was and how he or she influenced the field of early childhood education. Be sure to include your thoughts about what you learned.

Write a Review: Read a biography or autobiography of one of the educators mentioned in the chapter who has had an impact on the field of early childhood education. Write a review of the book. Include your thoughts about what you learned.

Observe a Classroom: Visit an early childhood program that might be traced back to the thought and writing of the educators described in this chapter. Observe classroom practices and analyze how what you observed might reflect the ideas described in the chapter.

BIBLIOGRAPHY

Antler, J. 1987. *Lucy Sprague Mitchell: The Making of a Modern Woman*. New Haven, CT: Yale University Press.

Aries, P. 1962. *Centuries of Childhood*. New York: Vintage Books.

Auleta, M. S. 1969. *Foundations of Early Childhood Education*. New York: Random House.

Braun, S. J., and E. P. Edwards. 1972. *History and Theory of Early Childhood Education*. Belmont, CA: Wadsworth.

Caplan, F., and T. Caplan. 1974. *The Power of Play*. New York: Anchor Press.

Clarke-Stewart, A. 1977. *Childcare in the Family: A Review of Research and Some Propositions for Policy*. New York: Academic Press.

Cleverley, J., and D. C. Phillips. 1986. *Visions of Childhood: Influential Models from Locke to Spock*. Rev. ed. New York: Teachers College Press.

Cremin, A. A. 1964. *The Transformation of the School: Progressivism in American Education, 1876–1957*. New York: Vintage Books.

Dewey, J. 1972. *Experience and Education*. New York: Collier Books.

Featherstone, J. 1971. *Schools Where Children Learn*. New York: Liveright.

Goffin, S. G. 1994. *Curriculum Models and Early Childhood Education: Appraising the Relationship*. Englewood Cliffs, NJ: Merrill/Prentice Hall.

Grubb, W. N. and A. M. W. Lazerson. 1988. *Broken Promises: How Americans Fail Their Children*. Rev. ed. Chicago: University of Chicago Press.

Gutek, G. L. 1972. *A History of the Western Educational Experience*. New York: Random House.

Haring, N. G., L. McCormick, and T. G. Haring. 1994. *Exceptional Children and Youth: An Introduction to Special Education*. 6th ed. Englewood Cliffs, NJ: Merrill/Prentice Hall.

Kramer, R. 1988. *Maria Montessori: A Biography*. Reading, MA: Addison-Wesley.

Lazar, I., and R. Darlington. 1983. *As the Twig is Bent: Lasting Effects of Preschool Programs*. Hillsdale, NJ: Erlbaum.

Maccoby, E. E., and M. Zellner. 1970. *Experiments in Primary Education: Aspects of Project Follow-Through*. New York: Harcourt Brace Jovanovich.

MacDonald, J. B. 1972. Introduction. In J. R. Squire, ed., *A New Look at Progressive Education.* Washington, DC: Association for Supervision and Curriculum Development.

Mace-Matluck, B. J., ed. 1992. *Follow Through: A Bridge to the Future.* Austin, TX: Southwest Educational Development Lab.

McKey, R. H., ed. 1985. Project Head Start, A National Evaluation: Summary of the Study. In D. G. Hayes, ed., *Britannica Review of American Education.* Chicago: Encyclopedia Britannica. 235–43.

McMillan. 1919. *The Nursery School.* New York: E. P. Dutton.

Montessori, M. 1965. *Dr. Montessori's Own Handbook.* New York: Schocken Books.

Montessori, M. 1967. *The Absorbent Mind.* New York: Holt, Rinehart & Winston.

Noonan, M. J., and L. McCormick. 1993. *Early Intervention in Natural Environments.* Pacific Grove, CA: Brooks/Cole.

Osborn, D. K. 1991. *Early Childhood Education in Historical Perspective.* 3rd ed. Athens, GA: Education Associates.

Roopnarine, J. L., and J. E. Johnson. 1993. *Approaches to Early Childhood Education.* 2nd ed. Englewood Cliffs, NJ: Merrill/Prentice Hall.

Schweinhardt, L. J., and D. P. Weikart. 1980. *Young Children Grow Up: The Effects of the Perry Preschool on Youths Through Age 15.* Ypsilanti, MI: High/Scope Foundation.

Shapiro, M. S. 1983. *Child's Garden: The Kindergarten Movement from Froebel to Dewey.* University Park, PA: Pennsylvania State University Press.

Silber, K. 1965. *Pestalozzi: The Man and His Work.* New York: Schocken Books.

Silberman, C. E. 1970. *Crisis in the Classroom.* New York: Random House.

Standing, E. M. 1959. *Maria Montessori: Her Life and Work.* Fresno, CA: Academy Library Guild.

Steiner, G. Y. 1976. *The Children's Cause.* Washington, DC: The Brookings Institution.

Steinfels, M. O. 1973. *Who's Minding the Children.* New York: Simon & Schuster.

Weber, E. 1969. *The Kindergarten: Its Encounter with Educational Thought in America.* Englewood Cliffs, NJ: Teachers College Press.

Weber, E. 1984. *Ideas Influencing Early Childhood Education: A Theoretical Analysis.* New York: Teachers College Press.

Weber, L. 1971. *The English Infant School and Informal Education.* Englewood Cliffs, NJ: Prentice Hall.

Williams, L. R. 1993. Historical and Philosophical Roots of Early Childhood Practice. *Encyclopedia of Early Childhood Education.* New York: Garland.

Zigler, E. 1992. *Head Start: The Inside Story of America's Most Successful Educational Experiment.* New York: Basic Books.

Zigler, E., and A. J. Valentine. 1979. *Project Head Start: A Legacy of the War on Poverty.* New York: Free Press.

CHAPTER THREE

The Field of Early Childhood Education and Care

It takes a village to raise a child.   African Proverb

This chapter is written to provide you with a perspective on early childhood education and care, the variety of programs available, and some of the critical challenges confronting the field. In it we give an overview of the field today, its current prospects, and future directions.

Early childhood education and care is a system that touches the lives of nearly everyone in our society. Those who are most intimately affected by it are those children and families served and the professionals who provide the services. Early childhood educators feel strongly that the work they do is valuable, even essential to the well-being of children, families, and society. They agree that family, program staff, and the community need to work cooperatively with one another to create high-quality programs. They also believe that programs best serve children and families when they are based on a profound respect for and appreciation of the diversity found among families in our society.

Families have immense challenges to meet, and they need support in the form of quality programs and thoughtful public policy if they are to do the important work of nurturing their children. Nearly every issue confronting families of young children has become more pressing in the 1990s. More mothers of young children work and need child care, more children are living in poverty, more children are without health care, more children are born to teenage mothers, and more children are victims of abuse and neglect.

Although early childhood education and care programs cannot solve all of the social, economic, and political ills of our society, they can do much to give children a good beginning and to meet the needs of families in which the caregiving adults are in the workforce. For programs to be beneficial they must be of high quality—organized thoughtfully and staffed by well-trained, sensitive professionals. Recent research on the long-term effects of high-quality early childhood education and care programs has brought a growing awareness of the impact on every individual and institution in our society. These programs are beneficial to children who learn to love learning and develop greater social and cognitive competence. They benefit society because children who participate in these programs require fewer special services during their

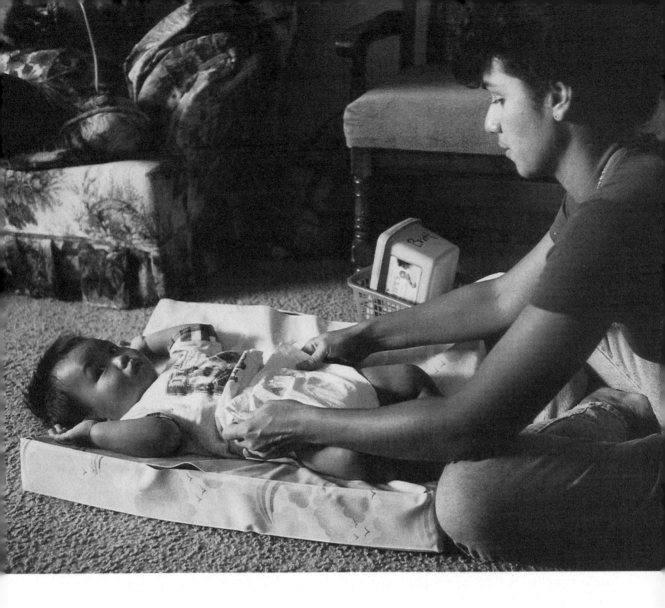

public school years and are more likely to graduate from high school. They benefit the family because its members can go to work each day knowing that their children are in good hands. And they benefit employers because their workers can focus on the job without worrying about the welfare of their children.

PROGRAMS FOR YOUNG CHILDREN

As you pursue your professional development you will learn about early childhood education and care programs, and you will have opportunities to experience them first hand. Your study of programs will enable you to see a range of professional roles and careers available to you in the field of early childhood education and care. Awareness of the diversity of programs for young children and their families can help you make decisions about the kinds of programs in which you are likely to feel most comfortable and in which you may want to work during your career.

The two primary purposes for early childhood programs are: (1) to support children's learning and development and (2) to provide child care for families while their parents are at work or are engaged in other activities. It is important to realize that care and education are inextricably linked and that child-care programs very often are a vehicle for delivering early childhood education. Early childhood programs also have secondary purposes: the education of parents, the provision of health and nutrition services to children, and the delivery of social services to families (Williams and Fromberg 1992).

A great variety of programs for young children are available today. Programs can be classified in a number of ways: in terms of their purposes, their sponsorship and funding, and their location and the duration of services offered. Sponsorship and funding may be public (federal, state, or local) or private. Private programs may be not-for-profit, basically intended to provide a service to children and their families, or for-profit, designed as a service-oriented business.

Early childhood programs may be found in centers or in homes—the family's home or the home of the caregiver or service provider. Center-based programs—those based in a specially designed or adapted facility—may be located in classrooms, churches, or synagogues; in community organization facilities such as the YWCA or YMCA; or in public housing complexes, public schools, or recreational facilities. Occasionally a facility is designed specifically for use as an education and care center. Many are full-day programs designed to meet the needs of families in the workforce, and some are part-day programs.

As an early childhood educator you may have opportunities to work in a wide variety of programs, some of which will be designed for a specific age group of children and others which will include a mixture of ages. Some programs will follow a particular program design or focus on a particular age group that will require that you receive some orientation or specialized training to be a staff member (for example, Home Visitor Programs, Montessori, Head Start, Healthy Start, and others). The descriptions that follow are organized by age groups to enable you to see the similarities and differences among programs across the entire early childhood education and care spectrum.

Infant-Toddler Programs—Ages Birth to Three

Children between birth and age three receive services in a variety of settings. Center-based care and family child-care homes are often used to meet the needs of families in the workforce. Other programs exist for the purposes of intervention and enrichment and may have as their primary aim to counter the negative effects of poverty, to deliver parent education to families who are potentially abusive or neglectful, or to address other issues encountered by families such as domestic violence, homelessness, and drug abuse. The sponsorship and funding sources are diverse and complex.

Center-Based Programs

During the past few decades licensing regulations in many states have been expanded to include provisions for infant and toddler center-based programs. This has enabled an increasing number of centers to add infant and toddler care services. These programs usually exist to provide child care for employed families and to enhance the development of children. In many places the demand for infant-toddler programs far exceeds the supply even though the cost is quite high compared to programs for preschool-age children. The cost is high because quality programs for infants require a ratio of one caregiver to every three infants to provide adequate attention to routines, maintain a safe environment, and promote frequent, responsive adult-infant interaction.

There are infant-toddler centers on military bases and in hospitals, high schools, colleges, businesses, churches, synagogues, and community agencies. Both public and private funding and a mix of the two is common. Often programs for infants, toddlers, and preschoolers will be provided by the same organization in the same facilities.

Home-Based Child Care

Home-based care is often chosen by families of infants and toddlers who prefer that their children be cared for in the smaller, more intimate environment of a home. Families may choose home-based care because in some cases it is less expensive and it is nearly always more flexible in scheduling hours of care and providing care to children during mild illnesses common during the early years.

Most infants and toddlers in home-based care are either in family child-care homes or in the care of relatives, with a few cared for in their own homes by someone hired for this purpose. Generally, the expense of in-home care is borne by the family. Public funding and support for home-based care has been minimal because regulation and licensing of in-home care is more limited than in center-based programs. Therefore in-home programs have difficulty meeting the accountability requirements for most forms of public funding. This is changing rapidly as both federal and state governments reevaluate social policies regarding child care. Also, people working in home-based settings have become aware that they are a significant force in meeting family needs and have begun organizing as early childhood education and care professionals.

Infant Intervention Programs

Infant intervention programs were originally conceived during the 1960s and 1970s to counter the negative effects of poverty. Like Head Start, these programs were based on the assumption that enriching experiences that involved the family would result in positive de-

velopmental outcomes for the child. One of the earliest infant interventions was the Head Start Parent-Child Center program (PCC), established as a demonstration program in the mid-sixties. PCCs were based on the same comprehensive model as the Head Start program for three- to five-year-olds. The Human Services Reauthorization Act of 1990 more than doubled the number of Head Start Parent-Child Centers. Throughout the nation there are numerous intervention programs based on the PCC model, with the purposes of preventing problems associated with poverty or intervening in families in which parenting behaviors might be detrimental to children's welfare. Such programs are most often funded by federal, state, and foundation monies and administered by government or community agencies.

A second source of public support for infant intervention programs is federal funding for services to children with disabilities or at risk for developing disabilities. The early funding mandating services for disabled children was for the three- to five-year-old group (P.L. 94–142). In 1986, P.L. 99–457 was enacted and includes infants and toddlers.

Preschool Programs—Ages Three Through Five Years

Preschool age children receive education and care services in a wide variety of settings, with diverse sponsorship and complex funding sources. They are often designed for a mix of purposes. Today most programs for preschoolers combine education and care and provide full day services. Some are primarily enrichment programs and others have as their primary aim to counter the negative effects of poverty or to address social issues faced by families.

Full-Day, Center-Based Programs

Contemporary, full-day, center-based programs combine aspects of the day-nursery, which

focused on the provision of care, and the nursery school, which had enrichment and education as its primary goal. Many such programs are called *child-care centers,* and they provide education and care for children when the caregiving adults are employed full time or are training to enter the workforce. These center-based programs are usually open from early morning until early evening and can be located in the wide variety of facilities.

Some centers are designed to provide special services for a particular population and may be open later hours or provide drop-in care according to family needs, such as hotel and hospital centers. Sick-child care is another special service program developed to respond to the growing number of working families and single-parent families. Programs for sick children help to lower absenteeism among employees with young children. In some communities a sick-child care ward is created in a hospital for use by hospital employees and community members. These centers are usually intended for children with mild, non-contagious illnesses. Some have isolation rooms available for more seriously ill children.

Child-care centers may be publicly or privately sponsored and funded or have a combination of funding sources. Employer-sponsored or subsidized centers provide care for employees' children and may have a combination of private and public funding sources. The U.S. Department of Defense may be the largest employer involved in the sponsorship of child care; it subsidizes child care for members of the armed services world-wide. Large corporations, hospitals, and government agencies have all become involved in the sponsorship of near-site or on-site centers. Some state university systems partially support child care for students and employees.

Many center-based programs in the U.S. receive increased federal funding through the 1990 Child Care and Development Block Grant administered through the states and aimed at expanding the quality and availability of child-care services for low-income families. The Family Support Act of 1990 is another federal source of funding for center-based child care for family members who are in programs to prepare them for entry into the workforce.

Most centers in the United States today are privately sponsored and rely on a variety of funding sources. The great majority of revenue in most programs is from tuition paid by families. Other funding may come from grants, fund-raisers, and some public funds for specific purposes. For-profit, franchised centers are becoming an increasingly common type of privately sponsored child care. Many new centers belong to nationwide chains that attempt to make child care affordable and profitable by using standardized building plans, bulk purchases of equipment and supplies, and a uniform curriculum. Quality in these programs has sometimes been sacrificed to profits, brought about by high child-to-staff ratios, low salaries, and the hiring of minimally qualified personnel.

Part-Day, Center-Based Programs

Part-day, center-based programs are designed to accomplish a wide range of purposes and are often referred to as preschools. However, the term *preschool* is also used by many centers that offer full-day education and care. They use the term in their name to denote the educational orientation of the program. Partial-day preschools are an outgrowth of the traditional nursery school, which focused on social-emotional development and provided learning through play for children three through five years of age. Traditionally, nursery schools were half-day programs that followed a public school calendar. They were common when most families did not need full-day care and mothers were available to pick up the children at midday.

Beginning in the late 1960s, nursery schools began to be called preschools as their programs were modified to recognize that important cognitive development occurs in the early years. Modern part-day programs may differ in their purposes. Some are focused on the enrichment of overall development, some on the socialization of children who have limited group experience, and others are aimed at preparation for academic success. Many programs in public schools, lab schools, and parent cooperatives still provide part-day options.

In many states, some four-year-old children are in preschool programs based in the public schools. Among these are early intervention programs for children considered "at risk" for school failure, federally funded prekindergarten programs for low-income children, special education classes for four-year-olds, some Head Start classes, and a few locally funded programs for prekindergarten children and children of teen parents.

Public sponsors of preschools include education and child development departments in colleges, universities, and some high school home economic departments. These preschools are laboratory settings for training students in education and child development while providing a service to the school and community.

Among privately sponsored programs are parent cooperatives (called *co-ops*). In these programs, an early childhood educator serves as teacher, director, and educational leader, and families commit themselves to regular, active participation in teaching and administering the program.

Head Start

The Head Start program, introduced in Chapter Two, is a federally funded, comprehensive program that began in the 1960s. It grew out of a recognition that many children in our society did not do well in elementary schools and that many of their problems could be traced to an early childhood in poverty. The program is designed to counter some of the negative effects of poverty. It offers low-income children developmentally appropriate educational experiences, as well as health screening and treatment, access to social services, and good

nutrition. An important component of the program is parent education and involvement of parents in policy decisions.

Preschool-age children and their families have participated in this part-day program for over thirty years. Current federal social policy regarding children and families in poverty and growing consensus at both the federal and state levels that we need a more effective approach to welfare reform has led to experiments in expanding Head Start. The provision of full-day programs in conjunction with the traditional Head Start part-day program will better enable families to pursue job training and employment opportunities. The expansion of Head Start is intended to help end the cycle of poverty.

In-Home Child Care

Throughout history, children have been cared for in their own homes and in the homes of relatives, friends, and hired caregivers. Today, child care in private homes provides an alternative to center-based care. In-home care is usually available from early morning to early evening and at special times to meet the needs of people who work unusual schedules.

Home-based care is the least visible, yet most prevalent, form of privately sponsored child care in the United States. Over 60 percent of the children under the age of five stay in someone else's home while their parents work. Family child-care homes (usually three to eight children) and group child-care homes (often twelve to fifteen children) provide care for nearly 27 percent of these children. Another 25 percent of the children in home-based care are with relatives, and the remaining 5 percent are cared for by an unrelated person in the child's own home. This latter arrangement is more in demand because many two-career families prefer to have a well-trained early childhood professional provide care for their children in their own home. A recent innovation in home-based services is the development of a system for providing in-home sick care for families who prefer that the child recuperate at home.

Kindergarten and Primary Programs—Ages Five Through Eight

Most five- to eight-year-old children attend kindergarten and primary programs in public or private school settings. Although home schooling has always been an option, interest in this alternative has increased greatly. In recent decades, before- and after-school programs for school-age children have become more widespread in response to the needs of working families.

Kindergarten

Traditionally, kindergarten has been a transition program for five-year-old children: a transition from home or an early childhood program to the more formal first grade classroom. Kindergartens range from informal programs stressing play, socialization, and the foundations for later school learning to highly structured academic programs that are almost indistinguishable from first or second grade classrooms. For many years, nearly all kindergarten programs were half day, but the percentage of full-school-day kindergartens is growing. A still more recent innovation is the extended-day program, designed to coincide more closely with the work schedules of families so that they do not need to make separate arrangements for the after-school care of their five-year-old children.

The kindergarten program is often a part of the public education system and is supported by public funds. However, unlike the primary grades, attendance has been optional and only recently has kindergarten become mandatory in a growing number of states. Privately operated kindergarten programs are often sponsored by or associated with religious organizations or other kinds of private schools.

Primary Schools

The primary school is generally thought of as the beginning of formal, academic schooling and covers the first three grade levels in the traditional elementary school. Most children begin primary school around age six following a year in a kindergarten class. Often first grade classes are in the same school and under the same sponsorship as the kindergarten. The look and feel of primary grade classrooms differ greatly from school to school and even from classroom to classroom in the same school because the purpose and focus of education for this age group is a subject of continuing debate. In some primary grade classrooms the curriculum is seen as preparation for the upper elementary grades and tends to be more formal and academic. However, many primary grade educators and administrators have become aware of the need to focus programs more on the development of the whole child in the context of the family. Because of this, more and more primary grade classrooms resemble those usually associated with developmentally appropriate early childhood programs.

In-Home Education

Prior to the advent of universal education in the United States, at-home education was the only option for families who lived in isolated locations. An increasing number of families today choose to do home schooling. In home schooling, a family member assumes responsibility for the education of the children. Families vary a great deal in their reasons for doing home schooling. Some wish to impart a value system they feel would be compromised in settings where diverse values and lifestyles are represented. In some cases the family disapproves of the instructional methods used in available programs. Others prefer home schooling because they believe they can do a good job of educating their children and wish to have this special relationship with them.

Many states have established standards and requirements that families must meet to do home schooling. These differ greatly across the United States. Some states and school districts require a particular curriculum or adherence to a previously submitted and approved plan of instruction.

School-Age Child Care

In times past it was assumed that children in most families had an at-home mother who would see them off to school in the morning and be waiting with fresh-baked cookies and milk when they returned mid-afternoon. The contemporary reality is that, in many families, all adults have work commitments. They require special arrangements for the care of their school-age children both before and after school hours, during school holidays, and during the summer months when schools are not in operation.

School-age child care is sponsored and organized in many different ways: by municipal parks and recreation departments, YMCA and YWCA programs, family child-care homes, elementary schools, religious organizations, child-care centers, and, more recently, state departments of education. Most of the options available for school-age child care must be paid for by the families who use them. In some programs the cost is partially subsidized by the sponsoring organization. The result has often been that those most able to pay have their children in supervised settings and those with more limited resources do not.

Parent Education Programs

Parent education acknowledges that parents are their children's primary educators in the early years. There are many kinds of programs available for parents of young children. These can take the form of parent classes and meetings dealing with topics such as child development, educational techniques, and child management; they can involve parents in working with children in early childhood classrooms; or they can provide trained visitors to work with parents and children in their homes. Programs for infants and toddlers that combine parent education with activities for children are becoming increasingly widespread due to increases in federal funding. Parent education, especially in combination with a good program for children, has proved to be very successful in producing developmental gains for young children.

The dramatic increase in births to teenage parents has major social and economic consequences for the teenagers themselves and for their children. Concern over this trend has led to the creation of new programs in schools and social service agencies. Parenting education programs for adolescents are being advocated as a necessary addition to the curriculum of intermediate and high schools. Some programs provide services for teen parents and their babies; others focus on just the parent or the child. Head Start is among the agencies responding with new approaches to young parents and children.

Program Regulation and Standards

Because young children are so dependent and vulnerable, families and society want to be assured that the programs to which they are entrusted will protect them and be committed to their welfare. Therefore, the great majority of center-based programs for young children are subject to some form of regulation. Whether you choose to work in a program for infants and toddlers or preschool-age children, become a family child-care provider, teach in a public school kindergarten or primary classroom, or run a school-age child-care program at the local YMCA, you are likely to find that the program is subject to some type of regulation based on identified standards. Two avenues commonly used to ensure a minimal

Reflect and write about . . .

programs you've known

Compare programs for young children in which you have observed or worked.

- What were the purposes of each program?
- How were the purposes similar/different?
- What was the sponsorship of each program?
- How was each program funded?
- How might parents and children be affected by each kind of program?
- What kind of program do you think you would like to work in and why?

level of quality in programs for young children are the regulation of the program, through registration or licensing, or the certification of the individuals who work in the program. A more recent trend for both centers and home settings is the establishment of accreditation that uses higher standards and indicates a higher quality of education and care.

Licensing and Registration

Private programs for children from infancy to kindergarten are subject to licensing standards in most places. Since early childhood programs have, until recently, been viewed as a social service for families, early childhood licensing is most often administered by departments of social welfare. Historically, licensing has focused on preschool programs, but recently licensing has become more prevalent for programs that provide infant and toddler and before- and after-school care. Most states have provisions for licensing or registering family child-care and group child-care homes, though requirements are difficult to enforce since the licensing agency may not know about the homes.

At a minimum, state licensing sets program standards to ensure that the physical environment is a safe and healthy place for children and that there are enough adults to provide supervision. Some also provide guidelines for program components in an attempt to ensure that all aspects of development are provided for.

Even with licensing, a wide range in quality still exists, from programs that offer excellent care and education to programs that provide unsafe and inappropriate care. In the United States there are no nationally mandated child-care standards, even for federally funded child-care programs. State standards for licensing centers and for enforcing these standards vary so greatly that licensure in itself is no guarantee of quality.

In 1984, the National Association for the Education of Young Children (NAEYC) issued a position statement on licensing, urging that licensing standards adopted by states cover all forms of supplementary care for children from birth through school age, with no exemptions for any program because of its sponsorship or funding. It called for vigorous enforcement of standards that are clear, well-publicized, and congruent with current knowledge about quality care. These standards have yet to be developed and implemented.

Other Standards

Programs that receive public funds may be subject to different or additional standards. Two examples are the Department of Defense regulations that are applied to early childhood programs run by the branches of the armed services for the children of military personnel and the Head Start Performance Standards that dictate criteria for all of the components of the program—health, social services, parent involvement, and education.

Public school systems use certification of teachers as a primary standard-setting mechanism. Certification standards are usually mandated by state departments of education. They are statements concerning what teachers should know and be able to do in order to receive a teaching certificate. Four-year college and university departments of education offer course work that enables you to meet the certification standards of the state in which you wish to teach.

Accreditation

A recent development in the profession's effort to improve the quality of programs for young children is the establishment of voluntary accreditation. Accreditation standards and processes for both centers and home settings generally require that the setting first be licensed or registered to meet the minimum standards for the state or community. The accreditation process uses criteria to determine if the program meets standards that the professional community agrees represent high quality.

In the early 1980s NAEYC established accreditation standards and procedures and a separate credentialing body called the National Academy of Early Childhood Programs. NAEYC's accreditation criteria were established by a process of consensus among many representatives of the field. The accreditation program enables programs to be identified as surpassing the minimum standards required by the licensing regulations. Center-based full- and part-day programs for children from birth through age five and before- and after-school care programs for school-age children are eligible for NAEYC accreditation. The process involves a careful program review, including a self-study that lets all of the program participants (parents, staff, administration) offer input.

A similar accreditation is available to family care providers through the National Association for Family Day Care. Like the NAEYC accreditation it is voluntary, involves standards that exceed licensing requirements, and involves self-study and peer evaluation.

SOCIETAL CHANGES IMPACTING ON THE FIELD

The early childhood education and care system is affected by cultural, social, political, and economic factors in our society. We have a diverse population that influences the demand for and nature of programs. Numerous forces affect children and families, including the economy, the unemployment rate, health care, media, drugs and violence in the streets, homelessness, and AIDS. Early childhood programs are a part of the support system for families who experience the stress of contemporary life. As a nation, we have yet to make children a priority and devise a coherent social policy to deal with the long list of problems that impact on children and families. Many of the federal initiatives begun in the early 1990s represent progress and the hope of more support for children, families, and the programs and professionals that provide services for them.

Knowledge of the social, cultural, political, and economic context in which early childhood education and care exists will help you to understand the field and to see the unique contributions you can make to the well-being of children and families. In response to changes in society, the field has undergone many changes in recent decades.

The Changing Family

As an early childhood professional, you must understand the changes that families are undergoing in order to understand the wide range of programs developed in recent decades to respond to their needs. It is also important to remain aware that you are very likely to be working with children and families whose cultural, ethnic, and lifestyle values differ from yours and that you have a professional obligation to them.

You may encounter a variety of family structures and lifestyles. The two-parent, intact family that was considered normal in preceding generations is now the exception. Many of the children you work with will live in single-parent homes. These can result from divorce, the birth of children to unwed teenage mothers, or to more mature women who chose to have children outside of marriage. Most single-parent families will be headed by a working mother, but some will be headed by a father, a grandparent, or a single foster parent. Other children will live in blended families resulting from the partnership of people who already have children from previous relationships, and an increasing minority will live in a two-parent family in which the parents are gay or lesbian.

In recent decades there has been an influx of immigrants and refugees from many parts of the world. Regardless of their place or circumstance of origin, you can be certain that immigrant families have undergone stress in relocat-

---

Reflect and write about . . .

program quality standards

Think back on programs in which you have observed or worked.

- What kinds of regulatory standards were used?
- Have you ever visited or worked in a NAEYC-accredited program?
- How might programs be different if they were not regulated?

ing and can benefit from the support of professionals who have some understanding of their life situation and appreciation for their heritage.

Though we like to think of America as the land of opportunity, the fact remains that you are likely to find yourself working with children and families who have had few opportunities. Millions of children live in poverty—sometimes in low-income working families; sometimes in families without jobs, homes, or health care. Many live in neighborhoods that are filled with drugs and violence. You may also find yourself working with children who are stressed by their families' unrealistically high expectations for their achievement.

The increased number of mothers of very young children in the workforce and the growth of dual-career families has led to a demand for programs. These families need more settings for the care of infants and mildly ill children and settings that accommodate variable work schedules. The changes in family structure and the increase in the diversity of lifestyles among families who are raising children has led to an increase in programs to provide respite to single parents and a broad range of social services to families who are experiencing stress. Families who suffer the consequences of poverty or dislocation benefit from intervention programs that provide them with guidance for acquiring health services, homes, literacy training, job preparation, child care, parenting education, and other forms of assistance.

The Changing Workplace

A steadily declining population and the growing number of youth who reach young adulthood without the knowledge and skills they need to function in the contemporary workplace raises concerns about whether we will have a viable workforce for the next century. Some leaders in the business community have begun to think seriously of ways to recruit and retain valuable employees and to consider ways in which government and business might work cooperatively to support families with children. Large and small businesses have begun to recognize that high-quality early childhood education and care programs are essential to a stable and efficient workforce, currently and for the future.

An initial response to the need for such programs was to create work-site child-care facilities. However, changing demographics of the workforce and the high cost of building and operating child-care facilities have caused employers to consider a variety of other solutions. Flextime—giving employees flexibility in arranging their own hours—may enable families with young children to coordinate their schedules so that they are less dependent on outside child care. Ever-expanding advances in communications make telecommuting—traveling to work via modern technology—a reality for more and more people. People who work in a home office are more available to their young children. For employees whose work is tied to the workplace, family assistance options such as child-care resource and referral services and partial subsidies of child care at existing child-care facilities are increasingly popular. Another approach is for several smaller businesses to form a consortium and jointly sponsor a child-care program. As many families seem to prefer flexibility and choice in child-care arrangements, it is most likely that employers will continue to subsidize a range of solutions rather than build costly child-care centers.

The Changing Society

Society in the United States is also changing in ways that can make life very difficult for families with young children. It is important to think about the nature of life in contemporary society so that you can understand some of the effects on children and families.

Many American families live in poverty. In 1992, for example, close to six million chil-

Reflect and write about . . .

programs and services in your community

What programs and services are provided for young children in your community? Based on your own experience and that of other people you know, what changes need to be made and new programs initiated to provide a comprehensive support system for families with children from birth through eight years of age?

dren under age six lived in poverty. Every night that year approximately 100,000 children were homeless and eight million were without health insurance. Children who live in poverty have parents who are jobless or have limited employment. Many were headed by a single mother, and even those with two working parents earned a low income. Children who live in the most precarious economic circumstances are often subjected to other stresses, such as living in neighborhoods with drug abuse and crime, domestic violence, and limited access to early childhood programs and other social services (Children's Defense Fund 1994).

Many children of more affluent families also experience stress. Domestic violence, child abuse and neglect, and exposure to drugs and alcoholism are present in every socioeconomic group although the causes may be different. Even families with high incomes may be unable to provide high-quality, consistent care for their children because care and education programs are not available or extensive enough to meet their needs.

Media is a powerful societal force that has an impact on early childhood programs. In their own homes, children learn about crime, violence, sex, drug use, and materialism through television, video games, and music. Numerous studies have linked the viewing of twenty or more hours of television violence per week to the predisposition to violence among children, youth, and in society in general (Children's Defense Fund 1994; National Association for the Education of Young Children 1990). The steady diet of television keeps children from active involvement in activities that support their development and leads to increased violence in their behavior.

It is unlikely that poverty, stress, or television will cease to exist. It is part of your responsibility as an early childhood educator to understand these issues and develop curriculum that helps children to cope with their impact.

ISSUES AND PROSPECTS FOR THE FIELD

In the first half of this century, most people believed that nothing important happened during the early years and that young children were not ready to learn until the age of six, when they entered formal schooling. It was generally accepted that all children needed prior to their sixth year was a home in which their physical needs were met. Even after Freud revealed that important emotional development occurs in the early childhood years, most people held the idea that anyone who worked with children under six was "only babysitting," a phrase that we sometimes still hear today.

During the last thirty years, research on the first years of life has shown that early experience has a great impact on all areas of a child's development. This suggests that the first teachers are extremely important people in children's lives. Yet, there is a gap between research and practice. In the United States today, programs for children under five are still inadequately funded. Most are privately supported, in contrast to fully state-supported programs for children aged five years and older.

Expenses for child care are now the average family's fourth largest expenditure. More affluent families can afford some type of early childhood program, and federal support for early childhood programs is available for families who meet poverty guidelines. But as more and more families fall beneath the poverty line, there are more children eligible for subsidized programs and services than there are openings in such programs. And for many lower-middle and middle-class families, paying for needed child care is an overwhelming burden. The alternatives are either no program or the least expensive, unlicensed, unmonitored care. Unfortunately, when child-care and education costs become prohibitively high, even middle-income parents turn to non-regulated sources of child care, which offer less assurance of quality.

Many of the issues in the field today are summed up by what is referred to as the "trilemma" of child care: the interrelationship of the need for quality programs for children, affordable child-care services for families, and adequate compensation for practitioners. The issue is also referred to as QCA—Quality, Compensation, and Affordability. The National Child Care Staffing Study indicates that program quality is affected by the education of teaching staff and the adequacy of their wages. It also found that funding for child care has decreased in the past decade and that during the same period staff turnover has nearly tripled (Whitebook, Howes, and Phillips 1989).

Because programs for children under the age of five are paid for directly by already overburdened families, salaries in privately supported programs for young children are much lower than salaries in publicly supported programs for comparable positions with comparable professional preparation. Without public understanding and acceptance of the importance of having well-trained, competent people working with young children, there will be no remedy to the current condition of low salaries and inadequate benefits. This makes it difficult to recruit and retain good early childhood practitioners. Few men choose to enter the field, even though many would find it rewarding. They are discouraged by the low pay and by the common stereotype that caring for young children is women's work. Other consequences of inadequate compensation are lower program quality and high staff turnover. High staff turnover is especially unfortunate, because it undermines the stability of adult-child relationships and thus affects children's ability to benefit from program experiences.

Lest you despair, there are some bright spots in the field. The steady growth of publicly supported programs for four-year-olds is a sign of increased recognition of the value of early childhood education. NAEYC's book *Developmentally Appropriate Practices in Early Childhood Programs* (Bredekamp 1987), has been influential in improving programs for kindergarten and elementary school children as well as younger children. More people and organizations have publicly acknowledged the importance of early childhood education and care. For example, the National Association of State Boards of Education (1988) and the National Association of Elementary School Principals have issued statements on the importance of developmentally appropriate early childhood education, and the Association of Teacher Educators and NAEYC issued a joint position statement on the certification of early childhood teachers (National Association for the Education of Young Children 1991).

There has been an increase in collaborative work between organizations concerned with the well-being of young children and families. This has resulted in extensive media and legislative attention to family-related issues during the last half of the 1980s and the beginning of the 1990s. More children- and family-related legislation has been introduced into Congress than ever before. There appears to be a momentum building at the federal and state levels towards action on issues related to children, which are now being defined as family and employment issues as well as child-care issues.

THE GROWTH OF PROFESSIONALISM

American attitudes toward the early childhood education and care field have been heavily influenced by the late nineteenth and early twentieth century origins of the field. This mixed heritage of the educationally oriented kindergarten and the care-oriented nursery has lent early childhood education and care and early childhood professionals a correspondingly mixed status, character, and reputation. This is reflected in the perception that pre-school and kindergarten are just preparation for the serious learning of first grade—they are not "real school." This same attitude influences pay scales; generally, the younger the children, the lower the status and salary of the educator.

The past decade has heralded major movement in the transformation of the early childhood education and care field from being primarily an occupation toward being a profession deserving of respect and compensation commensurate with the contributions it makes to society. Working with young children requires training and skill and has an impact on children, families, and society. However, as we have just pointed out, early childhood professionals are less likely than other educators to receive adequate compensation or have consistent training or opportunities for career advancement. In an effort to improve the prospects for early childhood educators, NAEYC, the Center for Career Development at Wheelock College, and many state and local organizations have begun working together to find solutions to these problems. This effort, known, as the *career development initiative,* seeks to achieve an articulated, coordinated professional development system. The system is intended to accomplish three things: (1) ensure that individuals from all groups in the early childhood education and care workforce have access to training and career mobility, (2) ensure a supply of qualified practitioners to work with young children, and (3) enhance the level of training of staff to improve the quality of care for children.

A growing sense of conviction about the uniqueness and importance of our field comes, in part, from NAEYC's efforts to clarify the nature and requirements of the field. Membership in NAEYC, the largest organization of early childhood educators, has grown dramatically (nearly 90,000 members in September 1993). NAEYC has become involved over the last few years in providing standards and mechanisms for the promotion of professionalism in the field. These include a model of professional development, guidelines for two-year and four-year teacher education programs, national accreditation of quality child-care programs, a Code of Ethical Conduct, and the National Institute for Early Childhood Professional Development. These efforts contribute to growing recognition of the field as a profession.

FINAL THOUGHTS

The field of early childhood education and care is constantly evolving. Many things that we considered best practices in programs for children and families even a decade ago have been reexamined and supplanted by new best practices. The rethinking of what we do in programs for young children and families and the kinds of programs we should be providing for them is based on a number of factors. Some of the reasons for change in practices and policies include: the changing circumstances of children and families in contemporary society, the developing public awareness of the early childhood years as the most important in the development of a person, reinterpretations of child development knowledge, new understandings gleaned from research on the effectiveness of quality programs, and the dramatically increased awareness of those who work with children and families of themselves as valuable professionals with important contributions to make to society.

As we grow as a profession, early childhood educators are becoming increasingly

---

Reflect and write about . . .

issues and trends

What early childhood education and care issues (for example, program quality, salaries, teacher qualifications and certification, and program availability) are being discussed in your community at present? What recommendations are being made, and what actions (if any) are being taken? What do you think society needs to know and do to improve the quality, availability, and affordability of early childhood education and care?

committed to child advocacy. We are becoming more sophisticated about the political process and are forming alliances with others with similar concerns in order to heighten community awareness and influence public attitudes and legislation on behalf of young children and families. Certainly there is cause for hope that the needs of young children and of those who work with them will someday receive the attention they deserve.

PROJECTS

Visit a Program: Observe and write a description of a program for young children in your community. Find out about its history, philosophy, sponsorship, tuition, ratios, provisions for parent involvement, teacher qualifications, salaries, and current concerns.

Program Quality Standards: Survey your community and report on the kinds of programs that are available for children from birth to eight years of age (preschools, child care, programs for low-income children, public school programs). Who is responsible for regulation of each kind of program? How do regulatory standards differ?

Learn About Training Opportunities: Research and report on training programs available for teachers of young children in your community, on how teachers are certified, and on typical salaries for teachers in different kinds of programs. What thoughts and issues are raised by your findings?

BIBLIOGRAPHY

Boyer, E. L. 1991. *Ready to Learn: A Mandate for the Nation.* Princeton, NJ: Carnegie Foundation for the Advancement of Teaching.

Bredekamp, S., ed. 1987. *Developmentally Appropriate Practices in Early Childhood Programs Serving Children From Birth Through Age 8: Expanded Edition.* Washington, DC: National Association for the Education of Young Children.

Caldwell, B. M. 1989. A Comprehensive Model for Integrating Child Care and Early Childhood Education. *Teachers College Record* 90(3):404–14.

Carnegie Corporation. 1994. Starting Points: Executive Summary of the Report of the Carnegie Corporation of New York Task Force on Meeting the Needs of Young Children. *Young Children* 49(5):58–61.

Children's Defense Fund. 1994. *The State of America's Children, 1994.* Washington, DC: Author.

Clarke-Stewart, A. 1977. *Childcare in the Family: A Review of Research and Some Propositions for Policy.* New York: Academic Press.

Costley, J. 1991. *Career Development Systems in Early Care and Education: A Planning Approach.* Boston: Wheelock College.

Feeney, S., ed. 1992. *Early Childhood Education in Asia and the Pacific: A Source Book*. New York: Garland.

Galinsky, E. 1989. The Staffing Crisis. *Young Children* 44(3):2–4.

Haring, N. G., L. McCormick, and T. G. Haring. 1994. *Exceptional Children and Youth: An Introduction to Special Education*. 6th ed. Englewood Cliffs, NJ: Merrill/Prentice Hall.

Johnson, J., and J. B. McCracken, eds. 1994. *The Early Childhood Career Lattice: Perspectives on Professional Development*. Washington, DC: National Association for the Education of Young Children.

Jorde-Bloom, P. 1988. *A Great Place to Work: Improving Conditions for Staff in Young Children's Programs*. Washington, DC: National Association for the Education of Young Children.

Kagan, S. L. 1988. Current Reforms in Early Childhood Education: Are We Addressing the Issues? *Young Children* 43(2):27–32.

Kagan, S. L. 1989. Early Care and Education: Tackling the Tough Issues. *Phi Delta Kappan* 7(6):433–9.

Kagan, S. L., and J. W. Newton. 1989. For Profit and Nonprofit Child Care: Similarities and Differences. *Young Children* 45(1):4–10.

Lazar, I., and R. Darlington. 1983. *As the Twig Is Bent: Lasting Effects of Preschool Programs*. Hillsdale, NJ: Erlbaum.

Mitchell, A. 1989. Old Baggage, New Visions: Shaping Policy for Early Childhood Programs. *Phi Delta Kappan* 70(9):664–72.

Mitchell, A., M. Seligson, and F. Marx. 1989. *Early Childhood Programs and the Public Schools: Between Promise and Practice*. Dover, MA: Auburn House.

National Association for the Education of Young Children. 1984. *Accreditation Criteria and Procedures of the National Academy of Early Childhood Programs*. Washington, DC: Author.

National Association for the Education of Young Children. 1988. Position Statement on Licensing and Other Forms of Regulation of Early Childhood Programs in Centers and Family Day Care Homes. *Young Children* 42(5):64–68.

National Association for the Education of Young Children. 1990. NAEYC Position Statement on Media Violence in Children's Lives. *Young Children* 45(5):18–21.

National Association for the Education of Young Children. 1991. Early Childhood Teacher Certification: A Position Statement of the Association of Teacher Educators and the National Association for the Education of Young Children, Adopted July/August 1991. *Young Children* 47(1):16–21.

National Association for the Education of Young Children. 1993. NAEYC Position Statement on Violence in the Lives of Children. *Young Children* 48(6):80–84.

National Association for the Education of Young Children. 1994. NAEYC Position Statement: A Conceptual Framework for Early Childhood Professional Development. *Young Children* 49(3):68–77.

National Association of State Boards of Education. 1988. *Right from the Start*. Alexandria, VA: Author.

Noonan, M. J., and L. McCormick. 1993. *Early Intervention in Natural Environments*. Pacific Grove, CA: Brooks/Cole.

Pittman, R. 1988. *Nannies.* Moravia, N.Y.: Chronicle Guidance.

Robinson, S. L. 1987. Kindergarten in America. *Phi Delta Kappan* 68(7):529–30.

Robinson, S. S. 1987. Are Public Schools Ready for Four-Year-Olds? *Principal* 66(5):26–28.

Schultz, T., and J. Lombardi. 1989. Right From the Start: A Report on the NASBE Task Force on Early Childhood Education. *Young Children* 44(2):6–10.

Seefeldt, C. 1990. *Continuing Issues in Early Childhood Education.* Englewood Cliffs, NJ: Merrill/Prentice Hall.

Smith, M. M. 1989. Confronting Tough Issues. *Young Children* 45(1):32–37.

Steinfels, M. O. 1973. *Who's Minding the Children?* New York: Simon & Schuster.

Whitebook, M., C. Howes, and D. Phillips. 1989. *Who Cares? Child Care Teachers and the Quality of Care in America: Executive Summary.* Oakland, CA: Child Care Employee Project.

Willer, B., ed. 1990. *Reaching the Full Cost of Quality in Early Childhood Programs.* Washington, DC: National Association for the Education of Young Children.

Willer, B., S. L. Hofferth, E. E. Kisker, P. Divine-Hawkins, E. Farquhar, and F. B. Glantz. 1991. *The Demand and Supply of Child Care in 1990.* Washington, DC: National Association for the Education of Young Children.

Willer, B. A., and L. D. Johnson. 1989. *The Crisis is Real: Demographics on the Problem of Recruiting and Retaining Early Childhood Staff.* Washington, DC: National Association for the Education of Young Children.

Williams, L. R., and D. P. Fromberg, ed. 1992. *Encyclopedia of Early Childhood Education.* New York: Garland.

Zigler, E., and S. Hunsinger. 1977. Bringing Up Daycare. *American Psychological Monitor* 7(March).

PART II

Understanding Children

This section includes chapters to help you understand children's development and the significance of their play. Because understanding children is of central importance to early childhood education and care, these chapters form an essential foundation for practice. Chapter Four, Child Development: Theory Into Practice, provides a basis for understanding young children. Chapter Five, Play, introduces a critical medium for children's development and discusses how you can support play. Chapter Six, Assessing Children, acquaints you with basic skills that you will use to observe individuals and groups of children and decide how to best support their development.

Child Development:Theory into Practice

In all the world there is no other child exactly like you. In the millions of years that have passed, there has never been a child like you. Pablo Casals

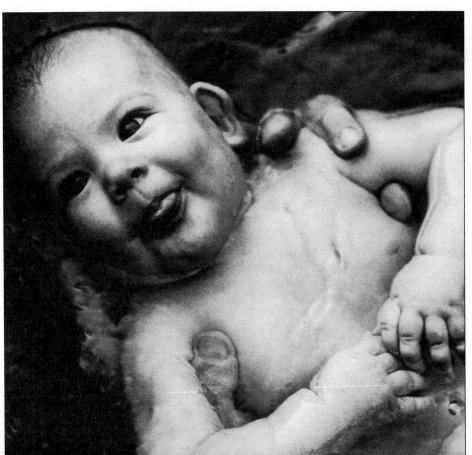

In this chapter we focus on how knowledge of child development can contribute to your understanding of children and your ability to support their growth and learning. We present some basic principles of development and discuss the significance and interrelationship of biology and environment in development. We also describe physical, social, emotional, and cognitive characteristics of children, from birth through the primary grade years, and explore some related research and theory.

The study of child development is one of the cornerstones of early childhood education and care. As we pointed out in Chapter Two, people have been studying children for centuries. Over the last three or four decades there has been a tremendous amount of new research and writing. Information about development tells us what young children are like and how they learn and grow. It also helps us to understand the ways that young children are different from older children and adults. We study child development to help us understand the children with whom we work and so that the programs we plan reflect this knowledge. Learning about children's growth and development is an essential part of becoming a competent early childhood professional.

In early childhood education we often refer to the development of the whole child. By this we mean that children use their bodies to move and their senses to explore the world (physical development); they learn to trust, to recognize and express their feelings, and to accept themselves (emotional development); they learn to relate to others and make moral decisions (social development); and they acquire and order information and learn to reason and problem solve (cognitive development). Although early childhood educators may differ in the emphasis they give to each of these aspects of development, they recognize their interconnectedness and the importance of each one in children's development.

As you study to become an early childhood professional, you will take courses in child development and child psychology. It may not always be clear how what you are learning relates to classroom practice—especially since the practical implications of the research are not always spelled out and some of the ideas are fragmented or contradictory. There are, however, aspects of this study that can be very helpful in working with young children. In this chapter we will share some of the research and theory we have found valuable and point out some implications for practice in early childhood programs. Knowledge of development in combination with your own direct experience in early childhood programs will give you a basis for understanding children and making informed choices in your work.

CHARACTERISTICS OF DEVELOPMENT

In the following sections we will describe some important characteristics of children's development and their implications for work with children. These characteristics include: the relationship between growth, maturation, and development; the directional sequence of development; and the order and rate of development.

Growth, Maturation, and Experience Are Interrelated

Development results from changes in the child that are based on the interplay of growth, maturation, and experience. *Growth* is primarily an increase in size; *maturation* is an increase in the complexity of organization, both physically and psychologically; and *experience* is all of a person's interactions with the environment. During the early childhood years, children's bodies grow—increase in size and mass. At the same time, maturation occurs—the child gradually develops control of his or her muscle system. Although it is not clear

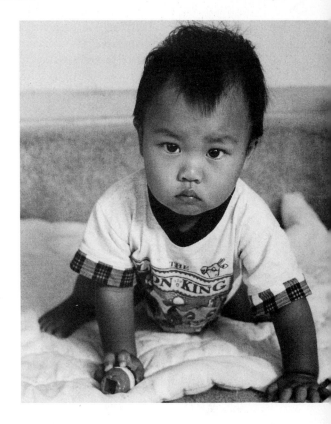

whether the rate of maturation can be increased through special training, it can be retarded by factors such as poor nutrition, serious illness, and the lack of opportunities to explore the world.

The same processes occur in psychological development. For example, infants lack the concept of object permanence—awareness

---

Reflect and write about . . .

your interest in child development

Where did your interest in young children begin? What did you notice about them? What interested you? How did the children you observed seem to be like you? How were they different? What did you think about their development?

that even when an object is not in sight it still exists. As the child matures, the concept develops, but no amount of training seems to be able to significantly accelerate its acquisition. A lack of experience with objects that can be seen, handled, and then removed may, however, result in the concept failing to develop.

Development Proceeds from Top Down and from Near to Far

All human development proceeds toward greater size and more complex organization and in an orderly and predictable manner. Physical development proceeds from the top downward (the *cephalocaudal principle*), seen most clearly in the development of the fetus. In the early stages of development, the head is half the length of the body, whereas at birth the head is one quarter the body length. This same top-down pattern is seen in motor development. The infant develops head control and reaching and grasping skill before sitting and walking. Growth and maturation also proceed from near to far (the *proximodistal law*). The large muscles closest to the center of the body grow and develop coordinated functions before the small muscles of the hands and fingers. This is reflected in children's developing skills in painting and drawing. Younger children paint or draw using their whole arm in large circular motions. As they get older they are better able to control the brush or pen and use their wrists and fingers to make more precise movements.

As children grow and mature they become more capable of coordinating their movements. It is important to be aware of physical capabilities so that you provide children with the challenges that they need to grow but do not frustrate them by expecting them to perform tasks for which they are not yet ready. An example of an inappropriate expectation that we often see is the expectation that all kindergarten children should be able to write with pencils within the spaces on lined paper.

Development Is Sequential and Cumulative

Since prior levels of size and complexity must precede later ones, development is sequential and cumulative. For example, before children can learn to write, they must have mastered the small-muscle coordination required to grasp objects; learned to use instruments like brushes, pencils, and scissors; had experiences forming shapes and letters; and seen and used written language.

New experiences that do not build from previous experiences can be meaningless or overwhelming to a child, while experiences that are not challenging or interesting may provoke boredom and restlessness. J. McVicker Hunt (1961) describes the concept of an *optimal match* between a child's present level of understanding or skill and the acquisition of a new knowledge or skill. New experience needs to provide just the right amount of novelty or challenge in order to interest the child. You can stimulate children's development by planning experiences that provide challenge and by avoiding experiences that children find frustrating (because they are too difficult) or boring (because they are too easy). The work of Lev Vygotsky, which we will describe later in this chapter, helps us to understand how adults can support children's emerging knowledge and skills.

The knowledge that development is a process that follows a sequential order, combined with information about the characteristics of each stage, lets you know what can generally be expected of children. You can then plan experiences for them based on this knowledge. Awareness of the cumulative nature of development helps teachers recognize that children cannot be expected to have knowledge or skill for which their level of development has not prepared them.

Rates of Development Vary

The child's actual age in years (chronological age) and stage of development are only approximately related. The direction and sequence of development are similar for every child, but each individual moves through stages at his or her own rate. Each infant enters the world with a unique biological endowment, and since the interplay of physical and environmental forces are different for every person, no two children (even from the same family) are exactly alike.

What a child can do and understand today is the basis of future development. If you are knowledgeable about the physical, social, emotional, and cognitive milestones each child must master before progressing to the next, you will be better able to plan a program that takes into account the wide variety of abilities you are likely to encounter, even among children who are very close in age. In order to have developmentally appropriate expectations, it is essential to observe and become acquainted with the competencies of each child in your group.

BIOLOGICAL VERSUS ENVIRONMENTAL INFLUENCES ON DEVELOPMENT

The history of thought about human development has been characterized by shifts in our beliefs about the relative impact of biological versus environmental forces on personality and behavior. Biological forces on development (sometimes referred to as *nature*) are genetic traits or inherited capacities and are expressed in the process of growth and maturation. Environmental forces (referred to as *nurture*) have to do with the kinds of interactions and experiences that enhance or restrict the development of biological potential. For example, every child is born with the capacity to learn any language but will only learn those that he or she hears spoken.

In the past there has been a heated debate (sometimes called the *nature-nurture controversy*) between people who felt that either the biological endowment or the environment was the primary force in shaping human behavior. Views on the subject shifted from the belief that all development was biologically determined to the opposing view that children were infinitely malleable and the environment was all-important in shaping later behavior and achievement.

Those who believe that inheritance is most significant maintain that there is a predominantly biological basis for personality, behavior, and intelligence. Arnold Gesell (whose work is discussed later in this chapter) was a leading proponent of the maturationist view that changes in children's physical and psychological development are a result of their genetic endowment. The opposing view comes from the behaviorist school of psychology, founded by John B. Watson and elaborated by B. F. Skinner (Nye 1986). These theorists state that all behavior is controlled by the environment and can be modified by the application of scientific principles of conditioning.

Scholars continue to debate the relative importance of biological and environmental influences, but there is some agreement today that they interact in complex ways and that each plays an important role in development.

Biological Factors

Today most child development specialists believe that biological factors have an important role in development. No one questions the hereditary basis of physical characteristics such as eye, hair, and skin color. Other characteristics —height, weight, intelligence, predisposition to some diseases, and temperament—are significantly determined by the individuals' inheritance but can be influenced by environmental factors such as diet, exercise, nutrition, health, and living conditions.

Research on inherited temperamental characteristics conducted by physicians Alexander Thomas and Stella Chess (1977), previously discussed in Chapter One, has influenced current views of the significance of biological inheritance. Thomas and Chess have shown that babies are not all alike at birth (something that parents have always known) and that there are distinct and observable differences in temperament among newborn infants that are fairly persistent over time. Thomas and Chess's work has given us valuable insight into the importance of what the child brings into the world at birth and how it interacts with the child's experiences.

According to Thomas and Chess, babies in their first days and weeks of life can be seen to differ in nine personality characteristics.

1. *Activity level:* the proportion of inactive periods to active ones.
2. *Rhythmicity:* the regularity of cycles of hunger, excretion, sleep, and wakefulness.
3. *Distractibility:* the degree to which new stimulation alters behavior.
4. *Approach/withdrawal:* the response to a new object or person.
5. *Adaptability:* the ease with which a child adapts to the environment.
6. *Attention span and persistence:* the amount of time devoted to an activity and the effect of distraction.

7. *Intensity of reaction:* the energy of response regardless of its quality or direction.
8. *Threshold of responsiveness:* the intensity of stimulation required to evoke a response.
9. *Quality of mood:* the amount of friendly, pleasant, joyful behavior as contrasted with unpleasant, unfriendly behavior.

Although these characteristics tend to persist over time, they can be modified by experience. For example, babies who tend to be fearful of novelty may adapt more easily if their behavior is understood and accepted by their parents and they are given support in developing new patterns.

We have found the work of Thomas and Chess valuable in helping us to understand the wide range of personalities in the young children we have taught and in understanding the interplay between children's characteristics and those of the adults who live and work with them.

Environmental Factors

Research has demonstrated that the experiences of the first five or six years of life have a critical impact on all areas of children's subsequent development. Until the 1950s and 1960s, the prevalent view was that people matured in predictable ways according to a biologically predetermined plan. In *Intelligence and Experience* (1961), Hunt cited many research studies that demonstrated the powerful effects of early

---

Reflect and write about . . .

your observations of temperament in young children

Think about the temperament of your own child, or a child with whom you have worked. What appeared to be the characteristics of the child's temperament? How do you think these influenced how other people responded to the child and how he or she functioned in an early childhood program?

experience on children's development. This book contributed significantly to the current view of the great importance of early experience.

Research has shown that in humans, as in animals, there are critical periods, times of physical or psychological sensitivity, during which the normal development of an organ or structural system must take place. If it does not occur during this period, permanent damage may occur or development may be retarded. Critical periods for development of physiological structures for vision and for brain growth occur prenatally. A comparable period for language development occurs during the first few years of life (Black, Puckett, and Bell 1992; Schickedanz, Hansen et al. 1993).

Research on the importance of early experience led to the idea that preschool programs might be an antidote for the deprivation associated with extreme poverty in young children, and hence compensatory education programs were developed. Research has made a persuasive case for the positive impact that early childhood programs can have on the lives of participating children (Lazar and Darlington 1983).

There is also evidence that human beings are resilient and can overcome adverse circumstances encountered in early life. A study of Guatemalan Indian children conducted by Jerome Kagan (1973) suggests that inadequate nurture and stimulation in the early years does not necessarily cause irreversible deficiencies later in life. A longitudinal study on children from the Hawaiian island of Kauai identified characteristics of children who are resilient in the face of adversity (Werner, Bierman, and F. E. French; Werner and Smith 1992). These include inherited characteristics, like optimistic personality, and environmental factors, most important of which is a long-term, trusting relationship with a caring adult. Although repeated experiences of extreme and early deprivation may cause serious damage to the developing

child, these studies suggest that human beings can be remarkably resilient, and early deprivation does not necessarily result in lifelong problems.

Foundations of Healthy Development

Research on child development and psychological theory offer useful insights into the necessary conditions for healthy development. We know that the foundation is laid down in infancy and that healthy development is likely to occur when infants have their basic needs met, when they are nurtured by the adults in their environment, and when they have adequate opportunity to explore the world. It is important to understand the nature of these early foundations to help children to function productively throughout the early years.

Meeting Basic Needs

Infants require consistent adult attention to their basic needs. Once viewed as passive organisms engaged primarily in reflex behavior during a relatively unimportant period, infants are described today as active beings who have the ability to react to sensory stimuli, to interact with others, and to be alert to and observant of the environment. Infancy is a crucial time for laying the foundation for later development. Understanding the importance of this period of development will help you to meet the needs of infants and see the continuity between infancy and the next stages of development.

Today's professionals who work with young children are increasingly aware of the importance of prenatal conditions including the health, mental health, and nutritional status of the parents. From birth throughout the early years it is essential that children have their basic physiological needs met. Appropriate nutrition is especially important. Most doctors and nutritionists recommend breast-feeding because mother's milk is the most nourishing food for an infant and apparently has a positive effect on the child's resistance to disease and allergy. Malnutrition in the infant and toddler has been shown to be associated with retarded mental and physical development and may be related to attention deficits. Brain development, particularly myelination (the laying down of myelin sheaths, the nerve insulation essential in sensory integration), is impaired in malnourished children. Children with good nutrition in infancy and early childhood tend to fare better in all areas of development.

The importance of providing for basic needs has a psychological as well as a physical dimension. Abraham Maslow, a major figure in humanistic psychology, focused his work on the actualization of human potential and suggested that there is a hierarchy of basic and growth needs (Maslow 1968, 1970). At the base of Maslow's hierarchy are the physiological needs for air, water, food, and shelter. If these needs go unmet or are only partially met, the individual may not survive or may focus all of their thought and energy on meeting these needs. When basic physical needs are satisfied, the urge to feel secure becomes more pressing. This need is met when people are free from fear of hazards and threats in their environment and when they are surrounded by others who are caring and predictable. When they feel secure, people are able to focus on giving and receiving love, the pursuit of an understanding of the world, and the self-knowledge that satisfies the highest human need—that of self-actualization. Maslow's work serves as a reminder that infants, toddlers, and young children must have significant others available to provide the conditions that free them to grow and learn.

Nurturing Relationships

The second prerequisite for healthy development is a warm, intimate, continuous relationship between the infant and his or her primary caregivers. Care given in the context of a loving relationship is essential to normal physical and emotional development and helps a child to learn that the world is a safe and trustworthy place.

Research motivated by observations of the high mortality rates of unhandled research animals has established the significance of comforting tactile experiences in the early development of all species of mammals. Harry and Margaret Harlow's classic research showed that baby monkeys had a marked preference for contact with a terrycloth surrogate mother, who provided contact comfort but no food, to a wire mother who had the advantage of providing milk but who had little else to recommend her in the eyes of the baby monkeys (Schickedanz et al. 1993).

Similar needs in humans are shown in research demonstrating that a large percentage of institutionalized human infants did not survive the first year of life when there was little or no opportunity for consistent, close contact to occur and where only the basic needs for nourishment and cleanliness were met. In institutions where caregivers provided frequent comforting physical contact, the mortality rate decreased sharply and infants developed normally. Other research on institutionalized and neglected children has demonstrated that those who suffer maternal deprivation in infancy often have problems in later development (Skeels 1966). Research and clinical observation reinforce our awareness of the importance of intimate contact between the primary caregiver and the infant, and how this connectedness (or failure to connect) influences all aspects of later development.

Research on child development clearly demonstrates that children can only thrive when adequate nurture is available. Early observation of the failure of institutionalized infants to develop normally (or even to survive) led to a concern with the social and emotional development of children who were cared for in child-care centers rather than by their mothers.

John Bowlby did work in the middle of this century that identified attachment to the mother as an essential prerequisite for normal social and emotional development (Bowlby 1951). Bowlby's work led to the conclusion that care outside of the home deprived children of this vital connection to their mothers and could result in serious psychological disorders and problems with interpersonal relationships.

Other researchers and theorists have revisited this topic in recent years and confirmed the idea that the nature of early attachments has a profound effect on development. Mary Ainsworth, an associate of Bowlby, conducted further research regarding the security of attachment of children to their mothers. She found that the degree of attachment between mothers and their children differed a great deal, from securely attached to those who had not attached at all. Her work confirms the belief that children must be secure in their primary relationships before they are able to fully explore the world. However, few early childhood specialists today believe that only a mother can serve this purpose. Children re-

quire consistent, warm, and responsive nurturing by a few intimate caregivers. They can be the mother, father, grandmother, uncle, family child-care provider, and/or one or two consistent, nurturing teachers in an early childhood education and care center. This "multiple parenting" can be just as effective as a single attachment as long as there are no more than half dozen people and all respond in a reliable and predictable manner to the child's needs. Attachment is a necessary condition of optimal social and emotional development. However, the precise form the attachment takes is not important as long as it provides a secure base from which infants can begin to explore the world (Clarke-Stewart, Perlmutter, and Friedman 1988).

Research on non-parental infant care has recently been extended into exploration of the effects of child care on development. A summary of current research on the effects of non-maternal care on development led Jay Belsky to caution that more than 20 hours a week of care outside the home may lead to heightened insecurity and aggression in children (Belsky 1988). Belsky's work led to lively debate regarding the pros and cons of group care for infants and pointed to the importance of the quality of the care and the importance of stability, acceptance, and emotional responsiveness in those who work with infants in group settings.

Psychoanalyst Margaret Mahler studied behavioral, social, and emotional aspects of infants and toddlers as they moved from the security of infancy to the relative independence of the preschool years. She introduced the concept that children are born first when they enter the world and a second time, psychologically, at about eighteen months when they begin to be aware of an identity separate from their mother or mother-figure. According to Mahler, the major developmental task of infancy is separation-individuation, the process of slowly differentiating the self from another and the acquisition of the sense of self (Mahler 1975). The period around eighteen months is very important. Although children begin to move away from their principal caregivers and gain a feeling of pleasure in mastery, there is a need to maintain connectedness and to have the caregiver appreciate developing skills and provide continuing support and reassurance. Some child development specialists urge parents not to place children in care situations out of the home before they reach this important developmental landmark. Mahler's work, like that of Bowlby, has been recognized as essentially correct but subject to refinement by new research that recognizes that the consistent nurture of children can be distributed between several adults without interrupting attachment and then separation-individuation.

A Stimulating Environment

The final important condition required for infants and young children to develop normally is an environment that provides them with novelty and stimulation and includes opportunities for sensory exploration. Interaction with people and objects in the course of play—the important work of infancy and childhood—has positive effects on subsequent intellectual development. For example, children who were given colorful objects to look at began reaching and grasping earlier than normal (Schickedanz et al. 1993).

Table 4.1 summarizes all these influences on development.

DEVELOPMENT OF THE WHOLE CHILD: RESEARCH AND THEORY INTO PRACTICE

Child development researchers gather information about how children grow and learn and create theories that attempt to explain what they have studied. A *theory* is a systematic statement of principles that organizes and explains what was observed. A theory shows us the relationship of facts and ideas and enables us to understand the past and predict the future. Theories aid us in understanding the world, but they do not represent a truth, which is static and unchanging. As we gain new knowledge, a theory may be changed or replaced by another theory that is simpler, more accurate, more comprehensive, or more useful.

Over the years a number of researchers and practitioners have developed theories about the development of children. These theories differ greatly in the aspects of development on which they focus, in their underlying assumptions, and in the subjects and methods used as a basis for their conclusions. No single theory explains all aspects of child development. Each is like a lens that focuses on some unique aspect of the whole. Knowledge of the-

---

Reflect and write about . . .

your own development

Reflect on what you know about your own development. What were you like as an infant and young child, physically, socially, emotionally, and intellectually? How do you think your characteristics as an infant/child relate to the adult you are today? How might this influence the early childhood educator you will become?

TABLE 4.1
Implications of biological and environmental factors influencing development

Developmental Factors	Implications for Practice
Heredity and environment interact to influence development.	Although there are some things about a child that you cannot change, positive interventions in the early years can make a lasting difference.
Some characteristics and conditions are inherited (eye, hair, and skin color, blindness, and deafness that appear before birth); others are primarily determined by inheritance (height, weight, intelligence, and temperament) and can be altered by experience	Accept and appreciate children as they are; be aware of the contributions you can realistically make to their development; provide appropriate referrals and resources if you feel there is a health or development problem that needs professional attention.
Early experience influences later development, but early deprivation can be compensated for.	Good quality early childhood programs and caring teachers can make a difference in a child's life.
Nutrition is a critical factor influencing early growth and development.	Make sure that meals and snacks provided in school are nutritious, avoid too many sweets in the classroom, and provide nutrition information to families.
Attachment to and loving contact with warm, responsive caregivers is essential to normal physical, social, and emotional development.	Have warm, physical contact with children; support positive relationships between children and their families; be sure that consistent, nurturing caregivers are available for each child; avoid inconsistencies in numbers and schedules of caregivers.

ory can help you to understand children and their behavior, but it is important to keep in mind that there is no single theory that is "right" and that ties up everything we know about children into one neat package. It is most often educators, not the theorists, who derive educational implications from child development research. It is important, therefore, that you read theory critically and that you choose to apply only those aspects of theories that support your values for the education of young children (Maier 1978; Nye 1986; Thomas and Chess 1977).

In the following sections we will discuss some ideas about development that are both theoretical and practical. For each aspect of development—physical, social, emotional, and cognitive—we give a profile of typical growth at different stages, describe the work of researchers and clinicians who have contributed to understanding this aspect of development, and explore possible implications of theory and research for work with young children. These descriptions will give you a framework for understanding and guiding children's behavior.

Physical Development

From birth to eight years of age, children undergo dramatic changes in their bodies and in their physical capabilities. Physical development is orderly and is marked by the change from undifferentiated to controlled activity. It can be observed in increased height and weight, altered body proportions, and changes in sleeping, eating, and toileting patterns. Sensory-perceptual skills develop; large muscles become strong, flexible, and coordinated; and fine motor strength and skill develops. Those who work with young children need to be aware that a child's physical competence influences other aspects of his or her development, especially self-concept. Physically competent children may advance more rapidly than others in the cognitive domain simply because they are likely to explore more aspects of the world at an earlier age and perhaps more extensively.

Stage-Related Characteristics of Physical Development

Knowledge of some typical aspects of physical development at different stages can help you to have realistic expectations and to design appropriate experiences for young children. The rate of physical development varies between children and can be related to biological inheritance, nutrition, and early opportunities for moving and exploring the environment. Following is an outline of some of the characteristics of physical development from infancy through the primary years.

Infants (birth through twelve months). Infants develop very rapidly. At birth children sleep and wake in unpredictable patterns, but within the year most are sleeping through the night and taking several naps. The toothless newborn eats every few hours and receives all nourishment from milk. By age one most children have a least twelve teeth and eat three meals of solid food plus snacks.

The grasping reflex of the newborn is largely accidental in nature—if an object comes into contact with the hand, the child grabs it. This reflex develops into the hand and eye co-

ordination that enables the one-year-old to meticulously pick up a pea from a plate.

At birth children have no control over head movement and are almost totally dependent on their caregivers for changes in position. Within a few months infants can lift their own heads to visually explore the world; by mid-year they can roll over, and some can stand; and by the end of the first year many children can walk.

Toddlers (twelve through thirty-six months). Toddlers refine and consolidate many of the motor abilities they have gained during the first year of life. At twelve months, fingers are tools for eating, and by mid-year children may enjoy using a spoon at least part of the time. By the end of the toddler stage most children have all twenty of their teeth. They are able to control elimination when awake and use the toilet with little assistance. Most toddlers sleep twelve or thirteen hours each day and most still need diapers at night.

During the second year children can scribble with crayons and pencils and learn how to turn the pages of a book. Hand preference emerges at this time. Toddlers are likely to spend a lot of time picking up small items like cubes and blocks and dropping them into containers, carrying them about, and dumping them out. At eighteen months most children can stack two or three blocks and by age two can manage a stack of six or more.

By fifteen months the vast majority of children walk. By age two nearly all can run, climb up and down stairs (the same foot forward one step at a time) with a firm hold on an adult or a rail, and throw a ball in a two-handed style. Between two and three years of age, children consolidate many skills and become much more independent in their ability to move about in the world and meet their own physical needs.

Preschool and Kindergarten Children (three through five years). Children this age are energetic and involved in practicing physical skills. They expend a good deal of energy, so most preschool-age children nap for an hour or two a day; many stay awake all day by the end of the preschool years. A young three-year-old may have an occasional daytime toileting accident, but by age four this will be a rare occurrence. Many children have night control of elimination by age four or five.

Zippers, snaps, and buttons can be mastered during this period, and children may enjoy dressing themselves. Although a pair of scissors may be a challenge for a young three-year-old, most four-year-olds use them with ease. Five-year-olds have developed considerable skill with paint brushes, pens, and pencils. Many children can learn to cut along a straight line and copy a drawing of a circle or square. Some will attempt to copy letters and numerals as they near the end of this period. Five-year-olds may be able to write with good control though not great precision.

At the beginning of the preschool years large-muscle development may still be toddler-like in nature. For example, a three-year-old can run but may not be able to stop and change direction with ease, while four-year-olds can run, vary speed and direction, and stop on a dime. During these years, children progress from throwing and catching with clumsily outstretched arms to the ability to throw a ball overhand with accuracy; from hesitant, awkward attempts at climbing to the ability to climb quickly and smoothly with alternating steps. By age three most children have learned to ride a tricycle, and by age four they have the strength and skill to make it go fast, turn sharply, and back up with accuracy and considerable speed.

Primary Children (six through eight years). Primary children are quite independent in their self-care. Toileting accidents are rare, naps are nearly unheard of, and eating patterns closely resemble those of adults.

During this period the rate of growth slows, handedness develops, and permanent teeth appear. Children have a good deal of fine muscle control and take great joy in practicing skills such as writing, drawing, and playing an instrument.

Height and weight vary greatly. Children tend to be energetic and are developing agility, stamina, strength, and skill in games, bicycling, skating, swimming, and dancing. At this stage physical skill becomes an important aspect of a child's self-concept.

Theoretical Contributions to Understanding Physical Development

Arnold Gesell (1896–1961), who pioneered the scientific study of child development, collected observational data on children and charted their growth patterns and behavior changes as they matured. Gesell and his associates, Frances L. Ilg and Louise B. Ames, identified and described the age or stage-related growth and behavior characteristics of children from birth through adolescence. They gathered information under ten categories on dozens of children at each age level and used the information to write summary descriptions of what the "normal" child was like at a given age. These are now called *developmental norms*. The resulting guidelines for what can be expected of children at various ages and stages of development serve as the basis for many developmental charts and screening instruments that are in use today (Gesell 1940; Gesell and Ilg 1974).

Gesell believed that maturation was the crucial factor in reaching new developmental levels. His maturation theory of development holds that growth is governed by heredity and proceeds in a genetically determined sequence; the individual rate is minimally influenced by experience. Because each person is genetically different, the rate at which they attain the growth and maturation necessary for learning skills and concepts varies. Gesell and his colleagues noted alternating years of positive and negative behavior ("terrible twos" and "tranquil threes") that they associated with periods of equilibrium and disequilibrium. This idea is still prevalent in early childhood literature.

Gesell's work led to the concept of readiness, a period of development in which a specific skill or response is most likely to occur. Maturational theory suggests that attempts to hasten development are futile because progress cannot be made until the prerequisite growth and maturation have occurred within the body and mind of the child. Critics of Gesell's work have cautioned that this can be taken to mean that environmental stimulation is not important. Although Gesell and his colleagues stress that development cannot be rushed, research on physical development suggests that it is most likely to occur when young children have many opportunities to engage in small and large motor activities on a daily basis.

Gesell's methods of data collection have also been challenged. The data on ages and stages was collected from a small geographic area and from a limited number of subjects who were of limited socioeconomic, racial, and cultural diversity. The critics say that it is not appropriate for this data to be used to assess children who have very different backgrounds.

The use of normative charts has led some people to associate average, age-related behaviors or growth levels with desirable degrees of development. Maturational scholars have taken great care to remind practitioners to avoid setting up unrealistic expectations and to remember that the sequence of development does not vary but that the rate may be different from child to child: All children crawl before they walk, but one child may begin to walk at eight months while another begins at twelve months. Each is progressing within the normal range of development. In spite of these cautions, children have been denied school entry and promotion based on their performance on developmental tests that use Gesell's norms.

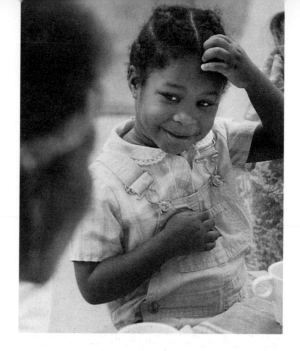

Implications for Practice

Information about developmental norms can help us to determine whether children are developing according to schedule and when we might be concerned with a child's overall progress or with a particular aspect of development. Developmental norms can guide our decisions about when children can realistically be expected to acquire abilities and to learn skills. Gesell and his colleagues were pioneers in the use of observation as a tool for the study of children. Observational methods are now central to the work of researchers and invaluable in the daily life of the people who work in early childhood settings (see Chapter Six on uses of observation). Gesell's descriptions of normal stages of development provide us with general guidelines for expectations. The developmental charts in the curriculum chapters of this book and many instruments for screening development are based on this kind of data.

Social Development

Social development in young children can be seen in their growing ability to relate to others and to become productive members of society. It includes how children learn expectations about behavior and their emerging skill in social relationships. A number of different aspects of social development have been explored by researchers and theorists. These include social competence, how effectively a child functions in society; the acquisition of social skills, behaviors that help a child in social situations; the development of social cognition, the ability to understand the thoughts, intentions, and behaviors of themselves and others; and the ability to engage in prosocial behavior, behavior that benefits others, such as sharing, helping, cooperating, empathizing, comforting, reassuring, defending, and encouraging. Another important aspect of social development is the acquisition of values and morality, the development of standards for judging right and wrong, and the ability to consider the needs and welfare of others.

These areas of social development are interconnected and are influenced by the kinds of experiences and social relationships that children have with their families and others and by their level of cognitive development. Current research points to the importance of fostering children's social development in the early years.

Stage-Related Characteristics of Social Development

During the early years children experience tremendous growth in their ability to relate to others. Knowledge of typical behavior at each stage can help you to understand children's actions and provide experiences that will support positive social development.

Social development involves a spiraling increase of knowledge about self and others. It is influenced both by the kinds of experiences and relationships that children have with significant adults in their lives and by their level of cognitive development. Four aspects of cognition are particularly significant: (1) movement from being egocentric—seeing the world only from one's own perspective—to the growing ability to understand how other people think and feel, (2) growth in the ability to understand cause and effect—to see the connection between one's actions and the consequences, (3) change from thinking concretely (you are my friend when you are playing with me) to thinking more abstractly (friendship is based on shared interests or attributes and persists over time), and (4) growth in cognitive complexity. Understanding others is not merely a matter of learning more, it requires organizing what one knows into systems of meaning or belief. As they grow, children become able to develop abstractions—first from direct experience of observable phenomenon (some people are called boys and some girls; boys play Power Rangers and girls play dress-up) and then from intellectual reflection on experience (if you are a boy, you can't be a girl; boys grow up to be men).

Infants need to forge strong bonds with the important adults in their lives and to develop basic trust. Secure connection of a baby to a "principal attachment figure" is essential to all subsequent social and emotional development. During infancy babies begin to orient to people in their environment; they become socially responsive, will return a smile, and by the middle of the first year participate in games such as this-little-piggy and peekaboo. They also become more selective about who they will respond to.

Toddlers are very concerned about the presence of the principal attachment figure. They worry when that person out of sight and use them as a base for forays out into the world, returning to safety when they get too far away from their reassuring presence. Early in the toddler stage children like to play on their own (solitary play) or to have the exclusive attention of favorite adults. As they approach their second birthday they remain very possessive of their belongings but begin to enjoy the nearby company of other children as they play (parallel play). At this stage we see vocal exchanges with turn-taking, social imitation, and conflicts over toys. Although it was previously thought that their relationships were limited to parallel play, today's toddlers who spend a good deal of time in group settings have been observed to develop genuine friendships.

Preschool and kindergarten children are better able to separate from the significant adults in their lives because they are able to visualize the behavior of these people even when separated from them. They are more flexible and are growing in the ability to recognize the needs and wishes of others.

Three-year-olds enjoy adult company, can play with other children (associative play), and are quite able to share belongings. Peers become very important to four- and five-year-olds. Children at this stage are learning to cooperate and negotiate with other children. Friendships are quite transient, depending on proximity and shared activities.

Prosocial behavior is increasing. Preschool children are likely to obey to avoid consequences. Four-year-olds base decisions on self-interest: "I should have it because I want it." Five-year-olds are more able to see the conflict between what they want and external rules. Moral judgments are based on the amount of damage done rather than on a person's intentions (for example, breaking several plates by accident is a worse moral transgression than breaking one on purpose).

Primary children begin to seek interactions with children rather than adults, and the peer group becomes a powerful force. Friendships are increasingly important and less transient. Increased self-awareness is accompanied by the tendency to be competitive and to make comparisons between self and others.

Gender identity is firmly established during the primary years and is often expressed in same-sex play groups that engage in gender-role stereotyped play (boys acting out superheroes and girls playing with dolls). Boys and girls continue to enjoy dramatic play and become very interested in sports and games. Games with rules lead to conflict and offer opportunities for children to learn to express their views of fairness and to negotiate.

Children are more independent at work and play and are mastering new skills. They often enjoy working cooperatively with peers, teachers, and parents. This gives them some of the positive human contact they need to feel good about themselves.

Research on moral development has shown that children at this stage respect authority because of the power of the authority figure. They have a view of strict equality, where everyone gets the same amount when resources are distributed. In their moral reasoning children are now able to take into account subjective factors like motivation (Kohlberg 1981).

Theoretical Contributions to Understanding Social Development

Constructivist theory, derived from the work of Swiss epistemologist Jean Piaget, is very helpful in explaining how social understanding comes about. This theory proposes that development takes place through interaction between the child and the environment and that the developing child constructs his or her own knowledge. Piaget's work will be described more fully in the section on cognitive development.

Although much of the writing based on constructivist theory has focused on how children develop physical knowledge, Piaget suggested that there were parallel structures and functions for the child's construction of knowledge of the social world (Edwards 1986).

Constructivist theory is particularly helpful in understanding a critical component of the understanding self and others, the development of social cognition. Social cognition refers to children's ability to understand and classify of their own and other people's characteristics, relationships, thoughts, feelings, and behavior.

During the early childhood years, children do move from an egocentric perspective toward an appreciation of the thoughts and feelings of others. They become capable of understanding the relationship between their own behavior and the responses of other people. They become capable of envisioning relationships as persevering over time.

Constructivist theory also contributes to our understanding of children's moral development. In the past people believed that morality was learned from "teaching." But we know today that it is actively constructed by the individual. The development of morality is a complex process that grows out of children's early social experiences in combination with their emotional and cognitive growth.

Understanding of children's moral development has been the concern of a number of researchers, beginning with Jean Piaget. In his pioneering work, *The Moral Judgment of the Child* ([1932] 1965), Piaget proposed that children develop concepts about morality through an interactive constructive process. Piaget's research demonstrated that children reason about fairness and justice in their daily encounters with peers. His ideas form the basis for most current research on moral development.

Piaget associated moral development with children's growing ability to interpret rules, and he described stages and a sequence of moral development. Children under six base their judgments about what constitutes naughty behavior on the amount of damage done and not on intention because their focus is on concrete and observable outcomes. By middle childhood, children are able to take intentions into account and to base their judgments on them. According to Piaget, both the child's stage of cognitive development and previous social experiences are precursors to moral development.

Piaget's research demonstrated that children move from the view that rules are unchangeable and derived from higher authority to a more mature perspective that rules are made by people and can be changed. This translates into two kinds of morality. The first is the morality of obedience, or heteronomy, which involves being regulated by others and conforming to rules that are accepted without question. The second, the morality of autonomy, involves being guided by oneself and by principles of moral conduct. A number of scholars today are continuing to study how children think about authority and fairness and how the development of morality can be supported by the adults in children's lives (Damon 1988; Edwards 1986; Eisenberg 1992; Lickona, Geis, and Kohlberg 1976).

Laurence Kohlberg's work on moral reasoning elaborates and extends Piaget's work to fo-

Reflect and write about . . .

supporting social development

What are some of the ways that you have observed adults in early childhood settings supporting the development of social skills among children in their groups? In programs you have visited, what examples have you seen of adults modeling prosocial behavior? What examples have you seen of children demonstrating their understanding of the concepts of fairness and justice?

cus on how people make moral decisions across the life span. Kohlberg described three levels of moral development that relate to the child's views of moral conventions; thus, the terms *preconventional, conventional,* and *postconventional* are used to describe them (Kohlberg 1981). People move from stage to stage as a result of their own reasoning power and see for themselves the contradictions in their own beliefs. A person must pass through each stage in order, and each is dependent on the preceding one (Figure 4.1).

Carole Gilligan and others have been critical of Kohlberg's work because the subjects were primarily male and because research was based on hypothetical and not on real-life situations. Gilligan's research led her to conclude that males are more oriented toward fairness and justice in their moral decision making, and females are more concerned with caring and responsibility (Gilligan 1982).

Implications for Practice

Getting along with others in a group is not an inborn trait but, rather, a slowly learned skill that occurs as a result of interaction between people. Young children are egocentric and slowly develop social and moral competence. Opportunities for social development can permeate the early childhood program as children are given many opportunities to cooperate, share, be helpful, understand the viewpoint of others and solve interpersonal problems. These things are not taught in isolation but can be integrated into everything that children do in the classroom.

When children feel a sense of security and control over their actions and their environment, they are more apt to behave in positive ways. Adults can assist children by offering nurturing and caring guidance and by providing many opportunities for them to engage in prosocial behavior. Modeling and pointing out children's prosocial behaviors when they occur, helping children to recognize the rights and feelings of others, helping them to understand the impact of their actions on others, and encouraging children to role play interpersonal problems are some things that early childhood educators can do.

Research has shown that the development of concepts of justice emerges during the pre-

Level One: *Preconventional Morality* (characteristic of children from two to seven)—moral decisions are based on self interest—on emotion and what the child likes. At this stage children have no personal commitment to rules that they perceive as external. They will do something because they want to, or not do it because they want to avoid being punished. By age four children begin to understand reciprocity—if I am nice to you, you might respond by being nice to me.

Level Two: *Conventional Morality* (characteristic of children between seven and twelve)—people choose to conform to and uphold the rules and conventions of society because they exist. They are concerned with group approval and consensus. Action is guided by concern with the general good and a desire to maintain the social order by doing one's duty.

Level Three: *Postconventional Morality* (adolescent and older, though not everyone reaches this stage)—people accept rules and laws that are agreed on in society and based on underlying moral principles. When the highest level is reached, individuals may make decisions based on conscience, which places universal morality above law or custom.

Source: L. Kohlberg, ed., *The Philosophy of Moral Development: Moral Stages and the Idea of Justice.* (San Francisco: Harper & Row, 1981).

FIGURE 4.1
Kohlberg's stages of moral development

school years and that young children are capable of recognizing the importance of fairness in their lives. According to Kohlberg, moral development is fostered when adult-child relationships are characterized by mutual respect: when children have opportunities to regulate their own behavior, to think independently and creatively, and to develop moral feelings of reciprocity. Demonstrating reflection on moral issues, using stories to promote thinking and discussion of moral issues, and discussing moral intentionality with children four years of age and older are some things you can do to guide children on the road to moral understanding.

Emotional Development

During the early childhood years, children develop as individuals who can be described in terms of their characteristic mood, ways of expressing feelings, and perceptions of themselves. Emotional development involves the development of sense of identity, self-esteem, impulse control, and the capacity for autonomous responses. It evolves from the child's inherited characteristics and, like other aspects of development, is influenced by experience and follows a sequence of growth.

Stage-Related Characteristics of Emotional Development

Each stage in childhood has distinctive characteristics of emotional development that affect how children will react to the experiences they encounter. Knowledge of these stage-related characteristics can help you to interact with children in ways that support their healthy development.

Infants need a primary nurturing caregiver, routines, and security. Their physical dependency requires a relationship with another person (often a parent) that lays the foundation for subsequent emotional and social development. The nurturing responses of a caregiver ensure the survival of the infant and provide the basis for his or her eventual perception of the world as a trustworthy place. Infants soon learn to express a wide range of emotions through body movements and facial expressions. They cannot tolerate frustration nor control impulses.

Some time between six and nine months of age most infants become somewhat anti-social and develop stranger anxiety, a highly predictable wariness of unfamiliar people. An approaching stranger evokes cringes, head hiding, and finally cries of protest. However, from the security of a primary caregiver's arms the feared newcomer can be observed carefully and may be judged as trustworthy—especially if the caregiver reacts positively. By the beginning of their first year, children will again be more accepting of new people and situations. One-year-olds are demanding but at the same

time are generally friendly, adaptive, and able to give up an assertive demand at the request of a loved adult.

Toddlers are on an emotional roller-coaster ride, from the amiability of the one-year-old, to the vociferous demands of the two-year-old, and finally back to the calmer sociability of a three-year-old. By age two, children begin to assert themselves much more strongly. They can seem stubbornly self-centered and resistant to change as they begin their quest for auton-omy. At this age children have little control of impulses and are easily frustrated.

Preschool and kindergarten children are beginning to be able to tolerate frustration and are developing self-control and a sense of humor. Three-year-olds tend to be curious and generally positive in disposition. Like age two, the fourth year is often a tumultuous one, during which children seem to display a different personality from minute to minute— joyful humor may be replaced by an explosive burst of temper with little or no apparent cause. By ages four and five children become more aware of the effects of their behavior on others and begin to clearly identify with their gender.

Primary children tend to be active, outgo-ing, and assertive. Children at this stage be-come very involved in mastering new skills and learning about the world in which they live. They may show off their accomplish-ments, and if their competence is challenged they can become defensive and argumentative. Young school-age children are becoming more independent, but new found autonomy can create feelings of insecurity. At this age chil-dren seem to feel the need to act grown up, so they may resist expressing their needs for af-fection and approval because they do not wish to be seen as "babies." They are able to ex-press and label a variety of emotions, and they are developing an understanding of right and wrong.

Theoretical Contributions to Understanding Emotional Development

Theorists associated with psychodynamic the-ory have addressed issues related to emotional development. The basic concepts underlying this theoretical approach were formulated by Sigmund Freud (1856–1939), a nineteenth-century neurologist and neuroanatomist. His theory of human development focuses on in-ner processes and on emotional development. Freud worked with emotionally troubled pa-tients during a period in history when their dis-turbances were believed to have an organic ba-sis. Freud put forth the revolutionary idea that unconscious psychological processes were the source of mental illness. He developed his ideas into a framework that was the first com-prehensive theory of human development de-scribing the stages of emotional development from infancy through adolescence.

Freud introduced the idea that behavior is influenced by unconscious factors, often sexu-ally motivated, originating in early experiences. Awareness of these is often lost to conscious memory through the mechanism of repression. Many of the researchers who later expanded the psychodynamic model de-emphasized Freud's discovery of childhood sexuality (de-spite the exciting stir it caused in nineteenth-century Vienna). The recognition that uncon-scious processes frequently play an important determining role in our thought and behavior has been tremendously influential and remains a hallmark of those who have used this ap-proach to understanding human development (Thomas 1985).

Freud's work provided the stimulus for more recent theoretical contributions to our un-derstanding of human development. Primary among those who have elaborated psychody-namic theory is Erik Erikson (1902–1994), whose work continues to be influential in the thought of early childhood educators today.

Erikson described a series of stages of social and emotional development that expand Freud's original psychosexual stages to include social influences (Figure 4.2). Erikson believed that basic attitudes are formed as individuals pass through the stages, and that serious problems at any stage lead to difficulty in reaching the next stage. Each stage is characterized by a major task or challenge. In infancy, the major task is the development of basic trust; for the toddler, it is the development of autonomy; for the preschooler, the development of initiative; and for the school-age child, industriousness (Erikson 1963).

For each stage, Erikson described the potential for healthy development at one end of a continuum and the potential for development of negative and self-defeating attitudes at the other. He saw development as a product of the tension between the two extremes, with more positive than negative experiences necessary for healthy progress.

Implications for Practice

Insights from psychodynamic theory have important implications for people who work with young children. The development of the child is seen as progressing through a series of stages that are predictable, continuous throughout life, and influenced by many forces. Because crucial aspects of the child's development occur in the first eight years when there is a great

---

Trust vs. mistrust (infancy): During the first stage of development, infants learn, or fail to learn, that people can be depended on and that they can depend on themselves to elicit nurturing responses from others. The quality of care an infant receives, especially in the first year of life, is essential to the development of basic trust. Through the love, nurture, and acceptance received, the infant learns that the world is a good and safe place.

Autonomy vs. shame and doubt (toddler): During the second stage of life, which begins at twelve to fifteen months, children develop a basic sense of autonomy—self-control and independent action. During this period they are growing rapidly, learning to coordinate many new patterns of action and to assert themselves. Conflict during this period centers on toilet training. If parents are accepting and easygoing and if they recognize the child's developing need to assert independence, the child will move successfully through this stage. If adults are harsh and punitive and if the child is punished for assertive behavior, then shame and doubt may become the stronger forces.

Initiative vs. guilt (preschool years): Three to six years of age is a period of interest, active exploration, and readiness for learning. Children need to express their natural curiosity and creativity during this stage through opportunities to act on the environment. If explorations are regarded as naughtiness and if parents or teachers are overly concerned with preventing children from getting dirty or destroying things, a sense of initiative may not be developed and guilt may be the prevalent attitude.

Industry vs. inferiority (school age): During the period between six years and puberty, children are ready for the challenge of new and exciting ideas and of constructing things. They need opportunities for physical, intellectual, and social accomplishment. They also need many and varied interactions with materials. Success and a feeling of "I can do it!" result in a sense of industry.

Source: E. Erikson, *Childhood and Society,* rev. ed. (New York: W. W. Norton, 1963).

FIGURE 4.2
Erikson's stages of childhood psychosocial develepment

dependency on adults, the relationships between children and significant adults in their lives is extremely important. Understanding that the young child is in the process of becoming a separate person can help kowledgeable caregivers to support the conflicting needs for connectedness and independence.

Psychodynamic theory has influenced educational programs through its emphasis on the significance of emotional development and its encouragement of creative expression as an outlet for children's feelings. By calling attention to unconscious forces that influence behavior, early childhood professionals have become aware that children cannot consciously control their thoughts, feelings, and responses and are therefore less harsh in their judgments. It has also made them increasingly aware of the importance of adult-child relationships and the importance of psychological health in the adults who work with young children. This approach also provides insights into causes of psychological disturbance in children and techniques for treatment.

Many practices found in high-quality early childhood programs support children in moving successfully through Erikson's developmental tasks. These practices include:

- Low ratios of children to adults and the designation of a primary caregiver in programs for infants and toddlers because contact with warm, caring, available people is a necessary condition for the development of the sense of trust.
- The provision of many opportunities for toddlers and young preschool-age children to make choices about play activities, materials, and playmates so they develop a sense of autonomy.
- Adequate time to explore and to plan and carry out play episodes so that the sense of initiative that is central to development during the preschool years can develop.
- Opportunities for school-age children to de-velop the sense of industry through experiencing success in many kinds of creative projects.
- Opportunities for preschool and school-age children to dramatize situations, learn to acknowledge and label feelings, hear stories, and relate how the characters felt and how the story relates to their own lives.

Cognitive Development

Cognitive development involves the development of thinking and reasoning abilities and the acquisition of knowledge about the world. The maturation that enables children to make sense of their experience evolves slowly over the first decade of life. During these years they come to understand a great deal about their world.

Stage-Related Characteristics of Cognitive Development

At each stage of development, children differ in their mental abilities. Infants reveal their understanding of the world through their actions. They are well equipped to collect information about the things that fall within their sensory range—things they can see, hear, smell, taste, and touch. As they grow older, children develop the capacity to organize and share their thoughts and feelings through the shared symbols of spoken and written language and number systems and through creative media such as music, art, dance, and drama. Knowledge of some of the hallmarks of cognitive development at different stages can help you to have realistic expectations and to design appropriate learning experiences for young children.

Infants explore the world with their senses—by looking, mouthing, and grasping. The primary caregiver is often the first object explored and the first person that the infant is able to tell from others. In the early months newborns gaze at some things for long periods of time and at the same time seem to ignore things and events that might attract their attention. It's as if the world is full of meaningless sensations and those that capture their interest are just random accidents. Later, after they have had many interactions with people and things, babies begin to make sense of happenings in their immediate world, and they begin to make some choices.

Infants soon discover that they can make things happen by their own actions. Within a short period after birth they come to some rudimentary understanding that a cry will often bring an adult. Before long the random batting at the crib mobile will be recognized as the cause of the ringing bells and be repeated for the effect. Sometime between the middle and the end of the first year infants demonstrate that they have begun to believe in the permanency of people and things (object permanence) by searching for them and protesting when they disappear from sight. Action-based problem solving appears at about the same time. Infants will retrieve a toy that has rolled behind something else by removing the obstacle.

Toddlers can crawl and walk so they are better able to explore and construct an understanding of the world. Like infants, they still rely on sensory information but are increasingly able to make use of mental images stored in memory to recall and anticipate events.

At one year of age most children have a few words available to represent the objects, people, and events with which they are most familiar. Toddlers come to recognize that actions, objects, and ideas are represented by words. They can often recognize and name a few colors, distinguish a few objects from many, and begin to understand aspects of space and time. For example, the park is near but mommy's office is far away; we are staying home today but will go to the park tomorrow.

Preschool and kindergarten children have developed many ideas about how the social and physical world works. During this period children become able to form more complex mental symbols of events and objects and use language to represent their ideas. Through this process, language becomes the tool for constructing and communicating concepts. By age three children have a vocabulary of over a thousand words that they use effectively for thinking and learning.

"What is it?" and "How does it work?" are frequently heard questions of three- and four-year-old children. As they pursue the answers, they construct many concepts about the qualities of things and learn to group objects by shared characteristics such as color, size, shape, and function. They explore quantity and learn that numerals (one, two, etc.) refer to a specific amount. They are still unable to relate numerals to more than about ten objects. By age five, most children understand the practical use of clocks and calendars and many associate specific events to times and days. Children are increasingly able to make and follow a plan and predict the outcomes of their own actions. Some older preschool and kindergarten children may begin to be interested in representing their ideas in writing. Most will represent quite sophisticated ideas through art media and dramatic play episodes. Play has taken on symbolic forms in which children can pretend that they are people other than themselves and in which objects can stand for something they are not.

Primary children are developing the ability to think logically. Symbols become effective tools for children as they develop thinking and literacy skills. Some six-year-olds will be reading with considerable skill while others may not master the skill by the end of the primary years. Early in this stage of development children judge quantity by appearance. For example, if you set out two glasses of juice, one in a short, wide glass and the other in a tall, narrow glass, many children will select the tall glass as the one that has more even when someone demonstrates that the amounts are the same. As they mature, children begin to realize that quantities remain the same even though the form may change and will no longer be fooled

by how things look. (This is called *conservation of quantity;* see the description of Piaget's stages in Figure 4.3.) Children also become able to visualize how something will appear if it is viewed from another position in space. They enjoy their ability to construct complex relationships between objects and may be interested in collecting, sorting, and classifying things in new ways. They are now able to sequence objects from short to tall and to arrange colors from light to dark. They take great pleasure in using these and other new skills.

Children at this stage have a more elaborated understanding of time—they can appreciate their own past, their family history, and historical events in their communities and the world. The ability to think logically leads to the

enjoyment of games that are governed by rules and a beginning understanding of societal concepts such as laws, rules, and justice.

Theoretical Contributions to Understanding Cognitive Development

Many early childhood educators today hold a constructivist view of the cognitive development of young children. The basic premise of this theory is that knowledge is built up over time as the child constructs knowledge through interaction with the environment. At every stage a person is engaged in the cumulative process of receiving and interpreting new information.

The best known explanation of cognitive development comes from the work of Jean Piaget (1896–1980), who devoted many years of his life to the study of children's thinking. He began his career as a biologist and later became an epistemologist, a philosopher who specializes in the nature of human knowledge. His youthful fascination with the biological adaptation of animal species evolved into an interest in how human beings adapt to their environments through their ability to use reason. The theory that Piaget developed focuses primarily on the nature and development of logical thought and on the construction of knowledge as an individual activity. His systematic, in-depth approach was based on case studies of individual children and interview techniques. Since the 1960s Piaget's work has had a major influence on early childhood programs in Europe and the United States (Flavell, Miller et al. 1993; Ginsburg and Opper 1988; Piaget 1966). Piaget postulated that children acquire three kinds of knowledge as they grow. The first, physical knowledge, consists of information about tangible aspects of the world gained by acting upon objects. It is best gained through first-hand experience. Social knowledge, the second kind, consists of information that society has agreed on. It includes language, social conventions, symbols, values, rituals and myths, and ideas about right and wrong and

Sensorimotor Stage: During the sensorimotor period (from birth to approximately two years of age), the child changes from a reflex organism to one capable of thought and language. Behavior is primarily motor and the child is dependent on physical manipulation to gain information about the world. During this period infants learn to differentiate themselves from others and to seek stimulation. They begin to develop the concept of causality. The ability to form mental images for events that cannot be readily heard, felt, seen, smelled, or tasted does not occur until age two.

The important developmental task of infancy that represents a shift in development and signals progress into the next stage is called *object permanence*. Children learn that objects exist in the world apart from their relationship to them and that an object may still exist even after it is out of sight.

Preoperational Stage: The preoperational period (between the ages of two and seven) is characterized by language acquisition and by rapid conceptual development. During this time the child evolves from a person who relies on actions for understanding to one who is able to internally represent events (think conceptually). Children learn labels for experience and develop the ability to substitute a symbol (word, gesture, or object) for an object or an event that is not present. Thought is based on how things appear to the child rather than on logical reasoning.

The early phase of this period is called *preconceptual*. Between the ages of two and four, children are egocentric; that is, they are unable to take the viewpoint of others. They tend to classify by a single salient feature. For example, they might classify all adult females as mothers. During the second, *intuitive,* phase of the preoperational period, between four and seven years, children are capable of more complex thought. They are less egocentric and more capable of social relationships. Moral feelings and moral reasoning begin during this stage.

The developmental hallmark of the early childhood period is conservation, the child's realization that the amount or quantity of a substance stays the same even when its shape or location changes. It is dependent on the child's growing ability to look at things from more than one point of view at a time.

Concrete Operations Period: During this period (between ages seven and eleven), children develop the ability to apply logical thought to concrete problems. Formal thought processes become more stable and reasonable even though children still have to think things out in advance and try them out through direct manipulation.

Formal Operations Period: During this final stage of cognitive development (between the ages of eleven and fifteen), children's cognitive structures reach their highest level of development and they become able to apply logic to all classes of problems. Children develop basic principles of cause and effect and of scientific experimentation. They can weigh a situation mentally to deduce the relationships without having to try it out.

Sources: H. Ginsburg and S. Opper, *Piaget's Theory of Intellectual Development,* 3rd ed. (Englewood Cliffs, NJ: Prentice Hall, 1988); B. J. Wadsworth, *Piaget's Theory of Cognitive and Affective Development,* 4th ed. (New York: Longman, 1989).

FIGURE 4.3
Piaget's stages of cognitive development

what is acceptable and unacceptable. It is learned by direct transmission through being told and by reading. The third kind of knowledge, logico-mathematical knowledge, is constructed by the child. It consists of processes used in operating on information, categorizing and ordering objects, and observation of relations. It is achieved as the child has opportunities to think and reason. Reflection is the important action. The gradual development of logico-mathematical knowledge enables children to move from reliance on manipulating objects to the ability to use symbols and to deal with abstractions.

Constructivist theory stresses adaptation as a result of the interaction between the individual and the social and physical environment. Piaget was interested in mental activity, in what the individual does in his or her interactions with the world. He believed that knowledge is not given to a passive observer; rather, it must be discovered and constructed by the activity of the child. Children have within themselves the capacity to adapt and change (Ginsburg and Opper 1988).

Through his observations of children, Piaget identified processes of cognitive development. As a result of interaction with the environment, the child develops organizing mental structures or concepts that Piaget referred to as *schemata*. Early schemata become the basis for more complex future mental structures. Piaget identified three complementary processes that children use to organize their experience into structures for thinking and problem solving.

The first process is assimilation, by which a person integrates new information or experience into existing schemes or patterns of behavior. Through this process the child fits new information into his own framework for understanding the world.

For example, the child who sees a goat for the first time and calls it a dog is trying to assimilate, or use a scheme he or she already has. Assimilation does not result in a change of schemes, but it does elaborate on an existing one and therefore contributes to development. When confronted with a new stimulus the child will try to assimilate it into an existing scheme.

If it is not possible to fit new information or experience in to existing schemes, the child engages in the second process, accommodation, the changing of an existing scheme to fit external reality more accurately or the creation of a new scheme. Through this process cognitive structures change and develop. The child has accommodated when she or he acquires the new scheme—goat. Schemata are constructed

by the child and reflect his or her understanding of the world.

The third process, equilibration, is based on the tendency for individuals to seek a dynamic balance between assimilation and accommodation. When there is a balance between assimilation and accommodation, the child is in a state of equilibrium. Imbalance between the two creates a state of disequilibrium. Equilibration is the process of moving from disequilibrium to equilibrium. It is through the tension and conflict of imbalanced assimilation and accommodation that intellectual growth (or adaptation) occurs.

Through the processes just described, children progress through a series of developmental stages that build from the interaction among three elements: existing mental structures, maturation, and experience. According to Piaget, each stage is distinct. Stages occur in the same predictable sequence for everyone, although the exact age at which a child enters the next stage varies with the individual and the culture. The characteristics of the stages are summarized in Figure 4.3.

Children in early childhood education and care programs will be in the sensorimotor and the preoperational stages of cognitive development. As they enter the preoperational stage, children are beginning to use symbols to represent experiences (words) in their thought processes. According to Piaget they are still bound to their perceptions and see things only from their viewpoint (egocentrism). The primary way that they learn is through direct experiences that involve sensory exploration and manipulation. During this period children are likely to focus on only one characteristic of an object or experience at a time, so they are easily deceived by appearances. One of our favorite stories that illustrates this concerns a child on his first plane ride who turned to his mother after the plane had completed its ascent and asked, "When do we start getting smaller?"

Piaget created a whole new focus and methodology for the study of children's cognitive development. Like any pioneering work it was neither complete nor fully formulated. The focus of Piaget's study was the structure of knowing and thinking. Less attention was paid to content. Moreover he did not address topics like the growth of the knowledge base, memory, and metacognition, the understanding of one's own mental processes.

The interest that Piaget's work has generated attests to its significance. His studies have been replicated in many settings and his work extensively critiqued. His careful observations of the strategies that children use in their thinking and his description of the processes and stages of development have made a tremendous contribution to our understanding of how young children learn and have generated much fruitful thought and research about cognitive development.

A number of researchers today are engaged in extending Piaget's work, especially in the area of children's interactions with people. They are taking a social interactionist perspective, which focuses on the role played by adults in facilitating young children's development. The ideas of Lev Semenovich Vygotsky (1896–1934), a Russian psychologist who wrote during the 1930s, have contributed to this interest in the social origins of language and thought. Vygotsky, like Piaget, was a constructivist. He believed that children are active in their own ongoing process of development. However, Vygotsky believed that the relationship with other people is the major process contributing to development. In his view, children develop in a specific social and cultural context, with early communicative interactions with adults becoming internalized to form the basis for speech and thinking.

Vygotsky distinguished between two types of development: natural, which is a result of maturation; and cultural, which involves language and reasoning ability and is culturally derived. Vygotsky described development as proceeding from the inter-psychic (between the child and other people) to the intra-psychic

(within the child) plane. Social experiences were seen as the foundation for human development. In Vygotsky's view the development of language is of primary importance because all human meaning is mediated by language.

If we accept Vygotsky's premise that knowledge is created through interaction with other people, it is not only important to look at the child, as Piaget did, but it is also important to focus on the interaction of the adult and child. Vygotsky believed that every function in development occurs first at the social level and then at the individual level. Children develop through what he referred to as the *zone of proximal development* or the point at which a child cannot accomplish a task alone but can do it with support. In *Thought and Language* he wrote, "What the child can do in cooperation today he can do alone tomorrow" (Vygotsky 1962, 104). In Vygotsky's view, children collaborate with others in co-constructing the structures of their minds. Social constructivism, as conceived by Vygotsky, regards knowledge and mind as deeply social and emerging from the mind of the child and of other people and out of the materials provided by culture, society, and nature (Williams 1992). Current research in child development, particularly in the areas of language and literacy development, reflects this social interactionist focus by exploring the relationship between thought and language.

Implications for Practice

Piaget's work has been extremely influential in early childhood education in the United States since the late 1960s. Its focus on the nature of children's thought has helped parents and professionals become aware that children's thinking is fundamentally different from that of adults. Another important lesson from Piaget's work is that we can learn a great deal about children's thought processes by paying attention to the line of reasoning they use in answering questions.

Reflect and write about . . .

your experience of child development theories in action

In what ways have you seen the developmental theories discussed in this chapter visible in the children you have observed and/or worked with?

Piaget's insistence that young children are always trying to construct a more coherent understanding of their world through their experience has led many educators to the belief that educational practices should allow ample opportunity for children to explore, experiment, and manipulate materials. Piaget was adamant that we cannot directly instruct children in the concepts that they need to move on to the next developmental stage. These concepts are acquired as a result of a complex interaction between experience, maturation, and adult mediation. Piaget was critical of what he saw as an American tendency to hurry development rather than to let it follow its own course. He was interested in the role of play in development and believed that it was the adult role to provide material and challenges and to facilitate the exchange of viewpoints between the players.

Vygotsky and others concerned with social interaction extend Piaget's perspective. They point out that educators play a vitally important role in young children's learning and development because they are actually helping them to construct meaning. They do this through conversation relevant to the particular child and by helping each child to find a personal meaning in the activities offered at school. This work makes us aware of the importance of the social context for learning.

FINAL THOUGHTS

We hope that this chapter has given you greater appreciation for the children you know

and a sense of the contributions that knowledge of child development can make to your work with young children. As you move ahead in your professional development we hope that you will keep two things in mind. First, keep learning about child development. Don't think that the information you get when you are a student is all you need. Knowledge about children, like the children themselves, is always growing and changing. New research is being conducted, old theories are being refined, and new ones created. And there is more knowledge available than any one person could read and absorb in their lifetime. If you are interested, it might give you more insight into the nature of the field of child development if you read some of the writings of the major theorists in the field and some of the original research in addition to other people's interpretations of this work.

Second, keep in mind that you are in the process of personal and professional development. As you study and as you work directly with young children, your understanding will grow. Your daily experiences and observations of children will combine with what you read to give you an every deeper and richer understanding. Working with young children involves a constant and dynamic interplay of information derived from the work of others and information you develop yourself based on your own experience and observation. Keep watching and listening to children and know that your understanding will continue to grow and that you can rely on your own conclusions as well as those of the experts.

Reflect and write about . . .

how you will apply child development knowledge

How do you think that your knowledge of child development might influence you in the classroom?

PROJECTS

Observe a Young Child: For at least two hours, observe a child. Interpret and report on his or her behavior in terms of Erikson's and Piaget's stages of development.

Review a Book: Write a review of a book dealing with one of the topics in this chapter that you want to learn more about. Describe the implications of what you learned as a person who works with young children.

Make a Poster: Elaborate on the content in the text and illustrate the hallmarks of development for one age group of children—infants, toddlers, preschoolers, kindergarten, or primary children—in one area of development—social/emotional, physical, or cognitive.

Make a Chart: List at least five characteristics in each area of development—social/emotional, physical, and cognitive—for one age group of children—infants, toddlers, preschoolers, kindergarten, or primary children. After each item list what adults can do or say to support children's development of this characteristic.

BIBLIOGRAPHY

Ainsworth, M. 1979. *Patterns of Attachment*. New York: Halsted Press.
Belsky, J. 1988. The Effects of Infant Day Care Reconsidered. *Early Childhood Research Quarterly* 3:235–72.
Berger, K. S. 1986. *The Developing Person*. 2nd ed. New York: Worth.
Black, J., M. Puckett, and M. Bell. 1992. *The Young Child: Development from Prebirth Through Age Eight*. Englewood Cliffs, NJ: Merrill/Prentice Hall.
Bloom, B. 1964. *Stability and Change in Human Characteristics*. New York: Wiley.
Bowlby, J. 1951. *Maternal Care and Mental Health*. Geneva: World Health Organization.
Clarke-Stewart, A., M. Perlmutter, and S. Friedman. 1988. *Lifelong Human Development*. New York: Wiley.
Damon, W. 1988. *The Moral Child*. New York: Free Press.

DeVries, R., and B. Zan. 1994. *Moral Classrooms, Moral Children: Creating a Constructivist Atmosphere in Early Education*. New York: Teachers College Press.

Donaldson, M. C. 1978. *Children's Minds*. New York: W. W. Norton.

Edwards, C. P. 1986. *Promoting Social and Moral Development in Young Children*. New York: Teachers College Press.

Eisenberg, N. 1992. *The Caring Child*. Cambridge, MA: Harvard.

Eisenberg, N., and P. Mussen. 1989. *The Roots of Prosocial Behavior in Children*. New York: Cambridge University Press.

Erikson, E. 1963. *Childhood and Society*. Rev. ed. New York: W. W. Norton.

Flavell, J. H., P. H. Miller, et al. 1993. *Cognitive Development*. 3rd ed. Englewood Cliffs, NJ: Prentice Hall.

Gesell, A. 1940. *The First Five Years of Life*. New York: Harper & Row.

Gesell, A., and F. L. Ilg. 1974. *The Child from Five to Ten*. Rev. ed. New York: Harper & Row.

Gilligan, C. 1982. *In a Different Voice*. Cambridge, MA: Harvard University Press.

Ginsburg, H., and S. Opper. 1988. *Piaget's Theory of Intellectual Development*. 3rd ed. Englewood Cliffs, NJ: Prentice Hall.

Honig, A. S., and D. S. Wittmer. 1992. *Prosocial Development in Children*. New York: Garland.

Horowitz, F. D. 1982. The First Two Years of Life: Factors Related to Thriving. In S. G. Moore and C. Cooper, eds. *The Young Child: Reviews of Research*. Washington, DC: National Association for the Education of Young Children.

Hunt, J. M. 1961. *Intelligence and Experience*. New York: Ronald Press.

Kagan, J. 1984. *The Nature of the Child*. New York: Basic Books.

Kohlberg, L., ed. 1981. *The Philosophy of Moral Development: Moral Stages and the Idea of Justice*. San Francisco: Harper & Row.

Kohlberg, L. 1984. *The Psychology of Moral Development: The Nature and Validity of Moral Stages*. New York: Harper & Row.

Kostelnik, M. J., L. C. Stein, et al. 1993. *Guiding Children's Social Development*. 2nd ed. Albany, NY: Delmar.

Lazar, I., and R. Darlington. 1983. *As the Twig Is Bent: Lasting Effects of Preschool Programs*. Hillsdale, NJ: Erlbaum.

Lickona, T., G. Geis, and L. Kolhberg. ed. 1976. *Moral Development and Behavior: Theory, Research and Social Issues*. New York: Holt, Rinehart & Winston.

Mahler, M. S. 1975. *The Psychological Birth of the Human Infant: Symbiosis and Individuation*. New York: Basic Books.

Maier, H. 1978. *Three Theories of Child Development*. 3rd ed. New York: Harper & Row.

Maslow, A. H. 1968. *Toward a Psychology of Being*. Princeton, NJ: Van Nostrand.

Maslow, A. H. 1970. *Motivation and Personality*. 2nd ed. New York: Harper & Row.

Nye, R. D. 1986. *Three Psychologies: Perspectives from Freud, Skinner and Rogers*. 3rd ed. Monterey, CA: Brooks/Cole.

Papalia, D. E., and S. J. Olds. 1993. *A Child's World: Infancy Through Adolescence*. 6th ed. New York: McGraw-Hill.

Piaget, J. (1932) 1965. *The Moral Judgment of the Child*. New York: Free Press.

Piaget, J. 1966. *The Origins of Intelligence in Children*. 2nd ed. New York: International Universities Press.

Schickedanz, J. A., K. Hansen, et al. 1993. *Understanding Children*. 2nd ed. Mountain View, CA: Mayfield.

Skeels, H. M. 1966. Adult Status of Children with Contrasting Early Life Experiences. *Monographs of the Society for Research in Child Development* 31 (Serial No. 105).

Thomas, A., and S. Chess. 1977. *Temperament and Development*. New York: Brunner/Mazel.

Thomas, R. M. 1985. *Comparing Theories of Child Development*. 2nd ed. Belmont, CA: Wadsworth.

Vygotsky, L. S. 1962. *Thought and Language*. Cambridge, MA: MIT Press.

Wadsworth, B. J. 1989. *Piaget's Theory of Cognitive and Affective Development*. 4th ed. New York: Longman.

Werner, E. E., J. M. Bierman, and F. E. French. 1971. *The Children of Kauai: A Longitudinal Study from the Prenatal Period to Age Ten*. Honolulu, HI: University of Hawaii Press.

Werner, E. E., and R. S. Smith. 1992. *Overcoming the Odds: High Risk Children from Birth to Adulthood*. Ithaca, NY: Cornell University Press.

Williams, L. R. 1992. Perspectives on Children. *Encyclopedia of Early Childhood Education*. New York: Garland.

CHAPTER FIVE

Play

Play is a child's life and the means by which he comes to understand the world he lives in.
Susan Isaacs

Through play, children learn what no one can teach them.
Lawrence Frank

In this chapter we review the role of play in the development and learning of children and present some of the ways in which early childhood practitioners can enhance and enrich the play of children in early childhood settings. We discuss several issues concerning children's play.

Do you remember the dizzy joy of rolling down a hill, the focused effort of building an elaborate structure with blocks, the exhausting satisfaction of learning to jump rope, or the prolonged concentration of pretending with friends? Whether rich or poor, in town or country, you played. Children all over the world play; they have always played.

Child development theory tells us that children learn best through direct, hands-on experience. Play is the ultimate realization of the early childhood educator's maxim of "learning by doing." Since the field began, early childhood educators have sought to understand and support this most natural of activities. Today, as in the past, belief in the value of play is a distinguishing characteristic of early childhood education. It is a link to our past and a bond between early childhood professionals. As an early childhood educator you must learn about young children and their development. Similarly, you must become knowledgeable about

play—what it is, how it develops, its function in growth and learning, its role in early childhood education and care, and the role of the early childhood practitioner in supporting children's play.

THE NATURE OF PLAY

What is play? What is its significance? Why is play so compelling to children? Reflecting on the play of children and your own childhood play can help you to realize that many things can be play. As you observe a child at play you may notice the characteristics of play. As you watch children of different ages you will see that play changes as children grow. And as you observe boys and girls with different temperaments, experiences, and abilities, you will see some of the individual differences in children's play. The characteristics and stages of play described by theorists and researchers can help you to understand what you see.

The Characteristics of Play

Ask an adult how they can distinguish children at play and they will likely tell you "when they are having fun" or "when they are enjoying themselves" or even "when I can't get their attention." Although there is no single agreed-upon definition of play, theorists, researchers, and educators have identified characteristics that distinguish play from other behaviors.

- **Play is intrinsically motivated.** Children play because it is satisfying, not because it meets a basic need or receives an external reward. It is the motivation and not the activity that makes something play. Walking on a balance beam as you traverse the playground is play; walking a balance beam as part of a gymnastics routine in an attempt to win a prize is work. The pleasure and focus brought to play is a sign of this personal motivation.
- **Play is freely chosen.** Children choose play. The play opportunity beckons and children decide to play. Adults may invite but never compel children to play. The moment compulsion enters and a task has been assigned it becomes work, not play.
- **Play is pleasurable, enjoyable, and engaging.** Pleasurable, focused pursuit of an activity is a hallmark of play in children and adults. Although play can be seriously pursued and there can be challenges, fears, and frustrations in play, it is the quality of enjoyment that stands out when we think of play. Activity that is not enjoyable most of the time will not be chosen as play.
- **Play is process oriented.** The activity, rather than the end product, motivates. Children are more involved in spontaneous discovery and creation (the process) than the eventual outcome. Play can have a product or goal, spontaneously decided by the players as part of play, which may change as the play progresses.
- **Play is active.** It requires physical, verbal, or mental engagement with people, objects, or ideas. Although we clearly recognize the rough and tumble actions of the young child as play, our own daydreams can also be called play, for they are freely chosen, pursued for their own sake, process-oriented, pleasurable, and engage our mental capacities.
- **Play is self rather than object oriented.** In play the basic question is, "What can *I* do with this object?" When confronted with a new or unusual object, the first order of business for most children is to find out the answer to the question, "What is this object and what can *it* do?" Play theorists and researchers call this *exploration* and distinguish it from play (Bergen 1988; Johnson, Christie, and Yawkey 1987).
- **Play is often non-literal.** It is pretend. Many activities are "playful," but it is non-literal pretend that is the pinnacle of play. Children suspend and alter reality for make-believe. The external world is temporarily set aside for fuller exploration of internal imagining. The players are often heard saying things such as: "Let's pretend . . . ," "I'll be the fireman and you be the baby trapped in the building," or (holding a block) "This can be the phone."

Children at play are powerful creators compelled by forces from within to create a world. Although the raw materials of their creations are their life experiences, the shape of their creations is their own. Play is simultaneously an attachment to and a detachment from the world—a time during which children can act autonomously and freely and experience themselves and the world with intensity every moment.

The Purpose of Play

As you read in Chapter Two, philosophers, theologians, educators, and psychologists have observed children at play for centuries and speculated about play's nature and purpose.

Reflect and write about . . .

your memories of play

When you were a child, how did you play? What made it play? As an adult what is your "play"? What are the characteristics of your play now?

There are several "classical" theories that, until recently, were used to explain why children play.

During the nineteenth and early twentieth centuries, a number of writers formulated explanations for the role of play in human development (Levy 1978). Johan Huizanga, a Dutch historian and educator, believed that among the essential components of civilization are certain forms of play—ritual, poetry, music, and dance. Herbert Spencer, a British philosopher and psychologist, introduced the surplus energy theory of play, which suggested that the purpose of play was to help human beings use energy they no longer needed for basic survival. Adults have work to do, but children need to expend their energy in play. The relaxation or recreation theory, posited by G. T. W. Patrick, held that play was an essential mechanism to relieve the stresses of work. The recapitulation theory, credited to G. S. Hall, maintained that during childhood the history of evolution is relived. Play rids the human race of primitive and unnecessary instinctual traits carried over by heredity from past generations. Instinct theory, developed by German philosopher and writer Karl Groos, suggested that play was a natural instinct, necessary for children's growth and development. The practice theory suggested that play was practice for adulthood. Children at play practice the tasks and roles of adults (Levy 1978).

When we observe a group of children, it is easy to see how these theories evolved. A group of energetic preschoolers cooped up on a rainy day certainly seem to have surplus energy. That same group, after an opportunity to run and yell outside, are much more relaxed when they come back in. A jungle gym full of climbing children is humorously reminiscent of our primate cousins and can seem to be replaying evolution. And it can be frighteningly apparent when we watch children playing house, school, or war that they are practicing adult roles.

There is still much to be learned, but recent theorists, researchers, and educators have expanded our understanding of why children play. Today we know that play is both a natural and instinctive activity that helps children to develop in all areas. Current theories of play strongly reflect the influence of Freud and Piaget.

Freud and his followers, particularly Erik Erikson, felt that play provided a catharsis, an emotional cleansing, to help children deal with negative experiences. In play children feel more grown up and powerful, exert some control over their environments, and can relieve anxiety created by real-life conflicts. Play therapy, based on this theoretical framework, uses play as a therapeutic mode for working through children's conflicts and problems (Schickedanz, Schickedanz, and Forsyth 1993).

Piaget and his followers believed that play both reflects and is the medium through which children develop cognitively (Athey 1984). Based on his observations Piaget described a set of stages in the development of children's

play. Many of today's early childhood programs have a Piagetian orientation to play. Children are allowed time and materials to play and their teachers trust they will "construct" their own knowledge.

Theorist Lev Vygotsky also believed that play served as a vehicle for cognitive develop-ment. Vygotsky saw the special role of play as creating a "zone of proximal development" that allows children to stretch or bridge from one level of thinking to a higher level of thinking. In Vygotsky's view, play provides an "anchor" between real objects and the ability to symbol-ize (Monighan-Nourat 1992).

The Stages of Play

As children grow and develop they engage in different and increasingly complex types or stages of play. Stages of play have been described by various developmental theorists. If you know that two five-year-olds can play happily building a road with blocks together and sharing a single vehicle but anticipate that two toddlers will play separately and each need their own truck, you have experienced and internalized some of the characteristics of children's stages of play (Figure 5.1).

The different play stages tend to parallel the stages of cognitive and social development. They are different, however, in that the appearance or dominance of one stage of play does not signal the extinction of the previous play stage. For example, a child will continue to enjoy sensory motor experiences typical of practice play (for example, playing with water and sand) even after cooperative play has become their dominant play. Indeed, we think of the companionable silence of sitting and reading a book near a friend as a grown-up version of parallel play.

Parten: Stages of Social Play

In the early 1930s, M. B. Parten developed categories of play that described the nature of the relationships among the players. Her categories of play continue to be used by early childhood educators. Parten identified six stages of social play that can be viewed as a continuum from minimal to maximal social involvement. The first two (unoccupied behavior and onlooker) are periods of observation preceding the venture into a new situation. The four remaining stages each dominate a particular age (although they occur at other ages as well), with children tending towards more and more social play as they get older.

- **Solitary play** (dominates in infancy). During solitary play, children play alone and independently with objects. Other children playing nearby go unnoticed. Although solitary play is dominant in infancy and is more typical in younger children, older children also may select and benefit from solitary play.
- **Parallel play** (typical of toddlers). In parallel play, children play side by side but still are engaged with their own play objects. Little interpersonal interaction occurs, but each may be aware of and pleased by the company of a nearby friend.
- **Associative play** (seen most in young preschool-age children). Parten identified two forms of group play. Associative play is the first. It involves pairs and groups of children playing in the same area and sharing materials. Interaction may be brisk, but true cooperation and negotiation rare. Two children each building a zoo in the block area, sharing animal props and talking about their zoo but *not* creating a joint zoo or negotiating what will happen at their zoo, are involved in associative play.
- **Cooperative play** (characteristic of older preschool and kindergarten/primary-age children). In the second and most social form of group play, children actively work together to create sustained play episodes with joint themes. They plan, negotiate, and share responsibility and leadership. For example, a group of children pretending to go on a picnic might cooperatively decide what food to take, who should attend the event, how to get there, who will drive, and what joys and catastrophes await them on their outing (Parten 1932).

Piaget and Smilansky: Cognitive Stages of Play

Jean Piaget looked at how play supported cognitive development. He developed a framework with three stages of play development that are analogous to his stages of cognitive development. In the late 1960s Sara Smilansky adapted Piaget's stages of play, based on her observations of young children from more diverse cultural and economic backgrounds (Smilansky and Shefatya 1990). She categorized play into four types, based on those of Piaget. Piaget's and Smilansky's stages are not mutually exclusive; they provide different ways of looking at similar play behaviors. Smilansky's work can be seen as building on Piaget's.

- **Practice** (Piaget) or **functional** (Smilansky) **play** (infancy to two years of age). In practice play, children explore the sensory qualities of objects and practice motor skills. This stage parallels Piaget's sensorimotor stage of development. Children who are engaged in functional play repeat actions over and over again, as if practicing them. A baby who repeatedly drops her toy over the side of the crib for you to pick up, or a toddler who dumps and refills a coffee can over and over, are engaged in practice play. These actions are viewed as explorations to learn about objects. Although practice or functional play is the common play of the first two years, it does not disappear. A preschooler repeatedly pouring water from one container to another and a teenager repeatedly combing his already perfect coiffure in front of the mirror are both involved in practice play.
- **Symbolic play** (two to seven years of age). In symbolic play, children use one object to represent another object and use make-believe actions and roles to represent familiar or imagined situations. Symbolic play emerges during the preoperational period as the child begins to be able to use mental symbols or imagery.

  There are different forms of symbolic play, which are further separated by Smilansky into two categories: constructive play, in which the child uses real objects to build a representation of something according to a plan (for example, creating a birthday cake with playdough and wooden sticks), and dramatic and socio-dramatic play, in which children create imaginary roles and interactions where they pretend to be someone (mommy, firefighter, etc.) and use actions, objects, or words to represent things or situations (a block for an iron, an arm movement for steering a truck, or "woof, woof" for the bark of a dog).
- **Games with rules** (seven to eleven years). In games with rules, children recognize and follow preset rules in the interest of sustaining solitary or group play that conforms to the expectations and goals of the games. During the concrete operational period, children's play is typified by games with rules, though they can be introduced to and enjoyed by much younger children. The ability to agree upon and negotiate rules is viewed as growing from the cooperation and negotiation that developed in cooperative play. Chutes and Ladders, dominoes, kickball, jump rope, and perhaps even peek-a-boo are examples of games with rules (Piaget 1962).

Sociodramatic Play. In her recent work concerning the nature and importance of dramatic and sociodramatic play, Smilansky points out that dramatic play represents a different and potentially a higher level of play behavior than any other play. "Dramatic and sociodramatic play differs from the three other types of play in that it is *person-oriented* and not material and/or object oriented" (Smilansky and Shefatya 1990, 3). Dramatic play is acting out human relationships using symbols—when I put on the big boots and hat I'm the daddy. It may be carried out in a solitary or parallel play style. Sociodramatic play involves the acting out of complex interactions in cooperation with others. There is a story line, roles to be assigned, and changes to be negotiated as the play proceeds—I put on the big boots and the hat and you can be the little boy and get in the car and

Parten/Piaget Scale			
Child's Name _____ Date _____			
	Solitary	Parallel	Group
Functional			
Constructive			
Dramatic			
Games			

FIGURE 5-1

Stages of play and stages of development table

Source: Adapted from J.E. Johnson, J.F. Christie, and T.D. Yawkey, *Play and Early Childhood Development* (Glenview, Ill.: Scott Foresman, 1987).

I'll drive you to the zoo. "Socio-dramatic play allows the child to be an actor, observer and interactor simultaneously, using his abilities in a common enterprise with other children" (Smilansky and Shefatya 1990, 3).

Smilansky identified the important elements of dramatic and sociodramatic play:

- **Imitative role-play.** The child undertakes a make-believe role and expresses it in imitative action and/or verbalization. (Miriam shows that she's a puppy by getting down on all fours and barking to ask for supper.)
- **Make-believe with regard to objects.** Toys, non-structured materials, movements, or verbal declarations are substituted for real objects. (Miriam uses a block as a pretend bone.)
- **Make-believe with regard to actions and situations.** Verbal descriptions are substi-

tuted for actions and situations. (Miriam acts out being scared of another child who she says is a mean lady who wants to steal puppies.)
- **Persistence.** The child continues playing in a specific episode for at least ten minutes. (Even though activity time is over, Miriam continues in the role of puppy and comes to circle time on all fours. She barks for the first song.)
- **Interaction.** There are at least two players interacting in the context of a play episode. (Miriam and Rivera both are pets, but Rivera is a kitty. They play together and meow, hiss, whine, purr, and bark to one another.)
- **Verbal communication.** There is some verbal interaction relating to the play episode. (Periodically Rivera gives Miriam directions on the next event in the play such as, "It's night time and the puppies and kitties

123

have to go to sleep for one hundred minutes.") (Smilansky and Shefatya 1990, 24)

Understanding the Stages of Play

Understanding the stages of play allows you to provide appropriate play experiences for children and helps you to appreciate children's play behavior. An awareness of Parten's stages makes it more likely that you will understand rather than be irritated by the infant whose solitary play takes the form of repeatedly banging a rattle on a tray and never seems to tire of dropping objects to the floor from a high chair. You will appreciate the movement toward social intercourse represented by the toddler who engages in parallel play by carrying the basket of cubes to the block rug to build beside a special friend. You will appreciate that two-year-olds might enjoy a game such as "ring-around-the-rosy," led by a teacher. You will understand that they are only just beginning to be involved in associative play on their own and would be unlikely to initiate such a group game. Likewise, you may be somewhat concerned about a four-year-old who rarely engages in the associative or cooperative play typical of her age, such as a lively interchange in the block corner, and never uses materials to pretend. Knowledge of the stages of play enables you to plan a program appropriate for the children in your class and gives you some important clues to use in observing the developmental progress of each child.

Gender and Play

Another characteristic of play has to do with differences between the play of girls and boys. Although the play of girls and boys has many similarities, particularly during the first three years of life, differences exist in the play behavior and characteristics of boys and girls. It is difficult to determine the source of these characteristics. Strong evidence exists for a biological basis for two commonly identified differences—better spatial ability and more aggressiveness in males—but the social environment also influences the expression of these characteristics (Schickedanz et al. 1993).

Some gender differences in play may be attributed to gender stereotyping. From birth, girls are described as little, soft, and pretty and boys as big, strong, and active, even when identical in size and activity level. Books and media given to children tend to depict boys as more active, competent, and adventurous while girls are depicted in supporting roles and are shown to need help to overcome incompetence and fearfulness. Many gender-related play characteristics may be influenced by both environment and inheritance, but it is difficult, at this time, to assign primary influence to one or the other.

Although the causes may remain a mystery, boys at all ages engage in active play of a rough and tumble nature, get into fights, use the outdoors, and play in groups more than girls do. Girls begin to prefer same-sex playmates earlier than boys, but both do so between two and five years of age. By age five, girls begin to be interested in cross-sex play, but boys tend to persist in their same-sex preference throughout the elementary years. The approach to materials and toys differs in both choice and uses. Girls generally prefer art materials, dolls, and small constructive toys and play with them in quieter ways. Boys generally prefer blocks and wheeled vehicles and play with them more noisily and repetitiously. Girls play with toys regardless of the gender category people ordinarily assign to the item; boys avoid "girl's toys." Boys appear to prefer larger groups of playmates from preschool age through the primary years, while girls show a marked preference for small groups.

Although these gender differences have been noted generally, all of us know many individual children who do not conform to these stereotypical play behaviors. Additionally it is important to remember that girls and boys both explore, build, and pretend and need our support in fully realizing their play potential. The similarities are more important than the differences.

THE VALUE OF PLAY

Children need to play. Play supports the development of the *whole child*—a person able to sense, move, think, relate to others, communicate, and create. It helps children to learn without direct instruction or time set aside for specific subject areas. The importance of play was recognized by the United Nations General Assembly, in November 1989, which approved a convention on the rights of the child that put forth that every child of the world must have the right to play.

Professionals have long been able to justify play's value in supporting physical, social, and emotional development. In recent decades early childhood educators have met with ever-increasing pressure to justify play in terms of how it contributes to cognitive, language, and creative development. It is of particular interest that researchers have begun to find positive relationship between the play abilities of children and their subsequent academic achievement and school adjustment. In their book *Facilitating Play: A Medium for Promoting Cognitive, Socio-Emotional, and Academic Development in Young Children* (1990), Sara Smilansky and Leah Shefatya describe many studies in which competence at sociodramatic play is highly correlated with cognitive, creative, and social abilities

Play researchers continue to discover how play facilitates the development of children in all areas. As an early childhood educator whose program provides opportunities for children to play, you are likely to have many occasions in which you will need to understand and explain the role of play in each of the four areas of development.

The Value of Play in Physical Development

Children learn best when they have bodies that are strong, healthy, flexible, and coordinated and when all of their senses are operating. Play contributes to physical development and health throughout the early childhood years. Children at play develop physical competency efficiently and comprehensively. No teacher or staff of physical education experts could devise a curriculum that would accomplish what children's own spontaneous play does naturally.

Newborns move their limbs and heads in quite random and uncoordinated ways and are unable to change position or location without assistance. Within a year many can walk and all can grasp and direct objects at will. During the second year, running becomes a favorite activity and all children, unless disabled, can turn the pages of a book. A developmental chart (see Chapter Eleven) that explains the physical milestones of development can give you an appreciation for the accomplishments of the early childhood years—from near immobility at birth to the physical skills of an aspiring gymnast by age eight, and from an inability to intentionally grasp to the ability by the end of the early childhood years to draw pictures, write, and even play the piano.

Infants discover their own hands and spend hours gazing at them, flexing the fingers, and waving them in front of their own faces. Later, they load a large hollow cube with toys, dump it all out, reload, dump, and repeat over and over. The older child will spend hours each day playing a favorite ball game and practicing the skills that the game requires.

Children have an innate drive to explore, discover, and master skills. The concentrated play of childhood leads naturally to the physical mastery toward which we humans seem predisposed and indeed is probably essential to our survival as a species. Play is of prime importance in the development of perceptual-motor coordination and in the attainment and maintenance of the good health that is essential if optimal development is to occur.

The Value of Play in Emotional Development

Therapists and educators have long appreciated the rich emotional value of play. Freud and his followers identified play as a primary avenue in which children express and work through their fears, anxieties, and desires. Contemporary therapists still use play as the medium for helping children deal with the feelings associated with traumatic events and disturbing situations in their lives.

Children at play devise and confront challenges and anticipate changes. In the process they master their fears; resolve internal conflicts; act out anger, hostility, and frustration; and resolve personal problems for which the "real" world offers no apparent solutions. It is no wonder children are highly motivated to play all day.

Those of us who work with young children value play for its role in normal emotional development. Children at play feel that they are in control of their world, are practicing important skills that lead them to a sense of mastery over their environment, and are building a sense of competence that heightens self-esteem and confidence.

The Value of Play in Social Development

From birth, children are enmeshed in a social environment. Survival depends on the care of adults from the moment of birth. Caregivers *play* with infants in a way that is unlike anything adults do in any other life situation. You will hear a grown-up addressing questions to the infant and then taking the infant's part to answer, "Now, don't you have about the most beautiful eyes in the whole world?" "Well, of course I do, I got them from my daddy." An or-

dinarily dignified adult will make undignified noises and facial expressions ("ZZZZZZZZZZ-ZZZZZZZZZZZZ Gotcha!") and respond with the greatest joy when the baby laughs aloud for the first time. Infant-adult play progresses to games like pat-a-cake and this-little-piggy.

All this social play leads to increased social interaction skills. Children learn how to initiate play with relatives, family friends, and peers. In early play encounters, children learn awareness of others, cooperation, turn-taking, and social language. They become aware of group membership, develop a social identity, and learn a lot about the rules and values governing the family, community, and culture. The play becomes increasingly complex and is sustained for greater periods of time. By the time children reach their second birthday, most are making rudimentary attempts to portray social relationships through dramatic play. By age four or five they will have learned all the things they need to know to enact the most complex of social relationships with their peers in highly developed sociodramatic play. Soon after, they become able to play rule-governed games, and through this play social concepts such as fairness, justice, and cooperation evolve and influence play behavior and other social relationships.

The Value of Play in Cognitive Development

Play is the primary medium through which young children make sense of their experiences and construct ideas about how the physical and social world works. The functional play that begins in infancy and persists through life is basic to the process of learning about the properties of objects and learning how things work. The constructive play of the toddler is the mode we use throughout life for discovering and practicing how to use unfamiliar tools and materials (for example, learning to use a new appliance). The dramatic (pretend) play of preschool children has a critical role in the development of representational or symbolic thought and the eventual ability to think abstractly. In sociodramatic play children develop understanding of the world by reenacting with playmates experiences (for example, a trip to the grocery store) they have had or observed. They alter their understandings based on the response and ideas of their friends ("I'm the store man and you have to give me fifty dollars for that orange. Oranges cost lots of money!") and then use the new meanings as they again experience the "real world" ("Mom, do we have enough money for oranges?"). This circular process is one in which information is constantly being gathered, organized, and used. It is one of the primary ways in which children construct their understanding of the world. We have found the following description of children's dramatic play to be useful in clarifying its significance:

> The familiarity of life's scripts is what makes the daily life of adults efficient. . . . We are free to think about other things. . . . We recognize this only when we find ourselves in an unfamiliar setting—driving a borrowed car, . . . placing a phone call in a foreign country. Young children . . . play in order to find their way around in what is for them the foreign country of adults, to master its daily scripts. (Jones and Reynolds 1992, 10)

Sociodramatic play is of particular interest to play researchers because of its significance in cognitive development. A high level of competence in sociodramatic play has been found to be associated with cognitive maturity (Smilansky and Shefatya 1990).

The Value of Play in Integrating Development

Throughout this book, we refer to the development of the *whole child*. At play, more than at any other time, children engage all aspects of themselves and most fully express who they are, what they are able to do, and what they know and feel. Blocks, dramatic play props, construction toys, art materials, books, puzzles, climbing structures, sand and water—equipment and materials found in almost every early childhood program are rich in their potential for supporting all aspects of development.

Three or four children building an office building in a block area near a shelf stocked with several hundred blocks of eight to ten different shapes and sizes, a few vehicles, animal and human figures, and a large stack of hollow blocks with boards have a full range of development and learning opportunities. They provide an example of how play supports development.

- **Physical development.** Coordination and strength are enhanced as the large, hollow blocks are lifted, carried, and stacked; small muscles are developed as children decorate the top of the building with a row of unit blocks; and sensory awareness is gained as they handle the blocks, feel the texture, and note the grain of the wood.
- **Social development.** Cooperation and negotiation skills are practiced as they work

Reflect and write about . . .

more memories of play

Reflect and write about a time when you developed or improved a skill or
learned through play. Did the activity take energy and work? Was it still play?

out how to share materials so that they can build both a garage and create the office building; interpersonal sensitivity is used as they decide how to include a latecomer.

- **Emotional development.** A sense of competence is gained as the children create the office building and a garage based on a plan and accomplish this in cooperation with friends.
- **Cognitive development.** Problem-solving skills are developed as the children solve the problems of balance and symmetry inherent in construction. And they plan and communicate as they to build the agreed-upon structures.

These are only a few of the things a group of children might be learning and developing as they play together in the block area. Such a list could be developed for every spontaneous play experience in an early childhood program.

Spontaneous play in learning centers also integrates curriculum areas. In the block play described above, the children are creating an office building with an attached parking garage. Below are a few examples of how you (and the children) might integrate curriculum based on the play experience.

You might introduce **social studies** concepts by suggesting to the children that they use what they know and create some ways for people to get to work at their office building. Children might then create roads and railways or build a bus by lining up a row of chairs.

Math is occurring when one child comes up with the idea of setting out enough seats for all the players. Observing children riding the bus might lead you to introduce **music, creative drama, and movement** experiences by singing and miming "The Wheels on the Bus" with them as they ride. A child might initiate a **reading/writing** experience by asking you to help make a sign to label the parking garage. You might suggest that children use **art** materials to make road signs.

Every play activity contributes to the developing child. Just as "transportation" became the curriculum in the above example, so could a curriculum focus—for example, on "community"—be introduced into the children's play opportunities. In the block area you might add street signs, trucks, cars, ambulances, planes, and other vehicles to suggest the building of a community's roads and streets. In the dramatic play area you might add cereal boxes, plastic food, a cash register, and a shopping basket to suggest the creation of a community grocery store.

SUPPORTING DEVELOPMENT THROUGH PLAY

Early childhood educators who study play come to understand it as a natural and compelling way for children to develop and learn. They then devise a variety of ways to support development through play. As an early childhood professional you have a significant role in children's play. By your attitudes and your actions you can support or discourage play. As you do so, you influence the nature of the play.

Supportive Attitudes

When you understand play's role in children's development and learning, you approach children at play with an attitude of respect and appreciation. You see play as your ally. When you understand that you have an important role to play in facilitating children's play, you approach it with an attitude of serious attention. You see the support of play as an important part of your job.

Some practitioners in early childhood education and care accept play as part of the "care" aspect of their work but fail to respect and trust it as a primary process in their "educator's" role. These individuals feel uncomfortable when children play in the educational part of the program and may try to intervene in play to make it seem more like "school". This lack of comfort with play indicates an incomplete understanding of play and of the nature of education and care.

Your view of play will be influenced by your professional setting and tasks. Those who work with infants and toddlers generally receive support and approval for giving play an important role in their programs. The same is true for many, though not all, who work with three- to five-year-olds. If you teach in an elementary school you may find that play is not understood and supported by your colleagues or the families of the children you teach. In this case your appreciation for play must be coupled with information that supports its importance.

Supportive Roles

Children play regardless of the circumstances. What you do before and during their play can make a vital difference in the quality of play and in what children gain in the process. Respect and appreciation for children's play brings with it the realization that in play children, not adults, are the stars. You can, however, fulfill many supporting roles that facilitate their play. The In Practice box is a diagram that we devised for our students that graphically depicts how you can support children's play. Your role begins by setting the stage but continues endlessly, repeating all the roles.

Stage Manager

The essential elements of play are *time, space, equipment,* and *materials.* Your first supporting role in children's play is providing these elements. Elizabeth Jones and Gretchen Reynolds (1992) refer to this important role as that of *stage manager.* Being a stage manager involves more than simply setting out materials for play. It includes selecting and organizing materials, space, and equipment so that they suggest play that is meaningful to the children. Children of all ages must have time to play. Early childhood educators who value play use time flexibly. They view children's play as more important than strict adherence to a schedule. You will learn more about creating an appropriate schedule and a stimulating play environment when you read Chapter Seven, A Good Place for Children, and Chapter Eight, The Learning Environment.

The artful arrangement of equipment and materials assists children in what Jones and Reynolds refer to as distinguishing figure ground relationships; in other words, distinguishing what you are looking at from the background (Jones and Reynolds 1992). Too much equipment, or equipment that is disorganized, may be confusing and inhibit play. The cycle of setting up, play, and reordering of the environment is an ongoing process in early childhood settings. Early childhood educators

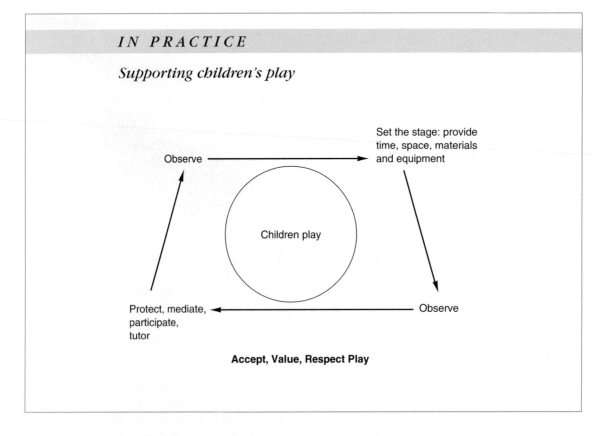

IN PRACTICE

Supporting children's play

---

participate in this process willingly and view it as critical to maintaining an environment that invites play.

Observer

Another important role you will have in children's play is that of observer. Thoughtful observation is the best tool that you have for coming to truly respect and appreciate play. When you observe carefully and assess what you see based on what you know about child development and play, you are better able to understand what is happening for children, what children might need, and how you can support them in play. This involves offering a child a space to play near but not with other children when you have observed that the child still

functions best in a parallel play mode. Or it could mean providing a length of cloth for a pretend cape when you observe a child dragging her blanket out of her cubby for this purpose. You will learn more about developing observation skill in Chapter Six, Assessing Children.

Systematic observation can yield important insight about play. Several checklists or scales have been developed for looking at play behavior. These can be used to increase your understanding of play. Johnson, Christie, and Yawkey (1987), in their book *Play and Early Childhood Development,* describe several scales in detail and give instructions for using them to gain valuable information about the play of children. The Parten/Piaget scale (found in Chapter Six) codes play on its social and cogni-

As a mediator you help individuals to work out conflicts and concerns when a neutral third party is needed. A mediator does not intervene when the participants can handle a problem on their own. Children's conflicts in play can give you an opportunity to teach peaceful conflict resolution skills (see Chapter Nine) that will assist children in handling problems on their own.

As a play *protector* you maintain the delicate balance between guidelines that support and sustain rich play episodes and over control that interferes with or limits play. You encourage the play but do not let it get dangerous or uncontrolled. The way you enter children's play to ensure safety and order needs to be sensitive and respectful of the play ("Excuse me, birds, would you like me to help you move your nest here under the table? I'm afraid it might fall out of the tree and the eggs will crack"), rather than intrusive, thus interrupting the play ("Get down from the table. Tables are not for playing on; someone might get hurt").

Dramatic play episodes that are prolonged and engrossing often attract late-comers who wish to join in. In this situation the play protector and mediator can observe carefully and assist shy or anxious children in entering the play. Delicacy is the order of the day. It is best if you can unobtrusively help the child find a role. For example, in a camp scene you might say, "Would you like to get some wood for the campfire? I think I know where we can find

tive dimensions and enables you to get a quick look at a child's level of play development.

Protector and Mediator

Children's play is most productive when they feel safe from harm and relatively free from interference. There is potential for disorder and disruption in group play. To support children's play you will sometimes take the role of play protector and play mediator. As opposed to limit setter, disciplinarian, or rule enforcer, a *mediator* collaborates with children.

Reflect and write about . . .

playing in school

Reflect and write about a time when you played in school. Where did you play? Who supported your play? How much time did you have for play? What do you think your teachers thought about your play? Why do you still remember this play today?

more wood." If the entering child is disruptive you may help to ease the child into the scene by setting a task that makes use of the high energy, such as chopping the wood, or suggesting an alternative play activity.

The hallmark of highly developed dramatic play is that the children use objects to represent things: a bowl becomes a hat, a plate becomes a steering wheel, a block becomes a telephone. This can make play a disorderly process as play materials for one type of activity are transformed in children's imaginative pretend. This presents a dilemma: If you are overly concerned about the proper use of equipment, you may curtail play and important learning; if you provide no limits, the resulting disorder can be overwhelming for both you and the children. Deciding on the best course requires sensitivity and judgment. It can help to see the use to which children are putting materials; if they are being used in a way that is important to extending a play episode, don't discourage the activity.

Participant

Until the 1960s the conventional wisdom in early childhood education was that teachers should not become directly involved in the play of children. Play was seen as the arena in which children were to be left free to work out their inner conflicts and exercise power over their environment. It was regarded as the duty of an adult to keep out of the child's play world so as not to interfere with important psychological development. The only valid role allocated to the adult was that of stage manager and observer. In recent decades research has pointed to reasons for joining in children's play as a *participant.*

Why should adults play with children? Research findings indicate that when adults play with children they lend support to the amount and quality of the play. Your participation gives children a strong message that play is a valuable activity in its own right, so they play longer and

learn new play behaviors from observing you. It also builds rapport with the children. As you learn more about their interests, needs, and characteristics you are better able to interact with them. When you participate, play lasts much longer, and it becomes more elaborate.

Of course, your participation must harmonize with the play of the children or else it will disrupt or end the play (Johnson et al. 1987). When you play with children, take your cues from the children and allow them to maintain control of the play. You limit your role to actions and comments that extend and enrich the play. When you join in, it is important that you do so in a way that supports ongoing play. Sometimes children offer a role to an adult. "Would you like a cup of coffee?" is an invitation to join a restaurant scene being enacted. If not invited, you might observe and then approach the player who seems to be taking leadership and ask to be seated as a customer and in this way gain entry into the play. As a customer you might inquire about the price of a cup of coffee, ask for cream to put in it, and praise the chef for the delicious pancakes she prepared. By asking questions, requesting service, and responding to things children have done, you introduce new elements into the play without taking over.

It is common for adults to intervene in children's play to teach concepts or vocabulary. We observed a teacher stepping into a play scenario to comment on the colors and shapes of the food being consumed at a pretend picnic. Just as this might interrupt the conversational flow at a real picnic, the interruption did not lead to a meaningful discussion of colors and shapes, and it stopped two players having a lively interchange on the merits of feeding hamburgers to the pretend dog. It is possible to help children to be aware of new ideas in play, but it takes skill to do so without manipulating and diverting the activity. For example, when joining the group at a pretend picnic it would be possible to comment, "Could you please pass me that red apple? It looks very tasty," rather than, "What color is this apple?"

Why play with children? Perhaps the best reason is because it is a way to share their world, to demonstrate your respect, and to renew your appreciation of the complexities and importance of children's play.

Tutor

Although children play naturally, not all children fully develop play skills. Children who have been deprived of opportunities to play or who are traumatized by violence on the streets, in the media, and in their homes may need the help of a *tutor* in learning to play.

A study conducted by Smilansky (1968) in Israel found that children from low-income families in which parents lacked a high school education engaged less often in dramatic and sociodramatic play than did children from more affluent families. Since then other researchers have found the same pattern in other countries. Intervention strategies were designed to teach the play skills that a child lacked. In this play tutoring, you demonstrate or model a missing skill until the child begins to use the skill in spontaneous play situations. For example, if a child is dependent on realistic props you might offer substitution ideas—"Let's pretend that these jar lids are our plates," or "Let's pretend that the sand is salt"—until the child begins to do so independently. It is important to note that the goal of play tutoring is to teach play skills in the context of the spontaneous play episode. The adult does not change the content of the play by introducing new themes or taking a directing role. Play tutoring has proven effective in improving the dramatic and sociodramatic play skills of children, which in turn has improved play skills to bring about gains in cognitive and social development.

Other children also benefit from play tutoring. Just as some children lack play skills because they are deprived of a safe physical and emotional environment in which to play, other children do not develop play skills because they are deprived of time to play. They are compelled to conform to adult standards of behavior, to excel academically at an early age, and to master skills typically developed by older children. To them play time is something they must "steal" from their busy schedule of dance lessons, soccer practice, birthday parties, and full-day school (Elkind 1981). Optimal development requires challenges, but it also requires relief from burdensome responsibility. Play may save these children from burn-out at an early age.

Violence and Children's Play

Children's play reflects children's experience. The prevalence of violence in society and in television programming (much of which is aimed at a child audience) make it almost certain that in any group some children will introduce violence and war play into dramatic play. Although early childhood educators generally encourage children's spontaneous dramatic play, it is common for gun play to be outlawed. The proscription of gun and war play reflects the way it tends to dominate otherwise peaceful classrooms. Additionally, in violent play children tend to imitate the stereotypic behavior of media characters and the violent story action of the programs. Imitation and repetition replace imagination and creativity (Carlsson-Paige and Levin 1987).

This introduces a dilemma. Should you prohibit children's violent play or allow children to play out any drama they choose? In deciding whether and how to intervene, it helps to understand some of the reasons that children are so attracted to war play.

- Young children are fascinated by heroes, weapons, and machines. In a world where they are virtually powerless, young children are drawn to power.

- Violent play involves fast action and a thrilling chase. Adults find this exciting, and so do children.
- Today's toy weapons and accessories are much more realistic than were those in previous years. This realism is tantalizing and often creates a strong response in other children and adults.
- Intense interest may be evoked by much more sophisticated marketing aimed at children through TV.
- Peer approval is important to young children in the preschool years. When one child has a highly prized toy, others want one.

There are several strategies for coping with violent play:

- Observe the violent play to help you understand what it means to the children.
- Participate in children's play by asking questions to increase empathy, such as, "How does the bad guy feel? Who does he play with when he goes home? What does he do on his birthday?" In doing so, it is possible to help children to think beyond stereotypes.
- Guide children in choosing times, places, and behaviors that do not interfere with the play of the group. For example, just as yelling and shouting disturbs others indoors, shooting and crashing is also disruptive. Ask children to think of where and when such play will not disturb other people.

In a society where violence is prevalent, we cannot eliminate children's fascination with violence. We can provide children with alternative models of human relationships and help them to learn to be responsible and thoughtful members of their community.

Gender-Stereotyped Play

As noted earlier, there are some recognizable and persistent differences in the ways boys and girls play. Since some of this is a reflection of the stereotypes present in the environment, we can support all children engaging in a diverse range of play activities. We believe it is reasonable for early childhood educators to take steps to overcome and avoid gender stereotyping in the books and materials offered to girls and boys—to make certain that both males and females are depicted in a variety of family and occupational roles in books and posters.

Similarly, the environment can be arranged to encourage children to play with a wide range of materials. One way to encourage more diverse play for both boys and girls is by integrating block (particularly hollow block) and dramatic play areas. Another important way to overcome gender stereotyped play is through your expectations and behavior. As you practice ball skills with girls and involve boys in cooking activities you are taking small, important steps toward breaking down the gender stereotypes that limit the choices of all children in our culture.

Reflect and write about . . .

play you've observed

Think about a classroom you recently observed. How did the children play? How did the adults facilitate play? What seemed to be their attitudes toward play? Did you observe violent play or gender-stereotyped play? How did it make you feel? How did the adults respond? How did this affect children?

FINAL THOUGHTS

Play is the heart of the early childhood program, the center of the curriculum. It brings together the child's world and the adult's. Play is the way children develop, the way they express their understanding of the world, and an important way for early childhood educators actualize the curriculum and learning goals.

The full realization of the learning potential of play ensures that you will value it in its own right and make a full use of it in your work with children. In this enthusiasm for play as a tool for promoting development, it is important not to lose sight of the exuberant, joyful, and nonsensical aspects of play. We urge you to value play. Treasure the creativity in fantasy and see worlds open up as children pretend. Appreciate the bravery, joy, and exhilaration as

children take risks, laugh hysterically, run, fall, tumble, and roll without restraint. The uninhibited, imaginative quality of play distinguishes child from adult, play from non-play. Adult restraint imposed on children is a sad sight when we appreciate and understand the power of play for leading children to a full realization of their human potential.

Become an advocate for children and play. This may sometimes be hard if other educators and children's families don't understand the value of play. We urge you to hold fast to your beliefs. Help others to understand play's importance not only in learning but as an inoculation against the stress and pressures that society imposes on children. The children in your care need the opportunity to play now. You can speak to protect, support, and ensure them this right. When you do, you give them a precious gift.

PROJECTS

Write an Article: Pretend you are writing for a school or classroom newsletter addressed to a group of families who have questions about the role of play in the early childhood program. Explain your rationale for making play an important part of the child's early childhood education.

Observe Two Groups of Children: Observe children of different ages, spending a half day in each group. Compare them and report on the following:

- The types of play in which the children engage.
- The stages of play shown by children.
- What the adult's attitudes toward and beliefs about play seem to be.
- What the adults do to facilitate play in their programs.

Interview Two Educators: Ask the educators about how they view play and re-port on their responses regarding:

- Their views of the role of play in their classrooms and in the development of the children they teach.
- What they do to support play in their program.
- How they handle the issues of war play and gender-stereotyped play in their program.

Create a Poster: Design a poster to educate others about the value of play. Choose a play material (for example, playdough); a type of play (for example, dramatic play); or a play experience (for example, jumping rope). Your goal for the poster is to help an average person (such as a parent) understand how this kind of play experience contributes to young children's development.

BIBLIOGRAPHY

Athey, I. 1984. Contributions of Play to Development. *Child's Play: Development and Applied.* Hillside, NJ: Erlbaum.

Bergen, D., ed. 1988. *Play as a Medium for Learning and Development: A Handbook of Theory and Practice.* Portsmouth, NH: Heinemann.

Bredekamp, S. 1988. *Developmentally Appropriate Practice.* Washington, DC: National Association for the Education of Young Children.

Bruner, J., A. Jolly, and K. Sylva. 1976. *Play: Its Role in Development and Evolution.* New York: Basic Books.

Caplan, F., and T. Caplan. 1973. *The Power of Play.* New York: Anchor Press/Doubleday.

Carlsson-Paige, N., and D. E. Levin. 1987. *The War Play Dilemma: Balancing Needs and Values in the Early Childhood Classroom*. New York: Teachers College Press.

Christie, J. F., and F. Wardle. 1992. How Much Time Is Needed for Play? *Young Children* 47(3):28–31.

Elkind, D. 1981. *The Hurried Child: Growing Up Too Fast Too Soon*. Menlo Park, CA: Addison-Wesley.

Johnson, J. E., J. F. Christie, and T. D. Yawkey. 1987. *Play and Early Childhood Development*. Glenview, IL: Scott, Foresman.

Jones, E., and G. Reynolds. 1992. *The Play's the Thing: Teacher's Roles in Children's Play*. New York: Teachers College Press.

Krogh, S. L. 1994. *Educating Young Children Infancy to Grade Three*. New York: McGraw-Hill.

Levy, J. 1978. *Play Behavior*. New York: Wiley.

McKee, J. S., ed. 1986. *Play: Working Partner of Growth*. Wheaton, MD: Association for Childhood Education International.

Monighan-Nourat, P. 1992. The Role of Play in Development. In L. R. Williams and D. P. Fromberg, eds, *Encyclopedia of Early Childhood Education* (229–31). New York: Garland Publishing.

Monighan-Nourot, P., and J. L. V. Hoorn. 1991. Symbolic Play in Preschool and Primary Settings. *Young Children* 46(6):40–47.

Monignan-Nourot, P., B. Scales, et al. 1987. *Looking at Children's Play: A Bridge Between Theory and Practice*. New York: Teachers College Press.

National Association for the Education of Young Children. 1990. NAEYC Position Statement on Media Violence in Children's Lives. *Young Children* 45(5):18–21.

Parten, M. B. 1932. Social Participation Among Preschool Children. *Journal of Abnormal Psychology* 27(3):243–69.

Piaget, J. 1962. *Play, Dreams and Imitation in Childhood*. New York: W.W. Norton.

Rogers, C. S., and J. K. Sawyers. 1988. *Play in the Lives of Children*. Washington, DC: National Association for the Education of Young Children.

Schickedanz, J. A., D. I. Schickedanz, and Forsythe 1993. *Understanding Children*. Mountain View, CA: Mayfield Publishing.

Smilansky, S. 1968. *The Effects of Sociodramatic Play on Disadvantaged Pre-School Children*. New York: Wiley.

Smilansky, S., and L. Shefatya. 1990. *Facilitating Play: A Medium for Promoting Cognitive, Socio-Emotional, and Academic Development in Young Children*. Gaithersburg, MD: Psychosocial & Educational Publications.

Trawick-Smith, J. 1994. *Interactions in the Classroom: Facilitating Play in the Early Years*. Englewood Cliffs, NJ: Merrill/Prentice Hall.

CHAPTER SIX

Assessing Children

Bring with you a heart that watches and receives.   Wordsworth

You see, but you do not observe.   Arthur Conan Doyle

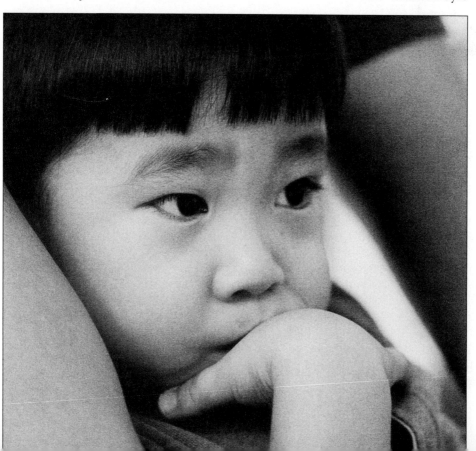

The purpose of this chapter is to help you to understand the process of assessment and to develop a range of skills for learning about children's development and learning. Guidelines are given for the use of observation tools, the selection of standardized tests, and the collection, organization, and use of the data in your work with children.

Children are ever changing and endlessly intriguing. Those who are interested in learning about them have devised many ways to study their growth and development, to evaluate the impact of their learning environments, and to appraise the quality of the interactions they have with the significant people in their lives. Methods for this type of study range from informal observations conducted during the course of daily life in early childhood programs to the use of formal assessment instruments administered under controlled conditions. All of these methods share the goal of helping us to better understand and serve children.

In this chapter we examine the process of assessment. Assessment is a four-part process that involves data collection, interpretation, judgment, and reporting. We use this process to learn what children can understand and do for the purpose of making decisions about how to best support their development. Used appropriately, the assessment process guides our de-cisions about program design and curriculum, helps us plan and make educational decisions for individual children, and serves as the basis for sharing what we have learned with others.

As an early childhood educator, you will observe children and gather and record information in a number of different ways. You will watch children carefully and write running records and anecdotal records describing what you saw. You will learn to select and use observation tools such as checklists, rating scales, event samples, and time samples that enable you to efficiently capture important information about children, relationships, and environments. You will learn how to select, collect, organize, and interpret samples of children's work. You will interview and collect information from family members. And you may learn how to use standardized instruments to gather information about a child or a group of children. All these different sources of information can contribute to your work with children and families.

LEARNING TO OBSERVE

Paul is a fragile-looking, curly haired, just turned three years old. He drags a laundry basket into the shade of a tree. He sits down in the basket and stretches his legs. "I fit! I'm three!" he says, holding up three fingers. Paul rocks his body and the basket back and forth: "I'm rocking the cradle. I'm rocking the cradle." He rocks and rocks till the basket tips, and with a look of surprise he spills onto the ground. Paul stands up and smiles. He turns the basket over and hits it on the top several times, listening to the hollow drumming sounds that his thumping makes. Then he lifts up the basket and crawls underneath. He crouches under the basket, peering out through the holes and announces, "I'm going to hatch the cradle." He stands up wearing the basket like a turtle's shell, "I hatched!"

Vivid descriptions of what children do and say, such as the one above, are one of the time-honored ways of collecting and recording information to assess the development of children. The ability to observe—to "read" and understand children—is one of the most important and satisfying skills that an early childhood professional can develop. It will help you to know and understand individuals, plan more effectively, and evaluate your teaching. More important, observation is the window that enables you to see into the world of the child. By watching Paul and his laundry basket with your heart and mind you learn about who he is, you know about how he is learning and growing, and you gain an empathy towards him that helps you to be his advocate and his friend.

Observation will provide you with information that helps you to respond effectively to the needs of a frightened or angry child, to intervene, to mediate recurring problems between two children, to let you know what a child is experiencing as a member of a family, and much more. Observation lets you know what children are learning and experiencing each day. It also helps you to identify a child who needs more stimulation, who might be troubled, have special needs, or be abused or neglected and in need of help. Observation will help you to communicate about children with other adults who share a concern about their well-being.

Observation is your most basic technique for understanding children, the foundation of all the other ways that you will learn about them. It is the most important technique because many things that children cannot express through spoken words can be inferred by watching them in their natural settings.

In the course of your daily work you will gather information to help you make appraisals regarding the development of children and your own work. The primary focus of this chapter is gathering information about individual children so that you can make plans to support their development. However, because children do not live in a vacuum it is equally important that you apply your observation skills to many other things that impact on their development. The information you gather about children will be used for a variety of purposes: to monitor the development and progress of individual children and to plan appropriate experiences for them, to learn more about problems and help to solve them, to collect data about children to inform discussions and make plans with family members or other professionals, as a basis for choosing and evaluating equipment and materials, to aid in decisions such as whether a child should be referred for further developmental assessment and it is time for the child to move on to another setting or program. Observation is the basis for much of your work with young children and their families, and it is used in some form in almost every chapter in this book. You will observe children, their environments, and their interactions with the significant people in

---

IN PRACTICE

What you gain from observation

Through observation you develop:

- In-depth understanding of individual children—how they think, feel, and view the world, and their interests, skills, characteristic responses, and areas of strength and weakness.
- Increased sensitivity to children in general--awareness of the range of development and a heightened awareness of the unique qualities of childhood and the world of children.
- Understanding of the kinds of social relationships among children and among children and adults and how these can be facilitated.
- Awareness of the environment; how well it is meeting the needs of children, families, and staff; and how it might be improved.
- Greater self-awareness.

their lives. In a less structured but no less important way, you also observe yourself, your values, your relationships, and your own feelings and reactions. When you apply what you know about observation to yourself, you gain greater self-awareness. It is difficult to be objective about yourself, but as you watch your own behavior and interactions you can learn more about how you feel and respond in various situations and realize the impact of your behavior on others.

The Observation Process

To observe is to take notice, to watch attentively, to focus on one particular part of a very complex whole. It means perceiving both the total picture and the significant detail. Learning to observe involves more than casual looking, and it is not nearly as easy as one might think. To make useful observations of children, their significant relationships, and their environments requires training and practice. You must be clear about why you are observing and be willing to gather information and impressions with a receptive eye and mind.

When you select a focus and watch children attentively, the information you collect increases your understanding and gives you insight into the meaning of their behavior and of the impact of relationships and environments on their development. The consistent practice of observation will help you develop *child-sense*—a feeling for how individual children and groups of children are feeling and functioning. This deep understanding is based on a great deal of experience in observing individuals and groups of children over time. Observing can generate a sense of connection and greater understanding, and hence empathy, caring, and concern. To observe more objectively and separate out feelings and reactions from what is actually seen, it is useful to divide the observation process into two components:

- Gathering information—what you see and hear.
- Interpreting information—what you think it means.

Gathering Information

Regardless of the information-gathering technique you use, the first and most essential step in the observation process is to watch and listen carefully, to experience as completely as possible while attempting to suspend interpretation and evaluation. This involves consciously focusing and quieting the inner voice that usually adds a running commentary that explains and evaluates. An effective observer of young children has the ability to wait and see what is really happening instead of drawing conclusions based on hurriedly gathered impressions. Such "intensive waiting" (Nyberg 1971, 168) requires that you suspend expectations and that you be receptive to what is really happening: behaviors, feelings, and patterns. This doesn't mean that you must become an impersonal machine, but it does require you to carefully separate what you see from what you might have wanted or feared to see.

To know what is actually taking place, you must avoid value judgments and try to reduce the distortions that result from biases, defenses, or preconceptions. Objectivity is difficult because you are a participant in the life of the children, families, and settings that you observe, and you both influence the people and things in it and are influenced by them. If you are aware of your impact on the situation and its impact on you, you can work toward becoming a more objective observer.

It is also helpful to be aware of your characteristics as an observer. When you realize what you tend to focus on, you can also get an idea of what you characteristically ignore. We have our college students observe a bowl of goldfish and describe what they see. Each student chooses one fish to write about. Some students describe the minute detail of the fish's anatomy as a biologist might, some look at the fish in the context of its environment (bowl, sand, water, and other fish), and some describe the interactions among the fish. Not only do students learn something about the features they tend to observe from this exercise, but they are surprised to find how different the observations of the same fish are and how much they attribute human feelings and motivations to them. By doing these kinds of observation exercises you increase the range of things that you attend to, become a more keen observer, and improve your ability to write more detailed and comprehensive descriptions. Millie Almy says of keen observers:

> They study facial expression, note the steady and the shifting look, the tightly or loosely held jaw and lips, the grimaces and the smiles. They hear not only words but tones, pitch, strain, hesitation, and pauses. They note body posture, slumping shoulders and puppet-on-a-string gestures, as contrasted with flowing, graceful movements and accurate, efficient coordination. They see all the details in relation to the settings where the behavior takes place. The clenched hands and intent frown seen in the reading period are different from the freedom and *joie de vivre* of the playground. These finer details, this attention to its quality, provide clues to the meaning of behavior. (Almy and Genishi 1979, 39–40)

As Almy and Genishi suggest, a good observer goes far beyond the obvious. The more teachers know about children, the more differentiated and refined their observations become. They focus on features of a child's body, build, posture, tone of voice, appearance, grooming, ways of moving and manipulating objects, mood, interactions with others, and many other attributes. Keen observers know that children communicate a great deal through their bodies—facial expression; body tension; the language of hands, fingers, and eyebrows; the tilt of a head or shoulder—as much as through their spoken words and obvious actions.

Interpreting Information

The second basic step in the observation process is to make an interpretation (sometimes called *conclusion* or *inference*) based on what you have seen and heard. Although behavior is observable, the reasons for behavior are not visible and may only be inferred. You need to observe closely and then seek the relationship between the observed behavior and its unobservable cause. You can never truly know why a child behaves as he or she does, but you will make decisions based on your understanding about children's behavior every day. It is important that you develop skill in making interpretations based on what you actually observe.

Understanding a child's behavior is difficult because many factors—stage of development, health, culture, and individual experience—combine in complex ways to determine how a child acts in a given situation. The same behavior can mean very different things in different children. Angelito's downcast eyes mean that he has been taught to show respect to adults by avoiding eye contact when spoken to, while the same behavior from Joanie means she is avoiding acknowledging what you are saying. Individual observers may interpret the same behavior or incident in dissimilar ways, depending on their knowledge and their own cultural and ethnic backgrounds. If your cultural and ethnic background is the same as Angelito's you are likely to understand his behavior, but if your background is more similar to Joanie's you might mistakenly assume he is trying to avoid hearing or acknowledging what you are saying.

We have seen situations in which several individuals observed the same incident and made very different interpretations. For example, several of our college students noticed a little girl lying in a large cement pipe in the yard of a program they were visiting. One thought she was withdrawn and antisocial; an

other was convinced she was lonely, unhappy, and in need of comforting; and the third felt that she was just taking a few moments for quiet contemplation. Obviously they needed more information about the child and the events that preceded their observation in order to make accurate and meaningful interpretations.

Writing Descriptions

Just watching carefully will often be enough to give you helpful information about a child or a situation. At other times you will need to write down what you have observed to have a permanent record for yourself or to share with families or other professionals. Learning to

write clear, concise, meaningful descriptions takes time, commitment, and practice. As a practicing professional you will usually have to observe while you are directly involved in interactions with children and families. It may be a rare occasion when you are called upon to get a more detached look at a child or situation. However, as a college student you should have many opportunities to really focus on a child or a group to develop your observation and description-writing skills.

There are a few things you should keep in mind each time you have an opportunity to observe and write descriptions of children. Learn to observe unobtrusively. Enter the situation quietly, sit at children's eye level, close enough to see and hear but not so close that you distract the children with your presence. Don't get involved while you are observing unless it is necessary to protect a child. Briefly answer children's questions about who you are and what you are doing ("I am learning about what children do") and try not to get involved in extended conversations. Take time just to watch; you will have other opportunities to get involved. Whether you observe children, adults in action, or program environments, it is important that you let everyone in the setting know that you are practicing writing descriptions based on observation and that you will protect the confidentiality of children, families, professionals, and programs whenever you share your writing in class or with your instructors.

When you write it is important to clearly separate what happened (description) from what you think it means (interpretation). Good description uses clear language and communicates enough information to convey the uniqueness of the subject of the observation. At first your writing may be awkward, and you may have difficulty deciding how much to record.

If you are writing for someone unfamiliar with the setting, begin with the context for the observation; where you are (school, home, playground, shopping mall, and so on), who and what you are observing (an individual child, a group of children, an adult-child interaction), and a brief description of the people and the situation. If your readers are familiar with the people and setting, simply note who or what you are observing, where, and the date and time.

The first thing to do in writing a description of a child is to note basic physical attributes that will help the reader to visualize the child: age, sex, size, build, facial features, coloring, and distinguishing markings. A plain physical description sets the stage but gives little sense of the distinctiveness of a child. For example:

"She is an Asian girl, approximately four years of age, shorter than her peers. She has a slight build, oval face, and brown hair and eyes." Your writing will communicate more if you elaborate the basic physical description with some of the child's unique personal qualities: body stance, way of moving, facial expression, gestures, tone of voice. This conveys a better picture of the child as a unique individual. It will take practice to find a balance of vivid imagery and objectivity. The following addition conveys a much more vivid sense of the child whose physical attributes were described above: "She has black eyebrows and lashes, brown hair, almond-shaped eyes, a fair, smooth complexion, pouting lips and a small up-turned nose. She is slim and almost fragile looking, and strolls from activity to activity with small light steps, her eyes alert and her head turning occasionally from side to side. Her arms hang slightly away from her body and swing with the rhythm of her stroll."

The next step is to describe what happens—the child's activities and interactions. The addition of expressive detail, including body language, and interactions with people and with materials communicates more than a bare-bones description. The language used in recording should capture the subtleties and complexities of children's behavior. Carefully chosen words convey the essence of the person and situation and are an important part of writing vivid descriptions. Adverbs and adjectives enhance our ability to visualize the subject of the observation: "He rushes from the block area to the easels" instead of "He walks very fast." In choosing modifiers, avoid words that have a strong emotional impact or bias built into them. Describe what a child *does,* instead of giving your views of what he or she *is, feels, wishes,* or *intends.* Opinions of children such as *pretty, cute, bright, attractive, good, messy, slow, mean,* or *naughty* are to be avoided in description (and in interpretation), as these are value judgments. Describing a child in these terms tells more about the values of the observer than the nature of the child. Since the descriptions you write may be shared with others, you have the responsibility to convey useful information that is as free as possible from personal bias or unsubstantiated evaluations.

A good description is specific, but does not give so much detail that the point is lost. Broad general statements do not convey much information and are not very effective in capturing important qualities of the child or interaction. For example, the statement that "John is stringing beads" does not tell the reader very much. We have a better picture of the child and situation when the observer tells us, "John has an intent look on his face, his tongue protrudes slightly from between his teeth, and it appears that all of his concentration is focused on the beads." Details such as when John worked with the beads, how long he worked, how he worked, who he worked with, and how he worked increases the reader's ability to understand the child and the situation.

Interpretations Based on Description

When you need to communicate information you have gathered about a child to another person, you will usually add your interpretations to your description. Interpretations based on written descriptions make it possible for others to read what you have written and decide whether or not they agree with your conclusions. When you share your descriptions and the interpretations you have made with others, they can then offer their insight and you benefit from the collective experience of all who review your writing. Descriptions of the same child or incident written by different observers can be helpful since each of us tends to notice different things. It is also eye opening to have several individuals interpret the same written description of a situation. Since two

people viewing the same child or incident (or reading about them) will often have different perceptions, it is best to be tentative in your interpretations. It is also helpful to discuss your interpretations with someone else. Becoming aware of different perspectives can help you to realize how difficult it is to interpret accurately. We encourage you to make liberal use of the words *might* and *seems to* in your written interpretations to underscore the tentative nature of conclusions about children's needs, feelings, and motivation.

The format in Table 6.1 is helpful for learning to write interpretation based on description. We recommend no less than a half hour for each observation of a child. During the actual observation, use the left hand column to record what you see. As soon after observing as possible write some tentative interpretations and note any feelings or other impressions in the right hand column.

With this format you are able to review your description, add other possible interpretations, and decide if you have enough data to substantiate your conclusions. If not, you can observe the child in other settings to see if the behaviors are repeated and characteristic or simply the outcome of a particular situation.

Your written summary should be based on several observations. State your conclusions concisely, and cite the descriptive data on which they are based. A teacher who has made several more observations of Joshua might summarize with: "Joshua appears to be a leader and to be well respected by the other boys. Although his behavior can appear 'bossy,' Sae Won and Thomas accept his directives and do not seem upset by, or resistant to, his stepping into their work. Joshua seems enthusiastic about learning, will stay with a task for a long time, and appears to dislike being diverted from it. He will cooperate with adults if he has warning and a little encouragement and if they show respect for his purposes."

TABLE 6.1
Interpretation Based on Description

Description	Interpretations/Inferences
Joshua enters the classroom well ahead of his father and makes a beeline for the block corner where Sae Won and Thomas have a large unit block structure well in progress. J. drops his lunch pail in the middle of the rug and begins issuing directions—"Make it go this way" as he takes a block from Thomas and begins a second wall at a right angle to the first. "Get more of the big kind," J. says to Sae Won.	excitement at being in school enters activity quickly a little bossy?
The two quickly join in and proceed with J.'s plan as J.'s father approaches, observes a few moments, and then interrupts to tell J. to take lunch pail to his cubby.	accepted as leader among his peers
J. acknowledges the request with an impatient glance and says, "Just a minute, Dad," and continues to direct the building with even more vigor and hurriedness.	expects to have a say in what happens to him
Father says, "You can come back to the blocks after you've. . . ." J. grimaces and scrambles over the wall, grabs the pail, runs to his cubby, and deposits the pail inside. It falls to the floor as he turns to rush back to the blocks.	follows through on request—retains focus on self-identified task
Father intercepts him half-way and points him back to his cubby and pushes him gently from behind. J. stops, looks up at Father, and laughs as if sharing a joke.	sense of humor trust in father

SYSTEMATIC OBSERVATION METHODS

To develop more awareness of a child or of a situation, it may be sufficient to simply take time to stop and mentally note what you observe. If your goal is to understand more for a particular purpose, such as to learn more about a child in order to make a referral, then some form of systematic data-gathering may be useful or necessary. Systematic recorded observations reveal trends and patterns in behavior. They enable you to increase your objectivity since conclusions based on recorded observation can correct for misperceptions and biases that can occur when conclusions are based on recall and memory alone. Anecdotal records, running records, event samples, time samples, checklists, and rating scales are some of the most commonly used methods of gathering information. They differ in the degree to which they are systematized, their most appropriate use, and their advantages and disadvantages. All observation techniques have the common characteristic of beginning with a focus (a child, behavior, interaction, practice, or situation). Some are very time consuming, but open ended and rich in detail; others are more narrowly focused and are quick and easy to use.

The particular method that you choose depends on what you want to know and how you think you might best find it out. If you understand what information each can give and think carefully about the purpose of the observation, you will be able to select an approach to generate the kind of information you need.

Systematic observation methods can help to gather more information about something you have noticed. For example, you may use a time sample to determine what percentage of the time a child who seems withdrawn is actually spending in passive activity and how much time the child is more actively involved. You might use a checklist to appraise the richness of a learning environment and a rating scale to guide your observation of the quality of adult-child interactions.

Anecdotal Records

A frequently used form of recorded observation is the anecdotal record—a brief narrative describing incidents, behaviors, and interactions (Figure 6.1). It is written after the fact in the past tense and can be open ended and rich in detail. Anecdotal records are essential tools for teachers of young children, home visitors, and other early childhood practitioners who need to document events and changes in children, families, and programs. It is important to learn to write them well.

You will write anecdotal records about some of the things that are important to understand in your work with young children and their families. For example:

- Behavior or interactions that seem typical for a child or family.
- Behavior or interactions that seem atypical for a child or family.
- The achievement of a developmental milestone for a child or a significant change in the way a family functions.

Child: Tina
Setting: Classroom/Playground at Preschool
Observer: Jackie S.

9/3/93—Tina came to school late today. She entered very reluctantly and had a crying spell as mom tried to leave. Mom told her how sorry she was to have to leave her several times. After the departure T. withdrew into the library area during the learning center period. She refused Jennifer's attempt to get her to read a book with her.

9/8/93—Tina came to school on time today. Mom left quickly because she was a little late for a meeting. T. seemed only a little sad about mom's departure.

9/9/93—Tina came to school with grandma today and said a hasty good-bye and quickly entered the finger-painting activity going on in the back yard.

9/10/93—Mom brought Tina to school today. After a tearful good-bye Tina went to her cubby for her teddy bear and spent most of the first hour curled up in the library. She finally was coaxed from this area by Jennifer, who wanted her to play dress-up with her.

9/14/93—Dad brought Tina to school late. T. began to cry as he said he had to leave. She stopped within a few seconds and skipped off with Jennifer and Star to the sandbox.

9/15/93—Mom came for Tina very early in the afternoon. T. refused to leave her activity willingly, so mom had to forcefully carry her from the school.

9/18/93—Tina's mother spoke with me today about Tina's refusal to stay with her grandmother on Saturday night—which she has always enjoyed doing in the past. Mother wondered out loud in front of Tina about whether it is connected to the new experience of being left at school each day. Tina began crying and struck her mother on the thigh with a closed fist.

FIGURE 6.1
An example of anecdotal record

- Incidents and interactions that convey the nature of social relationships and emotional reactions.
- Behavior or interactions relating to an area of special concern.

In our work with young children we have sometimes used sharing notebooks for anecdotal records. Each child had a notebook in which we wrote observations, and the child's family members were invited to comment.

It is valuable to write anecdotal notes on a regular basis. Anecdotal records can also be made with special emphasis on children or families about whom you have questions or concerns and those children who are "invisible"—so inconspicuous that they tend to be

forgotten. If possible, write some notes each day. They may be just words or fragments of information with details that you fill in later, but not more than a day later or you will have lost the details that make records useful. These records become part of your collection of information about each child and family and need to be filed with all other confidential records.

Running Records

A running record is a narrative account of behavior and events that is written at the time of occurrence in the present tense (Figure 6.2). These are open ended and very rich in detail, provided that the observer is skilled. The critical skill is the ability to write vivid description

---

Child's Name __Lani__ **Birthdate/Age** __4.5__
Observer __Gene__ **Date** __9/8/93__

Lani is playing by herself with plastic blocks, making guns. She walks into other room. "Sara, play Super Woman with me." They walk into the other room to the block table.

L: "I'll be Wonder Woman and you can be Super Woman."

S: "No, I want to be Wonder Woman."

L: "I ask you, so I get first choice."

Both L. & S. are sitting facing each other at the round manipulative table with their elbows planted firmly on the table surface. L. picks up the plastic blocks she had already assembled into a gun-like form. S. notices and quickly scoops a dozen or more blocks toward herself and begins to quickly create a gun for herself.

James approaches the table and shouts, "You can't make guns in school." The teacher approaches the table quickly. J. says, "Lani and Sara are playing guns." The teacher nods toward J. and stands by quietly as though waiting for comment from L. or S. S. says, "Lani made one first." L. says, "Sara made one too." The Teacher says, "I guess you both know it's not O.K. What can you do instead?"

L. turns to J. and says, "You be Batman so we can ride in the bat mobile." J. grabs a chair and places it in the middle of the floor area, sits down, and reaches his arms in front of himself as though preparing to drive a car. L. & S. drag their chairs into place behind him just as he makes a vocal noise that sounds like the starting of a car engine.

J. says, "Batman doesn't have to use a gun 'cuz he is super strong and really fast. Wonder Woman is weak." L. still has the plastic block gun in her hand. She glances toward S. as she points the gun at the back of J's head and pretend shoots him. S. says, "James, you're dead, Lani shot you dead." J. drops from his chair onto the floor and sprawls his legs and arms limply to either side of himself as though he has died. S. & L. laugh as L. takes the driver's chair and makes a noise to indicate that they are roaring away quickly.

FIGURE 6.2
An example of a running record

quickly while avoiding interpretation and judgment. Learning to do this well requires training and considerable practice.

Writing a running record is generally done for very special purposes and often by someone who is not responsible for what is happening in the program setting. It is usually too time-consuming to be done by those who are actively involved in interactions with children and families. As a student in the field of early childhood education and care you will have opportunities to practice and master the skill of writing running records as a way for you to develop sensitivity to and knowledge about children and families. As a practicing professional you will use this skill when you need to do an in-depth study of a particular child. For ordinary purposes you may select more efficient and less time-consuming methods for gathering information.

Time Samples

A time sample is a method for tracking behaviors that occur at regular intervals and in rapid succession (Figure 6.3). It is not a record of everything that happens but rather a system for collecting information of a predefined behavior or set of behaviors displayed by individual or groups. For example, you might use this technique to find out how often a particular behavior (hitting, fantasy play, thumb sucking) is actually occurring. A time sample will be conducted often enough to get a good idea of the frequency of the behavior—a minimum of three are needed as the basis for any interpretation. You may want to sample weeks or months later to determine if change has occurred.

A time sample uses a grid on which you can tally the occurrence of the particular behavior during a short time period. A simple checklist or code may be devised to help you quickly record what type of behavior is occurring. For example, *R* may stand for *rejects inter-*

action and *I* may stand for *initiates interaction*.

Time sampling is a very efficient method of gathering information. It can be used for observing more than one child at a time. The information from a time sample can be used as a basis for drawing conclusions about the frequency and relative importance of particular behaviors. However, the behaviors being studied must occur frequently. It is also important to recognize that the information about the cause of behavior is not included so you can not draw conclusions.

We once designed a time sample to test our belief that four-year-old Micah was initiating an excessive number of conflicts with others. Several staff members felt that they spent a great deal of time each day intervening in the conflicts that he provoked. Another teacher had difficulty understanding this because she perceived Micah as a very positive and cooperative

Child's Name __Jason__ **Birthdate/Age** __4.3__
Observer __Gene__ **Date** __10/93__

Instructions: Observe a different ten-minute play period each day for a week. Select a variety of times of day and places during the week. During that ten minutes watch the play of the child for fifteen seconds, then mark what type you saw. Wait for the remainder of the minute, then repeat the observation period and mark, and so on.

	Solitary	Parallel	Group
Functional			
	//	/	///
Constructive			
	////	/////	///// /////
Dramatic			
	//	/	///// ///// /
Games			
	/	///	///// //

FIGURE 6.3
An example of a time sample

person. The time sample was simple. We agreed to track how frequently Micah initiated interaction with two friends and whether it was positive or negative. The three fifteen-minute time samples uncovered that Micah had many more positive than negative interactions, as did his friends. We discovered, however, that Micah initiated interactions three times more frequently than his two playmates. This helped explain our different perceptions and helped us to understand why we felt taxed by our frequent interventions. Our increased understanding helped us to become more trusting and to allow Micah more opportunity to handle interpersonal problems on his own.

Event Samples

An event sample is used to understand more about a behavior (Figure 6.4). You watch for a particular behavior or interaction and then record exactly what precedes the event, what happens during the event, and the consequences of the event. The record of the event is made while it is occurring or immediately after. The purpose is to collect information about the

relationship between the behavior and the context of the behavior so that you can understand the cause and possibly devise a way to alter the course of events.

Like a running record, this type of observation relies on your skill in making detailed descriptions. For example, if you think a child has been engaging in a lot of aggressive behavior, you may want to write a description of what precedes every aggressive act, exactly what happens, and what follows the behavior. You may discover that the behavior is only happening before lunch or nap, at the end of the day, or is triggered by interaction with one child or group. Event sampling is not time-consuming, and it can provide useful information for figuring out the causes of behavior. It can be the basis for generating plans to change behavior.

Checklists and Rating Scales

Checklists are lists of traits, behaviors, concepts, and skills on which an observer puts dates or check marks next to each item to indicate if or when it is observed (Figure 6.5). Checklists are an efficient way of gathering in-

Child's Name <u>Jay</u>   **Birthdate/Age** <u>4.5</u>
Observer <u>Gene</u>   **Date(s)** <u>9/94</u>

Date/Time	Preceding Event	Behavior	Consequence
9.24.94/7:48	J. was pouring juice at the snack table. He tipped over the paper cup and spilled a small amount.	J. set down the pitcher and struck out at the stack of paper cups, knocking them from the table.	The student aide quickly grabbed him in her arms and said, "It's OK, it was just a little spill."
9.26.94/8:07	J. entered the block area and began placing trucks from the shelf on the structure Pua and Jenny were building. Pua said, "You can't play."	J. ran from the block area past the art area on his way out the back door. On his way past the watercolor table he made a wide sweep with his arm and knocked over a cup of water	Ginger, the teacher who witnessed the block corner scene, followed him out. She took him in her arms and told him, "I bet it made you made when Pua told you that you not to build with them."
10.6.94/7:55	J. placed his blanket in his cubby on top of a plastic container. The blanket fell out as he turned to walk away.	J. shoved the blanket back into the cubby and pulled the entire contents of the cubby onto the floor and ran out the front door to the gate.	Jim, who was greeting the children, followed him out and said, "Please let me help you get your blanket in straight."
10.8.94/8:15	J. was playing with the tinker toys. Jenny accidentally bumped his construction and several pieces fell off.	J. screamed at Jenny and said she was stupid. With a single sweep of his arm he knocked the pieces to the floor.	Lani, the assistant, joined him where he had thrown himself on the rug and gently rubbed his back until he calmed.

FIGURE 6.4
An example of an event sample

FIGURE 6.5
An example of a checklist

Child's Name <u>Henry</u>   **Birthdate/Age** <u>2yrs. 11mo.</u>
Observer <u>Iris</u>   **Date** <u>9/8-12/31/93</u>

Instructions: Enter the date on which you first observe the listed behavior.

___ / ___ / ___ Scribbles
___ / ___ / ___ Paints with whole arm movement
___ / ___ / ___ Turns door knobs
___ / ___ / ___ Holds crayon with thumb and fingers
___ / ___ / ___ Paints with wrist action
___ / ___ / ___ Cuts with scissors
___ / ___ / ___ Holds cup with one hand

TABLE 6.2
Selecting an Observation Method

In Order To:	Use:
Record a behavior or interaction or the achievement of a milestone.	Anecdotal record
Ascertain how often a type of behavior occurs	Time sample
Understand why or when a particular behavior occurs	Event sample
Gather information about children's play preferences, individual progress, how materials and equipment are being used	Checklist, rating scale

formation such as which children have acquired a particular skill or concept or which of a list of possible interaction skills are displayed by a professional. These are a useful, relatively simple way to find out what children are doing or not doing and what is working in the classroom. A checklist can also provide an informal profile of each child in a class if it constructed to cover the different areas in the usual sequence of development. Teachers can create their own checklists to help in assessing the progress of individual children. This is actually a very good strategy for reviewing the milestones of development. It also ensures that you have a systematic guide to observing and recording information about the aspects of development that you wish to emphasize in your program.

Rating scales are nearly identical to checklists in purpose and uses. The only significant difference is that a rating scale provides a mechanism for indicating the degree to which a behavior or characteristic is present in a person or a situation (Figure 6.6).

Table 6.2 will help you choose an appropriate observation method.

THE PORTFOLIO APPROACH TO ASSESSMENT

In the last several years there has been growing interest in the use of portfolios to organize assessment information about children's learning and development. In the elementary school, the portfolio represents an innovative alterna-

Reflect and write about . . .

observing children

Think about the programs you have visited or worked in. Did teachers regularly observe children? How were these observations recorded? Were any of the systematic observation techniques described above used? How was observational data used in program and curriculum planning? Do you think observing provided staff members with useful information?

Child's Name __Henry__ **Birthdate/Age** __2yrs. 11mo.__
Observer __Iris__ **Date** __9/8/93__

Indicate the degree of success the child has with the following by marking the place on the scale that best represents the current level of functioning.
Scribbles:

easily	somewhat easily	with difficulty	not able to do

Paints with whole arm movement:

easily	somewhat easily	with difficulty	not able to do

Turns door knobs:

easily	somewhat easily	with difficulty	not able to do

Holds crayon with thumb and fingers:

easily	somewhat easily	with difficulty	not able to do

Paints with wrist action:

easily	somewhat easily	with difficulty	not able to do

Cuts with scissors:

easily	somewhat easily	with difficulty	not able to do

FIGURE 6.6
An example of a rating scale

tive to traditional evaluations of children's progress, which have typically included testing and letter grades. In programs for younger children it is a logical extension of the observational approaches that have always been used.

To understand what we mean by a portfolio, keep the traditional form of a portfolio in mind. Artists, photographers, and writers compile portfolios of their work. Their contents are selected to demonstrate their capabilities in their particular field. In early childhood education and care settings, portfolios are thoughtfully organized collections of materials that represent a child's progress in all areas of development.

A portfolio is like an artist's gallery exhibition with paintings, sculptures, and descriptions of the artist's life and work. Just as the works in a gallery give a fuller understanding of the artist, so does a child's portfolio give a fuller understanding of who the child is and what the child knows. The portfolio is used to collect samples of work that provides evidence of a child's progress. The use of a portfolio builds on the practice of observing children in the context of their daily lives in early childhood settings. It broadens the range of information to give us a portrait of each child's development, and it provides a way to systematize the information to make it more useful.

Why Use the Portfolio Approach?

The purpose of a portfolio is to enable you to look back at observations and samples of children's work to gauge how they have developed—socially, emotionally, physically, and cognitively—and how you can best plan for their future growth. The portfolio approach is a systematic way to collect information about a child from many sources and organize it for later analysis and use. Among the important uses of portfolio collections are to:

- Plan for individual children.
- Plan meaningful activities and events for groups of children.
- Report on children's developmental progress to families and other professionals.
- Identify the need for special services.
- Evaluate how well a program is meeting its goals and objectives.

The Selection of Portfolio Contents

To make meaningful and useful decisions about what to collect for a child's portfolio, you must know the goals and objectives of your program, understand child development, and decide what materials and information will indicate progress. For example, if you teach preschool children and literacy is a program goal, you may plan ways to assess if individuals are developing literacy awareness and skill. You might collect periodic work samples in which a child has incorporated print or print-like marks, keep records of books read to or by the child, and write anecdotal notes to record when the child makes use of written materials or uses pens or pencils to communicate.

The amount of information you collect will depend on the requirements of your setting and your reasons for making the collection. It may range from making observations and gathering work samples on a regular basis, to making notes only when you observe new knowledge or skills emerging, or to note changes in children's behavior. Following is a list of the kinds of things that can be included in the portfolio.

- Anecdotal records
- Samples of drawings and paintings
- Samples of writing

- Photographs of constructions, clay and dough objects, block structures
- Developmental checklists
- Developmental rating scales
- Time samples
- Event samples
- Running records
- Lists of books read to or read by the child
- Audiotape samples of speech or musical production
- Videotapes of the child in action

Collect samples of each child's work on a regular basis. Be selective about items to include in a portfolio. The purpose is to collect items that represent the individuality of a child's development; therefore, samples do not need to be the same for every child. You may want talk with a child about which painting, drawing, or piece of writing they like best and would like to have you keep in their portfolio. Be sure to label and date all items before placing them in the portfolio.

How to Organize and Use a Portfolio

Many families keep a baby book in which they record first words, lists of favorite things, and significant milestones such as the date of the child's first steps. They may also collect and save samples of their child's school work, drawings, and paintings. These and other things may make it into a file folder or beneath a magnet on the refrigerator. Most families have photo collections that represent important events in the family and in the lives of the children. More and more people keep audiotape samples of a child's speech and videotapes of significant events. Some families have developed systematic ways to organize and store all these pieces of information; for others, these collections remain a jumble of notes and papers in desk drawers, photos in boxes, and tapes in closets with no easy way to locate and sort out what is interesting and meaningful.

Similarly, in early childhood programs information can be random and disorganized or it can be carefully selected and organized to provide a portrait of each child. For infant, toddler, and preschool-age children, a portfolio can be organized by the domains of development—physical, social, emotional, and cognitive. This organization can serve primary-age children well, but some teachers may wish to organize portfolios by subject or content areas such as social studies, science, literacy, and so on. Whether you organize by domains of develop-

ment or by subject areas, it is important to include items that are an authentic representation of the child's understanding and skill in the categories you have determined to be relevant and important. This means that your curriculum must be rich enough to provide opportunities for children to produce concrete representations of their abilities. A collection of completed worksheets organized by subject areas would not be adequate. Likewise, a large collection of a child's art productions might be useful to an adult who was interested in the developmental stages of art but would not give a very complete picture of a child's abilities and interests.

Regardless of your categories, it is essential that you develop a system that makes the filing and retrieval of contents easy. A large accordion folder that includes several file folders to organize different kinds of materials serves well as a portfolio. Some people use file boxes and others organize materials into notebooks that have folders and pocket sheets in which to store work samples. All of these systems work well for works in progress such as anecdotal records, checklists, and rating scales. Large items that must be stored elsewhere may be indexed in the system with a note about where it is stored. Whatever system you use, it is important that it work for you or you will not be as systematic in the collection and storage of materials as you need to be for the portfolio to accomplish its purposes for the child, staff, families, and program.

Reflect and write about . . .

portfolios

Have you used portfolios or observed early childhood settings in which they were used? How were the portfolios organized, and what information was included in them? How was the information from the portfolios summarized? How was it reported to families and other educators?

The portfolio weaves a rich tapestry of a child's life. From the data collected you will use your understanding of child development and early childhood education and care to create a deeper understanding of each child. This deeper understanding will enable you to select the appropriate next steps in support of their development, to share your understanding with families and other professionals, and to represent the child's strengths and potentials with the staff of the program to which the child moves next.

STANDARDIZED TESTS

A variety of assessment techniques can be used to monitor the developmental progress of individuals; to serve as the basis for planning for individuals and groups of children; to learn more about problems and develop strategies for solving them; to collect information about children to share with their families; and to make decisions about the design and enrichment of the learning environment. In the past, most of the information gathered about children in early childhood programs (especially those for children under five years of age) was based on observation. In recent years there has been a dramatic increase in the use of standardized tests for assessing young children. By a standardized test we mean a set of tasks or questions that has been designed to measure a child's functioning and that follows a prescribed procedure in administration and scoring.

Standardized tests have clearly defined purposes and can be useful for some of the same purposes as other information-gathering methods. They have some additional characteristics that set them apart from other approaches to studying children. Each item on a standardized test has been carefully studied to establish the dependability of the test. Two kinds of data are used to establish the dependability of these tests: *validity,* or accuracy, the degree to which

it measures what it claims to measure, and *reliability,* or consistency, how often identical results can be obtained with the same test. Standardized tests are either *norm referenced,* comparing an individual child's performance on the test with that of an external norm, established by administering the test to a large sample of children, or *criterion referenced,* relating the child's performance to a standard of achievement but not comparing the child to a reference group.

Tests are standardized on selected groups of children. They may not be as useful a measure for other groups of children with different cultures and different experiences. Traits that are related to culture or experience may seem to indicate a developmental problem where none exists. For example, a test used in Hawaii asked children to respond to questions relating to snowsuits, mittens, and snow shovels—their "incorrect" responses were not due to developmental delay but to lack of experience with the items.

A test also reflects the values of the people who created it—what they believe is worthwhile for a child of a particular age to know, to do, or to have experienced. If you are ever called upon to evaluate an instrument, you will want to determine if it is a good fit for your purposes and the child or children whom you wish to assess.

The kinds of standardized tests that are commonly used in early childhood programs include screening instruments, developmental assessments, diagnostic tests, and readiness and achievement tests. These are described in the sections that follow.

Screening Instruments

Screening instruments are brief evaluations that compare a child's development to other children of the same age. Screening is a relatively fast and efficient way to assess the developmental status of children. These instruments are designed to identify children who may need further assessment—they should not be used to determine individual development plans or as the basis for curriculum plans. Every child is screened, in some way, beginning at birth. The newborn is observed for obvious defects. Simple screening such as observation and testing of heart rate, muscle tone, and respiration occur in the first few minutes after birth. As children grow and develop, they encounter other forms of screening in the course of regular medical care.

Another important kind of screening occurs in school settings to identify children who might have developmental delays or conditions requiring correction such a vision or hearing impairment. The goal is to identify children who may need further assessment so that specialized services can be provided as early as possible.

Appropriate screening can bring about remarkable improvements in children's lives. Generations of children entering the Head Start program have been screened: those with hearing losses have discovered a new world of sound, those with visual impairments have been given the gift of good sight, and those with other medical conditions have had them treated. Some children who have been identified by the screening as at risk for learning problems have been evaluated and received special services to help them enter school able to keep up with their peers.

Screening instruments are relatively short, have few items, look at a number of developmental areas, and can be administered and interpreted by trained professionals or trained volunteers. Screening identifies children who need to be looked at more carefully. A child should *never* be labeled on the basis of screening since screening *cannot* predict future success or failure, prescribe specific treatment or curriculum, or diagnose special conditions. Even if no children are identified as needing further assessment, information from screening can help you to understand the range of development of the children in your program.

Examples of screening instruments include the Early Screening Inventory, the McCarthy Screening Test, Developmental Indicators for the Assessment of Learning (DIAL), the Minneapolis Preschool Screening Test, and the Denver Developmental Screening Test.

Screening services vary from community to community and from state to state. Many have Childfind programs to make parents and other adults aware of the importance of early identification. Some communities provide screening when children first enter kindergarten or first grade. As an early childhood educator you may participate in choosing or administering a screening instrument and be involved in follow-up. If formal screening is not available in your school or community, informal screening through sensitive observation can also identify children who need further assessment.

Children who are identified through screening as being at risk may be referred to a specialist for further testing, diagnosis, and intervention or to an interdisciplinary team for comprehensive assessment. Chapter Fifteen, Working with Children with Special Needs, provides more information on the referral process. Sometimes screening will indicate problems that are not severe enough to warrant special services through the schools but that do need to be acted upon by the child's family. Program staff are usually the ones who must inform families that their child needs to be evaluated further and follows up with and supports the family to assure that the child receives the needed service.

No method of screening is foolproof. Some children with developmental delays will remain undetected while others who have no serious delays will be identified as needing further evaluation. One criterion for choosing a screening instrument is how often children are missed or falsely identified. Be very careful in reporting screening results, since false identification may label children and worry families unnecessarily.

Good screening instruments are valid and reliable and focus on performance in a wide range of developmental areas (speech, understanding of language, affect, perception, large and fine motor skills). They are more likely to appropriately identify children if they use the language or dialect of the community since children not tested in their first language will not reflect their true abilities. Similarly, they should be adaptable to the experience and cultural background of the children. Good screening instruments also involve information from parents, since they know the child and have important information to contribute.

Developmental Assessments

Developmental assessment includes the various checklists and rating scales that have been created for appraising children's skills and abilities. They help you learn about children's actual functioning in the classroom by identifying patterns of strengths and weaknesses in a number of developmental domains. Developmental assessments give a profile of a child's abilities in a variety of tasks and settings. They are criterion referenced—that is, they reflect a child's degree of mastery over a skill or sequence of skills. Developmental assessments are not meant to label children; rather, they give you information so that you can design appropriate experiences for individual children and groups.

A developmental assessment is usually administered, interpreted, and used by program staff. It may take weeks or even months to completely administer a developmental assessment in a number of skill areas. In some settings it may be a process that continues throughout the school year. You may administer it early in the year to identify skills the child already has and then design experiences and activities to help the child to move to the next step. The child may be assessed again later in the year and the process repeated. Results may help you discuss program goals and content. They are a part of the information you will share with parents.

Developmental assessments often include guidelines for lessons and materials that are designed to develop specific skills. Although these may provide good ideas, they should be used in the context of activities that are meaningful to children. You should never teach assessment items in isolation or use them as the basis for curriculum. Examples of commonly used assessments include Learning Accomplishment Profile (LAP) and the Portage Guide to Early Education.

Developmental assessment may also serve a screening purpose, especially if no other screening has been done. Results can indicate that a child may have a problem. A very general guideline is that if there is a six-month lag in language or a one-year delay in any other area, the child should be carefully watched and receive special attention in the area of the deficit. If the delay is greater, the child may need a diagnostic evaluation.

Like screening instruments, developmental assessments only measure what can be observed and what their authors believe to be important. They may not assess what you or your colleagues value. If you feel that the use of a developmental assessment instrument is appropriate for your program, be aware of the limitations of the instrument and continue to use your own observations to create a more comprehensive picture of a child.

When you choose a classroom assessment, it is important to consider the use you wish to make of the results. With your purpose in mind, you can select an instrument will suit your needs and the needs of the children in your classroom. If you use information from assessment instruments in the design of your program, then the day-to-day reality of your program will be tied to that assessment. Used well, this can help you to create a program that is developmentally appropriate and responsive to the needs of individuals. Used incorrectly, children may be required to master items from the assessment in isolation and learning may turn into drudgery for them.

Developmental assessments can give you information that will be helpful in planning for children. Good developmental assessment instruments have goals for children that are similar to or compatible with the goals of your program. They provide guidelines for use and can be easily administered and interpreted by staff—criteria for success are clearly spelled out. They can be used with the language or dialect of the program's population and can be adapted to reflect the culture and typical experience of its children. Good assessments involve age-appropriate responses and timing (manipulative and verbal rather than written responses and short testing periods followed by rest intervals).

Diagnostic Tests

Diagnostic tests are in-depth evaluations used to assess what children actually can do in specific areas of development, identify children with special needs, and serve as the basis for making decisions about instructional strategies and specialized placements. These tests vary from those designed to help understand a child's functioning in a single developmental domain to others that are more general. For example, a speech-language specialist might administer a diagnostic test to determine a child's receptive language capabilities and a psychologist might administer a developmental inventory that assesses a half dozen or more domains.

Diagnostic tests are often conducted as a part of the comprehensive evaluation process carried out by an interdisciplinary team. The team may include a physician; psychologist; speech, hearing, and physical therapists; family members; and the classroom teacher. The team will evaluate whether or not a serious problem exists, what it seems to be (diagnosis), and the kind of strategies, placement, and services that would be most appropriate (treatment).

There are a dozen or more frequently used diagnostic tests. A few include the Kaufman Assessment Battery for Children, the Peabody Picture Vocabulary Test (PPVT), the Stanford-Binet Intelligence Scale—Fourth Edition, and the Vineland Social Maturity Scale. The selection of diagnostic tests will be dependent on the purposes of the assessment, which will be related to the nature of the information provided by the referring person or agency.

Readiness and Achievement Tests

Readiness and achievement tests examine children (individually or in groups) to assess their capability and achievement and to make judgments regarding their performance, based on the performance of others. They can be helpful in determining a child's readiness to benefit from a specific program or curriculum or to determine the level of school achievement compared to the performance of other children. They should not be used to reject, track, or retain children.

Readiness tests focus on existing levels of skills, performance, and knowledge. They are used to assess the child's ability to profit from a

---

Reflect and write about . . .

standardized tests

Why is it important to know about screening instruments, developmental assessments, diagnostic tests, and readiness and achievement tests? What experiences did you have as a child or teacher with these kinds of standardized tests? Do you think that these tests were used for the benefit of children? What are your feelings about them?

---

particular program of instruction, and their proper purpose is to facilitate program planning. Achievement tests measure what a child has actually learned—the extent to which he or she has acquired information or mastered identified skills that have been taught. Achievement tests determine the effectiveness of instruction.

Readiness tests that are commonly used in early childhood programs include the Metropolitan Readiness Test, the Cognitive Skills Assessment Battery, and the Gesell School Readiness Test. Achievement tests include the Peabody Individual Achievement Test and the Boehm Test of Basic Concepts.

Clarity of purpose, a clear manual with adequate information on standardization procedures, reliability and validity, clear directions, and appropriateness to the group of children to be tested should all be considered in selecting a standardized test.

ISSUES IN STANDARDIZED TESTING

Many early childhood educators have expressed concern and begun an important dialogue about the potential abuses of standardized tests when used with young children. They feel that the long history of child study based on observation is a more appropriate starting point for the assessment of young children. Those who advocate for the use of these tests maintain that hav-

ing comparative data and a national frame of reference is helpful in assessing the effectiveness of instruction and in making decisions about admissions and placements. They also claim that data on standardized tests are helpful in justifying programs and proving accountability to agencies that fund them.

Critics of standardized testing, including a growing number of early childhood educators (see Cryan 1986; Kamii 1990; Wortham 1990), raise many issues and concerns. Some of the most frequently cited are:

- Test results may not be valid and reliable because it is so difficult to administer tests to young children. They may be beyond children's developmental capabilities or their behavior may be unduly influenced by mood or by the test situation.
- Tests measure a narrow range of objectives, mostly cognitive and language abilities, and miss important objectives of early childhood education like creativity, problem solving, and social competence.
- Tests do not reflect current theory and research on how children learn. For example, research on literacy development indicates that a whole language approach is best for young children, but the tests focus on isolated skills that have little relationship to the development of reading and writing abilities.
- Most if not all tests are culturally and economically biased. If you are not a white,

middle-class citizen of the mainland United States you may not do as well on the tests.

- Tests are often inappropriately administered and interpreted because many early childhood professionals are not trained in the appropriate use and interpretation of standardized tests.

- Teachers who want children to do well on tests may introduce skills too early or alter their curriculum and "teach to the test," resulting in teaching methods and content that are inappropriate for young children.

- Tests are often used for purposes for which they were not intended: readiness tests are being used to identify children who need special services; test results are used to pass judgment (sometimes resulting in labeling of children) rather than for improving classroom practice; and results are being misap-

plied and used to keep children out of school, retain them in the same grade for a second year, place them in remedial classes, or make unwarranted placements in special education classrooms.

The National Association for the Education of Young Children has developed a position statement to address these issues and to help ensure that testing is used appropriately. Their position states:

> NAEYC believes that the most important consideration in evaluating and using standardized tests is the *utility criterion:* The purpose of testing must be to improve services for children and to ensure that children benefit from their educational experiences. Decisions about testing and assessment instruments must be based on the usefulness of the assessment procedure

for improving services to children and improving outcomes for children. (NAEYC 1988, 44)

They offer the following guidelines for decisions regarding testing in early childhood settings:

- All standardized tests used in early childhood programs must be reliable and valid according to technical standards of test development.
- Decisions that have a major impact on children such as enrollment, retention, or assignment to remedial or special classes should be based on multiple sources of information and should never be based on a single test score.
- It is the professional responsibility of administrators and teachers to critically evaluate, carefully select, and to use standardized tests only for the purposes for which they are intended and for which data exists demonstrating the test's validity.
- It is the professional responsibility of administrators and teachers to be knowledgeable about testing and to interpret results accurately and cautiously to parents, school personnel and the media. (NAEYC 1988, 44–45)

CONFIDENTIALITY AND USE OF ASSESSMENT DATA

When and how we share our assessments of a child's development with others, the degree to which we protect the information we collect, and the uses to which we put it are all important issues in early childhood education and care. In our decisions about the uses of the information we must consider our professional obligations to children, families, and society.

When a child enters a program, the family is asked to provide information. Some of the information may be required by law or regulation (such as immunization records), but some may be optional (such as family composition, the child's food preferences, and sleeping requirements). Much of this information becomes a part of the child's official record file and is considered confidential, as is all other information collected and recorded by program staff. All of these records should be stored in such a way as to protect the privacy of children and families. In most programs official files are stored in a locked file cabinet. A log is kept of every individual who is granted access to a file other than program staff, who are presumed to have a legitimate need to use the information. Generally, the only individuals who should have access to a child's record file are parents or guardians and those professionals with a legitimate need to have the information to serve the best interests of the child. The Family Education Rights and Privacy Act, Public Law 93–380 (1974), grants families the right to examine their child's official records and the protection of the privacy of the records.

Families want and need information about their child's experiences and progress. Most programs have some system for sharing information with them. A conference between families and staff is the time-honored way of sharing assessment information, discussing its interpretation, and planning how to mutually support the child's development. Many primary schools use regularly scheduled conferences also. Guidelines for conducting conferences are given in Chapter Sixteen: Working with Families. Conferences enable the participants to share informally and participate in a joint problem-solving process when necessary. They are often culminated with a summary of the discussion and decisions of the conference and are followed up with a written report. In some programs written progress reports are the primary way families receive information about their child's functioning, and they are asked to confer only when problems have been identified that require their participation to solve.

Written reporting methods that are frequently used include report cards and narrative summaries. Report cards are most commonly found in programs for primary-age children

Reflect and write about . . .

assessment

Think about the programs you have visited or worked in. How was information about children collected and stored? How were assessment results shared with families and others? What were your reactions to what you observed?

and are often criticized because they distill large quantities of information about a child into a single letter grade. In most early childhood programs some combination of conferences and written summaries are used to regularly report on a child's progress.

FINAL THOUGHTS

There are advantages and disadvantages, appropriate and inappropriate uses of each of the approaches to assessment described in this chapter. Observational methods are invaluable in helping early childhood educators to increase their sensitivity and to make sound educational decisions based on in-depth knowledge of children. They are useful because they are simple, flexible, and adaptable to a wide range of situations. Also, when educators observe, they can focus on what they are interested in and concerned about. Observation may need to be supplemented by other forms of data, but it is always the best beginning point for learning about children.

When the primary purpose of assessment is to identify developmental problems, to determine levels of achievement, to compare the individual to a large group of peers, or to gather information about children's progress in a systematic way, then standardized tests may be called for. Properly chosen and administered, screening instruments can point to children whose problems might not otherwise be discovered until they were having serious problems in school. Unfortunately, standardized testing is too often used at present to determine which children fit existing programs and to exclude those who do not "make the grade," rather than to make educational programs responsive to all children's needs and developmental stage.

No one instrument or occasion will disclose everything that you need to know about a child. Early childhood educators need to be aware of the many different ways of gathering and using information, to know the advantages and disadvantages of each type, and to remain sensitive and flexible in the ways they assess children.

PROJECTS

Observe a Child: For a period of at least half an hour, observe a child and describe:

- The physical attributes of the child.
- Some of the child's unique qualities.

- The activities and interactions the child engaged in during the period of the observation.

- Your inferences regarding what the child might have been thinking, feeling, and doing.

- Note any strong feelings and reactions elicited by the observation.

Assess a Child: Use a standardized test instrument to assess a child. If the instrument has a large number of items, assess the child in one developmental area. Describe the experience and answer the following questions:

- What does the assessment tell you about the child?

- What doesn't it tell you that you might want or need to know?

- To what extent were the assessment results consistent or not consistent with your observations of the child?

- What does this experience suggest to you about the possible advantages and/or disadvantages of using commercial instruments?

Use Systematic Observation Methods: Use several of the systematic observation methods described in the chapter to collect information about one child. Include several half-hour-long observation periods during which you use the running record system of recording your observations. Follow up by using at least two other types of systematic observation methods to study some aspect of the child that you wish to explore further. For example, you may wish to use a time sample of the kinds of play the child engages in and a developmental checklist. Write a brief interpretation of what you learned about the child. Include:

- A profile of the child's physical, social-emotional, and intellectual development.

- The child's development in terms of norms for his/her age group and in comparison to his or her peers.

- How you see the child progressing developmentally (strengths and weaknesses). Include your impression of how well the setting is meeting the child's needs and what could be done to better meet them.

BIBLIOGRAPHY

Almy, M., and C. Genishi. 1979. *Ways of Studying Children.* Rev. ed. New York: Teachers College Press.

Bagnato, S. J., J. T. Neisworth, and S. M. Munson. 1989. *Linking: Developmental Assessment and Early Intervention.* Rockville, MD: Aspen.

Bailie, L., S. Bender, C. Jackson, C. Watada, and J. Zane. 1980. *A Manual to Identify and Serve Children with Specific Learning Disabilities: Ages 3–5.* Honolulu, HI: Department of Education.

Beaty, J. J. 1994. *Observing Development of the Young Child.* New York: Macmillan.

Benjamin, A. C. 1994. Observations in Early Childhood Classrooms: Advice from the Field. *Young Children* 49(6):14–20.

Bentzen, W. R. 1993. *Seeing Young Children: A Guide to Observing and Recording Behavior.* Albany, NY: Delmar.

Cryan, J. R. 1986. Evaluation: Plague or Promise? *Childhood Education* 62(5):344–50.

Gullo, D. F. 1994. *Understanding Assessment and Evaluation in Early Childhood Education.* New York: Teachers College Press.

Genishi, C., ed. 1992. *Ways of Assessing Children and Curriculum: Stories of Early Childhood Practice.* New York: Teachers College Press.

Genishi, C., ed. 1983. *Observational Research Methods for Childhood Education.* New York: Free Press.

Hills, T. W. 1993. Assessment in Context—Teachers and Children at Work. *Young Children* 48(5):20–28.

Kamii, C., ed. 1990. *Achievement Testing in the Early Grades.* Washington, DC: National Association for the Education of Young Children.

McAfee, O., and D. Leong. 1994. *Assessing and Guiding Young Children's Development and Learning.* Needham Heights, MA: Allyn & Bacon.

Meisels, S. J. 1993. Remaking Classroom Assessment with the Work Sampling System. *Young Children* 48(5):34–40.

Meisels, S. J. 1989. *Developmental Screening in Early Childhood Education* 3rd ed. Washington, DC: National Association for the Education of Young Children.

The National Association for the Education of Young Children. 1988. Position Statement on Standardized Testing of Young Children 3 Through 8. *Young Children* 43(3): 42–47.

The National Association for the Education of Young, Children. 1991. Guidelines for Appropriate Curriculum Content and Assessment in Programs Seering Children Ages 3 Through 8. *Young Children* 46(3):21–38.

Nicolson, S., and S. G. Shipstead. 1994. *Through the Looking Glass: Observation in the Early Childhood Classroom.* New York: Macmillan.

Nyberg, D. 1971. *Tough and Tender Learning.* Palo Alto, CA: National Press Books.

Puckett, M. B., and J. K. Black. 1994. *Authentic Assessment of the Young Child: Celebrating Development and Learning.* Englewood Cliffs, NJ: Merrill/Prentice Hall.

Schweinhart, L. J. 1993. Observing Young Children in Action: The Key to Early Childhood Assessment. *Young Children* 48(5):29–33.

Seefeldt, C., ed. 1990. *Assessing Young Children.* Englewood Cliffs, NJ: Merrill/Prentice Hall.

Williams, L. R., and D. P. Fromberg, ed. 1992. *Encyclopedia of Early Childhood Education.* New York: Garland.

Wortham, S. C. 1990. *Tests and Measurements in Early Childhood Education.* Englewood Cliffs, NJ: Merrill/Prentice Hall.

PART III

Living and Learning with Children

This cluster of chapters focuses on the knowledge and expertise that you must have to create a nurturing and stimulating program for young children. Chapter Seven, A Good Place for Children, explores the importance of meeting children's basic physical and psychological needs. Chapter Eight, The Learning Environment, looks at how you can structure the use of space and provide the equipment and material necessary to support children's development. Chapter Nine, Relationships and Guidance, deals with how you can develop positive relationships with children and help them learn to work and play in a group setting. These are essential aspects of the program for children. They are based on the knowledge you gained in the previous chapters and are the necessary foundation for curriculum as it is described in the chapters that follow.

CHAPTER SEVEN

A Good Place for Children

We must have . . . a place where children can have a whole group of adults they can trust.
Margaret Mead

This chapter explores factors to be considered in meeting the physical and emotional needs of children in early childhood programs. First we look at the ways in which a program for young children ensures their safety and health. Then we look at ways you can help children with the first separation from their parents when they enter your program. Guidelines are provided to help you to design and handle routines and transitions each day and throughout the year. We also look at endings and what you can do to help children adjust to a new class or program, the transition to their next school, or the departure of their teacher.

Early childhood programs are children's second homes, and early childhood educators and other children their extended family. This may seem obvious for children in full-day programs and for very young children. However, it is true for all children in early childhood settings. All young children, even those in partial-day programs, kindergartens, and primary grades, are vulnerable. They need to be safe and secure and form close attachments to the adults and children with whom they spend time. What do we want for children in their second homes? What do they need to thrive?

A good place for children is flexible enough to be responsive to their needs, yet stable enough to provide security over many hours. The quality of relationships, the safety and design of the environment, and the program schedule will make—or fail to make—the program a place where development and learning can occur.

A SAFE AND HEALTHY PLACE

Although there are many important aspects of an early childhood practitioner's job, maintaining safety and health comes first in the eyes of the world and the families served. Regulations for safety and health are a part of all program licensing standards. Meeting these standards is critical in creating a good program for young children.

Safe and healthy environments protect children from hazards and ensure that they have the elements needed for health. As you focus on the important goals of helping young children learn and develop a positive sense of self, you need to make sure safety and health are not overlooked.

When children know that both you and the environment are trustworthy, they can direct their energy to exploring and experimenting in a setting designed to help them learn and develop. When you know that children are safe

and healthy in the environment that you have designed, you are able to devote your energy to helping children to benefit from your program. We recommend that you use a resource such as *Healthy Young Children* (Kendrick, Kaufmann, and Messinger 1991) or *Caring for Our Children* (APHA and AAP 1992) to gain awareness of the broad scope of safety and health concerns in programs for young children.

Psychological Safety and Health

It is fundamental that a program be both psychologically and physically safe and healthy for children. Psychological health and safety involve the child's perceptions. Children can tell when and where they are welcome. They know they are in a safe place when their needs are cared for and when adults show respect in the way they listen to and talk with them.

In psychologically safe and healthy programs, children do not fear rejection or humiliation. They are comfortable and feel secure. This sense of safety is dependent on warm, consistent adults who provide positive and respectful physical contact such as gentle carry-

ing and rocking for an infant or toddler, a friendly hand on the shoulder or pat on the back, or an appreciative hug for an older child.

You contribute to psychological health by being encouraging and by believing in children's competence. You support this belief by creating environments in which it is safe to experiment and acceptable to make mistakes. You accept children as unique people with their own pace and stage of development.

A Safe Place

A safe environment for children has sound facilities, equipment, and materials that do not present hazards. It has equipment to prevent accidents such as gates, railings, and impact-absorbing surfaces under play equipment. It is arranged to minimize hazards and ensure protection. Adult-child ratios are low enough and group size small enough so that staff can always supervise children well (see Table 7.1 for recommended ratios).

It is important to be aware of and committed to program safety. This means that you attentively supervise children at all times and are continually aware of potential hazards. Because young children are vulnerable, it is critical that all staff of early childhood programs perceive safety as *their* responsibility. An identified safety hazard should be removed or fixed as soon as it is noticed. Waiting for someone else to take care of a problem can put children at serious risk.

Early childhood is a time of inevitable scrapes and bruises, but the majority of serious injuries are foreseeable or preventable with preparation and attention. Preparation enables you to minimize potential dangers. Problems can then be taken care of before they exist or handled effectively when they are unavoidable. Prevention of accidents includes such things as locking away hazardous substances, doing a daily informal safety check in which play areas are surveyed for broken or hazardous equip-

173

ment or dangerous debris, and making sure that pathways and exits are uncluttered. Preparedness involves anticipating such situations as fires and accidents by having first-aid training and supplies, knowing how to use fire extinguishers, having a plan for an unexpected trip to the hospital, and practicing emergency evacuation with children.

Keeping children safe also involves making sure that the program is secure. Yards, gates, and doors must ensure that children do not leave without supervision. We know of resourceful three-year-olds who have climbed fences and opened "childproof" locks to attempt a trip home. It is also critical that the threshold of the program is crossed only by those who should enter. This helps to ensure that children do not leave with strangers or non-custodial adults. In most programs for children under five and in some kindergartens, families sign their children in and out.

Your training as an early childhood professional gives you both resources and responsibility in regard to children's safety. As a trained professional you will be expected to know about and maintain a safe environment for children.

Additionally, as a trained professional you may incur liability (that is, you may be sued and be required to make financial restitution) if you fail to supervise children or take reasonable steps to ensure safety and a child is seriously injured as a result of your negligence.

The checklist in Figure 7.1 outlines the safety aspects of the program with which early childhood practitioners need to be concerned. It can help you to quickly evaluate the safety and preparedness of an early childhood setting.

It is important to remain attentive to safety not only as you design the environment but in everyday practice. Children need information in new situations, such as on trips and when new equipment, materials, or experiences are introduced. You can help them to recognize hazards and activities that may be dangerous

and teach them procedures for handling potential hazards. For example, this is how we have discussed using a knife with four-, five-, and six-year-olds: "This is a knife. One side is sharp and the other side isn't. When you cut with a knife it's important to have the sharp side down and to make sure that your fingers aren't under the cutting blade. Hold onto the blade with one hand and use the other hand to push down—that way you won't accidentally get cut." An explanation for toddlers would necessarily be simpler and accompanied with close supervision and physical protection: "The pot is hot. Let's just look till it cools down." (Place the pot out of reach and place your body between the pot and the toddlers.)

When children understand precautions, they are usually willing to cooperate. It is more effective to tell children what to do and why rather than insisting that they stop something that is dangerous: "Please climb on the jungle gym instead of the table. The table could tip from your weight and you might fall."

Some precautions change as children reach new developmental stages. For example, covering electric outlets is essential with mobile infants, toddlers, and young preschoolers and generally unnecessary with kindergarten and primary school children. The characteristics that typify each stage of development are often the ones that make children victims of accidents. Infants and toddlers explore the world by putting things in their mouths—so choking and poisoning are common hazards. Three- and four-year-olds are curious and active—so falls and scrapes during active exploratory play happen. Kindergarten and primary school children can do many things on their own and have well-developed motor skills and infinite confidence in their own abilities—so injuries during the creative exploration of materials and equipment are likely. If your program includes children with special needs, you will need to evaluate the safety of the environment in terms of these children. For example, a child who has

This checklist can be used to evaluate the safety of an existing environment for children or to plan an environment.

Program name _____ **Date** _____
Number of staff _____ **Number of children** _____ **Age of children** _____
Use the following code as appropriate: $\sqrt{}$ = yes/adequate   − = no/inadequate

General

___ Program is licensed or meets licensing standards.

___ Enough attentive adults are present to supervise children at all times.

___ Building and equipment are structurally sound and free of rust, peeling paint, and splinters.

___ Bolts and rough edges on equipment and furniture are recessed or covered.

___ Entrances and yard are secure. Staff can monitor strangers entering the facility.

___ Arrival and departure procedures ensure children are safe from traffic and from leaving with unauthorized persons. Sign-in/out procedure is followed and well known to staff.

___ Floors where water is used and entrances have non-skid surfaces.

___ Inside and outside are free of debris.

___ Sharp tools and glass items are out of children's reach.

___ Stairs, ramps, lofts, decks, and platforms above 20″ have stable guard railings.

___ Stairs, ramps, lofts, and platforms are kept free of toys and clutter.

___ Equipment is free of entrapment hazards (openings are less than 3.5″ in width or more than 9″).

___ Medicines, cleansers, pesticides, aerosol sprays, and other hazardous items are locked out of children's reach.

___ Equipment and furniture is appropriately sized for the children enrolled.

___ Pathways between play areas are kept clear of toys and equipment to prevent tripping.

___ Kitchen, storage closets, gardening sheds, and other areas with hazardous materials are secured from children.

___ Procedure for regularly surveying and maintaining program safety is in place.

___ Shooting or projectile toys are not permitted.

___ Plastic bags and balloons are kept out of children's reach.

Emergency Prevention and Preparation

___ A telephone is accessible with emergency numbers posted nearby.

___ Records for each child include permission for emergency treatment and health records.

___ A medical practitioner and facility are prepared to provide emergency care and advice.

___ At least one supervising adult is trained in first aid and CPR. Certificates are current.

___ There is a procedure for handling first aid known to staff.

___ A first-aid kit is adequately stocked, easily available, and marked for visibility.

___ A first-aid kit is carried on trips.

___ A first-aid handbook is available.

___ Injury reports are written and an injury log is kept.

___ A plan for handling medical emergencies is in place and is known to all staff.

___ Emergency exists are clearly marked and clear of clutter.

___ An emergency evacuation plan is posted. The fire department has evaluated it.

___ Emergency evacuation procedures are practiced monthly.

___ Emergency procedures include a plan for children with special needs.

___ A plan for civil defense emergencies exists and is known to staff.

___ Smoke detectors are installed and functional.

___ A fire extinguisher is available in each room, it is annually tested, and staff know how to use it.

___ A plan exists for safe classroom coverage in case a child must be taken to the hospital.

___ Children are appropriately, legally, and safely restrained in cars.

FIGURE 7.1 (pp. 175-176)
Saftey checklist

Inside

___ Walls and ceilings are free of peeling paint and crumbling asbestos.

___ Environment is arranged so all areas can be easily supervised.

___ Furniture is stable.

___ AV equipment is secured so that it cannot be tipped over and is put away when not in use.

___ Equipment is unbroken and in good working order.

___ Low windows, doors, and mirrors have safety glass or Plexiglas.

___ Glass doors have stickers to ensure that children do not walk into them.

___ Heaters, radiators, pipes, and hot water tanks are inaccessible to children.

___ Hot water taps are turned off or are turned down so that hot water does not scald.

___ Unused electric outlets are covered in programs for children under the age of five.

___ Electric cords do not cross pathways.

___ Rugs are secured or backed with non-skid material.

Outside

___ Outdoor play area is protected by fences and has child-proof gates.

___ No poisonous plants are growing in the yard.

___ Permanent outdoor equipment is securely anchored and movable equipment is stable.

___ Manufactured rubberized surfacing or 8"–10" of non-compacted sand, woodchips, or pea gravel is beneath all climbing, swinging, and sliding equipment, extending through fall zones.

___ Swings are attached with closed fasteners, not open S hooks.

___ Swing seats are constructed of soft or lightweight material.

___ Swings are away from pathways, and barriers prevent children from walking into the path of a swing.

___ Metal slides are located so that they are shaded to prevent burns.

___ Equipment has no places where pinching or crushing of fingers, etc., can happen.

Special Precautions in Infant-Toddler Programs

___ Cribs, gates, and playpens have slats less than 2-3/8" apart or mesh less than 1/4" in diameter.

___ Cribs, child gates, and playpens have locking devices that work.

___ Furniture that can be climbed is securely anchored.

___ Furniture has rounded edges or edges are cushioned.

___ Mattresses fit snugly in cribs.

___ Dangling strings do not hang from cribs, playpens, curtains, etc.

___ There are no dangling appliance cords.

___ High chairs and walkers are stable and are used in locations away from stairs and doors.

___ Strollers and carriages are stable and have adequate brakes.

___ Strollers, high chairs, and walkers have restraining straps.

___ Toys are at least 1-1/2" diameter.

___ Swings support children on all sides.

___ Stairway gates are locked when children are present.

___ Separate space is provided for non-mobile infants.

___ Diaper supplies are kept within reach of the changing table.

___ Nuts, popcorn, raisins, hotdogs, and other food that might cause choking are not served.

FIGURE 7.1 *continued*

developmental delays may explore in ways that are more typical of a younger child, requiring different precautions.

Awareness of safety hazards changes with time. For example, recent analysis of childhood accidents has identified the unsafe nature of most playgrounds constructed prior to 1990. Much of the equipment was designed for older children and does not meet today's safety guidelines. Familiar pieces of equipment have proven to be hazardous for young children. Merry-go-rounds and seesaws often contain mechanisms that can crush fingers. Jungle gyms are often so high that serious injuries result when children fall. Many slides are constructed so that children's clothing can catch, causing strangulation. The Consumer Product Safety Commission *Public Playground Handbook for Safety* (CPSC 1991) can provide guidelines to help you know what is currently viewed as safe. Since understanding of safety changes with time, it is important to keep up to date on new information. Periodicals such as *Child Health Alert* can provide you with this information.

We cannot protect children from all hazards. Many safety measures are absolutely necessary for the well-being of all young children, but others are not as clear-cut. In the real and complex world of an early childhood program, we must often make choices between greater safety and learning. The learning and joy gained by climbing a tree and sitting among its branches must be weighed against the damage that might occur if a child falls out of the tree. Safety choices are influenced by the age, experience, temperament, and skills of the children, the size of the group, the adult-child ratio, the situation, the purpose and policies of the program, and the philosophy and beliefs of the staff. For example, a walk to the store with a group of eight six-year-olds and one teacher that includes crossing a busy street seems safe and reasonable. That same walk with six toddlers and one teacher would be unsafe. Typical

concerns include the use of potentially hazardous tools (like sharp knives and scissors), exposure to challenging environments (like an inclined trikeway), and the restriction of common materials and equipment (such as electric outlets and sticks). As you consider these gray areas you must make safety decisions consciously and not simply react to an immediate concern or embrace an easy solution to a current problem.

A Healthy Place

Healthy environments are clean and provide children and adults with the necessary facilities, materials, and routines for maintaining health: water, washing and toilet facilities, good light, ventilation and heat, and nutritious food. Early childhood practitioners ensure health by attending to routines (such as diapering and hand washing), keeping health records, and having plans and policies concerning health routines and emergencies.

The first early childhood programs usually emphasized health. As more attention was paid to children's intellectual and social growth, less attention was paid to health. Health problems and epidemics today have been traced to child-care centers, and public health practitioners have pointed to the need to look at the fundamentals of health in early childhood environments. When programs are evaluated by measures such as the accreditation standards of the National Association for the Education of Young Children, health standards are one of the most frequent areas where problems are encountered.

Every early childhood educator needs to have basic training for maintaining a healthy environment, coping with minor health emergencies such as fevers and vomiting, recognizing when a child needs to be referred to a health practitioner, and knowing when a child should be isolated from others for health reasons. In some programs a nurse or health aide will attend to health emergencies; in others you will be responsible. In general, the younger the children, the greater the need to be health conscious in group settings.

Communicable illnesses and conditions are spread from one person to another. To be transmitted, bacteria, viruses, or parasites (known as pathogens) must be present and must be transmitted to a child or adult who must be susceptible. In early childhood programs people have close contact with one another. The most common ways that communicable conditions are spread are through the air, through fecal-oral transmission, and through direct and indirect contact.

Airborne pathogens cause such conditions as flu, colds, and chicken pox. Fecal-oral transmission, the result of inadequate sanitary precautions in hand washing, diapering, and toileting, cause diarrheal diseases, pinworms, hepatitis, and giardiasis. Direct physical contact with an infected individual can transfer such conditions as impetigo, conjunctivitis, and lice. Indirect contact occurs when objects or food become contaminated with a pathogen.

Infant-toddler programs provide special challenges to early childhood educators. Infants and toddlers are more vulnerable and at the same time present greater health hazards in group settings than do older children. Children under the age of three are smaller and have immature organs and body systems, have less immunity, and are at greater health risk because they explore the world by touching and mouthing. Infants and toddlers wear diapers, and many diseases—some minor and others life threatening—can be spread through unsanitary diapering.

You can control communicable illness by eliminating pathogens and the ways they can be transmitted and by decreasing the susceptibility of children and adults. Susceptibility to disease is decreased by improving overall health. Good nutrition, exercise, reduced stress, and good psychological health all improve resistance. Another way to minimize illness is by removing sick children and adults from the early childhood setting. Recognizing early signs of illness in children and having good policies and procedures for exclusion helps to prevent the spread of infection. NAEYC has recently published *Model Child Care Health Policies* (Aronson and Smith 1993), which gives useful guidelines for health policies.

The most effective and important measure for preventing the spread of disease is conscientious and thorough hand washing. Early childhood practitioners, especially those who work with infants and toddlers, always seem to be washing their hands. In doing so they help to limit the spread of disease. It is recommended that you wash your hands when you arrive at work, before handling food, before and after feeding children, before and after changing diapers or assisting a child with toileting, after using the toilet yourself, before and after giving a child medication, and after any contact with mucus, urine, feces, vomit, or

---

Reflect and write about . . .

childhood dangers

Remember a time in your childhood when you did something that was unsafe. Why did you do it? What happened? What would have helped you to have a good experience that was safe?

blood. When you work with young children, you are at high risk of contracting disease—so conscientious hand washing is also self-protection. Children also must wash their hands and younger children must be assisted with hand washing. To make hand washing effective in preventing disease, it is important to use running water, use soap, rub hands together vigorously, wash all over from fingertips to wrists, dry hands on a disposable paper towel, and turn off the faucet with a towel so as not to recontaminate hands.

Another important technique for preventing the spread of disease is the regular cleaning and sanitation of equipment. Whatever the age of children, tables should be disinfected prior to meals with a sanitizing solution (the most common is one tablespoon of bleach in a quart of water). Toys, mats, and furniture should be sanitized whenever they are mouthed or contaminated by saliva, urine, blood, or feces. Regular

sanitation of all toys, furniture, and equipment used by infants and toddlers is recommended. In some programs this is done daily; in others it is done once or twice a week.

Concerns with very serious diseases such as hepatitis and AIDS have led to the common recommendation that "universal precautions" (wearing disposable latex gloves and sanitizing all contacted surfaces) be taken whenever caring for a bleeding child or material contaminated by blood. Some programs extend this caution to handling other body fluids, and gloves are worn for diapering as well.

Recently educators have become aware of pollutants that are prevalent in program environments. These pollutants are of particular concern because young children are more vulnerable because of their size and stage of development. Early childhood educators need to be particularly concerned with making sure that asbestos, lead, pesticides, and other chemical

toxins are absent from the settings in which they teach. Additional information about lead and other pollutants can be found in *Healthy Young Children: A Manual for Programs* (Kendrick et al. 1991).

The early years are a critical time for developing good health habits. Awareness of and concern for health can be promoted as you help children learn to make wise nutrition and exercises choices and develop healthy habits like hand washing and tooth brushing. In Chapter Eleven, The Physical Development Curriculum, we discuss ways that you can help children learn about health and nutrition.

The checklist in Figure 7.2 will help you to evaluate health practices in your own and other early childhood programs.

Helping Children Learn To Be Safe

Traffic and water accidents, fire, and accidental poisoning are the most common causes of death in young children. Young children are also frequent victims of abuse. All of us want to prevent children being hurt or killed in accidents or abuse. Because it is not possible for young children to protect themselves from the hazards of the natural and human environment, adults must provide this protection. Some hazards, however, can be made less threatening with education. For example, children who are familiar with the appearance of a fully outfitted

fire-fighter will not be as frightened should a Darth Vader look-alike come toward them in a smoke-filled room. Tragically, many children die in fires because they hide from rescuers whose protective gear looks threatening.

It is possible to help children begin to learn ways in which they *can* protect themselves. Effectively helping children to be safe requires understanding hazards and the ability to consider the world through children's eyes. Your goal is to enable children to participate in their own protection. This involves providing information children can understand in a way they can remember and helping them learn skills they can master.

It is tempting to teach safety as series of warnings—don't play with matches, don't go near the water, don't run in the street, don't talk to strangers. Unfortunately, *don'ts* often don't work since taboos are alluring. (The story of Pandora's box is one of many myths based on the human desire to try what is forbidden.) Instead, you can help children learn things they *can* do and help them understand *why* they should do them. Affirming children's ability to take part in their own care and assuring them of your commitment to take care of them makes you partners in the effort to assure safety.

Young children begin to be able to keep themselves safe when you help them learn to:

- Ingest only good foods and safe medicines that are given to them by trusted adults, avoiding other substances.
- Wear a seatbelt, avoid street-crossing unless they are with an adult, use crosswalks, and obey traffic signals.
- Give matches to adults, stop-drop-and-roll if their clothing catches on fire, recognize and trust firefighters in firefighting gear, and practice safe ways to evacuate home and school buildings in cases of fire and other emergencies.
- Play in pools and other bodies of water only when they are with a supervising adult.

This checklist can be used to evaluate the healthfulness of an existing environment for children or to plan an environment.

Program name _____ **Date** _____
Number of staff _____ **Number of children** _____ **Age of children** _____

Policies and Procedures

____ Program is licensed or meets licensing standards.

____ Health records are well organized and accessible.

____ A basic manual of childhood health and disease is available.

____ Program has written health policies, which are given to staff and parents.

____ A policy and procedures exist for isolating sick children within the setting or for removing them from the setting.

The Environment

____ Clean drinking water is available to children at all times.

____ Toilet facilities are clean and easily accessible to children at all times.

____ Stable step stools are provided if children must use adult toilets, sinks, or water fountains.

____ Tissue, soap, paper towels, and toilet paper are available where children can reach them.

____ The temperature is regulated as necessary.

____ Floors are mopped and rugs are vacuumed daily.

____ There is adequate light for children to see easily as they work without areas of darkness or shadows falling on children's work. As much as possible, light is from natural sources, with incandescent or full-spectrum fluorescent light used when necessary.

____ Windows and doors are opened regularly to let out pollutants.

____ Air conditioners, air filters, humidifiers, and dehumidifiers are cleaned often to minimize pollutants.

____ Animal cages are cleaned frequently.

Health Practices

____ Children's clothes are changed as necessary. There are extra clean clothes kept for children.

____ Soiled clothes are stored in closed plastic bags away from children's play areas.

____ Toys are washed or sanitized when dirty.

____ Nutritious foods are chosen for meals, snacks, and cooking activities.

____ Food is not withheld as punishment or used as a reward.

____ Children and adults wash their hands after toileting and before handling food.

____ Tables are cleaned prior to meals, snacks, and food preparation.

____ Children brush their teeth after meals, and toothbrushes are stored hygienically.

____ There are clean, individual napping arrangements for each child.

____ Trash cans are lined, kept covered, and emptied daily.

Practices Specific to Infant-Toddler Programs

____ Toys are sanitized regularly (e.g., daily or weekly) and when soiled or mouthed.

____ Healthful diapering procedures are known and practiced.

____ Changing tables are covered with paper during use and cleaned with disinfecting solution after each use.

____ Bottles are kept refrigerated.

____ Pedal opening trash cans are available for diaper disposal.

____ Daily records are kept on children's food intake and other health concerns. This information is shared with parents.

____ Each child has own sleeping arrangements and bedding. Linens are changed weekly or when necessary.

FIGURE 7.2
Health checklist

IN PRACTICE

Helping Children Avoid Abuse

Provide Choices: Offer children opportunities to make choices, including the choice to say no—to an activity, food, or suggestion. This includes the right to reject physical contact. You teach this by asking or alerting children before you touch or pick them up by saying things like: "May I give you a hug?" "Would you like me to rub your back?" or "I'm going to pick you up and put you on the changing table," rather than doing so without warning.

Develop Body Awareness and Appreciation: Provide many ways for children to appreciate their bodies through routines, games, songs, movement, and stories. Use correct names for body parts. When children are taught to value their bodies, they are less likely to passively allow themselves to be hurt.

Encourage Children to Express Feelings, Needs, and Ideas: Emphasize understanding feelings and encourage self-expression through words, stories, music, art, movement, and puppetry. Children who can express their ideas, needs, and feelings are better equipped to handle situations in which they are uncomfortable.

Integrate Safety Education: Integrate safety into topics and activities through discussion, role playing, and dramatization so children learn things they can do to be safe in many contexts—crossing the street, riding in cars, at the beach, at the shopping mall, answering the phone, with a stranger, and with a friend.

Distinguish Surprises From Secrets: Explore differences between secrets and surprises to help children understand that *surprises* are things you are waiting to share to make someone happy (like a birthday present), and *secrets* are things that someone wants you to hide that feels dangerous, wrong, or scary.

Build Positive Self-Esteem: Help children to feel good about themselves—their characteristics, abilities, and potential. Recognizing and valuing differences and affirming individuality through song, celebration, and activities help children to feel that they are worthy of protection.

- Say *stop* if someone wants to hurt or touch them in ways that feel bad and to tell a teacher or parent or other adult if someone has hurt them.

Young children learn about safety in the context of daily life. As you prepare for a field trip, children can help you to make up safety rules. The day before a fire drill you can talk about it and have children help to decide how to have a safe one. Safety concepts can be integrated into activities that you are already doing. For example:

- As you sing Woody Guthrie's song "Riding in My Car," you can modify a verse—"Spree-i-spraddle in the front seat, spree-i-spraddle in the back seat. Lock the door, Put on your seatbelt. Take you riding in my car!" (Blood-Patterson 1988).
- Add a painted crosswalk to the trike path for practice.

- Include props and pictures of firefighters in full regalia in the dramatic play area.

You can also teach children about safety through planned curriculum on fire, home, and traffic safety or taking care of yourself. All of these can be appropriate and integrate curriculum in preschools, kindergartens, and primary schools.

Abuse Prevention

All early childhood educators have a responsibility to protect the children in their care. This includes helping children to avoid abuse. The heart of an effective child-abuse prevention curriculum is you, a trained, skilled early childhood educator, who shows respect and appreciation for children. You help prevent abuse when you are respectful of and able to relate to the needs of children and families, and when you accept their feelings, ideals, choices, culture, and values. The quality of the relationships that you establish with families will enable them to feel that they can turn to you with questions and problems concerning their children.

It is essential for children to know that it is okay for them to resist physical intrusion and say, "No, I don't want you to do that to me!" to other children and to adults. This means that *you* must respect children's feelings and invite their cooperation rather than insisting on their compliance. Physical force (for example, picking children up and forcing them to be where they do not want to be) can be used only when a child's safety is at stake.

It is impossible to "abuse-proof" very young children. There is no lesson, curriculum approach, or defensive strategy that will guarantee children's safety. Although there are several popular approaches specifically designed to prevent child-abuse by focusing on the concept of private parts, or the idea of good touches, bad touches, or stranger danger, these may mislead, alarm, or arouse the curiosity of

children and tend to place responsibility on the relatively powerless child instead of on the adult. Adopting such a curriculum may lead to a false sense of security, thus endangering children.

Effective child-abuse prevention is an ongoing part of children's learning rather than a one time "inoculation." It uses the basic principles of early childhood education and development. The In Practice box on p. 182 gives you ideas for effective child-abuse prevention.

GOOD BEGINNINGS

Beginnings are times of change, excitement, and hope. They are also times of stress, fear, and anxiety. They are a time to say farewell to the security of the familiar and to go forward to meet new challenges. Life is composed of many beginnings; some are large and stressful, and others are small and easy to deal with. You can help guide children over the sometimes rocky paths of the transitions between home and classroom and the transitions within and between phases of the early childhood program.

The Transition From Home

During infancy children have a limited sense of themselves as individuals. They bond with and feel they are part of their primary caregivers. Between the ages of eighteen and thirty-six months, children forge their sense of themselves as individuals who are separate from their parents. Achieving this sense of separateness can be an anxiety-fraught experience filled with frightening realizations ("I can exist separately from my parents; they can exist without me!"), unnamed fears ("Will I be abandoned? Am I a bad child who deserves abandonment?"), and sometimes of frighteningly intense anger ("I hate my parents, who refuse to perfectly understand and meet my needs"). Although there are individual variations, generally by the time children are three years old their initial sense of separateness and identity is formed. They begin to understand that neither their parents, the world, nor they themselves are either all good or all bad.

All of us can recall the anxious feelings that we had when separating from the familiar: leaving our childhood homes, moving to a new city, starting a new job, becoming a parent. With a lifetime of experience behind us, we can still remember the stomach-clutching anxiety that accompanied those changes. When young children enter your program, they face an unfamiliar world. They are assaulted by sensations: new people, noises, objects, smells, and activities. They may have had little experience with being parted from their parents, with being among many children, or with making choices. This strangeness is made less traumatic when you and parents work together.

You can help children and their families to realize that the bonds that exist between them are strong enough to thrive despite separation. At the same time, you need to help children to build relationships in the new setting. When children trust you and feel assured of their own competence, they become comfortable enough to benefit from their school experiences. They adapt more easily when they know that their parents have confidence in the program and in you.

Young children make the transition from home best when the introduction is gradual and when they have an opportunity to integrate familiar aspects of their homes into their new lives in an early childhood program. One way to accomplish this is a home visit before the child's first day in the program. Such a visit gives the child the opportunity to experience you from the security of their own home. During visits, you build the base of later relationships with children and learn about their homes and families. Such visits are also opportunities for families to get to know and to develop confidence in you.

Classroom visits by parents and children are another way to provide the information needed for children to feel comfortable and competent in the new setting. It is essential that all children entering a program for the first time experience their classroom in the company of a familiar adult. A visit orients the child to the set-

Reflect and write about . . .

a separation

Recall a change in your life that involved separation from friends and family or a familiar place. How did you feel? What strategies did you use to cope with this transition? How might you apply this to children who are undergoing separation?

ting, the staff, and the materials. In some programs, initial visits occur during the course of a regular day: The child and parent sit in on an hour or two of the program. In other places, a special orientation for several new children or individual parent-child visits outside of regular program hours may precede the child's first day. Whatever its form, the initial visit helps prepare both child and family for the new experience. Visits like those just described are essential for infants, toddlers, preschoolers, and kindergarten children. A child entering a primary grade has had at least a full year of school. These children handle the transition to a new class or school with much greater ease. An orientation visit is still a valuable opportunity to get to know the teacher and the environment without the pressure of also beginning school work and establishing new relationships with other children.

First Days and First Weeks

Your goal for the first day is to begin to know children and to help them to get to know you, one another, and the routines of the program. Because adjustment on the first day can be difficult, a family member is often asked to spend part or all of the day with their child. Some programs require parents or other familiar caregivers to stay for several days with the child. In general, toddlers and young

preschoolers have a more difficult time making a transition to a new setting than do infants or older children. It is not uncommon for the family of a toddler to spend a week gradually preparing to leave their child for a full day. It is equally common for a four-year-old to pointedly ask a parent when they're going home at the end of the first hour. Each child responds in an individual way. We have worked with toddlers who had no difficulty saying good-bye to their parents after only minimal preparation and four-year-olds who wept and clung each day for months. The temperament and experience of both the family members and child will interact with the kind of preparation that you provide to make each child's entrance into your program smooth and suited to the individual. In our experience, the time and energy spent are well worth it.

Individual children react differently on their first day; some want to touch and try everything, some are cautious observers, and others want to stay close to their parents. All children will carefully observe your behavior and the arrangement of the environment to understand what is expected of them and to find out how you will react. It is especially important to be aware of what you say and do those first days. You will want to be calm and caring, letting children know that you will help and protect them in this new, and possibly scary, place. Since so much is unknown, the environment, the activities, and the schedule of the first

IN PRACTICE

Suggestions for the First Days

- Have the child begin with a short first day. Children who have little experience in group settings may have absorbed all they can in an hour.
- Encourage a parent or familiar caregiver to spend all or part of the first day with their child.
- Greet children and their family members by name each day as they arrive and say good-bye as they depart. Keep families informed of how their child is adjusting.
- Show children the location of the toilet and the water fountain and how they work on the first day, and accompany them when they seem uncertain.
- Stay close to children who need extra reassurance (infants, toddlers, and young preschoolers may need to be held).
- Show clearly what you expect of children but do not be overly concerned if children cannot meet simple expectations.
- Encourage children to bring a special toy or comfort object to help provide a tangible bridge between home and school. Some children are comforted by a photograph or tape recording of family member.
- Allow children to borrow a book or toy from the classroom to provide a bridge when they return to their homes.
- Provide an interesting but limited number of age-appropriate materials.
- Provide soothing, open-ended materials like water, sand, and dough.
- Provide time for independent exploration of materials.
- Help preschoolers, kindergartners, and primary children to feel that they are a part of a group by introducing a group activity like a song or story. Sing name songs to help children to get to know one another and to acknowledge each child
- In the first weeks avoid abrupt or major changes and excitement (fire drills, films, trips, room rearrangement). Help children to know their environment by taking small excursions to important places: the parent room, the play yard, other classes, the library, the office, and the kitchen.

day should be simple to allow children to focus on a few new experiences at a time. This will allow them to understand what is happening without being overwhelmed or fearful of doing the wrong thing.

Almost all children experience anxiety the first time they are left at school. Some children overcome this easily; others express their anxiety through tears, tantrums, or angry words; and still others become despondent and quietly wait while sucking thumbs or holding comfort objects. Some, not as visibly upset, may have toilet accidents, nightmares, or angrily reject their parents when it's time to go home. A few will appear fine for a few days or a week and then will react very strongly as if it was the first

Reflect and write about . . .

the first day of school

Remember your first day of school or your first day in a new school or class. What stands out in your memory? What was most reassuring? What was most frightening? Why? Which of these things will you make sure to do when you are working with children? What do you want to make sure not to do? Why?

day. Our interpretation of this delayed response is that, as the novelty of the new experience wears thin, the child realizes that going to school will henceforth be a perpetual part of life—one that involves little personal choice. If a reaction persists or is extreme, it may mean that the child needs a more gradual or a delayed entrance into the program.

Many toddlers and young preschoolers need the reassurance of physical contact with an adult during the first days and weeks. If you work in a program where many children enter

at the same time, you may sometimes feel like a mother opossum moving about the classroom with the small bodies of children clinging to you. As they become comfortable, most children will find more interesting things to do. For many children, a treasured blanket, stuffed animal, or piece of clothing is important in the separation process. These very personal possessions are comforting reminders of home that help them to feel secure. It is important that children be allowed to keep them near. With time, comfort objects become less evident and may only be needed when a child is under stress or at nap times.

During the first days and weeks, children begin to adjust and learn to trust and feel competent. They become accustomed to the daily rhythm of activities linked by transitions, learn that they can care for many of their own needs, and discover that you will be there to help when needed. The most important tasks of this time are to develop trust, build relationships, and establish routines. This *is* the curriculum. You will want to ensure that children's successes outnumber their failures and that your expectations of them are realistic. It is a time when you learn what children can and cannot do.

As children become more comfortable, you can begin enriching the environment with materials, activities, and trips that might have been overwhelming at first. By understanding and supporting children as they go through the separation process during first days and weeks, you help prepare them to be active and competent learners.

A GOOD DAY

A typical day in any program for young children is an artful blend of routines and learning experiences linked by smooth transitions. We think of the daily ebb and flow of learning activities and routines as being part of a larger experience of living and learning with children.

A day for children in a good early childhood program has a relaxed pace. Children are not rushed from activity to activity. There is lots of child choice and large blocks of time (at least one hour long) in which to fully explore the activities chosen. Although there are great differences depending on the age of the children and the characteristics of the program, there are also great similarities. Nine-month-old Camille delightedly crawling from shelf to shelf and exploring toys until she tires and crawls to her teacher for a cuddle and seven-year-old Harrison writing a story about tigers during learning center time over several days are both making choices and governing their own use of time.

The Program Day

The structure of the program day is influenced by the needs and developmental stage of the children and your observations of individuals; by your values and the values and concerns of parents, community, and the school administration. It is influenced by the physical setting, the length of the program day, and the time of year.

Both spontaneous and planned activities occur daily in every carefully prepared program for young children, but spontaneous activities and an emphasis on play predominate. In all developmentally appropriate programs for infants and toddlers, and in many preschools, curriculum evolves from the interests and experiences of the children. The daily schedule in a primary school program is influenced by the size and philosophy of the school. Many elementary schools impose a structure of weekly assemblies, special classes, and scheduled lunch and recess times. Within this structure you can plan a good day for the children in your class. Your role is to build routines that allow for maximal independence and ritual that bring a sense of security for the children you teach. A good way to start each day in a primary class is with a group gathering to share news, sing a song, and map out the day's direction. A good way to finish each day is listening to a chapter from a book.

Children's Needs and Developmental Stage

Early childhood programs must include provisions for children's needs and take into account developmental differences. All children need time for rest, nourishment, and personal care. It is important that there are periods of vigorous activity and quiet and daily times when choice is permitted to allow for individual interest and attention. The younger the children, the more flexible you will remain since younger children's needs vary greatly. At ten-o'clock in a group of toddlers we visited, Aimee was lying down and drinking a bottle, Ian was having a nap, Walden was looking at books, Nadine was cuddling on a teacher's lap, and Jonathan was using the toilet. A rigid schedule could not meet such diverse needs and would inevitably lead to frustration for adults and children. As children mature you can gradually forgo planned toileting and naps. Typical schedules for different age groups have the following characteristics:

>**Infants:** Each child regulates him or herself—meals, rests, active/quiet times
>
>**Toddlers:** Regular meals, snacks, and rest with active/quiet times occurring in response to children's needs and interests
>
>**Preschoolers and Kindergartners:** Scheduled eating and rest times and flexibly scheduled group and outdoor times
>
>**Primary Children:** Routines scheduled as above with closer adherence to plans for group and activity times.

Your values and goals are among your most important considerations in planning your schedule. If you value creativity, independence, and the development of responsibility, you will allow large blocks of time (one to two hours) during which children choose their own activities while you work with individuals and small groups. Without considering your values and the implications of your scheduling decisions, you may inadvertently fail to foster the very things you most care about.

The Physical Setting

The building in which you work will influence how you structure the day. If it houses only your program and has sufficient space for younger children to be separated from older ones, it is relatively easy to schedule the day to meet the basic needs of all age groups. Where space is limited or facilities are shared, you may need to work out ways to accommodate the eating and resting schedules, separation of rest and activity areas, and use of bathrooms and playgrounds for different groups of children. If the bathroom or playground are located at a distance from the classroom, you will have to take this into account in planning. Young children are not ready to use the toilet on a schedule and will require some supervision if they need to walk any distance to use the bathroom, so you may have to plan frequent trips to make sure that children's needs are met. Even older children who are capable of going on their own may require supervision to ensure safety and security.

The Length of the Program Day

However long the day, early childhood programs must provide for the needs of children. A full-day program must provide lunch, a midday rest, and snack periods to avoid overstimulated, hungry children. Children in a full-day early childhood program spend up to 60 percent of their waking hours in an institution. This is a significant portion of a young child's life, and the program is very much a second home. In full-day settings it is especially important to pay close attention to the quality of relationships, the design of the environment, and scheduling.

Children in full-day programs may stay six to eleven hours, but the staff in such programs generally remain for only six to eight hours. The children may spend significant time with two separate groups of staff. The coordination of this transition must help children to maintain their sense of trust if they are to benefit from the experiences offered. There is often a misperception that anyone who cares for young children in the afternoon has a less important job than those who perform similar tasks in the morning. Children do not make this distinction. They learn and need nurturing throughout the day. Involving afternoon staff in planning and recognizing the vital tasks they accomplish is one way to maintain program quality throughout the day.

In some preschools and kindergartens, children arrive in the morning after a good night's sleep and a hearty breakfast and depart in time to eat lunch and take an afternoon nap at home. In these programs, scheduled rest time is unnecessary, and a light snack is usually sufficient. An enforced rest period will probably meet with resistance and is a waste of limited time. In a short program, a good blend of outdoor activity and indoor activities with a short snack break will provide for a pleasant, productive half-day experience.

After-school programs for kindergarten and primary children have a distinct mission. They are designed to ensure children's well-being while parents are at work and to provide appropriate activities for children who have had a full day of school. There is growing recognition that children continue to need high quality care and education throughout the day, and after-school programs are losing their custodial status. However, children who have been in structured school settings all morning require a different, more relaxed afternoon. Good after-school programs address children's needs with opportunities for play, socialization, and self-selected work. Although many see after-school programs as homework mills, and some home-

work can be incorporated, primary school children need the opportunity to play in the second half of their days away from home.

Staff-Child Ratio and Group Size

The number of staff members in relation to the number of children is an important factor in how you structure the day. In a program with an adult-to-child ratio of one to seven, events, routines, and activities can be scheduled with more flexibility than if you work in a program with one adult for every fifteen children. With lower ratios you need not personally meet the needs of so many children and so are free to be more spontaneous and to plan for activities that have an unpredictable time-frame or that require more intense adult-child interaction.

The size of the group will also influence the day. With smaller groups you can make spontaneous changes without disrupting others. You are able to give your full attention to individuals because there are fewer children to attend to. Larger groups require more advance planning for the use of facilities (like playgrounds, vans, and lunchrooms), and with them you must stick more closely to the schedule. Beyond a certain group size, no matter how low your ratios, you meet with inevitable problems. Large groups of young children are noisy, overstimulating, and stressful.

The National Association for the Education of Young Children, which credentials early childhood programs, has set standards for adult-child ratios and group size in high quality early childhood care and education programs (Table 7.1).

The Time of Year

A program day may differ greatly from the beginning of the year to the end. During the first days and weeks, your program day must allow time to help children become accustomed to routines and new activities. As the year progresses, children will have mastered routines and become accustomed to program expectations. They will have developed new skills and abilities. A clinging toddler may have become a bold explorer, an uncooperative preschooler may have become a group leader, and a shy first grader may have developed poise and confidence. Your schedule can be adjusted to recognize children's new competencies, cooperativeness, and skills. Group times may last longer as children come to enjoy group activities. Scheduled routines, like toileting, may be omitted as children become independent and no longer require support and supervision.

Routines

Regardless of whether your program lasts for three hours or ten, there are some recurring events in the basic structure of a day for young children. Arrival must provide a smooth transition from home. There must be opportunities for nourishment, rest, diapering/toileting, and learning experiences. The end of each child's day should provide a sense of closure.

TABLE 7.1

NAEYC Standards for Child-Staff Ratios and Group Size

Age of Children	Group Size*										
	6	8	10	12	14	16	18	20	22	24	28
Birth–12 mos.	3:1	4:1									
12–24 mos.	3:1	4:1	5:1	4:1							
24–30 mos.		4:1	5:1	6:1							
30–36 mos.			5:1	6:1	7:1						
3-year-olds					7:1	8:1	9:1	10:1			
4-year-olds						8:1	9:1	10:1			
5-year-olds						8:1	9:1	10:1			
6- to 8-year-olds								10:1	11:1	12:1	
9- to 12-year-olds										12:1	14:1

*Smaller group sizes and fewer children per staff have been found to be strong predictors of compliance with indicators of quality.

Source: S. Bredekamp, ed., *Accreditation and Criteria Procedures,* rev ed. (Washington, DC: National Academy of Early Childhood Programs, 1991), 54.

Early childhood educators have long accepted the routine parts of daily living as important aspects of the child's experience. They recognize that children must have their basic needs met and must feel safe, secure, and accepted before they can begin to learn. They have understood that a primary task of young children is to develop competence in independently meeting their physical and social needs. As an early childhood practitioner, you will want to give routines, the regular and more or less unvarying parts of classroom life, attention and thoughtful planning, just as you do the other aspects of the program. When daily routines are predictable, children know what to expect and have the resources they need for ordering and understanding their experiences. When you communicate your good reasons for establishing a routine and your commitment to having it work, children will usually cooperate and participate willingly. See the In Practice box on p. 194.

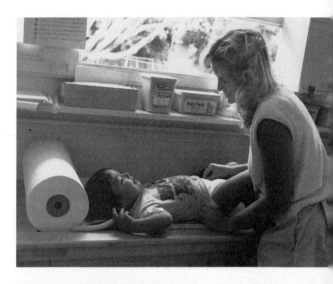

Arrival

Arrival each day should be a friendly, predictable event. It is important to establish a routine in which every child is greeted. An arrival period during which you personally greet and talk briefly with families and children sets a relaxed tone. At this time, you can notice if each child is in good health and appears ready to participate in the daily program. Arrival time may be one of the few regular contacts you will have with children's families, and it can be a good time for exchanging information. In some programs, one or two staff members greet families and help each child make the transition into the classroom.

Toileting, Diapering, and Toilet Learning

When you work with young children you have no choice but to be concerned with some very basic aspects of life. These include the healthy management of diapering and children's development of toilet skills. Early childhood educators have a serious, professional need to understand the process of diapering and toileting.

Diapering is a multi-step process that includes health practices such as washing hands before and after, carefully cleaning children, using disposable paper on the changing surface, disinfecting diapering surfaces to prevent contamination and the spread of disease, and sanitary disposal of diapers. It also includes an important psychological component. Young children's emotional health, self-image, and ability to become independent are intimately tied to how they are treated during diapering and how they are helped to develop toilet skills. A positive, relaxed attitude toward diapering and toilet learning makes it a pleasant opportunity to interact with children.

Children only gradually become self-reliant in using the toilet, but there is no set age when all children are ready to learn this skill. Between the ages of two and three young children generally are ready to begin to learn to use the toilet independently, but fears and reluctance to use the toilet at school are not uncommon and some children do not manage it until well into their third year. Children have an easier time using toilets when fixtures are child-sized and when clothing is manageable. They are more likely to become comfortable when you are patient and when attention is paid to making the bathroom pleasant. You may need to accompany reluctant or inexperienced children to the toilet to reassure them. Stable step stools to enable children to comfortably reach toilets and washbasins are essential if there are adult-sized fixtures.

Even among older children, toilet mishaps can be a normal part of life and may be a regular feature of your day. A child who is genuinely upset by an "accident" may need to be sheltered from public awareness and given help with cleanup. Other children may only need a small amount of direction and encouragement to take care of their own change of clothes. If your classroom of older children includes children with special needs who still wear diapers or have toilet accidents, you may need to take particular care to minimize potential humiliation and increase peer acceptance. A matter-of-fact attitude of acceptance on your part can make a great deal of difference.

Mealtimes and Snacks

Some of the nicest moments in an early childhood program occur when adults and children sit down and eat together. Snacks and meals are pleasant when they are orderly enough to focus on eating and casual enough to be a social experience. Independence can be fostered as children participate in meal preparation and serving. For example, children can set the table, spread their own peanut butter on a cracker, or pour their own juice. Children gain self-help skills when meals are served family style, passing bowls of food and small pitchers so that children can serve themselves.

Resistance to foods is common. You should neither force children to eat nor deny them the opportunity to eat. Food should never be withheld from children as punishment nor used as a reward. Young children become restless and irritable when they are expected to wait until everyone is served or while others finish. They may become anxious and unable to eat if they are hurried. Many problems can be avoided if you have a set routine for children who have finished eating before the rest of the group—for example, allowing them to leave the table to read a book or to play quietly with a game or toy.

In most programs children will have an opportunity to eat a morning breakfast or snack as well as a mid-day meal. In full-day programs they will also have an afternoon snack. Some full-day programs provide an additional snack toward the end of the day. This helps children and families to have more pleasant departure times without the "arsenic hour" syndrome of tired parents and hungry, whining children.

Not all families are able to feed their children nutritious foods. Because of this it is important that the snack or breakfast served in the morning is nutritious and that meals are planned to meet children's daily nutritional requirements. In many states the USDA food program guidelines form the standard for meals and snacks provided in early childhood programs. If families provide children's food, you will need to give culturally sensitive guidance concerning appropriate meals brought from home.

IN PRACTICE

Suggestions for Routines

- Give children several minutes' warning before a transition to the next part of the program day. Accommodate children who wish to finish an activity by extending activity time, providing additional time later, or by allowing them to return to the activity the next day.
- Be flexible about time while maintaining the usual sequence of events. (Activity time might be lengthened if it doesn't mean skipping another important activity.)
- Offer help when children request it or show unusual frustration, even if the task is one you know they ordinarily can do independently.
- Acknowledge cooperation by commenting on individual and group efforts rather than making negative comparisons. ("Thanks for the help, Hur Youn!" not "I wish everyone cleaned tables as well as Hur Youn.")
- Ignore noncooperation as much as possible, or give an alternative that is neither punishing or rewarding. ("If you are not helping, you may wait at that table." "Please come stand by the door. I'm afraid someone will be hurt when you push in the bathroom.")
- Maintain your communication style and tempo of movement during routines. (It is disruptive if you suddenly start giving orders and rushing around.)
- Avoid having children wait in lines or large groups with nothing to do.
- Give clearly stated reasons for routines. ("We'll all clean up now so that we can sit down to lunch together.")
- Offer choices only when there really is a choice. Avoid offering choices you are unwilling to allow. ("It's time to go inside now," not "Would you like to go in?")

Reflect and write about . . .

routines

What routines do you have in your own life? How do you feel when the rhythm of daily routines is disrupted? What do you like about your routines? What routines have you observed or implemented in programs for young children? When did these seem to harmonize with the activity of the classroom? When did they seem to be a disruption?

Good snacks for young children should consist of minimally processed foods that are low in fat, salt, and sugar. Fresh fruit or vegetables; whole-grain bread or cereal; and milk, cheese, or peanut butter are all components of healthful snacks. Because children's nutritional requirements are proportionately higher than or equal to adults but their calorie intake is smaller, young children's diets have less room for poor food choices. When children eat foods that have little food value, they have to eat more calories to meet needs for other nutrients. With, proportionately higher vitamin and mineral requirements and lower calorie requirements, young children's diets are more likely to contain excessive calories or to be deficient in vitamins and minerals than the diet of an adult.

Cleanup

Cleanup prepares the classroom for the next activity and is a natural and necessary part of living with others. Children begin to understand that they are members of a community and that they need to share in the responsibility for maintaining cleanliness and order. All adults who work with young children find themselves doing a good deal of tidying of toys and equipment. As you straighten and reorder the environment you are helping children to see learning possibilities, what Elizabeth Jones and Gretchen Reynolds refer to as part of "clarifying figure-ground relationships" (1992, 16). In doing this, you also help children to understand the process of maintaining order.

Although cleanup is seldom a favorite activity, it need not be hard or unpleasant. Much of the drudgery that often surrounds cleanup comes from the attitude that is projected by adults. When you participate in cleanup with an attitude of expectant good will (I feel good about doing this and I expect that you share my feeling), children are generally also cheerful and cooperative. Often teachers make cleanup the punishment that children must endure for the pleasure of play—such an attitude discourages not only clean up, but play itself. Children frequently resist cleanup when they are forced to straighten large messes without assistance: To a young child, such a mess may appear large and impossible to clean. Although it may seem easier to "do it yourself," it is important to persist in engaging children's participation.

Your expectation and firm but gentle follow-through will help children become able and responsible members of a group.

Rest Time

Rest time can be a positive experience if children are tired, if the environment is made restful, and if children understand the importance of relaxing their minds and bodies. As with other routines, it is essential that children feel secure. If they are fearful of the school setting, they will be unable to relax. Most children under the age of five, and many five-year-olds, sleep if the environment is soothing and comfortable. Every child in a preschool or kindergarten needs a mat or cot for sleeping. Infants need the protection of an individual crib or other sheltered sleeping space. To create an atmosphere conducive to rest and sleep, dim lights, play quiet music, and allow children to cuddle personal comfort objects such as a favorite stuffed toy or blanket.

When you are helping children to fall asleep it is important to be calm. Focus on children as they begin to rest, gently rub their backs, avoid speaking to others, and whisper when you must speak. Wait until most of the children are sleeping before you begin any other tasks. Children who nap will generally do so for at least one hour. When they are finished resting, children should be free to put away their mats and play quietly.

Children who do not sleep will respond to rest time positively if, after an initial rest, they are allowed to look at books and quiet relaxing play is allowed. Children who regularly do not sleep can rest away from others so their activity is not disturbing. Preschool children who are unable to sleep can rest but should not be required to lie down for more than an hour. The length of rest for non-sleeping children should be based on their needs and ability to relax.

Five- to eight-year-olds also benefit from short quiet times in their day. In many programs this is combined with an opportunity for Sustained Silent Reading, or SSR time.

The length of nap and rest periods should be based on children's needs. It may also provide a quiet period for teachers to collect themselves and do some planning or preparation, but this is not the primary purpose.

Transitions

Each time a scheduled activity or routine ends, there is a transition, a time of gathering children or of movement into a new activity. Transition times can be smooth and relaxed if they are well planned and if children are prepared for them.

Adults and children may perceive transitions very differently. You have responsibility for moving children from one activity or routine to the next according to a plan you have made. Children who do not know the reasons for the changes may respond to transitions as interruptions of things they would prefer to continue doing.

In nearly all programs, transitions take up between 20 percent and 30 percent of the total time (Berk 1978). Transitions can be pleasant and unobtrusive, or they can be times of frustration and conflict. Transitions in which many children are gathered together can be difficult for children and adults. They can often be avoided by having children go on to the next activity independently—for example, by letting children go outside after they have finished cleaning up their area rather than waiting for the entire group to finish. If children must gather or wait, the waiting can be turned into productive time. Use the time to share songs and fingerplays or games or to listen to relaxing music or look at books.

When children are leaving a group to go on to the next activity you can use techniques

IN PRACTICE

Some Ideas for Transitions Between Activities

- **Clues:** Give a clue about the child's family, vacation, pet, or home. "A child whose mom is named Donna and whose dad is named Skip can go."
- **Riddles:** Ask a riddle game about something related to the curriculum theme: What grows in the ground, gives shade to sit in, makes a good place to climb, and is a place for birds to build their nests? The guesser can go.
- **Verse:** Sing "Old MacDonald" (or a similar endless song). Ask children to think of a verse, and they can go when their verse has been sung.
- **Props:** At activity time bring an item from each center for each child. As you bring out the item ask a child to describe it, name its place, and take it there to play.
- **Friends:** Select a child to pick a friend with whom to leave the group.
- **Games:** for example: the lost and found game. Choose a child. Say, "Police Officer Maya, there's a lost child who's wearing blue shorts and a Batman t-shirt. Can you help me find him?" When Maya finds the child she leaves, and the found child becomes the police officer.
- **Name Songs:** Sing a name song like *"Get On Board Everybody"* or *"Hello"* and have children leave when their name is sung. The bibliography at the end of Chapter thirteen lists several song books that provide many ideas for name songs.

that avoid a chaotic stampede or excessive regimentation. You may use chants and songs that include a child's name and what to do next, such as singing "This is the way *John* washes his hands everyday at lunchtime" (for older children the name can be spelled out), or "Everyone wearing red (or stripes) can hop like a bunny to the playground."

Sometimes children must move to another area of the school as a group. The practice of lining up and walking silently can be difficult for young children (it is even challenging for adults!). In early childhood programs it is almost always unnecessary. To be a young child is to hop, skip, giggle, shout, jump, and run. You can encourage children to be safe by walking where running is hazardous, courteous

by being quiet where others are working, secure by staying with the group, and attentive in a fire drill or emergency. Encouraging children to do all these things as necessary is reasonable and appropriate, but precision marching for an ordinary walk to the playground imposes an unnecessarily difficult task.

Experienced teachers design many creative ways for making transitions smooth, interesting learning experiences. You may wish to collect such ideas and invent your own.

Departure

The end of the program day should provide a smooth transition back into life at home. Departure time can provide an opportunity to talk to families about children's experiences. Sharing this information helps families to know what kind of a day their child has had and to understand the behavior and needs the child may have when they get home. For example, a child who usually naps but does not one day may be unusually irritable, and a parent who knows this may respond with an early bedtime. Sharing some basic information about the child's day with families is essential in programs for infants and toddlers. Parents need to know about feeding, elimination, rest, and variations in the normal activity and behavior of the child.

If all the children leave at the same time, departure can be structured to provide closure. You may read a story, go over events of the day, and plan for the next day. If children leave at different times throughout the afternoon, a staff member should be available to share information with families and say farewell as they leave.

GOOD ENDINGS

In every classroom for young children, there are endings. Just as beginnings require special thought and planning, so endings require special care. The relationships that children build during their early childhood program experiences can be very close, and it can be painful when they finish. For many children, this may be the first time that an important tie has ended.

Changing Classes

When children remain in a program for more than a year, they will usually experience at least one change of class or teacher. In programs that follow a ten-month or public school calendar, this will occur in September after a long summer vacation. In full-year programs, this change may occur when you feel that a

child is ready for a new group or when space is needed in your group for younger children entering the program.

Although many children are ready and eager to move on to a new class, some are not. Making the transition to a new group requires the cooperation of both the staff and families. The change to a new class can arouse feelings of anxiety similar to those experienced during the initial days of school, and similar techniques can help make a bridge between the old and new class. This transition is easier when children know about their new class, when they can carry something familiar with them into the experience, and when the transition can be gradual. It also helps if children feel their parents and you have confidence in the new group and teacher.

Allow children in transition to make visits to their next class accompanied by you or a special friend. Let them visit for an activity that they especially enjoy, perhaps circle time one day and choice time another day, so that they can discover new materials, activities, and companions. On the official day of transition, have the child take responsibility for transferring personal belongings and setting up a new cubby or locker. Going back to the old room to share lunch or nap or simply to visit for a few minutes helps the child feel secure.

When You Leave

Like children, you will take vacations, become sick, and will eventually leave your job. These events sometimes take place during the course of a year. When you leave a group of children, either permanently or for an extended period of time, children experience feelings of loss. They may be sad that you are leaving and angry with you when you return. They may be fearful of the change and feel less secure until they build relationships with new staff. In programs for young children that have a team of staff in each class, the upsets of absences and departures are minimized. When children relate closely to two or more adults in the school, it is less traumatic when one of them must leave.

When you know that you or someone you work with will leave, it is important to consider the impact on children in planning and preparing for the transition. In one program we know, a teacher announced she would leave her job the same day that the co-teacher was going on a planned six-week leave. The impact on children was serious. The three- and four-year-olds in the class were plagued by nightmares, bedwetting, and fears about school. Another teacher we know learned that her husband was to be transferred and she would have to leave when her co-teacher had planned to move. This teacher talked about the change with her co-teacher and decided to leave the program six weeks early to give another teacher a chance to start so that both teachers would not leave at once. When you understand and take seriously your responsibility to children, you consider the impact of your personal decisions on children and adjust them to cause minimal distress.

Leave-taking is a natural part of relationships. Young children can accept this more easily if adults do. When a teacher leaves, minimize changes in the environment and routines. Most importantly, help children understand that adults leave programs because of changes in their own lives and not in response to the behavior or actions of children or their families.

The Next School

Children in early childhood programs go on to other schools that can be very different from

your program. One of your jobs is to prepare the children in your class for the transition to the next school.

Children may anticipate starting their new schools with both interest and concern. You can aid in the transition by helping to strengthen children's sense of themselves as competent, successful individuals by acknowledging their growth and by mentioning how the skills they have gained and the knowledge they have acquired will be useful in their new school ("You know how to take care of your own lunch now, Tyrone—you're going to be able to handle it all by yourself in kindergarten").

Early childhood programs should not be boot camps or training grounds for the next school! The time that children spend in early childhood programs should be spent on experiences that are appropriate for the early years. During the last few weeks before a transition to a new school, it may be beneficial to help children learn skills they will need. The more that you know about the schools in your community, the better able you will be to prepare children. If they will be expected to know about changing classes in response to a bell, standing in lines, getting their lunch from the cafeteria, doing work sheets, or raising hands, you can help children to learn these skills in a short time. At the end of the program year, when they are more mature, children will be more able to learn them. If you are in contact with the teachers in the next school, you may be

able to get more specific information or even take the children to see their prospective school and teacher. Tell the children that they are practicing for their next school and role play some of the routines that they will be expected to follow. Kindergarten and primary children often look forward to new events in their lives—new teachers, new classes, new challenges. Familiarity with the changes about to take place and time to talk about them and to consider their hopes and fears will fill endings with promise.

Everyone experiences some trepidation anticipating change. Whether the children are moving to a new class or a new program, or you or a colleague are leaving, you can work to turn endings into beginnings filled with enthusiasm and hope.

FINAL THOUGHTS

A good place for children, and a good place for adults, feels comfortable, feels like home. Safety and health, beginnings and endings, schedules and routines are the framework around which you will create a program for children. Alone they are not enough. Without them, your program will flounder. When the framework is sound, the experiences you provide are supported and your goals for children can be achieved. They are important foundations of your program day and of children's lives.

PROJECTS

Separation Journal: Observe and keep a journal on a child during the first days and weeks of his or her school experience. Report on the child's responses to the school, the techniques used by the staff to support the child, and the family's reactions to the experience. Describe what you learned from your observation and its possible implications for you as an early childhood educator.

Classroom Observation: Observe and describe an early childhood classroom focusing on schedule, routines, and transitions. Comment on their effectiveness. What changes would you suggest to better meet the needs of the children? Why? What are the implications of what you learned for you as a future early childhood educator?

Interview an Educator: Interview an early childhood educator about how he or she handles children entering their program, issues of separation, and ways of preparing children for the next class and program. Report on what was said and comment on how these compare to what is written in your text. Comment on what you learned and its implications for you as a future early childhood educator.

Health and Safety Interview: Interview two early childhood practitioners concerning health and safety. Ask what issues they have dealt with. How did these issues become known? How were they dealt with? What community resources were used? What did they learn? Report on what was said. Compare the two situations and suggest the implication for you as a future early childhood educator.

Health and Safety Checklist: Use the health and safety checklist to evaluate an early childhood program. Report on and evaluate what you found. Describe your thoughts about the relative safety and health of this program and the ways in which the staff could make it a safer and healthier place for children.

BIBLIOGRAPHY

American Public Health Association and American Academy of Pediatricians. 1992. *Caring for Our Children.*

Aronson, S., and H. Smith. 1993. *Model Child Care Health Policies.* Washington, DC: National Association for the Education of Young Children.

Berk, L. E. 1978. How Well Do Classroom Practices Reflect Teacher Goals? *Young Children.* 33(1).

Blakely, B., R. Blau, et al. 1989. *Activities for School Age Child Care.* Washington DC: National Association for the Education of Young Children.

Blood-Patterson, P. 1988. *Rise Up Singing.* Bethlehem, PA: Sing Out Corp.

Bowlby, J. 1973. *Attachment and Loss.* London: The Hogarth Press and the Institute of Psycho-Analysis.

Bredekamp, S. 1987. *Developmentally Appropriate Practice in Early Childhood Programs Serving Children from Birth Through Age 8.* Washington, DC: National Association for the Education of Young Children. Expanded Ed.

Bredekamp, S., ed. 1991. *Accreditation Criteria & Procedures.* Washington, DC: National Association for the Education of Young Children.

Christie, J. F., and F. Wardle. 1992. How Much Time Is Needed for Play? *Young Children* 47(3): 28–31.

Chun, R. 1994. *Capturing Childhood's Magic: Creating Outdoor Play Environments for Hawaii's Young Children.* Honolulu, HI: Hawaii Association for the Education of Young Children.

Click, P. 1994. *Caring for School-Age Children.* Albany, NY: Delmar.

Consumer Product Safety Commission. 1991. *Public Playground Handbook for Safety.* Washington, DC: Government Printing Office.

Crosser, S. 1992. Managing the Early Childhood Classroom. *Young Children* 47(2): 23–29.

Ecels, S., S. Aronson, et al. 1993. *Preparing for Illness: A Joint Responsibility for Parents and Caregivers.* Washington, DC: National Association for the Education of Young Children.

Frost, J. L. 1992. *Play and Playscapes.* Albany, NY: Delmar.

Galinsky, E. 1971. *School Beginnings: The First Day.* New York: Bank Street College of Education.

Galinsky, E. 1971. *School Beginnings: The First Weeks.* New York: Bank Street College of Education.

Gareau, M., and C. Kennedy. 1991. Structure Time & Space to Promote Pursuit of Learning in the Primary Grades. *Young Children* 46(4): 46–50.

Gonzalez-Mena, J., and D. W. Eyer. 1989. *Infants, Toddlers, and Caregivers.* Mountain View, CA: Mayfield Publishing.

Harms, T., and R. Clifford. 1980. *The Day Care Environment Rating Scale.* New York: Teachers College Press.

Hirsch, E. n.d. *Transition Periods: Stumbling Blocks of Education.* New York: Early Childhood Education Council of New York.

Jacobs, N. L. 1992. Unhappy Endings. *Young Children* 47(3): 23–27.

Janis, M. G. 1965. *A Two Year Old Goes to Nursery School: A Case Study of Separation Reaction.* Washington, DC: National Association for the Education of Young Children.

Jervis, K., ed. 1984. *Separation: Strategies for Helping Two to Four Year Olds.* Washington, DC: National Association for the Education of Young Children.

Jones, E., and G. Reynolds. 1992. *The Play's The Thing: Teacher's Roles in Children's Play.* New York: Teachers College Press.

Jordan, N. H. 1993. Sexual Abuse Prevention Programs in Early Childhood Education: A Caveat. *Young Children* 48(6): 76–79.

Kaplan, L. J. 1978. *Oneness and Separation: From Infant to Individual.* New York: Simon & Schuster.

Kendrick, A. S., R. Kaufmann, and K. Messinger. eds. 1991. *Healthy Young Children: A Manual for Programs.* Washington, DC: National Association for the Education of Young Children.

Koralek, D. G., L. J. Colker, and D. T. Dodge. 1993. *The What, Why, and How of High Quality Early Childhood Education: A Guide for On-Site Supervision.* Washington, DC: National Association for the Education of Young Children.

Marotz, L. R., M. Z. Cross, and J. M. Rush. 1993. *Health, Safety & Nutrition for the Young Child.* Albany, NY: Delmar.

Moravcik, E. 1981. *Good Snacks for Hawaii's Young Children.* University of Hawaii at Manoa.

Moukaddem, V. 1990. Preventing Infectious Diseases in Your Child Care Setting. *Young Children* 45(2): 28–29.

National Association for the Education of Young Children. 1993. The Effects of Group Size, Ratios, and Staff Training on Child Care Quality. *Young Children* 48(2): 65–67.

Pantell, R. H., J. F. Fries, and D. H. Vickery. 1984. *Taking Care of Your Child.* Reading, MA: Addison-Wesley.

Stevens, J. H., and M. Matthews. 1978. *Mother/Child Father/Child Relationships.* Washington DC: National Association for the Education of Young Children.

Stonehouse, A. 1990. The Golden Rule for Child Care. *Child Care Information Exchange* (November–December): 63–68.

Stonehouse, A., ed. 1990. *Trusting Toddlers: Planning for One- to Three-Year-Olds in Child Care Centers.* St. Paul, MN: Toys 'n Things Press.

Strickland, J. 1988. Do You Have Swiss Cheese Liability Insurance. *Child Care Information Exchange* 62: 75–77.

Strickland, J., and S. Reynolds. 1988–1989. The New Untouchables: Risk Management of Child Abuse in Child Care, Parts 1–4. *Child Care Information Exchange.* Issues 63–66.

CHAPTER EIGHT

The Learning Environment

There is no behavior apart from environment.   Robert Sommer

In this chapter, we discuss the environment of the early childhood program and its influence on children's development. We explore how an environment communicates to children and offer guidelines to help you design spaces and choose equipment and materials. We discuss evaluating and modifying environments so that they better meet children's needs.

The environment speaks to children. When they enter the classroom they can tell if it is a place intended for them and how it is best used. A cozy corner with a rug, cushions, and books says, "Sit down here and look at books." A climbing structure with ladders, ramps, slides, nets, and a bridge suggests, "Climb up, go across any way you can think of, and come down a different way." An airy environment with light, color, warmth, and interesting materials to be explored sends a clear message: "We care—this is a place for children." In such settings, there is enough space to move comfortably, the furnishings are child-sized, and the arrangement suggests how materials can be used.

Young children are learning all the time. The environments of their early childhood programs are more than safe and comfortable places to be. They are children's textbooks and learning labs. The environment is the tool that helps you to do a good job. For families it is the outward and visible sign that you are providing appropriate experiences for their children and meeting their needs. And since you too spend long hours away from home here, the environment contributes to whether you feel good about your work.

Learning environments can meet the needs of children and support your values and developmental goals. You make choices as you design the environment that influence the quality of the child's relationship to other people and to learning materials. In making these choices, you need to consider three very basic questions:

1. Is the environment appropriate for the developmental stage of the children?
2. How does the environment affect human relationships—among children, among adults and children, and among adults?
3. How does the environment facilitate children's learning and development?

THE BUILDING

The building itself is the first aspect that influences the learning environment you create. In the design of facilities, early childhood programs have frequently been afterthoughts and were housed in buildings created for other purposes. Although these settings may not be ideal, they can be workable and even charming. We have known and loved programs in converted homes, church sanctuaries, basements, apartment buildings, offices, coffee houses, and storefronts.

Design of a building may suggest certain types of use. The way you and children actually use the space may be different. Buildings with self-contained classrooms are designed so that single classes work within four walls where most of the materials needed for learning will be found. Each group of children is intended to spend most of the time in "their" room. Self-

contained classrooms can also be used by teams. Each room then is given particular functions (for example, one room may be the messy activity room with space for art and sensory activities). Groups of children have access to more than one room, and there is a larger amount of space within which to create a learning environment.

Open-design buildings, whether created for classrooms or converted, are constructed so that many people (sometimes all of the children in the school) will be within one room most of the time. Teams can arrange large interest centers throughout the open room, or self-contained "classrooms" can be created using dividers, furniture, and taped lines to suggest walls.

Extremes are not optimal. We have seen children confined in classrooms that were little larger than closets, and rooms housing over a hundred children where noise and confusion made conversation or concentration impossible.

207

Reflect and write about . . .

your first school

Remember your first school (or any school that was important to you during your childhood). What about the environment stands out in your memory: the classroom, the playground, the equipment and materials, storage and distribution of materials, the beauty of the setting? Why were those things important to you? What did you like? What do you wish had been different? How do you think the environment affected learning and relationships?

Research suggests that program size and group size are two of the most important indicators of quality in early childhood programs. Smaller programs and smaller group size have a positive effect on children. It is possible to gain the advantages of a small program and small group in programs with many self-contained classrooms; it is much more difficult to do so in open-design programs where a single large room holds several groups and many children.

Both self-contained and open-design classrooms offer advantages, and both have drawbacks. Self-contained classrooms offer a homelike atmosphere, a pride of ownership in the classroom, and a feeling of security and belonging that is especially beneficial for very young children. Some self-contained classrooms are not large enough to provide the variety of experiences that older children may need. Large open-design classrooms offer more space, more variety, and more diversity. They are usually noisier and may be distracting to children and frustrating if you prefer to have greater control over the use of space. Large rooms with many children are inappropriate for infants and toddlers, who thrive in environments that are more sheltered from stimulation and that are more like homes.

Program environments vary in the degree to which they can change, but the building structure is not flexible. Your first thoughts in accepting a job may not be about the environ-

ment. However, since this is a place where you will spend many hours of your waking life, it is important to make sure that it is one in which you can work effectively and comfortably.

THE CLASSROOM

Your knowledge of child development can help you design a classroom that gives children opportunities to move, interact, explore, and manipulate. The developmental needs of young children require that they move their bodies frequently. They learn through physical interaction, manipulation, and sensory experience and not through paper and pencil tasks. An atmosphere of warmth and informality meets the social-emotional needs of young children.

We call classrooms in which arrangement allows activities to occur simultaneously with maximum child-direction *child-centered*. These settings tend to be natural, casual, relaxed, and spontaneous. A child-centered environment is a classroom where children work either individually or in small groups. Both quiet and noisy activities happen throughout much of the day. *Content-centered* early childhood programs are represented by classrooms where teacher-selected and teacher-directed learning prevail. In these environments there is less variation in activities since they lack the spontaneity, unpredictability, and freedom characteristic of more child-centered settings.

The organization of the learning environment can be viewed on a continuum from child-centered to content-centered.[1] The extreme, and inappropriate, content-centered end of the continuum is represented by programs where children spend much of their day seated at tables or desks while the teacher lectures or provides seat work. The extreme, and also inappropriate, child-centered end of the continuum is a center where materials are provided with little organization and minimal planning or adult-child interaction. Classrooms for young children fall in many places between these extremes but are most appropriate when they are informal in structure and rich in materials *and* when there are many and diverse planned experiences for children. We will discuss how this continuum can be applied to curriculum in Chapter Ten, Planning Curriculum.

Organizing the Environment

Organizing an appropriate environment for young children will be different for different ages, but there are some similarities across the early childhood age span. All young children need a clearly defined "home" space for their group or class. They also need an outdoor play area with access to nature and space for active play that can be used year round. There needs to be enough space indoors and outdoors. Accessibility to children and family members who use walkers or wheelchairs needs to be provided.

Every early childhood environment must be arranged so that it can be easily supervised, cleaned, and maintained. Every early childhood program should include indoor and outdoor space for play. The way space is organized for

different kinds of routines and learning will vary with age. For example, infants and toddlers need special areas to be changed and washed, to sleep, and to eat. Preschoolers and kindergarten children need spaces for books, blocks, toys, art, and dramatic play. School-age children need spaces for table activities, group projects, reading, and gathering. Additionally, all young children benefit if there are soft areas for cozy cuddling, resting, and relaxing and quiet, private spaces where they can escape from the din of the class.

Organizing Environments for Infants and Toddlers

Infants thrive in environments which, like homes, have fewer people and are sheltered

---

[1]Our use of the terms *child-centered* and *content-centered* came after considerable debate. We rejected *open* vs. *closed,* since this often refers to architecture or the arrangement of space, and *structured* vs. *unstructured,* since we feel that all programs have structure that may be more or less visible.

from stimulation. Because there are more adults per child, more space is required (typically 50 square feet per child). A classroom for infants has separate areas for routines and activities. Since children under eighteen months do not eat or rest on a schedule, there must be separate areas for sleeping that are quiet and shielded from stimulus and eating areas somewhat separate from play areas. There must be protected areas for immobile babies. Since diaper changing is a prominent feature of the daily program, a changing area with a sink and hot water must be close at hand and separate from eating and play areas. A stable, comfortable chair or couch is a must so that adults can sit and hold children. It also contributes to a home-like atmosphere and provides good climbing experiences and excellent handholds for beginning standers and walkers.

Play areas in programs for infants and toddlers must be very flexible. They should include clean, carpeted surfaces for playing and crawling and different levels to crawl and climb on. Several play spaces need to be available for mobile children so that different kinds of play can occur at once. A large central space in a classroom with smaller areas surrounding it (Figure 8.1) is a good arrangement for infant and toddler programs.

A room for infants will be divided into areas. A program for toddlers can include a sensory, manipulative, block, dramatic play, book, and art area. Toddlers are climbers, so safe places for toddlers to climb are a must, both indoors and out. It is essential to assume that anything that can be climbed will be climbed—high and unstable shelves must be eliminated from toddler environments.

Organizing Environments for Preschool, Kindergarten, and Primary Programs

Preschool, kindergarten, and primary programs are often organized into interest or learning centers (sometimes called *areas*). These are de-

fined spaces within a classroom. A learning center is usually enclosed on two or three sides by walls, shelves, or dividers. These may include areas for blocks, books, dramatic play, manipulative toys, art, music, writing, science, and math.

When you design a classroom with learning centers, it is a good idea to begin by defining areas for different types of activities: messy, active, quiet, large group, or small group. Areas that have particular requirements can be located first. Quiet areas should be separated from noisy areas. The art area should be near water and will be easier to clean up if it has an uncarpeted floor. The block area should be set out of pathways between centers. It needs space to encourage complex building. Other areas can be arranged in the remaining space, keeping in mind their purpose and requirements. The library area will require good lighting and some shelter from noise and activity. The science area may need an electric outlet for an aquarium. The tape player in the listening or music center will also need access to electricity.

The space between centers must also be considered. There should be pathways that give access to all the centers. Paths will invite running if they are too long. Work will be interrupted if they lead through areas where children are working. Space for groups to meet and space for movement activities will also be needed. Private space is also important. Children who spend long hours away from home need a place to be alone.

The floor plan in Figure 8.2 illustrates one way that a classroom with interest centers might be arranged.

In programs for primary children, space for individuals to work alone and in small groups is also very important. Space for the group to come together to think, plan, and work on a project will be essential. Comfortable places for reading, working, and playing; places to be alone or work with a friend; and space for on-

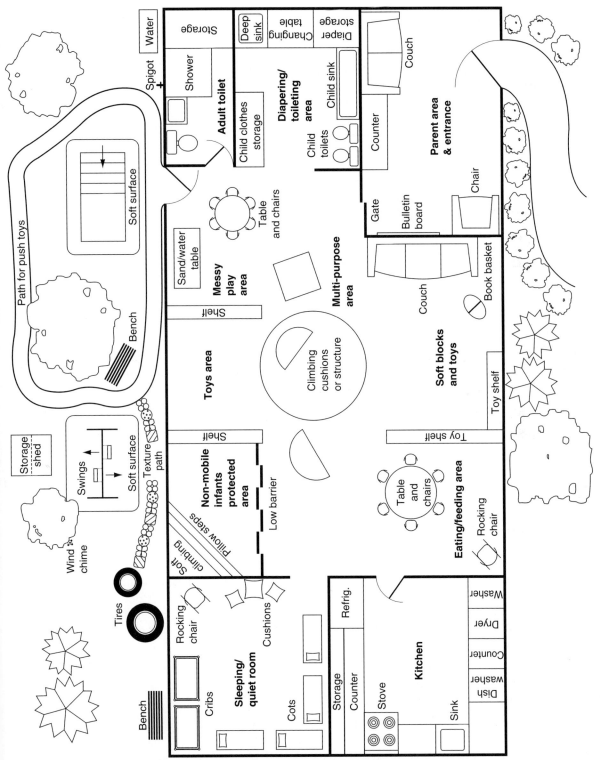

FIGURE 8.1
Infant and toddler program floor plan

211

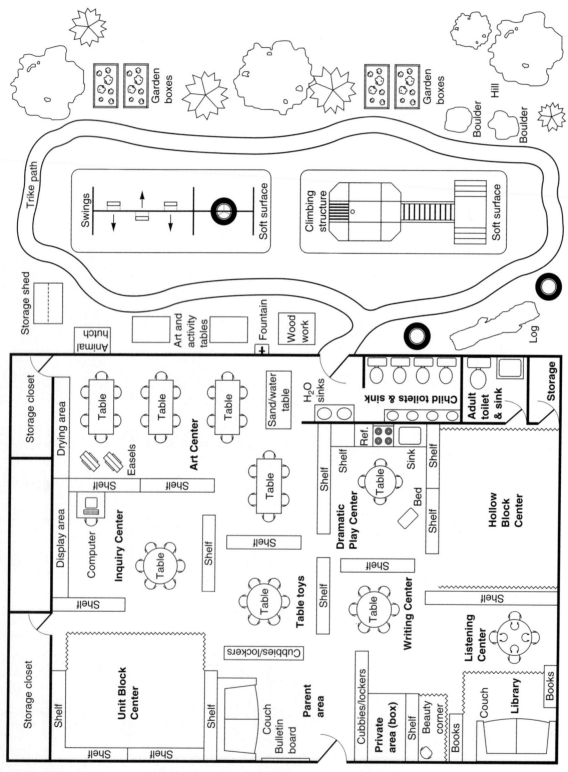

FIGURE 8.2
Preschool/kindergarten floor plan

going projects are other important elements in a primary classroom (Figure 8.3).

If your classroom includes children with special needs you may need to make some adaptations in the arrangement of your environment. For example, doors, pathways, centers, tables, and play materials must accommodate adaptive equipment such as wheelchairs and walkers. Often small rearrangements of the furniture are enough to make your classroom a place for all children.

Your classroom is first and foremost a place for children, but it is important not to forget adults when you design the space. Create a place where you and other adults can sit comfortably. You may want to put this near the sign-in area or the library so parents feel invited to participate. Chapter Sixteen, Working with Families, gives you suggestions for a family area in the classroom. You will also need a place where you can keep your own things safely, keep confidential records, and prepare materials.

Aesthetics

Aesthetics should be considered in arranging a classroom. We believe that children's classrooms should be beautiful places. Attention to the aesthetic quality of the environment means looking for ways to make aspects of the classroom harmonious (for example, by paying attention to color and design and by grouping shelves or chairs of the same color or design in one area) and by eliminating clutter. The In Practice box gives suggestions for the aesthetic enhancement of environments for young children.

Equipment and Materials

Equipment and materials suggest direction and provide raw materials for children's exploration, development, and learning. Generally *equipment* refers to furniture and other large and ex-

pensive items such as easels and climbing structures. *Materials* usually refers to smaller, less expensive items such as puzzles, books, games, and toys. Consumables like paint, paper, glue, and tape are referred to as *supplies*. Through interaction with well-designed equipment and materials, children develop large and small muscle coordination, concepts about the world, creativity and self-expression, social skills, and self-awareness.

Furniture

Environments for young children require furnishings that support classroom activities and respond to the needs of children. We favor wood because of its aesthetic appeal and stur-

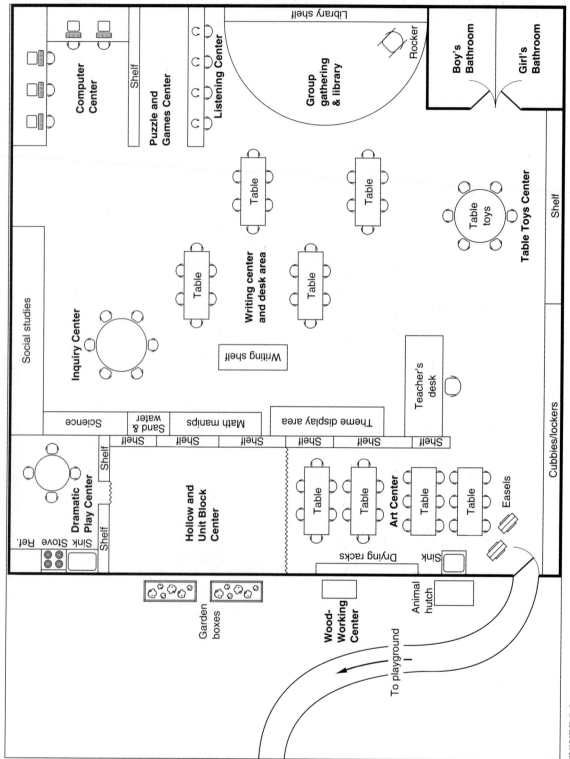

214

FIGURE 8.3
Primary classroom floor plan

IN PRACTICE

Suggestions for Aesthetic Enhancement of Environments

Color: Bright colors will dominate a room and may detract from art and natural beauty present. If you have a choice, select soft, light, neutral colors for walls and ceilings. Try to color coordinate learning centers so that children begin to see them as wholes rather than as parts. Avoid having many different kinds of patterns in any one place—they can be distracting and overstimulating.

Furnishings: Group similar furniture together. Keep colors natural and neutral to focus children's attention on the learning materials on the shelves. When you are choosing furnishings, select wood rather than metal or plastic. If you must paint furniture, use one neutral color for everything so that you have greater flexibility in moving it from space to space. Have a cleaning day periodically— give children brushes and warm soapy water and let them scrub the furniture on a sunny, warm day.

Storage: Rotate materials on shelves rather than crowding them together. Crowded shelves look unattractive and are hard for children to maintain. Baskets make excellent attractive storage containers. If you use storage tubs, try to put all the same kind together on one shelf. If you use cardboard boxes for storage, cover them with plain-colored paper or paint them.

Decoration: Mount and display children's artwork. Provide artwork by fine artists and avoid cartoons, advertisements, and garish, stereotyped, faded, or tattered posters. Make sure that much artwork (both by children and adult artists) is displayed at children's eye level. Use shelf tops as places for displaying sculpture, plants, and items of natural beauty like shells, stones, and fish tanks. Avoid storing teacher's materials on the tops of shelves—if there is no other choice, create a teacher "cubby" using a covered box or storage tub.

Outdoors: Design or arrange play structures as an extension of nature rather than an intrusion upon it. If possible use natural materials like wood and hemp rather than painted metal, plastic, or fiberglass. Provide adequate storage to help to maintain materials. Involve children, parents, and other staff in keeping outdoor areas free of litter. Add small details like a garden or a rock arrangement to show that the outdoors is also a place that deserves attention and care.

---

diness and because it is easier to maintain than plastic or metal. Furniture must be stable, portable, and have rounded corners and edges. It should be proportioned to the size of the children. Toddlers are better able to manage squat, four-legged stools than chairs, which tend to tip. Children can be comfortable and can focus when seated at tables if their feet touch the floors and their elbows can rest comfortably on table tops. Small tables where several children can sit provide greater flexibility than large tables and leave more space free for diverse activity than a room filled with desks for each child.

Every child needs space for the storage of clothing and personal belongings. Cubby holes meet this need. Cubby holes can be manufactured or improvised using such materials as dishtubs, sweater boxes, cardboard boxes, or commercial five-gallon ice-cream tubs. Low open shelves are essential for storing materials that children use independently. If children can see over shelves they are less likely to climb on them. Storage of this kind allows children to make choices and encourages them to become responsible for clean-up. A shelf especially designed for books invites reading by displaying the books with their covers facing the children. Since it is relatively easy for young children to return the books to such a shelf, it helps to protect books.

Infant-toddler programs also require:

- A sturdy changing table at a comfortable height for adults.
- A secure crib or sleeping area for each infant in the program.
- Lower shelves that toddlers can see over.
- Smaller dramatic play furniture without doors that pinch fingers.
- Comfortable adult chairs for holding and rocking children.
- Stable furniture and rails for infants to pull up on.
- Squat, four-legged stools or chairs for toddlers and tray chairs for infants.
- Very low, stable tables with rounded corners.

Arrangement and Storage

Attention to storage can contribute to the smooth functioning of a classroom as well as to its aesthetic quality. Uncrowded materials that are stored in attractive containers contribute to an orderly environment that is a pleasant place in which to live and work. A thoughtfully organized classroom helps children to understand and maintain order.

When children look at the environment they should be able to tell at a glance what materials are available to them. If materials are stored on low, open shelves, they tell children that they are available for their use. Materials that are reserved for use by adults need to be stored so that they are out of children's reach and view. Cleaning supplies, files, first-aid equipment, and staff personal belongings need secure storage within the classroom or nearby areas.

Low, open storage encourages independence and responsibility by allowing children to choose and return materials on their own. You may wish to aid this independence by creating a system to help children to understand and participate in classroom organization. Materials can be stored in containers labeled with pictures of the contents. Shelves and materials can be coded with self-adhesive colored dots. Outlines of equipment can be drawn on shelves to help children match the equipment to its proper place.

Keep in mind that your classroom's primary function is to encourage children to engage with materials, a sometimes disorderly process. Avoid being excessively concerned with maintaining constant order while children are working because such concern can be constricting. Instead, work on building routines that help children understand that cleanup is a part of each activity.

Toys

Think of a toy you loved when you were a child. Chances are good that you remember what it looked like, how it felt, what it did, and how you used it. You may even know where it is today. Good toys are good learning materials and they influence children. They are attractive. They have sensory appeal and feel good to touch and hold.

Good toys are sturdy and not easily broken. Since they are the tools of learning, they must be kept in good repair, work properly, and fit children's size, abilities, and interests. They must be non-toxic, adequately clean, and free of hazards like broken, sharp parts. An environment that supports the development of young children will have many different toys organized in play areas.

Setting Up Learning Centers

Learning centers are appropriate for children from toddlerhood throughout the early childhood years. Common to the arrangement of all learning centers is the idea of partial seclusion. Each center is partially secluded from the rest of the classroom with shelves and dividers. This allows children to concentrate in each workspace.

Block Centers

Unit blocks and hollow blocks help develop motor coordination and strength, enhance imag-

ination, and provide opportunities for children to work together. They provide learning experiences in measurement, ratio, and problem solving.

A set of hardwood **unit blocks** is an essential part of a learning environment for young children from toddlerhood on. Children building with blocks gain experience in abstract representation that contributes to the ability to read and write. Children also learn about mathematical relationships when they experience that two blocks of one size are equivalent to the next larger size blocks. Blocks serve as a vehicle through which children can express their growing understanding of the world. They provide raw materials out of which children can recreate developing ideas.

A unit block area for preschool, kindergarten, and primary children begins with a set of hardwood unit blocks. A basic set includes at least one hundred blocks and eight shapes (often called a nursery school set). Older children will benefit from larger and more complex sets of blocks (often called a kindergarten set).

For blocks to be used well, children need adequate space and sufficient time for block play. A daily self-selected activity period that lasts for at least an hour provides time for children to benefit from blocks. The block area should be large enough so several children at a time can build. A smooth floor or low pile carpet will enable children to build without structures tumbling down. Block storage shelves should be spacious enough so that each type of block has its own individual place that is clearly marked with an outline to enable children to more easily find the appropriate blocks for their constructions and to take more responsibility for cleanup.

You can enhance and extend unit block play by adding toy vehicles, doll houses, small human and animal figures, and other props. Provide special storage baskets and separate labeled space on the shelves for props.

Hollow blocks allow children to build a world that they can physically enter. Because of this, they inspire and contribute to rich dramatic play. Hollow blocks can be made of wood, cardboard, soft foam, or hard plastic. Wooden blocks are sturdier for building, and most sets include short and long boards for making roofs and platforms. A hollow block area should have enough blocks for a child to build a structure that can be climbed on or entered (at least fifteen big blocks).

Hollow blocks require a good deal of storage space. They can make a good addition to a dramatic play area or can be used in a separate hollow block area. We find that hollow blocks are used for more elaborate building and for more sociodramatic play if they are separated from unit blocks. Space for building with hollow blocks can be set up on a porch or in the play yard if you have sheltered storage. As with unit blocks, children will be more self-sufficient if storage is marked to indicate where to put away blocks. Good props for hollow blocks include hats, sheets, and lengths of colorful chiffon or gauze, which you can store in bins, boxes, or baskets nearby.

Hollow blocks for toddlers must be lighter than those for older children. Light plastic, foam, or cardboard hollow blocks work better for toddlers than heavy hardwood hollow blocks.

Table blocks are sometimes also used in classrooms for young children. These smaller blocks provide opportunities for intricate building for preschoolers, kindergarten, and primary children. They also work well for infants and toddlers since they are lighter. To be useful with young children, table blocks must have large pieces that cannot be swallowed and must withstand frequent sanitizing.

Dramatic Play Area

Dramatic play is one of the most important forms of play for young children. Children imitate the actions of the very important grown-ups in their lives and thus learn about how different roles might feel. When they take on roles and use materials to pretend, they learn to symbolize and practice the skills of daily living. Manipulating the physical environment, such as putting on clothes with buttons and zippers, and managing relationships are both skills learned in part through dramatic play.

Dramatic play materials can be organized in an interest center (often called home, housekeeping, dress-up, pretend, or fantasy area). Dramatic play centers are frequently organized into a "home" area, emphasizing domestic activity. The home theme relates to the most common and powerful experiences in children's lives, but children find new ways to vary this theme. In one classroom we observed children become a family of spiders when they spread a crocheted shawl between chairs to become a giant web. Home areas can be changed to present other options: a post office, hospital, store, bus, farm, camp, or restaurant.

A dramatic play area requires sheltered space and simple child-sized furniture typically including a stove, sink, and a table with chairs for two to four children. To give children motivation for elaborate dramatic play, add dress-up clothes. Dress-up clothes for both boys and girls should reflect different kinds of work and play, different cultures, and different ages. You may have to seek out props for the dramatic play area that suggest diversity of age, sex role, and cultures. Dolls representing a variety of racial backgrounds and common objects of daily life such as kitchenware, books, furnishings, and tools also form a part of the equipment of the dramatic play area.

Open shelves, bins or baskets, or hooks on the wall provide storage for dramatic play props. To prevent clutter, props can be stored in sturdy, attractive, lidded boxes organized by occupation, situation, or role. These can then be brought out to fit the children's play. Arrange materials so they are easy to find. Make picture labels for storage shelves.

In programs for toddlers' dramatic play materials are simpler, fewer in number, and include duplicates. Furniture must be smaller without cupboard doors that pinch fingers. A good selection might contain: hats, clothes with few fasteners, purses, dolls, lightweight aluminum pots, and wooden or plastic stirring spoons. Toddlers will incorporate manipulative toys in their first efforts at symbolic, dramatic play.

You can respond to children's dramatic play by adding appropriate materials when you observe a new interest developing—for example, by contributing fire hats, a rain slicker, boots, and a length of hose when the children are pretending to be firefighters rescuing the baby.

Manipulative Toy Center

Manipulative materials like puzzles, beads, Legos, Bristle Blocks, and pegboards give children practice in hand-eye coordination and help develop the small muscles of their fingers and hands. These experiences are important preparation for writing, and they expose children to such concepts as color, size, and shape, which help in the ability to recognize letters and words. In play with manipulative toys, children also have opportunities to cooperate, solve problems, and be creative.

For infants and toddlers, manipulative materials must be large so they do not present a choking hazard and sturdy enough to withstand frequent sanitizing. They can include homemade toys like plastic bottles with clothes pins to drop inside and commercially made equipment like busy boxes. Duplicate toys placed side by side on the shelf will encourage parallel play and reduce conflicts. Infants and toddlers often interpret everyday objects as manipulative toys, so it is essential to keep unsafe or inappropriate items out of their reach.

Manipulative toys for primary children can include more complex games and toys such as jigsaw puzzles. Equipment for developing fine motor skill can be combined with cognitive tasks such as following pattern cards for geoboards, attribute blocks, and beads. Primary children also enjoy the challenge of duplicating the complex structures portrayed on the boxes and in the direction pamphlets that often come with manipulative toys.

An organized and clearly marked manipulative toy area invites children to play productively. If pieces are jumbled, broken, or missing and if materials are crowded on the shelf, children will have difficulty playing and will not be able to put materials away in an orderly fashion. An open shelf provides good manipulative toy storage. A soft, clean carpet provides a comfortable place to work. Baskets, tubs, and boxes hold toys so that they are easy to find and put away. Arrange the materials on the shelf so that there is a choice of different materials at any one time. Make sure materials are not crowded and it is easy to see where each toy or game goes.

Picture labels for the tubs and for the shelves help children to put things away. A puzzle rack makes it possible to store many puzzles in the classroom, although these make it hard for children to see the puzzles and can be hard for them to manage.

Sensory Play Areas

Most early childhood classrooms have materials that clearly contribute to sensory development: water, sand, mud, dough, and clay. They are usually found out of doors but can also be provided indoors with tubs and water tables, often in the art area. If you have room in your classroom or playground, a special area can be provided for sensory play. Set up the sensory area near a sink or on a porch so that spills can be cleaned up more easily.

Natural materials like sand and water suit a wide range of developmental stages and abilities. They provide children with rich sensory experiences and an opportunity to learn about mathematical concepts like volume and

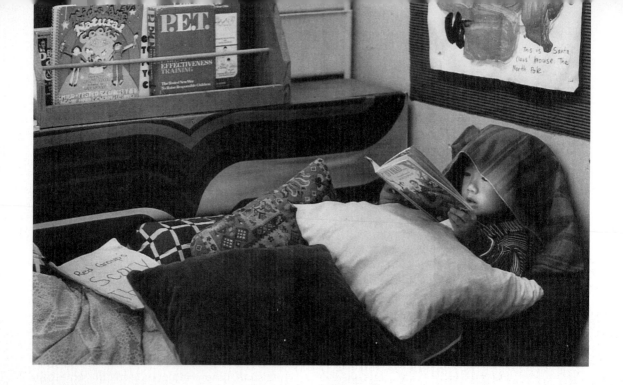

measurement. Observation of almost any child will tell you that these are satisfying play materials. They are open-ended and can be used in many ways. Children learn about the properties of substances through pouring, feeling, and mixing. They may soothed by the responsiveness of the materials and can safely vent strong emotions in their play with them. Cooperative and imaginative play is fostered as children work together with them.

Natural materials are generally safe and are particularly satisfying for infants and toddlers. The younger the children, however, the more you will need to supervise. Since very young children are likely to put things in their mouths, you may wish to substitute dough for clay, and flour, cornmeal, oatmeal, or rice for sand.

Primary children tend to use sensory materials in more task-oriented ways. For example, they might compare and contrast different natural materials and record the differences. Water might be channeled with pipes and tubing, and the workings of a waterwheel or an aqueduct can be explored. Clay is likely to be used to construct objects that can be fired.

Principles of claywork can be learned. Sand might be closely observed and different sands examined.

Art Center

Art materials provide media with which children can create, based on their experiences. In the art area, children can work with full concentration, with materials and equipment that are developmentally appropriate, functional, and satisfying to use.

An art area requires work tables and easels that are sized to the children (they should be able to reach the top of the easel) and cleanup facilities near by. Old or second-hand furniture minimizes concerns about inevitable paint and glue spills. Additionally it is important to have open shelves for child-accessible supplies, closed storage for adults-only supplies, open wide shelves children can reach for drying and storing work still in process, and smocks to protect clothes.

Art materials provide opportunities for creative expression, problem solving, and physical and sensory development. These may include crayons, scissors, tempera paint, water colors, water color markers, non-toxic glue and paste, construction paper, food color, crewel needles, yarn, clay, clay boards, clay tools, fabric, small containers for water, and brushes. Chapter Twelve provides a more detailed explanation of art materials and their uses for different age groups.

Writing Center

Preschool, kindergarten, and primary classrooms need a writing center where children can explore, write messages and stories, and draw. Children are encouraged to write to communicate when writing supplies are available and there are written words to look at and think about. In the writing center children can record, report, and create based on their experience.

A writing center needs an open shelf for storage, a child-proportioned table with chairs, baskets or boxes to hold paper and writing materials, different types and sizes of paper and envelopes, note cards, paper notepads, pencils, erasers, markers of various widths, crayons, a set of wood or plastic letters (both upper and lower case) for constructing words and sentences and for tracing, a letter-stamp set for printing, and staplers and hole punches for binding books. Kindergarten and primary children will enjoy keeping journals in the writing center. A typewriter or a computer with a simple word-processing program designed for children is also useful. Other ideas about things children can do and learn in the writing center will be described in Chapter Twelve.

Library Center

The best way to help children to learn the joy of reading and become motivated to read is to have good books available and to read to children often. Every classroom for young children should have a large selection of books. Children need many opportunities to look at books, to hear stories, and to see adults using and enjoying books.

Children feel invited to use well-cared-for, appropriate books displayed with the covers visible on an uncrowded book shelf at their eye level. From toddlerhood on, a book area that is comfortable, quiet, well-lit, and stocked with a selection of quality children's books is an important part of a classroom. (Infants also need, enjoy, and benefit from books each day, but do not require a library area.) Locate the classroom library area in the best-lit, quietest corner of the classroom and include soft pillows or a big chair or sofa. In programs for infants, a book shelf can become a hazard, so age-appropriate books can be provided throughout the room flexibly, where it seems

---

Reflect and write about . . .

a classroom

Think about an early childhood program you attended, observed, or worked in. Describe the arrangement of the classroom, the playground, the equipment and materials, space for children's belongings, storage and distribution of materials, and the aesthetics of the setting. What was included? What was omitted? How did the arrangement of the learning environment effect the experience of children?

appropriate. Additionally, in programs for preschoolers and older children, books can be integrated throughout the classroom. For example, science books might be kept in the science area, picture dictionaries in the writing center, and the phone book, newspapers, and magazines might be located in the dramatic play area.

Children are drawn to the library area when there is a supply of interesting and attractive books that are in good repair and that are changed on a regular basis. In most locales, the public library will supply you with a selection of books at no cost. In Chapter Thirteen we describe criteria for selecting good books for children across the early childhood age span.

Inquiry Centers

Inquiry centers can include work areas for science, math, and social studies. These are laboratories for exploration and discoveries. Where did the new child come from? What does an earthworm need to survive? Who is taller, Kane or Yoon Ki? Children solve problems based on observations and research, using tools and books you provide in inquiry centers for science, math, or social studies. If you have space in your classroom, you can create activity centers devoted to each of these subjects. If not, you can join two or all three together.

A **science center** is a home for the tools of exploration and for ongoing projects such as aquariums and terrariums, animal families, and plants. You can also include science games, collections of objects and pictures, and science reference books. Arrange your science area in a place in the classroom that has access to electricity and water. Define the space with low, open shelves for storage and a low table or counter for investigation. Set tables for displays against a taller shelf or wall. Set up a shelf with tools for investigation: sorting trays, plastic tubs and pitchers, aquariums, insect and animal cages, airtight containers for storage, balances, scales, measuring cups and spoons, and magnifying glasses. Select materials for investigation, sorting, collections (like buttons or rocks), machinery to investigate and disassemble, information books, and photographs and posters that illustrate science concepts.

The processes of comparison, classification, and measurement, as opposed to rote counting and computation, are the basis of math in early childhood. A **math center** contains materials such as scales, balances, lotto, objects with different attributes, and matching games. It is a place where you provide games that encourage children to experiment and think.

Materials like attribute blocks, colored cubes, parquetry blocks, board games, and seriation materials like stacking cups are designed to enhance learning. Many of the materials based on the work of Maria Montessori found in the math area are also designed to teach young children math concepts through the manipulation of attractive materials. Additionally, many early childhood educators make simple materials like button sorting, lotto games, and matching activities to foster math development. With all of these toys, children compare, classify, sort, seriate, measure, count, and create patterns. Chapter Fourteen provides information about these materials.

In a **social studies area** children compare and contrast the attributes of the human and natural environments and how these effect people. In a social studies area you will include special displays and activities, bulle-tin boards, artifacts, learning games, maps and globes, and books related to social studies. Pictures, posters, and children's work relating to social studies can also be exhibited here. You might wish to use a single bulletin board or display area to attractively mount one type of work (for example, maps children have drawn) or set aside space for each child's work.

Technology and Early Childhood Environments

Technology is becoming an ever-increasing part of our lives. Television is in the homes of virtually all children in our society. It is a powerful force in their lives. Computers have become commonplace. Both of these technologies have potential uses and some problems in early childhood classrooms. You will have decisions to make regarding how and if to use them in your work with children. Because of this, it is important for you to understand the issues involved.

Some educators have embraced the television and computers in the early childhood classroom with great enthusiasm and see them as an important tools. Others fear that children may be robbed of the critical concrete learning opportunities of early childhood if symbolic and abstract media are introduced too soon. Although there are few absolute answers, it is clear that the abstract nature of television and computers makes them inappropriate as *principal* educational tools before the age of five. These technologies spark debate about the goals of education, appropriate methods of instruction, and the issue of *hothousing*—rushing young children.

Television and Video

Most children will spend far more time in their lives watching television than they will in school. There has been a long-term debate over the negative effects of television and general agreement that some programming can be harmful. Programs created for children can be thoughtfully produced or they can be marketing devices for selling breakfast cereal and promoting toys. Television and its servant, video recorders, can be used as a "plug-in drug" to keep children entertained and quiet in lieu of appropriate learning experiences, or they can be used carefully as a tool with appropriate content and active teacher involvement.

If the use of television and video is a choice in your setting, you can thoughtfully evaluate its use. Reject the use of television if:

- It is to be shown to children on a regular basis for segments of more than ten or fifteen minutes.
- You do not know or have no control over the programs watched.
- Programs include violent content, talk down to children, or are designed for an older audience.
- It is used as a babysitter.

Consider including television if:

- It is to be shown to children in short segments that you have previewed.
- Programs contribute to educational goals.
- You sit and watch with a small group of children and talk with them about what they have viewed.
- Programs address children respectfully and are geared to their age.

As more and more schools have video cameras and recorders, it becomes possible to use television to serve the curriculum. New technology in the form of interactive video/computer programs also hold exciting possibilities for primary children.

Computers

Although they are not a substitute for the traditional play materials of early childhood educa-

tion, computers can contribute to children's development. Computers are powerful tools, not electronic sorcerers. They can free beginning learners from the tyranny of rote memorization and painful drill by teaching repetitive skills in entertaining formats. Some children with disabilities may be able to be included in a regular classroom thanks to computer technology that allows them to communicate through the use of point and touch screens. As children begin to write they can make extensive use of computers in the classroom. Young children learning to write are often much more fluent with the assistance of computers than without. We have seen creative writing and "publishing" occurring among primary-school children that would not have been possible without the assistance of computers.

Self-selected learning and choice are important elements of early childhood education. Early childhood educators trust children to select learning experiences. Eager learners of all ages have embraced computer use when it meets their needs. Research suggests that children's response to computers varies with their developmental stage. Children who have yet to begin symbolizing are more interested in and need concrete play materials. Computers in their classrooms are of only momentary interest. Children ages five and above may become fascinated by computers with age-appropriate programs and are delighted to control them.

Although the technology of computers is innovative, many programs are simply electronic workbooks. They do no more than develop rote learning. Appropriate programs for young children help them to develop critical thinking skills and creativity and help them to learn to be confident members of the community of computer users. You will need to find software (programs) that is appropriate and consistent with your values. What makes software appropriate for young children?

- Concepts are *developmentally appropriate;* that is, relevant and concrete. For example, children learn how to create a picture, open a window, or initiate a train of interesting activity rather than learning to repeat a correct answer to a math problem.
- Programs are *open-ended.* They allow a great deal of child choice and child direction.
- The *pace* is set by the child and not by the program.
- Programs have an intrinsically appealing *process* (such as exploring an environment) rather than a extrinsic reward (such as a smiling face for giving the correct answer to a problem).

THE OUTDOOR ENVIRONMENT

Every program for young children needs an outdoor play area. When you recall your own childhood play experiences, you probably will remember outdoor play. Inside play is

restricted—*walk slowly, talk softly, don't break it, don't get it dirty.* But outside the loud, active, enthusiastic play of children is safe and permitted. The historical roots of early childhood programs reflect the importance of outdoor play—the first nursery school designed by Rachel and Margaret MacMillan was an outdoor school and emphasized children's health.

Since we know children are learning all the time, not just when they are in the classroom, outdoor space and equipment should support a range of developmental goals: physical, social, cognitive, and creative. It can be used for an endless variety of learning activities. Animals, gardens, sandboxes, and water play areas located outdoors can be the source of science, math, language development, and creative activities. Messy art materials like clay and fingerpaint are especially well suited to outdoor use. Many learning experiences take on new dimensions when they go on outdoors. A story about trees, for example, read in the shade of an oak carries new meaning. And, of course, it is in the outdoor environment that children have the opportunity to engage in vigorous physical activity that builds skill, strength, stamina, and coordination.

Just as there is variety in buildings that house programs, there is also variety in outdoor space. Unfortunately, spacious yards carefully designed for young children are the exception rather than the rule. In a program located in the business district of a big city, play space may be a porch, a rooftop, or a paved parking lot. In a suburban or rural setting, it is likely to have a grassy yard with some play equipment. Whether your outdoor space is a rooftop or a garden, there are things you can do to enhance the space to meet children's needs.

In designing an outdoor environment you need to make sure that there are opportunities for a number of different kinds of experiences.

These include opportunities for active play with appropriate and increasingly challenging experience, sensory play with natural materials like sand and water, constructive play where children can use equipment to build, pretend and dramatic play, quiet activities like painting and working with clay, and places to comfortably think, relax, and daydream. Creating a well-designed and safe outdoor play environment can be a major effort that will be greatly assisted by involvement of parents and community.

Arrange materials in the yard so that the equipment is located where it is safe and appropriate for children to use it. If possible, provide comfortable surfaces for sitting and lying, and water for drinking and play. The outside environment should not be static. Just as you have different indoor experiences for children each day there should be special activities for children to do outside every day.

Equipment for Active Play

The outdoor area is typically used as a site for climbing structures and other equipment that offers opportunity for vigorous movement and exploration. Active play helps children develop and explore their physical limits, develop creativity, release energy, and learn many spatial concepts (up, down, under, over) by experiencing them with their bodies. Swings, slides, bal-ance beams, trampolines, rocking toys, wheel-barrows, wagons, trikes, and scooters offer opportunities to use and develop the large muscles of the arms and legs and provide experience in balance and coor-dination.

Active play materials and equipment range from simple inexpensive toys like jump ropes, parachutes, and balls, to elaborate and costly play equipment with slides, ramps, platforms, steps, and ladders, called *superstructures*. Playground equipment and superstructures are very important components of the outdoor environment and should be designed thoughtfully with safety and developmental goals in mind.

Wood, hemp, and rubber are aesthetically pleasing and safer than harder materials but are more prone to disintegration in a shorter amount of time. As described in Chapter Seven, play equipment needs to be sized for the children and installed over safe surfacing like sand, woodchips, or rubber to cushion children from falls. In play yards that are used by children with a wide range of ages and different degrees of strength and ability, there should be equipment that provides challenge and success at a number of different levels.

Wherever you work, some equipment for active play will probably exist. Most play equipment in use today is viewed as unsafe, inadequate, or inappropriate. The safety checklist in Chapter Seven and the In Practice checklists

---

Reflect and write about . . .

dimensions of teaching learning environments

Use Figure 8-4, *Dimensions of Teaching Learning Environments,* to reflect on a childhood classroom or your college classroom. How might the dimensions be used to generate changes that would make the learning environment more effective?

at the end of this chapter give you some measures for evaluating your playground. The standards established for play equipment, developed by the Consumer Products Safety Commission (1991), will also be helpful. If the play equipment in your program is inadequate, you can create additional active play experiences with simple inexpensive equipment such as sturdy wooden boxes, cable spools, planks, tires, cargo nets, marine rope, cardboard cartons, and natural structures such as logs, trees, and boulders. Whether the equipment is purchased or improvised, this part of your environment requires thoughtful planning and evaluation on a regular basis.

Infants and toddlers require different challenges than older children. Play structures need to be low to the ground, stable, wide (to accommodate a child who needs time to climb up or down), and less steep. They enjoy wide ramps and entrances and exits to be climbed into and out of. Infants and toddlers may make many false starts before they actually feel confident enough to slide down the slide or climb to the top; therefore, there should be few irreversible choices (such as tall slides from which you can't back down). Push vehicles and pull toys that are stable without joints that pinch, low belt swings, and swings with seatbelts are appropriate for younger children.

Primary children require greater variety and more challenge in their play yards. They are able to go higher, jump further, and learn new skills such as sliding down long poles, balancing along high balance beams, and turning on parallel bars. Primary children also will need additional movable equipment such as hoops, bats, and balls for organized games, and hard surfaces for rope jumping and ball bouncing are needed.

It is important to adapt the outside environment, equipment, and activities so that children with physical challenges can also partici-

pate fully. Adaptations can be relatively simple. For example, the range of a child in a walker or wheelchair will be extended by creating conveyer-belt walkways across grass and sand (using recycled conveyer belts donated by airports or large stores). A sling swing or hammock can

be substituted for a child who does not have the upper body strength required to use a conventional swing.

MAKING THE ENVIRONMENT WORK

Designing a learning environment is not a one-time event; it is an ongoing process. As you live and work with children you will wish to remain sensitive to the ways their needs change as they grow and learn. Any setting can be modified and improved. The perfect arrangement for this year's class of children may not work as well for a new group. Plan on regularly reevaluating and changing the environment.

When you are planning an environment, you need to consider the kinds of experiences you want children to have. When problems arise—for example, if children consistently fail to get involved in activities—you may want to look first at the environment to see if it is part of the cause of the problem. Robert Sommer, a psychologist who has studied the effect of environment on behavior, has said, "There is no behavior apart from environment, even in utero" (Sommer 1969, 19).

Look at the space and the equipment that are available and consider what you wish the environment to communicate to children. Keep in mind their age and experience. Create interest centers and make the environment as safe, aesthetic, and appropriate as you can. Since adults will spend time in the classroom, address their needs, too. Create a corner where they can sit and relax on an adult-sized comfortable chair or couch.

Before you finish arranging your classroom and outdoor space, and whenever you are about to change the environment, observe from the viewpoint of a child by sitting on the floor or the ground. From this perspective, observe from the entrance and each of the areas. Notice what you can see in each location, what is most attractive, and what is most distracting.

This may be quite different from what you perceive from your regular height and will help you to design an environment that works for children.

Using a checklist, like those in the In Practice boxes at the end of this chapter that we designed for our students, or the Harms-Clifford Early Childhood Environmental Rating Scale (1980), and reviewing accreditation guidelines designed by NAEYC, can help you to take a structured approach to this part of your work. We have found it helpful to use specific dimensions or attributes described by Elizabeth Jones in *Dimensions of Teaching-Learning Environments* (1977) as another kind of lens through which to observe and evaluate our environments (Figure 8.4).

FINAL THOUGHTS

What do you want your environment to say to children and their families? How can you make it say "Welcome! I care. This is a place for you."? As you arrange the learning environment you create children's experiences, write their textbook, design a learning laboratory. Through it you will be showing families that you know how to do your job, and you will meet children's needs. You will also create the tool that will help you do your job. And you are creating your own work environment.

Your home changes as you change. It reflects your needs, tastes, activity, and lifestyle. It grows with you and your family. Creating an environment for children and making it work is also a process of growth. It allows you to use your knowledge of children's development, your sensitivity in observation, and your creativity. As you gain greater skill and information, and as you devote time, energy, and resources to the environment, it will better meet children's needs. This kind of creation is a challenging and very satisfying aspect of the work of a teacher of young children.

Hard-Soft Softness changes the environment and what happens in it. Softness contributes to productivity, craftsmanship, motivation and morale, and lower absenteeism. Homes have soft furnishings, carpets, decorations, and lighting. Early childhood classrooms need to reflect softness of homes. Hard environments with indestructible materials like cement, unattractive colors, and harsh lighting are seen as serious and are created because the clients (children, prisoners, the public) are expected to damage vulnerable settings. You can soften an environment with comfortable furniture, pillows, rugs, grass, sand, furry animals, soft toys, sling and tire swings, dough, fingerpaint, clay, mud, and water. Warm, physical contact also softens the environments.

Open-Closed The degree to which the environment and materials restrict children is called Open-Closed. Children have changing needs for open and closed experiences. Materials can be viewed on a continuum with closed materials such as puzzles (which have only one right way of being used) on one end and open materials with unlimited alternatives on the other. Open materials inspire innovation. Open-closed does not mean good-bad. Materials that are closed can be rewarding when they provide both challenge and opportunities to succeed. Overly difficult materials cause frustration. Younger or less experienced children require more open materials. Older, more experienced children also need and enjoy open materials but enjoy closed challenges. When children appear bored or frustrated the cause might be in the balance of open/closed experiences.

Low Mobility–High Mobility Activities can be characterized by physical involvement and motion. High mobility involves active motion. Low mobility involves sedentary activities. It is important to provide opportunities for both. Early childhood programs should provide opportunities for movement and access to outdoor play. Quiet activities like painting, books, and table games can be provided outdoors where low mobility is often neglected.

Simple-Complex Materials can have one or more uses. *Simple* materials have one obvious use. They include: trikes, slides, puzzles, concept games like Snakes and Ladders. *Complex* materials allow children to use two different play materials together making play less predictable and more interesting; they hold children's attention for a longer period of time. They include: a sandbox with tools, blocks with props, collage with paint. *Super* materials offer the larger number of possibilities and hold children's attention much longer. They include: climbing structures with the addition of hollow blocks, sand with tools and water, dramatic play area equipped with furnishings, dress-up clothes, props, and dolls. Classrooms for inexperienced or less mature children need to be simple to help them focus and make choices. Older children can handle more complexity which can be added by materials or people.

Intrusion-Seclusion Who and what crosses boundaries between spaces is reflected in this dimension. Intrusion adds novelty and stimulation that enrich learning. Children learn from intrusion; from visitors, trips, and other experiences with the world outside the classroom. Seclusion from stimulation provides the opportunity to concentrate, think, and be alone. When opportunities for seclusion do not exist, children often create their own seclusion by hiding or by withdrawing emotionally. Tables or easels set up against walls provide partial seclusion, insulated spaces with protection on three sides, allow a small group to share privacy, hiding spaces, cozy closed places in crates, lofts or under a table allow children to escape the stimulus of the classroom.

Source: E. Jones, *Dimensions of Teaching Learning Environments: Handbook for Teachers.* (Pasadena, CA: Pacific Oaks, 1977).

FIGURE 8.4
Jones's dimensions of teaching-learning environments

IN PRACTICE

Infant-toddler learning environment checklist

This checklist can be used to evaluate an existing environment for children or to plan an environment. No program will have everything, but the * items are essential and are found in most high quality programs for young children.

Program name _____ **Date** _____

Number of staff _____ **Number of children** _____ **Age of children** _____

Use the following code as appropriate: + = present/exceptionally rich
√ = present/adequate   √− = minimal/inadequate   − = not present
n/a = not applicable to this environment

OVERALL ATMOSPHERE AND ARRANGEMENT

Room Arrangement*
_____ Well lit with natural light if possible*
_____ Drinking water, sinks, and toilets accessible*
_____ Sheltered from outside noise and stimulus*
_____ Orderly and attractive*

_____ Ventilated and temperature controlled*
_____ Separation for non-mobile children*
_____ Paths that don't lead through areas
_____ Separate play and rest areas*
_____ Separate storage for staff*

Activity Areas
_____ Area for sleeping*
_____ Area for diapering*
_____ Area for toileting*
For older toddlers and twos
_____ Block area*
_____ Library area*
_____ Dramatic play area*

_____ Area for seclusion
_____ An outside play environment

_____ Manipulative toy area*
_____ Art area

Organization & Maintenance
_____ Space for eating*
_____ Space for small groups to play (2–3 children)*
_____ Space for active play*
_____ Space for messy activities*
_____ Uncluttered shelf tops
_____ Environment cleaned each day

For older toddlers and twos
_____ Space for larger groups (3–8 children)

_____ Clean cages or aquariums for pets*
_____ Plants/animals fed, watered, protected*
_____ Equipment/materials complete/ working
_____ Equipment washable, can be sanitized

*Category/area is essential in all environments for infants and toddlers or item is essential in this area

Furniture

_____ Low, open shelves for each play area*

_____ Equipment for each play area*

_____ Comfortable, clean carpets*

_____ Toddler-sized tables and chairs

_____ Adult-sized chairs or sofa*

_____ High or closed shelves or closets for staff*

_____ Variety of levels for crawling and climbing

_____ A locked cabinet for hazardous materials*

Schedule

_____ Infants are allowed to regulate their own schedule*

_____ Toddlers' schedules are flexible with general times for predictable routines*

Aesthetics

_____ Orderly and attractive*

_____ Neutral color walls

_____ Patterns, colors, and storage coordinate

_____ No promotional or media products or characters

_____ Items of beauty such as flowers, plants, or sculpture provided

_____ Pictures and displays at infant and toddler eye level*

_____ Areas decorated with art prints, photographs, children's work, book covers, and displays

_____ Many pictures and displays at infant and toddler-carried eye level*

_____ Provision of appropriate music (e.g., soothing music for nap)*

ROUTINE AREAS

Entrance and Departure Area

Location & Space

_____ Located where families enter and exit

_____ Childsafe gates/doors

Materials

_____ A clock

Furniture

_____ Comfortable seating for adults*

_____ Cubby shelf for children's things

_____ Adult-height counter/table for dressing/undressing children

Organization & Maintenance

_____ Cubbies labeled with names and pictures*

_____ Bulletin boards and mailboxes for communication between families and staff.*

Food Preparation/Eating Area*

Location & Space

_____ Located in or near the room

_____ Clean-up equipment such as sponges, brooms, mops, etc.*

Furniture & Equipment

_____ Adult-height counter/table
for preparing food*

_____ Sink for washing hands and
rinsing dishes*

_____ Adult seating for comfortably
holding children*

_____ Necessary appliances
(refrigerator, stove or
microwave, washer/dryer)*

_____ Dishwasher or triple sink if
dishes washed*

Organization & Maintenance

_____ Hazardous equipment stored
in childsafe cupboards

_____ Shelves and cupboards
labeled to facilitate clean-up

_____ Poisons stored in locked
cupboards*

_____ Equipment and materials
stored in an orderly manner*

Materials & Supplies

_____ Clipboard or notebook to
record eating

_____ Pots, pans, etc., for cooking
and play*

For toddlers

_____ Toddler-sized tables and chairs

Sleeping Area*

Location & Space

_____ Located near the play room*

Materials

_____ Mirrors, pictures, etc.
where children can see them*

Furniture

_____ Cribs for infants*

_____ Storage for blankets and toys
from home

_____ Mats or cots for toddlers*

_____ Storage shelves/bins for linens*

_____ Rocking chair*

Organization

_____ Equipment and materials
stored in an orderly manner

_____ Shelves and cupboards
labeled to facilitate clean-up

_____ Clipboard or notebook to
record sleeping

Changing/Toileting Area*

Location & Space

_____ Located next to or near the
play room*

_____ Low toilets and sinks for
toddlers or stepstools to make
toilets and sinks accessible*

_____ Adult-height sinks for adults,
with warm water for hand
washing

_____ A lidded garbage can for soiled
diapers*

Organization & Maintenance

_____ A supply of plastic bags for
soiled diapers and clothes*

_____ Area clean and pleasant and
sanitized daily*

_____ Sanitizing spray and paper for
changing surfaces*

_____ A shelf above or beside
changing table for easy
organization, locked for
ointments, etc.*

_____ Clipboard or notebook to
record diapering/toileting*

Furniture
_____ Adult-height counter or
changing table*
Materials & Supplies
_____ Labeled boxes or bins for each
child's diapers and clothes*

PLAY AREAS

Sensory Play* (sensory play will take place throughout the room)
Location & Space
_____ Within classroom close to   _____ Washable/non-staining floors*
sinks/washing up facilities*
Furniture
_____ Toddler-sized table and chairs   _____ Toddler-sized watertable
for messy play
Materials
_____ Mirrors (unbreakable)*   _____ Wall hangings (textured and
_____ Music boxes   touchable)
_____ Record/tape player and   _____ Sand/water play with lots of
recordings*   containers*
_____ Non-toxic materials such as
cornmeal and flour
Organization
_____ Materials orderly and attractive _____ Duplicates of items and 2–3
_____ Containers labeled with   choices per child
pictures   _____ Sets stored separately, not
jumbled

For infants and young toddlers
_____ Mobiles   _____ "Peek-a-boo" toys
_____ Jack-in-the-box   _____ Rattles and bells
_____ Squeeze toys   _____ Toys for sucking and teething
_____ Texture balls
For toddlers and twos
_____ Rhythm instruments   _____ Paint
_____ Clay and dough   _____ Soap and goop

Manipulative Play
Location & Space   _____ Push and pull toys
_____ Within classroom   _____ Nesting containers (plastic
_____ Enough space for at least two   bowls, cups)
children to work*   _____ Dumping containers
(baskets, buckets)
Furniture
_____ Low, open shelves for storage   _____ Comfortable carpets or mats
of materials*

Materials
_____ Shape sorting boxes   _____ Pop-up toys
_____ Large snap beads   _____ Containers and shelves labeled
_____ Stacking toys   with pictures
_____ Boxes with lids   _____ Busy boxes
For toddlers and twos
_____ Jumbo wood beads with strings
Organization
_____ Shelves close to work space*   _____ Pegboards and pegs (jumbo
_____ Materials uncluttered and   size)
       orderly*   _____ Simple-to-put-together toys
_____ Sets of toys stored separately,   _____ Complete puzzles with 1–8
       not jumbled*   pieces*

Library
Location & Space
_____ Lighting even so shadows do   _____ Decorated with art prints, book
       not fall on pages*   covers, posters
Furniture
_____ Clean pillows and carpets   _____ Big comfortable chair or couch
Books and Materials
_____ Cloth or cardboard picture books*   _____ Multiethnic and multiage
_____ Picture collections (mounted   non-stereotyped characters*
       and covered)   _____ Not based on commercial
_____ A variety of styles of illustration*   products
_____ Homemade books with   _____ Nursery rhymes
       photographs of the children   _____ Wordless books and books
       and things they know*   with text
_____ New and classic books   _____ Mood and concept books*
For toddlers and twos
_____ Low bookshelf that displays   _____ Sturdy books that are not board
       covers   books
_____ Simple stories with plots
Organization & Maintenance
_____ Books are in good condition*   _____ Books are neat and orderly*

Large Muscle Play*
Location & Space
_____ Within classroom and outside
Materials & Equipment
_____ Riding toys to propel by feet   _____ Cars and trucks
_____ Small climber with slide   _____ Wagons and buggies to push
_____ Tunnel (purchased or   and pull
       homemade)   _____ Soft balls of various sizes
_____ Large boxes to crawl through   _____ Soft pillows to climb on
Furniture
_____ Carpets or mats to cushion falls   _____ Steps, stable sofas, cruise bars,
                                                      platforms, or climbers*

Organization

_____ Duplicates of toys
and several choices (2–3)
per child

_____ Materials arranged neatly
_____ Different materials are stored
separately, not jumbled up

Outside Environment*

Location & Space

_____ Space to run and play*
_____ Fenced for protection*
_____ Gates have childsafe locks*
_____ Hard surface for vehicles away
from other play
_____ Natural features such as
boulders, hills, and trees
_____ Access to toilets and sinks*
_____ Shelter from sun, wind, rain*

_____ Sand and dirt for digging*
_____ Located near the classroom
_____ Levels and textures to touch,
crawl, climb on*
_____ Comfortable places to sit and lie*
_____ Access to water for drinking
and play*
_____ Separation for non-mobile
children*

Materials & Supplies

_____ Clean sand in plentiful supply*
_____ Clean water in plentiful supply*

_____ Toys arranged in an orderly
and attractive manner

Equipment

_____ Portable equipment for
climbing
_____ Equipment for climbing,
sliding, swinging with safe
surfacing underneath and to 6'
beyond (10" sand, woodchips,
etc., or 2" rubber matting)*
_____ Large playground balls that
bounce*
_____ Hoops, parachutes, rope, cones
_____ Water play toys (cups/spoons,
basters, funnels, pitchers,
tubing, water wheels, etc.)
_____ Sand toys (cups/spoons, pots
cars, buckets, trowels, etc.)
_____ Wading pool

_____ A line/rack to hang clothes and
art work
_____ A covered sandbox or alternative
_____ Wagons and buggies to push
and pull
_____ Toddler height sand/water
table or tub
_____ Shed or other secure storage
for outdoor supplies
_____ Natural or manufactured
balance beams
_____ Mud toys (shovels, pots, etc.
pans, buckets, trowels)
_____ Riding toys to propel by feet
_____ Storage for vehicles

For toddlers and twos

_____ Space for dramatic play
_____ Tables for outdoor table
activities

_____ Space for art
_____ Wheeled pushing, pulling, and
child-sized riding vehicles

Organization & Maintenance

_____ Water, sand, mud toys separate
from one another

_____ Storage near the sand, water,
mud areas for toys* labeled
with pictures and words

AREAS FOR OLDER TODDLERS AND TWOS

Block Area

Location & Space

_____ Space for 2–4 children to work*

_____ Posters or photographs of buildings

Furniture

_____ Low, open shelves where blocks can be stored*

_____ Low napped carpet or clean floor*

Materials

_____ Unit blocks (100 blocks in 5–10 shapes)

_____ Large figures (animals/people) and vehicles

_____ At least 20 cardboard, plastic, or light wood hollow blocks

_____ Table blocks

_____ Large soft blocks

Organization

_____ Blocks stored in an orderly fashion*

_____ Shelves labeled with pictures

_____ Blocks clean and unsplintered

Art Area

Location & Space

_____ Located near sink or water source*

_____ Floor is washable/non-staining

_____ Inside or outside if climate permits daily use

Furniture

_____ Painting surfaces—table, wall, or easel (toddler-sized)

_____ Low tables and chairs*

Materials & Supplies

_____ Tempera paints in at least primary colors (red, yellow, blue), black, and white*

_____ Brushes in a variety of sizes: wide and narrow with long and short handles*

_____ Base or paint for finger painting*

_____ Dough boards and tools*

_____ Large paper for easel painting*

_____ White paper, clean on one side*

_____ Recycled materials (card, styrofoam, paper, ribbons, fabric, plastic jars and lids)*

_____ Large non-toxic unwrapped crayons and felt pens

_____ Food color

_____ Bowls, spoons, and measuring tools

_____ Wide-weave fabric

_____ Collection of textured materials (fabrics, etc.)

_____ Yarn, string, ribbons

_____ Smocks or old shirts (to protect clothing)*

_____ Clay boards and clay tools*

_____ Special papers (construction, tissue)

_____ Trays and plastic cups or containers*

_____ Blunt playdough

_____ Potter's clay*

_____ Playdough*

_____ White glue and paste*

Organization
_____ Storage shelves close to table/
easel
_____ Brushes clean and stored
upright

_____ Materials orderly and attractive*
_____ Floor and table coverings
(plastic or old tablecloths)
available

Dramatic Play Center
Location & Space
_____ Space for 4 children to work*

Furniture
_____ Child-sized table and chairs*
_____ Sturdy "bed" for a child
and dolls

_____ Open shelves for storage*
_____ Small cupboard
_____ Full-length unbreakable mirror

Materials
_____ Clothes and props reflect
children's families*
_____ Uniforms, clothes, and props
that reflect a variety of cultures,
jobs, and fantasy roles*
_____ Two telephones*

_____ Pots and pans
_____ Unbreakable dishes
_____ Large wooden or plastic
utensils
_____ Pictures depicting family life
and other scenes

Organization & Maintenance
_____ Clutter minimized*
_____ Props and costumes
stored in an orderly fashion*

_____ Duplicates of items and several
choices (2–3) per child
_____ Extra props stored and rotated

IN PRACTICE

Preschool/primary learning environment checklist

No program will have everything. Items with * are essential and found in most high quality programs.

Program name _____ **Date** _____
Number of staff _____ **Number of children** _____ **Age of children** _____

Use the following code as appropriate:
√ = present/adequate   + = present/exceptionally rich
√− = minimal/inadequate   − = not present
n/a = not applicable to this environment

OVERALL ATMOSPHERE AND ARRANGEMENT

Room Arrangement

_____ Arranged in learning centers*
_____ Arranged for easy supervision
_____ Noisy and quiet areas are separate
_____ Paths do not lead through centers*
_____ All areas useful (no "dead" space)*

_____ Sheltered from outside noise and stimulus
_____ Well lit* with natural light if possible
_____ Ventilated* and temperature controlled
_____ Drinking water, sinks, and toilets accessible*

Learning Centers/Areas

_____ Unit block*
_____ Hollow block
_____ Library*
_____ Dramatic play*
_____ Manipulative toy/game*
_____ Art*

_____ Writing (may be in art)
_____ Inquiry (science, math, social studies)
_____ Private area for children
_____ An outside play environment*

Organization & Maintenance

_____ Each center has equipment/materials complete, working, and in good condition
_____ Space for large group gathering*
_____ Space for messy activities*
_____ Space for active play*
_____ Space for eating snacks/meals (may be in cafeteria for primary children)

_____ Space for resting (* in full-day programs)
_____ Shelf tops are uncluttered
_____ Pets have clean cages or aquariums*
_____ Plants and animals are fed, have water, and are protected*
_____ Space for small group gathering

*Category/area is essential in all environments for children age 3 through 8 or item is essential in this area

Furniture*

_____ Low, open shelves for each center*

_____ Comfortable, clean carpets

_____ Low tables and child-sized chairs

_____ Adult-sized chair or sofa

_____ Chairs and tables for all children in the class

_____ High or closed shelves or closets for staff*

_____ A locked cabinet for hazardous materials*

Aesthetics*

_____ Orderly and attractive*

_____ Neutral wall color

_____ Patterns, colors, and storage coordinates

_____ Areas decorated with art prints, photographs, children's work, book covers, and displays

_____ Provision of appropriate music (e.g., soothing music for nap)

_____ No promotional, or media products or characters

_____ Items of beauty such as flowers, plants, or sculpture

_____ Most pictures and displays at child's eye level*

Schedule*

_____ Includes large blocks of time (at least 1 hour in morning and afternoon) for child-selected activity in both learning centers and outside*

CLASSROOM AREAS

Unit Block Center*

Location & Space

_____ Enough space for at least 4 children to work*

Furniture

_____ Low, open shelves for storage of blocks*

Organization & Maintenance

_____ Blocks stored in an orderly fashion*

_____ Blocks clean and unsplintered

For primary children

_____ At least 200 blocks, at least 15 shapes

Materials

_____ At least 100 hardwood unit blocks* for small areas (1–4 children); 200 or more for larger areas

_____ Posters or photographs of buildings

_____ Low napped carpet or clean floor*

_____ Shelves labeled with pictures and words

_____ Additional props such as signs

_____ Paper and pens for writing signs

_____ At least 10 shapes

_____ Figures and vehicles as props*

Hollow Block Center
Location & Space
_____ Enough space for at least 4 children to work*
_____ Inside, on a covered porch, or outside

_____ Located near dramatic play area for more diverse and cross-gender play
_____ Posters or photographs

Furniture
_____ Space for all blocks to be stacked easily*

_____ Low napped carpet or clean floor*

Materials
_____ At least 15 hollow blocks* and 6 planks
_____ At least 3 shapes

_____ Hats, sheets, and lengths of fabric as props*

Organization & Maintenance
_____ Blocks stored in an orderly fashion*
_____ Blocks clean and unsplintered

_____ Shelves labeled with pictures and words

Dramatic Play Center*
Location & Space
_____ Within classroom and additional center outdoors*
_____ Enough space for at least 4 children to work*

_____ Located near hollow block area for more diverse and cross-gender play

Furniture
_____ Child-sized table and chairs*
_____ Low, open shelf to hold props*
_____ Small cupboard with doors
_____ Pretend stove/sink unit

_____ Clothes rack
_____ Full-length unbreakable mirror
_____ Sturdy "bed" to hold a child and dolls

Materials
_____ Clothes and props reflecting children's families*
_____ Uniforms, clothes, and props reflecting various cultures, jobs, and fantasy roles*
_____ Two telephones*

_____ Pots and pans
_____ Unbreakable dishes and utensils
_____ Props for multiage pretend play
_____ Pictures depicting family life and other scenes

Organization & Maintenance
_____ Clutter minimized*
_____ Extra props stored in kits and rotated with children's interests and themes

_____ Props and costumes stored in an orderly fashion*
_____ Shelves and racks labeled with pictures and words

For primary children
_____ Prop boxes accessible to children
_____ Hand-held mirror

_____ Boxes, etc., for children to create stage sets

Art Center*
Location & Space
_____ Located near sink or water source*
_____ Floor is washable/non-staining

_____ Inside or outside if climate permits daily use

Furniture
_____ An easel adjusted so the smallest child can reach the top of one side*

_____ Low tables and chairs*

Materials & Supplies
_____ Tempera paints in at least primary colors, black, and white*
_____ Brushes in a variety of sizes*
_____ Wide-weave fabric
_____ Clay boards and clay tools
_____ Non-toxic felt pens*
_____ Unwrapped non-toxic crayons*
_____ Watercolors
_____ Playdough
_____ Large paper for easel painting*
_____ Scissors for either hand
_____ Dough boards and tools
_____ Recycled materials (cardboard, styrofoam, wrapping paper, fabric, plastic jars and lids)*
_____ Collection of textured materials and fabric

_____ Yarn, string, ribbons
_____ Smocks or old shirts (to protect clothing)
_____ Base or paint for finger painting*
_____ Food color
_____ Potter's clay*
_____ White glue and paste*
_____ White paper, clean on one side*
_____ Trays and plastic cups or containers*
_____ Bowls, spoons, and measuring tools
_____ Special papers (construction, tissue)

Organization & Maintenance
_____ Floor/table coverings available
_____ Materials orderly and attractive*
_____ Storage shelves close to tables/easels*
For primary children
_____ Pencil crayons

_____ Brushes clean and stored upright
_____ Containers and shelves labeled

_____ Oil-base modeling clay

Library*
Location & Space
_____ Lighting even so no shadows fall on pages*

_____ Decorated with book jackets/ posters and reading-related art prints

Furniture
_____ Low bookshelf that displays covers*
_____ Comfortable, clean pillows and carpets or chairs where children can sit and read*

_____ Big, comfortable chair or couch where an adult can sit with a child and read

Organization & Maintenance

_____ Books are in good condition*   _____ Books uncluttered and orderly*

Books

_____ Appropriate for developmental   _____ Not based on commercial
stage*   products

_____ A variety of styles of   _____ Fiction: realistic and fantasy*
illustration*   _____ Informational books*

_____ Multiethnic and multiage   _____ Mood and concept books*
characters in non-   _____ Poetry*
stereotyped roles*   _____ New and classic books*

_____ Females and males in various   _____ Child-authored books
roles*

In primary school environments

_____ Listening center with book-   _____ Big books and a big-book shelf
tape sets

Writing Center (* in primary classrooms)

Location & Space

_____ Even lighting so shadows   _____ Decorated with writing
do not fall on work*   samples, posters, etc.

Furniture

_____ Low tables and chairs*

Materials & Supplies

_____ Peeled crayons*   _____ Sharpened primary pencils*

_____ Non-toxic felt marking pens*   _____ Paper cut in uniform sizes*

_____ Hole punch   _____ Yarn

_____ Rulers, protractors   _____ Recycled envelopes

Organization & Maintenance

_____ Baskets, jars, or cans for pens,   _____ Storage shelves close to table*
crayons, etc.*   _____ Materials stored in an orderly

_____ Containers and shelves labeled   manner*

In primary school environments

_____ Pencils and thin wax crayons   _____ Lined paper

_____ Dictionary or word file   _____ Staplers

Inquiry Centers*

Location & Space

_____ Located near electric outlets*   _____ Located near sink

_____ Located near window*

Furniture

_____ Water/sand table* (may be   _____ Low table or counter*
found outside or in messy
play area—tubs/basins may be
used instead)

General materials

_____ Sorting trays*
_____ Plastic tubs and pitchers*
_____ Measuring cups/spoons
_____ Balance and scale
_____ Photographs and posters to illustrate concepts

_____ Trays*
_____ Information books* (may be found in library)
_____ Sorting collections (buttons, rocks, etc.)

Math materials

_____ Materials with sequence and proportion
_____ Attribute beads or blocks

_____ Concept games
_____ Colored cubes

Social studies materials

_____ Globes and maps
_____ Social studies games and puzzles

_____ Bulletin board displays
_____ Artifact collections

For primary children
_____ Tools like knives and scissors

Science materials

_____ Magnifying glass*
_____ Machinery to investigate and disassemble

_____ Aquariums and animal cages
_____ Airtight containers for storage
_____ Probes

Woodworking Center

Location & Space

_____ Located so it can be supervised*

_____ Located where it is non-disruptive*

Furniture

_____ Low, sturdy table for woodworking*

_____ Tools arranged in an orderly manner (e.g., a storage rack labeled with pictures and words)*

Materials & Supplies

_____ Small working hammers, saws, drills, vise*

_____ Wide-headed nails*
_____ Soft wood scraps*

Organization & Maintenance

_____ Storage boxes for wood pieces*

_____ Storage rack for tools close to table*

Manipulative Toy Area*

Location & Space

_____ Within classroom

_____ Space for at least 2 children*

Furniture

_____ Low, open shelves for storage of materials*

_____ Comfortable carpet or low tables and chairs*

Materials

_____ A variety of materials requiring different skills*

_____ Complete puzzles with 8–25 pieces*

In primary school environments

_____ Puzzles with 25–100 pieces

_____ Large sets with wheels, gears, etc.

_____ Several choices for every child the area accommodates (2–3 per child)*

_____ Directions and patterns to use with toys

Organization & Maintenance

_____ Shelves located close to work space*

_____ Multi-piece sets stored separately, not jumbled*

_____ Containers and shelves labeled

_____ Materials uncluttered, orderly*

_____ Trays or space where children can save and display completed work

Outside Environment*

Location & Space

_____ Space to run and play*

_____ Fenced for protection*

_____ Located near the classroom

_____ Hard surface for vehicles away from other play

_____ Comfortable places to sit and lie

_____ Access to water for drinking and play

_____ Space for art and woodworking

_____ Plants, grass*

_____ Sand and dirt for digging*

_____ Gates have childsafe locks*

_____ Space for group play

_____ Natural features such as boulders, hills, and trees

_____ A place to garden

_____ Access to toilets and sinks

_____ Shelter from sun, wind, rain

_____ Space for dramatic play

Equipment

_____ Play structures for climbing, sliding, swinging*

_____ Surfacing underneath and to 6′ beyond structures (10″ sand, woodchips, etc., or 2″ rubber matting)*

_____ Tables for outdoor table activities*

_____ Wading pool

_____ A covered sandbox or appropriate alternative*

_____ Trikes and wagons sized for the children*

_____ Sand/water table or large tub*

_____ Portable equipment for building and climbing

_____ A line/rack to hang clothes and art work

Materials & Supplies

_____ Clean sand in plentiful supply*
_____ Clean water in plentiful supply*
_____ Natural or manufactured
balance beams*
_____ Materials to encourage active
play: hoops, parachutes,
rope
_____ Sand toys (cups/spoons, pots,
cars, buckets, trowels, etc.)

_____ Large balls that bounce*
_____ Hoses and big buckets*
_____ Water play toys (cups/spoons,
basters, funnels, pitchers,
tubing, water wheels, etc.)
_____ Kits for bubble play
_____ Mud toys (shovels, pots and
pans, buckets, trowels)

Organization & Maintenance

_____ Water, sand, mud toys separate
from one another
_____ Baskets and bags for ball
storage
_____ Shed or other secure storage
for outdoor supplies*
_____ Storage for trikes and wagons*

_____ Storage near the sand, water,
mud areas for toys* labeled
with pictures and words
_____ Parking area for vehicles near
the riding surface
_____ Toys stored in an orderly and
attractive manner

For primary children

_____ Cargo nets and ropes
_____ Bikes and scooters
_____ Equipment for organized games

_____ Hard surfaces for hopscotch,
jump rope, etc.

PROJECTS

A Child's Eye View: Observe a classroom from a child's perspective by kneeling or sitting on a low chair. Observe from this viewpoint from the entrance and the interest centers. Write down all that you can see in each location. Go back to each position and observe it again from your regular height. Write a short (three- to five-page) paper in which you describe your experience. How did you experience the environment differently when viewed from a child's perspective? What did you learn about this classroom? What did you learn about the design of environments for children? What changes would you make in this classroom based on your experience? If you are working with children, use your own classroom, make changes, and report on what happens.

Dream Program: Imagine that you have the resources to create a perfect early childhood learning environment. Select the age and number of children in the class. Using the principles you have read about in this chapter, plan an ideal environment for them. Make a diagram of the indoor and outdoor space. You may wish to create a shoe box model. Go through educational supply catalogues and select equipment and materials you would purchase and plan the equipment and materials you would find or create. Describe your environment and explain your decisions in terms of children's needs and your values and your goals. Explain how you will address features of *Dimensions of Teaching-Learning Environments* in your environment.

Environment Observation: Visit an early childhood program and observe the environments in one classroom for the same age children. Complete the Learning Environment Checklist. Write a short (three- to five-page) paper with your evaluation. What is present and what is missing? Analyze the strength of the environment in supporting children's physical, creative, language, and cognitive development. Decide in what ways it is appropriate for the age and needs of the children. Sketch a floor plan of the environment. You may wish to include a few photographs. Discuss your thoughts about the environment and how you might change or modify it to better support children. Summarize your personal feelings about the environment you observed.

Environment Comparison: Repeat the preceding assignment in another classroom of children of the same age. Compare and contrast the two.

BIBLIOGRAPHY

Bredekamp, S. 1987. *Developmentally Appropriate Practice in Early Childhood Programs Serving Children from Birth Through Age 8.* Washington, DC: National Association for the Education of Young Children. Expanded Ed.

Bredekamp, S., ed. 1991. *Accreditation Criteria & Procedures*. Washington, DC: National Association for the Education of Young Children.

Burns, M. S., L. Goin, and J. T. Donlon. 1990. A Computer in My Room. *Young Children* 45(2):62–67.

Chandler, P. A. 1994. *A Place For Me: Including Children with Special Needs in Early Care and Education Settings*. Washington DC: National Association for the Education of Young Children.

Chun, R. 1994. *Capturing Childhood's Magic: Creating Outdoor Play Environments for Hawaii's Young Children*. Honolulu, HI: Hawaii Association for the Education of Young Children.

Click, P. 1994. *Caring for School-Age Children*. Albany, NY: Delmar.

Consumer Products Safety Commission. 1991. *Public Playground Handbook for Safety*. Washington, DC: Government Printing Office.

Crosser, S. 1992. Managing the Early Childhood Classroom. *Young Children* 47(2):23–29.

Feeney, S., and M. Magarick. 1984. Choosing Good Toys for Young Children. *Young Children* 40(1):7–15.

Feeney, S., and E. Moravcik. 1987. A Thing of Beauty: Aesthetic Development and Young Children. *Young Children* 42(6):7–15.

Frost, J. L. 1992. *Play and Playscapes*. Albany, NY: Delmar.

Frost, J. L., and S. C. Wortham. 1988. The Evolution of American Playgrounds. *Young Children* 43(5):19–27.

Gandini, L. 1984. Not Just Anywhere: Making Child Care Centers into Particular Places. *Beginnings* Summer: 3–8.

Gareau, M., and C. Kennedy. 1991. Structure Time & Space To Promote Pursuit of Learning in the Primary Grades. *Young Children* 46(4):46–50.

Gonzalez-Mena, J., and D. W. Eyer. 1989. *Infants, Toddlers, and Caregivers*. Mountain View, CA: Mayfield Publishing.

Greenman, J. 1988. *Caring Spaces, Learning Places: Children's Environments That Work*. Redmond, WA: Exchange Press.

Gross, D. W. 1972. Equipping a Classroom for Young Children. *Ideas that Work with Young Children*. Washington, DC: National Association for the Education of Young Children.

Harms, T., and R. Clifford. 1980. *Early Childhood Environment Rating Scale*. New York: Teachers College Press.

Haugland, S. W., and D. D. Shade. 1988. Developmentally Appropriate Software for Young Children. *Young Children* 43(4):37–43.

Henniger, M. L. 1994. Planning for Outdoor Play. *Young Children* 49(4): 10–15.

Hignett, W. F. 1988. Infant/Toddler Day Care, Yes; But We'd Better Make It Good. *Young Children* 44(1):32–33.

Hill, D. M. 1977. *Mud, Sand and Water*. Washington, DC: National Association for the Education of Young Children.

Hirsch, E. 1984. *The Block Book*. Washington, DC: National Association for the Education of Young Children.

Jones, E. 1977. *Dimensions of Teaching-Learning Environments: Handbook for Teachers*. Pasadena, CA: Pacific Oaks.

Jones, E., and E. Prescott. 1978. *Dimensions of Teaching-Learning Environments II: Focus on Daycare*. Pasadena, CA: Pacific Oaks.

Koralek, D. G., L. J. Colker, et al. 1993. *The What, Why, and How of High Quality Early Childhood Education: A Guide for On-Site Supervision*. Washington, DC: National Association for the Education of Young Children.

Kritchevsky, S., E. Prescott, et al. 1969. *Physical Space: Planning Environments for Young Children*. Washington, DC: National Association for the Education of Young Children.

National Association for the Education of Young Children. 1993. The Effects of Group Size Ratios and Staff Training on Child Care Quality. *Young Children* 48(2):65–67.

Phillips, D. A. 1987. *Quality in Childcare: What Does Research Tell Us?* Washington, DC: National Association for the Education of Young Children.

Prescott, E. 1978. Is Day Care as Good as a Good Home? *Young Children* 33(2):16–23.

Readdick, C. A. 1993. Solitary Pursuits: Supporting Children's Privacy Needs in Group Settings. *Young Children* 49(1):60–64.

Sommer, R. 1969. *Personal Space: The Behavioral Basis for Design*. Englewood Cliffs, NJ: Prentice Hall.

Stone, J. G. 1970. *Play and Playgrounds*. Washington, DC: National Association for the Education of Young Children.

Stonehouse, A., ed. 1990. *Trusting Toddlers: Planning for One- to Three-Year-Olds in Child Care Centers*. St. Paul, MN: Toys 'n Things Press.

CHAPTER NINE

Relationships and Guidance

Nothing I have ever learned of value was taught to me by an ogre. Nothing do I regret more in my life than that my teachers were not my friends. Nothing ever heightened my being or deepened my learning more than being loved.

J. T. Dillon

This chapter is about some of the most critical aspects of working in an early childhood program: developing positive relationships with children, managing a classroom to support learning and relationships, and handling the conflicts that inevitably occur among young children. In it we focus on approaches that enhance children's self-concepts and help them to learn to live and work productively in group settings.

Creating caring, supportive relationships with children is one of your most essential and rewarding tasks as an early childhood educator. Your skill in building relationships and providing guidance will influence children's self-concepts, determine the quality of their experiences, influence their learning and relationships with others, and contribute to their deciding if school is a safe and trustworthy place. Although most children enter early childhood programs with lively and inquisitive minds, only some come to feel good about themselves, love learning, and regard education as a rewarding experience. When you base what you do on genuine appreciation and respect for children and sound knowledge of development and early education, children are likely to retain the eagerness and curiosity with which they enter your program.

VALUES AND BELIEFS

Relationships and the ways practitioners guide young children are based on values and beliefs widely held by early childhood educators, including the authors of this text. We value childhood and believe children have a right to be childlike. We try to understand how children's development affects their behavior. We gear expectations to reflect how children grow and learn. We know that children learn through experiences appropriate to individual age, temperament, interest, culture, and learning style.

Respect for children, families, colleagues, and self is a core early childhood value. It effects every aspect of the program. Early childhood practitioners share a fundamental belief that the quality of relationships is critical. Because of this, they are attentive to relationships with children, families, and staff and evaluate guidance strategies to see whether they are supportive of relationships. Time and attention are given to social and emotional development because they are as important as the development of concepts and skills.

Early childhood educators also believe that children must construct knowledge, including social knowledge. Children learn about relationships through being part of a group and interacting with people and the environment. They learn through play and exploration. Children and adults in early childhood programs are given freedom to make choices and responsibility to respect others. They are not asked to blindly obey rules. Instead, they are given opportunities to make choices that exercise social learning and moral development. This demonstrates trust that every child can learn to be a cooperative, productive person.

SELF-CONCEPT

As children develop, they form concepts about the world and how it works. They also form concepts about themselves. *Self-concept* is the total picture children have about themselves, based on their perceptions and on what others tell them. Self-concept includes perceptions of the physical self, social and cognitive qualities, and competence. It influences children's ability to develop meaningful relationships with people, ideas, and the physical world.

Children's self-concepts are subject to change. They are greatly influenced by the "mirror" held up by significant people in their lives— family members, peers, and other adults. Self-concept begins to develop in the first days of life and continues to build and change. Families are children's first and most influential sources of information about who they are. It is from families that children begin to establish their identities as individuals of a gender, race, and culture.

Self-esteem, a child's internal appraisal of his or her own worth, is also based on the

messages that families give. Children learn whether their identity is desirable or undesirable, whether they are acceptable or not. Their first appraisal of their potential and whether they are likely to succeed also comes from their families. Indeed, low self-esteem seems to be "catching." When family members judge themselves negatively, they tend to judge their children negatively, and eventually children may judge themselves the same way. Affectionate care and attention from adults who feel good about themselves help children to conclude that they are attractive, competent people.

One of the goals of early childhood education is to help children develop strong, positive, and realistic self-concepts. This is not the same as encouraging narcissism, which is excessive preoccupation with oneself to the exclusion of others. Instead, it means helping children appreciate who they are and what they can do and to accept what they are still learning to do.

As an early childhood educator, you will be a significant person who has the power to influence children's self-concept and who can help families view their children positively. What you do, how you do it, and when you do it can be of great importance in children's perceptions of themselves as competent and attractive.

For you to be able to enhance the self-concept of children, you must yourself possess a positive self-concept.

> Affirmation of self precedes affirmation of others, and an authentic adult can do much to induce and bolster a child's affirmation of himself by displaying rich and open feelings toward him, by showing unyielding confidence in him, and by providing and sharing with him genuine human encounters. (Yamamoto 1972, 17)

You need not view yourself as perfect in order to have a positive self-concept. We all have self-doubts and awareness of our own faults. Instead you must appreciate your strengths, acknowledge your weaknesses, and have an inner acceptance of who you are. If you are unable to accept yourself, you will have difficulty being truly accepting of children, however much you may want to help them.

*Enhancing Se
and Self-Estee*

Self-concept and s _____ the experiences childr _____ early childhood programs. Viewed broadly, this entire book is about experiences that enhance children's self-concepts. Children come to accept and appreciate themselves in a positive social climate in which you help children to know that they are worthwhile and respected. You arrange environments to provide positive experiences and encourage independence and responsibility. You create routines to ensure each child feels safe, secure, and capable. You design curriculum in which every child has the opportunity to be challenged and successful. Most importantly, you relate to children, manage the group, and deal with interpersonal problems in ways that help children view themselves positively.

At different ages and stages, educators use different techniques to help children to develop positive self-concept. Frequent, affectionate physical and verbal contact, responsiveness to a baby's needs, and the provision of attractive, appropriate materials provide a sense of being

valued. A comfortable environment with many safe yeses and few noes, with enough toys, laps, and hugs, and a positive view of their struggle to explore and do things for themselves help toddlers to feel good about themselves. Preschoolers come to have a positive self-concept when they are valued for what they can do, are given many opportunities to do things for themselves and lots of interesting things to do, and are forgiven for their lapses into asocial behavior. Lots of affectionate contact and adults who appreciate them, respect them, and provide clear limits complete the picture. Primary school children feel good about themselves as they take on more and more real and meaningful learning and work. They respond well to guidance from warm, consistent adults who appreciate their abilities and worth.

A critical part of your task in guidance is to develop knowledge, skills, and sensitivity so that your efforts are appropriate for the individual and supportive of children's positive sense of themselves. If you work with infants and toddlers, they are developing their initial sense of self. Your primary guidance task will be to help them to feel safe, secure, and lovable—the foundation of positive self-concept and self-esteem. Preschoolers and older children are developing their sense of themselves in terms of their relationships with other people and the world. As you work with them, you will help them to see themselves as competent, worthwhile, and productive. Young children's sense

Reflect and write about . . .

how you feel about yourself

Recall an experience at school that made you feel good or bad about yourself. What happened? What role did your teacher play? How did this effect how you felt about school, your teacher, and learning?

of self is inextricably linked to their sense of family and culture. Acknowledging and appreciating children's backgrounds supports their sense of self.

Young children need educators who accept them as they are and who encourage them to value and positively evaluate themselves. It is not necessary to love all the children you work with all the time, nor is it realistic to expect to. It is essential, however, to

---

IN PRACTICE

Ways to enhance self-concept and self-esteem

Help Children Feel Likable and Appreciated

- Make positive contact with every child often each day.
- Give each child smiles, hugs, a hand on a shoulder, or a pat on the back. Infants and toddlers need to snuggle and have close physical contact.
- Be sensitive to feelings and aware of cultural values relating to touching and eye contact.
- Avoid giving excessive attention to some children and limited attention to others.
- Give genuine encouragement and acknowledge children's strengths. Avoid insincere or manipulative praise.
- Consciously and obviously appreciate differences.

Help Children Feel Competent and Capable

- Allow children to do things themselves.
- Be promptly responsive to infants' and toddlers' needs, requests, and communication—they feel competent if they have an effect.
- Provide appropriate challenges and many guaranteed successes. Ap-

preciate attempts and near misses as well as successes. Show that you noticed!
- Store materials so children can help themselves whenever possible.
- Recognize children's accomplishments.
- Identify positive behavior (catch them being good).
- Avoid criticism. Talk about mistakes as learning opportunities.
- Tell children what they can do rather than saying "no" or what they can't do.
- Admit it when you make a mistake.
- Emphasize a range of skills (social, creative, physical, verbal, intellectual).
- Teach strategies for success (e.g., turn the puzzle piece so it's easier to see).
- Resist the urge to label children's work (good, bad, etc.). Allow children to evaluate themselves.

Demonstrate Respect for Child and Family

- Have positive relationships with family members. Greet them by name.

- Express a sense of trust in children verbally and through your actions.
- Acknowledge children's needs, fears, and concerns as legitimate.
- Provide choices for children.
- Ask for children's thoughts, ideas, and opinions and listen to them attentively.
- Crouch or sit at children's level when you talk with them.
- Notice and accept the way a child looks, feels, responds, and thinks by saying things like, "Max likes to play his way."

- Follow the guidelines and rules you expect children to follow.
- Be flexible and willing to try alternatives.
- Accept security items such as blankets and stuffed animals in the classroom.
- Provide quiet space in the classroom where a child can be alone.
- Allow children to pass or observe an activity if they prefer.

communicate genuine respect and caring. The suggestions in the In Practice box give ideas for practical ways you can help young children develop positive self-concept and self-esteem.

These strategies can help a child who enters a program with negative feelings about themselves to exit with a more positive view. We recall 3½-year-old Becky, who started preschool unspeaking, thumb-sucking, and unwilling to engage with children or attempt simple activities. She responded to most activities with a defeated "I can't." Her teachers encouraged her, allowed her time, and made sure she had an opportunity to try activities. They noted what she could do well and sent other children to her as a resource. Becky gradually became more comfortable, gained friends, and spent less time sleepily sucking her thumb. By the end of the year she was a quiet but enthusiastic participant in the group.

BUILDING RELATIONSHIPS WITH CHILDREN

Caring and supportive relationships form a foundation from which children explore, create, discover, communicate, and relate to others. Research supports the view that good relationships are of primary importance in effective teaching (Gazda 1975). Good relationships between children and early childhood educators, like all good relationships, are characterized by honesty, empathy, respect, trust, and warmth. They are authentic and not forced or artificial. In good relationships children feel safe from fear of physical and psychological harm. No one can be productive when they feel threatened, anxious, or uncertain. Relationships and children's feelings about education, teachers, and learning can be irreparably damaged by tactics such as corporal punishment and humiliation.

The most effective early childhood educators we know like children, feel good about their work, and have clear, developmentally appropriate expectations of children. They enjoy and often share in young children's viewpoints and are playful. They gain children's willing cooperation without demanding unquestioning obedience. In fact, they welcome questions as signs of growth. They see children as partners, not adversaries, and view the process of helping children grow, through difficult as well as pleasant times, as central to their job.

Relationships

Since each child is unique, your relationship with each individual will be unique. You are also an individual, so you will have your own unique style of relating with and responding to children. With capable and confident children you may be exuberant and join their play. With hesitant or awkward children you may simply add an encouraging presence, a word of confidence, a touch, or a shared joy in success.

Early childhood educators who love their work genuinely enjoy relating to children. Relating to a child requires some special techniques and an investment of time and attention. Since there is a size difference that interferes with adult-child relationships, get down physically to the child's level. Because young children communicate through physical interaction as well as through words, consciously pay attention to smiles, facial expressions, sounds, body posture and tension, hugs, and touches.

There are no age limitations on relating to a young child. When you relate to infants and toddlers you communicate with your whole being—voice, body, and heart. A relationship with an infant involves being attentive and responsive to them by returning coos, smiles, and babbles. The best educators of that we know relate to even the youngest child with the respect they would use with a friend. They always explain what they are doing before they move a child and give time and attention to each interaction from play, to feeding, to diapering.

A good relationship with an infant involves being responsive and really attending to the signals given. It is impossible to "spoil" an infant by responding to his or her needs (something some adults fear). By being responsive to non-verbal messages, you are giving the child exactly what is needed and building a positive relationship. This does not mean jumping at every cry. Instead, by knowing the infant and his or her typical needs and behavior, you can acknowledge feelings and create routines and activities that meet the baby's needs.

Relationships are built on the small, shared individual experiences you have with children each day. Reading a story, having a conversation, feeding a guinea pig, watching the goldfish swim, digging in the sand, taking a walk around the yard to look for bugs, or singing a song together are the kinds of experiences that build relationships.

When relating to a child, look at the individual and speak in a relaxed and natural voice using words and a style of speech not unlike the way you talk with friends. The emotional tone need not be highly modified for children.

Because of the differences in experience, you cannot share the adult aspects of your life, nor can you fully share the experience of being a child. But it is possible to have worthwhile and enjoyable relationships built on shared interests and experiences. The workings of the plumbing, the quality of the easel paint, the traits of a favorite character from a story, home, family, the world, and thousands of other shared experiences make up the content of conversations you can have with children. Frequently adults make contact with children only to give directions, handle problems, pronounce facts, or teach skills and concepts. These will be part of your day, but they are not the stuff of which genuine relationships are built.

You can even relate to infants in this same way. Although the words may be one-sided, the relationship is mutual. Just as with older children, you will build a relationship based on the things you do together instead of words. You will read non-verbal messages. You will also acknowledge, interpret, and provide a scaffold or bridge as sounds turn to talk. Not only does this build relationships, it is the way that human beings learn language.

Barriers to Relationships

Relationships are facilitated when you make the environment a comfortable place. Barriers to relationships include physical distractions, personal bias, and inappropriate or disrespectful ways of communicating. Distractions in the environment can create barriers. If it is too noisy, crowded, or uncomfortably hot or cold, it is difficult to focus on another person. When you are aware of those things that get in the way of good relationships, you can work to avoid them.

Strong feelings about an individual's appearance, race, culture, or personality also hinder relationships. As we discussed in Chapter One, everyone has some biases, but these need not damage relationships. You can be aware of and thoughtful about your own strong feelings with the goals of not allowing them to affect children and with becoming more tolerant of others. Your example will help children and other staff members learn to be accepting as well.

Relationships can be damaged when you are unaware of the effect of your words and behavior on others. It is not respectful or appropriate to talk to other adults about children in their presence or to talk through a child for the benefit of the adults or other children who might be listening. Similarly, sarcasm and humor at children's expense while pretending to talk with them is disrespectful.

Communication

The quality of your relationships with children will be based to a great extent on your skill in communicating. Respectful communication conveys to children that you value their feelings and thoughts and you trust their capacity to grow and learn. Adults often speak to children in ways that are condescending and insincere or brusque, bossy, and rude. You may have felt insulted when someone spoke to you "as if you were a child." When you talk to children "like people" you will find that you enhance communication and relationships, although it may feel awkward when you first try. You can even communicate in this way with infants.

Basic abilities that will help you to be effective in communicating with children include: the ability to listen and perceive their meanings accurately, the capacity to respond clearly and authentically, awareness of barriers to communication, and willingness to try to overcome these barriers. There should be plenty of time and opportunity for children to talk. Adults often talk a great deal and leave very little time for children's responses. This may be because they feel that it is a part of their role, because they are uncomfortable with silence, or because they are disinterested in what children have to say. Continual talking gives little opportunity or encouragement for children to express ideas and feelings.

Another barrier to communication can be the manner in which you speak to children. "Cute," condescending, or artificially sweet ways of talking send the message to children that they are not worthy of sincerity and respect. Educators who have a genuine interest in children speak to them without such artificiality and never cut a conversation short because the subject matter isn't "nice."

Listening

Listening means to pay attention to the message another person is communicating. Although it seems commonplace, listening requires concentration and effort. The essential skill needed for good communication is the ability to listen. Listening well can be almost magical in building relationships with children and creating a peaceful, productive classroom. In our work with college students and parents we have consistently found that as we teach listening skills they report how important and powerful a tool it becomes to them.

Listening well requires that you pay very careful attention to words, gestures, body stance, movement, and tone of voice. One message can be sent by a person's words while their body and expression convey something else. Non-verbal messages are frequently your best source of information about children's thoughts and feelings. If you work with infants and young toddlers, they will be your only source. Even highly verbal preschoolers were non-talkers only a year or two ago. It is easy to be misled into thinking that language is their first mode of response. And despite their sophisticated language, primary children also speak with their bodies. Whatever age you work with, it is critical to listen with your eyes as well as your ears.

The more you know about a child (age, social and language habits, culture, family background and experiences), the better you will be at really understanding the child. The combination of general knowledge plus attention to the immediate situation will enable you to understand the meaning behind words and behavior. We once observed three-year-old Noa at the beginning of the school year. The morning was punctuated by bouts of crying, "I want my Mommy!" As children left circle time to play, Noa's crying started again, and the cry for Mommy took on a new and more desperate tone accompanied by a dance-like motion. His observant teacher approached him, spoke with him quietly, and then led Noa to the bathroom. Her observations, her awareness of his day at school, and her knowledge of three-year-olds helped her to understand what the problem really was.

Listening means being obviously attentive to a child's meaning and feelings. You can demonstrate attentiveness and "listen" better if you look at a child, crouch or sit at his or her level, and give responsive verbal and non-verbal feedback that communicate that you really heard. Timing, the quality and register of your voice, facial expression, gestures, and body posture often convey more to a child than the words you use.

When a child talks to you, an appropriate response can be to sit down close and acknowledge you heard with a nod, smile, or word of encouragement. This gives the child time to express ideas and feelings and gives you time to try to piece together words and body language. Use words of encouragement to invite further communication. Statements like, "I see," "Tell me more," "Yes," "Is there anything else you want to tell me?" and "Thank you for telling me" are encouraging responses.

It is tempting to jump to conclusions when children talk. Sometimes, despite our best efforts to understand, we misinterpret. To avoid this, restate or ask a question to confirm what you think a child has said (called *reflective listening*). This allows the child to correct any misunderstandings. For example, we recently heard a child say, "I want poopoo." Her teacher asked, "Are you looking for the purple pen?" The child smiled and nodded.

It is useful to think of words and body language as a code for feelings as well as thoughts. *Active listening* is a term we learned from Thomas Gordon in his book *Teacher Effectiveness Training* (1974). It describes a process in which you listen and respond to the feeling as well as the content of a message. By asking a question or making a statement, you give the child the opportunity to clarify the meaning and express the feelings involved. Here are two examples of situations where a child's words and actions had different meanings and the teacher used active listening.

Situation 1: Two-year-old Sango, during the first month of school, was absentmindedly stacking blocks. Her teacher walked by and

Sango said, "When my Mommy come?" Sango's face and body slumped and her voice sounded worried and sad. The teacher responded, "It sounds like you wish you could see her right now." Sango nodded and a tear spilled out. She whispered, "I miss Mommy."

Situation 2: Four-year-old Chloe, during her fifth month of school, was intently building an elaborate block structure. The teacher walked by and Chloe said, "When is my Daddy coming?" Chloe's body was tense her eyes focused on her structure, and her voice was high pitched and anxious. The teacher responded, "Are you worried you'll have to stop before you're finished?" Chloe said, "Yeah, when I want to finish building Daddy always wants to hurry up."

Active listening is even appropriate with infants and young toddlers who have few words to communicate their feelings. For example:

Situation 1: Torin, a twelve-month-old child who was familiar with his caregiver, reached for her new glasses. The child touched them, wrinkled his brow, and said, "Ga?" Torin's face and body were relaxed. The caregiver smiled, "You're touching my new glasses. I look different." The child smiled and touched the glasses again.

Situation 2: Six-month-old Cameo reached for the glasses of her caregiver. She touched them, then grabbed on, pulled, and vocalized. The caregiver smiled, "Those are my glasses. They're nice to touch but I need them to see." Then she handed Cameo a rattle. "You can play with the sun rattle." Cameo gurgled and chewed contentedly on the rattle.

The educators in these examples used knowledge of individuals as well as observation of non-verbal cues to make inferences regarding each child's feelings. Active listening helped them to understand that the child was trying to communicate and enabled them to support children to express their concerns and needs. When you use active listening, you help the child to express feelings and needs, think, discuss, question, and explore. Active listening is especially valuable because it demonstrates to children that you really pay attention to how they feel.

What happens when you don't listen to feelings as well as words? Communication can be blocked and eventually relationships can be damaged. You can tell someone is not listening to you when their responses don't acknowledge your feelings and concerns, deny or fail to acknowledge your feelings, or address their concerns instead of yours. Gordon calls these responses *roadblocks* (1974). Instead of responding with words that show you were paying attention to feeling and meaning, they tell the person you are communicating with that his or her ideas are unimportant, unacceptable, or irrelevant. Recognizing roadblocks and understanding how they stop communication helps you observe your own responses and learn new ways of listening and responding. The In Practice box gives examples of roadblocks.

As you read the roadblocks in the In Practice box on p. 260, you may wonder "Why are these so bad?" or "What can I say that would *not* be a roadblock?" Even when offered with the best of intentions, as many roadblocks are, they ignore the child's feelings and concerns and reflect the adult's point of view, needs, and feelings.

When you respond to children's concerns by telling them what to do or by warning them about the consequences of their actions, it can create a dependency on you to solve their problems or may make them angry and defensive. If you attempt to persuade them to your viewpoint, you may discourage exploration as well as communication. Similarly, evaluating children (positively or negatively) can effectively halt their attempts to share. Criticism or ridicule makes all of us feel foolish and unacceptable. Avoiding talking about feelings or problems by analyzing them or by distracting or humoring the child may communicate disregard for the child's true feelings. All keep you from focusing on what the child is really trying to communicate. Some of these responses (such as questioning, interpreting, or giving advice) may be used profitably once you really understand what is happening.

In contrast, a listening response will help you understand the child's feelings and ideas without leaping to conclusions or solving the problem for the child. Effective responses respect and acknowledge children and allow them to tell you what they are feeling. For example:

Child: "I want to climb. I don't like to go inside."

Teacher: "Really? Do you want to tell me about that?" or "You really like climbing and you don't like being interrupted to go inside."

The challenge is to be aware of the ways you talk and respond. Notice when children re-

---

Reflect and write about . . .

roadblocks you have experienced

Remember a time when someone didn't listen to you when you were trying to communicate a problem or concern. Did they use a "roadblock"? What did it feel like? Why do you remember this situation? How did it affect your relationship? What might have been different if they had listened?

IN PRACTICE

Roadblocks to avoid in communication

Situation:

Jasaré is climbing on a piece of playground equipment and will not come inside at the end of an outdoor play period. She says, "I want to climb. I don't want to go inside."

Some roadblocks give **orders, advice,** or attempt to **convince.**

1. Ordering, commanding, directing: "You have to come in right now."
2. Warning, threatening: "If you don't come inside you won't get a snack."
3. Moralizing, preaching, giving "shoulds" and "oughts": "Nice girls come in with their friends."
4. Advising, offering solutions or suggestions: "If you come inside you can play with your friends and have fun."
5. Teaching, lecturing, giving logical arguments: "You're going to miss activity time and you'll be all alone with no one to play with."

Some roadblocks **evaluate** or **interpret** based on your values.

6. Judging, criticizing, disagreeing, blaming: "Why are you so difficult?"
7. Name calling, stereotyping, labeling: "Only babies want to play outside all the time."
8. Interpreting, analyzing diagnosing: "You must wish you had a friend."
9. Praising, agreeing, giving positive evaluations: "You are such a good girl. I know you want to come in."

Some roadblocks **avoid** the problem.

10. Reassuring, sympathizing, consoling, supporting: "I know how you feel."
11. Questioning, probing, interrogating: "Are you feeling sick?"
12. Withdrawing, distracting, humoring, diverting: "Have you seen the new puzzles we just got? You're really going to like them."

spond eagerly and contrast it with the times when a child withdraws or rebels. Be aware of the times when you feel threatened or "turned off" by other people and try to learn from these situations.

Praise versus Encouragement

For many years educators were taught to use praise generously with children in their classrooms. Praise was viewed as a tool to make children feel good about themselves and motivate good behavior and learning. Because it was seen as desirable, many educators began to use praise to manipulate children's behavior. The excessive and manipulative use of praise made this technique lose much of its true value. Today many psychologists and educators question this use of praise. Excessive and inappropriate praise is now seen as ineffective with possible negative consequences (Hitz and Driscoll 1988).

IN PRACTICE

Differences between encouragement and praise

ENCOURAGEMENT	PRAISE

Content

Encouragement is specific.	*Praise is general.*
"Thank you. You helped pick up all the blocks and put them away where they belonged."	"That's beautiful!"
Encouragement is descriptive and non-judgmental.	*Praise makes a judgment.*
"You did the pilot puzzle. It's a tricky one."	"You're a great puzzle solver."
Encouragement concerns internal feelings and motivation.	*Praise concerns external products or rewards.*
"It's really satisfying when you finish a painting that you have worked on so hard, isn't it?"	"I'll put the best paintings on the bulletin board to show the parents."
Encouragement is thoughtful and individual.	*Praise is the same for all and holds little meaning for the individual.*
"That was the first time you slid down the twisting slide by yourself."	"Great job! Great job! Great job! Great job!"

Focus

Encouragement focuses on the process, experience, and effort.	*Praise focuses on the person or outcome.*
"You really worked hard on scrubbing that table."	"That's the best job of cleanup I ever saw."
Encouragement focuses on growth of the individual.	*Praise compares children.*
"You wrote the names of everyone in our class. I remember when you could only write your name."	"You're the best printer in our class."

Source

Encouragement originates with the child (you evaluate yourself).	*Praise originates with the one who praises (I evaluate you).*
"It looks like you feel proud of that picture."	"I love your picture!"

Impact

Encouragement supports independence.

Encouragement motivates exploration and experimentation.

Encouragement sustains involvement.

Praise often promotes dependence.

Praise often motivates imitation and repetition.

Praise often limits involvement.

Delivery

Encouragement is given in a natural tone of voice.

Inauthentic praise is often delivered without expression or in a false voice.

Praise implies evaluation. It can create anxiety and invite dependency on adult judgment and fear of negative appraisal. It is not conducive to self-reliance, self-direction, or self-control. We often see praise used in classrooms not as genuine recognition of positive behavior but as manipulation. The statement, "I like how Amy is sitting!" is often meant to spur another child who is not sitting to conform. This can generate negative feelings toward the child who is being commended, and it dilutes the value of authentic praise.

Praise that is not genuine ("That's beautiful!" used for every picture) and praise used to manipulate behavior can result in lack of faith or even evoke defensiveness and hostility. Genuine praise, sometimes called *encouragement* to distinguish it from judgmental or inauthentic praise, gives children information and encourages internal sources of evaluation rather than reliance on external judgments.

Because both praise and encouragement often feel good and are usually given with positive intentions, it can be difficult to distinguish them. The distinctions and examples in the In Practice box are designed to help you provide encouragement to children.

GUIDING A CLASSROOM OF YOUNG CHILDREN

If you decided to enter early childhood education because you enjoy being with children and want to help them develop and learn, it can be surprising to discover that much of your energy and time must be spent maintaining classroom order and addressing conflicts among children. Guiding a group of young children, sometimes called *classroom management,* is an art that requires knowledge, skill, sensitivity, and self-confidence. Like any art it is one that you will acquire through training and experience, and it becomes easier with practice.

Becoming Comfortable with Authority

By virtue of your role as an educator, society confers on you a certain authority: the rights to exercise power, make decisions, take action, give commands, and expect obedience. The most obvious source of this authority is adulthood. You are larger, stronger, and older, so children acknowledge your right to give direction. Although authority is conferred by society as a part of your role, it is strengthened by your education, knowledge, skill, experience, and commitment.

There are many ways to exercise authority and use power. Most of us have encountered teachers, bosses, family members, or others in authority who were harsh, punitive, or unfair and who in other ways could be described as abusing their position. Most of us have also experienced people in authority who were unclear and inconsistent, who thus abdicated authority and left us without a sense of what was acceptable. Neither of these uses of authority are beneficial. Instead, early childhood educators strive to use authority humanely, fairly, and with clarity.

Becoming comfortable with authority is one of the first issues that faces any prospective educator. Our college students often struggle with authority as they learn to work with children. The way they approach authority involves their values and expectations. Some try to deny their authority. They behave as if they were one of the kids and become confused and frustrated when children do not respect them or cooperate with their requests. Others expect children to grant them authority simply because they are the "teacher." They make demands without first building respectful relationships and are surprised when children are rebellious and resistant.

We have found the concept of *natural authority,* described by George Dennison in *The Lives of Children* (1969), helpful in defining authority that feels natural and that has positive effects on children.

> Natural authority is a far cry from authority that is merely arbitrary. Its attributes are obvious; adults are larger, more experienced, possess more words, and have entered into prior agreements among themselves. When all this takes on a positive instead of merely negative character, the children see adults as protectors and as sources of certitude, approval, novelty, skills. (Dennison 1969, 124)

Authority that is authentic and lasting is based on mutual respect and not on coercion or abandonment of responsibility. It is used wisely and with compassion. There is no single right way to exercise authority and no one way that is appropriate for each age and individual. Some early childhood practitioners invite children's cooperation with a shared joke and a smile and children seem delighted to join them. Others clearly and calmly state appropriate expectations in a friendly, no-nonsense voice and gain willing compliance. Still others almost silently step in to redirect children with a word or gesture and like

---

Reflect and write about . . .

teacher authority

Think about a teacher you liked and a teacher you didn't like. How did each exercise authority or power? Did he or she win your respect and gain your cooperation? If so, how? If not, why not? How did this influence what you learned and who you are today?

magic prevent a blow, encourage a friendship, or assist in a routine. Each of these approaches, and other successful variations, are grounded in respect, clarity, knowledge of children, and positive relationships.

Your first experiences in trying to manage a group of children are likely to be somewhat challenging. Children will test you to find out what they can expect from you so they can feel secure. Experienced teachers are usually clearer about their expectations of children and communicate these with authority from the very beginning in words, body language, and behavior. Children quickly become "well behaved" with them. Less experienced individuals often hesitate and send mixed messages. Children respond with more testing. When you are clear on your expectations and communicate them with authority, your work becomes much easier. Authority comes with time, practice, and patience.

Anticipating and Preventing Problems

Before your first day working with children, there are important things you can do to ensure that problems will be minimized. You can make sure children have appropriate and interesting things to do, sufficient time to do things, and enough adults to supervise. An orderly environment with well-defined space, appropriate materials, and a schedule geared to the needs of children with well-organized routines and transitions will contribute greatly to order and calm and help to minimize conflicts. When you provide these things, children are likely to enjoy their day and play productively.

The guidelines for arranging the environment and schedule provided in Chapters Seven and Eight help to prevent problems. When problems do occur, it is useful to look first at the environment and schedule to eliminate obvious problems. For example, in a preschool class we know, the block center was in the center of the room. To get to any other area children had to walk through the block center, often bumping into structures. Children whose buildings were knocked down responded by using blocks as defensive weapons, and children who walked through the block area regularly picked up blocks as props for other centers and deposited them far away. Creating a more sheltered block area reduced these problems. In a toddler program we recently observed, staff provided few duplicate materials and toddlers were often in conflict over toys. Replacing highly prized single toys with similar toys in pairs minimized conflicts. And in a primary program where children often misbehaved during two consecutive and lengthy seated activity periods, behavior improved when time outside and in centers was interspersed.

The In Practice box contains strategies that can help you plan a classroom where problems are minimized.

Managing Group Dynamics

Managing a group requires specific skills and understanding that help children to stay on task and meet expectations. They help you to minimize disruption from the minor problems that occur in every classroom. Skills held by teachers who have well-managed and productive classrooms have been described by researchers (Kounin 1970) as:

1. **With-it-ness:** Being aware of what is going on in the classroom and dealing with inappropriate behavior quickly and effectively.
2. **Overlappingness:** Dealing with a number of events at the same time.
3. **Flow or momentum:** Keeping activities moving in a smooth flow without digressions and distractions.
4. **Group focus:** Awareness of the group at all times, alerting the group before changes, and keeping all children involved rather than focusing on individual children and losing track of the group.

In practical terms this means being highly attentive to everything that is happening in your

IN PRACTICE

Anticipating and preventing problems

Arranging the Environment

- Set up well-defined centers separate from one another.
- Provide space for children to work sheltered from the group.
- Make sure there is enough space for children to play (35 sq. ft. of space for every child over 2, and 50 sq. ft. for children under 2).
- Keep activity centers out of paths between areas, doors, or bathroom.
- Eliminate corridors, which invite running and noise.
- Position library and writing centers so you can work in them and see the rest of the room.

Planning the Schedule

- Include opportunities for both energetic physical activity and quiet activity frequently.
- Include time for self-selected activity and group activity in preschool/primary programs.
- Have a flexible schedule for younger children, self-regulated for infants and young toddlers, and highly flexible for older toddlers.
- Maintain well-organized routines and transitions every day. Be flexible in duration.

Selecting and Arranging Materials

- Make sure there are several appropriate and appealing choices for each child in the room.
- Introduce several new or appealing activities at once to make sure there are materials for every child to use the day they are introduced.
- Clearly mark shelves so children know where materials belong.
- Avoid crowded shelves.
- Remove broken or damaged materials.
- In programs for toddlers make sure duplicates or similar materials for each choice are available together.

Managing Your Time and Behavior

- Model what you want children to do.
- Think through activities, materials, and events to anticipate problems.
- Talk about feelings spontaneously and as part of curriculum.
- Teach cooperation and non-violent conflict resolution before problems occur.
- Focus on the children. Do other tasks outside of class time (e.g., phone calls, planning).

classroom. For example, in a typical preschool or kindergarten class you might need to attend to all of the following situations at once:

Yoon Ki and Michael building a large block structure and wearing the construction hats they use for playing police, which often leads to rough and tumble play.

Teale and Harrison painting at the easel, giggling with one another as they look at one another's work while Harrison holds up a wet paintbrush and drips purple paint on the floor.

Sarah, Tyrone, Billy, and Yukiko listening to a story read by Tyrone's mom in the library corner.

Kellen, Max, and Nermeen in the dramatic play area, dressed up in finery, feeding the dolls when Kellen announces, "No boys!"

John and Tiffany staring intently at Squeakers, the mouse, while Tiffany pokes a piece of tinker toy in at Squeakers.

Anna, Mishka, and Sasha at the writing center calling you enthusiastically to come write dictation.

You would then need to make an on-the-spot decision in response to what children need, what will help individuals, and what is needed for the class as a whole. You will have to continue to attend to the rest of the group after you have made your decision, and you will need to have an interesting alternative ready for each group of children as they are ready for a change.

The In Practice box on p. 265 lists some techniques that we have found helpful over the years in managing a group of young children.

Managing Large Group Gatherings

In working with preschool and primary programs, additional skills are needed when you lead a group. Group times work best when they have a wide appeal, allow children to be active, and are relatively short (ten to fifteen minutes for younger preschoolers). As children grow older, their ability to participate meaningfully and for longer periods of time increases (up to half an hour for primary children). Structured group activities are not appropriate for infants and toddlers although a group may gather spontaneously if you do something highly interesting, such as playing a guitar, reading a story, or bringing in a puppy to visit.

Advance planning and a few key skills will help you to make group times enjoyable for you and children. Group times should be purposeful. Some good reasons to bring together a group of young children include: to help children develop a group identity, to learn group roles and behavior, to present activities like singing and creative movement that are more enjoyable in a group, to introduce activities, and to efficiently make sure all the children have the same experience or information.

Group times work when children are comfortable (which means not too hungry, tired, crowded) and group size and ratio are appropriate to age and abilities (see Chapter Seven). Consider children's development and interests in selecting group activities so that they match children's ability to participate. For example, a typical group of three-year-olds will be more interested in moving and making noises like animals than in discussing how their family recycles. A group of seven-year-olds might feel exactly the opposite.

Appropriate group activities for preschool and primary children have the following characteristics:

- They encourage participation.
- They include physical activity.
- They include something to look at or explore with other senses.
- They contain an element of novelty.

Singing songs, doing fingerplays, reading stories, presenting flannelboard stories or puppets,

IN PRACTICE

Suggestions for group management

- Position yourself so you can see what is happening throughout the room.
- Get children's attention by moving close to them, crouching down, and speaking directly to them. Avoid shouting across the room or yard or addressing the group about a problem with an individual.
- Use children's names positively and frequently so that they don't fear something negative when you address them by name.
- Indicate what to do rather than what not to do when correcting behavior. Children often feel rebellious and challenged when told what not to do.

For	Substitute
"Don't run with the scissors."	"Please walk when you carry scissors so no one will get hurt."
"Don't get paint on your clothes."	"Wear a smock so you won't get paint on your clothes."
"Don't tear the book."	"Turn the pages carefully."
"Don't poke the guinea pig."	"Use very gentle pats and quiet voices so you don't scare the guinea pig."

- When a child doesn't respond appropriately to the above examples, give two acceptable choices. Choices help children to feel powerful and in control.

   "Please walk when you carry scissors so no one will get hurt. I'd be happy to carry the scissors while you go outside to run."

   "Wear a smock so you won't get paint on your clothes. You may use pens or crayons if you don't want to cover up your new overalls today."

   "Turn the book's pages carefully—you can use newspaper if you'd like to tear."

- Avoid giving children choices that you are unwilling or unable to allow. "Would you like to give me the knife?" is not appropriate when you mean, "I must have the knife right now; it is dangerous!"

creative movement activities, writing group stories, playing group games, and discussing something that is of interest are all potentially good activities for group time.

When leading a large group, you are the center of the learning experience and the children respond to your direction. Your sensitivity to their mood and energy and your ability to respond to it will determine whether the children stay involved and cooperative. A large group will fail if it requires too much waiting or if children lack interest. When you reach the limits of children's interest you need to say, "That's all for today." Learning to read and respond to a group takes time, experience, and self-confidence.

Young children who are not ready for group experiences will tell you by wiggling, getting up, lying down, or walking away. When they do, they are giving you valuable feedback—something, the activity or the timing, is not appropriate to the needs of the group. Sometimes one or two children have difficulty while the rest enjoy group time. If so, have a simple alternative available for these children. Both you and children will have a better time if expectations are appropriate and clear and if there are alternatives for children who aren't ready for group.

When group time works it can seem like magic, and like all magic, it is based on carefully practiced illusions that experienced educators use, without being aware they are doing so. The In Practice box suggests some ways to make group times successful.

IN PRACTICE

Group-time magic

Have a Good Attitude. If you present a group activity as something that is fun and desirable and you expect everyone to cooperate, the children are likely to believe you're right.

Be Positive. Focus on the things children do right; don't focus on the negative.

Be Prepared. Plan the place, the activities, and the time to minimize distractions. Always have a fail-safe activity to do if something doesn't appear to be working.

Be Dramatic. Use your voice for effect (change volume and pitch to catch interest). Use your face to communicate—eyes, eyebrows, and mouth can express feelings and ideas without words. Some practitioners even dress to focus children. A teacher we know has a collection of interesting t-shirts and earrings that she wears to go with the day's activity.

Direct Attention. Direct children's attention to what's happening by keeping the activities moving without long pauses, include lots of movement, and do different things.

Be Flexible. Make changes in response to what children do. Cut out an activity, add movement, or insert a song or fingerplay as you notice children's responses.

Use the Unexpected. See the classroom from a child's point of view, anticipate what's going to interest children, and incorporate it into what you are doing. If a firetruck drives by or a visitor walks in, make this a part of the group activity.

Quit While You're Ahead. Instead of doing an interesting activity over again, save it for tomorrow. Group times often fall apart when they go on too long.

Creating Appropriate Guidelines

Clearly stated expectations for behavior enable people to exist together in harmony. A *rule* is a statement of expectations and limits, usually phrased as behavior that is required or prohibited. The word *rule* suggests something that is inflexible and imposed, so we prefer to use the words *guideline* or *agreement,* which imply flexibility and cooperation more consistent with our values and beliefs.

Whatever they are called, guidelines protect rights and property, make the program predictable, and help children to respect and get along with others. When fairly and consistently applied, they help children to feel safe and comfortable. Guidelines for young children need to be simple enough so they can be easily understood, few enough to remember, and general enough to apply to a wide variety of situations.

A few general guidelines that address im-portant principles are better than a laundry list of rules that address every conceivable situation. Good guidelines help young children to know what to do rather than denying them an activity. They are reasonable in terms of the developmental level of children. For example, it is unreasonable to require any young children not to move or talk, to insist preschoolers keep their clothes clean, or to require toddlers not to put toys in their mouths. Whatever the age, it is appropriate to have the following guidelines:

> Take care of yourself.
>
> Take care of others.
>
> Take care of toys, books, and the environment.

These three guidelines are stated by early childhood educators in different ways—for example: treat yourself gently, treat one another gently, treat our school gently; or be safe, be kind, be thoughtful. The adults and children together can then decide what constitutes safe, kind, thoughtful care for people and the environment they share.

Older preschool and primary children can participate in creating and modifying guidelines or agreements. Agreements created by the group are not permanent; instead, the group considers them and changes them in response to changing situations. As they do so, they are likely to develop greater commitment to following agreements as well as developing understanding of the principles of group living.

You will need to communicate your expectations regarding guidelines with clarity and simplicity. Problems often arise when children lack information or understanding. Children are likely to respect guidelines when they understand the reasons for them and when the behavior required is within their ability. Following are some examples of guidelines and their reasons:

Guideline: We will treat one another gently.

Reason: No one can work and play if they are afraid of getting hurt.

Guideline: We will use toys, books, and games carefully.

Reason: Toys, books, and games can get lost or damaged. Then we would not have them to use anymore.

Guideline: We will put toys, books, and games away when we are done.

Reason: When they are not put away it's difficult to find them.

In the best of situations, guidelines for behavior are accepted, understood, followed, and supported by all of the adults and children in the class. They are clearly stated and consistently enforced. Through them both you and children make a commitment to the safety and well-being of the individuals and the group. You can help children to understand the underlying principles of your guidelines by repeating the

reasons for them and by helping them to understand that they are there to protect all of the children—including themselves.

Problems with Guidelines

We have observed two kinds of problems with guidelines in early childhood programs. Problems occur when there are too many, or when guidelines are vague, unclear, or inconsistently enforced. When there are too many guidelines, it is difficult for children to remember them. Adults then spend much of their time enforcing guidelines or else enforce them sporadically without clarity about what is important.

When guidelines are ambiguous, children fail to understand and follow their direction and limits. Such a guideline as, "Blocks are for playing," fails to address the issue of using blocks as weapons or missiles and hence can be misunderstood. A clearer guidelines would be, "Use blocks only for building, not throwing or hitting."

Although there will be differences in values, beliefs, and perceptions among the staff in an early childhood program, it is critical that all the adults who work with a group of children agree upon rules, limits, or guidelines to be followed. Problems occur when there is a lack of consistency among adults. For example, in a school we know adults did not agree on ways to use outdoor equipment. Children were told they must follow the rules of the teacher on duty. This gave little information to children who engaged in a range of unsafe behavior regardless of who was on duty, perhaps in an effort to try to figure out what was acceptable.

Dealing with Conflicts and Problems

Problems and conflicts are an inevitable aspect of group life, both in and outside of early childhood programs. The way you deal with conflict provides an important model for young children. They can experience that conflict is a part of life that, while not pleasant, is an op-

---

IN PRACTICE

Ways to help children understand and express feelings

- Accept and name children's feelings for them: "You feel disappointed that Calder has the ball you wanted."
- Model expressing your own feelings: "When it's noisy I feel frustrated because you can't hear me."
- Invite children to talk to you and to one another about how they feel.
- Point out similarities and differences in feelings: "You both like to read stories. Briana likes to read by herself. Aaron wishes he had company."
- Provide opportunities for children to identify and express feelings through conversations, art, music, movement, dramatic play, and writing.
- Rehearse expressing feelings through activities like role-playing

---

portunity for problem solving rather than something that is violently disrupting and harshly controlled.

How you feel about conflict is a reflection of your experiences, values, and culture. Reflecting on how you feel about and deal with conflict in your own life may be helpful in considering what you will model for children. Do you tend to avoid conflict? Do you try to impose a solution? Do you tend to let go of what you want or need so relationships will not be damaged and the problem will go away? Or do you work collaboratively to find mutually satisfactory solutions?

Conflict can be difficult to deal with because it is often accompanied by anger, a powerful emotion that can be hard to understand and express. Anger is a second level reaction—a response to hurt, threat, frustration, disappointment, and anxiety. Young children may not know words to express the feelings that lay behind their conflicts or may have been told not to express feelings. Before you can help children learn to resolve conflicts peacefully, you must help them to identify and acknowledge their feelings. The In Practice box suggests some ways to help children understand

and express feelings as a prelude to conflict resolution.

When disputes between young children occur, it is wise to watch first and refrain from intervening too soon. Children who are not hurting one another can then try to work out their own solutions. Although it is tempting to step in to solve problems for them, this does not help them to learn to be problem solvers when an adult is not there to help. With practice, children can learn to tell each other how they feel and what they want instead of striking out when a confrontation occurs.

When conflict threatens to cause serious harm, however, you must act. When you must intervene in children's conflicts, it is more effective to ask *what* can be done so that children can return to their activities than to ask *why* they came into conflict or who hit first. Causality is usually complex, and if you didn't see the confrontation you are unlikely to get an accurate picture of what occurred. In the long run it is more productive to help the children to find a solution to their problem than for you to try to judge the situation.

You show respect for children by helping them to understand the possible consequences of undesirable behavior and giving them the option of controlling behavior themselves. Such an approach indicates that you see them as mature and intelligent enough to control their own behavior. Acknowledging acceptable behavior and communicating clearly when and how a behavior is unacceptable are effective management strategies and help children to develop self-control.

Even very young children can be given time and opportunity to deal with conflict. We recently observed a teacher of toddlers simply put her arm between two toddlers who were hurting one another. She kept her arm there, saying little except, "You both want the white purse, but there's just one here," and "I can't let you hurt one another."

When children are "stuck" and cannot reach a solution on their own, a well-timed word can sometimes help two children to resolve the conflict. The suggestions in the In Practice box can give you ideas of things to say when children are having problems and you need to intervene.

Your job as an early childhood educator is to ensure that children behave in ways that are safe and that contribute to the learning and well-being of everyone in the group. Guidance strategies (techniques to help children behave in appropriate ways) can reflect your values and goals for children. In addition to helping you to ensure that children are safe and behave in ways that are acceptable, they also serve as an important teaching tool. We believe guidance should help children to become more competent, responsible, and caring. Attention to the learning potential in each guidance situation is one of the hallmarks of an early childhood professional (Katz 1984).

A variety of guidance strategies can take into account individual needs, show respect for children, and help them learn. No successful early childhood educator uses one strategy exclusively; instead, the child, situation, family, learning potential, and program are all considered. Before we begin our description of guidance strategies it may be helpful to look at the differences between guidance and punishment.

Guidance is a process designed to help children develop self-control—to understand and use constructive behaviors instead of mis-

---

IN PRACTICE

Examples of ways of talking with children in conflict situations

"Stop. I won't let you hurt Harrison. You can tell him that it makes you mad when he takes your truck. Ask him to give it back to you."

"I can see you're angry about what happened. What do you want to tell her?"

"Hitting hurts. Let's think of some other ways to handle this problem."

"That hurt Althea's feelings and she's really sad now. Please stay with me— maybe we can help her feel better."

"There isn't room for five children on the tire swing. Would you like to choose who goes first? Shall I help?"

"What can we do to solve this problem so you can go back to building your tower?"

behavior. The dictionary defines *guidance* as assisting or leading to reach a destination. Appropriate behavior resulting from guidance is the result of thought and internal control.

Punishment is defined as a rough or injurious penalty. It is designed to stop unwanted behavior by inflicting retribution that is painful or unpleasant. It does not teach alternatives or enhance understanding. "Good" behavior resulting from punishment is the outcome of fear. Punishment, by definition, is painful. Physically painful or corporal punishment is never acceptable in an early childhood program because it demonstrates that it is all right to hurt someone if you are big enough. Additionally, although children who have been physically punished may behave appropriately when there is an adult watching them, at later times they tend to show increased aggressive behavior (Honig 1985).

It is more consistent with the early childhood values of respect, trust, and appreciation for childhood to choose strategies to guide behavior rather than techniques that are punitive. It is important to keep in mind the fit between what you do and your long-term goals for children. Without this awareness you can accumulate a "grab bag" of techniques that "work" (that is, control immediate behavior problems). Your decisions about the success of guidance techniques should focus on whether the outcome is likely to have long-term positive effects rather than on whether the technique is effective at that moment.

Different approaches to guidance vary in the degree of adult control that they involve. These approaches are based on different views of child development, which are then translated into ways of dealing with problems.

Problem Solving

The values of positive self-regard and individual responsibility are emphasized in the **humanistic** approach to guidance, based on the work of Carl Rogers as applied to guidance by Thomas Gordon (1974). In this approach children are viewed as partners with an interest in participating in good relationships with adults and other children. Your central task in this approach is based on the development of good relationships between individuals and within groups and to help children realize their potential and see the world and themselves positively. Good relationships are developed as you use the open, honest, and authentic communication we described earlier in this chapter. When problems arise you send non-judgmental messages to children about the effects of their behavior and involve children in finding peaceful and mutually acceptable solutions to problems.

You demonstrate understanding of children's problems through your willingness to listen to them and hear their feelings. You demonstrate respect when you allow them to participate in generating solutions to classroom problems. When you have a problem, your needs and rights are being violated, or a situation makes you uncomfortable or unhappy, you have an opportunity to model interpersonal problem solving. Feelings, especially unpleasant ones, can be difficult to share, but collected negative feelings can come out harshly and may damage relationships. If you don't maintain your own rights in the classroom or if you try so hard to be nice that your needs are not met and respected, you may find yourself disliking children.

Sending an **I-message,** another technique described by Gordon, is a way to communicate your problems and feelings without criticizing or blaming children. You invite them to participate in solving the problem rather than telling them what to do. When you give an I-message, you maintain your rights, get your point across, and avoid hurting children or your relationship with them. An effective I-message has three elements:

- It states the specific condition or behavior that is problematic.

- It states your feelings.
- It explains why you feel that way.

For example, a teacher who is having trouble reading a story to a group in which some children are making noise might give the following I-message: "When there is so much noise during story, I feel frustrated because it's hard for everyone to hear." This statement does not send a negative evaluation and it leaves the solution in the hands of the child. A more common response than the above example might be to respond with a roadblock: "Stop talking! You're bothering everyone. You will have to leave if you can't be quiet." Such a you-message denies the child the opportunity to solve the problem. It focuses on the child's behavior in a blaming or evaluating manner, ignores the effect of the behavior on others, and imposes a solution on the child.

I-messages communicate that, even if you don't like a particular behavior or situation, you trust that the child is caring enough and capable of helping to solve the problem. Often the behavior will stop once the child knows that it causes a problem. The order and wording of an I-message is not as critical as communicating the three pieces—behavior, feelings, and effect—and the implied invitation to the child to engage in problem-solving to find mutually acceptable solutions. For example:

> "It's hard for everyone to hear when there's so much noise. It makes me feel bad if I have to shout so you can hear the story."
> "I'm feeling frustrated. There's too much noise for everyone to hear the story."

Even very young, non-English speaking, and pre-verbal children benefit from this approach. For example, a toddler with minimal language who pulls your hair can be told "Ouch!"—with an exaggerated sad expression. "It hurts when you pull my hair," is followed by a gentle guiding of the hand in a patting motion and a smile: "I like it when you touch me gently."

When a toddler behaves in an unacceptable way or an infant's action must be stopped, teachers who understand development very gently and clearly explain what must be done and why. "I can't let you pull my hair. That hurts me. Here, you can pull the raggedy doll." Do the children understand? Infants and toddlers, like the rest of us, understand kindness and respect; understanding the words may come much later.

Peaceful Conflict Resolution

We want children to learn to be cooperative and solve problems peacefully even when we are not present. By guiding children repeatedly through the process of peaceful conflict resolution, teaching negotiating skills, and offering encouragement, we can enable them to reach this goal. Peaceful conflict resolution begins by guiding children in the problem-solving process described below.

- **Define the issue.** Figure out what the problem is and what needs to be solved without making judgments. "Olivia and Stacy want to play in the home area. Jayson and Paul say 'No' because they're playing Power Rangers."
- **Identify the underlying feelings, worries, concerns, and values.** These things must be acknowledged before solutions can be generated. "Olivia and Stacey are worried they might not get a turn if they don't play now. Jayson and Paul like playing here too. They're afraid they won't get to play Power Rangers if you join them."
- **Develop alternative solutions.** Ask the children what they can think of to solve this problem. "Olivia thought of two plans: Jayson and Paul can play Power Rangers outside, or she and Stacey can be Power Rangers, too. Paul thought of two plans, too. He thinks that Olivia and Stacey can play in the block area and play in the pretend area tomorrow, or they can play in the home area in ten minutes."

- **Choose an alternative that is acceptable to all individuals.** "What do you want to try? What do you think might work for all of you?"
- **Act on the solutions.** "Okay, Olivia and Stacey will try playing Power Rangers in the home area for ten minutes with Jayson and Paul. Then they will play another game."
- **Talk about what to do next time so the problem will not occur again.** "What do you think we could do so that this problem doesn't happen again? . . . The next time someone wants to play in the home area, we'll try to find a way for each person to be part of the game."

We find young children often interested in and able to go through this process. When we have consistently involved children in handling problems with us we have found that they also start to do this quite effectively in their own problems with peers.

Used consistently with goodwill, the problem-solving approach builds relationships, teaches skills for negotiation and peaceful conflict resolution, and deals effectively with everyday upsets and problems with many children. This approach works well when children have few deep-seated problems and are used to dealing with adults in reciprocal relationships.

Natural and Logical Consequences

Problem solving works when children are willing and able to engage in a process of thinking through a problem. It can be less effective with children who are not used to this kind of activity. When problem solving does not work, another effective and respectful technique that is often used in early childhood care and education programs involves the use of **natural** and **logical** or **"related"** consequences.

This is sometimes known as the **democratic** approach to guidance. It is based on the work of Alfred Adler, interpreted and applied to classrooms by Rudolf Dreikurs (1969). In this approach, children are viewed as social beings with a strong desire to be part of a group. Children become discouraged and disrupt the group or misbehave when they do not know how to be positive and cooperative members of the class. The central task in this approach is to help children discover appropriate ways of gaining approval and becoming responsible members of a group of peers. The democratic approach can help children understand the mistaken strategies that they have adopted and allow them to redirect their behavior more positively. This approach is consistent with Piaget's view of guidance. Piaget suggests that adult responses to misbehavior should assist children in understanding the reasons for rules and limits to help them move toward moral autonomy (Fields and Boesser 1994).

Some consequences are the **natural** result of a child's actions and require no intervention on the part of an adult. For example, if a child pours his yellow paint down the drain, the natural consequence is that there is no yellow paint. Children who hurt others may find themselves being rejected by the children they hurt, another kind of natural consequence.

Natural consequences allow a child to learn from experience. Your task is to allow the child to experience the result of his or her action. This is appropriate when the result does not endanger a child and when it does not unfairly penalize another person or the group. Natural consequences seem simple, but they require restraint. It can be hard to see a child naturally disappointed, hungry, or unhappy. It is also can be difficult to refrain from voicing a smug "I told you so" when a child experiences natural consequences you foretold. For a natural consequence to be effective, you must accept and support children while allowing them to learn from experience. We find that reflective listening is a good response in these kinds of situations. For example, "You wish you had more juice but it's all gone," or "You'd really

like to play with them but they don't want to play with you now."

Sometimes there is no natural or acceptably safe consequence for misbehavior. In this situation, as the leader of a group, you guide a democratic process with respect and group cooperation and participation in decision making. Agreements for group living are first established. Along with the agreements, you create **logical** or **related** consequences for breaking the agreements. If you are working with older children you can do this as a process with the group. For example, in an after-school group the children got tired of not being able to find pieces of board games because they were often not put away. They decided the consequence for leaving a game out would be no games for the rest of the week. By confronting the direct consequences of their behavior, children learned the laws of living as a member of society.

With younger children you might decide on some basic guidelines and simple consequences. For example, if a child hurts someone else the logical consequence might be to lose the opportunity to play with that child or in that area. In following through on a consequence, you would be calm and simply say, "You may not be in the block area with Yusuke now. You hurt him. You can come back when you are ready to play without hurting." Logical consequences must be reasonable, fair, and very clearly related to behavior: "You threw the books off the shelf. When you are calm you can put them back on the shelf." Such consequences are consistent with the values of justice and responsibility.

The use of time-out as a consequence comes from this approach. An appropriately used time-out gives a child who misbehaves an opportunity to leave the group and return *when he or she feels ready.* In time-out, the child is in control. Providing a safe space away from others for a child to regain composure can be helpful. Time-out as an island for calm reflection can be an effective and humane way to help children gain self-control. The key elements in time-out are that it is not punitive and that it is self-regulated—the child determines when to return to the group. Allowing the child to be in control of time-out expresses your trust in the child and teaches self-control. If a child returns to the situation before he or she can behave appropriately, you can give the child criteria for readiness: "When your body is relaxed and you can keep your hands from hitting other people then you will be ready to come back." We have often observed time-out used incorrectly as a punishment: "Sit in the time-out chair and think about what you did until I tell you to get up." If the child's experience of a consequence is as punishment, then it fails to achieve the goal of helping children to become self-regulated group members.

Used well, the democratic approach to guidance is respectful. If it relies heavily on adult control of the consequences or on consequences that are unrelated to behavior, it is not effective. To be effective with young children, rules must be few, consequences very clear, and follow-through consistent, timely, and just.

Reinforcement

Sometimes, despite many repeated efforts at problem solving and the use of natural and logical consequences, you will find that a child has trouble cooperating, and destructive patterns develop and become habitual. When this happens, the consistency and power of reinforcement techniques can be an effective guidance strategy.

Reinforcement techniques developed by B. F. Skinner have been interpreted and applied to the classroom by many theorists and educators. This approach is known as *behaviorism*. In this approach, children are viewed as learners who have learned to misbehave. Behavior-

ists believe children misbehave because they have been taught to do so by improper rewards, or *reinforcement*. To change or *extinguish* old behaviors, new ones must be taught and rewarded.

All early childhood educators use behaviorist principles some of the time. When you smile at a shy child who attempts a new activity, you are providing reinforcement. When you ignore a child whose demanding behavior is disruptive, you are avoiding reinforcing it. The phrase "catch them being good" is a simple way of suggesting that you encourage, reward, or provide social reinforcement to children for desired behavior.

Behaviorist principles are useful in terms of the awareness that they bring. Adults can become aware that they may inadvertently teach misbehavior by giving attention or reinforcement to inappropriate behavior and ignoring appropriate behavior. For example, we observed a teacher who rarely gave children physical affection take a child on her lap and stroke his back while explaining why he should not hit. If she had realized this child was using negative strategies to gain her attention, she might have taken special care to be affectionate with him when he was doing something positive. You will want to make changes if you notice you are spending a lot of time attending to misbehavior and little time with children when they are responsible, productive, and positive.

Although all early childhood practitioners knowingly or unknowingly provide social reinforcement, the behaviorist approach to guidance involves more than this. It includes techniques for shaping children's actions so they behave according to the prescriptions of the adult. The adult decides which behavior is to be reinforced and which is to be extinguished through structured use of reward and punishment.

Systematic reinforcement can be effective, but it is also highly manipulative and counter to our values of respect and freedom of choice. We do not believe that it is appropriate for normal young children, who will respond to approaches more consistent with the values and goals of early childhood education. It can be effective when problems have become habits or for children who have severe behavior problems. Katz (1971) reminds us that behaviorist techniques are only appropriate when behavior is an outcome of conditioning.

In many elementary schools, Lee Canter's assertive discipline, based on behaviorist principles, is in use. Teachers who use this method record children's unacceptable behavior on the chalkboard, using a system of checkmarks. Consequences for each checkmark are predetermined. Early childhood educators (Gartrell 1987a, 1987b; Hitz 1988) have serious reservations about this approach. They question the equity of a system in which every infraction of rules is treated in exactly the same way in spite of intent, severity, and consequences. This, like other behaviorist techniques, does not actively involve children in becoming responsible for their own actions.

Choosing Guidance Strategies

All of these guidance strategies can be used in ways that take into account individual needs and that are respectful of children. Each has value in different kinds of situations. The communication and skills used in the problem-solving approach are helpful for building relationships and dealing with everyday upsets and problems. They work well when children have few deep-seated problems and are used to dealing with adults in verbal reciprocal relationships. This approach is less immediately effective with children who are not used to this kind of relationship or with very young children who have limited verbal ability. Other strategies may, at least initially, need to be employed with these children.

When conflicts arise, the use of logical and natural consequences may help children under-

stand the mistaken strategies that they have adopted and allow them to redirect their behavior more positively. And when destructive patterns have developed and become habitual, the consistency and power of reinforcement may be effective in changing or eliminating the behaviors. In our opinion, behaviorist techniques are called for only after humanistic and democratic approaches have failed.

Reflect and write about . . .

guidance and punishment

How were conflicts and misbehavior dealt with in your school experiences? What techniques or strategies were used? Were they effective? What were your feelings about them? Recall an incident in which you were punished in school. What happened? How did you feel? What were the effects on you? What do you wish had happened? How did the teacher's ways of handling problems effect how you felt about your teachers, school, and learning?

The Difficult Child

A child's repeated inability to behave productively in a group and failure to cooperate with reasonable expectations is often indicative of a deeper problem. It may suggest stress in the home or inconsistency between the discipline used in home and school. Every early childhood educator will encounter "difficult" children. Sometimes it will be a child who is having a bad day, sometimes one who is going through a hard time, and at other times a child who has serious problems beyond the scope of your training and resources. (See Chapter Fifteen, Working with Children with Special Needs, for more information about identifying and working with children with severe emotional problems.) These problems can take the form of rudeness, resistance, rebellion, and even violent outbursts. It can be frustrating and it can make you angry when a child hurts others or refuses to cooperate with reasonable classroom rules. Children are referred to as *difficult* not only because they misbehave but also because they can make you feel incompetent.

In dealing with such a child, first remember that all behavior has a cause. Try to look at and understand the behavior from the child's point of view. When you do so, you will almost always recognize stresses in the child's life that make the behavior understandable. Children

who have frequent problems and outbursts may be telling you that they need help. Educators, families, administrators, and local mental health professionals need to work together to make sure that a child who is in emotional distress receives help.

For many years we have found the ideas in Bruno Bettelheim's book *Love Is Not Enough* (1950) helpful for handling destructive behavior and for reassuring violent children. Bettelheim suggests telling these children that you will not allow them to hurt themselves or other people, nor will you let anyone hurt them. As children learn that their feelings will be respected, their needs met, and that they will be protected from retaliation, they may turn less to destructive behavior.

A child who is lashing out will usually stop this behavior given time and space to calm down. If there is danger of the child hurting self or others, you sometimes may need to use physical restraint. This can be done gently and firmly. Hold the child from behind so that you can contain flailing arms and legs. Speak calmly and let the child know that as soon as he or she regains self-control you will let him or her go. If your environment contains safe open space away from others, you might wish to take an out-of-control child to a space where the angry feelings can be worked out in vigorous physical activity that does not harm anyone. Violent outbursts are usually short lived, especially if you help children learn to control themselves—and if you believe that they can.

In addition to helping a child negotiate problems, you can provide alternatives to disruptive behavior. This is especially important if the behaviors have been found useful in other settings or have been used to fulfill basic emotional needs. Children may need time, courage, and your persistent encouragement to change from old reliable behaviors to new untested ones, even when the old behaviors no longer work.

The guidance techniques that work with other children in a classroom will work with difficult children—but you will find yourself more challenged in trying to apply them. Change does not happen overnight, and you may find yourself needing support as you help a child to become a functional member of the group. In addition to being clear, consistent, and following the other strategies previously mentioned in working with a difficult child, we find it helpful when we:

- Identify things we genuinely like about the child—and tell him/her.
- Identify for the child what he or she is doing right.
- Let the child know we are committed to helping them make it in the classroom and that we believe that will happen.
- Have sincere, positive physical contact with the child every day.
- Notice our own aggravation and find ways to release it away from children.
- Find a co-worker to talk to during the days when the child's behavior is giving difficulty.

There may be some children about whom you can't find positive qualities to like, in spite of your best efforts. They may be children who have characteristics that are distasteful to you; they may seem manipulative, mean, or hurtful to others. In this case, it's a good idea to find another adult, or possibly another class, that

can give the child genuine appreciation. If the child must stay in your class it is essential that you make sure you are just in your treatment of the child, whatever your own feelings.

You may also encounter children who need more intensive supervision and help than you are able to provide in a regular classroom. You need to try your best to help all children learn to function in your program. But when a child fails to do so in spite of your best efforts over a significant amount of time, you will need to work with the family and get the assistance of a mental health specialist. Together you can then plan for appropriate curriculum, family involvement, or even to make a referral to a setting that can better meet the needs of this child.

FINAL THOUGHTS

Early childhood educators attend to creating good relationships with children, perhaps because they can see things from a child's point of view. Building positive relationships with children and guiding them so the program runs smoothly is a foundation for your work. As you make decisions about the strategies and techniques you will use to build relationships and guide children, we urge you to give thoughtful consideration to your values and the ways you want to use authority. We hope you will be able to select from a variety of guidance strategies to meet children's individual needs. We encourage you to be mindful of supporting children's self-concepts. We recommend that you attend to developing skills in relating to and communicating with children, anticipating and preventing problems, managing a group, and guiding children's behavior.

Working with young children is a voyage of discovery. The ways you relate to and guide children will determine whether it is a peaceful voyage taken with friends.

PROJECTS

Observe an Early Childhood Educator: Visit someone who has been working with young children for several years. Observe him or her working with children for at least two hours. Describe his or her communication and relationships in the following situations: with one child at play, with a child during a routine, mediating or preventing a dispute, and leading a group activity. Include what the practitioner and children said and did; how she or he listened, responded, and communicated problems; and any barriers or roadblocks to communication you observed. Comment on the goals and values that this practitioner might hold and how he or she appeared to influence children's self-concepts, relationships, and feelings about school and learning.

Interview an Early Childhood Educator: Talk to an educator who has been working with young children for several years. Ask him or her about: the guidance strategies most frequently used, where they were learned, why they were chosen, the most frequent guidance problem encountered, the resources called upon when confronted with a difficult problem, and what he or she thinks is the most important thing learned about guiding young children. Comment on how this practitioner might influence children's self-concepts, relationships, and feelings about school and learning.

Compare Two Early Childhood Educators: Observe and/or interview two early childhood educators using the above assignments and compare the strategies, goals, values, and impact of each educator. Describe your impressions and which seems to best meet the needs of children.

BIBLIOGRAPHY

Bettelheim, B. 1950. *Love Is Not Enough.* New York: Free Press.
Bredekamp, S. 1987. *Developmentally Appropriate Practice.* Expanded Ed.
    Washington, DC: National Association for the Education of Young Children.
Canter, L. 1988. Assertive Discipline and the Search for the Perfect Classroom.
    Young Children 43(2):24.
Combs, A. W., A. C. Richards, and F. Richards. 1976. *Perceptual Psychology.* New
    York: Harper & Row.
Crosser, S. 1992. Managing the Early Childhood Classroom. *Young Children*
    47(2):23–29.
Dennison, G. 1969. *The Lives of Children.* New York: Vintage Books.
Dillon, J. T. 1971. *Personal Teaching.* Englewood Cliffs, NJ: Merrill/Prentice Hall.
Dreikurs, R. 1969. *Psychology in the Classroom.* New York: Harper & Row.
Erikson, E. H. 1963. *Childhood and Society.* New York: Norton.

Essa, E. 1990. *A Practical Guide to Solving Preschool Behavior Problems.* 2nd ed. Albany, NY: Delmar.

Faber, A., and E. Mazlish. 1980. *How to Talk So Kids Will Listen and Listen So Kids Will Talk.* New York: Avon.

Fields, M. V., and C. Boesser. 1994. *Constructive Guidance and Discipline: Preschool and Primary Education.* Englewood Cliffs, NJ: Merrill/Prentice Hall.

Gartrell, D. 1987a. Assertive Discipline: Unhealthy for Children and Other Living Things. *Young Children* 42(1):55–61.

Gartrell, D. 1987b. Punishment or Guidance? *Young Children* 42(2):55–61.

Gazda, G. M. 1975. *Human Relations Development.* Boston: Allyn & Bacon.

Ginott, H. 1972. *Teacher and Child.* New York: MacMillan.

Gonzalez-Mena, J., and D. W. Eyer. 1989. *Infants, Toddlers, and Caregivers.* Mountain View, CA: Mayfield.

Gordon, T. 1974. *Teacher Effectiveness Training.* New York: David McKay.

Greenberg, P. 1987. Ideas That Work With Young Children: Child Choice— Another Way to Individualize—Another Form of Preventive Discipline. *Young Children* 43(1):48–54.

Greenberg, P. 1988. Ideas That Work with Young Children: Avoiding Me Against You Discipline. *Young Children* 44(3):24–29.

Greenberg, P. 1991. *Character Development: Encouraging Self-Esteem & Self-Discipline in Infants, Toddlers, & Two-Year-Olds.* Washington, DC: National Association for the Education of Young Children.

Greenberg, P. 1991. Why Not Academic Preschool? Part 2. Autocracy or Democracy in the Classroom? *Young Children* 47(6):27–81.

Greenberg, P. 1992. How to Institute Some Simple Democratic Practices Pertaining to Respect, Rights, Roots, and Responsibilities in Any Classroom. *Young Children* 48(6):10–17.

Hitz, R. 1988. Assertive Discipline: A Response to Lee Canter. *Young Children* 43(2):25.

Hitz, R., and A. Driscoll. 1988. Praise or Encouragement: New Insights Into Praise. *Young Children* 43(5):6–13.

Honig, A. S. 1985. Compliance, Control and Discipline. *Young Children* 40(3):47–52.

Jones, E., ed. 1978. *Joys and Risks in Teaching Young Children.* Pasadena, CA: Pacific Oaks.

Jones, E., and G. Reynolds. 1992. *The Play's The Thing: Teacher's Roles in Children's Play.* New York: Teachers College Press.

Katz, L. G. 1984. The Professional Early Childhood Teacher. *Young Children* 39(5):3–10.

Katz, L. G. 1971. Condition with Caution: Think Thrice Before Conditioning. *Preschool Education Newsletter* (February).

Kounin, J. 1970. *Discipline and Group Management in Classrooms.* New York: Holt, Rinehart & Winston.

Malaguzzi, L. 1993. For an Education Based on Relationships. *Young Children* 49(1):9–12.

Marion, M. 1987. *Guidance of Young Children*. Englewood Cliffs, NJ: Merrill/Prentice Hall.

Maslow, A. 1968. *Toward a Psychology of Being*. New York: Van Nostrand Reinhold.

Miller, D. F. 1990. *Positive Child Guidance*. Albany, NY: Delmar.

Oken-Wright, P. 1992. From Tug-of-War to "Let's Make a Deal": The Teacher's Role. *Young Children* 48(1):15–20.

Readdick, C. A. 1993. Solitary Pursuits: Supporting Children's Privacy Needs in Early Childhood Settings. *Young Children* 49(1):60–64.

Stone, J. G. 1979. *Discipline*. Washington, DC: National Association for the Education of Young Children.

Stonehouse, A., ed. 1990. *Trusting Toddlers*. St. Paul, MN: Toys 'n Things Press.

Weber-Schwartz, N. 1987. Patience and Understanding. *Young Children* 42(3):52–54.

Weichert, S. 1989. *Keeping the Peace*. Philadelphia: New Society Publishers.

Yamamoto, K., ed. 1972. *The Child and His Image*. Boston: Houghton Mifflin.

PART IV

The Curriculum

The five chapters in this section deal with aspects of the curriculum in early childhood programs. Chapter Ten, Curriculum Planning, presents a framework for thinking about and designing meaningful and appropriate learning experiences for young children. Chapters Eleven through Fourteen deal with four broad areas of early childhood curriculum: physical development, the arts, language and literacy, and cognitive development. In each chapter we provide you with a lens through which to view effective practice.

CHAPTER TEN

Planning Curriculum

Awareness of alternatives and the bases of choices distinguishes the competent teacher from the merely intuitive one.　　　Elizabeth Brady

In this chapter, we explore early childhood curriculum as a dynamic process that reflects values, is responsive to the learner, has content that is worth knowing, and involves developmentally appropriate processes. Guidelines for thematic planning are given.

A companion to the question, "Who am I in the lives of children?" is "Why am I involved in the lives of children?" or, put another way, "What am I trying to accomplish—for children and for society?

Young children are learning all the time and from all of their experiences, both in and out of school. Early childhood educators need to ask, "How, when, and in what ways do I want to support and extend this natural process?" Because children are so interested in the world around them, the choices about the curriculum you provide in an early childhood program are almost infinite. Nevertheless, choices must be thoughtful and appropriate for the children with whom you work. Planning is essential.

WHAT IS CURRICULUM?

Two different but related definitions of curriculum are often used in early childhood pro-

grams. The first focuses on what the child perceives and experiences throughout a day, planned and unplanned, sometimes summed up by the phrase, *Curriculum is what happens* (Jones and Nimmo 1994). We call this the *experienced curriculum*. The second definition focuses on intentions and defines curriculum as planned learning experiences. We refer to this as the *planned curriculum*. The term *curriculum* is used as well to refer to a product (often commercial) that provides specific materials for presenting topics and skills, or to refer to the entire course of study of a school or program.

In this chapter we will focus on how an early childhood educator can design experiences that enhance children's social, emotional, cognitive, and physical development and give an overview of the curriculum development process. In the four chapters that follow, we discuss in more detail how you can plan for all of the learning areas that are generally included in early childhood programs.

and interests provided an alternative to the joyless academics that were prevalent during the first part of the century. The 1950s saw a return to a more academically focused curriculum as a reaction to the belief that progressive schools lacked rigor and didn't give children the knowledge and skills that were needed to be competitive with Russia in science and technology. In the 1960s and early 1970s, many American educators traveled to England to observe the child-centered project approach of the British Infant Schools and then adopted this approach in the United States as an alternative to the academic focus of the schools of the time. This was followed by a period of political conservatism that influenced the "back to basics" movement with its emphasis on the three Rs, traditionally taught, as the most desirable approach to education. Today early childhood educators' views of "developmentally appropriate practice" are having an impact on education, and there is a movement to focus public school programs on the needs and interests of children.

Curriculum is based on a vision of society, on a philosophy of the role of education, and on some structured way to translate this vision into learning experiences. It can originate from three broad sources: (1) beliefs about what is true and important to know, (2) learners and their patterns of development, and (3) knowledge or subject matter (Armstrong 1989).

Curriculum is also a product of its time. As a society changes and as knowledge of children and learning evolves, so does the content of education change. Educational values and practices are profoundly influenced by social and political forces. We have, over the years, observed an "educational pendulum" that swings, over a period of about a decade, between an emphasis on the nature and interests of the learner and an emphasis on the subject matter to be taught. Each swing is a reaction of a group of people to their perception of the shortcomings of the prevalent educational approach. The progressive education movement with its emphasis on the learner's needs

The field of early childhood education, as we discussed in Chapter Two, The Historical Roots of Current Practice, has always been characterized by a humanistic and child-centered approach. Over the years the majority of programs for children under five have based their teaching on this philosophy, while public school programs have been subject to the pedagogical swings just described. Today the pendulum continues to swing. Just as early childhood views of developmentally appropriate practice have had an impact on public education for children between the ages of five and eight, so have the public school requirements for children to enter kindergarten ready for academic demands brought pressure on preschool programs to require worksheets and other academic tasks. Awareness of the tendency for pendulum swings between emphasis on the learner and on the subject matter may enable future educators to find a middle position that takes both into account.

Elements of Curriculum

In planning curriculum, it is important to be aware of three interconnected elements: the nature of the learner *(who),* the content or subject matter *(what),* and the process or the actual engagement of children with planned learning opportunities *(how).* Learner, content, and process are linked together and each needs to be carefully considered in designing meaningful learning experiences for children. Early childhood educators whose professional preparation emphasizes child development tend to place greater emphasis on children and educational processes than on content. In contrast, in elementary and secondary schools where teacher education places more emphasis on curriculum subject areas, there tends to be a greater emphasis on what is taught and less on the learner and the process. Thus, your educational background may have an impact on the curriculum choices that you make.

Some essential elements should receive careful attention in the process of planning curriculum:

- A statement of purpose that involves reflection on educational mission. Statements of purpose may include *aims* (inspirational ideals based on philosophy and values), *goals* (broad desired learning outcomes), and *objectives* (intended learning outcomes stated in specific terms).
- Selection and organization of content.
- Strategies or methods: ways of delivering the curriculum. These may include the design of the learning environment or planned activities.
- Evaluation: some method of determining what the child has learned. In early childhood settings this is most often done by observing children and making anecdotal records of the observations.

These elements interact with each other; decisions made in one area will impact upon the others.

The Early Childhood Perspective

In early childhood education and care, views of curriculum are guided by our values and by beliefs about children and learning that characterize the field. These include the view that learning occurs best when children construct knowledge themselves as they explore the world they live in, that classroom experiences should be meaningful, and that play is one of the most important vehicles for children's learning. Early childhood educators believe that the curriculum of an early childhood program should nurture the natural curiosity and exuberance of childhood, that it should be meaningful and intellectually stimulating, and that it should combine child-chosen play in a planned learning environment with planned, developmentally appropriate activities. Our goal is to help you learn to design curriculum that reflects these views.

When you observe programs, you will probably see many different approaches to curriculum. Some will be guided by the ideals we have just described; others may be based on different values and beliefs or may provide a grab bag of unrelated activities with no underlying rationale. You may observe programs that fail to provide stimulation and rely on a few unvarying play areas and materials, or those that have mishmash of unrelated activities that don't make sense to children or adults. You will probably encounter some programs that use workbooks or prepackaged materials that focus on isolated skills and concepts. Although these may appeal to adults, they are not appropriate for young children who need meaning and active engagement in their learning. For them, abstract tasks unrelated to real-life applications have little or no meaning.

CRITICAL CONSIDERATIONS IN PLANNING CURRICULUM

You will make many decisions as you plan curriculum for children. You will choose the content to be taught, how it should be organized, and how it should be presented to the children. As you make decisions it is important to take several critical elements into account: the philosophy and goals of the program in which you work; the nature of the children, families, and community; knowledge of child development; and consideration of the value of the content for the children.

Goals, Values, and Program Philosophy

What you teach and how you teach it must reflect your values for society and your long-term goals for children's development. It is best to begin the curriculum development process by reflecting on these things. Think about what knowledge and skills your group of children will need to function effectively in society as it exists now and as well as what they will need to be productive citizens in the future.

As Barbara Biber points out, programs for young children are a powerful force in influencing "not only the excellence of intellect but in shaping the feelings, the attitudes, the values, the sense of self and the dreaming of what is to be, the images of good and evil in the world about and the visions of what the life . . . might be" (Biber 1969, 8). Because of the important impact of early childhood programs, one of the most basic challenges for education and for those who work to further it is to become clear on our educational goals.

Many early childhood programs have a statement of philosophy that makes clear their purpose, goals, and underlying values and assumptions about children and learning. The program's statement of philosophy and your own values and goals can provide valuable guidance in making decisions regarding what you do with children.

Programs vary in the extent to which they place emphasis on social, emotional, intellectual, and physical goals. Some educators believe that we must begin with feelings and relationships; others believe that it is more important to begin with skills and concepts to be learned. As we visit programs we see a wide range of practices and curriculum content. Curriculum decisions vary from setting to setting. There is room for a range of differing perspectives, but remember that whatever you choose to teach, you owe it to the children to have given it careful thought.

Curriculum choices can be placed on a continuum between two poles—*child-centered* and *subject-centered*. Educators on the child-centered end of the continuum focus on the total development of the child and believe that children are capable of making their own choices in a planned learning environment. They feel that educational experiences should be personally meaningful for children, that the process of learning is more important than the product, and that education *is* life and not just preparation for later schooling.

Educators closer to the subject-centered end of the continuum place more emphasis on what is taught—the fields of study. They tend to be

---

Reflect and write about . . .

the role of education in shaping the future

What do you want the world to be like in the future? What kind of people will be needed for the world you envision to exist? What must early childhood programs and curriculum be like to help to develop these people?

more concerned with what is learned and place emphasis on the acquisition of specific knowledge and skills that they believe are important for children to learn.

Every early childhood educator and program will balance these dimensions in different ways, though the age of the children and the values and philosophy of the individual and program will influence on which side of the spectrum the majority of choices fall. When the way children develop is not adequately considered, programs may emphasize content without regard to children's needs, or they may fail to provide adequate support for children's learning. These programs are not developmentally appropriate. On the child-centered end of the continuum are laissez-faire programs that do not give the structure, stimulation, content, and guidance that children need to grow and learn. On the content end of the continuum are rigid programs that stress mastery of specific tasks to the exclusion of other goals and that tend to regard children as machines to be programmed rather than thinking and feeling human beings. Between the two extremes lie a range of alternatives that can contribute positively to children's learning and development (Figure 10.1).

Your personal values, the values of your program and community, and the age and abilities of the children you teach will influence where on the continuum your choices will fall. The child-centered emphasis is essential for infants, toddlers, and young preschoolers. Subject-centered approaches are more typical of and more appropriate for programs for older children.

Good programs for young children are based on articulation of values and goals. Al-

though it is important to begin with values, it is not always an easy matter to agree with families and other staff members on which values are most important and which should guide practice. We live in a society that is characterized by diversity in every arena of life, and one of the places in which this is most apparent is in people's educational values and goals. There are many different and contradictory points of view regarding what is best for children and how they should be educated. Differences should not be ignored. They need to be discussed and reconciled whenever it is possible to do so.

Knowledge of Child Development

An important hallmark of the field of early childhood education is that program practice is based on knowledge of child development. This knowledge enables educators to plan activities for children at the appropriate level for their age and for their individual needs, backgrounds, and interests.

According to NAEYC's influential document *Guidelines for Developmentally Appropriate Practice* (Bredekamp 1987), developmental appropriateness has two dimensions: age appropriateness and individual appropriateness. *Age appropriateness* refers to the universal, predictable sequences of growth and change that occur in all children during the first eight years of life. Knowledge of typical development of children within the age span served by a program provides a framework from which educators prepare the learning environment and plan appropriate experiences. *Individual appropriateness* refers to the fact that each child is a

Child-centered   Content-centered

Laissez-faire – – – – | ————————————————— | – – – – **Rigid**

Inappropriate   **Developmentally appropriate for young children**   Inappropriate

FIGURE 10.1
Child-centered versus content-centered program continuum.

unique person with an individual pattern and timing of growth as well as distinct personality, learning style, culture, and family background. Both the curriculum and adults' interactions with children should be responsive to individual differences in interest, style, ability, and culture.

Just as educational experiences for individual children within a group will differ, planning for the range of age groups is markedly different. For infants and toddlers, you develop very broad general goals that are applicable to all children based on your knowledge of their stage of development. For example, knowing that toddlers are developing a sense of themselves as capable individuals means that a curriculum plan in any toddler room needs to include lots of opportunities for looking into mirrors, at books with pictures of toddlers, and at photo albums with pictures of themselves. They also need to sing name songs and talk about themselves, push buggies, turn on faucets, pour water, and move toys from one part of the room to another. Curriculum should meet individualized goals for particular children. If Janelle is afraid of monsters, opportunities need to be available for her to express that fear. If Matthew is having difficulty saying good-bye to his mom, it means including lots of talking about how mommies always come back. Most planning will be done on a short-term rather than long-term basis.

The younger the children, the more child-centered the program should be. The majority of the program day should consist of play and routines. Children's spontaneous exploration is the core of the curriculum for two- and three-year-olds.

For older children, planning can be done further in advance and will be more elaborate. Four- through six-year-old children benefit from planned learning experiences based on carefully chosen themes that supplement their play and exploration. Planning for preschoolers should take into consideration the predictable characteristics of a group. Most

preschoolers will at first be intensely involved with exploring the environment and in testing the challenges and limits of the setting. They are likely to have some difficulty working as a group and staying together. As they become accustomed to routines, preschool children develop confidence in the adults and the environment and gain a sense of membership in the group. As the year progresses, they learn to work together and will enjoy more complex challenges. They will also seek new stimulation, and, if it is not provided in the context of the planned curriculum, they may supply it in unexpected and undesirable ways. Knowing this will help you to begin with fairly simple and predictable activities and to add complexity as the year progresses.

For primary age children, learning is more purposeful, more project oriented, and more structured. They do more elaborate planning for play episodes, are anxious to accurately represent what they have learned, and may seek out resources to make sure that they are doing it "right." Young primary school children are able to think more abstractly—to represent verbally and through other symbols the things that they are striving to understand. For example, we once observed a class of second graders studying the harbor. After talking and reading about the harbor and shipping, they took a trip to the harbor where they were able to visit a cargo ship. When they returned to the classroom they marked the harbor on a city map, wrote stories and painted pictures about their experiences, built ships and harbor buildings out of cardboard, and reenacted the roles of harbor master, chandler, ship's agent, captain, and dock worker.

What's Worth Knowing?

Choosing content is a vital task because curriculum will have little value if what you are presenting isn't worth knowing. What is worth knowing when you are one, two, three, four, five, six, seven, or eight years old? This crucial

question has guided the ways in which we have thought and written about curriculum since we first heard it posed in conversation by Lilian Katz a number of years ago.

Children want to know many things about the world they live in. They want to know about themselves, about how to get along with others and care for their own needs, about their families and communities, and the natural and physical aspects of their environment. We can see this as we watch a two-year-old's triumphant, "Me can!," a three-year-old's passion for pretending to be a firefighter, or a five-year-old's fascination with babies and animals. What about learning shapes, colors, numbers, classification, seriation, conservation of volume, the alphabet, phonics, or prepositions? These are isolated skills and fragments of knowledge. It is valuable to know these things, but they can be learned as children pursue tasks and learn about things that are interesting and meaning-

ful to them. In isolation, they have little significance or relevance to children's lives.

Families and Community

Your curriculum must also be considered in terms of the background of the children and families, their culture, and community characteristics and values. Before you choose, reflect on the families of the children in your class. You might want to ask yourself some of the following questions: What are their views about what is important for children to learn? Are there subjects or activities with which they might be uncomfortable? Are families willing and able to share things from home and/or participate in the program by coming in as resource people or participating in class trips? The answers to these questions will help to guide you in choosing and adapting curriculum.

Sometimes you will have to do a difficult balancing act, for what families want you to teach may not be what is best for children. Pressure from families for schools to emphasize academic skills is a frequently occurring issue in early childhood education today. Such pressure is felt in programs in which economically disadvantaged families see early academics as a road out of the cycle of poverty. The pressure is also felt in "exclusive" programs where families want their young children to gain admission to highly competitive private schools. You can be respectful of the wishes of such families by making

---

Reflect and write about . . .

what you felt was worth knowing when you were a child

Think back to the time you were about the age of the children with whom you wish to work. Was there anything you were vitally interested in, something you wanted to know about or be able to do? Reflect on what that was, why you think it was important to you, what you learned about it, and how you learned it.

Reflect and write about . . .

curriculum you experienced as a child

Recall your earliest school experience and share your memories about the kinds of learning experiences that your teachers provided. What was the balance between play and teacher-directed activities? Do you think that what was taught was developmentally appropriate and worth knowing?

---

your academic content more visible than you otherwise might. But don't let pressure push you into developmentally inappropriate practice. Remember, you have knowledge and skills from your professional training that families do not have. Ideas found in the curriculum chapters can serve as the basis for explaining good early childhood practice to families so that they can see the ways children's experiences are contributing to their development and learning.

The cultures of the children in your program and events in the community and geography will influence your choices. A curriculum that promotes acceptance of diversity is desirable in every program. If most of the children in your class come from one cultural group, this culture might be the starting point for many activities. In order for children to gain understanding and acceptance of others, it is important to provide experience with other cultures as well as their own.

Weather and events in the community can also provide the impetus for what you study. In Hawaii, when the air is filled with volcanic haze or the TV news is filled with stories of eruptions, volcanoes are a natural and important topic of study. The study of earthquakes might well be the most relevant curriculum in the days following a major quake. Similarly, construction of a new park in your neighborhood or a celebration in your community might spark the interest of a group of children and serve as the starting place for exploration and learning over a number of weeks.

SELECTING, ORGANIZING, AND PRESENTING CURRICULUM

We believe that children learn best when decisions about curriculum are made by those who work with a group on a daily basis and who know them well. Sometimes a program administrator or education specialist will participate in the process of deciding. They may be a valuable source of assistance but are most effective in the role of consultant to the planning process, not as the prime decision makers. In some preschools and many elementary schools, curriculum decisions are made by curriculum committees, administrators, and boards of education. This approach to decision making may support coordination and articulation between classes, but the needs of a particular group of children can easily be lost in a top-down decision-making process. Even if you work in a setting in which curriculum is chosen by others, you still have choices about the method you will employ and the relative importance that you place on the different aspects of the curriculum.

Organizing Learning Experiences for Children

There are a number of ways to organize learning experiences for children. The three approaches that are most well known are: (1) subject-centered organization, (2) learner-centered organization, and (3) integrated or thematic organization.

Subject-Centered Organization

Historically, education has focused on the attainment of knowledge, and the curriculum of the school has been presented by subject areas (math, science, social studies, reading, language arts). Each subject is regarded as having its own distinct content and method. This design is prevalent in most elementary and high schools in which subject matter teaching is generally organized into discrete blocks of time (reading 9:00 to 9:45, math 10:00 to 10:30). Sometimes two or more disciplines—for example, math and science—are combined for instruction. Organization by subjects is a useful framework for assuring that all areas of content will be given attention in the program, but it does not help children understand relationships that exist between subjects.

This traditional approach may work in settings for older children, adolescents, and adults. It is not appropriate for young children who want to learn about the world they live in and understand it best as a whole.

Child-Centered Organization

A second major way to organize learning experiences is based on the developmental stage, needs, and interests of the learners. Learning is based on children's purposes, on their natural inclinations and ways of learning. Some advocates of this approach believe that all learning experiences should be based on children's interests and that the curriculum must emerge from daily occurrences. The developmental early childhood program in which children have large blocks of activity time to play and explore in a planned environment is an example of a learner-centered curriculum design. Planned activities emerge from observations of children and are based on their interests.

This approach is appropriate in early childhood classrooms and is the best way to plan for infants, toddlers, and young preschoolers. Because it is limited by what children bring to the educational experience, it may not provide enough intellectual stimulation for older preschoolers, kindergartners, or primary-age children.

Integrated or Thematic Organization

It is possible and often desirable to combine aspects of these two approaches through the use of integrated or thematic planning. We use the word *theme* to refer to a topic that provides an organizing framework—a focus for the curriculum. Using a theme as the hub around which appropriate activities are planned allows you to integrate several different subject areas into meaningful and worthwhile experiences. Children engage in in-depth exploration of the topic over a period of time. The terms *unit* and *project approach* are also used to refer to this type of curriculum.

Children's interests or your ideas about what children would enjoy or benefit from can be source of the theme. Exploration of a topic can be tailored to fit the learning styles of a group of children and of individual children in the group. This is an approach to structuring curriculum that we have used and found effective over the years, especially for children four years old and older. The use of integrated themes has helped us to think in new and creative ways and has taken us on learning adventures with children. Later in this chapter we will describe how you can plan curriculum using an integrated approach.

Presenting Curriculum

There are several ways to present curriculum to young children. These include allowing them to engage with materials in a planned learning environment, one-to-one interactions, small groups, and large groups.

Play in a Planned Environment

Through their exploration and self-initiated play activities, children construct knowledge and develop individual skills and interests. Young children need many opportunities to learn and discover through their play each day. Play is the most appropriate learning medium when you want children to explore and discover for themselves. The power of play is that through it children develop skills and knowledge of many kinds simultaneously. At the same time they enjoy themselves and become motivated to keep exploring and learning.

As we have said in Chapter Five, Play, and Chapter Eight, The Learning Environment, blocks, sand, water, art materials, dramatic play, manipulatives, woodworking, and outdoor play are the cornerstones of the early childhood curriculum. You can provide additional play materials and self-directed activities that support the learning objectives and themes that you have chosen.

One-to-One Experiences

When you want a child or group of children to acquire a specific concept or skill, it is often useful to plan an activity to present to the children one at a time or to the child who has a specific need or interest. These special one-to-one experiences permit you to concentrate on the child's learning process and participate in a learning dialogue. They allow you to observe and assess a child's knowledge and skill and modify what you do based on the child's response. Large blocks of time for child-chosen activities enable you to engage in planned or spontaneous interactions with individual children while the rest of the group engages in activities. One-to-one instruction is most appropriate in helping children to refine a physical skill, learn a new skill or technique (a painting technique, forming letters), for conversation, for literacy activities like key vocabulary and dictating stories (see Chapter Thirteen, The

Communication Curriculum), and for exploring and discussing scientific phenomena like why an object floats or sinks.

Small Group Activities

Small group activities in which you work with two to ten children enable you to present concepts, facilitate an exchange of ideas between children, and have meaningful personal contact with each child. This approach reduces waiting time and works best in activities that involve turn taking, manipulation of materials, and teacher assistance. You are able to attend to the way children respond and can evaluate and modify.

Small groups work best for games like "I Spy," reading stories where you want to generate a lot of discussion, acting out stories, creative movement activities, cooking projects, and field trips, especially to places like concerts and museums where it will be more meaningful if an adult can discuss the experience with the children.

Small groups can also meet together for special activities on a regular basis. These experiences can help children to develop some important skills including the ability to listen and talk in a group, solve problems and make decisions democratically, take leader and follower roles, and accept responsibility for the outcomes of their decisions. Small groups develop an identity of their own. When they select a name for their group, they further cement feelings of belonging and responsibility.

Large Group Activities

Large group activities are valuable when you want children to share a common experience or to hear the same thing. (We use the term *large group* to describe a group of more than ten—usually a whole class.) They are most appropriate for giving information that is needed by all of the children, singing, stories (told or read), demonstrations, and to meet with visiting resource people. They are also effective for group games like dodge ball and for field trips to a familiar place like a park. Large groups are economical in terms of your time but are not appropriate when you want to attend to individual needs and responses, when you want children to explore and discover, or for activities like cooking where you want children to be active participants.

Choosing Between Child Choice and Teacher Direction

Although much of what young children learn grows out of their day-to-day play experiences, there is more that they can learn. There is other information and experiences that are interesting and valuable for young children. These can often be presented through teacher-led experiences that provide stimulation and focus. People who are accustomed to traditional schools may think that learning involves a teacher in front of the room addressing a large group of children. In fact, this is the teaching approach that is used the least in good programs for young children. Indeed, it is apparent to children: four-year-old Jasmine recently commented when Eva referred to herself as a grown-up, "No, you're a teacher—you listen to us. Grown-ups just talk."

The relative balance of child-chosen exploration in a planned environment and teacher-led experiences will vary based on the age and characteristics of the children as well as on the philosophy and characteristics of the program. Both processes have advantages and disadvantages and are most appropriate for different kinds of content. For example, it is unlikely that a five-year-old would spontaneously learn to read a clock or tie shoelaces without direct teaching. Similarly, it is unlikely that any amount of planned activity would teach that same five-year-old to climb a rope although she might learn to do so in focused, self-directed play.

Infants, toddlers, and young preschoolers can learn very little through direct instruction. Both you and the child will feel frustrated if you try. But as children get older they will gradually become more able to learn through direct teaching when they are interested and motivated. Every educator will seek an optimal balance between child-chosen and adult-directed activity. As you plan you need to ask yourself which best meets the developmental characteristics of the children and your educational purposes. The answers to these questions will help you find the right balance for your group.

THE PLANNING PROCESS

Every educator wants to help children learn important things. But what guides you as you de-

---

Reflect and write about . . .

your observations about how curriculum is selected, organized, and presented

Reflect on early childhood programs you have observed or worked in. Do you know how the curriculum was chosen? How was curriculum organized in terms of subject matter? How was it communicated to the children? What seemed to be the balance between child-chosen and teacher-led experiences?

cide what is important and how to help them learn? As we have said, choices should be tied to your values and your views of what children and society need now and will need in the future. As you begin to think about what to teach, reflect on your values and on the purpose and goals of the program in which you teach. You will also want to think about the children, their developmental stage, interests, backgrounds, and the kinds of activities they respond to best. And you will want to think long and hard about which of the myriad of possible learning experiences that you can offer will be of most value to this group of children.

Starting Places

It is important to be aware of your starting point for planning. We have found it useful to think of the planning process as having several possible beginning places. You can base your planning on your observation and assessment of children's interests, needs, abilities, and concerns; with an activity that seems appropriate and relevant to the children; or with a set of

learning objectives that are selected based on what is known about the developmental stage of the children and the goals of the program.

Observation and assessment of the children in your group will give you valuable information about the kinds of learning experiences from which they will benefit. Observe their strengths and abilities as well as areas that need special attention. Watch to find out the things they are interested in and the kinds of activities they enjoy. And be sure to observe their spontaneous play—it will give you information about issues in their lives, their perceptions of people's roles, and how they interact with each other. You might choose to focus your curriculum on an interest of the children (insects, pets, dinosaurs, machines at a construction site) or a concern or issue in some of their lives (changing families, moving, making and keeping friends). You may incorporate an area in which the children need to develop skills as a focus of your curriculum (for example, by providing activities that involve lots of oral language for a group in which many children do not use language fluently).

Long- and Short-Term Plans

Planning creates the context for learning to occur. All educators plan. You will choose how much you will plan, in what detail, and how far in advance. Most early childhood educators make very general plans for a long period, a year or a month, and more detailed weekly or daily plans.

Long-term plans give a sense of direction. They are useful for thinking though the topics that you might want to introduce during a semester or year. Long-term plans help you make decisions about ordering material and planning trips. It is useful to be able to share general directions with families so that they have advance notice of events that call for their participation. It is best if these plans are quite flexible. If you find out that your advance planning was inap-

Reflect and write about . . .

the planning process

Describe the planning process used in a program you have observed or worked in. What do you know or would you infer about how planning occurred? To what extent were the learning experiences that you observed related to the needs and interests of children? To what extent were they based on predetermined objectives? What are your thoughts about each?

propriate or if you discover unanticipated interests or resources, you can change with little inconvenience.

You will also do short-term planning that sketches out the major activities of each week and each day. The schedule of daily activities such as story time, circle, and outdoor time and regular events such as cooking and field trips can provide the structure for your plan. As you plan, you will deliberate about the skills and concepts that you want children to develop throughout the days and weeks ahead. You will think about ways to include learning centers such as art, science, math, blocks, and dramatic play. For preschool, kindergarten, and primary children, you also think about how the theme you are studying and subject areas such as literature and science will be addressed (Table 10.1). Next you will write a tentative plan that includes a sequence of activities to support the children in acquiring skills and concepts and review it to see if it is practical and appropriate. And finally you will write a version that you can use and share with other staff members and families.

Thematic Planning

We think that the best organization for curriculum in a program for preschool and elementary-age children is to integrate activities by using a theme as an umbrella to coordinate different developmental and subject areas. A theme can simultaneously contribute to children's growing awareness and understanding and can provide opportunities for children to learn by doing and to have many direct experiences with the world. Children can reflect on, represent, and recreate experiences through discussions, writing, drawing, art, music, movement, measuring, graphing, mapping, block building, and dramatic play. Through their involvement with a topic, children will acquire knowledge of all of the subject areas generally taught in early childhood programs and develop skills in sensing and moving, thinking and problem solving, communicating, creating, and working and playing with others. Theme possibilities are rich and varied. Used well and thoughtfully, thematic planning helps children to understand that learning is connected to life. Themes make planning easier and more fun. In the sections that follow, we describe how to develop thematic units that are worthwhile and appropriate.

Selecting a Focus[1]

The first step in planning is the choice of the theme (topic). This involves thoughtful consid-

---

[1]Our continuing dialogue with Elizabeth Jones has contributed to our thinking about the appropriate use of themes and to this section.

TABLE 10.1
Week Plan for Families Unit—Week Two

Time/Activity	Monday	Tuesday	Wednesday	Thursday	Friday
Circle Time	**Music:** Songs: "You Are the One Your Mommy Loves" Lullabyes to sing to Max's baby. **Discussion:** What do mothers and children do together?	**Music:** Song: "House That's Made of Love" **Discussion:** How are homes the same/different?	**Music and Physical Development:** Finger-play songs: "Here's a Family" "One Little Bird"	**Trip Preparation:** Song: "House That's Made of Love" **Discussion:** What kinds of homes might we see?	**Visitors:** Max's mom and their baby. We will sing lullabyes to the baby and talk to his mom about taking care of the baby.
Activity Time 9:00–10:00 Special activities available in centers, every day.	**Blocks:** Block families and doll house	**Home Area:** baby care box **Science:** visiting mouse family	**Toys and Games:** Duplo farm family games	**Field Trip:** Neighborhood walk to observe different kinds of homes where families live	**Cooking:** Najeda's favorite spaghetti
Art Activities 9:00–10:00 Easel, drawing materials, and clay always available	My home—box construction	Finger painting	Families magazine collage	Remind parents to send shoes, backpack, school shirt, drink	Sponge printing
Outside Time 10:00–11:00	Obstacle course	Game: Mother May I?	Hoops and balls		
Small Groups 11:00–11:30	Group book on how family members take care of each other		Family graph		Baby doll and clothes washing
Lunch 11:30–12:00					Illustrating family recipe
Books/Stories 12:00–12:30	*Your Family, My Family*	*Are You My Mother?*	*Big Sister, Little Sister*	*A House Is a House for Me*	*A Baby Sister for Frances*

301

eration of the values and goals of the program, observation of children's interests and concerns, consideration of your own interests and skills, and attention to coming celebrations and events in your community. A list of possible themes is then generated and each item is evaluated.

A theme must be appropriate for the group of children for whom it is planned—it should reflect their interests, abilities, and issues of concern to them. It should include concepts and skills that provide the right level of challenge. See Chapter Fourteen, The Inquiry Curriculum, for a discussion of how to evaluate the developmental appropriateness of various concepts.

Meaningful themes help children make connections. They reflect life and are not separate from it. Children's lives and their environment—their families, cultures, community, or geographical locale—are good sources of themes. A team of kindergarten teachers we know chose a unit on marine life for their class when they observed that several of the children were captivated by this topic (one that is relevant and motivating in Hawaii but that would probably not be appropriate in a state with no seashore). When a swarm of bees settled in their tree house, this same team, after thoughtful deliberation about the potential for generating productive learning, abandoned their plans to begin a unit on gardens and embarked on a study of bees that they felt could accomplish many of the same educational goals. The children's fear of the bees gave way to fascination as they learned about the social structure of the hive and the production of honey and watched the beekeeper relocate the hive to a site further removed from the classroom. Themes that we have seen developed for successful integration of subject areas and meaningful learning for children include: life cycles, produce from garden to market, space, the farm, marine life, family, rain, insects, the hospital, trees, and the community. Exploration of this kind of topic can

contribute to children's awareness and understanding of the world and themselves as well as heightening their sense of uniqueness and pride in their families and community. While these larger goals are being realized, children are exploring, experimenting, discussing experiences, building with blocks, manipulating materials, writing, and cooking. They are simultaneously developing fine motor and hand and eye coordination; understanding of letters and numbers; discrimination of size, shape, and color; and a myriad of other skills and understandings.

Remember that you and the children will live with the topic that you choose for a period of time, so it should be worthwhile for everyone involved. Questions to ask that will help you to choose wisely include:

- Are the topic and the central concepts interesting, meaningful, and worth knowing? Will study of this topic help children to acquire greater understanding and appreciation of some aspect of the world in which they live?
- Are the underlying concepts developmentally appropriate for young children? Are the required skills within their grasp? Can they be organized to move from more simple to more complex and from concrete to abstract? Can this topic be taught through direct experience? Can children explore it with their senses?
- Can many things be experienced and learned about this topic? Can it generate a variety of activities and learning in all areas of development and in a broad range of subject areas?

Make sure that the theme you chose is complex and interesting enough to be explored in some depth. Plan to use the theme for several weeks to several months and then stay open to possibilities that emerge from children's or adults' ideas and interests. In most cases themes used

for a week or two promote a once-over-lightly view of content.

Observe the children each step of the way and adapt and change according to their responses to the material. No plan implemented with real children will end up looking as it was originally visualized. Don't get too attached to your plan. We once planned and began teaching a unit on feelings for a group of young three-year-olds. While reading a story about a baby who thought her mother didn't love her, we found that the children were extremely concerned with the issue of parental love and care. We realized that the stress of separation was high and that dealing with this dramatic transition in their lives was the real "curriculum" for these children. We refocused the curriculum on the study of families to help the children connect their experiences at school with their lives at home.

Be sure that the theme is a source of genuine learning and not just a way to sugarcoat traditional academic subject matter. Using dinosaurs, bears, or bees on the pages to make worksheets more palatable is not even distantly related to the meaningful learning that good thematic planning can generate. Sometimes the theme gives a surface appearance of connecting ideas but is not meaningful to children and does nothing to enhance their understanding of the world. We observed a group of three year olds "studying" the letter *M* by making *magazine* collages and *muffins* and by coloring a picture of a *monkey*. When we asked the children what they had been doing, they responded that they had been cooking, gluing paper, and coloring. Their teacher quickly corrected them saying that they had been studying *M*. This approach failed to integrate children's learning because the central concept was not relevant to this lively group of three-year-olds.

Be careful about using holidays as the basis for thematic planning. Some holidays have an impact on children's lives and can be studied in terms of the joys of family celebrations. They are often are made trivial and inappropriate by focusing on a few songs and look-alike craft activities that are devoid of meaning to the children. Other holidays can be used as the basis for significant learning. For example, Halloween can be used as a springboard for discussing fears and the distinction between fantasy and reality. Holidays that do not have an impact on children's lives such as President's Day and St. Patrick's Day have little or no appropriate content for young children. Although holidays are times of excitement, they do not necessarily make worthwhile themes for integrating learning and development. Your desire to celebrate holidays may stem from the welcome relief they brought to the hard, colorless institutions of your elementary school days. In a beautiful and everchanging classroom designed for young children, such relief is unnecessary.

Creating a Thematic Plan

Although you can plan on your own, we have found it more rewarding to work with other members of a teaching team. For many years, to generate thematic plans we have used a chart system that involves placing the theme name or topic in the center of a large piece of chart paper, off of which numerous lines are drawn to map ideas related to the theme. We use this system to brainstorm ideas for all elements of the plan: the purposes, goals, major ideas, and activities in each area of curriculum and what will be included in each interest area in support of the theme (such as books and dramatic play props). These charts are referred to by several names including *sunbursts, curriculum maps,* or *webs.* For a sample of how a curriculum map or web might look, see Figure 10.2, A Curriculum Map.

Whether you use mapping or simply make an idea list, creating a thematic plan involves the interconnected steps that follow:

- Choose the theme using the criteria described. If the subject is unfamiliar, background reading will help you to learn.
- Once it has been selected, think through and, if appropriate, write the rationale for the plan describing why this topic is meaningful to young children and why you are choosing it for this group of children at this time.
- Brainstorm the topics and activities that might grow out of the theme.
- As you assess the value of different activities, consider your goals and decide on the major understandings that you wish children to acquire. This is a step that is often omitted in the tendency to generate lots of interesting activities. As we have added this step to our own planning we have found that we are more focused on helping children gain meaning from a thematic unit.
- Collect teaching materials and resources and develop your initial plan, making sure that you have included activities that support each of the major understandings.
- Schedule activities into weekly plans (see Table 10.1), schedule trips and resource people, and begin to write any necessary activity plans.
- Once you have planned, you will implement, keeping in mind the importance of being open to changes in children's interests and to fortuitous events.
- As you complete activities, assess children's learning and evaluate the unit. There are many ways to evaluate whether children have acquired the major understandings you have targeted. You can observe their play as it pertains to the unit or have children discuss the topic, dictate stories, or write in their journals as a way for you to assess what they have learned. Children who make representational drawings may spontaneously, or upon request, draw pictures that demonstrate their understanding. For example, following a unit on volcanoes two preschoolers

(ages 4-½ and 5) were asked to draw a picture (content unspecified) to illustrate the school newsletter. Kerri drew the picture in Figure 10.3 on p. 306, which illustrates an erupting volcano, its caldera, and the lava tube that feeds it. Partner drew the form of a piece of lava. Both of these children were providing visible proof of the internalization of concepts relating to a volcano. Similarly the drawings in Figure 10.4 on p. 307 were kindergarten children's responses to their teacher's request at the end of a unit to draw and label a picture of an insect.

- Store the materials so you can easily retrieve them. Cardboard banker's boxes work well for this purpose. It may be a year or several years before you open the box, but when you do the materials will be there. You will probably make changes based on new ideas, interests, and materials, but you will not have to start over again from scratch.

Figure 10.5 on p. 308 summarizes these planning steps in outline form. Figure 10.6 on p. 309 presents several parts of the outline for a unit on families.

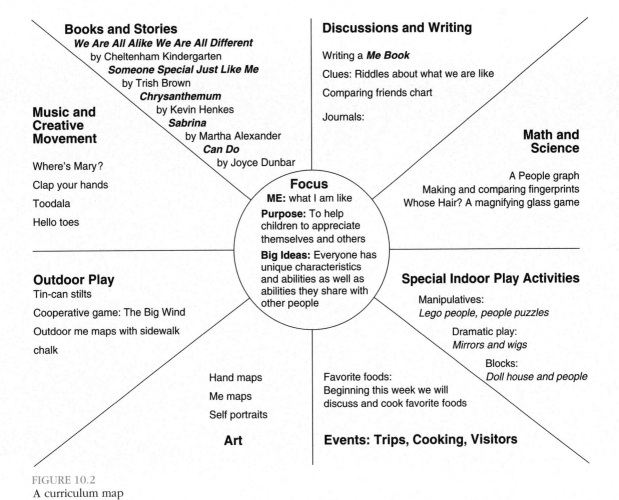

FIGURE 10.2
A curriculum map

FIGURE 10.3
Drawing by a preschooler showing understanding of a volcano

Activity Plans

Activity plans for a single instructional event include a statement of goals or purpose, specify intended learning outcomes, list needed materials, describe teaching procedures, and have provision for evaluation. These are called *lesson plans* in elementary schools and special education settings. We prefer to call them *activity plans,* suggesting a somewhat less formal planning approach.

Lesson plans include objectives that describe intended learning outcomes in terms of what the children are expected to know or do as a result of experiencing a lesson. Objectives stated in very precise terms, called *behavioral objectives,* are sometimes used by elementary school and special education teachers. These objectives de-scribe the desired child behavior in observable terms; for example, the child will cut along a straight line or will identify three shapes. Evaluation of lesson plans appraises the degree to which the specific learning objectives were met.

Behavioral objectives enable you to assess whether your objectives have been met. But under most circumstances their use is not compatible with the philosophy of early childhood education.[2] They predetermine learning, so there is not room for individual choice; they require all children to be at the same place at the end of a given lesson; and they do not allow

[2]Personal correspondence with Marjorie Fields, professor of education at the University of Alaska, has contributed to our thinking about behavioral objectives in early childhood education.

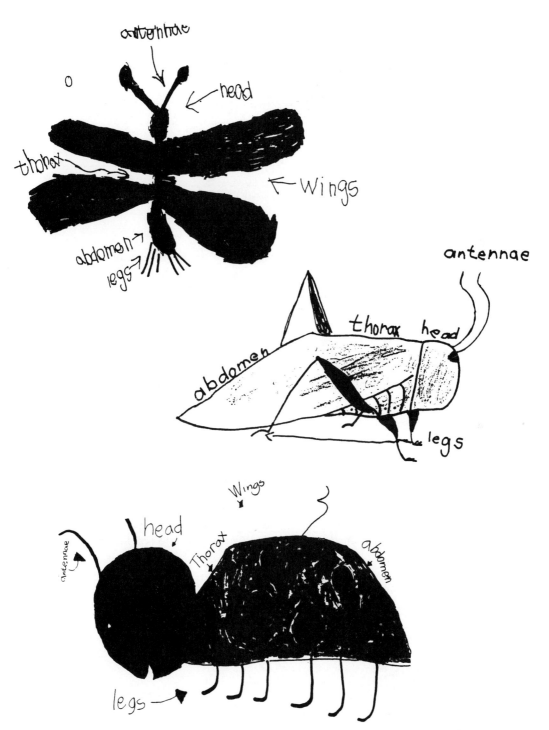

FIGURE 10.4
Drawings by kindergarteners showing their understanding of the parts of an insect

Title: _____
(theme/topic/subject)

Children: _____
(age/#/backgrounds/interests)

Purpose: _____
(why you selected the topic)
_____

Goals: _____
(what you want children to experience/develop/learn)
_____

Big Ideas: _____
(4–6 major understandings/concepts that you would like children to acquire)

Resources: _____
(children's books, records, anthologies, songs, poems, other resources)
_____
_____

Environment Additions: _____
(theme-related materials for the learning center)

Activity Ideas: _____
(specific experiences to accomplish the goals of the theme)
_____
_____
_____

Introduction: _____
(how to introduce the theme/capture the children's interest)

Culmination: _____
(wrap up of theme/review/reflect on experiences/assess learning)
_____

Assessment: _____
(samples to collect for child's portfolio)
_____

Evaluation: _____
(what worked/what didn't)
_____

FIGURE 10.5
Outline for thematic plan

Theme Topic: Families

Children: A preschool class of four- and five-year-olds from diverse ethnic and socioeconomic backgrounds.

Purpose: The family is essential to the child's physical and emotional well-being. Children are innately interested in family roles and relationships. Much of the young child's learning begins at home within the family environment. The theme was chosen because the teachers had observed a lot of interest in family relationships in the dramatic play area and because two of the children recently experienced changes in their families—a divorce and a new baby.

Goals:
- To help children understand the basic unit of human relationship.
- To make a link between children's homes and school.
- To help children realize that differences are acceptable and desirable.
- To help children to learn about the importance of nurturing others and of the critical role that they as family members play now and will play in the future.

Big Ideas:
All people come from and/or live in a family.
All families try to provide for their members' basic needs.
Family members have roles and responsibilities.
There are differences between families.
Families change.

FIGURE 10.6

Rationale, goals and big ideas: families unit

for spontaneity or creativity. Moreover, behavioral objectives are not consistent with the belief that children must construct knowledge from their own active involvement with materials and experiences (Lawton 1988).

The objectives in activity plans also focus on what the child is expected to gain from the lesson, but they may be broader and include involvement, awareness, and appreciation as well as concepts, understandings, and skills to be acquired. Evaluation is based on observation of what children do and say during and following the activity rather than determining if specific outcomes have occurred.

Written activity plans are useful and may be necessary when clarity and sequence are crucial or where procedure or content is complex or

unfamiliar. An activity, such as reading a simple, familiar story, will be included in a weekly plan but generally does not call for a detailed written activity plan. Locating the book, reviewing it, and spending a few moments thinking about how to structure discussion may be enough preparation. During your preparation to become an early childhood educator you will likely practice writing activity plans in great detail until you master the process. As you gain experience, you will be able to use a much simpler planning process. Eventually, with sufficient experience, a few notes may be enough to guide you through most activities. As you present activities you will observe children's responses, experiment with variations, and modify or drop activities that are not successful.

Writing Activity Plans

Activity plans are guidelines for thinking and for action and can also be used to preserve good ideas that can easily be forgotten if they are not recorded and stored. Carefully thinking through the purpose and sequence of an activity helps to ensure success. We strongly encourage beginners to use the sequence in Figure 10.7 for planning activities. When your planning is good you will express yourself clearly to children and feel more comfortable.

The first step in the creation of the plan is to decide on your purpose and then choose the activity. We ask our college students, "Why this activity with this group of children at this time?" Next, think about the concepts, skills, and knowledge you want children to acquire and write your objectives based on these.

Think through and list all of the materials that you will need for your activity. Carefully spell out the procedures. Include a plan for introducing the activity and all of the steps in the presentation, transitions, and closure. Without adequate introduction, a good activity may never get off the ground. Without smooth transitions your purpose may get lost in a trample of children, and without a well-thought-out closure it may just fizzle out. The major steps should be simply described without so much detail that you get bogged down trying to follow it but with enough information that you will be able to use it again at a later date. Be sure not to make assumptions about what children know. Think through what they need to understand in order to do the activity and introduce unfamiliar words and concepts.

Activity Name: **Theme:**

Brief Description:

The Children:

Purpose: (your goals)

Objectives: (specific awareness, understanding, or skills you want children to acquire)
As a result of this activity, the children will:

What you need (all materials and supplies):

Space (where will you present the activity?):

What you do:

    Introduction

    Procedure

    Closure

For the portfolio: (representative samples of child's work)

Evaluation/Follow-up (How did it go, and what changes might you might make next time? What might be possible next steps based on what happened?):

FIGURE 10.7
Activity plan outline

Gather the materials and present the activity. If it involves an item that is novel to the children, try to let them get acquainted with it before you begin teaching. (We once planned a sorting activity using different kinds of nuts. Our objective was delayed as we spent several days cracking and eating nuts with the children before we were able to move on to the activity we had planned.)

The plan provides guidelines, but try to remain flexible. If children are interested in different things or if you sense that the plan is not going well, redirecting or changing often helps. As you gain confidence and experience, you will find yourself able to adapt more easily to children's needs and interests. Be ready to change your plans based on shifts in children's interests, a new insight, or a serendipitous event.

When you are finished, evaluate the activity to see if your goals and objectives have been achieved. There is no better way of evaluating than sensitively observing children. You can ask questions, observe if and how the material is incorporated in their play, or ask them to draw or write about the topic. These samples can be included in the children's portfolios.

Be sure to jot down your thoughts concerning what worked, what didn't work, and your ideas for next time. Keep all of your activities and store them where they can be easily retrieved. You will be glad to have your plans and will be able to make use of them in the future (Figure 10.8).

When you begin to use written activity plans, you may want to follow them closely. Know the plan thoroughly so that you can con-

Activity Name: Family Graph

Theme: Families

Subject Area(s): math and social studies

Brief Description: a bar graph to compare the number of members in a family

The Children: 8 four-year-olds in the Blue Room Class

Purpose: to help children to understand two of the major concepts in the families unit: **1) All people come from and/or live in a family** and **2) There are differences between families.** I hope to have children come to realize that there are many ways to be a family.

Objectives:
As a result of this activity the children will:
1) Gain understanding of some differences between families
2) Develop awareness of the words *big* and *small* to refer to quantity
3) Have an experience that contributes to positive self-concept and family pride
4) Gain understanding of the use of a bar graph to compare quantities
5) Experience working together in a group and listening to each other

What you need •1 sheet butcher paper approximately 30″ divided into 2 1/2″ squares, children's names written beneath columns •pictures drawn in advance on several squares of paper to show the teacher's family members •lots of 2 1/2″ square pieces of paper (50 or so) •7-8 paste pots with applicators •2 sets narrow tip markers •yardstick.

Space: Carpeted area near the bulletin board

What you do:

Introduction: Show pictures of my family; talk about what a little family I have. Name the people in my family. Paste on graph, show how pictures take up one square. Say, "I wonder how many squares your family will make and if you live in a little family or a big family."

Procedure: Pass out squares and have children draw a picture of each family member (discuss with them). As they finish, write the child's name on each square and show them how to glue the picture in the column with their name on it.

Closure: When all of the pictures are glued on, have the children find the columns that are biggest, littlest, the same (use yardstick). Have children tell who is in their family.

For the Portfolio: Note children's comments comparing/contrasting families to include in their portfolios.

Evaluation/Follow-up: From their discussion, I could see that the children understood the concepts. They seemed to enjoy it quite a bit, worth repeating. Make a separate graph or color code the squares for pets next time: Lani had eight dogs.

FIGURE 10.8
Activity plan: families unit

centrate on how children respond. Sometimes what appears to be a disaster in planning may be the result of materials that are too stimulating, mistakes in timing, room arrangement, an activity that is not challenging enough or too challenging for the developmental level of the children, or insufficient opportunities for physical activity or rest when they were needed. Tried again with an appropriate modification, the plan may prove sound. We like to write a

Activity name:_____

- What It Is: (description)

- What You Need: (materials/space)

- What You Do: (procedure)

- How You Assess: (items for portfolio)

- Comments: (include activity source)

FIGURE 10.9
Shortened planning form

shortened form of our plans on 5×8 cards and store them in notebooks, file boxes, or on metal rings. This way they can be easily retrieved and used again. Experienced teachers often find the shortened version adequate for recalling and implementing activities that they have tried, heard about, or seen others use (see Figure 10.9).

FINAL THOUGHTS

The choices you make about the curriculum you provide to children are among your most important professional decisions. Although it is important that the curriculum be developmentally appropriate and interesting for children, it is even more important that it be worthwhile. Worthwhile curriculum contributes to all aspects of development and provides opportunities for children to encounter many meaningful concepts and to practice useful skills.

Some of the most exciting curriculum we have seen integrates the child's experience as a participant in a family, a community, and a culture. This allows for and encourages family input and participation. As an early childhood educator your challenge is to engage the children with whom you work in a variety of experiences that will result in them constructing an understanding of the physical and social world and developing the abilities they need to live fulfilling and productive lives.

PROJECTS

Observe a Teacher: Observe a teacher-directed learning activity. What do you think the goals and objectives of the activity might be? How does the activity contribute to accomplishing the goals? Do you believe the activity was successful in accomplishing its purpose? If not, why not?

Interview a Teacher: Interview a teacher about his or her program goals. Ask about how these are modified or influenced by the community, the interests of children, the concerns of parents, the school administration, and educational trends. How does this effect the experience of children?

Interview a Teacher II: Interview two teachers about the kinds of planning that they do regularly, how much time it takes, how important it is in program success, and so on. Compare their responses. What are your conclusions?

Develop a Plan: Choose a theme from science or the social studies area as described in Chapter Fifteen. Use it as an integrating theme for a week's plan for a class of young children three years of age or older. Decide on appropriate concepts and relate activities to the theme and concepts. Using the process described in this chapter, plan for daily large group and small group activities, relevant materials for interest centers, outside play, and integration of other subject areas.

BIBLIOGRAPHY

Armstrong, D. G. 1989. *Developing and Documenting the Curriculum*. Boston: Allyn & Bacon.

Barclay, K. H., and W. C. Breheny. 1994. Letting the Children Take Over More of Their Own Learning: Collaborative Research in the Kindergarten Classroom. *Young Children* 49(6):33–39.

Biber, B. 1969. *Challenges Ahead for Early Childhood Education*. Washington, DC: National Association for the Education of Young Children.

Bredekamp, S. 1987. *Developmentally Appropriate Practice in Early Childhood Programs Serving Children from Birth Through Age 8*. Expanded ed. Washington, DC: National Association for the Education of Young Children.

Bredekamp, S., and T. Rosegrant, eds. 1992. *Reaching Potentials: Appropriate Curriculum and Assessment for Young Children, Volume 1*. Washington, DC: National Association for the Education of Young Children.

Chenfeld, M. B. 1994. *Teaching in the Key of Life*. Washington, DC: National Association for the Education of Young Children.

DeVries, R., and L. Kohlberg. 1990. *Constructivist Early Education: Overview and Comparison With Other Programs*. Washington, DC: National Association for the Education of Young Children.

Dittmann, L. L., ed. 1977. *Curriculum is What Happens: Planning is the Key*. Washington, DC: National Association for the Education of Young Children.

Edwards, C., L. Gandini, and G. Forman. 1993. *The Hundred Languages of Children*. Norwood, NJ: Ablex.

Jones, E., and J. Nimmo. 1994. *Emergent Curriculum*. Washington, DC: National Association for the Education of Young Children.

Katz, L. G., and S. C. Chard. 1989. *Engaging Children's Minds: The Project Approach*. Norwood, NJ: Ablex.

Krogh, S. 1990. *The Integrated Early Childhood Curriculum*. New York: McGraw-Hill.

Lawton, J. T. 1988. *Introduction to Child Care and Early Childhood Education*. Glenview, IL: Scott, Foresman.

McCracken, J. B. 1993. *Valuing Diversity: The Primary Years*. Washington, DC: National Association for the Education of Young Children.

Mitchell, A., and J. David, eds. 1992. *Explorations with Young Children*. Mt. Rainier, MD: Gryphon House.

Ornstein, A. C., and F. P. Hunkins. 1988. *Curriculum: Foundations, Principles, and Issues*. Englewood Cliffs, NJ: Prentice Hall.

Saylor, J. G., W. M. Alexander, and A. J. Lewis. 1981. *Curriculum Planning for Better Teaching*. 4th ed. New York: Holt, Rinehart & Winston.

Schwartz, S. L., and H. F. Robison. 1982. *Designing Curriculum for Early Childhood*. Boston: Allyn & Bacon.

Seefeldt, C., ed. 1992. *The Early Childhood Curriculum: A Review of Current Research*. New York: Teachers College Press.

Spodek, B., and O. Saracho, eds. 1991. *Issues in Early Childhood Curriculum*. Yearbook in Early Childhood Education. Vol. 2. New York: Teachers College Press.

Wiles, J., and J. C. Bondi. 1994. *Curriculum Development: A Guide to Practice*. 4th ed. Englewood Cliffs, NJ: Merrill/Prentice Hall.

Wortham, S. 1994. *Early Childhood Curriculum: Developmental Bases for Learning and Teaching*. Englewood Cliffs, NJ: Merrill/Prentice Hall.

CHAPTER ELEVEN

The Physical Development Curriculum

And look at your body . . . what a wonder it is! Your legs, your arms, your cunning fingers, the way they move.
Pablo Casals

In this chapter we discuss the importance of young children's physical development and some of the ways you can support it and help them learn how to be healthy.

The body is a young child's connection to the world. Unlike other animals, human beings are completely helpless at birth and spend years gaining full command of their bodies. To develop their fullest potential for sensory and motor competence, young children need opportunities to move, to explore and manipulate materials. As they gain physical skill, children become increasingly able to care for themselves and move beyond the limits that are imposed by their dependency on others. As they gain the ability to control, care for, and use their bodies, they become more confident and independent. The maintenance of physical well-being is essential to all other aspects of development. A sensitive, strong, flexible, coordinated, healthy body allows a child to function competently in the world. It is essential for learning and development to occur.

Sensory and motor development are prerequisite to many areas of competence. To learn to read and write, children must first develop the ability to make fine visual and auditory discriminations. Writing requires fine motor skill that emerges from years of practice in the control of the muscles of the fingers and hands. To appreciate the order and beauty of the world, children must have the ability to perceive it. To translate ideas and feelings into words or art, children must first have a foundation of many real experiences.

In this chapter we discuss how early childhood educators can support children's sensory, small muscle (sometimes referred to as *fine motor*), and large muscle (sometimes referred to as *gross motor*) development. As children grow and develop they learn about how to care for themselves, so we include a section on health and nutrition, covering some things children can learn about caring for their bodies. Information about physical development, health, and nutrition can help you to design and plan appropriate experiences for children.

318

Reflect and write about . . .

your experiences in school with physical education and health education

How were physical education, health, and nutrition taught in the schools of your childhood? What do you remember most vividly? Did these experiences influence what you do as an adult? Is there anything that you learned that you use in your life today?

A DEVELOPMENTAL PERSPECTIVE

The work of Arnold Gesell and his associates, begun in the 1930s, provides much of the information about physical development currently used by early childhood professionals (see Chapter Four, Child Development). Gesell believed that inheritance and maturation determined a major portion of an individual's development but that environmental factors could influence it positively or negatively. For normal growth and maturation to proceed, children must have adequate nutrition, affectionate human contact, and regular opportunities to exercise. Children need protection from disease, injury, and environmental hazards. Day-to-day care needs to be supplemented by periodic medical examinations to make sure that a child's growth patterns are normal and his or her health is good.

Because physical development follows a predictable sequence you will be able to plan activities that help children move on to the appropriate next steps. The infant develops head control and reaching and grasping skills before sitting and walking. The large muscles closest to the center of the body grow and develop coordinated functions before the small muscles of the hands and fingers. Because mastery of the muscles of legs, arms, and torso must be accomplished first, good early childhood educators provide many opportunities for active movement. Growing mastery makes large muscle activity enjoyable to young children, and it is a feature of much of their play. They gradually go on to develop small muscle control. The arms, legs, and trunk must work in concert before a child can pump on a swing; scissors cannot be used until the hand's coordination and strength is well developed.

ROLE OF THE EARLY CHILDHOOD EDUCATOR

Early childhood educators have a vital role to play in supporting physical development. Many of the skills that young children need to develop are available as part of the daily activities and routines of an early childhood program. They need regular opportunities to use their senses and to exercise their large muscles. Teachers need to plan for these things as thoughtfully as they plan any other aspect of the daily program for children and to be attentive to the balance and scope of physical experiences.

Sensory and large muscle activities seem so natural for children that it is easy to take them for granted, and planning may seem unnecessary and be overlooked. It is unnecessary and inappropriate to plan physical education experiences like gymnastic classes and complicated games for young children. Small muscle development opportunities are more frequently planned as part of the curriculum. Activities that develop coordination and control of the hands and fingers are obviously prerequisites to small muscle tasks like writing, using keyboards, and using tools. For this reason they are more often included in planning the early childhood programs.

Daily routines offer another avenue for physical development. Children involved in self-help activities are mastering essential physical skills. To realize this you need only to observe the delight on the face of a two-year-old who has used the toilet unassisted for the first time; the struggle of a three-year-old attempting to button a shirt; or a four-year-old laboriously

cutting the vegetables for a cooking project. You will see that these children are involved in challenging, serious work that will eventually result in gratification and mastery.

In supporting physical development, your first important role is to carefully observe your group of children and to notice the range of physical skills, attitudes toward physical tasks, areas of strength, and areas in which more practice is needed. Your second important role is to plan a well-rounded program. This includes designing the learning environment to support sensory exploration and large and small muscle activity, providing interesting activities, and communicating with children to encourage their involvement. It is also impor-

tant to be able to clearly articulate to families, administrators, and other staff members the rationale for the physical development components of your daily program.

SENSORY DEVELOPMENT

Learning depends on sensory input—hearing, smelling, seeing, touching, moving, and tasting. We are not born with the ability to fully discriminate between different sensations but must learn to be aware of them. Therefore sensory experience should be at the core of the early childhood curriculum for very young children. Every child needs opportunities to learn to perceive using all of the senses. The obvious joy a child shows when rolling down a hill, playing with water, smelling a rose, or rubbing his or her fingers along a soft piece of velvet are the observable evidence of how important sensory experience is.

Looking and listening are generally considered acceptable ways for children to find out about the world. Although these are valuable, they should not be encouraged to the exclusion of taste, touch, smell, and physical manipulation. By the time children come to your early childhood program they may have already been taught to avoid some of these sensory avenues to learning. Touching, smelling, and tasting are often particularly restricted, even in children as young as two. They have been given messages like: "Don't taste—it's dirty," "Don't touch—it's dangerous," and "Don't touch—you may break it." If children are to gather and use the information available to them in the world, they need opportunities to fully develop each of their senses.

In the sensorimotor period (from birth to two years), the senses are the child's primary mode for gathering information and learning. Infants and toddlers learn by experiencing many things through touch, taste, and exploration. Young preschoolers are in the transi-

tional stage between sensorimotor and preoperational modes of learning. If a child's ability to receive and use sensory input is impeded, normal development may be retarded. For this reason, all early childhood programs should include a strong sensory component.

The Organizing Framework

The senses give you a natural framework for thinking about what should be included in the sensory component of your program. The *kinesthetic* sense is an internal awareness of movement, touch, and gravity. It is probably the first sensation that human beings experience. Indeed, the survival of an infant has been demonstrated to be dependent on tactile and kinesthetic stimulation. Children have kinesthetic experiences when they engage in movements like swinging and rocking and when they are touched and held. To remain upright and to make judgments on how we move, we need to have the ability to discriminate and control using the kinesthetic sense.

The *auditory* sense, hearing, also begins before a child is born. Differentiating between sounds is a major developmental task. Learning to screen the auditory environment—to exclude irrelevant sounds and to attend to what is meaningful—is an important part of language development. In a typical noisy early childhood program, it is easy to become insensitive to subtleties of sound. We can help children to attend to and differentiate between sounds in music, language, and the natural world around them.

The sense of touch, or *tactile* sense, is a primary mode of learning for young children. The organ of touch is the skin, which by its all encompassing nature makes touch a dominant aspect of our lives. We get information about the world from touching things. And this tactile sense allows us to make decisions about comfort and safety. Experiences in early childhood programs can help children learn to identify

Reflect and write about . . .

sensory experiences you enjoy

Think of a sensory experience that you especially enjoy (a hot bath, a walk in the woods, the feel of sand on your bare feet, putting up a Christmas tree). What do you feel or think of as you recall this experience? What might be some implications of this memory for your work with young children?

and discriminate between tactile sensations so they can make judgments about the world based properties such as texture, temperature, and pressure.

We make many decisions based on our sense of smell—the *olfactory* sense. We smell bread baking and decide to eat; we smell a rose and bask in the sensation; we smell a dirty diaper and know that it is time to change it. Very young children have limited olfactory experience and may not be able to make clear judgments based on smells. This is one of the reason that they sometimes drink poisonous substances like ammonia. Older preschoolers make many choices based on the smell of things and often reject experiences because of an odor that is unfamiliar or that they judge unpleasant.

The sense of taste is sometimes called the *gustatory* sense. There are actually only a few taste characteristics—sweet, sour, salty, and bitter. Eating is a multi-sensory experience—taste characteristics, together with the aromas of food, create the multitude of flavors that we experience. Texture and temperature (elements of the sense of touch) also influence how we experience food. Infants and very young children explore everything with their mouths, and they do not confine their exploration to things that are edible. In early childhood programs children can be provided with a range of taste experiences and can develop an understanding of which things are unsafe or unhealthy to put in their mouths.

The sensory mode that we most commonly associate with learning is sight. Learning to make visual discriminations begins early in life. From infancy we use visual information to make judgments, but the ability to make fine discriminations takes many years to develop. *Vision,* like other senses, requires opportunities for practice. Children develop visual discrimination as they engage in activities that are regularly found in early childhood settings—putting together puzzles, sorting buttons, looking at books, and building with plastic snap-together blocks. It is rarely necessary to provide tasks that are exclusively designed to teach visual discrimination.

Although it may be useful to think in terms of planning for development of each of the senses, it is important to realize that they need not be learned in isolation. Children involved in making pancakes touch and compare the flour and salt, smell the banana as it is mashed, experience resistance when the thick batter is stirred, see the bubbles that form as air is beaten in, hear the sizzle as batter is poured in the pan, and taste the finished product. To separate these would be difficult and unnecessary—children learn from the entire sensory experience.

The Environment

Early childhood educators who recognize the importance of sensory experiences can create environments that support the development of the senses. Most early childhood programs have materials that clearly contribute to sensory development: water, sand, mud, dough, and clay. You can add other activities that have a sensory focus. Consider what you could provide to stimulate each sensory modality. Include materials such as sound cans, sorting boxes, texture boards, pegboards, puzzles, collage materials, and blocks. Many games and materials designed for young children help them to focus on sensory variables. For example, materials designed by Maria Montessori are intended to encourage sensory development. These include cylinders that vary in only one dimension—diameter, circumference, or height—and the colored chips that children can arrange by gradations in shade and hue. You can also create games to develop sensory awareness. These might include sound cylinders, color matching games, and "feely" boxes.

Everyday objects and activities can also encourage sensory exploration. An orange, an interesting piece of driftwood, the texture of a piece of cloth all give children a chance to use their senses. Collections of natural objects like rocks, shells, leaves, beans, and seeds give children opportunities to look, touch, and sort.

Materials designed for other curriculum areas are also sensory in nature. The colors in a beautifully illustrated children's book, the different weights and sizes in a set of unit blocks, the sound differences of rhythm instruments, the feel of moving through space on a swing, the cool mush of fingerpaints or clay, the tastes and smells as children cook applesauce—all are sensory highlights of activities that have other purposes. As you provide experiences to children you can point out aspects and encourage their sensory exploration and involvement.

In our own teaching we have used sensory activities that were readily available in our environment. We have enjoyed tasting and smelling days when children brought their favorite items to savor, listening walks when we went to hear what we could hear, and color days when we all wore the same color. When a small group of children and their teachers move beyond the classroom, they encounter many experiences that heighten sensory awareness such as the smells and tastes of the neighborhood bakery and the textures, sights, and sounds of a local park.

Supporting Learning

Sensory experiences are essential for young children. If you work with children under three you will be involved in both planned and spontaneous sensory explorations. If you work with children over the age of six you may find that you are confronted with the challenge of encouraging them to continue with sensory exploration as a valid mode for learning about the world.

Learning and development are intimately tied to sensory experience during the earliest years. When we provide for sensory experience and exploration, we nurture curiosity and learning in infants and toddlers. Children at this stage will transform the most ordinary daily experiences into sensory exploration activities. The ripe banana served to an infant is squished between fingers and smeared on the face—turned into a tactile, taste, and smell experience. The ensuing mess should not interfere with our ability to see that the child is learning about the properties of substances.

Feelings of security and well-being are gained as an infant strokes the surface of the satiny border of a blanket or the soft fur of a stuffed animal or experiences a gentle powdering after a bath. Children become attuned to sound as caregivers talk, sing, recite nursery rhymes, and join children in responding with wonder to unanticipated sounds like the passing fire truck, the boom of thunder, or the creaking of the tree limbs in the wind.

A well-equipped preschool or kindergarten class can be a wonderful laboratory for sensory experience. Children are developing their senses as they paint; manipulate clay and dough; play in sand, water, and mud; play with clay; feel the shape, weight, and texture of the blocks; observe the fish in the aquarium; feel the rabbit's fur and feel its heart beating; listen to stories; move to music; sort objects by shape, color, and size; and cook and taste what they have made. Your role is to provide space that can be used without fear of mess and materials that can be fully explored. You can also help children focus on sensory aspects of materials and experiences by the ways you call attention to them. For example, you might help children to notice the cool, smooth texture of a polished rock by saying things like, "How does it feel in your hands?" "What do you notice when you rub it against your cheek?" "What does it remind you of?"

Activities that can be messy such as sand, mud, water, clay, and fingerpaints are sometimes rejected by fastidious children, particularly when these activities are available only occasionally for short periods. Reluctant children are more likely to learn to use and enjoy materials if they observe other children enjoying them. It also helps when the use of materials moves in a sequence over several weeks or even months, from structured and contained to more open and unrestricted. For example, fingerpaints might be presented first

on a cafeteria tray with individual pieces of paper, small amounts of paint, and protective smocks. Later activities might involve a group mural fingerpainting on the tables on the playground, perhaps with sand and gravel added.

Primary-age children should continue to have experiences that build sensory awareness and appreciation of the world. It is important to plan experiences for them that employ

Reflect and write about . . .

sensory experiences that were a part of school

Think of a sensory experience that you had in school (cooking, exploring a sensory material, looking at something beautiful, making music). What do you feel or think of as you recall this experience? How did it effect your perceptions of school?

324

senses other than the ones traditionally used in schools—looking and listening. They need frequent opportunities to explore and create with art media such as paints, clay, and collage materials. Field trips into natural environments provide a variety of sensory experiences. Visits to view works of art in the community and the display of photographs, prints, sculpture, pottery, and paintings heighten appreciation of beautiful and interesting creations. Gardening and cooking are activities to learn from and to give sensual satisfaction. No eating experience is better than the peas from your own patch or the tortillas you make with your classmates as a part of a study of bread. Sensory learning is valuable independent of other educational goals, but it often deepens and enriches other learning experiences. And there is an important aesthetic aspect of sensory development. We live in a world that needs people who can appreciate the beauty and variety of nature, art, and music; the sights, sounds, smells, and flavors of a variety of cultures; and all the other sensory joys that contribute to our humanity.

LARGE MUSCLE DEVELOPMENT

Human beings come into the world unprepared to stand upright or to move through space in a coordinated way. Some masterery over the large muscles must precede almost any other development. The large muscle curriculum—that part of the early childhood program that is concerned with the development of children's strength in arms, legs, and torso—is designed to help children gain and maintain physical skills and abilities as they work and play.

Physical activity is essential for lifelong health. Attention span and concentration increase as children use their bodies in challenging physical movement. Exercise helps to release tension and promotes relaxation. Children's early physical development experiences will influence how competent they feel and whether they will enjoy physical activity throughout their lives.

The Organizing Framework

To become physically competent, children must develop kinesthetic awareness, strength, flexibility, coordination, and agility. These are the basis for experiences that support development of the large muscles.

Kinesthetic awareness is stimulated through activities such as climbing, running, jumping, and rolling. They lead to the ability to balance, identify one's position in space, and control physical motions. Swinging, turning somersaults, walking on a beam, and jumping on a

---

Reflect and write about . . .

your favorite large muscle activity

Think about your favorite large muscle activity—walking, jogging, swimming, tennis, dancing, backpacking, and so on. What makes the activity enjoyable to you? How did you learn to do this activity? How did you feel while you were learning? How do you think you could best bring different kinds of large muscle experiences to young children? How might you help them develop positive attitudes about physical activities?

trampoline are skills that depend on kinesthetic awareness and control.

Strength is the physical energy available for movement or resistance. *Stamina* or endurance is the capacity for the sustained use of strength or physical energy. Older children generally are stronger and have greater and more predictable endurance. Strength and stamina increase as children exert energy and effort for prolonged periods of time in challenging activities like group games, walking, running, swimming, and dancing.

Flexibility concerns the ease and range of movement. Physical suppleness lessens with age as the muscle system becomes less elastic. An infant easily brings toes to mouth, but this flexibility wanes as children get older. One of the goals of the physical development curriculum is to help children retain flexibility while developing muscular strength.

Coordination involves being able to move different body parts in relation to one another. A child pumping a swing pulls arms and legs forward and backward in unison. A baby crawling or a young child climbing on a jungle gym moves arms and legs in opposition. Young children learn to coordinate their actions first by experimenting, imitating, and exploring movement to gain control. Repetition then internalizes a new skill. Regular opportunities for children to move freely encourage experimentation and practice.

Agility refers to the ability to stop abruptly and change directions. It requires flexibility, strength, coordination, and a well-developed kinesthetic sense. As children gain speed, grace, and precision they feel a sense of mastery. Much of the pleasure children find in large muscle play stems from the enjoyment of growing agility. Like other areas of physical development, the development of agility requires ample opportunities for children to use their bodies in ways that are both challenging and lead to success.

Large Muscle Skills and Activities

When children engage in a range of large muscle activities, they develop in each of the areas of physical competence. Children should have frequent opportunities to do all of the large muscle activities listed below. There should be space, time, and equipment for children to develop each skill.

Balancing	Twisting/turning
Walking/running/stopping	Stretching
Galloping/skipping	Rolling
Jumping/hopping	Crawling
Pedaling vehicles	Catching
Climbing	Punting/striking/kicking
Pulling/pushing	
Swinging	Throwing
Swaying/rocking	Bouncing/dribbling

Table 11.1 summarizes some important milestones in large muscle development from infancy through age eight.

The Environment

Children need equipment for climbing, swinging, throwing, digging, hammering, balancing, and exploring space with their bodies. Large muscle development opportunities abound in a well-designed play yard. An ideal outdoor space for a group of young children would include a hill for climbing and rolling, large flat areas for running and galloping, paved areas for wheel toys, dirt and sand for digging, and trees for shade and for climbing. The most important and versatile piece of equipment for large muscle development is a well-designed and constructed climbing structure. Tricycles, blocks, sand and water tables, climbing structures, and rocking boats are valuable for physical development. If your program budget does not allow for the purchase of equipment for large muscle develop-

TABLE 11.1
Milestones of Large Muscle Development

Age	Developmental Milestones
Infant (birth–18 mos.)	Holds head erect and steady Elevates self by arms Rolls from side to back, then back to side Sits alone Crawls Pulls to standing holding low, stable objects Stands alone Walks alone Walks up stairs with help Climbs onto furniture and up stairs (as an outgrowth of creeping) Throws objects from crib Rolls a large ball using hands and arms
Toddler (18 mos.–3 years)	Walks up and down stairs with some assistance Walks backward Walks on toes Runs with little control Jumps down from low object Jumps off floor with both feet Pulls and drags toys Picks up objects from floor without falling Kicks large ball and catches a rolled ball Throws ball with forearm extension Awaits thrown ball with arms outstretched Sits on riding toy and pushes with feet
3-Year-Old	Walks on a line without watching feet Walks backward Runs more smoothly and with more control Jumps in place with two feet together Jumps over low objects Broad jumps about 1 foot Climbs stairs with alternating feet, holding on to handrail Climbs up slide and comes down Balances on one foot Throws ball overhand Catches with arms fully extended Pedals and steers tricycle
4-Year-Old	Walks, heel to toe Runs with leg-arm coordination Changes direction while moving and stops quickly Gallops Jumps skillfully Climbs jungle gym skillfully Climbs stairs with alternating feet Balances on one foot

TABLE 11.1
Milestones of Large Muscle Development *continued*

Age	Developmental Milestones
	Walks awkwardly on balance beam
	Throws ball overhand
	Catches ball with hands
	Rides tricycle rapidly, steers smoothly
5-Year-Old	Walks backward with heel-toe pattern
	Descends steps with alternating feet
	Runs, gallops, and skips with increasing speed and fluidity
	Does standing and running broad jump
	Jumps rope
	Climbs a rope, a ladder
	Walks securely, alternating feet on balance beam
	Turns somersaults
	Rides bicycle with training wheels
Primary School Child (6–8 years)	Skips (coordination of a step forward with a hop)
	Running speed increases
	Distance jumped increases
	Jumps rope
	Throws with speed, accuracy, and distance increase
	Improves catching ability
	Bats a ball
	Dribbles a ball
	Rides a small bicycle

Sources: L.E. Berk, *Infants and Children: Prenatal Through Middle Childhood,* 2nd ed. (Boston: Allyn & Bacon, 1994); J. Black, M. Puckett, and M. Bell, The Young Child: *Development from Prebirth Through Age Eight.* (Englewood Cliffs, NJ: Merrill/Prentice Hall, 1992; B.J. Cratty, *Perceptual and Motor Development in Infants and Children,* 3rd ed. (Englewood Cliffs, NJ: Merrill/Prentice Hall, 1986).

ment, then recycled materials can be used to build equipment that can substitute for more costly items. See Chapter Eight, The Learning Environment, for more information about equipment and materials for active play.

If the climate dictates that you spend long periods of time indoors, you will need to find ways to provide large muscle development experiences on a daily basis. Portable equipment that can be used indoors when outdoor play is not possible will be an important addition to these programs.

Supporting Learning

Between birth and age eight, children make tremendous strides in their ability to use their bodies. Their large muscle development at different ages requires quite different kinds of support from early childhood educators.

At birth children have little mobility. It is important that they be held and carried, for this is how they begin to develop a sense of their position in space and of their bodies as separate from the bodies of their caregivers. From newborns who are unable to lift their heads or roll over to toddlers who have the ability to walk, run, jump, climb stairs, and push a trike is journey of only thirty-six months.

Within months of birth most babies like to be held upright and push themselves up and down on the laps of willing adults. This helps the infant build the strength and coordination that will enable independent standing. Infants need space in which to practice crawling and stable furniture or stationary cruise bars to hold firmly when they are ready to stand upright and take their first tentative steps.

Older infants will begin walking by holding on to furniture or a friendly hand. Toddlers will still be wobbly when they first attempt stairs. A play structure with two or three broad steps and several safe ways to get back down to ground level will be used well in a toddler room and on the play yard. Pushing or pulling wagons loaded with toys and friends builds strength. By age three many toddlers will have learned to pedal a trike, throw a ball, and run and stop at will. You support this development by providing space, time, equipment, a helping hand, and lots of encouragement.

Preschool and kindergarten children develop their large muscle skills through their own natural activity and through teacher-led activities. The role of the early childhood educator is to provide an environment rich in equipment and materials, enough time and space for exploration, planned physical experiences, and guidance and encouragement. You support safe, productive, physical activity when you make sure that there is plenty of space for children to run and play and when equipment is free of hazards, appropriately placed, and sufficiently challenging. You also need to watch carefully so that you are aware of children's growing skill and are available to help as needed.

Children need periods of free play in an appropriate environment several times a day. They need optimal challenge—equipment, materials, and activities that provide the right degree of difficulty—to develop the skill that is just within their reach. Children can be discouraged from climbing, sliding, and swinging by adults who are overly concerned about possible injury. A useful guideline is that if children are willing to attempt using a piece of equipment, they can usually manage it. Occasionally a challenge will be beyond a child's capabilities, and you will need to

provide assistance. If a child climbs onto something and is not able to reverse the process, you can give instruction and encouragement: "Put your foot on the bar and move your hand down a little bit—now you can step safely." Or you can lift the child back to the ground without admonishing the failed attempt. As children get older they need increasing challenges and continued opportunity for physical activity.

Many children develop physical competence from their self-directed play, but others will need a good deal of support. It is important to observe so that you can encourage reticent children to practice skills they lack and so that you can provide adequate challenge for those who are more skilled. It is also important to provide special opportunities and encouragement for those children who might never choose to practice a particular skill or those for whom vigorous physical activity is never a choice. Children who have definite developmental lags in physical ability may require direct intervention in the form of formal instruction or one-to-one practice. All direct physical training and intervention needs to be carried out in pleasurable play situations so that the child's attitude will be positive and physical activity will become gratifying.

How you talk can encourage or discourage children's engagement in physical activities. It is best to avoid comments that create comparison and competition between children. Saying "Look how high Sam can climb" to the group may encourage Sam, but other children may attempt to reach dangerously beyond their current skill level in order to please you or may feel inadequate because they cannot achieve the standard Sam has set. Real encouragement relates only to the individual's accomplishment: "Sam, that's the highest I've ever seen you climb. You're becoming a very strong person." It acknowledges effort and new accomplishments and avoids implying everyone else should be able to do the same thing.

Children benefit from your active involvement in their play—they need someone to toss a ball or to play follow the leader with them, to play guitar and sing as they play a circle game like Ring-Around-the-Rosie, to explain the rules of Red-Rover, Red-Rover, or to share their triumph as they acquire new skills. By playing *with* children, you encourage and support their activity and you provide a model of an adult who is physically active—a powerful demonstration that being active is natural and pleasurable.

Adult-led activities like creative movement, simple yoga, group games, and exercises provide focused practice in developing physical competencies. All children, not just those who are physically competent, will participate if you minimize competition and win/lose situations in games and other physical activities. We enjoy teaching and playing cooperative games with children. Cooperative games give them opportunities to experience the benefits of cooperating while developing physical skills. Unlike traditional games where someone wins and others lose, these games promote the idea that

when everyone works together everyone wins. (The In Practice box has suggestions for some cooperative games.)

Primary age children also need to have daily periods of directed physical activity as well as periods of time each day for free play. Even though they may take dance lessons, play organized sports, and ride bicycles, the general physical condition of many children today suggests that they do not get regular large muscle exercise and have not become skilled at organized games or sports. In many schools large motor activity is confined to short "recess" periods. In some states no provision is made at all for regular physical development activities for primary school children (Javernick 1988).

You can strive to make physical activities an integrated and pleasurable part of school life. Children can enjoy and benefit from calisthenics done to music, creative movement or yoga sessions, obstacle courses, and climbing structures. Organized games, like the cooperative games described in the In Practice box on p. 332-333, have appeal and can be done by small groups or a whole class. Primary children benefit from skill practice (throwing, kicking, and catching balls, jumping, running relays) if it is conducted in a spirit of play and effort is appreciated as much as success. Field trips can provide exercise in the form of walking and climbing. An occasional teacher-led jog can be a playful deviation from the usual routine. Physical development should go beyond the physical education class and recess time; physical activity should be built into your daily life with children.

SMALL MUSCLE DEVELOPMENT

Learning to coordinate the hands and fingers begins when babies in their cribs reach out to feel, grasp, and manipulate. Those initial impulses will eventually lead to the competent use of tools—spoons, crayons, hammers, and

Reflect and write about . . .

physical development in early childhood programs

Think about how physical development was supported in a program for young children where you worked or observed. How did the learning environment provide support? How did the staff encourage children's growth? What particularly impressed or concerned you? How do you think this program influenced children? What else might be done to support physical development?

keyboards are all tools that need to be manipulated by the hands and fingers. Planned activities in early childhood programs can make an important contribution to this area of development.

The Organizing Framework

All small muscle activities involve control, agility, strength, and coordination. This combination of elements is involved in the multitude of skills that children need to develop. The elements described here provide a useful framework for planning and presenting experiences designed to develop children's skills in using their small muscles.

Small muscle *control* involves knowing what you want your hands and fingers to do and being able to direct them to do it. Preschool children can make more precise movements than toddlers can because they are increasingly able to control an object by using the fingers rather than the wrist or arm. Children gradually learn to control the direction, size, speed, shape, and force of hand movements. To be able to pat a cat and beat a drum requires conscious differing of the force, direction, speed, and size of a similar movement. Time, practice, and many diverse experiences are required to develop this competence.

Agility concerns the ability to move in a precise and intentional way at a desired speed.

Toddlers and older infants can use their hands and fingers to hold objects and release them, to wave and point. But they don't have much flexibility in their use. However motivated and intelligent they are, they can rarely master skills such as touch typing, playing the piano, and knitting. Before children can become agile they

IN PRACTICE

Cooperative games

Group Games

Animal Families: It's feeding time on the farm and the animals need to find their families for supper. Whisper the name of an animal (duck, cow, sheep, pig) in each child's ear. When you say, "Animals find your families," children make their animal's sounds and try to find their families by the sounds. When families are found, do it again or go on to a new activity. Have older children close their eyes or wear blindfolds and locate their family through sound only.

Bean Bag Freeze: To the beat of a drum, children walk around the room balancing bean bags on their heads. If a bean bag falls off, the child must freeze until another child can carefully crouch down, pick up the bean bag, and return it. When everyone is frozen the game is over.

Big Turtle: A group of children get on their hands and knees and a teacher places a "shell" on their backs. The shell can be a gym mat, a blanket, or sleeping mats. The big turtle attempts to move around without losing its shell. (An obstacle course can be made for the turtle.)

The Big Wind Blows: Using a parachute, the group holds the edges and lifts the parachute up to billow. They chant, "Blow, blow, the big wind blows. Who oh who does the big wind blow?" The teacher calls out categories, such as "Everybody wearing red." Those children run underneath the parachute and across to find a place to hold on the other side.

Cooperative Duck Duck Goose: In this version no one ends up in the center of the circle. Instead, two children are tappers, and if the chaser catchers a tapper he or she joins the tappers.

Cooperative Musical Chairs: No one is eliminated. Each person finds a chair when the music stops for as long as interest holds. Another alternative is **Musi-**

Reflect and write about . . .

your small muscle skills and abilities

What talents that involve small muscle skills have you developed—playing the piano, cooking, sewing, auto mechanics, calligraphy, typing, drawing, crocheting, and so on. Think about the kinds of motions that are involved in them. How did you become proficient in the skill? How long did it take? What it hard or easy to develop? What implications might your experiences have for your work with young children?

cal Laps. When the music stops, everyone must find a chair or a lap to sit in if there is no chair. Each time the music stops one chair is eliminated and the pile up on the laps is greater (best with smaller groups if children are young).

Partner Games

Obstacle Course: Children create an obstacle course with their bodies by making tunnels, bridges, and rocks. One partner closes their eyes and the other leads the "blind" partner through an obstacle maze. Then they switch and other children take turns.

Stick Together: Ask partners to pretend they have sticky bodies, and when you name a body part you want them to stick their body parts together and move in ways you direct. Give instructions that require cooperation. "Your hands are stuck together; walk with sticky hands. Your elbows are stuck together; jump with sticky elbows. Your legs are stuck together; march with stuck legs." After a couple of directions, have children change partners.

Person to Person: Have children walk around in the circle in a random fashion. Play the drum to a walking beat. With a hard beat say, "Person to person" and ask children to find a partner near them. Then say the name of a body part, such as "Knee to knee." Children touch knees and then continue walking and do the activity again.

Balloons in the Air: Give pairs of children a balloon. Have partners try to keep their balloon in the air by hitting it, blowing it, or catching it in a big scarf or piece of cloth that both hold.

Stand Up: Partners sit back to back with elbows linked. They try to get up without letting go. This can also be done with three or four friends.

Musical Partners: Partners walk around the room back to back as music plays. When the music stops, switch partners.

Sources: T. Orlick, *The Cooperative Sports and Games Book.* (New York: Pantheon, 1978); J. Sobel, *Everybody Wins: Noncompetitive Games for Young Children.* (New York: Walker, 1983).

must gain a great deal of control over the size, direction, shape, force, and speed of other less complicated movements.

Strength concerns the stamina and force that is available to apply to and sustain movement. Children growing up with normal abilities and opportunities to use their hands also develop the strength required to do most small muscle activities. As children persist at these activities they develop greater strength and stamina.

Coordination means being able to control the interrelationship of hands, fingers, and other body parts. It involves sensory and muscular interplay—hand-eye coordination, moving hands based on visual data, and coordination of the two hands based on visual and kinesthetic awareness (sensing where the hands are in space). Clapping hands, moving spoon to mouth, and stringing beads are examples of activities that require coordinated movement.

Small Muscle Skills and Activities

The equipment, materials, and activities that you present to young children should provide opportunities for all of the skills listed below to develop.

Grasping and releasing–
    whole hand and pincer
Dumping/pouring/spooning
Twisting/turning
Folding/tearing
Pulling
Stringing/sewing
Tying/buttoning/zipping
Writing/drawing/painting
Tapping/striking
Clapping/slapping/patting
Rubbing/rolling
Pointing/fingering
Cutting

As we created this list we were astonished by the complexity of the movements involved and by the sheer quantity of small muscle tasks that young children need to develop. We thought about which elements and discrete movements were involved in each task. For example, cutting involves all of the elements (strength, control, agility, and coordination) and consists of grasping, directing, releasing tension but not releasing grasp, and twisting and turning the opposing hand. No wonder it's hard for young children! Simply feeding oneself requires control and coordination and involves grasping, directing, and releasing an object with enough finesse to avoid spills. The significance of a two-year-old's grasping and dumping can be more readily appreciated as a learning task when viewed as an important step in the mastery of some complicated fine motor skills. Table 11.2 summarizes some important milestones in small muscle development from infancy through age eight.

The Environment

Every program for young children needs to have toys and materials that build small muscle skills. Many early childhood classrooms have an area exclusively for construction and manipulative toys such as pegboards, puzzles, and Legos. These need to be sized for the age of the children: Younger children need fewer, larger pieces that cannot be swallowed and are easier to manipulate.

Other curriculum materials contribute to small muscle development as well. As children cook, use math materials like Cuisenaire rods, build with blocks, investigate science materials, do fingerplays, play instruments, and turn pages in a book they are practicing fine motor skills. Art activities support small muscle development. Clay and dough are especially versatile materials that involve almost every small muscle skill. The tools and materials commonly found in writing centers (paper, pencils, pens, crayons, hole punches, staplers, rulers, scissors, stamps, and so on) also develop these skills.

As children learn to serve their own food, pour their own beverages, use the water fountain, put on their shoes, and fasten their clothes they are not only gaining independence but are practicing physical skills. The challenge of opening a lunchbox or thermos points out the real-life significance of fine motor development. Teachers can add pouring activities and lacing frames to help develop these same skills. The materials which are found in the practical life area of a Montessori classroom such as pouring from pitchers and using tongs can be added to any classroom.

Sufficient time, variety, and quantity of materials are needed for children to develop the use of their hands and fingers. The time spent is valuable and children are not "just playing." Children's obvious delight in fine motor activity is a good indicator of their interest

TABLE 11.2

Milestones of Small Muscle Development

Age	Developmental Milestones
Infant (birth–18 mos.)	Grasps objects Drops and picks up objects Pours objects from containers Builds tower of cubes (2 at first, later 3–4) Points to things Plays pat-a-cake Takes off shoes and socks Feeds self with fingers Uses spoon Uses cup
Toddler (18 mos.–3 years)	Strings large beads Holds crayon in fist Scribbles Places large pegs in board Turns pages of book, 2–3 at time Opens door by turning knob Puts on and removes simple items of clothing Zips and unzips large zippers Manages spoon and cup
3-Year-Old	Puts together 3–6-piece puzzles Uses scissors to cut paper Copies vertical line and circle Imitates shapes in drawing Handles books efficiently Builds tower of 8–10 cubes Fastens and unfastens large buttons Dresses and undresses with assistance Uses fork and spoon Serves self food without assistance
4-Year-Old	Cuts with scissors following line Copies simple shapes Dresses and undresses without assistance Gains proficiency in using fork and spoon
5-Year-Old	Copies numerals and letters Uses knife to cut soft food
Primary School Child (6–8 years)	Masters printing Begins to play musical instruments Uses a keyboard Makes models and does crafts Ties shoes (about age 6)

Sources: L.E. Berk, *Infants and Children: Prenatal Through Middle Childhood,* 2nd ed. (Boston: Allyn & Bacon, 1994); J. Black, M. Puckett, and M. Bell, The Young Child: *Development from Prebirth Through Age Eight.* (Englewood Cliffs, NJ: Merrill/Prentice Hall, 1992; B.J. Cratty, *Perceptual and Motor Development in Infants and Children,* 3rd ed. (Englewood Cliffs, NJ: Prentice Hall, 1986).

and need for frequent and prolonged practice through play. Daily choice times of at least an hour should include access to manipulative and other materials that support fine motor development.

Supporting Learning

From infancy through adulthood, people make use of the small muscles of their hands and fingers on a daily basis. To support the development of these muscles, you need to understand the developmental sequence for the emergence of small muscle skills. You need to observe children in a group and to be sensitive to individual differences. Educators can interpret each child's level of development and provide materials and activities that present optimal challenge. It is essential that children have adequate space, materials, and time to practice using their small muscles.

Newborns will cling tightly to a finger. Soon they grasp and pull, grasp and release, then pat, slap, bang, and drop objects within reach. Later babies begin to drop toys from their cribs and food from their high chairs and wail to have the items returned to them so that they can grasp and drop again. Although the behavior may frustrate adults, it is important small muscle development and deserves our cooperation and participation.

Educators who work with groups of infants and toddlers can provide experiences and materials that will help them to develop small muscle skills. Infants also enjoy games and songs that are a part of caregiver behaviors in every culture. Pat-a-cake and clapping hands to music are among the important educational games of infancy. Push-pull toys fascinate infants and toddlers, and they enjoy banging on a drum with a stick or on a food tray with a spoon. Toddlers will fill containers with objects and dump them out and repeat the sequence over and over again. They also begin to master the finer small muscle control and hand-eye co-

ordination required to stack small blocks, use a spoon, and direct a paint brush or a marking pen on a piece of paper. Manipulating play-dough can build strength and coordination while giving sensory pleasure.

Preschool and kindergarten children need many opportunities to develop small muscle coordination and control. These early years of repetitious small muscle practice are essential for the development of the skill level that enables adults to do things like sewing and using a computer. Each day they can practice buttoning, pouring, tying shoes, putting together puzzles, cutting, stringing beads, using table blocks and construction toys, writing and painting, and playing with dough. Cooking is a good activity for small muscle development if children are given ample opportunity to participate in cutting, kneading, shaping, and stirring.

If a child becomes frustrated or bored with an activity you can support his or her continued involvement by offering assistance, encouragement, or a greater challenge. For example, if a child is having trouble cutting you might say, "I see that paper is hard to cut. Would you like to use construction paper? Maybe it won't flop so much." You might also want to be sure to stock the shelf with a variety of different weights of paper and see if you need more functional scissors.

It is important to design experiences that will build prerequisite skills for more challenging small motor tasks like cutting. The child who hasn't yet mastered scissors needs plenty of grasping, tension/release, coordination, and strength-building experiences. Providing dough and clay to build strength and tools like tongs, hole punches, tweezers, and staplers that require similar motor action will contribute to this emerging skill. You may sometimes need to demonstrate and instruct to help children learn complex fine motor skills.

Most primary grade children know how to write, print, and cut accurately with scissors

and knives. Some children of this age will have had experiences with a computer keyboard; others may be skilled as pianists and sculptors.

A classroom filled with tools, materials, games, and activities that develop fine motor skill is essential for this stage of development. Children can be interested in and challenged by mastering the use of a typewriter or computer, playing a simple tune on a recorder or piano, or learning to weave on a simple loom. Provision of art materials, carpentry tools, and writing and drawing supplies and allowing time and space for these activities help children continue to refine their small muscle abilities.

SUPPORTING PHYSICAL DEVELOPMENT IN CHILDREN WITH SPECIAL NEEDS

The physical development curriculum offers joys and challenges to all children. When there are children with special needs in your program, you will want to think about whether you will need to make adaptations to include them in this essential part of your curriculum. As you do so, it is important to make activities for these children as similar as possible to those activities for other children. Adaptations should not be so visible that they single out a child or cause embarrassment.

For almost all children, sensory activities provide success and positive feelings. Sensory experiences are especially valuable for children with special needs. These experiences are soothing and can be used at any ability level. If a child should be fearful of or physically uncomfortable with sensory experiences, they may at first need gentle guided opportunities to interact with sensory materials.

Early childhood educators can support children with disabilities in their struggles for competence and self-sufficiency. Like all young children, those with impaired motor control or limited use of arms and legs are struggling to master basic movement skills. It may take them longer and be a little harder than it is for other children. You may be tempted to protect them from awkwardness and struggle, but it is best not to do too much for them. They need to master skills for themselves and that takes practice.

Children with physical disabilities will be more self-sufficient if their clothing is adapted to their skills—for example, shirts and skirts fastened with Velcro and zippers with large rings inserted through the tabs so they are easier to manipulate. Some children will be able to balance better while dressing themselves if they do it from a sitting rather than standing position. Others may be able to function more independently if they are given eating utensils and toothbrushes with extended or thickened handles. A stool in front of a toilet will make access easier.

Opportunities for large muscle development can be provided for children with special needs. First the teacher must observe the child and consider his or her abilities and then make appropriate adaptations. For example, a child with cognitive deficits may need more encouragement than other children. For a child with visual disabilities, you should be attentive to lighting conditions and can provide balls and other objects in bright colors. Auditory problems will not limit physical activity, but you will need to

be certain that the child can hear directions. Children with physical disabilities can participate, but some adaptations such as placing some playground equipment low to the ground and using large soft balls can be made. A special education, physical education, or physical therapist can help you to make appropriate adaptations for the needs of each child.

HELPING CHILDREN LEARN TO BE HEALTHY

Young children are intrigued with learning about themselves and their bodies. Early childhood is the time when the foundations of understanding are formed and the underlying skills and dispositions for health are established. You have an opportunity to interest children in a topic that will be important to them throughout their lives.

How do children learn to care for themselves? Until recently, they learned through the daily experience of watching their family members care for themselves and for their children, and then by becoming responsible for younger siblings. Today, adults' daily lives are often far removed from their children's lives and children may not often observe parents caring for themselves and others.

Children can learn important things about good health habits in their early childhood programs. This learning occurs in the context of daily routines and activities. All daily routines—dressing, washing, toileting, eating, resting, and exercising—teach children about their bodies and habits of caring for themselves.

As children experience classroom routines related to the provision of good health and as you discuss these things with them, they begin to acquire some important understandings and skills. They can begin to understand human growth and development, body parts and functions, and the value of cleanliness, medical care, exercise, rest, and good nutrition. As they learn about these things they will come to appreciate their bodies and develop positive practices and habits that may continue throughout their lives.

Personal Care

Teaching children about health and self-care takes quite different forms for different age groups of children. Infants and toddlers learn through routines that caregivers provide. When adults allow infants and toddlers to control what is happening to them as much as possible and explain what they are doing and why, they help these very young children begin to become knowledgeable and competent.

As you engage in daily routines with preschoolers, you can model and discuss the reasons for what you are doing. Children will learn from repeated practice and discussion that hand washing can keep you from getting sick, that tooth brushing and regular dental check-ups help to keep your teeth strong and healthy, that rest helps your body to calm down and gives you energy for vigorous activity, and that exercise helps your muscles grow and get stronger. Each time we discuss these things with children we have an opportunity to remind them that they can participate. When you discuss practices that build health and those things that are harmful, you are helping children develop concepts that may keep them from later substance abuse.

Preschool children are fascinated by their bodies. They only gradually learn to feel that physical functions are private or shameful. People who work with young children need to react to their interest in body parts and functions in supportive ways. All body parts and physiological processes have names—*shin, finger, knuckle, buttocks, knee, forehead, digestion, urination, saliva,* and so on. The words are innocuous and easy to use. Children who learn accurate terminology in a low-intensity, supportive emotional climate are bet-

ter equipped to understand and care for themselves. If all subjects can be discussed seriously, children are given an important message: Your body is okay; it is safe to talk with adults about it. Comfort with their bodies and the ability to talk about them unashamedly may help children to identify things that do not feel good to them and give them vocabulary for telling an adult about unwanted contact if it should occur.

Primary age children can learn about caring for themselves as interesting subject matter. For these children, health education is empowerment; it helps them feel responsible and is a first step on the road to being grown-up. They benefit from information that is presented in a straightforward, non-scary manner and from many opportunities for discussion. As they learn about caring for themselves they will share their ideas with you, and you may find that they have many misconceptions. Their eagerness to learn can provide valuable opportunities for you to support their development (Figure 11.1).

Nutrition

During the early childhood years, we can help children to understand that their health is affected by the food they eat and that they can make food choices that will help them to grow and be healthy. We have placed nutrition with physical development curriculum, but clearly it is part of other curricula as well. It connects physical, cognitive, social, and creative development. Because it is used to teach other subjects, nutrition content can get lost. Nutrition in itself is an important part of the curriculum, something that it is worthwhile for young children to know about (Figure 11.2).

People's health is linked to their diet. Children may learn to choose a healthier diet if we help them to appreciate the high-fiber, low-fat foods that have been demonstrated by research to contribute to good health. By expanding

- People's bodies are all very much alike.
- Body parts have names and functions.
- People differ depending on their age, size, gender, and state of health.
- Children and adults can do things to take care of themselves.
- All people need exercise, rest, food, and cleanliness.

FIGURE 11.1
Personal care concepts for young children

children's food horizons, we help them to discover new foods and make wise food choices. Much of what adults experience as children's reluctance to try healthful foods may be the product of their own expectations and biases. Children usually enjoy fruits, vegetables, brown rice, and dishes like borscht, tofu with broccoli, and ratatouille if they participate in preparation and if they know that they will not be forced to eat.

Nutrition can be a part of every day's experience. You can teach nutrition by providing planned experiences that will help children to develop skills and understand concepts. Take advantage of daily events that involve food like snacks and lunches, through cooking in the classroom, and model behavior and attitudes that encourage health-supporting habits.

A few simple concepts form the base of early childhood nutrition education. These do not involve memorizing lists of vitamins and minerals or the four basic food groups. Instead, they involve an awareness of food, the value of good nutrition, and the realization that food affects feelings, behavior, and development. Even young preschoolers can come to understand some very basic nutrition concepts, although they may not be able to verbalize them.

You can model appreciation for healthful foods and give children time and several opportunities to try any new or unusual food. When a new, healthy food appears in the cafeteria lunch, you can say something like, "We never had this for lunch before. I'm looking forward to trying it," rather than pushing the plate away and commenting negatively on the cook's choices. If children see adults making food choices that help maintain health and avoiding non-nutritious foods, they gain nutrition awareness. Poor habits can also be taught

- All people need food to live, grow, stay healthy, and have energy for work and play.
- Different foods have different substances that are needed for health and growth. Children over the age of four can learn that these nutrients are called *protein, vitamins, minerals, carbohydrates,* and *fat.*
- People need to eat a variety of foods to get all of the nutrients they need.
- All people need the same nutrients but they need different amounts depending on their age, size, gender, and the amount of activity they are involved in.
- There are many different kinds of foods that can provide the different nutrients.
- The way that food is grown, processed, stored, and prepared influences its nutritional value.
- Some foods provide many nutrients, and some provide very few (for example, sodas provide only calories, but fruit juice provides vitamins, minerals, and carbohydrates as well).

FIGURE 11.2
Nutrition concepts for young children

IN PRACTICE

Handy hints for cooking with children

Children enjoy cooking; it helps them to feel confident and competent. Cooking in your program will work well if you follow a few guidelines:

- Choose recipes that are simple and safe.
- Make sure there are things for every child to do.
- Plan well and be well organized.
- Invite an extra adult to volunteer to help out.
- Try recipes out ahead of time at home.
- Make a pictorial recipe chart to follow.
- Check in advance that you have all the ingredients and equipment and that appliances and utensils work.

Involve children in every aspect of a cooking project, including:

- Finding and carrying ingredients to the cooking area.
- Opening boxes, bags, and packages.
- Counting quantities.
- "Reading" a pictorial recipe chart.
- Measuring and adding ingredients to a bowl or pan.
- Stirring and mixing (involve children who are not stirring by having them help you count stirs as other children work).
- Grating and cutting.
- Spooning ingredients from one container to another.
- Observing changes as foods combine and cook.
- Reminding you when it is time to take food out of the oven or refrigerator.
- Serving the food to classmates.
- Washing dishes and cleaning up the cooking area.

by modeling. For this reason you should restrict non-healthy foods like soft drinks, French fries, donuts, and candy bars to times when you will not be with children. Better yet, learn to substitute foods that are better for your health and that will give you more sustained energy.

Preparing Food

Young children can begin to learn skills surrounding food choice and preparation, including: selection, planning, following recipes, stirring, pouring, measuring, and serving. Becoming competent at these things also fosters feelings of self-confidence and positive attitudes towards nutritious foods and cooking. We have been delighted at the competence of experienced cooks aged three and four and surprised at the lack of confidence and skill in first and second graders who had not been given cooking opportunities.

Cooking experiences can be integrated into the curriculum. As children cook, they become aware of the properties of food and how it contributes to their lives. And when they experience the food of other cultures, they are enhancing their appreciation of all people.

It is best to work with small groups to prepare food. The younger the children are, the smaller the group should be. Choose activities where children can do most of the work and remember that everything from set-up to clean-up is important. Reduce tasks to child-sized activities to ensure a successful experience. Use tools that work well. Knives that cut, eggbeaters that don't stick, and graters that grate properly are more satisfying to use and safer than those that are dull or don't work. It is a good idea to try all recipes before using them with children.

Cooking helps children to feel responsible, independent, and successful. It is a very important vehicle for teaching about nutrition. You can take note of the nutrient contributions of the foods that are being prepared: "The raisins in the trail mix will help to give you energy on our hike." You can help children to notice differences in tastes: "Some of us like the carrots best; other people prefer the celery."

Simple nutritious snacks make rewarding "cooking" experiences for young children. For example, spreading peanut butter on a slice of celery is not usually thought of as a cooking activity, but it involves food preparation skills that young children need practice to master. Allowing children to become actively involved instead of remaining passive recipients helps them begin to develop the skills and attitudes they will need to help take care of themselves (In Practice box).

The times that children are actively involved with food and nutrition—during meals,

snacks, and cooking, and while shopping, gardening, or feeding pets—are good times to talk about nutrition. Children are interested in talking about where food comes from and how it helps their bodies to grow. They often echo the information that they have heard. For example, many children have been told that milk makes them strong or big. You can help to develop the concept by adding a short informative statement like, "Yes, milk has calcium in it. It helps your bones grow and be strong."

During the early childhood years you can help children to understand that health and nutrition are important to them today and throughout their lives. This foundation can help them to respect their bodies, take responsibility for their health, and develop positive practices and habits that may continue throughout their lives.

FINAL THOUGHTS

Children grow and develop as they have opportunities to move, explore, and manipulate materials. It is satisfying and exciting to contribute to children's physical development. Whether you are providing an eight-month-old with the encouragement and opportunity to pull up and take her first steps, enabling a two-year-old to experience the messy joys of fingerpainting, providing a preschooler with a challenging new manipulative toy, or observing a six-year-old as he learns to write, you are making an important contribution to their growth into people who are skilled, able to care for themselves, and independent.

PROJECTS

Observe a Program: Use the Environment Checklist from Chapter Eight to observe an early childhood program. Report on the extent to which the program seems to support children's physical development. Suggest ways to provide some additional experiences from which children would benefit.

Observe a Child: Observe a child for a morning and focus on how she or he is involved in sensory, small muscle, and large muscle activity. Report on:

- The ways the child moves and explores sensory materials.
- How the environment supports the child's sensory, small muscle, and large muscle development.
- How the staff supports this child's physical development.
- How the program might be modified to enhance this child's physical development.

Observe an Educator: Observe an educator for a morning and then interview her/him about techniques to help young children's sensory, small muscle, and large muscle development and how to teach about health. Report on:

- The activities and routines that you saw that contribute to children's development in these areas.
- Any evidence you saw of planning for physical development.
- The educator's goals for children in the areas of physical development and health.
- The ways in which what the teacher perceives and what you actually observed match or appear differ.

Design an Environment: Design an ideal early childhood environment for the support of physical development. Describe what you included and why. Share your plan with an early childhood educator and a member of a young child's family and describe their response and suggestions.

Plan for Physical Development or Health: Write and implement a plan for an area of physical development or health using the activity planning format (Figure 10.7). Report on how children responded and on how you felt about what you did. What worked? What might you do differently next time? How might you expand on this experience for children?

Compare Two Programs: Compare how two early childhood programs approach sensory and physical development and health. Report on the ways that the two address these areas—their similarities and differences. Which program seems to best meet children's needs and why? What implications does this have for your future work?

Compare Two Ages: Observe two programs, one preschool and one for infants and toddlers or for primary school children. Report on how they are similar and different and how each enhances children's physical development. Talk to the educators about how they make their curriculum choices in this area. Do you think the programs were providing developmentally appropriate physical development opportunities for the children? If not, what changes would you recommend?

BIBLIOGRAPHY

American Academy of Pediatrics. 1988. Physical Fitness Facts. *Young Children* 43(2):23.

Berger, K. S. 1986. *The Developing Person Through Childhood and Adolescence.* 2nd ed. New York: Worth.

Berk, L. E. 1994. *Infants and Children: Prenatal Through Middle Childhood.* Boston: Allyn & Bacon.

Black, J., M. Puckett, and M. Bell. 1992. *The Young Child: Development from Prebirth Through Age Eight.* Englewood Cliffs, NJ: Merrill/Prentice Hall.

Chun, R. S. B. 1994. *Capturing Childhood's Magic: Creating Outdoor Play Environments for Hawaii's Young Children.* Honolulu, HI: University of Hawaii at Manoa.

Cratty, B. J. 1986. *Perceptual and Motor Development in Infants and Children.* 3rd ed. Englewood Cliffs, NJ: Prentice Hall.

Curtis, S. R. 1982. *The Joy of Movement in Early Childhood.* New York: Teachers College Press.

Frost, J. L. 1992. *Play and Playscapes.* Albany, NY: Delmar.

Gearheart, B. R., and C. J. Gearheart. 1989. *Learning Disabilities: Educational Strategies.* Englewood Cliffs, NJ: Merrill/Prentice Hall.

Goodwin, M. T., and G. Pollen. 1981. *Creative Food Experience for Children.* 2nd ed. Washington, DC: Center for Science in the Public Interest.

Harris, A. C. 1993. *Child Development.* 2nd ed. Minneapolis/St. Paul: West.

Hill, D. M. 1977. *Mud, Sand, and Water.* Washington, DC: National Association for the Education of Young Children.

Javernick, E. 1988. Johnny's Not Jumping. *Young Children* 43(2):18–23.

Miller, K. 1985. *Ages and Stages: Developmental Descriptions and Activities Birth Through Eight Years.* Chelsea, MA: Telshare.

Miller, K. 1989. *The Outside Play and Learning Book: Activities for Young Children.* Mt. Rainier, MD: Gryphon House.

Orlick, T. 1978. *The Cooperative Sports and Games Book.* New York: Pantheon.

Oyemade, U. J., and A. V. Washington. 1989. Drug Abuse Prevention Begins in Early Childhood. *Young Children* 44(5):6–12.

Papalia, D. E., and S. J. Olds. 1993. *A Child's World: Infancy Through Adolescence.* 6th ed. New York: McGraw-Hill.

Poest, C. A., J. R. Williams, D. D. Witt, and M. E. Atwood. 1990. Challenge Me to Move: Large Muscle Development in Young Children. *Young Children* 45(5):4–10.

Riggs, M. L. 1980. *Jump to Joy.* Englewood Cliffs, NJ: Prentice Hall.

Rowen, B. 1982. *Learning Through Movement.* New York: Teachers College Press.

Skeen, P. G., A. Payne, and S. Cartwright. 1984. *Woodworking for Young Children.* Washington, DC: National Association for the Education of Young Children.

Sobel, J. 1983. *Everybody Wins: Noncompetitive Games for Young Children.* New York: Walker.

Stinson, W. J., ed. 1990. *Moving and Learning for the Young Child.* Reston, VA: American Alliance for Health, Physical Education, Recreation, and Dance.

Torbert, M. 1980. *Follow Me: A Handbook of Movement Activities for Children.* Englewood Cliffs, NJ: Prentice Hall.

Wanamaker, N., K. Hearn, and S. Richarz. 1979. *More Than Graham Crackers.* Washington, DC: National Association for the Education of Young Children.

Witkin, K. 1977. *To Move to Learn.* Philadelphia: Temple University Press.

CHAPTER TWELVE

The Creative Curriculum

Every child is an artist. The problem is how to remain an artist.

Pablo Picasso

This chapter concerns the arts—music, art, and creative movement. In it we discuss the development of skills, creativity, and aesthetic awareness. We provide frameworks for thinking about and planning creative arts experiences. We also look at ways to support children's learning through the environment, interactions, and activities.

In all societies people create and appreciate art, music, and dance. The fundamental human need to express ideas and feelings through the arts has existed from the dawn of human history. The arts are vital in the development of children who can feel as well as think and who are sensitive and creative. They nurture an awareness of aesthetics (the appreciation of beauty) that can be destroyed in the pervasive grayness of factories, freeways, and institutional buildings.

The three subjects described in this chapter are grouped together because they all help children come to recognize and express their feelings and responses, communicate their ideas in new forms, and develop their senses. Although the arts can be a vehicle for all kinds of learning—physical, social, emotional, and cognitive—and although creativity is not confined to the arts, we link the arts with emotional development and creativity in this chapter. They are especially powerful in fostering these aspects of development.

Experiences in early childhood programs help young children to retain their innate responsiveness to the arts and to develop their natural expressiveness.

Through arts experiences, children come to:

- Feel good about themselves as individuals.
- Develop the ability to observe and respond sensitively.
- Develop skill and creativity in art, music, and movement.
- Develop beginning understanding of the arts disciplines.
- Become appreciative of music, art, and dance from their own and other cultures, times, and places.

Creativity, or originality, is not confined to artists or to people who have great talent or high intelligence. All people are creative when they put together what they know and produce something that is new *to them:* an idea, process, or product. The arts are a primary avenue for developing the ability to think and act creatively. Creativity is easy to see in the arts, but it also occurs in other activities typically found in early childhood programs such as building with blocks and construction toys, dramatic play, writing stories, playing with words, solving problems, and inventing games. The creativity of play leaves no lasting product but is important to recognize and acknowledge. It is also important to keep in mind that children are not always being creative when they are involved in the arts. If they are afraid of not being accepted or feel that their work must meet adult standards, they may make stereotypic "acceptable" products or responses to receive approval and praise.

The pre-primary schools of Reggio Emilia are internationally noted for the creative behavior and expression of their children. The philosophy of the Reggio Emilia schools points to some important considerations for early childhood educators in designing curriculum for creativity. Loris Malaguzzi, the founder of the schools, includes:

- Creativity should not be considered a separate mental faculty but characteristic of our way of thinking, knowing and making choices.
- Creativity seems to emerge from multiple experiences with a well-supported development of personal resources, including a freedom to venture beyond the known.
- Creativity seems to express itself through cognitive, affective and imaginative processes. These come together and support the skills for predicting and arriving at unexpected solutions.
- The most favorable situation for creativity seems to be interpersonal exchange with negotiation of conflicts and comparison of ideas and actions being the decisive elements.
- Creativity seems to find its power when adults are less tied to prescriptive teaching

methods but instead become observers and interpreters of problematic situations (Edwards, Gandini, and Forman 1993, 70).

Understanding how young children develop helps you to provide a climate that supports creativity, imagination, and self-expression. Satisfying and successful experiences with the arts occur when you understand what you can reasonably expect of children and when you provide activities that match their needs and abilities. When children's unique expressions are acknowledged, they become aware of their value as individuals, and their self-concept is enhanced. For young children, the most important aspects of the arts are the development of awareness, new skills, and feelings of self-worth. To support creativity it is important to give children many choices in their work, to provide a variety of creative materials (some constant and some changing), and to support children's efforts without being too directive.

Neither children nor adults create in a void; creative expression is an outgrowth of other life experiences. Your role is to provide experiences that heighten children's awareness and provide them with inspiration for artistic expression. These may be as simple as the careful examination of an apple, visiting a baby, or taking a trip to the beach. Creative expression is also stimulated by experiences with the arts. When children have opportunities to view artwork of many kinds, to listen to music, and to attend dance and drama productions, they begin to understand the potential communication power and joy of the arts.

We often hear our students despair of their ability to make meaningful creative experiences a part of their programs because they do not feel they are talented or creative. It is not necessary to be an artist, musician, or dancer to help children have good experiences with the arts. Children are not harsh critics and will learn from your participation and enthusiasm. Even if

Reflect and write about . . .

your experiences with the arts in school

What experiences did you have in school with the arts? How did your teachers support or discourage creativity and individuality? How did this effect your feelings about your creativity and ability as an artist, musician, or dancer?

you do not feel that you are talented in the arts, you have a responsibility to include them in your curriculum. You can develop a receptive attitude towards the creative expression of children and towards the arts in general. Every community has resources—artists, educators, reference materials—that can guide you in providing good arts experiences for children.

ART

Art provides opportunities for children to explore and manipulate materials and express their feelings and understanding of the world. The primary purpose of an early childhood art program is to enhance artistic and creative development. Its sensory and physical nature makes art especially appropriate for young children. The sensory pleasure of the art experience and the process of exploration are the primary motivation for very young children's involvement in art. As they mature, children use art to express ideas and to communicate with others, but throughout the early childhood years, they continue to enjoy the satisfaction of "messing about" with materials. The value of a final art product is its relation to the feelings and awareness that it generates in the child. For very young children the process is the whole of the art experience and product is not important (for example, toddlers enjoy painting on plexiglass easels which are hosed off after they are done). As children grow older, they begin to

take pride in their artistic efforts and want to share them with others.

Creative art activities reap educational benefits besides those associated with the arts. As children use art media they develop motor control and perceptual discrimination. Language is often inspired and experiences with new vocabulary are provided. Children learn about the characteristics of materials as they work. Confronted with challenges in artwork, children develop problem-solving strategies. Working with others, their social skills are enhanced. Developing aesthetic awareness and appreciation for the natural world and human creations are very direct and important benefits of art experiences.

Through their artwork, children can disclose private thoughts, feelings, and ways of perceiving. They can only risk this when they feel safe, valued, and encouraged. You support children's creativity by accepting *all* of their feelings, ideas, and creative expression, whether or not they are "nice" or "pretty" by adult standards. Those things that move children and adults are not always the most pleasant aspects of their lives. Nevertheless, if they have the power to evoke strong feelings, they are important, and important parts of life are a part of art (Figure 12.1).

Art and Development

The simple, nonrepresentational character of young children's art and the sequence of chil-

FIGURE 12.1
My mommy is mad at me: drawing by a four-year-old

dren's growth as artists is closely correlated to development. Every child throughout the world follows the same sequence of drawing, whether they use sticks in the dirt or a mouse and a computer drawing program (Figure 12.2).

The sophistication of the finished product is determined by the child's strength, motor coordination, and cognitive development. Young children view the world simply and attend only to those aspects that currently command their attention. For example, though most four-year-olds are aware of the existence of arms, legs, fingers, and toes, they often create portraits that omit these features and that consist exclusively of a smiling head—the most important feature of a human being and the one they were thinking of as they worked.

Infants and toddlers experience the world and art as color, texture, form, movement, temperature, and taste. Art is not distinguished from other sensory experiences and is enjoyed in the same ways. An infant may enjoy the colors and forms in a Mary Cassatt painting of a mother and child as much as the photo of the baby on the disposable diaper box. The Mary Cassatt print will certainly enhance the atmosphere for adults and may build positive feelings for fine art in the children. Toddlers may begin

Basic scribbles (often random)

dots   lines   multiple lines   zig-zags   roaming lines   whorls   loops   circles

Combined Scribbles (controlled)

crosses   mandalas   stars   closed shapes

Suns

Sun Faces

Human Figures with Limbs

Human Figures with Torsos

Human Figure with Limbs Used in a Drawing

by a Four-year Old.

FIGURE 12.2
Stages of development in children's drawing

Reflect and write about . . .

art in your childhood

Reflect on the way you experienced art in your childhood. Where did you experience art? Did you enjoy it? Who provided this experience? How did your teachers and family respond to your artistic efforts? What else could have supported your artistic development?

to examine the work more closely and begin to appreciate it.

Art media can offer wonderful, developmentally appropriate experiences for even very young children. Infants do not derive any real benefit from art activities, but toddlers will enjoy the sensory pleasures of art and the sense of empowerment that accompanies acting on

art materials. We have sometimes seen adults in infant classrooms holding children's hands and "helping" them to smear paint across the paper, then proudly presenting the result, saying, "Andy made this for you today." A year later, twenty-month-old Andy may take paintbrush in hand and delight in the color and texture of the paint and in the power that he has to mark the paper. He still will not have deliberately made anything *for* anyone, but he will have enjoyed the process and his family can enjoy the results.

A toddler first makes a mark on paper at around eighteen months of age, but the sensory-motor exploration that precedes this is essential. Children's first marks on paper are often referred to as *scribbling* although adult associations of the word *scribble* do not do justice to children's often thoughtful exploration. Children in this stage respond to the world as an extension of themselves. They touch, taste, and smell everything. Creating is very much a kinesthetic experience. Arts experiences must be correspondingly safe, sensory, and flexible. We think of scribbling in reference to drawing, but the characteristics of scribbling are also present in children's work with paint, clay, and even collage.

Appropriate activities for toddlers consist of frequent experiences with materials such as large, stubby crayons and watercolor markers with big pieces of paper, easel painting and fingerpainting, paste and paper, and clay and dough. Food used as an art medium is not appropriate because toddlers are just learning to distinguish between what can be eaten and what cannot be eaten.

Daily experiences with art media and an environment that is filled with objects of beauty provide appropriate experiences for preschool and kindergarten children. By age three, children are interested in exploring and manipulating art media. They view the world from their own perspective and have difficulty understanding that the experience of others may be different from their own. At age three children often begin to control and name their "scribbles," but representation is an afterthought. Adults are often eager to hurry children into representational art because it is easier to identify and understand what children are communicating in a representational work. A smiling face says more to us than a series of lines of different lengths, widths, and direction though the meaning to the child may be very much the same. Older preschoolers and kindergartners spontaneously represent their feelings and aspects of the world that they know and care about. Development in art at this stage has been referred to as *pre-schematic,* which means that children represent their world but have not yet developed the regular recurring symbols that will mark the next stage of art development. Sensory experience and exploration continues to be a motivation for involvement in the arts. The easier give-and-take of relationships and eagerness to involve others in their work leads to cooperation with peers.

By the primary grades children have developed a good deal of skill using the basic materials of art and enter the *schematic* stage of art. This stage is named for the recurrent symbols (or schema) that children develop in their work. For example, a crowd of people in a drawing would consist of a group of more or less identical figures. Work is more realistic in terms of proportion and color. This is a particularly fascinating stage of artistic development that seems to recapitulate art history in that

children's work often is reminiscent of artwork from early historical periods. Work often includes a "base line," which defines the bottom of the picture, and the rest of the work relates to this line. Perspective may shift within a piece of work. Events in time are often presented across the length of the work and an "x-ray" view allows the artist to represent what is hidden.

Primary-school children enjoy and can use fully open-ended art experiences. With regular access they will develop more and more sophisticated artistic skill. Six-, seven-, and eight-year-olds are also ready for additional challenges. You can begin to teach techniques that require group participation (for example, mural painting or large construction) or that use more difficult or dangerous materials and require greater motor strength and agility (for example, batik or soap carving). You can include projects that take more planning (for example, building a bird feeder), and teach processes that have many steps that must be carefully followed (for example, pottery).

Because of their growing understanding of the world and their increased ability to understand the perspective of others, children at this stage of development can begin to have a more sophisticated appreciation of the work of others and can begin to distinguish art styles and techniques (Table 12.1). They may be particularly appreciative of trips to art galleries or books about artists. We have enjoyed sharing styles like pointillism and expressionism, which children then may integrate into their own work.

The Organizing Framework

Curriculum for art consists of two kinds of experiences. Studio experiences, where children explore and create using art media, and "discipline-based" experiences, where children have opportunities to encounter, discuss, appreciate, and think about art. Both are valuable and can

TABLE 12.1

Development of Creative Expression in Art

Age	*Characteristics as an Artist*
Infant/toddler (birth–3 years)	Scribbling stage in art • Experiences art as sensory input • Explores media through all senses • Draws for the first time between fifteen and twenty months following the universal developmental sequence (see Figure 12.2)
Younger preschooler (3–4 years)	Scribbling stage in art continues • Explores and manipulates materials • Experiences art as exploratory play discovering what can be done with color, texture, tools, and techniques • Often repeats an action • Perceives shapes in work • Begins to name and control scribbles • Process not product important; may destroy work during process • Work may not be pleasing to adults
Older preschooler and kindergartner (4–6 years)	Preschematic stage in art • Creates definite forms and shapes • Represents feelings and ideas • Represents what is *known* and *what is important to the child* not what is *seen* or *important to adults* (may not be recognizable to adults) • Work becomes more and more detailed • Preplans and implements • Rarely destroys work during the process • Relationship between aspects of the work
Primary-school child (6–8 years)	Schematic stage in art • Serious effort to master skills • Evaluates own products critically • Uses recurrent symbols in work • Work more realistic in terms of color and proportion • Begins to use different perspectives in work • Use of a baseline to define pictures • Use of "X-ray" view

be a part of the regular program for young children.

Studio art experiences for young children can be designed to help them to become aware of and explore the elements that make up works of art. We help children to think about art by being aware of and talking with them about these elements. We also design art experiences so the children have opportunities to experience the basic processes of artistic expression.

The Elements of Art

Every work of art is composed of visual, graphic, and other sensory elements. We experience these elements long before we are consciously aware of them or learn to talk about them. Much of the creative process of art for young children is exploration of the elements of art. Realizing this can help you appreciate children's early artwork and their artistic exploration of art elements.

Line. Line is a part of every painting, drawing, collage, print, or sculpture. Line can be described by kind or quality: straight, curved, wandering, wiggling, jagged, broken, zig-zag, heavy, light, wide, thin. Every linear aspect of a piece of art has length, a beginning and end, and direction (up/down, diagonal, side to side). Lines have relationships with one another and other parts of the work. They can be separate, parallel, or crossed. When children fill their paintings and drawings with many different kinds of lines they are exploring this element.

Color. Colors have qualities and can be referred to by name or hue—red, scarlet, turquoise, magenta. These color names add richness to our experience of color. They can be pure—primary colors (red, blue, yellow), white, and black—or mixed. Different colors are considered to have temperature—coolness at the blue end of the spectrum, or warmth at the red end of the spectrum. They have different degrees of intensity or saturation (brightness or dullness) and value (lightness or darkness). Colors change as they mix. They are related to one another (orange is related to red) and look different when placed next other colors. Children who combine colors in painting or coloring with chalk or crayons are exploring the nature of this element. Discovering color by mixing takes much experimentation.

Shape. Shape or form in art is far more than geometric shapes like circles, squares, and triangles. Children and artists only rarely fill their work with regular geometric shapes. Instead, they combine these shapes with irregular shapes. The forms in artwork can be thought of as filled or empty. In relationship to each other they may be separated by space, connected or

overlapping, or one shape may be enclosed by another. When the boundaries of a shape are completed, the shape is closed; if the boundary is left uncompleted (like a *U* or a *C*), the shape is open. Shapes in three-dimensional art may be solid (like a ball) or may use empty space as part of the form (like a tire).

Space. The distance within or between aspects of a piece of artwork is the element known as *space*. The location of a line, shape, or color is part of the work—center, top, bottom, side, left, right. Space can be crowded and full, sparse or empty, and these give feelings of freedom or cramped enclosure to the work. The space can have balance with other spaces or forms. Boundaries in a work and ideas like inclusion and exclusion are a part of the spatial qualities of artwork.

Design. Design refers to the organization of a piece of work. Children initially work without plan or artistic purpose—art is sensory and exploratory. Nancy Smith refers to children's approach to paper in painting at this stage as a place "to play, a sort of two-dimensional park" (Smith 1983, 33). As they gain experience they become aware, and the elements of design enter their work. There is awareness of the unity of the work or of a division of elements. A planned, organized piece of work may have a concept (like a circular shape) repeated or varied. The way color, line, shape, and form are placed may give the work an actual texture or the impression of texture. Elements are used with an awareness of their relationship to one another although effects may be unexpected. Symmetry, balance, and alternation are some of characteristics found in design.

Art Processes

The studio art program for young children has five distinct processes. In talking to many teachers we have found that these five are the essential activities included in most good early childhood programs and that children can enjoy again and again over time. These basic media are used by child artists and adult artists alike, although there are differences in the complexity of the processes that each employs.

Children benefit from using the same media over and over and find the same basic activities satisfying over long periods of time. It takes many experiences with the same materials to fully explore their possibilities—clay and paint and crayons, for example, can be available every day.

In a desire for novelty we have found that many educators seek out more and more unusual art activities for children. Children do not seek constant novelty; they enjoy the stability of coming back to a familiar activity and developing skill. Always providing novel art activities may create a situation in which children are kept perpetual state of exploration without allowing them to gain the deeper skill and understanding from repeating the same activities many times, using familiar media to express ideas and feelings. Variations, such as those suggested in the In Practice boxes, can be presented when children have thoroughly explored basic processes and seek variation on their own. Each process can be varied in ways that build on existing skills while heightening interest and providing appropriate challenges. Variation can be provided by:

- Changing the *materials and tools* (a new type or shape of paper, the addition of real potter's tools, making homemade paste).
- Changing the *setting* in which the work is done.
- Providing a *motivating experience* (collecting collage materials on a walk, playing music while children work, painting outside, setting a vase of flowers on the table).
- Varying the *technique or task* (showing children how to spatter instead of brush paint, adding a saw to the woodworking materials, instructing children in the use of rolled clay to make coil pots).

Art processes can be varied to give children different experiences and expand their artistic vocabulary. Young children benefit when you demonstrate the use of tools and materials in different art techniques and when you show examples of fine artists' work (including illustrators of children's books) who have used the technique. The purpose is to show possibilities. Do not provide a specific model to be copied since by doing so you limit the child's creativity and can induce feelings of failure.

Drawing. All children draw. They draw with their fingers and sticks in sand, dirt, snow, fogged windows, fingerpaint, and flour dropped on the table. Drawing involves creating a line or figure on a surface with an implement. Drawing materials are nonfluid. They need no additional material to mark a surface and so are easy for young children to control. Thick primary crayons provide excellent first drawing tools. They can be used with greatest facility when they are short and chunky to fit small hands without encumbering paper wrappers that prevent use of the whole crayon. Felt markers are another good first drawing medium for young children. They require less

IN PRACTICE

Drawing variations

Offer a variety of drawing materials—crayons, chalk, pastels, felt-tipped marking pens, and colored pencils—demonstrate their use.

Crayons

- Unwrap crayons and use them on sides. Cover paper with wide swipes of color.
- Cover light colors with dark and scratch though the top layer with a toothpick.
- Crayon resist: Paint over light colored crayon drawings.
- Layer light colors to create new colors.

Felt-Tipped Marking Pens

- Use black pens after drawing or painting to create a black outline.
- Use only black pens and create pen-and-ink-style drawings. Provide black pens of different widths (ultra-fine to thick).

Oil pastels

- Use a finger or a soft cloth to blend two colors at the edges to make a third color.
- Use a watercolor wash over a white oil pastel drawing.

Chalk

- Use one color and smudge outwards to soften the edges. On top draw with hard lines.
- Use chalk on wet paper to enhance color brilliance or dip chalk in water.
- Use chalk dipped in milk to resist rubbing off, and make colors that are more brilliant.

Charcoal

- Explore charcoal and the shades it can create, from dark black to pale gray.
- Use charcoal briquettes to draw on the sidewalk to introduce artist's charcoal.

---

strength than crayons to use successfully and they produce bright appealing colors.

Painting. The application of a liquid medium to a surface with a tool like a brush or sponge is called *painting.* It is most important to provide primary colors (red, yellow, and blue—or the tones that are used by printers and photographers: cyan, magenta, and yellow) as well as black and white since these colors can be mixed to create all other colors. The In Practice box outlines many appropriate painting experiences for young children, but one of the most important is painting at an easel because it involves the large muscles of the arms and shoulders over which children first develop control, as well as the small muscles of hands and fingers.

IN PRACTICE

Painting Variations

Painting can be varied by offering different kinds of paints, different shades of paint, and different techniques for painting. Show children some of the following:

Using Brushes

- Make thin and thick lines, splotches and blots, wiggles, smears, drops, loops, twirls, and swirls. Talk about what a brush can do.
- Use a variety of objects for brushes: cotton swabs, feather dusters, feathers, frayed bark, straw, fur, grasses.

Fingerpainting

- Have a tray and paper. For each painting use a liquid soap, finger paint base, and tempera paint (or a commercial fingerpaint).
- Have children fingerpaint directly on the trays and make prints by placing paper on the image.
- Add textured materials to the paint—salt, sand, sugar.
- Make mud fingerpaint.

Color Combining

- Talk about the ways colors effect one another and changes as they are mixed.
- Provide experiences using limited combinations of colors.
- Provide experiences using paint with various shades of a single color.

Water Colors

- Wet the brush, rub brush in paint, paint, wash brush, and dry on the sponge; choose new color.
- Wet paper and drop on small amounts of paint; move the paper and let paint flow. Let two colors "marry" and become a new color.
- Use diluted food color instead of paint.

Textures

- Add sand, sugar, salt, or other substances to the paint to create textures in the paint.

In addition to easel painting, provide experiences with fingerpainting, watercolor painting, painting with large brushes and water on a fence or wall, string painting, and other variations. We are especially fond of palette painting (using small containers of red, blue, yellow, and white paint to mix on a tray to create a palette of colors) since this technique allows children to create their own colors and is like the process that artists use as they paint (see In Practice box on palette painting). Smith's excellent book, *Experience and Art* (1983), gives a

How to Palette Paint

Palette painting is a technique in which children have primary colors (red, blue, and yellow or cyan, magenta, and yellow), white, and black paint in small quantities along with a mixing surface (or palette). It enables children to discover elements of color and how they change.

Children mix the colors that they want for painting. You need the following materials for each palette:

- 5 small containers for the paint (furniture casters work well, as do the lids from baby food jars)
- A cookie sheet or cafeteria tray
- A small sponge
- A small brush
- A cup for water

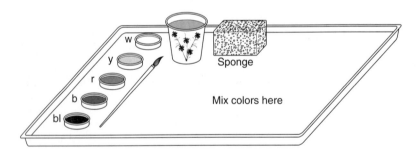

The only instruction that children need to succeed with palette painting is to learn to wash their brushes in the water when they change colors and to dry the brushes on the sponge before using a new color.

Note: Often children focus on color mixing for quite a while and will move on to painting when they have experimented enough. We have observed children explore a single color group for many days. You might ask children to make as many shades of blue, yellow, or red as they can and discuss how they made them and how they are different. The color swatches can be torn or cut to use for collages. A side benefit of palette painting is that it is a very efficient way to use the paint with little waste.

IN PRACTICE

Printmaking Variations

Printmaking can be varied by offering different objects with which to print, different inks and paints, and different techniques for print making. Show children some of the following.

Stamps

- Use one or two colors of paint in shallow trays. Add simple objects for printing—toilet paper rolls, fruits and vegetables, sponges, corks, styrofoam.
- Use objects that all have a similar shape or origin—round shapes, cookie cutters, kitchen utensils, citrus fruit.
- Use stamp pads with fingers, small objects, or simple rubber stamps.
- Carve shapes in a potato or similar vegetable to use as a stamp.
- Roller print by inking a round textured object like an ear of corn, a toy tire, or a spool and roll a print.

Stencils

- Use pieces of flat paper or cardboard for stencils. Place them on paper and brush or spatter paint over them. Children can cut shapes out of heavy paper to make their own stencils.

Embossed Prints

- Create a raised design on a piece of card or wood by setting down or gluing flat objects or making a design in glue. Use this to make a print by laying paper over the surface and rubbing the paper with chalk or crayon.

Monoprints

- Make a monoprint of a fingerpainting by laying down a piece of paper on the painting and lifting a print.
- Make a monoprint of a wax crayon drawing by laying a second piece of paper on top of a crayon drawing and using a warm iron to transfer the print.

Etched Prints

- Etch a design into a piece of cardboard or styrofoam with a pencil. Roll a layer of ink on it with a brayer. Place paper over the design and lift a print.

detailed explanation of the palette painting technique.

Print Making. Print making involves applying paint or ink to an object and imprinting a surface to make an image, or by rubbing a flat textured object beneath a surface. Anything that will hold the ink or paint—corks, hands, cookie cutters, spools, feet, paper rolls, fruits, vegetables, and many other things—will make a print (In Practice box). For rubbing, a flat, textured object or surface is used beneath a paper or similar material and the image is impressed using crayon, chalk, or charcoal. Leaves, surfaces of sidewalks and rocks, fabrics, boards, coins, inscriptions, and any other interesting surface will make an interesting rubbing. The creative aspect of print-making involves the selections children make as they choose what to print with, the colors to use, and how they arrange prints on paper.

Collage and Construction. (Combining two and three dimensional materials is called *collage* and *construction*. Collage involves attaching relatively flat materials like tissue paper, magazine pictures, cloth scraps, macaroni, ribbons, yarn, leaves, sticks, and sand together with paste or glue. Sturdy construction paper, cardboard, wood scraps, and similar materials make good bases for collage. The skills of cutting, tearing, and folding are often employed in collage. Construction involves three-dimensional materials like paper towel rolls, wood scraps, cardboard boxes, cans, toothpicks, and styrofoam. Sturdy bases are required for glued construction. Woodworking, stitchery, weaving, sculpture, and paper-maché are construction techniques that involve other kinds of materials and skills.

Modeling and Sculpting. (Modeling and sculpting involve molding a soft material or carving a hard one to create a three-dimensional work of art. Materials include potter's clay, flour and salt dough usually called *play-dough,* and oil-based modeling media (sometimes called *plasticene*). Children form shapes out of these malleable three-dimensional substances. Potter's clay, the most versatile of these, can be used over and over again, can be reconstituted with water, and can be fired (baked in a kiln) for a permanent product. For very young children who do not have adequate strength to manipulate potter's clay, homemade dough provides an introduction to modeling. Children should be give plenty of opportunity to work with model-

ing materials, sculpting only with their hands. When they are ready for a more complex experience, blunt knives, rounded sticks, and lengths of dowel for rolling make excellent tools. Cookie cutters and similar pattern shapes do not offer a creative experience since they prescribe and limit.

Pattern Art

In their efforts to make families happy, early childhood educators sometimes resort to pattern activities (often based on holiday themes) that they call "art." Creative expression should be a reflection of the child artist's ideas and abilities—not patterns from a teacher's magazine or book. Prepared patterns to be copied by children and coloring books have nothing to do with the development of creativity or self-expression—in fact, they can be destructive to children's feelings of competence and self-worth. The skills and understanding that they require are almost always developmentally inappropriate and can lead some children to feelings of failure and dissatisfaction. The activities take up valuable time that children should be using to develop other skills, awareness, and ideas. They are not a part of good early childhood programs. Viktor Lowenfeld and Lambert Brittain in their classic work on art education *Creative and Mental Growth* have said:

> Art instruction that includes these kinds of activities is worse than no art at all. Such predigested activities force youngsters into imitative behavior and inhibit their own creative expression. These activities make no provision for emotional growth because any variation the child makes can only be a mistake; they do not promote skills, because skills develop from one's own expression. Instead, they condition the child to accept adult concepts as art, art that the child is unable to produce, therefore frustrating normal creative urges.
>
> *(Lowenfeld and Brittain 1987, 179)*

Similarly, children may sometimes ask you (or other adults in your classroom) to draw a picture for them to color or to take home. Their appreciation for your efforts may tempt you to draw or paint for them. This has the unintended consequence of discouraging children's creative work and encouraging stereotypes. Since they do not have adult sophistication or skill, they find their own work less and less satisfactory and creativity and learning are sidetracked. When you understand the importance of creativity and art you will not draw, paint, sculpt, or make collages for children although you may participate in art activities side by side with children to demonstrate technique and model your own enjoyment of working seriously at art.

The Environment

The work of an artist, child or adult, requires a special kind of environment that supports artistic expression, enabling the artist to work with full concentration on the process of creation. It includes materials and equipment that are appropriate to the task, that are functional, and that inspire use. An environment for artistic expression also requires sufficient time and space for exploration. For young children especially, the environment may be a source of motivation.

An interesting model for an environment for artistic expression can be found in the schools of Reggio Emilia, Italy. Each of these pre-primary programs includes an *atelier,* a workshop in the school where children come to create art and work with an *atelierist,* an art specialist. It is also a place where children's work and their process is documented (Edwards, et al. 1993).

When designing an art area for children you may find it useful to think about an artist's studio: a place designed primarily for art. In a studio the amount of external stimulation is controlled—people, objects, and sound are brought in when desired as models or for motivation. The work area is well lit, usually with natural light. Materials are organized so that they can be found easily. Work tables and easels are a comfortable size for the artist and the work. Floors, walls, and furnishings are sturdy and washable. Storage is easily reached, smocks are available to protect clothes, and facilities for cleaning up are nearby. Space is set aside for drying work and storing art that is still in process.

In most early childhood programs it is possible to include many of the important features of a studio. Locate your art area near a window, a sink, and on tile or linoleum. Carefully arrange and maintain storage so that all materials and tools are within children's reach. If these are clearly organized and uncrowded children will be able to put things away. Make sure that furniture is the correct size for the children. Use old or second-hand furniture or cover tables and floors so that inevitable spills are not tragic.

Select art materials that are of good quality and proportioned to the size of the children. Make sure there are enough materials available and that they are stored so it is easy for children to get them and put them away. If materials are scarce, children may focus on obtaining and hoarding rather than on creative expression. Concentration is encouraged when the space is neither too noisy nor too crowded.

For child artists, like their adult counterparts, the impulse to create may not occur on a schedule. Include basic media (easels, clay, crayons) in the free choice of activities daily and provide other materials several times a week so that children can express their creative ideas as they occur. In our own work we make available a daily smorgasbörd of basic art activities, including easel painting, palette painting, drawing, collage, and clay as well as a special activity such as stitchery, construction, or print making. We offer the same special activity for several days to enable children to experience it in depth. Great complexity or novelty in art materials is not necessary. Children develop creativity as they find new ways to use the familiar.

Time to use art materials must be long enough for children to thoroughly explore the nature and possibilities of the activity or material and become involved. Little of creative significance occurs if access to art materials is limited to under an hour a day. Children who are repeatedly frustrated at having to leave activities just as they are getting involved may become unwilling to invest energy in art.

Supporting Learning

Your role in art is to provide an environment, materials, experiences, and relationships that support creative development and aesthetic appreciation. A classroom that provides for all of these needs has a creative climate: an atmosphere where creative expression is nurtured and where creativity can flourish.

Although it is not necessary for you to be an artist to help young children enjoy art, it *is* necessary to believe that experiences with and participation in art are valuable. Begin by reflecting on the role of art in your life. Treat yourself to an afternoon at a gallery or of quiet perusal of books of art prints at your library. Become aware of the art you enjoy and share this enjoyment with children.

As you look at and talk with children about art, remember to discuss color, shape, space, line, form, design, and effect—the elements of art. You might say, "You used hundreds of dots to fill in that shape—it stands out on your paper." You may want to write down all the words you can think of to describe an element of art; for example, line—jagged, broken, wide, narrow, short, long, curved, flowing, wavy, zigzag, curly, twisted, straight, upright, leaning, turned. These kinds of words give you important things to say with children about their work. "You used lots of lines in your work—short narrow ones, wide jagged lines, and there are even two wavy lines!"

As children work, it is best, especially at first, to offer only minimal input. Comment on children's effort, innovation, and technique. Avoid asking children *what* they have created. They may have had nothing particular in mind and the question implies that they should have. Instead you can ask them if they wish to tell you about what they have done and accept it if they do not. Children's creative expression is supported when you demonstrate your genuine appreciation and when your appreciation is broad enough to include the range of children's development. If you reserve appreciation and acknowledgment for work that meets adult standards, you communicate that you are looking for correct, rather than creative, responses. Indiscriminate or insincere praise, however, is not an appropriate alternative. It renders your comments meaningless. As you gain understanding of the meaning of children's stages of development in art and are

Reflect and write about . . .

your observations of art in early childhood classrooms

Reflect on programs that you have observed. How much time was allowed for
art experiences? What kinds of art materials and experiences were available?
What kinds of access did children have to them? Was artwork displayed? How
did staff talk to children about their creative efforts? What changes do you think
could have been made to better support children's artistic development?

charmed by their fresh, non-stereotyped efforts,
you will find it easy to be genuine in your appreciation of their work.

Acknowledge children's works by commenting on effort, "You worked hard"; innovation, "You tried it a new way"; or technique,
"You covered the whole paper." Refrain from
evaluative responses such as *good, bad, ugly,
beautiful,* and *messy* and instead help children
to become their own evaluators: "What do you
like best about it?" "When you do it again what
will you do differently?" Children who are encouraged rather than evaluated develop skills
that help them create their own standards and
meet their own goals. When finished artwork is
mounted carefully and prominently displayed in
the classroom, it also demonstrates to children
(and their families) that you appreciate the work.

Time, acceptance, and encouragement are
needed for some children to discover an interest in art. A long period of disinterest or observation may precede participation. A child may
simply be more interested in different activities
or alternative ways of being creative. They may
not want to attempt art activities because they
already feel they cannot measure up to their
teacher's or parent's expectations.

Helping Families Understand Children's Art

It can be hard for families to accept the messiness and non-productive nature of young chil-

dren's artistic expression. One of your essential
roles is to allow this messiness and to help families to understand the importance of their children's art process. As you explain what their
children do and what their work means, you
are helping them to understand the development of their child and your work. Carefully
packaging children's work for the journey
home also conveys a message. One teacher we
know uses ribbon to tie children's paintings in
a neat roll. To both the families and children
this says "This work is valuable."

MUSIC

Music is pervasive. In the heart of a city we experience the "song" of traffic, footsteps, and
voices. In the solitude of the country we listen
to the harmony of birds, wind, and water. Even
before we are born we experience the music of
a heartbeat. Music has been called a universal
language. It can make us happy or sad, calm or
excited, and has been used to evoke feelings of
patriotism, sanctity, love, and empathy.

The most important reasons to provide music experiences to children are that they provide a powerful and direct link to emotions;
that listening to and making music brings pleasure; and because sharing music with others is
an important way to be a part of your culture.
Music can also be a path to many other kinds

of learning. Because it is an enjoyable experience it can be an excellent vehicle for developing problem solving skills ("How could we make motion for a mouse?") and language ("The song says that Aikin Drum played upon a ladle; have you ever seen a ladle?"), and even for pleasantly remembering facts that might not otherwise be easy to recall. (Many of us have sung the ABC song to ourselves to remember whether or not Q comes before R.)

How do we learn to take pleasure in making music—to sing, to play, to create? A hundred years ago there were no radios, no TVs, no record players, and few musical superstars. But every town had musicians, most homes had pianos, guitars, or fiddles, and most people made music. People sang and played with and for each other as entertainment. Singing, like talking, was something that everyone did. Today many adults are musically mute and passive because of our technology. Our children will also be mute and passive if we fail to give them music.

Music and Development

Young children's musical responses are strong (Table 12.2). From the first moments of life they are soothed by quiet music and respond to a distinct beat with strong, rhythmic movement. Music evokes and describes feelings and provides an emotional outlet. As they grow, children may come to express feelings of joy or sadness with a song or aggressive feelings in a dance to rhythmic or dissonant music. They can come to understand, in simple terms, the elements that make up the discipline of music.

Even from infancy, children are active explorers of music. They respond to it physically, enthusiastically, and frequently. Crying is a baby's first sound. Pitch, loudness, and rhythm are aspects of a song and a cry. Their first vocalizations are akin to song and are called *lalling* and *trilling*. Favorite toys are often objects that make sounds: rattles, chimes, bells, drums, and music boxes. By ten months infants indicate preferences for music by rocking, swaying, or clapping hands to a favorite tune and by quieting to a favorite lullaby.

By approximately eighteen months, toddlers begin to sing and explore sound. Nursery rhymes and songs are much enjoyed. From age two they "dance" with swaying bodies, bending knees, and swinging arms. Two-year-olds sing within a limited vocal range and move to music at their own tempo. Through two years of age music and movement are almost inextricable—to listen, sing, or play an instrument is to dance.

Infants and toddlers are active explorers of music but cannot focus on group activities. Provide toys and other objects that make sounds. Sing and play songs and lullabies. Encourage infants' vocalizing and sing with them as they begin to sing. Explore sounds in the environment. Say nursery rhymes and songs. Play

TABLE 12.2
Development of Creative Expression in Music

Age	Characteristics as a Musician
Infant/toddler (birth–3 years)	• Is receptive to music • Responds to music by listening and moving (from birth) and vocalizing (from 6 months). • Sings for the first time at approximately 18 months • Uses objects as sound makers
Younger preschooler (3–4 years)	• Is particularly responsive to strongly rhythmic music • Moves and sings to music • Sings spontaneously in play • Has small comfortable singing range (D to A above middle C) • Enjoys repeating same song many times • Enjoys using instruments • Responds at own tempo
Older preschooler and kindergartner (4–6 years)	• Can participate in group music activities and games • Can enjoy focused listening activities • Increased singing range from A below middle C to C# an octave above middle C • Increasingly accurate in matching pitch and tempo • Can synchronize movement with music • Can identify and use simple instruments appropriately
Primary-school child (6–8 years)	• Expends serious effort and ability to master musicianly skills • Able to learn to use adult instruments • Evaluates own music critically • Can sing accurately with sensitivity • Strong sense of rhythm • Enjoys rehearsal and performance • Begins to identify harmony • Can begin to learn notation • Can begin to sing music with "parts"

recorded music for listening and dancing. Since toddlers have a limited vocal range, choose many songs that have a small range such as "Twinkle Twinkle Little Star." Appropriate music activities for toddlers consist of frequent experiences with music that use the whole body such as finger play and action songs.

Three- and four-year-olds have a great deal more physical coordination and language skill than toddlers. Their ability to participate in group music activities is much greater. They can reproduce tunes but cannot match their pitch to others. Like toddlers, they have a lim-

ited singing range and sing best from about D to A (the range of the "teasing" chant—"Nani nani boo boo, you cannot catch me"). Young preschoolers are among the most active of song creators and they often make up repetitive, atonal songs as they go about their daily activities. Movement songs are especially enjoyed by young preschoolers. You may observe the strong influence of media or pop culture as we did a few years ago when a group of three-year-olds each day built a stage out of hollow blocks, dressed in the flashiest clothes from the home corner, and performed "La Bamba."

Rhythm instruments can be played appropriately by young preschoolers who have been given instruction and guidance.

By age four and a half or five, given opportunity, encouragement, and sufficient musical experience, most children sing tunefully in a range that exceeds an octave, understand basic music concepts, remember elaborate songs, move rhythmically to music, and play simple instruments appropriately. If they have had limited music in their lives they will need additional experience to develop these skills. Four- and five-year-olds can discuss their musical experiences in terms of the impact it has on them.

Six-, seven-, and eight-year-old children clearly enjoy musical challenges. Learning to sing songs that have parts (such as *"There's a Hole in the Bucket"*), songs that are complicated (like *"Puff the Magic Dragon"*), or that show a sense of humor (like *"The Quartermaster's Store"*) make good choices for singing activities. Increasing competence can be a matter of great pride for primary children, and they often choose to practice and perform music and skits with music for others. Primary-school children have the capacity for learning to play chorded instruments like autoharps and ukuleles and can begin to learn to read notation. Older children enjoy having a voice in choosing songs. Listening to recorded music is appreciated when there is a related challenge ("Listen for the oboe making the sound of the cuckoo in this piece—how many times does the cuckoo call?"). As children get older, they may become more self-critical and as a result more self-conscious regarding their music.

The Organizing Framework

We use a framework that describes the music curriculum as consisting of two parts: the elements, which make up all works of music, and the processes used by musicians. Understanding both the elements of music and the processes of musicianship gives you the basis for an appropriate music curriculum for young children.

The Elements of Music

Elements such as beat, pitch, and phrase are the raw materials out of which every piece of music is made. It is useful for teachers to understand these elements, although they are not meaningful to children isolated from active music involvement. Children can be helped to respond to the elements in their daily experiences with music. As they participate in music activities they can come to recognize and label some of these concepts ("Let's clap to the beat!" "We sang that song faster than we usually do").

Rhythm.   Rhythm involves the characteristics that relate to the movement and time of a piece of music. It includes *beat,* the musical pulse that we respond to by tapping our toes, swaying, or clapping. *Melodic rhythm* is the rhythm of the melody or words in a piece of music. When you clap to every syllable of a song as if you were singing it, you are demonstrating the melodic rhythm. Speed in music is called *tempo.* Songs vary in their fastness and slowness, and children can sing songs at different tempos. The points of silence in a piece of music are called *rests.* Children recognize these more easily when they are very distinct, as in the rest that occurs just before the last line of the chorus of "This Land Is Your Land" by Woody Guthrie.

Tone.   Tone concerns the musical notes. It involves *pitch,* which is the highness or lowness of the notes, and *melody* or *tune,* which is the arrangement of notes into a singable sequence. Tone also involves the way that musical notes sound. *Tone color* or *timbre* (pronounced *tamber*) refers to the characteristic sounds that musical instruments create. Difference in tone color (for example, between a violin and a flute) is one of the elements to which children first respond in infancy and which they strongly respond to throughout early childhood. Children are also very responsive to the loudness or softness of tones, called *dynamics*.

Form. The structure of musical pieces is called *form*. Children learn to respond to an introduction when you play several chords or the first part of a tune to establish the pitch and tempo of a song before you start to sing. Structurally, all songs are composed of phrases, short but complete musical ideas; for example, the first line of "The Eency Weency Spider." Repetition occurs when identical musical phrases occur in a song, as in the first and last lines of "Twinkle Twinkle Little Star." When similar phrases occur in a song (as in the first two lines of "Shoo Fly"), it is called *variation*. A phrase that is obviously different from the ones that came before provides *contrast*—for example, the third line of "Happy Birthday to You."

The Processes of a Musician

As you plan and participate in musical activities with children, you help them to develop the skills and attitudes of a musician. Making music can be both individual self-expression and participation in a social event. It need leave no lasting product: It is valuable for the pleasure that it brings the individuals and the group. The elements of music are used and controlled as children sing and play instruments.

Singing. Singing offers many opportunities for children to experience music and to develop musical skills. The songs that you teach will contribute to musical growth and will be more successful if they have aesthetic value (beautiful melodies and words). Children will have an easier time learning songs if they are relatively short and simple and have a distinct rhythm. An appropriate vocal range for young children from the age of four is approximately the octave from middle C or slightly lower, to C an octave higher; the younger the children, the more narrow the range. Your repertoire of songs should include pieces with a variety of moods, subjects, and tempos and should reflect a diversity of styles.

Singing in the preschool needs to be primarily a music experience. Although songs may teach concepts, that should not be their primary purpose. Children are being cheated if their music has limited value and is really just a drill on color names, the alphabet, or counting. Excessive use of "limited value" songs dilutes the quality of the music experience.

Many good songs for young children touch on sensitive subjects, the hard edges of life that adults sometimes try to eliminate from the classroom: death, loneliness, fear, and anger. Children demonstrate by their obvious interest in such songs that they do not need their songs sanitized and cute. However, you should be

sensitive to children's response to songs that have a strong emotional impact. We once observed a child who became very upset when "John Henry" was sung, perhaps because of the line "He laid down his hammer and he died." It would have been insensitive and disrespectful had the teacher gone on singing this song in his presence

Playing Instruments. Regular experience playing simple instruments helps young children to acquire musical skills. The custom of giving each child a rhythm instrument on which to bang is neither necessary nor desirable. It tends to create noise and chaos instead of music. Instead, introduce instruments singly to small groups of children. Let each child have a turn to play and give instruction in the care and handling of the instrument. The musical elements provide a useful framework for learning about instruments. Comparing the sound of a triangle and tone block, for example, and using them to accompany different verses of "Froggie Went a-Courtin'" gives children an experience with timbre.

Composing and Improvising. The musical skills acquired in singing, movement, and playing instruments are used creatively when children compose and improvise music. For young children these are very simple variations of musical ideas. You help children to improvise when you ask them to think of something to do besides clap their hands in "If You're Happy and You Know It." Composing is more complex. It requires creating and preserving a new composition. Notation is too abstract for preschool children (and requires greater musical sophistication on the part of the teacher), but a tape recorder works well to make a record of a child's musical creation. *Musicplay* (Burton and Hughes 1981) gives a number of suggestions for helping children to develop their own notation.

Listening. Children can appreciate and enjoy music made by others. Recordings can provide

experiences with talented musicians, symphonic music, and music from many cultures. Since recorded music is commonplace, it often is treated like audible wallpaper—it is ignored. Although background music at naptime or to create a pleasant ambiance in your environment can have value, it is important to also use recorded music as a music listening activity. When you use recorded music with children, make your choices carefully and present them as important. To help children to be attentive listeners to recorded music, ask them to listen for a sound, move to the music, or notice what feelings the music creates in them. Short, evocative pieces of music are best able to hold children's attention.

Recordings are not a replacement for real people making music. When you play instruments and sing in the classroom you prove that music comes from people, not mechanical boxes. Have musicians visit your classroom to play short pieces of music for children. They need not be professionals; your next-door neighbor's daughter who is studying the clarinet, the high school string quartet, or a parent who plays the banjo will provide a listening experience with live music and real instruments that will impress itself indelibly in the minds of the children you teach. If possible, children should be allowed to gently try the visitors' instruments themselves.

Performing. Singing, moving to music, or playing instruments for the pleasure of others is performance. Because the goal of music education is to help children to become comfortable with musical expression, performance is the least important part of the music curriculum for young children. Younger children who have lots of opportunities to explore and share music may feel unself-conscious about making music for others. As children get older, they may come to enjoy the challenge of putting together a "show." In early childhood, though, performance should always be secondary to other goals. For preschool children, "performances" where families and other visitors important to the children are invited to participate in a daily music time are preferable to staged presentations where children are on display. Performances for primary children are more worthwhile when the children have been given the opportunity to work together to create their performance.

The Environment

Your program can be filled with music. Daily experience with music enables children to gradually build and practice a repertoire of skills and songs. These will form the base for individual exploration and appreciation. Schedule music at a regular time each day for ten to thirty minutes, depending on the age and development of the children.

Every early childhood classroom needs a serviceable sound system and an eclectic collection of recorded classical, folk, jazz, and other kinds of music. Your choices help make children aware of musical alternatives. Your responsibility is to acquaint children with a range of good music, not merely what is most familiar to you. Children may have plenty of exposure to Top Forty, Barney, and Muzak but may never have heard chamber music, folk music, bluegrass, jazz, Gregorian chants, Gamelan, symphonic music, classical guitar, flute, sitar, or opera. Most public libraries have a selection of different kinds of recorded music available for borrowing, and you can pick up a new recording when you borrow new books.

A collection of simple rhythm instruments that children can play is also essential. Good quality instruments are well made, have good tone, and are satisfying to play. They must be sturdy enough to take the enthusiastic handling of many young children. They are a worthwhile investment that must be stored and handled carefully like any other piece of valuable equipment. Tossed into a box and grabbed out again the next time or left lying on the floor to be stepped upon, they will have a short life span. A music center that is carefully arranged with one or two musical instruments and activities to explore makes a good addition to a classroom for children ages four and older.

Supporting Learning

You support children in music through an environment, experiences, and relationships that support musical development and appreciation. A *creative climate* for music, where musical expression is nurtured and creativity flourishes, means that music is frequently present. When music-making is a part of classroom, home, and community, children become spontaneous music makers. They hum tunes, make up songs, explore sounds, create rhythms, move to music, and use music to communicate. An environment that supports children's development in music must include live people making and responding to music.

You can help children to be comfortable with music by bringing it informally into the classroom and by formal planned music experiences. You need not be limited to songs or movement activities that are already created or topics that someone else has chosen. By modifying songs and activities you know and new ones that you can create, you can sing and dance about anything! A teacher we know improvises a song for each of the children in his group, which he then sings to them during activities during the day (for example, he sang new words to Michelle to the tune of "Michelle, Ma Belle," and to Katarina to the tune of "La Cucaracha").

The easiest way to enable yourself to sing about your day-to-day life with children is to use "zipper" songs,[1] predictable song templates with lyrics that can be changed to suit circum-

---

[1]*Zipper songs* is an expression used by Pete Seeger in his book *Where Have All the Flowers Gone: A Singer's Stories, Songs, Seeds, Robberies* (1993). He attributes the phrase to Lee Hays.

stances. A simple example that you probably know is "Old MacDonald Had a Farm." Most of us sing about different animals and the sounds that they make. Sometimes teachers add local animals to regionalize the song. You can also sing the song with lyrics that talk about the things children do, for example:

> The Blueberry room had some kids, E-I-E-I-O
> And in that room there was Alice, E-I-E-I-O
> She built blocks here, and she built blocks there
> Here she built, there she built,
> Everywhere she built with blocks
> The Blueberry room had some kids, E-I-E-I-O

Zipper songs like "Mary Wore Her Red Dress" are greeting songs in which children's names and attributes are inserted. The beginning of the day as children arrive is one of the times to sing zipper greeting songs. You can also sing them and other songs like "Get on Board Everybody" when children gather. But they can also be sung during the day as children are playing. You can use many other zipper songs throughout the day's routines and transitions. If you make up or improvise songs and chants as you work with children, they will follow suit. Another teacher we know always sings a simple tune she created to her class when it's time to go in: "Three-year-old class, it's time for snack. Hurry to the gate so you won't be late." In like manner the children in her class often sing about what they are doing.

Although there is much to be gained from spontaneous, informal music, a special time for music each day is essential. The age appropriateness of your plans, your sensitivity to children's responses, and your awareness that music can be very stimulating will contribute to positive, easily managed music sessions. One day this might be a carefully structured lesson to teach a musical concept using rhythm instruments. The next might be a spirited sing-a-long of everybody's favorite silly songs. *What* the content is is not nearly as important as making sure that music happens daily.

Group music times are most successful when you sit with children as you sing. If you can accompany the singing with a guitar, auto-harp, or ukulele, this will add to the experience. If not, clap your hands, keep time with a drum, or sway as you sing. Piano accompaniment does not offer the intimacy and accessibility of sitting near children and singing with them and is difficult to manage with groups of young children.

Moving to music is a natural response—our toes tap, our heads nod, and our bodies sway almost without our realizing it. Movement helps young children to concentrate on a music session. Hand gestures and fingerplays illustrate songs and help children to understand the meaning of the words. Use body movements with songs and encourage children to think of new ways to move.

Reflect and write about . . .

music in programs you have observed

Reflect on programs that you have observed. How much music did you observe? What kinds of music experiences were provided? How did educators respond to children's musical efforts? Did you observe children making music spontaneously? What could better support children's musical development?

CREATIVE MOVEMENT

Movement is one of the first ways that adults interact with children—holding, rocking, and bouncing are the earliest movement activities. Young children are nearly always moving. As they move, they learn. Concepts such as *jump, slide, run, creep,* and *push* must be experienced before they can be understood. Children move to play, to express feelings, and to communicate. Creative movement helps young children to express ideas and feelings through body movement.

When is movement creative? When ideas and feelings are expressed through movement in individual ways, children are using their bodies as an art medium. This is different from, and not a substitute for, large muscle activity on the playground or games and exercises such as the "Hokey Pokey." It differs from dance, in which a teacher formally instructs in specific, predetermined ways of moving. In a creative movement activity, children interpret and fol-

low suggestions and are encouraged to find their own personal, creative, and innovative ways of moving. During these activities, children discover joy and satisfaction in expressing ideas with their bodies and develop a repertoire of movement possibilities. Creative movement offers challenges and new ways to use and practice developing physical skills. As you direct children in movement, you encourage them to make suggestions and express ideas in innovative ways. This supports children's developing imagination and positive self-concept. It is this focus on individual ways of moving that makes it *creative* movement. Social development is enhanced as they learn to move with respect for the group and come to appreciate the creativity of others.

In working with young children, creative movement and drama are closely tied to one another. The motivation for movement activities is often the suggestion to act like a character, animal, or object. Children naturally take on roles in their play and dramatize stories and

Reflect and write about . . .

dance and creative movement in your childhood

Reflect on the way you experienced dance/creative movement in your childhood. Where did you experience it? Did you enjoy it? Who provided this experience? How did your teachers and families respond to your expression? What could have better supported your development?

scenes. With very young children, creative drama and movement are often part of the same activity. As you guide children in creative movement, you may alternate between directions that are exclusively related to body movement ("Bounce"), to those related to a dramatic idea ("Bounce like a ball" or "Hop like a rabbit"), to directions that are dramatic ideas as a part of a story or scenario ("The rabbit is hopping slowly. Now he hears something. Quickly hop away to your burrow").

Creative Movement and Development

All children move. In fact, movement characteristics are among the primary ways we define and describe children's development. Most children come to early childhood programs delighted with movement and actively seeking ways to explore, express ideas, and develop physical competence (Table 12.3).

Infants respond to the world physically. Learning to control movement is their first challenge. The sequence of physical development from lifting the head to walking takes the bulk of the first year of life. Once walking starts, at about one year of age, further movement challenges commence. These children are developing basic movement skills. You can provide space and activities that encourage them. Take delight in infants' exploration as they learn to move in new ways and participate with them by encouraging them to try new movement challenges.

Toddlers begin to "dance" with swaying bodies, bending knees, and swinging arms. They learn to manipulate objects in their environment and to catch and kick a ball, balance, climb, and gradually put into place the physical skills that they will need for later development. Appropriate movement activities for toddlers consist of frequent experiences with moving and music. The younger the children, the simpler the activities must be. Creative movement activities for toddlers are best provided through simple movement songs and games (like "Jack in the Box" and "The Eency Weency Spider") and by allowing space and freedom to move in response to music. Sustained interest of a group should not be expected, but a group may spontaneously move along to music.

Three- and four-year-olds can hop, gallop, run, broad jump, and catch large balls. Their ability to participate in group activities is much greater than it was when they were toddlers. They begin to be able to cooperate with their peers and enjoy repetitive, familiar movement activities. Three- and four-year-olds are very active, and they often dance and dramatize in play. At this age you may first see children who are too shy to actively participate and who are more comfortable observing. By age four and a half or five, children have gained a great deal of balance and control. They can move their body parts in isolation, can follow most directions, can begin to synchronize movement to music, and can respond quickly and skillfully

TABLE 12.3
Development of Creative Expression in Movement

Age	Characteristics as a Mover
Infant/toddler (birth–3 years)	• Enjoys movement games like This-little-piggy • Gradually develops the ability to creep, crawl, stand, walk, tiptoe, and jump and begins to run • First "dance" at about two–swaying, bending, enjoys moving to music • Begins to try to catch and kick a ball • Can walk on a low balance beam by age 3
Younger preschooler (3–4 years)	• Enjoys repetition of movement activities • Enjoys directed movement activities • Learns to hop on one foot • Begins to gallop • Runs efficiently but cannot stop or turn quickly • Jumps for distance • Catches large balls
Older preschooler and kindergartner (4–6 years)	• Can move body parts in isolation with practice • Can participate in group activities and games • Can synchronize movement with music • Runs quickly; controls speed, stopping, and turning • Understands and can move forward, backward, sideways, up, down, fast, slow, lightly, heavily • Gallops skillfully • Skips skillfully by age 6 • Catches small balls • Kicks balls in mature style • Balances on one foot
Primary-school child (6–8 years)	• Can do a forward roll • Has a strong sense of rhythm • Understands almost all verbal directions • Enjoys new challenges • Can learn dance and movement patterns • Enjoys rehearsal and performance

to a change in directions. Four- and five-year-olds are beginning to have the ability also to understand their role in group activities and can cooperate in group efforts although they continue to have moments when it is difficult.

Primary-school children have developed many skills and enjoy movement challenges like gymnastics and team sports. They have a strong sense of rhythm and a great deal of physical control. They can learn simple folk dances and gymnastics routines. (Make sure that they are not risking any injury as they attempt gymnastic exercises such as a forward roll or headstand, both of which can result in neck injuries.) Since they enjoy working together, integrating music, drama, and movement for performance is an enjoyable way to use creative movement in the primary grades. At this age children may be self-critical. For this reason it is important to avoid adding pressure and to respect children who need time to get involved.

The Organizing Framework

The different elements of movement provide a base that enables you to plan and guide creative movement activities that help children to become confident, creative movers.

The Elements of Movement

Body Awareness. (Knowing where you are and where your body parts are in space is called *body awareness*] In order to feel comfortable with expressing ideas through creative movement, children need to develop awareness of where they are in space *(location),* the shapes they can create, the ways they can travel from one place to another, called *locomotor movement,* and the ways they can move while staying in the same place, or *nonlocomotor movement.* Among the most difficult skills for young children to develop is the ability to move one part of the body while keeping the rest still, called *body isolation.*

Space. (The setting in which movement occurs is called *space.*] Space is viewed in terms of direction (forward, backward, sideways) and level (high, middle, low). Personal space is the space right around you, defined by your presence. General space is used by the whole group. Activities can help children to use all of their personal space—up high, down low, to the side, in back—and to learn to share the general space. Boundaries (for example, a chalked circle) can define the space for children to move within and around. Space may be filled in different ways while children stay in one place. Images motivate and encourage children to use space in diverse ways. Invite children to think about moving and filling space like balloons, fish, worms, trees, bubbles, or birds.

Time. Time concerns the tempo or speed of the movement. As you guide creative movement activities you can include suggestions that encourage children to move at different speeds and levels without touching or bumping anyone else. Young children experience tempo, or time, through a contrast of fast and slow movements. They generally find it easier to move quickly since slow movements require greater concentration and body control. Slow movement is sustained; fast movement can be jerky. Speed can be contrasted by moving body parts at different tempos (raise your arms slowly, shake your hands quickly) or moving the body as a whole at different paces (run, creep, trot, slowly unbend, jump). Imagery of animals, plants, and machines can encourage exploration of speed, and the use of a drum beat or music can help children learn to move to a particular tempo.

Force. (The amount of energy used in movement is another element to be explored] Some movements, such as stamping heavily or punching into the air, require a lot of force. Others, such as tiptoeing or jumping lightly, use less. Young children find strong, forceful movements very satisfying, but they also enjoy developing the control needed to move lightly. Activities that involve force may contrast heavy and light movement (stamping and then tiptoeing) and can involve isolated body parts or the whole body while in motion or stationary. Music can evoke heavy or light movements as can images of animals and fantasy creatures (elephants, butterflies, bears, birds, monsters, fairies, giants, ghosts).

Creative movement activities can be quite structured (as when children move parts of their bodies to the beat of a drum) or more open-ended (as when children are invited to explore all the ways they can move to music with a scarf). Children will respond with greater enthusiasm if you weave a story around your creative movement activity. We find the work of Ann Barlin (Barlin 1979; Barlin and Kalev 1989) and Mimi Brodsky Chenfeld (Chenfeld 1983, 1994) to be very useful in designing creative movement activities

Reflect and write about . . .

your observations of creative movement in early childhood programs

Reflect on programs that you have observed. Did you observe any creative movement? In what ways did teachers encourage or discourage children from being creative? How did teachers manage movement activities? What changes do you think could have been made to better support children's creative movement?

The Environment

An environment for creative movement must be both safe and conducive to creativity. Uncluttered open spaces with clear boundaries are needed. Wood or low pile carpeted floors provide the best movement surface. If you use a room filled with furniture, create a safe, open, inviting space. Whatever space is used it is important to think about how you wish it to be used ahead of time.

The ideal group size for creative movement is from five to twelve children. If you work with larger groups, have the children alternate between moving and being the audience. Regularly scheduled movement activities at least twice a week help children develop skill and build on previous experience. When movement activities occur only infrequently, children do not develop skills and tend to be over-stimulated by the rare event.

Supporting Learning

You can provide a safe, encouraging, and stimulating atmosphere within which children may experiment in creative movement. Movement activities must match the level of physical and language development of the children. Successful movement experiences take thoughtful planning. An awareness of the goals of creative movement can guide you. Basic rules for safety

need to be established (no pushing or bumping, and so on) and an attitude of respect for individual interpretations and skill levels is essential. We find it useful to have a written plan

to use as a "map" to guide us as we lead children in creative movement activities.

Children's literature can offer motivation for creative movement and drama. A rabbit may become Peter Rabbit fleeing from Mr. MacGregor. Leo Lionni's story *Swimmy* is another example that intertwines the story of a fish with descriptions of the movements of sea creatures and serves as an excellent outline for a movement/drama session. Creative drama for young children involves their interpretations of story lines and ideas, not memorization of scripts, and should be outgrowths of children's ideas, not production efforts put on by staff for families. Some older children do become entranced by performance, however. With a skillful teacher they can begin to extend their developing skills in performing arts into dance and drama productions.

As children develop confidence and movement skills, they will become able to use movement to express creative ideas with little direction. In the beginning, however, you will need to provide a good deal of guidance. Most children will be delighted to participate in creative movement, but a few will hesitate. Children should never be forced to participate in a creative movement activity or ridiculed or criticized for the way they move.

When you first begin creative movement with a group, establish a signal like a hard drumbeat to tell the children to freeze. Practice stopping to this signal as a game until they understand it as an integral part of every movement activity. This will help you to maintain control of the group and help children to focus their movement. Alternate vigorous and quiet activities, and begin activities sitting down or standing still before inviting children to move freely around the room. When you have reached a planned or natural ending place, it is best to finish the activity while it is still going well. End sessions in a way that provides a transition to the next activity: "Tiptoe to the playground when I touch you on the shoulder."

Managing creative movement sessions can be challenging for beginners—children or their teachers. Although every group of children is different—some need very specific limits and others need lots of opportunity to explore—it is usually best to begin with short (fifteen minutes or less), simple, well-planned, and fairly structured activities moving on to more open activities later. Children who have had little experience with structured movement activities can become overexcited and uncontrolled, and this can be difficult to handle. If a movement session does not go well, do not blame children or yourself. The learning that comes out of these experiences can be valuable for you as a teacher.

AESTHETICS

Every human being has the potential to develop sensitivity to beauty and the heritage of the arts. Teachers can help young children develop this potential. *Aesthetics* refers to the love of beauty, to cultural criteria for judging beauty, and to individual taste. Malcolm Ross says,

> Aesthetic perception involves the capacity to respond to the uniqueness, the singular quality of things—to value individual integrity and to reject the cliché and the stereotype.
>
> *(Ross 1981, 158)*

Most definitions of aesthetics involve the capacity to perceive, respond, and be sensitive to the natural environment and human creations. For several years we have been concerned with the topic of aesthetic development in early childhood because we were worried that children were not being encouraged to develop their ability to perceive aesthetic qualities. If much of what they were exposed to was without aesthetic merit, they might not learn to appreciate or produce beauty. Why should you

Reflect and write about . . .

aesthetics in your life

Think of a place that is beautiful to you, that restores your spirit. What kinds of things do you find there? What makes it special to you? How could elements of this place be a part of an early childhood program?

be concerned with aesthetics? One reason is that it is important to model and teach about those things that we value. If appreciation of beauty is important in your life, then you will want to share this with children. Another reason is that aesthetic experiences, like play, have intrinsic value. They allow appreciation of a moment for itself. Responding to a lovely sunrise, a painting, or a piece of music requires no coercion. Aesthetic enjoyment provides an avenue through which people can find focus and achieve balance and tranquillity in an increasingly fast-moving world. Moreover, children who learn to love beauty in nature and in the arts are likely to want to protect and nourish these valuable resources.

Yet a third reason for being concerned with aesthetics for young children is because it reflects our high value for children and childhood. The arts are considered to be the best that our culture has to offer, and that is what we wish for our children.

You can support aesthetic development through the experiences that you provide for children. Classroom activities can be designed to help children learn about elements of aesthetics. For example, postcards and calendars of the work of fine artists (available in museum and gallery shops) can become lotto and card games that children can sort and classify by subject matter, technique, color, or personal preference (Wolf 1984), and beautiful music can be played in the classroom.

Primary-school children can also begin to learn more about art history and criticism. Art postcard games (as described in *Mommy It's a Renoir* by Wolf [1984]) are particularly appropriate for primary school children. Trips to exhibits and museums and thoughtful presentation of an artist's work can be a valuable part of the curriculum. A seven-year-old friend of ours, for example, became entranced by the work of Van Gogh. He could easily distinguish Van Gogh's work from that of other painters and was particularly fond of the print of Sunflowers that his teacher had shared. When introducing children to art, it is important to guide them in a way that helps the art to be more personal and meaningful. For example, you might ask children to talk about what they see in the different parts of the picture and what the artist might have been thinking and feeling when she or he created the work.

With a little attention you can create an environment that helps children learn to appreciate art. Your walls can be adorned with art. The work of fine artists and the work of children, both carefully displayed, can help children to look and focus. A particular piece of work can be featured and given special prominence. Areas that feature flowers, art prints, sculpture, and beautiful natural objects can create an island of calm and heighten aesthetic awareness.

Books are an especially appropriate way of presenting aesthetic experiences. Books introduce children to different styles and techniques of art (for example, representational, impressionism, cubism, watercolor, printing, collage). They can also be used as a vehicle for discussing aesthetic impact and children's tastes in art. Consider carefully what you select to put on the library shelves of your classroom. The quality of the illustrations and the design should be important criteria in the selection of good books for young children.

Experiences in the natural world also nourish children's aesthetic sense. On a walk in the park or trip to the tide pools, stop and help children to reflect on colors, patterns, and textures, focus on tiny flowers, or watch a spider spin a web. Special places can be visited over and over again so that children can reflect on the changes in nature over time. These experiences can help them learn to cherish the beauty around them, whether it is found in isolated locations or in rich abundance. They also heighten children's senses and powers of observation and give them the raw material to convert into their own artistic products.

Trips to works of art in your community (for example, to see a sculpture that adorns a public building) and to galleries and exhibits make worthwhile trips for young children. In almost every community there are galleries and museums where works of art can be visited and artists and crafts people who are willing to share their work with children. For young children the best experiences with art take place when there is understanding of and arrangement for their developmental needs. It is best if

paintings and drawings can be viewed closely and if objects such as sculpture can be touched. We enjoy taking children to experience beautiful architecture and outdoor art such as large sculptures and murals since these are created to endure hard use and can be freely explored. Children may want to visit special places many times.

Children need exposure to beautiful environments and to good art and time to reflect on these things with a caring and thoughtful adult. The way that children are introduced to aesthetic experiences may be as important as the experiences themselves, and the early years may be the optimal time to lay the foundation for a lifetime of pleasure and enjoyment.

FINAL THOUGHTS

You have many gifts to give children. Being able to create and appreciate art, music, and dance and to express ideas and feelings through the arts is a gift. You give this gift as you support young children's creative and aesthetic development through experiences with beauty and the arts, an environment that supports creative expression, and supportive relationships. As you do so, you nurture children's innate responsiveness, develop their natural expressiveness, and help them to be sensitive, creative individuals who can give the gift of creative expression and appreciation back to others.

PROJECTS

Observe a Program: Use the Environment Checklist from Chapter Eight to observe an early childhood program. Report on the extent to which the program seems to support children's artistic and creative development. Suggest some ways to provide additional experiences from which children would benefit.

Design an Environment: Design and draw a floor plan for an ideal early child-hood environment for the support of creativity and the arts. Describe what you in-cluded and why. Share your plan with an early childhood educator and a member of a young child's family and describe their response and suggestions.

Observe a Child: Observe a child for a morning with a focus on creativity. Notice how the child engages with art, music, and movement experiences. What other kinds of creativity do you observe (including creative thinking)? Report on:

- The ways and the circumstances in which he or she creates.
- How the environment supports the child's development in this area.
- How the staff support this child's development.
- What might enhance this child's learning.

Observe an Educator: Observe an early childhood educator for a morning and then interview the educator about how he or she provides art, music, and move-ment and supports children's development of creativity in all areas. Report on:

- The activities and routines that you saw that contribute to children's learning in these areas.
- Any evidence you saw of planning for creativity and aesthetic awareness.
- The educator's goals for children's development of creativity and artistic ap-preciation and expression.
- The ways in which the goals and what you actually observed match or don't match.

Plan for the Arts: Write and implement a plan in art, music, or creative movement, using the activity planning format (Figure 10.7). Report on how children responded and on how you felt about what you did. What worked? What might you do differ-ently next time? How might you expand on this experience for children? Describe what you learned about yourself, children, creativity, the arts, and teaching.

Compare Two Programs: Compare two early childhood programs in creative curriculum areas. Report on the ways that the two address each area—their simi-larities and differences. Which program seems to best meet children's needs and why? What implications does this have for your future work with young children?

Compare Two Ages: Observe two programs, one preschool and one for infants and toddlers or primary-school children. Report on how each enhances children's creativity and supports the development of each age group. Talk to the staff about how they make their curriculum choices in this area.

BIBLIOGRAPHY

Andress, B. 1991. From Research to Practice: Preschool Children and Their Movement Responses to Music. *Young Children* 47(1):22–27.

Barlin, A. L. 1979. *Teaching Your Wings to Fly.* Santa Monica, CA: Goodyear.

Barlin, A. L., and N. Kalev. 1989. *Hello Toes! Movement Games for Young Children.* Pennington, NJ: Dance Horizons, Princeton Book Co.

Bayless, K. M., and M. E. Ramsey. 1987. *Music: A Way of Life for the Young Child.* Englewood Cliffs, NJ: Merrill/Prentice Hall.

Bos, B. 1982. *Don't Move the Muffin Tins: A Hands-off Guide to Art for the Young Child.* Roseville, CA: Turn the Page Press.

Burton, L., and W. Hughes. 1981. *Musicplay.* Menlo Park, CA: Addison-Wesley.

Burton, L., and K. Kuroda. 1979. *ArtsPlay: Creative Activities in Dance, Drama, Art, and Music for Young Children.* Menlo Park, CA: Addison-Wesley.

Chenfeld, M. B. 1983. *Creative Activities for Young Children.* New York: Harcourt Brace Jovanovich.

Chenfeld, M. B. 1994. *Teaching in the Key of Life.* Washington, DC: National Association for the Education of Young Children.

Cherry, C. 1990. *Creative Art of the Developing Child: A Teacher's Handbook for Early Childhood Education.* 2nd ed. Belmont, CA: Fearon.

Cole, E., and C. Schaefer. 1990. Can Young Children Be Art Critics? *Young Children* 47(2):33–38.

Curtis, S. R. 1982. *The Joy of Movement in Early Childhood.* New York: Teachers College Press.

Edwards, C. 1990. *Affective Development and the Creative Arts: A Process Approach.* New York: Teachers College Press.

Edwards, C., L. Gandini, and G. Forman. 1993. *The Hundred Languages of Children.* Norwood, NJ: Ablex.

Edwards, L. C., and M. L. Nabors. 1993. The Creative Arts Process: What It Is and What it is Not. *Young Children* 48(3):77–81.

Feeney, S., and E. Moravcik. 1987. A Thing of Beauty: Aesthetic Development in Young Children. *Young Children* 42(6): 7–15.

Gandini, L. 1993. Fundamentals of the Reggio Emilia Approach to Early Childhood Education. *Young Children* 49(1): 4–8.

Gardner, H. 1980. *Artful Scribbles: The Significance of Children's Drawings.* New York: Basic Books.

Gardner, H. 1989. *To Open Minds.* New York: Basic Books.

Hitz, R. 1987. Creative Problem Solving Through Music Activities. *Young Children* 42(2): 12–17.

Isenberg, J. P., and M. Jalongo. 1993. *Creative Expression and Play in the Early Childhood Curriculum.* Englewood Cliffs, NJ: Merrill/Prentice Hall.

Jalongo, M. R. 1990. The Child's Right to the Expressive Arts: Nurturing the Imagination as Well as the Intellect. *Childhood Education:* 66: 195–203.

Jenkins, P. D. 1980. *Art for the Fun of It.* Englewood Cliffs, NJ: Prentice Hall.

Kellogg, R. 1982. *Analyzing Children's Art.* Palo Alto, CA: Mayfield.

Lasky, L., and R. Mukerji. 1980. *Art: Basic for Young Children.* Washington, DC: National Association for the Education of Young Children.

Lowenfeld, V., and W. L. Brittain. 1987. *Creative and Mental Growth.* 8th ed. New York: Macmillan.

MacDonald, D. T. 1979. *Music in Our Lives: The Early Years.* Washington, DC: National Association for the Education of Young Children.

Marlay, A. 1993. The Importance and Value of the Development of Aesthetic Awareness in the Education of Young Children. *Professional News* 1(2): 19–27.

Mitchell, A., and J. David, eds. 1992. *Explorations with Young Children.* Mt. Rainier, MD: Gryphon House.

Moffat, M. 1993. How Do Young Children View Their Own Art and the Art of Others. *Professional News* 1(2): 2–5.

Rockefeller, D. J. 1977. *Coming to Our Senses: The Significance of the Arts for American Education.* The Arts Education and Americans Panel. New York: McGraw-Hill.

Ross, M. 1981. *The Aesthetic Imperative: Relevance and Responsibility in Art Education.* Oxford: Pergamon Press.

Rowen, B. 1982. *Learning Through Movement: Activities for the Preschool and Elementary School Grades.* New York: Teachers College Press.

Seefeldt, C., ed. 1992. *The Early Childhood Curriculum: A Review of Current Research.* Early Childhood Education Series. New York: Teachers College Press.

Seeger, P. 1993. *Where Have All the Flowers Gone: A Singer's Stories, Seeds, Robberies.* Bethlehem, PA: Sing Out Corp.

Shirrmacher, R. 1993. *Art and Creative Development for Young Children,* 2nd ed. Albany, NY: Delmar.

Smith, N.R., C.L. Fucigna, M. Kennedy, L. Lord. 1993. *Experience and Art: Teaching Children to Paint.* 2nd ed. New York: Teachers College Press.

Sullivan, M. 1982. *Feeling Strong, Feeling Free: Movement Exploration for Young Children.* Washington, DC: National Association for the Education of Young Children.

Wolf, A. D. 1984. *Mommy, It's a Renoir!* Altoona, PA: Parent-Child Press.

Wolf, A. D. 1990. Art Postcards—Another Aspect of Your Aesthetics Program? *Young Children* 45(2): 39–43.

Wolf, J. 1994. Singing with Children Is a Cinch! *Young Children* 49(4): 20–25.

Wortham, S. 1994. *Early Childhood Curriculum: Developmental Bases for Learning and Teaching.* Englewood Cliffs, NJ: Merrill/Prentice Hall.

Zeitlin, P. 1982. *A Song Is a Rainbow.* Glenville, IL.: Scott, Foresman.

CHAPTER THIRTEEN

The Communication Curriculum

Experience needs language to give it form. Language needs experience to give it content.
                                                                  Walter Loban

This chapter concerns communication—talking, writing, and reading. In it we discuss the development of language and literacy and the role of the early childhood educator in the development of language, literacy, and the appreciation of literature.

To understand the world and function in it, we need to be able to communicate with others. The strong desire and ability to communicate unites human beings in a common bond. Language is the systematic and symbolic form that represents human thinking. All languages are infinitely variable and can be used to communicate almost any experience or information. Learning language is one of the characteristics that unites people and one of our most important challenges.

This chapter concerns communication. Language, talking and listening, comes first and is of primary importance in the communication curriculum. Literacy (the name by which educators refer to the developmental process of learning to write and read) is the tool that extends language over distance and time. Literature is the art form that uses language. All are dependent upon a base of language. Together these are sometimes referred to as *language arts,* and today they are integrated in what is known as *whole language.*

The goal of the language, literature, and literacy curriculum areas is to help children become enthusiastic, competent communicators who use and enjoy spoken and written language. Early childhood programs can foster children's natural desire, ability, and pleasure in communicating with others. Your job as an early childhood educator is to provide relationships that are supportive, caring, and filled with language in all its forms. As you speak to children honestly and respectfully and listen to them attentively, you are encouraging language use. As you use language to mediate problems, communicate information, and share feelings and ideas, you are demonstrating the usefulness and value of oral language.

In a similar way the value of written language is demonstrated to children as you use it in your daily activities. When you write a note to a child or parent, a grocery list, or a thank-you letter or read a recipe, story, poem, or book, you model the importance of writing and reading. When children see significant adults in their lives using reading and writing, it provides them with a powerful incentive to begin learning these skills.

An environment that is rich in language, writing, good books, and other reading experiences is vital. It includes ample opportunities for each child to use language and written words for a variety of purposes, with lots of experiences with talk and print. Good literature will come to be appreciated as children are introduced to many well-written books.

Just as it would be inappropriate to expect every child to master the same physical challenges, so is it inappropriate to expect every child to be able to follow the same verbal directions, enjoy the same books, or have the same interest in written words. A single group of young children may include a range from nonverbal to beginning readers.

LANGUAGE

Language is a shared system of symbols that has structure, rules, and meaning that are accepted and unconsciously known by those who use it. The symbols can be combined, organized, and enlarged to convey an infinite variety and complexity of messages. Except for a few routine phrases like "Have a nice day," language is creative. Most utterances have not been spoken or written in just one way before.

It is fascinating to keep in mind that language itself is dynamic and growing. New words come into being every day in response to a changing world. The vocabulary that you use today is slightly different than that which was spoken when you learned to talk (twenty-five years ago it was uncommon to hear words like *burnout, networking, yuppie,* and *interface*). The language we use today is different than it will be when today's preschoolers reach adulthood.

Learning to understand and use language is one of the most significant accomplishments of early childhood. Almost all children acquire language without any formal teaching before they enter school; it is a skill that appears to be "caught, not taught." As they forge their language, children develop an inseparable part of themselves, as well as a tool for communication, self-expression, and learning.

Young children learn the customs for language that are familiar in their own homes and communities. They learn to select speech appropriate to the setting: They speak differently in the classroom than on the playground and differently depending on to whom they are speaking and why. Children learn very early to include nonverbal social features such as gestures, facial expressions, body position, and intonation in their style of speaking. They come to understand the expectations and signals for turn-taking in conversations. These unspoken ways of communicating are highly dependent on culture. In a culturally diverse society you can expect that young children in a group will have different nonverbal customs such as whether or not to make eye contact during conversations with adults. Part of your role as an educator is to have sensitivity to and awareness of these kinds of communication differences.

Both developmental stage and the desire to communicate influence language learning. Children learn the complex structure, rules, and meanings of language and develop the ability to create speech, read, and write their own words through processes that are still not completely understood. We know that children need language experiences that are meaningful to them and appropriate to their developmental abilities. For young children social, physical, and sensory activity is an essential underpinning for talking.

Language and Development

Language development, like physical development, follows a predictable sequence. It is related, but not tied to, chronological age.

Regardless of the language being learned or the culture in which it is learned, language develops at generally the same stage of life and through the same processes. Within any group of young children of a similar age, there are differences in language facility and individual style (Figure 13.1).

Although individuals vary in the speed of language acquisition and in how much they speak, the language-learning process is universal. Psychologists and linguists have long theorized how children learn language. The behaviorist view, popular until the late 1950s, that language is gradually built up through imitation and reinforcement is now regarded as inadequate to explain the creative nature of speech. The predominance of children's invented words

and phrases unlike any spoken by adults are among the many clues that children play a creative role in constructing their own language and do not simply learn by rote.

Linguist Noam Chomsky (Bruner 1983) proposed that humans must have an innate ability to process language, which he referred to as a *language acquisition device* (LAD) to explain why children are able to produce word forms and sentences they have never heard. Chomsky's work sparked interest in finding out what young children naturally understand about the structure of language when they start to talk—for example, identifying similarities in the ways all young children combine words or use grammatical forms. Although this research helped scientists and educators understand the formal

Sounds: From birth infants make and respond to many sounds. Crying, gurgling, and cooing are important first steps in the language-learning process.

Babbling: All of the sounds found in all languages are encompassed in children's first babbling. Gradually, babbling becomes more specific with native language syllables being consistently practiced. Before the end of their first year, children engage in pseudo-language, babbling that mimics the native language in its intonation and form.

Holophrases: The first word evolves to many single words or syllables that stand for a variety of meaningful sentences or phrases in different situations. *Car* said while looking out the window may mean, "Look at the car outside"; *car* said while standing next to the toy shelf may mean, "I want my toy car." A vocabulary of holophrases enables children to communicate with familiar caregivers. Children use successive holophrases to increase their communicative power: *Car* (pause) *go* to indicate "I want to go for a ride."

Two-Word Sentences: Two-word sentences appear between eighteen and twenty months of age and express ideas concerning relationships: "Mommy sock" (possessor-possession), "Cat sleeping" (actor-action), "Drink milk" (action-object), and so on. A vocabulary of about 300 words is typical.

Telegraphic Sentences: The next stage of language are sentences that are short and simple. Similar to a telegram, they omit function words and endings that contribute little to meaning: "Where Daddy go?" "Me push truck."

Joined Sentences: As language development proceeds, children join related sentences logically and express ideas concerning time and spatial relationships. They come to understand social expectations for language use and begin to use adult forms of language. Vocabularies expand rapidly, the ability to use words increases, and children intuitively acquire many of the rules of language. By age three children have vocabularies of nearly 1,000 words.

Overgeneralizations: As children become more sophisticated in their language, they overgeneralize rules in ways that are inconsistent with common usage; for example, "I comed home" for "I came home" (sometimes called *creative grammar*). Correct forms are temporarily replaced as rules are internalized.

FIGURE 13.1
Stages of language development

features of language, or *what* children do, it did little to explain *how* young children learn to speak.

Language and thought go hand in hand; however, the exact nature of the relationship is not clear. Jean Piaget and Lev Vygotsky, two developmental theorists, both studied children's language development and have helped early childhood educators to understand the relationship of children's cognitive growth and the development of language.

Piaget was concerned with how language influenced the development of thinking. He observed that preschool children's speech was more often egocentric (talking aloud to oneself) rather than socialized speech (dialogue with others). He suggested that egocentric speech is merely an accompaniment to activity—it reflects thinking rather than expanding it. That is, children become capable of acquiring and using language *only* as they develop

concepts. In this view, experience is most important. Language is acquired in social contexts *after* concepts are in place.

Vygotsky (1962, 1978) argued that children learn language as an interaction between innate maturation and the stimulation of social experiences. The development of language allows children to organize and integrate experience or, in other words, to develop concepts. Vygotsky observed the egocentric speech of childhood (which he called *external* speech) but interpreted it as the *means* by which children develop concepts and plan actions. In this view language is essential for understanding and organizing experiences. Communication with others is vital because children develop language in relationships with more competent speakers (adults and older children).

Although there are clear differences between these two views, both agree that a strong relationship exists between thinking and language, between concepts and the words used to express them. There is also agreement that children's development of language is part of an active mental process. It involves constructing intuitive rules that guide behavior. The work of these theorists suggests that experiences with the world *and* language-filled relationships are vital.

Before they speak, children make and respond to many sounds. Crying, gurgling, babbling, and cooing are important parts of the language-learning process. Caregivers respond to the sounds infants make, and important language abilities are established. Current theories of language development proposed by Jerome Bruner (1983) and Gordon Wells (1985) follow Vygotsky's view that early social experiences form the basis for language development. Bruner proposes that these experiences form a language acquisition support system (LASS) to assist Chomsky's LAD (Bruner 1983).

The communication between infant and caregiver helps us understand how children

---

Reflect and write about . . .

talking and listening

When do you talk and listen to other people? Do you think of yourself as a competent, skillful verbal communicator? When do you feel most comfortable expressing yourself verbally? Do any situations make you uncomfortable? Why?

---

learn to talk. Adults act as informal guides to support and foster language learning through these interactions. Routines are the major context for language learning: "dialogues" between adult and infant during feeding and changing, games like peek-a-boo, naming objects and events as they occur, picturebook reading, and nonverbal play. By their first birthday children generally speak their first word, and more words soon follow. Bruner suggests that caregivers provide a temporary framework or scaffold for language by assuming young children intend to communicate, by listening carefully, and by assisting only as much as needed. In early conversations caregivers provide some of the child's responses. As the child's ability to participate is demonstrated, the adult adjusts, gradually permitting the child to take over on his or her own.

As children learn language, they master a complex task that involves a system of speech sounds (phonology), grammatical forms and relationships (syntax), meaning (semantics), and socially based customs for language use (pragmatics). Exposure to everyday speech and a desire to interact socially contribute to children's construction of understanding of language principles. Many experiences with language used in context help children to understand and use new words. Vocabulary grows quickly.

Experimentation with all of the language elements is essential. Over-extensions of a particular word are common. For example, a toddler

of our acquaintance called the family cat *keycat* and over-extended the word to label the neighbor's dog, a furry toy, and the lady across the street who had three cats. Similarly, preschoolage children overgeneralize grammatical rules: "I holded the baby bunny." These are natural parts of children's active language development that help us realize that children analyze and construct language rather than merely imitating or learning by rote. This process of exploration is not affected by instruction or correction, but by speaking and listening. By the age of five or six, most children have mastered the basics in all of these areas in their native tongue; they have "learned language."

Language and Culture

Culture, as well as developmental difference, affects language use. School customs can be quite different from those of home and may require a greater adjustment for children from some social and cultural groups than for others. As an early childhood educator you will need to be aware of and sensitive to the social customs for talking that children have learned. Children from some cultures learn to show respect for adults by remaining silent and looking away; those from another cultural background learn to maintain eye contact and speak up. Anthropologists of education (Bryce-Heath 1983) have found that children from different cultural backgrounds learn different ways of talking about and expressing the meaning of events. Ways of telling stories, looking at picture books, and asking or answering questions may also be affected by cultural differences.

There are variations in the way individuals speak. Some are personal, relating to word and phrase preferences and individual characteristics such as voice quality. Other variations relate to the language that is used, valued, and taught in a particular locale. In the United States, Canada, Australia, and Great Britain, for example, English is spoken as the primary language, but there are regional differences. When the differences are distinct, these are called *dialects*. Dialects vary from the dominant language in vocabulary, pronunciation, and grammatical rules. Often they vary in the rules for forming plurals, negatives, and past tenses: *ain't* for *isn't*.

In the United States, there are variations of English that have roots in other languages. These variations use English words but are sufficiently different from Standard English to be considered separate languages. These include the Creole languages, Gullah in South Carolina and Georgia, and Pidgin in Hawaii. They use some non-English words, substantially different grammar, and are quite difficult for most Standard English speakers to understand.

Black English, spoken among the African-American population of urban ghettos in the northern United States and throughout the south, uses elements of southern dialects and words and structure that reflect a Creole language. Although it has greater differences from Standard English than most dialects, it is not considered a separate language.

Language differences have deeper implications, however, than simple grammatical or pronunciation variations. Because language is intimately connected to the way we live, a language expresses a particular culture's unique perception of the world. Certain languages, for example, have fewer names for colors than English; hence, colors themselves are probably perceived differently. The Inuit culture of the

Arctic, to point to another example, has many different words to describe snow. Many more properties of snow are perceived by the Inuit than by those of us with less experience with snow. Language, then, is more than written and spoken communication. It is an intrinsic part of our culture and reflects a distinctive vision of the world.

For children to become confident, effective communicators, they must first feel comfortable speaking. Whatever language they speak, it is vital that you accept and respect their language. Although dialects have sometimes been characterized as inferior, they are in fact simply different. Like Standard English, they are flexible, capable of expansion, rule-governed, and expressive. Dialect speakers communicate effectively in day-to-day interactions in their own communities. Standard English (sometimes called the *school dialect*) has no inherent superiority for communicating or for thinking. It is, however, widely used and understood as the language of education, literature, business, and technology. Because of this, educators are generally expected to provide a model of Standard English. Programs aimed at changing oral language through drill and practice separate talk from meaning. They are likely to be ineffective and may have a negative effect on children's self-concepts by demeaning their natural expression.

In our diverse society you may have children in your class whose first language is not English. At one time these children were considered disadvantaged and the job of the educator was to develop the child's skill in English while decreasing the use of the native tongue. Knowledge of two languages is now generally viewed as advantageous, and continued development in *both* languages is an important goal in the education of these children.

To support bilingualism, you need to actively value the child's first language and culture. The basis for teaching young children whose first language is not English must be re-

---

Reflect and write about . . .

experiences with other languages

Remember a time when you were in a place where you did not speak the language or when you watched a movie or TV program in a language you did not understand. How did it feel? What did you do to try to understand what was being said? What did you want or need?

---

lationships within a program for total development, ideally involving adults who speak both languages. This view of second language learning is consistent with knowledge of language development, but it is not always possible. Indeed, we have experienced classrooms with children from eight different language backgrounds. A United Nations translator would have been the only solution.

Creative monolingual educators can work successfully with the non-English-speaking children in their classes by using the resources available to them. They learn key words and phrases in the child's language; have children use their first language to teach the group words, songs, and games; and encourage bilingual family and community members to participate in the classroom. Most importantly, they can build strong relationships with the children and their families and help them feel comfortable sharing their language and culture. Reading, home visits, and discussions with the family will help you develop understanding of children whose backgrounds are different from your own.

The Organizing Framework

Language is used for a variety of purposes—to share ideas, direct others, express needs, direct one's own behavior, establish and maintain relationships, or call attention to oneself. Language can also be used to ask for and give information and interpret our experiences, to play, and to create imaginary scenes or think about events that are not happening in the present. Most young children have ample experience using language for directing behavior and other interpersonal purposes. When they first come to your program, some children may have had little opportunity to use language to describe and explain their experiences or to talk about things beyond the "here and now" of immediate events. Differences will reflect the wide range of possible ways language was used by individual families and social groups. When you become familiar with the different uses of language, you will be able to see where children's usual purposes for talking might be extended and to ensure that a range of language opportunities are encouraged in your program.

Informative Language

Informative language is used to share facts and opinions with others. Children, as well as adults, need opportunities to practice using language to exchange information. You may need to provide a model of this kind of talk and a great deal of encouragement. You must be a careful and respectful listener. Children who learn that you will listen to them and take them seriously will come to feel pride and delight in their own abilities. These children may be the ones that often say, *"My mommy says . . .,"* *"Did you know that . . .?"* and *"I saw. . . ."*

Descriptive Language

As you work and talk with young children, there will be many chances to describe experiences in words. Many adults naturally model the use of descriptive language, particularly with very young children. They talk about what is happening, giving a running commentary as they go through an activity: "Dylan sure seems to be enjoying himself on the trampoline. Look how his hair flops up and down as he jumps." Skillful educators make sure ample time is left for children to contribute. Children may need your help to become specific in their talk. For example if a child says, "I got the stuff," you can expand by saying, "Oh good, you brought the sawdust and scraper. Now we can clean the mouse cage."

Reasoning Language

Reasoning language, the language of cause and effect, helps children to understand the relationships between actions ("If we go out while it's raining we'll get wet") and relationships between people ("If you invite him over he may play with you"). Young children need help as they learn to use language for reasoning and solving problems. Early childhood educators often instruct children to substitute specific words or phrases. They suggest alternative ways to express problems ("Tell him you want him to stop taking your blocks") and model problem-solving language ("Please don't put that bucket on my lap, it's getting me wet"). Children then try out the new language in their play situations.

The Language of Imagination and Recall

Children first talk about the here and now. Eventually they begin to talk about things they remember, things that happened outside of school or in the past. Some children learn to use language to build imaginary scenarios for their play; others have little experience with this kind of talk. If children are not familiar with this kind of language use, they will need adult modeling and support to learn to talk to create or recall things not present.

Language Play

Young children often use language in playful ways. They invent silly words, use "naughty" language, and state things they know to be incorrect as a joke (Adult: pointing to a new hat the child is wearing, "What's that?" Child: [giggling] "A watermelon"). They may experiment with sounds and make up rhymes ("Swinging, ringing, pringing, flinging, minging"). Language play may help children begin to develop a conscious awareness of language itself, the kind of thinking about language they will need as they learn to read. Thinking and talking about language requires greater sophistication than using language to communicate. Playing with language may help children to develop this important awareness. Nonsense words, rhymes, jokes, tongue twisters, and "silly talk" in literature and conversation foster language play.

The Environment

Since most children learn language so well at home in their interactions with family members, we can draw on this natural environment as a model for a classroom that supports language development. In a natural language environment people communicate about meaningful events; real people use real talk about the real things they are doing. A classroom language environment can be very different than a home environment because of the high child-adult ratio (a relatively low preschool ratio of six to one would be a very high ratio for a home), so there may be fewer opportunities for children to talk with adults. To support language development in an early childhood program, you need to make time and create an environment where

conversations between adults and children and among children are encouraged.

The overall organization of your program will influence children's talk. You set the stage for language development by preparing a language-rich environment filled with interesting things to do, see, and talk about. Plan activities that will enable children to see connections with similar experiences at home (for example, cooking, gardening, caring for pets), and they will have much to talk about. Provide enough time and space for children to come together and converse as they work and play. Value the buzz of conversation and do not demand silence as an indication of order. Let the children know that talking to each other is worthwhile and something that you want them to do. Engage in conversations with children that are dialogues, not adult monologues. Use volunteers such as family members or students to increase the opportunities for extended conversations between children and adults.

Routines and daily activities also provide opportunities for language development. Lunch,

snack, and transitions are also conversation times. Music, movement, meetings, art, and storytimes involve language.

Supporting Learning

Children learn language by having many opportunities to engage in meaningful conversations. You will not actually instruct children in a subject called language (a discipline studied by linguists and other scholars). Instead you will help children develop language by using it. Like a family member in a home, you will try to know children well and converse with them often. Studies indicate that there are often far fewer opportunities for conversation in schools than there are for children in homes and that conversations are brief, less complex, and tend to be more adult-dominated than conversations at home (Wells 1985). Your goal therefore is to provide an environment and relationships within which conversations will occur with the richness and frequency of a language-rich home.

394

When you work with infants and toddlers you have dialogues with them that include words, sound, and action. You will spend focused time learning to understand a few very young children's unique ways of communicating and conversing with them. Like their families, you will be among a small group of adults who knows their special language of gesture, facial expression, vocalization, behavior, and individually meaningful words.

When you work with preschool children you also have conversations that support language development. You can encourage them as they use language throughout their daily activities. As they act out roles in block and dramatic play areas, they will develop variety and complexity in their language. As they work together on group projects, they will use language to plan, compare, and describe. You will provide comfortable areas in which they can talk and materials like picturebooks, puppets, dramatic play props, language games, flannelboards, and art projects to motivate language. When you take children on trips you provide them with shared experiences to talk about.

In primary school the language-teaching task remains a natural part of your daily interactions with children, and you will do many of the things just described to support language in preschool children. Because of their growing ability to think about language, you can begin to talk to children about words. Language games, language challenges, and humor like puns and riddles can add great richness and excitement to the curriculum. Primary-school children take special delight in learning the particular vocabulary of their intense interests. You can plan activities that help to develop language such as creating a web of words to describe the frog that is visiting the classroom (Figure 13.2). Knowing the long and complex scientific names of the dinosaurs, the words of complicated jump rope rhymes, and the intricate descriptions of the paraphernalia of a fantasy character all are examples of the power of language and the new abilities of children in the primary grades.

Whatever the age of the children, your program can be filled with language. Conversations between children and adults as well as between children can abound. The kinds of language described in the curriculum framework can be used as a guide to ensure that you are using language for a number of different purposes. Use variety and specificity in the words you choose to direct or describe: "It's on the top shelf next to the striped basket." Ask

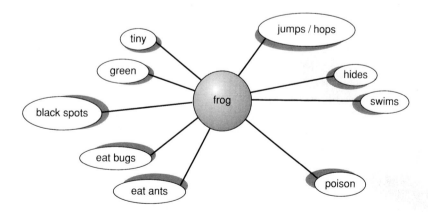

FIGURE 13.2
Word web

Reflect and write about . . .

communicating as a child

How did you feel about communicating with other people when you were a child? When did you feel most comfortable expressing yourself verbally? Did any situations make you uncomfortable? Why? How do you wish your family or teachers had supported you in becoming a good verbal communicator?

open-ended questions (those that do not require a particular answer—see Chapter Fourteen for examples) and expand children's language naturally without being distracting or making corrections.

Explore words and play with language. As children show interest in words, talk about them. In our own teaching we use a vocabulary that is slightly more complex than the children's (and only slightly less complex than the language we use in talking to one another) to help them learn, in context, new words and to help them to become curious about language. Recently, in talking to a group of four-year-olds, the word *distressed* was used ("Katherine is too distressed to come to circle right now.") Four-and-a-half-year-old Ben asked, "Why do you use words we don't understand?" The response was "So that you can learn them too— what do you think *distressed* means?" Ben answered, "Sad and mad."

Trust that all children (unless handicapped in some way) have language facility you can nurture. Hesitant or shy children may require a longer time to speak or answer questions, and it is important to be patient and give them enough time. You must plan for language, but you also must take advantage of the unplanned moments when language can occur.

How you talk with children is important. Children need a chance to express their ideas, to tell about the things they know and that are important to them, to be able to make sense of their experiences. In conversations

you can help children by allowing them to take the lead and then following their topics, showing interest and encouraging them to continue the discussion. It is not necessary to plan specific questions to use when you have conversations with children. Questioning by adults may seem like a test, and some children will focus on finding the answer expected by the adult, rather than on doing their own thinking.

LITERACY

Reading and writing are facets of communication, tools to unlock ideas, and adventures. *Literacy* describes the interconnected processes of reading and writing. *Emergent literacy* is the evolving process by which children become literate without formal instruction. The period of emergent literacy can be called the span "between birth and the time when children read and write in conventional ways" (Teale and Sulzby 1986, 1).

Until recently, an intense debate over whether young children should be taught to read was common. Proponents of more academic programs for young children argued for drill in phonics and other skill-oriented procedures. Another view presented reading and writing as requiring instruction in a set of skills that could not be taught until children had demonstrated certain "readiness" behaviors—for example, large and small muscle skills, visual and auditory

> ### *Reflect and write about . . .*
>
> ### *learning to read and write*
>
> What do you remember about learning to read and write? Were you self-taught or did a teacher or family member help you learn? Was learning to read a struggle or was it easy for you? What made it enjoyable or unpleasant? What connection can you see between how you learned to read and your feelings about reading today?

discrimination, sequencing ability, and the ability to follow a left-to-right orientation. Readiness skills, and not reading and writing, were viewed as appropriate preschool activities, and teachers were warned away from encouraging children's interests in written language.

Today some radically different ideas have been accepted. Educators now acknowledge that preschoolers in our society come to our programs with many ideas about reading and writing. Good educators have always provided some experiences for young children that contribute to their emerging concepts about reading and writing. However, it is not drill, rote learning, or workbooks that provide meaningful literacy education for young children. Much more than isolated skills to be mastered, reading and writing are in programs for young children because they are part of children's lives and the lives of their families who live in a literate world.

Literacy and Development

Children who live in our print-filled world have early awareness of written language and develop concepts about it from a very early age. Learning about reading and writing does not wait for children to be declared officially "ready."

Young children learn to speak at an early age, a complex and difficult task. They learn through everyday experiences with language with adults who pay attention to their growing skills. It is becoming clear that the foundations for making sense of written language start long before reading with early social uses of print. Everyday experiences and supportive adults who interpret and call attention to print give children opportunities to actively explore and think about written language.

Today we look for what happens before writing and reading and how literacy is supported in children's social interactions to guide us in planning for literacy development. Children begin to formulate ideas about written language before they receive formal teaching. Some even begin to read and write without instruction, although careful investigation shows that they usually live in homes where many experiences with written language are available and they have much adult support.

Stages of Literacy Development

Current research suggests that literacy follows a sequence in which social interaction about print plays an important role. Like oral language development, expression (writing) is as important as reception (reading), and like language learning it is an active process where children construct rules or models that help them make sense of experiences with print.

Although there are strong parallels, there are also ways in which language and literacy are different. Almost all children develop language with no formal instruction, but, though children in literate homes may be aware of print, only some will teach themselves to read. Language is essential for communication with other human beings, but literacy merely enhances communication. In some cultures, emphasis on an oral tradition replaces literacy.

Exploring and Refining. Children who are cared for by literate adults have many experiences with books and writing before they have the ability to hold a book or pencil. In homes where books and writing tools are available, they are both children's toys and the everyday objects used by adults. Like other toys and everyday objects, they are *explored* by children from the time they are allowed to hold them. They are looked at, felt, mouthed, shaken, and thrown. Family members and other important caregivers in a child's life model and teach the behavior that is appropriate with these raw materials of literacy. Observing this modeling, children at an early age come to *refine* their understanding of how books and writing work. From about the time they begin talking, around their first birthday, many children start to demonstrate that "book behavior" involves looking at pictures and not playing with or manipulating the books as toys. They learn that writing occurs on paper and has special characteristics.

Cultural Relevance and Conventions. Researchers have found that children begin to grasp principles of how print works as they explore and attempt to create graphic forms that resemble letters (Clay 1975). In their early concepts of writing, children rarely look for connections between spoken words and their written forms. They explore the graphic features of print, finding that it follows certain rules such as linearity, repetition of individual elements, directionality, variation of symbols, and arrangement and spacing of letters on a page. Children who grow up with print may distinguish their "writing" scribbles from their drawing scribbles.

Writing often consists of more regular and more individual marks than drawing. Like the sequence of drawing, children follow a sequence in learning to write, and many three-year-olds start to distinguish letters and letter-like forms from scribbles.

The two-year-old son of a graduate student we know was amply supplied with crayons, markers, and paper. At times he would use these and scribbled in typical toddler fashion. He often chose, however, to use the pens with which his father wrote drafts of his papers. These were used quite differently. He held them tensely and made tiny lines that squiggled and ran from one side of the page to the other. This child demonstrated that he had developed concepts about writing.

Children make guesses or assumptions about how print works as they explore; for example, many young children believe that a certain number of characters (at least three or four) must be written before a message or "word" can be read. These early concepts must be revised as the child's thinking progresses, to accommodate new information. In this way the meaning of writing is "constructed" by each child.

Many young children from all socioeconomic backgrounds in the United States "read" print as it appears in their environment; for example, they read the golden arches of the McDonald's sign and they understand the purpose of the red, white, and blue US Mail symbol (Harste, Woodward, and Burke 1984). This kind of reading is called *contextualized* or *environmental,* and it is one of the first signs that children are beginning to attend to print and understand the purpose of reading and writing.

Books, too, have a specific mode of use. Children learn to start at the front cover and go through page by page. With many enjoyable everyday experiences they develop a positive regard for books (and a predisposition to read and write). As children develop understanding of books they demonstrate awareness of basic

story structure by retelling familiar stories and pretending to read books to themselves or others using language forms which sound like "book language." Understanding the purposes and characteristics of books and the ability to comprehend and find personal meaning in story reading are essential underpinnings for later reading success. How well young children understand the conventions of print used in books is the best way to predict later success in reading (Wells 1985).

Invented Spelling. As children begin to recognize a connection between speech and print, they construct rules to explain this relationship. For example, a four- or five-year-old child who knows a few alphabet letter names may begin to write "words" by matching letter names with sounds in speech (for example, *M* to stand for

mommy). As children gain greater sophistication they might write one letter per syllable (*ME* to stand for *mommy*), and later one letter to stand for each sound (*MME* might now stand for *mommy*). Many children independently produce readable written messages, using this invented spelling, before they receive formal instruction in writing. A child we know wrote "hp vlnti" on a valentine. Children's invented spelling often uses the sounds of the letter name. For example, *engine* might be spelled *NJN* and *dress* might be *GS*—the sound of the "dr" in *dress* is often identified with the letter *g*. The first conventionally spelled word a child writes is likely to be his or her own name. Invented spelling continues to be an important process in children's learning throughout the early grades. Unlike the "social" knowledge of rote memorization, which is known only because others say it is true, the successive approximations of children's writing demonstrates that they are constructing internal knowledge of reading and writing. Children gradually develop rules and generalizations about written language for themselves, often proceeding through stages where they hold inaccurate or partially accurate concepts as they attempt to sort out how written language works.

Formal Reading and Writing. There is no one moment when children make the transition to formal reading and writing. The stages described above are a part of an ongoing process. For one child the progress from thinking about written words to adult-like reading and writing may be astonishingly rapid; for another it may be an agonizingly slow process. We have known children who seemed to be almost fully self-taught readers; they needed such limited assistance for such a brief period of time that their learning could hardly be followed. We have also known children who took a very long time and needed a great deal of support. However long the journey to literacy, it is a trip that brings a lifetime of benefits and one in which you can share the joy and wonder.

The Organizing Framework

Literacy is acquired because it is meaningful. Each child learns to read and write as an individual, putting together ideas in ways that make sense and that is personal and pleasurable. The curriculum for literacy must be similarly individualized. Before you plan curriculum it is important to understand how each child is thinking about the relationship between print and meaning.

Adult-conceived reading tasks, such as matching upper case to lower case letters or tracing letter forms, frequently do not match child concepts about written language. Reading and writing require conceptual development that is not compatible with direct teaching. Instead, knowledge construction depends on ex-

periences that are within a child's understanding.

The elements of the literacy curriculum are straightforward and consist of four major parts that are discussed in the following sections on environment and teaching. Literacy curriculum consists of:

- Providing experiences with the written word.
- Reading with children.
- Writing with children.
- Talking with children about print.

The Environment

You support emergent literacy by including reading and writing throughout the classroom—for example, by having a name label on the rabbit's cage or by labeling shelves and containers with pictures of the contents. Similarly, decorations can heighten print awareness. Alphabet charts and posters that include writing, signs, and book covers put reading and writing into the environment. With older preschoolers and kindergarten-aged children, use print throughout the classroom for purposes that will make sense to them. In addition to labeling items in the classroom, have name cards to read, copy, and use in activities. Use lists that include children's names; put up signs for various areas of the classroom and refer to them; use charts with recipes, stories, directions, songs; and read poems that include both print and pictures.

As children begin to notice the graphic elements of print they will incorporate them into artwork. Children's own writing can also decorate and label the classroom. We observed a preschool classroom where a child made a poster showing step by step how to make a new art project that he had invented. His teacher wrote the steps as he dictated them, and the other children came and followed his words and drawings. On the door to the bathroom in this same classroom one of the children had written a request: "Pls REBR To FH tiLT" (please remember to flush the toilet).

A Writing Center

Every classroom for preschool and primary children needs many different kinds of writing materials that are readily available so children can try writing on their own. You will need a variety of materials, including different types and sizes of paper (include envelopes, note cards, paper to be made into little "books," notepads) and different writing tools (pencils, erasers, markers of various widths, crayons). Other materials might include sets of small plastic letters (both upper and lower case) for constructing words and sentences, three- or four-inch wooden letters for tracing, a letter stamp set for printing, and a typewriter or a computer with a simple word-processing program designed for children.

Children can use these materials for exploring or for producing messages, artwork, or self-selected writing practice. Older preschoolers may begin to write the words they know (their names and words like *love*) and use invented spelling. Classrooms where writing supplies are available to children and where there are words to copy encourage children to write to communicate.

Books Throughout the Environment

Literature stimulates children's interest in words and in reading. In preschool and primary programs, reading materials like newspapers and books and writing experiences like making out a receipt can be incorporated into the dramatic play area. Reference books can be part of the science area; newspapers, cookbooks, and stories can be kept in the dramatic play area. Writing materials can be available in blocks or science so that children can label their work, draw or write about their experiences, or ask an adult to take their dictation. Books of all kinds, magazines, and newspapers can be kept as reference material throughout the classroom, as well as in the library area. Be sure children understand that they have permission to explore the books and that they are not just for adult use. Include books that adults use—encyclopedias, dictionaries, and some books with few or no pictures, as well as those specifically written for children—so children will have a broader exposure to what "reading" means. Include child-made "books" in the classroom library or book area.

Puzzles and Games

Children who are beginning to be interested in reading will enjoy using puzzles and games that use letters and print. Some of these materials can be open ended, like a set of alphabet letters that can be spread out on the floor or a basket of wooden letters for tracing and coloring. Other more defined tasks for children from preschool on include homemade games where small items are sorted by beginning sounds. These activities have the kind of personal "fit" needed by young children in various stages of literacy development. Avoid group lessons, which present isolated language tasks out of the context of children's real-life experiences.

Supporting Learning

Literacy is sometimes said to begin at birth. Literacy education continues throughout the years of schooling. The approach to literacy varies with children's developmental needs and interests.

Infants and toddlers gain powerful messages from adults and the environment. A program for even the youngest children should have books and words throughout. If you work with infants or toddlers, you can be a model of a person who loves and uses reading. Toddlers can be fascinated by the magic of the printed word when it applies to them. We once observed two-year-olds looking at a "pocket chart" with their names in a program office. They were anxious to find themselves and stopped to touch their names when they went past.

There are many different ways children show you their developing awareness of written language. Some begin to take an interest in favorite storybooks as they read along, point to the print, or retell the story. Others recognize or discuss the meanings of signs or labels frequently encountered. Most children are exposed to symbols, signs, and printed messages all around them in the form of traffic signs, logos for products on packages, and in television advertising. Children's first interest is often in their own names, which they recognize and wish to write, or they may print their initial, saying, "That's my J." Some children will pretend to write and read messages in their play. Familiar books may be "read" to a group by a child who pretends to be the "teacher."

All of these are evidence that print has been noticed and is being explored. In most programs for four- and five-year-olds, some children will be actively interested in learning about written language, while others will display little interest. Interest in print is sometimes demonstrated even by very young children. We recently observed a two-and-a-half-year-old laboriously writing "names" (written strings) on the paintings of all of the children in her group.

To support children in becoming literate requires a watchful eye and sensitive ear so that you notice children's efforts and know the children with whom you work. For example, we recently observed nearly four-year-old Loleine and her teacher sitting in the sandbox making birthday cakes. When Loleine traced an *L* in the sand, her teacher commented that *L* was the beginning of *Loleine*. Loleine printed the rest of her name. The two then entered into a play dialogue in which each took turns printing and reading letters and words in the sand.

Supporting literacy requires really knowing and attending to children so that you remember important events that are likely to become a part of initial writing and reading. The parallel with language can be made: Caregivers who really know a beginning talker will understand that "Nini" means a special blue ribbon. Similarly, adults who really know a beginning writer will be able to read the "writing" in Figure 13.3 and know that it spells *Theresa*.

Programs for primary age children generally have well-defined curriculum for literacy. If the curriculum includes the whole language teaching philosophy and techniques that emphasize emergent literacy, you will need to make sure to include reading and writing opportunities across the curriculum and recognize the importance of and encourage children's inventive writing. If your program uses a traditional basal reader or workbook-based reading and writing curriculum, you will want to also incorporate more developmentally appropriate techniques. We have known creative teachers who offered the required workbooks and readers as a choice for children in addition to a rich, appropriate whole language classroom. They won over amazed principals and families when

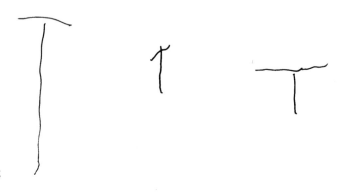

FIGURE 13.3
Sample of beginning writing

the children learned to read and write and, more importantly, wanted to!

Experiences with Writing

As young children experience print in their day-to-day lives, they gain literacy concepts. They learn that print communicates and that a collection of increasingly recognizable letters tends to be connected with the same word time after time. They also learn to view themselves as a part of a community that uses print.

Reading with Children

Children who are read to frequently and spend time with books during their early years often become successful readers. They begin to see that what is read must make sense and to be able to make connections between their own experiences and books. Hearing stories read gives children familiarity with the elements of a story and with "book language," which is different and more formal than day-to-day speech. Today researchers are looking at the concepts children gain as they are read to and at the kinds of supportive adult interactions that take place as children learn to read.

Children develop an appreciation of books when they experience them in the company of an adult who makes reading a time of warm sharing. As they hear books read, children become familiar with the print, match spoken to written word, and relate the illustrations to the text. When you read to individual children you will have an opportunity to talk about the books and print at the level of the child's interest and understanding and will be able to assess their understanding. The section that follows on children's literature describes how you can select a wide variety of good books for children.

When you read to the group, you are ensuring that all the children have an experience with books, and you are demonstrating that reading is a worthwhile part of the program day. A recent innovation for emerging literacy, the Big Book, is designed so that children in groups get some of the benefits of being read to one-on-one.

There are many things you can do to help children develop concepts about print. Let children "read" familiar picture books to you and to classmates. Encourage children to match print to known messages; for example, reading along with the words of familiar songs, rhymes, poems, or tapes and records. Provide storytelling, puppets, flannelboard stories, and dramatizations of books as other ways to help children begin to understand books and experiment with creating stories. The In Practice box on p. 404 suggests some things to do as you read with one or two children at a time to help them build concepts about books and print.

Writing with Children

One way children come to see that print is a way to communicate is through dictating to adults. As a group or as individuals, children can create stories and books based on trips or familiar experiences. These can then be illustrated and hung on charts or bound in books for the classroom library. This technique is called *language experience*. It helps children understand the connection between written and spoken language, and builds a sense of what it feels like to be a reader and a writer. We have seen it successfully used in many preschool, kindergarten, and primary-grade classes.

Creating a book or story using children's words can be successful even with very young children. We recently observed a classroom for two-year-olds where the teacher created small books of photos of each child's family and home. As she looked at the book with the child, she wrote down what the child said. The next time they brought out the books, the child's words were the text of the story. When you are taking dictation for a story with older

---

IN PRACTICE

Reading with children to develop concepts about books and print

- Keep favorite books in the classroom over time and re-read favorite stories.
- Talk about the author; show them where the author's name is.
- Read so that the child can see the print.
- Let the child turn the page as you read.
- As you read to children, comment on the words themselves to help children understand that print conveys meaning—e.g., "They wrote the words GREAT BIG CATERPILLAR in great big letters."
- Sometimes point out words or punctuation like ! or ?
- Talk with the child about the story, its meaning, and the child's own experience.
- Refer to books after you have read them at other times, making connections to life.
- Point out the front of the book and the back of the book.
- Turn the book upside down and talk about how it silly it looks and why you can't read it like that.

---

children, write so they can see what you are doing. When you are recording a child's language, talk about the words as you write, pointing out words or letters as you take dictation. Write what the child says, using his or her natural form of expression.

Another technique that uses the words of the child to develop reading skills is called *key vocabulary*. It is described by Sylvia Ashton-Warner in her book *Teacher* (1985). Key vocabulary involves having children dictate and keep a file of words that have special meaning to them, such as *Mommy, Daddy, kiss,* and *rocket.* As children become familiar with the words and want to use them in their writing, they can create personal dictionaries.

Writing children's dictated stories is another way to give them the experience of talk written down. Many preschoolers enjoy creating stories in this way when they are assisted by a teacher who helps them to think of "what comes next." *Storyplaying* is a technique evolved by Vivian

Paley and described in her book *Wally's Stories* (1981). A child dictates a story, which he or she later directs as the teacher reads it aloud and other children act out the parts. Storyplaying contributes to children's language ability, their creative imagination, and their emerging literacy as well as being a powerful outlet for feelings.

An excellent and highly motivating way to involve children in literacy activities is to build them into the dramatic play center. Suggest that the children write labels, lists, signs, or whatever fits the situation as they act out scenes from life. A lot of writing can be found in a home or the other dramatic play scenes that children create such as hospital, barber shop, or even jungle photographic safari.

You encourage children's attempts to produce writing and explore reading when you provide time and acceptance of their "free" writing, including scribble-writing and pretend-writing. Help them write their own names when they show interest in doing this. Encourage them to "Try and write all by yourself" or "Pretend you can write it." Children may wish to copy (or even trace) print that is of interest to them. One of us came into a classroom one day to discover four-year-old Anna copying the names of all the children and staff in her class onto a diagram of a circle—to show them all where they should sit.

As children begin to understand more about written language, you can support their efforts to communicate through writing. You can focus on the process—on what children are doing and how they are doing it—and on the *ideas* they are trying to express. Encourage them to write with "invented" spelling. Assist children who are beginning to write on their own by answering questions and providing specific information or help. Accept efforts and focus your comments on their approximations of print. Your most essential contribution is to encourage children to try to write. You can do this by inviting them to write for themselves to their families and friends or to you.

To help children understand reading, encourage them to read back the messages they write, and "read" dictation you have written for them. Often children will be able to convey the sense of what has been said if not the exact words. Feedback that has personal meaning seems to be the most effective way to help children begin to develop literacy concepts. For a child who expects adults to be able to read anything that looks like print, specific feedback such as "This doesn't look like any word I know" provides new information that conflicts with the child's expectations. Such conflicts require the child to adjust his or her thinking to make sense of this new information.

Base any help you provide on a child's requests and immediate needs within self-selected writing or reading tasks. Respond to children's thinking and questions as they are pursuing their own ideas about written language. For example, a child who is trying to find a friend's name on a list may read "Sue" as

"Steven" because he is looking only at the first letters. You could point out what the child knows, "You're right! There's an *S* in both names," and also call attention to the differences, "But Steven's name is a lot longer than Sue's."

Modeling

It is also important that you visibly enjoy reading and writing yourself. Adults who enjoy and use reading and writing for themselves provide a powerful model for children. Adults often write and read in the classroom and comment on their use of books as resources: "I wonder what ingredients we'll need for the lasagna. I'm going to look it up here in my cookbook." Your appreciation of children's literature and your visible enjoyment of reading demonstrate that it is a worthwhile and pleasurable experience. Some teachers have a short quiet time set aside when everyone, adults included, takes out a book and reads.

Take advantage of every opportunity to use print in the natural ongoing activities of your classroom, encourage the children's interest, allow them to explore print and writing on their own, and provide follow-up activities. You might also create simple stories for the children, and talk about your thinking as you write.

Show your writing to children when they express interest, tell them what you are doing, and answer their questions so they will begin to understand adult purposes for writing. Recently, while one of us was writing an observation, a child questioned, "What are you doing?" This led to a conversation: "I'm writing about the things that children and teachers are doing so I can remember and talk with your teacher later." The child looked at the writing, asked about specific words, and later in the day brought her own written "message" to share.

LITERATURE

Children who love books come to love reading. Children who have many positive experiences with literature come to love books. Literature is not merely the carrot with which we motivate children to read; in a very real way, it is the most important reason for learning to read. Through good literature, children experience both language and art and learn about the world and relationships. It can provide information and motivate exploration, creativity, a concern for others, and a love of reading.

Not all books are literature, and not all children's books contribute to development. *Literature* can be defined as "work of excellence that has permanent value: the poetry, stories, and other writing that we will continue to use over the passage of time" (*Webster's II New Riverside Dictionary* 1984). Children's literature is relatively new. Time has not yet defined which books will endure.

Until the twentieth century children's literature was not recognized, either academically or by publishers, as a separate or important part of literature. Most of "classic" picturebooks were written in the last fifty years. The last twenty years has seen an explosion of children's literature. Some of the new books are works of artistry that delight children now and will for generations to come.

Good literature for young children has the qualities that we look for in all literature. It shows respect for the reader; is not condescending; does not stereotype, preach, or moralize; has integrity (that is, honesty and truthfulness within the context of the story); uses aesthetic language; and in some way helps the reader to understand and feel more deeply. Good literature teaches by example. *The Story of Ferdinand*'s message about peace and nonviolence is positive and not overstated. Illustrations are essential in children's books and should enhance and enlarge experience of the words. They should be executed beautifully, with care and craftsmanship, in a medium that is appropriate to the content of the book.

Children generally are not able to purchase books or make unlimited use of libraries, so it is up to adults to present a range of quality literature from which children can make choices.

Reflect and write about . . .

the things you read and write

What are the things you read and write as an adult? Do you do a lot of reading and writing? How much is for work and how much for pleasure? How do you feel about literature and about the other reading and writing you do? How do you think your feelings are affected by your experiences as a child in school?

Since many families are not acquainted with the qualities that characterize good literature for children, the task of providing guidance often falls to early childhood educators. As children's literature has become an accepted product it has also become a vehicle for marketing. Most grocery stores, variety stores, and even bookstores have a shelf of children's books that accompany television shows and movies. These are advertisements, not literature, and do not belong in early childhood programs.

Literature and Development

The best, most honest, and most beautiful children's literature may not be best for every child. It is important to provide variety that is appropriate for the developmental level of the children.

Toddlers and very young preschoolers have not yet developed the fine motor skills necessary for turning pages carefully, have an attention span that is relatively short for seated activities, are limited in experience and vocabulary, and are primarily interested in their own experience of the world. Oral literature, like nursery rhymes and fingerplays, provided in the day-to-day context of play and routine are an important literature experience for these children. For infants and toddlers, books should be durable with heavy pages and hard covers (board and cloth books for infants and young toddlers), relatively short, and concerned with experiences that the child knows or can relate to. For example, *The Runaway Bunny* by Margaret Wise Brown deals with feelings of anger, love, and security that all children have experienced. It is best if books for young preschoolers are written in a straightforward manner with easy-to-interpret words and illustrations.

If you work with older preschoolers or kindergartners, you can include stories that deal with events and characters beyond their realm of experience, longer stories with more complex words and plots, and more intricate and subtle illustrations. Older children will also have more distinctive personal likes and interests. Although a book like *Where the Wild Things Are* by Maurice Sendak seems to have almost universal appeal because of its illustrations of monsters and its underlying subject matter of power, anger, fear, and belonging, other books appeal to some individuals more than others. Some children are moved and entranced by the moody poetry of *Dawn* by Uri Shulevitz; others enjoy the rhythmic silliness of Beatrice Shenck de Regnier's *May I Bring a Friend?*; and still others enjoy a well-told tale like William Steig's *Sylvester and the Magic Pebble*. Many children will be fascinated by books that deal with important issues in their lives such as *Julius, Baby of the World* by Kevin Henkes, which deals with the birth of a new baby, or *Charlie Anderson* by Barbara Abercrombie, which includes two children who live in a divorced family. Knowing children, their interests, their developmental level, their attention span, and the day-to-day events in their lives will help you to pick books that are appropriate and meaningful.

If you work with primary school children, the literature teaching task is much broader. They enjoy picturebooks they can read themselves like Arnold Lobel's *Frog and Toad* and Else Minarik's *Little Bear* series, and predictable books like Bill Martin Jr.'s *Brown Bear, Brown Bear*. Because of their greater attention span they can appreciate listening to longer picturebooks such as Chris Van Allsberg's *The Polar Express* and books with few pictures like Mary Norton's *The Borrowers*, Laura Ingalls Wilder's *Little House on the Prairie*, and E.B. White's *Charlotte's Web*.

Even after children begin to read, it is essential that we continue to read to them. Since the development of reading ability varies, this enables all children, not just the eager readers, to enjoy books. Additionally, reading to primary children provides pleasure and shared experience and helps children enjoy books that are beyond their reading skill and within their comprehension.

The Organizing Framework

Every classroom needs a variety of different kinds of books that change regularly. Part of what creates active, eager readers is the sense of adventure that accompanies making a choice and opening a new book. Make sure that the books represent diverse ethnicities, lifestyles, cultures, appearance, race, age, and activities among people. Mothers should not be cast solely in the role of nurturers. Families should include single parents and only children. Minorities should appear in many professions and activities. Girls as well as boys should be adventurous, outgoing, feeling, and creative, such as the children in Miriam Cohen's books about a first-grade class, *It's George!, So What?,* and *Jim's Dog Muffin.* Elderly people should sometimes be attractive and active as well as aged and infirm, such as the strong grandmother in Ann Grifalconi's *Osa's Pride.* People with disabilities should be portrayed as being more like other people than different, as they are in Fran Ortiz's *Someone Special Just Like Me.*

We find it useful to think of the following categories of books to help ensure that we provide a variety for children. Each kind of book serves a different purpose and appeals to different children at different times, supporting their existing interests and helping to build new ones.

Fiction

Fiction for young children can illustrate life, enchant, instill a love of literature, entertain, and bring pleasure. To be effective the author must respect childhood and children's lives. The author's ability to communicate in ways that create memorable, believable characters and the illusion of reality in time and place (even in a fantasy) develop an understanding of life's experience. A story's plot is more than a mere recounting of events. It encourages children to understand the reasons behind events. The

point of a good story need not be heavy handed; stories that preach or devalue their experience will not appeal to children. Both fanciful fiction or fantasy (real people doing fantastic things and fantastic characters doing real things) and realistic fiction are important and belong in early childhood programs.

Fantasy can be specially written for children or a retelling of a traditional story. Fantasy is among the most important of childhood activities, so it should come as no surprise that fantasy comprises much of the literature of childhood and the traditional literature of cultures and nations. Characters in fantasy have fantastic adventures but personalities very like children and adults that readers know. And it is this familiarity, coupled with pretend, that makes fantasy so appealing to children. Although by definition it cannot be real, fantasy delights because it has its own logic and rules that remain true for the story. Sylvester, the unfortunate donkey in *Sylvester and the Magic Pebble,* finds a pebble that grants wishes when held. He can turn himself into a boulder but cannot transform himself back without touching the magic pebble. The realism within the fantasy allows children to put themselves into the story.

Folklore is a part of our heritage that children can begin to enjoy in early childhood. Folktales touch on themes and questions that have universal appeal and universal similarity— magic, good and evil, joy and sorrow, the origins of the world, and the people and animals that inhabit it. Folktales are satisfying in their construction, have a clear beginning and ending, and are concise. They appeal to children's sense of justice and humor. Retellings of familiar fairytales like Susan Jeffer's lushly illustrated *Snow White* and of less familiar folktales like Verna Aardema's *Why Mosquitoes Buzz in People's Ears* are an important part of the classroom library.

Realistic fiction is a more recent addition to the literature of childhood. Authors of good realistic fiction write of childhood with an affectionate, unsentimental voice. Lucy Sprague

Mitchell, who influenced so much of today's early childhood education, was one of the first to call for realistic stories for preschool children (Sutherland and Arbuthnot 1986). Books like Margaret Wise Brown's *The Noisy Book* and Marjorie Flack's *Angus and the Cat* are two of the now-classic stories that were written in the 1930s (sometimes called the "golden age" of children's literature) in response to this new awareness of the importance of the "here and now" in children's literature.

In the past, realistic fiction failed to pay adequate attention to minorities, those with disabilities, and other groups of children, and in so doing gave them no one to identify with in the books that they read. If we are to lead all children to a love of reading, we need to include books that reflect children and their lives in ways that are positive and affirming. If we are to support the development of children who appreciate the common humanity they share with people who are different, they need books that include a range of diverse characters.

Today a wealth of stories include characters who are disabled, poor, or ethnically diverse and who live in families as varied as those of real children. An important characteristic of these books is that the plot is relevant to children and central to the story and not just a vehicle for a well-meaning message. Ezra Jack Keats's *Peter's Chair* is about a little boy who does not want to give up being the baby of the family. He happens to be African American and live in large urban setting. Anne Herbert Scott's *On Mother's Lap* depicts a similar theme, only the main characters happen to be Inuit and live in an arctic village.

Informational Books

All children are curious. They explore the world and want to know how things work and why. Informational books written in understandable, direct language; aesthetically worded and illustrated; and related to the experience of children can broaden their understanding. To teach and entertain they must be factually accurate, current, and not overgeneralized or filled with half-truths. To enhance interest and not bore, they must be well-paced and skillful in their presentation of concepts. Illustrations help to convey more than the words alone can. To be appealing and accurate without being demeaning or insincere is the great challenge of informational books for young children. Gail Gibbons, Milicent Selsam, and Aliki are a few of today's authors who have written informational books for young children that are direct, accurate, and appealing.

Informational books can be a vehicle to promote a host of goals. Some address scientific, social, and environmental concerns once thought inappropriate or too controversial for the young—concepts like birth, death, sex, racism, aging, war, and pollution. When well written and illustrated, these books help children to understand aspects of their lives about which they

Reflect and write about . . .

the books you loved as a child

What books did you love when you were a child? What did you love about
them? Why were they important to you? How did you discover those books?
When was the last time you read one of them? How have you shared these
books with children?

have vital concern. Others, written to meet a societal demand for curriculum material on a
current issue or fad, may be inappropriate for young children. Some seem to suggest
that it is children's responsibility to handle the
problems that generations of adults have created. They are often promoted as a cure for social ills or for the troubles of today's society or
children. Good literature must provide more
than a "band-aid." If the book was produced
hurriedly to address a short-lived concern, the
language used and style of illustration may be
sentimental, stereotyped, or carelessly executed.
If the subject matter is inappropriate, the books
generally treat the subject in a superficial, sim-
plistic, or inaccurate manner. "Band-aid" books
that purport to teach children how to avoid sexual abuse or drugs or fix the problems of pollution or the disappearing rainforest do more to al-
leviate the concerns of adults than to solve the
problem or ensure the welfare of children. They
should not be confused with literature or solutions to problems.

Mood and Concept Books

Mood and concept books sensitize children to
ideas, feelings, and awareness. They help to expand the realm of an individual's experience.
Into this category we place books that use organizing frameworks like the alphabet, aesthetic
experiences, and elements of design, colors,
shapes, and numbers. Wordless books are generally a part of this category. They encourage

children to think and use language. Concept
books are most valuable when they provide a
sense of joy and wonder in the world and are
not used to drill children on concepts. There are
a wealth of choices in this area; Jan Ormerod's
beautiful wordless book about a child's morning, *Sunlight;* Anita Lobel's *On Market Street;*
Mitsumasa Anno's *Topsie Turvies;* and a host of
beautiful photography books by Tana Hoban
such as *A, B, See!* are a few of our favorites.

Poetry

Poems appeal to young children, who have a
natural response to rhythm and rhyme and often speak in the sing-song cadences of Mother
Goose. Rhymes and finger games are nearly
universal forms of literature passed down from
adult to child around the world. Collections of
rhymes and poems belong in every program.
Nursery rhymes of all cultures include common
themes—animals, unusual or grotesque people,
street cries, games, fantasy creatures, clapping
and fingerplay, riddles, tongue twisters, nonsense, counting rhymes, proverbs, and simple
verse stories.

   Many books for young children are written
in poetry. Poetry that is sometimes, but not always, rhythmic and rhymed presents mood and
melody in language in a natural and unforced
manner. Poetry helps to enhance children's understanding of the world and develops their sensitivity to language. It can inspire and move children or calm them. Poetry is more than rhyming

words. Poetry consists of words carefully chosen that remain in memory long after they are gone, words that have music and power. Children are surprisingly interested in hearing poems, and an illustrated anthology of poems for children in the classroom library may become a favorite book. *Tomie dePaola's Book of Poems* and *The Random House Book of Poetry for Children,* edited by Jack Prelutsky, are two good examples. Individual poems illustrated as books like Clement Moore's *The Night Before Christmas* (a particularly appealing version has been illustrated by Tomie dePaola) or Arnold Lobel's *The Microscope* make a good introduction to poetry. Robert Louis Stevenson's *A Child's Garden of Verses,* Edward Lear's *Book of Nonsense,* and A. A. Milne's collections *When We Were Very Young* and *Now We are Six* are other good choices to share with young children.

The Environment

A comfortable, well-stocked library area in the quietest corner of the classroom provides a good setting for children's experience with books. A low shelf designed to display the front covers of books enables children to select and replace books themselves. Soft pillows, artwork, a rocking chair, and an adult lap to sit on attract children to the library corner. A quiet area of the classroom with adequate lighting and comfortable seating is the best place to read to groups. It enables children to hear the words and see the pictures and sets the stage for positive literature experiences.

In programs for infants and toddlers you can share books frequently with one or two individuals and may find that a small group gathers round when you start to read. This will create a short-lived but enjoyable group book experience. In preschool and primary programs you should provide ten- to twenty-minute group book times at least once or twice daily. Books can be read to a full class of fifteen to twenty children, but smaller groups will have more pos-

itive and longer book times. For children to fully benefit from being read to, they must first be interested and able to focus. Anxious, uncomfortable, hungry, or overtired children will not be able to lend their attention to books.

Supporting Learning

Helping young children to understand and love literature involves choosing books thoughtfully and designing space for group reading and independent exploration of books as we have just described. It is also important to learn to read to children with skill and responsiveness and to design experiences to expand on literature. Another important way to support children's learning is to help families to make literature a part of their children's lives at home.

Reading to Children

There are different ways of reading to children, depending on the age and experience of the children, your purpose, and the type of book you are reading. It is best to read the words as the author has written them. This gives children the experience of rich language, one of the most important parts of literature. Children who are beginning to attend to reading also will develop understanding of the constancy of print. It is usually best to read the text continuously without interruption. This helps children to develop the sense of the story and the flow of the book's language and helps groups of children to remain attentive.

With very young, non-English speaking, or inexperienced children you may find books that are valuable but too wordy or difficult for your children to understand. In this case you may just wish to talk about the pictures, convey the story in simpler words, or select alternative books that match your children's needs.

More personal connection and dialogue is possible when you read to one or two children at a time. When reading a book with one or two children, comments and questions can help de-

---

IN PRACTICE

Reading to a group

- Prepare by becoming well-acquainted with the story and the children.
- Sit on a stool or low chair to help children to see.
- Make frequent eye contact while reading to keep you in touch with children's responses.
- Speak in a clear, audible voice and make your expression relate to the content of the story.
- Use a natural conversational tone with the distinct differences and nuances that you use as you talk with other people.

---

velop understanding of the story experience by enlarging on events in the books: "I wonder what the Gunniwolf wants. The little girl seems to be going deeper into the jungle. Why do you think the Gunniwolf talks like that?" Such interaction can help you to become better attuned to children's needs, feelings, and interests. Questions and comments can also serve as a bridge between the child's life and the book: "Little Sal is filling her bucket with blueberries just the way we filled our buckets with crabapples when we went to the farm." One of your most important goals in presenting literature to children is to help them to develop understanding and love of books. They should never feel pressured by questions about books. If they feel that story-time is quiz time, they may avoid reading altogether. Reading a story to a group requires skill and practice. The In Practice box above makes some suggestions for reading to a group of children.

Literature is enhanced when it is not isolated from other classroom experiences. It can be a launching point for many other kinds of activities. For example, a memorable phrase such as, "Cats here, cats there, cats and kittens everywhere, hundreds of cats, thousands of cats, millions and billions and trillions of cats" (from *Millions of Cats* by Wanda Gag) may be

the perfect response to a squirming litter of kittens if children know and love the book.

Books and poems have tremendous potential for motivating children in creative drama and movement. It is a rare group of young children, for example, that does not spontaneously begin to take on the role of the monkeys in Esphyr Slobodkinas's *The Peddler and His Caps* after hearing it one or two times. With the addition of a few props and some adult direction you can introduce a new dimension to children's innate dramatic sense. Flannelboards and puppets are effective ways to present literature to very young children. They also contribute to the experience of older children who appreciate props that can be manipulated and who enjoy using the materials for their own storytelling.

Poems that are "stuck" in books may never make their way into your mouth or children's hearts. We have used poetry posters, developed by our friend Kay Goines, as a way to bring poetry into the classroom. A poetry poster is a poem written on a piece of poster-sized paper, illustrated by a staff member or family member and hung in the classroom to bring the poem to the children and you.

Some recorded stories and poems for children add an extra dimension to a familiar book.

We like recordings of authors reading their own work. It is vital to remember that no recording, however good, is a substitute for daily reading time. Many recordings are made without aesthetic awareness or respect for children and are not appropriate classroom materials. These often have been designed to be sold in grocery stores and seem to be the literary equivalent of the candy and junk food displayed at checkout stands.

Similarly, there are many fine films and videotapes of good children's literature and others that do not contribute to children's development. Videotaped books are certainly preferable to typical children's television programming, but we do not believe that either deserve a regular role in the classroom. Occasionally, after a child has had exposure to a book, a short film or videotape of the book can add new dimensions and enlarge on children's experience. Only the very best of these should be included in your program. They must be thoughtfully conceived and well executed, making use of the talents of artists and storytellers. For example, we were recently charmed by the extremely well crafted videos of Rudyard Kipling's *Just-So Stories* narrated by Danny Glover and Jack Nickolson and accompanied by the music of the South African a cappella chorus, Ladysmith Black Mambazo, and Bobby MacFarrin.

Although children's literature can be expanded into many other areas of classroom life, it is important not to turn literature into reading texts or use it as a basis for worksheets and tests. When children's literature is "basalized" in this way, there is a very real danger of squelching children's inherent love of books.

Helping Families Provide Literature to Children

One of the important things you can do is to help families use and choose good books for their children. Few families have spent time learning about good literature for young children. Some may not understand the importance of adults reading to children. In some families, adult illiteracy is a barrier, often accompanied by a sense of shame, that prevents adults from attempting to read to children. Family literacy programs that combine early childhood and adult literacy education may be available in your community.

You can help children's families to provide good literature to their children. Feature a review of good books for children in your newsletters to families. In communities where families are financially able you may wish to introduce one of the paperback children's book clubs that sell good quality paperbacks for a few dollars.

A simple and effective way to encourage families to read to their children is to make good classroom books available for overnight borrowing. A selection of wordless books and simple repetitive books can help adults for whom reading is difficult. Your careful explanation of how important reading is to children

---

Reflect and write about . . .

the role of literature in your family

How important was literature in your family? Do you remember being read to? What effect did this have on you? How did your family's interest or lack of interest in literature influence your attitudes and values?

and how special the books are to you will help ensure that they are returned undamaged. Special book-borrowing envelopes or bags can be used to record the titles of the books borrowed and to protect them as they travel to children's homes and back to school again in the morning. The establishment of this routine will help children later on when they begin to use public libraries. You can also encourage families to take regular trips to the library with their children to borrow books and to attend library-sponsored story hours.

FINAL THOUGHTS

Young children need and want to communicate with others. As you work with children, you will help them to take on a most important challenge and share a bond with the rest of their human family. Through language, literacy, and literature curriculum, you can help them to become confident talkers, attentive listeners, enthusiastic readers and writers, and life-long lovers of literature.

PROJECTS

Observe a Program: Use the Environment Checklist from Chapter Eight to observe an early childhood program. Report on the extent to which the program seems to support children's language and literacy development. Suggest some ways to provide some additional experiences from which children would benefit.

Observe a Child: Observe a child for a morning, focusing on communication and literacy. Notice how the child communicates and engages with books and print. Report on:

- The ways and the circumstances in which the child communicates or engages with books and print.

- How the environment supports the child's development in this area.

- How the staff supports this child's development.

- What might be done to better enhance this child's development of language, literacy, and appreciation of literature.

Observe an Educator: Observe an early childhood educator for a morning and then interview her/him about how she or he provides opportunities and supports children's development in language, literature, and literacy. Report on:

- The activities and routines that you saw that contribute to children's learning in these areas.

- Any evidence you saw of planning for language, literature, and literacy.

- The educator's goals for children's development of language, literature, and literacy.

- The ways in which the goals and what you actually observed match or don't match.

Design an Environment: Design an ideal early childhood environment for the support of language, literacy, and literature. Describe what you included and why.

Share your plan with an early childhood educator and a member of a young child's family and describe their response and suggestions.

Observe a Program: Observe an early childhood program with regard to the language, literacy, and literature experiences it provides. Report on the way that it addresses each area. Does the program meet children's needs and why? What implications does this have for your future work with young children?

Compare Two Programs: Observe a second early childhood program with regard to the language, literacy, and literature experience it provides. Compare and contrast it with the first program.

Compare Two Ages: Observe two programs, one preschool and one for infants and toddlers or primary-school children. Report on how each enhances children's language and literacy and supports the development of each age group. Talk to the staff about how they make their curriculum choices in this area.

Plan for Language, Literature, or Literacy: Write and implement a plan in language, literacy, or literature using the activity planning format (Figure 10.7). Report on how children responded and on how you felt about what you did. What worked? What might you do differently next time? How might you expand on this experience for children? Describe what you learned about yourself, children, language, literacy or literature development, and teaching.

BIBLIOGRAPHY

Ashton-Warner, S. 1985. *Teacher.* New York: Simon & Schuster.

Bissex, G. 1980. *Gnys at Wrk: A Child Learns to Write and Read.* Cambridge, MA: Harvard University Press.

Bruner, J. 1983. *Child's Talk: Learning to Use Language.* New York: Norton.

Bryce-Heath, S. 1983. *Ways With Words: Language, Life and Work in Communities and Classrooms.* New York: Cambridge University Press.

Butler, D., and M. Clay. 1983. *Reading Begins At Home.* Portsmouth, NH: Heinemann.

Cazden, C. 1975. Play with Language and Metalinguistic Awareness. *Dimensions of Language Experience.* New York: Agathon.

Cazden, C., ed. 1981. *Language in Early Childhood Education,* Rev. ed. Washington, DC: National Association for the Education of Young Children.

Chomsky, N. 1971. Write Now, Read Later. *Childhood Education* 47:296–99.

Clay, M. M. 1975. *What Did I Write? Beginning Writing Behavior.* Portsmouth, NH: Heinemann.

Cochran-Smith, M. 1984. *The Making of a Reader.* Norwood, NJ: Ablex.

Ferreiro, E., and A. Tebrosky. 1979. *Literacy Before Schooling.* Translated by K. G. Castro. Portsmouth, NH: Heinemann.

Fields, M. V. 1989. *Literacy Begins at Birth.* Tucson, AZ: Fisher Books.

Fields, M. V., K. L. Spangler, and D. Lee. 1991. *Let's Begin Reading Right: Developmentally Appropriate Beginning Literacy.* 2nd ed. Englewood Cliffs, NJ: Merrill/Prentice Hall.

Genishi, C. 1988. Children's Language: Learning Words From Experience. *Young Children* 44(1):16–22.

Gonzales-Mena, J. 1981. English as Second Language for Preschool Children. *Language in Early Childhood,* Rev. ed. Washington, DC: National Association for the Education of Young Children.

Graves, D. H. 1984. *Writing: Teachers and Children at Work.* Portsmouth, NH: Heinemann.

Harste, J., V. Woodward, and C. Burke. 1984. *Language Stories and Literacy Lessons.* Portsmouth, NH: Heinemann.

Hymes, J. L. 1958. *Before the Child Reads.* Evanston, IL: Row, Peterson.

Jacobs, L., ed. 1965. *Using Literature with Young Children.* New York: Teachers College Press.

Jalongo, M. R. 1988. *Young Children and Picture Books: Literature From Infancy to Six.* Washington, DC: National Association for the Education of Young Children.

Jones, E., ed. 1988. *Reading, Writing and Talking with Four, Five and Six Year Olds.* Pasadena, CA: Pacific Oaks.

Meek, M. 1982. *Learning to Read.* Portsmouth, NH: Heinemann.

Moskowitz, A. 1979. The Acquisition of Language. *Scientific American* 239(5):82–89.

Neuman, S. B., and K. A. Roskos. 1993. *Language and Literacy Learning in the Early Years: An Integrated Approach.* Orlando, FL: Harcourt Brace Jovanovich.

Paley, V. G. 1981. *Wally's Stories.* Cambridge, MA: Harvard University Press.

Roskos, K. A., and S. B. Neuman. 1994. Of Scribbles, Schemas, and Storybooks: Using Literacy Albums to Document Young Children's Literacy Growth. *Young Children* 49(2):78–85.

Sawyer, W. E., and J. C. Sawyer. 1993. *Integrated Language Arts for Emerging Literacy.* Albany, NY: Delmar.

Schikedanz, J. 1986. *More Than the ABCs.* Washington, DC: National Association for the Education of Young Children.

Schikedanz, J. A. 1978. Please Read That Story Again! Exploring Relationships Between Story Reading and Learning to Read. *Young Children* 33(6):48–55.

Sumison, J. 1991. *Playing With Print.* Watson, ACT, Australia: Australian Early Childhood Association, Inc.

Sutherland, Z., and M. H. Arbuthnot. 1986. *Children and Books,* 7th ed. Glenview, IL: Scott, Foresman.

Teale, W., and E. Sulzby. 1986. *Emergent Literacy: Writing and Reading.* Norwood, NJ: Ablex.

Tough, J. 1977a. *The Development of Meaning.* Boston: Allen & Unwin.

Tough, J. 1977b. *Talking and Learning: A Guide to Fostering Communication Skills in Nursery and Infant Schools.* Portsmouth, NH: Heinemann.

Vardell, S. M. 1994. Non-fiction for Young Children. *Young Children* 49(6):40–41.

Vygotsky, L. S. 1962. *Thought and Learning.* Cambridge, MA: MIT Press.

Vygotsky, L. S. 1978. *Mind in Society: The Development of Higher Psychological Process.* Cambridge, MA: Harvard University Press.

Waring-Chaffee, M. B. 1994. RDRT . . . HRIKM (Ready or Not Here I Come): Investigations in Children's Emergence as Readers and Writers. *Young Children* 49(6):52–55.

Wells, G. 1981. *Learning Through Interaction: The Study of Language Development.* New York: Cambridge University Press.

Wells, G. 1985. *The Meaning Makers.* Portsmouth, NH: Heinemann.

Wilkinson, A. 1971. *The Foundations of Language.* London: Oxford University Press.

Williams, R. P., and J. K. Davis. 1994. Lead Sprightly Into Literacy. *Young Children* 49(4):37–41.

CHAPTER FOURTEEN

The Inquiry Curriculum

It is little short of a miracle that modern methods of instruction have not already completely strangled the holy curiosity of inquiry, because what this delicate little plant needs most, apart from initial stimulation, is freedom; without that it is surely destroyed.   Albert Einstein

The universe is the child's curriculum.   Maria Montessori

In this chapter we will focus on how the early childhood curriculum can be designed to support children's growing understanding of the world in which they live. In it we discuss inquiry processes that are the building blocks for children's construction of knowledge and how these contribute to concept development. We look at the curriculum areas that are most directly involved with cognitive development: math, science, and social studies. Although the primary focus is on cognitive development, the social studies component has to do, in large part, with social and emotional development as well.

Young children have a compelling curiosity to figure out why and how the world works. They learn by doing—by observing and manipulating concrete materials and interacting with their environment. Through play they acquire and order knowledge. From their earliest months they observe phenomena, discover relationships, search for answers, and communicate their discoveries. They construct knowledge as they explore, experiment, and act upon their environment.

Math, science, and social studies extend into every aspect of curriculum and of life. Children inquire and develop concepts as they play and participate in all curriculum activities. Experiences in mathematics, science, and social studies are uniquely suited to the development of thinking and problem solving and are the areas of the curriculum in which cognitive development is a primary emphasis.

A DEVELOPMENTAL PERSPECTIVE

How children's thinking changes is a fascinating area of child development. The work of Jean Piaget and his followers is enlightening because of their careful observations of the characteristic ways that children think and develop concepts. Piaget observed that children's thinking is very different from the logical thinking of adults and relies on direct, repeated sensory experiences. As children have these experiences they construct their own knowledge.

Piaget's work has helped educators to understand that children's cognitive development proceeds through stages, just like their physical development. It is as foolish to attempt to rush a child into thinking like an adult as it would be to attempt to teach a crawling infant to high jump. Although cognitive development cannot be rushed, research suggests that it can be impaired. Children need intellectual stimulation to learn to think and reason (Healy 1990).

Reflect and write about . . .

a time when you were excited about learning

Think of a time when you were really curious and excited about learning something. What made it interesting? What did you do to find out more about it? Do you still remember what you learned? How do you use it?

Piaget described three kinds of knowledge. *Physical knowledge,* the knowledge of external reality, is the understanding that is gained from doing things or acting on the physical world. For example, by holding and playing with a playground ball, children experience and learn about its properties—its texture, its shape, its weight and squishiness, and its tendency to roll away and bounce.

Logico-mathematical knowledge is the knowledge of logical relationships. Children observe, compare, and think. For example, children will observe the relationship between a tennis ball and a playground ball. Both have similar shapes and roll and bounce. There are also differences observed in size, color, texture, and weight. Logico-mathematical knowledge requires direct experience but is based on the internal process of reflection on what is experienced. Through the experience of many balls, a child develops the idea of *ball* as a single category based on shared characteristics. Logico-mathematical knowledge is dependent on one's own observation, experience, and reflection. It is not arbitrary or dependent on others and it cannot be taught.

The last kind of knowledge is *social knowledge,* which depends on what is learned from others and not on direct experience of objects or events. It is based on what people decide. For example, children learn that balls are used to play games, that different kinds of balls are used for different games, and different balls have different names.

In traditional educational settings teachers have often taught math, science, and social studies as social knowledge rather than providing experiences that allow children to develop physical or logico-mathematical knowledge. Information like this shape—8—is called *eight;* the earth goes around the sun; Boise is the capital of Idaho.

Piaget's description of cognitive development as constructed knowledge suggests that for children to really understand math, science, and social studies, they must have opportunities to explore and act on the real world to establish relationships and construct their own knowledge.

Concept Development

Through activity, children develop concepts to help make sense of experience. A concept is a mental image or word picture that is communicated in a single word or combination of words—it has a general, not a specific meaning. As a child repeatedly experiences the characteristics of an object, animal, person, or event and mentally combines and organizes these, he or she is constructing a concept. For example, an infant may have constructed the concept *door* based on many repeated experiences, including: a slam, mother returning through this spot, the way to get where you want to go, pinched fingers, a light source at night, and the barrier to what is desired. Concepts are generalized as children recognize the common attributes of objects, people, ideas, and experiences. In the door example, the initial concept of door may only refer to the door of the bedroom. As many doors are experienced, the concept is generalized and different doors are recognized: the door of the family car, of grandma's house, the automatic door at the supermarket, and finally doors in general. Although the doors differ greatly, the common characteristics are recognized and the concept is established.

A child's ability to understand and develop a concept depends on cognitive maturation and the availability of relevant experiences. Concepts differ in how difficult they are for children to understand. Whether or not a concept is likely to be understood is related to its degree of abstraction and complexity.

Concepts can be thought of as existing on a continuum from concrete to abstract. The *concreteness* of a concept refers to whether it can be directly experienced or observed. Concrete concepts are accessible to children. They can be experienced through the senses—seen, heard, held, felt, touched, tasted. Concepts that depend on information outside of direct experience are abstract and cannot be completely understood by a young child regardless of how hard an adult may try to provide the experience through language, books, or pictures. This makes times, events and places that cannot be directly experienced in some way—a trip to the moon, World War II, and abstract concepts like social justice and liberty, for example—mostly meaningless to young children.

The *complexity* of a concept—the amount of information needed to define it—is the second quality that affects a young child's ability to understand. Children acquire concepts of low complexity more quickly than those of high complexity. Some concepts are available to children through direct experience but involve many interrelated ideas. These cannot be understood since young children's capacity for creating and retaining connections between

such ideas has not yet developed. The concept of *wind* is both relatively simple and concrete, defined primarily by one's experience of it against the skin and its ability to move objects about. The concept of a weather system, however, is complex and requires the grasp of numerous other supporting concepts including evaporation, wind patterns, cloud formation, low- and high-pressure areas, and precipitation. Young children will not understand the phenomena of a weather system because the overall effect requires attending to a variety of attributes simultaneously. Providing children experiences with some of the components of

Reflect and write about . . .

a time when you made a discovery

Think of a time when you discovered something. What did you discover? How did you discover it? Do you still remember what you learned? How did you feel when you discovered it?

weather will, however, lay a foundation for later understanding of the complex concept.

Inquiry Processes

The processes that a child uses to learn about the world and construct concepts are referred to as *inquiry processes*. To *inquire* means to ask, to discover, to think, to take risks, to make mistakes, and to learn from them. Inquiry does not mean learning right answers. If we teach science, math, and social studies as predetermined answers that must be acquired by rote, then we do not help children to develop higher level thinking skills or learn to inquire. Inquiry for a young child involves the organization of experiences through exploration. An inquiring child uses sight, sound, taste, smell, touch, and the kinesthetic sense to gain general and specific information that will contribute to the development of concepts. Curriculum specialists identify between ten and fifteen distinct inquiry processes, but the In Practice box on p. 424 applies best to young children who learn from concrete experience.

ROLE OF THE EARLY CHILDHOOD EDUCATOR

Children approach the world with a sense of wonder and an almost infinite curiosity. Your role is to create the climate in which each child can discover the power of ideas and generate concepts about the world. It is important to be responsive to children and open to the many aspects of life in which they are interested.

Although all children are curious and actively try to understand the world, it is possible to destroy the delicate flower of inquiry. Children learn and inquire when they are encouraged to be autonomous, ask questions, and ponder creatively. If, instead, they are convinced that all the answers are already known and will be fed to them by an adult, they come to see learning as memorizing facts without thinking, and they lose their curiosity. This is the great danger of telling what we know instead of encouraging children to find out on their own. In so doing it is possible to limit children's intellectual growth.

For thinking and problem solving to take place, you must provide a learning environment that is both stimulating and reasonably ordered. There must be space, interesting equipment and materials, and lots of time to explore how things work and to develop and test ideas. Activities that stimulate inquiry and lead to concept development can arise spontaneously and from carefully planned curriculum. When you design learning experiences, you will want to think about the developmental appropriateness of your expectations so that the concepts that you want children to learn are concrete and appropriately simple.

Many important kinds of learning can take place outside the confines of the classroom. The world beyond the program walls provides

---

IN PRACTICE

Inquiry processes used by children

- *Exploring:* Using the senses to observe, investigate, and manipulate.
- *Identifying:* Naming and describing what is experienced.
- *Classifying:* Grouping objects or experiences by their common characteristics.
- *Comparing and contrasting:* Observing similarities and differences between objects or experiences.
- *Hypothesizing:* Using the data from experiences to make guesses (hypotheses) about what might happen.
- *Generalizing:* Applying previous experience to new events.

---

more than a pleasant vacation from routine. It is vital for children to see and experience the real world. This is particularly true if you work in a setting where children have had limited experiences. A teacher we know took her class to see the ocean—a two-hour bus trip that had never been made before by the majority of the poor, inner-city first graders in her class. At the shore one of the children came to her barely able to speak he was so excited, saying, "Robin! . . . water! . . . sand! . . . moving!" He had not known that the ocean moved. His understanding of *ocean* and *shore* would have been mere social knowledge without this direct experience. It takes effort to take children on learning trips. They can take extra personnel, money, and special planning, but they are worth the effort.

Communication that Supports Inquiry

Talking with children as they explore and discover is one of the most important things you will do to help them learn to think. Skilled educators target their comments, questions, and activities to support the natural curiosity of children. You can make statements about your own wonder and curiosity. Supportive com-

ments about children's discoveries and explorations encourage further inquiry. Questions help children to notice detail, make comparisons, and come to conclusions. For example, if a group of children are exploring what happens when they narrow a faucet with a finger, making the water spray out, you might comment: "I wonder what makes that happen? You found a way to change the water flow. Can you make it come out slower (faster)? What do you have to do to change it? Why do you think that happens?"

You can express a sense of curiosity about and appreciation of the world in statements like: "I wonder why the clouds are moving so quickly?" "Look at how different each shell is." "The baskets all nest together, the little ones inside the big ones." "I wonder why cats purr." "What do you think would happen if people purred?" "The mother bear is looking after her cubs—every mother seems to do that." "I can feel the rabbit's heart is beating quickly and hard. Why do you suppose that's happening?" Statements like these model an inquiring mind. They help children to form concepts but do not hand them pre-formed ideas.

Children learn to inquire and become active problem solvers when they are encouraged and supported in doing so. They need to understand that it is desirable to think creatively about problems, acceptable not to have an answer, and okay to give the "wrong" answers.

Giving information is not your most important role. Facts pronounced by adults deprive children of the opportunity to learn through inquiry. For example, we once observed a child who found a praying mantis and eagerly asked his teacher what it ate so that it could be kept alive. The teacher explained that she did not know but asked, *"How can we find out?"* This resourceful four-year-old questioned other adults, looked through a book about insects in the science area, and found a photograph of a praying mantis. He took it to his teacher, and she read to the group about the insect. They proceeded to offer the praying mantis ants and beetles and discovered its preferred foods. Had the teacher simply said, "It eats bugs," the learning would have been much less meaningful to the child.

Open-ended questions encourage children to think. They say to the child, "Tell me more." Questions are open when they can be answered in a number of different ways and have more than one correct answer. You can develop skill in asking open questions by practicing until you can ask them with comfort. The following are the beginning phrases of some open questions.

What would happen if . . . ?

What do you notice (see, hear, feel, smell)?

How are these the same (different)?

What do you think . . . ?

How do you know . . . ?

How could we find out . . . ?

A closed question has only one correct or acceptable answer, for example, "What color is it?" "What is the name of this shape?" Closed questions can help you to learn whether children have acquired a concept or piece of information, but they do not stimulate inquiry, and sometimes they squelch it. In most classrooms, educators use a mixture of open and closed questions. The kind of mix is influenced by values, objectives, and the nature of the particular situation. Awareness of the purpose of each type of question can help you to make conscious choices about which to use. If you wish to stimulate children to inquire, you will ask many open-ended questions.

To help children think flexibly, it is useful to ask questions that have many possibilities. Jane Healy, in her book *Is Your Bed Still There When You Close The Door?* (1992), suggests many creative thinking questions that adults can ask children, such as: How many things could you do with a balloon? If you had a pair of magic wings where would you fly? What would happen if everything was yellow?

The silence that you allow between statements or questions is also an important factor in how children respond. Researchers have found that three to five seconds is the average amount of silence that occurs between adult questions and the child's response or a follow-

Reflect and write about . . .

asking open questions

Try asking a child some open questions. What happened when you used this approach? How was it different from other kinds of interactions? What did you learn from the experience?

up comment. They found that if the adult waits only one or two seconds, one word responses are most frequent. If the wait lasts for several seconds longer, children respond with whole sentences and complex thoughts that represent more creativity and increased speculativeness (Costa 1974).

MATHEMATICS

Mathematics is a way to structure experience to form ideas about the quantitative, logical, and spatial relationships between things, people, and events. During the early childhood years, young children come to think of themselves as part of a community of people who use number to order and communicate about their world. In the same way that young children will pretend to write and read, they will label distance and ages with numbers *("My doll is twenteen" "It's thirty-fifty miles")*.

The development of mathematical thinking is a long process that consists of far more than simply knowing how to count and calculate. Math concepts must be constructed. They appear to evolve as children mature and have many real-life experiences.

The conceptual underpinnings of adult skills like using money, balancing a check-book, and reading a clock are based on many years of concrete experiences that may not seem to relate to mathematics. Concepts such as more and fewer, far and near, similar and different, short and tall, now and later, first and last, over and under precede later mastery of complex mathematical concepts. Educators participate by providing an environment, materials, and activities that support children's inquiry into math.

Math and Development

The work of Piaget and others has led to an investigation of the kinds of math concepts children can construct and the ways they best construct them. Traditional beginning math education has often been taught as "social knowledge" through repetitious drill and the memorization of number facts. Instead young children need opportunities to be active in constructing ideas about number, space, and logical relationships.

The discovery of what young children can learn has led to a rethinking of the traditional content of math curriculum. Math education for young children should lead toward the ability to think logically and to creatively solve problems found in daily life. Counting and shape and numeral recognition are no longer considered sufficient content for a preschool or kindergarten math program.

There are many misconceptions about what *number* is in the early childhood years. The ability to count and understanding *number* are not the same thing. Being able to count reflects the ability to memorize and mimic certain behaviors (touching and saying a number). It is a rote activity unless a child has a concept of number (oneness, twoness, threeness, and so on). Only then does a child understand that the name represents a specific quantity. A parent of our acquaintance proudly told us that her four-year-old child "knew" numbers up to twenty. Indeed, the child could recite the words *one, two, three,* and so forth in proper order. However, when asked, she could not point to a stack of six blocks from among several piles of six or less. Despite her rote counting skill, she clearly demonstrated that "sixness" was not a concept she had acquired. It's easy to understand how confusing number must be when we think of the many ways adults use number words (You can have three crackers. Mommy will come get you at three. You can go on the big slide when you are three).

Children only gradually come to really understand number despite rather easily learning to count using number names in the correct order. They use counting as a reliable tool when underlying number concepts are in place—usually around the age of seven. Children do not understand number until they understand that:

- There is a one-to-one correspondence between each number name and an object in the set being counted.
- The number name applies not only to the last object named but to the entire set of objects.
- Other number names mean more or less than the number.
- Number is the same regardless of the objects counted.
- The physical arrangement of the objects does not influence how many there are.

Numeral recognition is a visual perceptual task that is unrelated to the concept represented by the numeral. Until children develop the number concept and understand that the word represents the concept, they are not able to understand the meaning of the symbol *even if they know its name.* Numerals and their names comprise social knowledge—useful for communicating once the underlying concept is in place. Although young children may appear to be reading numerals, a closer look at their understanding will usually demonstrate that they are naming the shape of the numeral rather than understanding the number concept.

Children who are beginning to identify numerals and letters often add these to their paintings and drawings because they enjoy their new-found ability to identify and make these shapes—they are design elements rather than symbols for quantity or sound. Just as print literacy begins with play with letters in print, so numeracy includes play with numerals. And similarly an environment that includes numerals—for example, used in recipe charts, on the phone in the dramatic play area, or on a sign indicating the number of children an area can accommodate—gives children important experiences with how numerals are used in our society.

The practice of memorizing shape names *(triangle, circle, square)* is a sensory-perceptual and labeling task that is a minor part of geometry. Names of shapes are often taught without connection to the larger world of mathematics. This kind of rote learning does not help children to gain the concepts that are needed for later mathematical and logical thought. Although it is appropriate to use shape names when you are discussing shapes with children—"Would you bring me some triangle blocks for the roof of my building?" or "We have circle-shaped paper to paint on today"—it is not necessary or appropriate to focus your curriculum on learning shapes. Instead you can remember that children are learning about shape as they experience form in relation to their world through such activities as building with blocks, painting, working with clay, and playing with manipulative toys and puzzles.

Children are discovering math concepts in the course of the ordinary activities and routines of classroom living. You can help them develop these concepts by providing a math-rich environment in which each child has the raw materials needed for understanding important mathematical concepts and relationships. You also plan specific activities to give children a broad range of math experiences.

The Organizing Framework

The math content of our childhoods—addition and subtraction facts—is no longer regarded as a good foundation for children's learning about mathematics. What is the foundation that young children need to help them to make sense of the physical and social world and to master abstract mathematical concepts later in their school careers? Young children can develop concepts of classification, space, number, seriation (ordering), patterning, measurement, and time. These basic concepts can provide the basis for the math curriculum for young children.

Classification

One of the ways that we organize and understand daily life is by classifying. To classify means to sort or group people, objects, ideas, or events by shared characteristics. As children come to understand that they can group things together based on the ways they are alike and exclude them based on the ways that they are different (negation, or "not like"), they have developed the basic concept of classification. As they become more sophisticated and flexible in the categories they use, children are developing more profound understanding of classification. Children are learning to classify things according to common attributes when they hang up all the dresses; place all the dishes in the cupboard; put all the large beads in a basket and all the small beads in a can; and sort buttons by size, shape, color, or number of holes. When all the children with blue sneakers want to sit together, they are demonstrating the ability to classify.

Seriation

When objects are ordered in a sequence based on a difference in the degree of some quality such as size, weight, texture, or shading, they are arranged in a series or seriated. Children gain experience in seriating when they arrange things in their environment: for example, themselves from shortest to tallest, balls from smallest to largest, or a set of color chips from palest to darkest.

Patterning

Another form of ordering based on repetition is called *patterning*. When children create bead necklaces with alternating colors, arrange parquetry blocks, or sing the chorus after every verse of a song, they are experiencing patterns.

Measurement

Measurement is the process of comparing size, volume, weight, or quantity to a standard. Adults use numerically expressed standards such as meters, ounces, or dollars. Measurement is a very practical part of math that we use with children informally all the time. ("We need three cups of flour in this playdough recipe." "I bet you grew two inches last month." "We need another foot of ribbon.") Measurement for children involves making comparisons of things in the immediate environment. They discover the concept of measurement when they experiment to find how many unit blocks equal the width of the carpet, count how many cups of water fill a large container at the water table, or compare their height to the heights of their friends and teachers. Children need experience comparing length, mass (heavy/light), capacity, and temperature. Older children will also begin to use money—another, more abstract standard.

Number

Number is actually several complex, related ideas that concern quantity and order. One-to-one correspondence is a precursor of counting and understanding of number. Children must first learn that objects matched one for one (for example, a napkin for each person) share the same quantity before they can understand number.

Quantity, or the amount, is what we usually think of when we refer to number. A set of objects has a certain quantity that is unchanging and unrelated to the physical act of touching and naming (1-2-3) the objects. This characteristic is sometimes referred to as *cardinal* number, *many-ness,* or *quantity.* Children can learn to compare quantity and to determine more, less, fewer, or the same amounts.

Children can also come to understand number as it relates to the order of objects or events (first, second, third). This number concept is sometimes called *ordinal* number. When you talk about which ingredient in a recipe comes first or when a child complains that she doesn't want to be last, this is ordinal number.

Today's world is filled with numerals that give information. Children learn about numerals as labels (Room 3 is our room). As they reach the primary grades and develop understanding of number concepts, they can begin to use numerals as symbols for quantity and order.

Young children learn about number by exploring and describing arrangements and combinations of objects. Repeated opportunities to use many kinds of objects in play and in practical life situations are important so that children can manipulate and talk about number, and so that they begin to understand that number is unrelated to specific objects and instead is a tool to describe and understand many aspects of the world.

Time

As children notice the sequence of events in their daily lives they are learning about time. For example, lunch is always followed by rest time, and a story about zoo animals is read be-

fore a visit. Duration is another time-related concept. Children begin to understand as they notice such things as outdoor play lasting a long time in comparison to booktime, which lasts for a short period.

Space

Concepts of space have to do with the way objects relate to others based on position, direction, arrangement, and distance (or proximity). Children develop these ideas as they observe spatial relationships between people and objects. The concept of position may be developed when children are involved in day-to-day activities such as putting away the blocks: the long on the *bottom* shelf and the short on the shelf *above,* the block people in the basket *next to* the trucks. The concept of direction may be discovered as a child first drives a tricycle forward and then backward. When a child kicks a ball to a nearby child and then to a faraway child, the concept of distance is being explored.

Shape

Shape or geometry refers to two- and three-dimensional objects and their properties. It is easy to think of shape as simply referring to the Euclidean shape names we know well (for example, circle, triangle, rectangle, square, and so on). Shape also involves how shapes are constructed (for example, two C-shaped blocks can be put together to create a circle), topological characteristics such as whether a shape is open or closed (a *C* is an open shape and an *O* is a closed shape), how the appearance of shapes changes based on how we look at them (for example, the table top looks thin from the side and round from above), and how shapes can be manipulated while retaining their characteristics (a round ball of clay retains some of its roundness even when squashed flat into a pancake). Geometry in early childhood education is a real-world experience. Children can identify how objects are similar and different in shapes and properties. As they manipulate blocks, puzzles, games, and toys, they are learning about geometry.

The Environment

A math area can encourage children to experiment and thus discover many math concepts. Purchased equipment like wooden beads, attribute blocks (shapes that vary in size, thickness, and color), parquetry blocks (regularly shaped colored pieces of wood that can be arranged in patterns), Cuisenaire rods (small colored rods that are numerically related), colored cubes, pegboards, measuring tools, and seriation materials like stacking cups are designed to enhance math learning. Unit blocks are essential math materials that provide excellent experiences for the development of number, spatial, seriation, and classification concepts.

Homemade materials like button sorting, lotto games, and matching activities foster mathematical learning. Good sources for ideas for homemade math games are Mary Barratta-Lorton's books, *Workjobs* (1972), *Workjobs II* (1979), *Math Their Way* (1976), and *Explorations* (Harcourt 1988). Math learning opportunities occur throughout the classroom and the program day. Manipulative games, water play with measuring cups and containers, dramatic play, and outdoor exploration where spatial concepts like top/bottom, in/out, and up/down are experienced all teach mathematical concepts.

Computer programs are starting to be developed that provide math experiences for young children that are more than rote drill. Some allow children to program, and some provide experience with patterning, seriation, and number. Computers can be very motivating and if the software is thoughtfully and appropriately designed can supplement manipulative materials-based math program for young children.

Supporting Learning

Although you cannot teach the concepts directly, you *can* plan for math experiences and support children as they construct math concepts for themselves. It is important to be aware of when and how mathematics is meaningful to children. A child who is comparing and arranging the dishes in the dramatic play area and setting the table for the other children is using ideas of classification and quantity and providing you with important information. Based on your observations of children you can add additional activities and ask stimulating questions that will provide opportunities to help them learn.

Even infants and toddlers are learning about math. They do so by being free to explore in their natural, instinctive way. When six-month-old Emily reaches and touches a mobile, she learns about space and distance. As eighteen-month-old Severn gives one floppy toy dog to each caregiver, he learns about quantity. Fitting a block into a sorting box is a lesson in geometry. Looking at a book about animals and using the category "Mooo!" to describe all the large four footed animals and "Bow-wow" to describe all the small furry animals is a sorting experience. Putting on grownup's shoes is an experience in measurement. You can support them in their self-initiated exploration by providing materials and by saying things like, "There's lots of blocks to play with" or "You and Tona both have big trucks."

Help preschool children by encouraging them to question, think, and share ideas with one another. Ask questions that encourage mathematical thinking: "What shall we put next in our pattern?" "How could we find out who's tallest?" and be prepared to forego questioning when children do not appear interested. Providing children with many opportunities to manipulate objects, including those made as "math" teaching equipment (like Unifix cubes or Cuisenaire rods) and other equipment that lends itself to mathematical relationships (like blocks and button collections), supports the development of math concepts. They also learn about math in their relationships with their peers. With other children they will be challenged *("You got more than me!" "I don't want to be second!"),* and they will need to work out mathematical problems in very meaningful and very concrete ways. Math experiences like graphing to compare quantity are appropriate for children four years of age and older.

You support children in their development of time concepts by encouraging them to be aware of the ways that many kinds of things (objects, actions, and events) relate to one another—snack comes before circle time; fish, birds, and mice are all alive; grown-ups are bigger than children; running is faster than walking.

The world and our daily lives are filled with math. Children can become math conscious. Talking about time, dates, ages, amounts, size, money, and other math ideas is both natural and a necessary preparation for later understanding. Children who have a background with the concrete experiences upon which math is based come to see themselves as individuals who use numbers and measurement as important tools in daily life.

Using math ideas in daily conversation will help children to become aware of them: "Would you like your cracker whole or in two pieces?" Set math tasks and ask children questions: "Which beads do you think belong together? Why?" "Can you find me a doll that is smaller than this one but larger than this one?" "Can you cover the mat with blocks? What kind will you use? Why?" "How many cubes do you think will fit along the side of the box?"

Children learn about math as they handle the routines of the day. When each child has one cracker and rests on one mat, one-to-one correspondence is experienced. As they learn the sequence of the daily schedule, learn to

pour half a glass of milk, or cut their apples in two parts, they are using math.

Older children are eager to learn to use math in the practical ways that grown-ups do. They want to be competent in making number, measurement, and time work for them and continue to need the base in real experience with sand, water, blocks, and manipulative toys. If you work with older children, help them to start to use math in real life. For example, in cooking they can use standard measurement and note its usefulness. Just as younger children needed repeated experience of three things to comprehend threeness, older children will need many opportunities to manipulate sets of twelve things to comprehend that twelve really breaks down into sets of three and four. Otherwise, like one of the authors of

---

Reflect and write about . . .

how math was taught in your schools

How was math taught in the schools of your childhood? What do you remember most vividly? Did these experiences influence what you have done as an adult? How do you use what you learned in your life today?

---

this text, they may believe until adulthood that multiplication tables are magic formulae to be memorized and not logical aspects of reality that can be understood.

These are only a sample of the potential of the early childhood program environment for supporting math learning. Look closely at how the learning environment of the center in which you work supports children's construction of math concepts so you can better evaluate what you might do to expand and enrich the possibilities.

SCIENCE

Young children are natural scientists. Scientific exploration does not wait until children are old enough to sit still for a lesson or are competent enough to manage a Pyrex beaker. Their play is full of scientific exploration. This is true for an infant who is learning about physiology as she first discovers her toe and physics as she drops a bottle from a highchair. It is also true for a third-grader carefully observing and drawing the parts of a wildflower.

For many adults science is a scary, mysterious field involving a collection of facts and complex concepts that are learned by rote from a teacher or a textbook. For others it is specific information that adults know and that must be told to children. Educators who have maintained their own playfulness and enthusiasm for science view it as a process of exploration

and experimentation through which they and children together find out about the world.

Your own spirit of scientific inquiry will effect what is learned and the attitudes that children develop about science. We once observed a group of children and a teacher who were fascinated and curious about an animal skeleton they had found along the side of the road. They took the bones back to the classroom for further exploration. Another teacher responded to their find with repulsion. Fortunately, the group was not deterred, and they spent several days examining, reassembling the skeleton, counting the bones and teeth, and figuring out that it had been a dog—a wonderful lesson in scientific inquiry!

Science and Development

In early childhood programs, science is the process of exploring the environment and the creatures that live in it. Science, like play, is an active process that involves thinking fluently. Severeide and Pizzini compare play and science:

> Play is fanciful, divergent, and subjective. Scientific inquiry is logical, linear, systematic, and objective. Yet scientists often solve problems most effectively and innovatively when they pursue solutions in the spirit of play. (Severeide and Pizzini 1984, 58).

One of the ways that science educators have helped us to remember that science is indeed an active process is by referring to it as *scienc-*

ing. Sciencing is active; it implies trying things—things that work and things that do not work. It means a joyful risk-taking approach to learning.

The task for early childhood educators is to recognize what is most appropriate sciencing for the stage of development and interests of the children. This is as true for the teacher of a toddler who plays endlessly with water faucet as it is for the teacher of a second-grader who catches tadpoles after school.

It is useful to remember that science itself is not a collection of static facts. It is growing and changing as scientists explore and experiment, as they question and learn. In early childhood science education, it is more important for young children to feel confident enough and curious enough to wonder, explore, and ask questions than it is for them to know answers.

The Organizing Framework

The processes of exploring, identifying, comparing, contrasting, classifying, experimenting, hypothesizing, and generalizing are critical in young children's science curriculum. Science is a large field, encompassing almost every aspect of life. Although it may not be clearly divided into separate subjects for young children, it is important for you to recognize the diverse experiences that can offer scientific learning opportunities. As you think about the many kinds of experiences that you might provide for children, you may find it useful to think about three broad categories: physical science, earth science, and life science.

Physical Science

The study of matter, form, and change is called *physical science*. Children explore and observe the properties of substances—reactions to temperature and force and interactions. Concepts basic to physics and chemistry are experienced and explored by young children in the course of daily activity. Their curiosity is aroused when these have personal impact.

Physical science activities are related to the formal study of physics (energy, motion and force) and chemistry (the composition, properties, and transformation of matter). When children explore objects and act to create or alter speed, leverage, and balance they are involved in physical knowledge activities, and they are experiencing physics. When they act to make substances change by combining, heating, or cooling, they experience chemistry. Physical science for young children involves the exploration of the commonplace.

Physical science activities are uniquely appropriate to young children because they involve action and observation. Children first become aware of the physical properties of the world through their exploratory play. A ball rolls across the floor. An unbalanced pile of blocks collapses. A rock dropped into a pond makes rings of ripples. The playdough disintegrates when left in the water play table. The oil separates from the rest of the salad dressing. The glass of milk left in the sun curdles. The ice in the water table melts. These are children's first science experiments. Many repeated experiences such as these help children to anticipate the predictable phenomena that can be generalized.

In programs for young children you can provide physical knowledge experiences. First, you can provide many safe, appealing objects that children can pick up, stack, drop, throw, roll, push, pound, and manipulate in other ways. You can plan activities such as water play and cooking that provide opportunities to observe transformation through the use of heat, moisture, and the combination of substances. You can also be open to children's curiosity and allow them opportunities to experiment and try things out. For example, you can have them combine common substances like salt and ice and observe the results. As children reach the primary grades, they can begin to experiment purposefully and record the results of their work.

Earth Science

Children experience earth sciences when they observe, explore, and wonder about the common features of the earth, sky, and ocean such as sand, dirt, water, and rocks, and natural phenomena like shadows, sunsets, frost, and streams. There are a host of earth sciences including geology (the study of the origin, history, and structure of the earth), meteorology, and astronomy.

Basic concepts of earth science are experienced and explored by young children in the course of daily activity. When children ask questions like "Where does the sand come from?" "What made the mountains?" "Where did the sun go?" "Where did the snow come from?" you will know that they are curious about this aspect of science.

Children's curiosity is aroused by these subjects when they have personal impact. As they walk over hills and look at the layers of rock formations, they are experiencing geology. If they pound sandstone into bits, they are making geologic experiments. When they observe the moon hanging in the sky above the playground in the morning, they are observing astronomical phenomena. When they guess that dark clouds in the sky hold rain, they are making meteorological predictions. Young children's concepts of earth sciences are limited to what they can see and experience. Children will be curious about these phenomena, and in school they can have a place to talk, write, and read about them.

We are dependent on the resources of the earth for survival and, consequently, have responsibility for it. We are teaching ecology when we help children to understand that animals and people need clean air and water and a safe healthy environment and that they can participate in taking care of the environment. Because of its critical importance, ecology is increasingly a part of the curriculum. You teach it as you read, observe, and talk about people's effect on the environment (for example, noticing where people have trodden the grass away, or where they have planted a garden), when you observe how garbage is collected and disposed of, when you notice the effects of litter, and as you observe the impact of people on animals and plants in your environment. A visit to the zoo to see animals that are in danger of extinction and, for older children, learning about the kinds of habitats that they need and how they are threatened are also lessons in ecology.

Life Science

Children are naturally curious about living things: what they are, how they live, how they move, and their life cycles. Many life science concepts can be explored, discovered, and validated by young children in their daily experiences in your early childhood program.

A young child may wonder about where the butterfly came from, how a bean grew into a plant, how the bulging mother mouse got the babies inside her, and why the dog has four legs and the spider has eight. Life science involves the structures, origins, growth, and reproduction of plants and animals. The raw materials abound in and around the classroom. As you work with children you will help them to observe, compare, and contrast living things, and to ask questions about what they see. As children observe the transformation of a caterpillar into a butterfly, the seed into a plant, and the pregnant mouse into a family, they are having concrete experiences with biology.

Starting with their own bodies, young children may notice functions such as breath, movement, sensation, and digestion. Interest in their own growth can lead children to explore and learn about physiology. Children's fascination with their own bodies and with animals at home, in the classroom, and in nature can be used as the springboard to further discovery. Infants and toddlers experience physiology as you play games with fingers, touch and name body parts, and talk about eating, drinking, digestion, elimination, breathing, and sleeping ("You drank a lot of water and now your tummy is really full. The cold water feels good going down." "Sheila has toes and Max has toes. Everybody has toes!").

The Environment

The program environment will affect the scope and variety of your science curriculum. An outdoor play area with trees, grass, sand, dirt, water, insects, and other creatures provides a laboratory for science experiences. Earthworms dug from the ground, a millipede discovered beneath the overturned rock, or seedlings growing after a rain are ideal starting places for exploring living things. Children on a seesaw may discover concepts about balance and leverage. The frozen water puddle in the early morning that melts by noon and is miraculously gone as children leave for home provides a chemistry lesson. If you look and listen to children as they interact in the outdoor environment, they will provide you with many ideas for science experiences that you can explore together.

Just as an art area can be modeled after an artist's studio, a science area can be like a laboratory. If an earthworm is brought into the area, a science problem is posed: What does this creature need to survive? Together, you and the children may solve the problem based on your observations or by referring to books or resource people. Tools and materials for exploration can be stored in a science area: magnifying glasses, magnets, dissection equipment, trays, bug boxes, animal cages, tools for manipulating and taking apart a clock or radio, and measuring equipment like scales and rulers.

The area can include ongoing projects such as aquariums, terrariums, animal families, and plants. Learning materials, such as a sink and float game, and picture collections for sorting and describing may be stored and used in the science area. The area can also contain science reference books. In programs for infants and toddlers, special care is needed to make the living plants and animals accessible to view and safe for and from children.

Some appropriate and worthwhile science experiences require moving beyond the walls of the early childhood program. Science learning trips can be as simple as a nature walk in the neighborhood or can involve visits to locations like the zoo, aquarium, preserve, farm, museum of natural science, forest, seashore, or mountains. Whether your trips are nearby and spontaneous or more distant and carefully planned, they will promote more science learning if there is enough time for children to learn by discovery. This is facilitated by allowing small groups of children to visit sites where they can explore and discuss experiences as they occur in an unhurried fashion.

Supporting Learning

It is not necessary to be a scientist to offer science experiences in your classroom, but you do need to appreciate the value of science and be aware of subject matter suitable for young children. Science for young children can, and should, be much more than a fish tank and a rock collection in a corner of the classroom.

Your main role in science education is the preservation and encouragement of the natural curiosity of children. To maintain children's attitude of playfulness toward science you need to view their difficult questions as an opportunity to model the attitudes of the scientist: curiosity, questioning, openness to exploration, and problem solving. Together you will work to figure out how to learn the answers to questions through observation, research, or experimentation.

Children's natural curiosity is the beginning place for your science curriculum, but it is not the end. The framework described above provides you with a tool for thinking about the kinds of experiences that you will provide. When there is a subject about which children are interested, you can plan specific activities. We have observed educators and children conducting experiments on the needs of seedlings (what happens if one is kept in the dark?), the effect of time on a carrot, keeping track of the progress of monarch caterpillars, exploring the environment and needs of earthworms, and composting garbage to make soil for a garden.

In planned or spontaneous science activities, you can guide children's curiosity and help turn a pleasant experience into one that has deeper learning potential. For example, a small group of children looking a squirmy family of baby mice will be delighted by their tiny pinkness and their mother's felicitous care. They may not spontaneously realize that the babies are seeking milk, that their eyes are closed, or that these babies are like many other babies, including human infants, in some ways. Asking children questions like "Why do you suppose the baby mice were squirming?" "What do you think will happen if their mother goes and runs on the wheel?" and "What do the babies remind you of?" encourage thinking and concept development. Part of your role is to find resources (books, people, or media) to expand their knowledge.

Primary children, too, learn best when science continues to be a form of play. This is quite different from a traditional model where children may do "hands-on" experiments only to duplicate the results in the textbook rather than to explore and find out. Wasserman and Ivany's lovely book on science curriculum, *Teaching Elementary Science: Who's Afraid of Spiders?* (1988), describes the *Play-Debrief-Replay* model for teaching sciencing. In this method the teacher sets up a science play center with materials to explore. Children "play"—explore the materials freely, "debrief"—discuss what they have done with a teacher who assists children in reflecting on what they have observed, and then "replay"—try it again with the same materials. As you model an inquiring and respectful attitude toward the world, you help children to think like scientists. Science, rather than being scary or mysterious, is everyday, accessible, infinitely interesting, and definitely worth knowing.

SOCIAL STUDIES

Social studies concerns relationships among people and between people and the world in which they live. It is an umbrella term that includes many fields. In an early childhood program it can involve aspects of: psychology (the

---

Reflect and write about . . .

how science was taught in your schools

How was science taught in the schools of your childhood? What do you remember most vividly? Did these experiences influence what you have done as an adult? How do you use what you learned in your life today?

mind, emotions, and behavior), sociology (society, its development, and organization), cultural anthropology (the way people live in different cultures), economics (how people consume, produce, and deliver goods and services), political science (how people are governed and the use of power to make and enforce decisions), geography (the earth, its features, and the effects of human activity), and history (the events that make up the past of humankind).

You may remember social studies as a dull subject, unrelated to the real world, requiring the memorization of dates, names, and places. If so, your learning may have been fragmented and the relevance of social studies to your life may not have been clear. You may have other memories of interesting and exciting social studies experiences. If so, they were probably taught in pleasant and memorable ways. If your recollections vary it may be because a number of different fields are included in what we call social studies, and there is a wide range of methods by which it is taught.

There is a good deal of interest today in teaching young children the social, political, and economic concepts that have an impact on people's lives. This social studies content goes well beyond the traditional disciplines and includes topics like: understanding feelings; awareness of aging, the elderly, and death; caretaking and compassion; developing positive self-concept; learning about disabilities; racial differences; cultural differences; resisting stereotyping; and cooperation and conflict resolution (Derman-Sparks and A.B.C. Task Force 1989; Edwards 1986; Hopkins and Winters 1990; Kendall 1983; Seefeldt 1993; Sunal 1990).

Social Studies and Development

Effective social studies experiences for young children are relevant to their lives and interests and appropriate to their stage of development. They help children to see some of the signifi-cant patterns in people's lives and the world. Their own lives, families, communities, and environments can provide the first subjects to be explored. In this way social studies is not a subject to be learned in isolation but a part of life and a personal exploration.

The goals of social studies in early childhood education can include helping young children to:

- Accept, appreciate, and respect themselves, other people, and their culture and environment.
- Explore, understand, and experience social aspects of the world that lay the foundation for later comprehension of the social sciences.
- Develop a sense of belonging to and responsibility for their family, community, and environment.
- Develop skills in a range of subject areas.
- Deal with some of the important issues in their lives.

Like math and science, social studies concepts are learned best when they are directly experienced. Knowledge of social aspects of the world, like physical knowledge, must be constructed by children from the materials and experiences that are available to them. This involves taking children out into the world of people and relationships or bringing the world to them. It may take more thought and planning to provide direct experiences with social studies than it does to put out math manipulatives or set up a science corner, but because social studies topics are so vital and meaningful, it is very rewarding.

The Organizing Framework

Social studies content can be structured in many ways. In the public schools it has historically been organized into an "expanding horizon" approach in which children's social studies experiences began with the child, family, and neighborhood and only moved to include other topics like the state, the nation, and the world when children were in the upper elementary grades. In today's world, immigration, technology, travel, and media cause children to experience diverse people and places. It seems certain that this tendency will continue in the future. It is therefore important to help young children to understand and appreciate people from other places and other cultures at an early age.

Social studies content for young children has also been based on the social science fields and on topics that have been regarded as important for young children to learn such as community helpers, self-esteem, and cultural studies. This way of organizing social studies fails to help children to understand relationships between topics.

Social studies experiences for young children must be meaningful. For a number of years we have based social studies content in our classrooms on a curriculum framework that uses the question "Who am I?" to relate social studies learning directly to young children's lives (Feeney and Moravcik 1995). "Who am I?" is a question of vital importance to young children. It can provide the core of the social studies curriculum based on four different aspects of the question:

Who am I as an individual? *(self)*

Who am I in my *family?*

Who am I in my *community?*

Who am I in my *environment?*

The questions are worth posing and exploring because they are universally relevant and have an impact on all children. Every child is an individual and lives in the context of a family, a community, and a geographical location. Social studies experiences based on these questions can contribute to children's understanding and appreciation of the social aspects of the world in which they live, engage children's interest,

involve their minds, and help them to understand themselves, other people and cultures, and the world in which they live.

The questions incorporate the social science disciplines as outlined in Table 14.1.

Who Am I as an Individual? *(Self)*

All children are interested in themselves, so the study of self is meaningful and appropriate. To really understand self, a child must compare and contrast him or herself with others. A growing understanding and appreciation of similarities and differences between people contributes to an emerging positive sense of self as well as awareness and appreciation for others.

The study of self relates to the behavioral science field of psychology. Experiences help children to gain awareness of their own abilities, feelings, and reactions. They can come to understand that it is natural and acceptable to have many feelings, both pleasant and unpleasant, and that everyone has much the same feelings. Related to this area children learn to distinguish fantasy from reality, an important task of the early childhood years.

As children learn about differences in people, they acquire a foundation for later understanding of cultural anthropology. People speak and do things in different ways but have the same basic needs and share a common hu-

TABLE 14.1
Who am I questions and related social science fields

Question	Related social science field	What children can learn
Who am I as an individual? (self)	**Psychology:** mind, emotions, and behavior	What I am like, what I do, and how I feel. How I am similar to or different from others.
	Cultural Anthropology: the way that different groups of people live	The common needs of all people and the different ways that they meet these needs.
	History: the past	How I have changed over time.
Who am I in my family?	**Sociology:** the functioning of human society, its development, institutions, and organization	What my family is like and the things they do with and for each other. How my family is similar to or different from other families.
	Cultural Anthropology: the way that different groups of people live	The common characteristics of all families and the different forms and functions of families.
	History: the past	How my family has changed over time.
Who am I in my community?	**Sociology:** The functioning of human society and its development, institutions, and organization	What my school and neighborhood are like, how people work together, and their roles and responsibilities. What other communities are like.
	Political Science: The government and political institutions and the use of power to make and enforce decisions	How the people in my school and neighborhood make rules, choose leaders, and provide services.
	Economics: The production, distribution, and consumption of goods and services	How the people in my school and community get, share, and use the things they want and need.
	Cultural Anthropology: the way that different groups of people live	The common characteristics of all houses and homes and the different forms and functions of houses and homes.
	History: the past	How my school and neighborhood have changed over time.
Who am I in my environment?	**Geography:** the earth's surface and its natural features, climate, resources, population, and the effects on it of human activity	What the place I live is like. How it is similar to and different from other places.
	Ecology: the interaction and relationships between living things and their environment	How my life is affected by the place I live. How the place I live is affected by people.
	History: the past	How the place I live has changed over time.

Source: S. Feeney and E. Moravcik, *Discovering Me and My World*. (Circle Pines, MN: American Guidance Service, 1995), 3.

manity. From the age of three or four, young children are aware of racial differences and begin to have positive and negative attitudes about them. Since thinking is still based on perception and not on logic, they may believe racial characteristics such as skin color are caused by external factors such as dirt, paint, or exposure to the sun. They do not understand that race is permanent and determined by heritage. Similarly they may understand that being a boy or a girl is mutually exclusive but may not understand that gender is unchanging and based on anatomy. Often they will look at clothes or the length of a person's hair to determine if that person is a boy or a girl.

Attitudes are heavily influenced by the adults in young children's lives. By the age of ten attitudes about race are formed and very resistant to change. Because of this, early childhood is the appropriate time to develop understanding and appreciation of others. Some issues related to culture and ethnicity are difficult for young children to understand. They can begin to develop awareness of prejudice and discrimination in the context of stories and class discussions. Concepts like racism and oppression are quite complex and cannot be readily understood by preschool and kindergarten children.

Who Am I in My Family?

The answers to the question "Who am I in my family?" are central to answering the larger question, "Who am I?" Families determine almost everything about children's day-to-day experience. Because of this, family is a topic of great interest and one that can have a strong emotional impact. Within their families children develop a sense of who they are and who they may become. Their first experiences with nurturing, roles, responsibility, values, culture, conflict, and justice come through families.

The primary purpose for having children engage in the study of family is to help them to

recognize the worth and dignity of their own family. A second goal is to help them begin to appreciate the value of other families. The study of family lays the foundation for later understanding of the social science field of sociology. This includes the study of ways people live together in families, the roles and responsibilities people have in families, and the ways decisions and rules are made.

The study of family helps children to understand that although families may do things in different ways they have the same basic needs and share a common humanity. They can come to appreciate that people in all families have similar needs and ways of living their lives and looking after one another. They come to understand the functions of family, forge a positive sense of their own and other families, and are assisted to become responsible members of their present and future families.

Since culture shapes many things about families, young children learn about cultural anthropology as they explore family patterns, rituals, and celebrations. An understanding of history is developed as children observe change in families over time and learn about the history of their own family. This is an appropriate way for children to learn about history. They can learn about the history of their own family through learning experiences like having their family members write the story of their own birth or arrival in the family.

Figure 10.8 gives examples of a plan for curriculum about families.

Who Am I in My Community?

Young children are intrigued by events and people in the community that they live in. You may notice this as you observe a two-year-old's fascination with the garbage collector, a four-year-old's reenactment of the grocery store checkout, or a six-year-old's careful drawing of a nearby construction site. They are keen observers who come to programs with many experiences, ideas, and attitudes about the way their community functions. They recognize symbols like the flag and conventions like using money. They understand that some people have power and authority. They can understand concepts that are relatively simple when they have concrete experiences through play, hands-on classroom activities, and trips (in Practice box on p. 442).

The study of community is an excellent way to introduce children to the study of social science fields like economics and political science. Children can begin to learn some economics concepts like production and scarcity and political science concepts like authority and rules, citizenship, and democratic decision making. They develop understanding of sociology as they experience interdependence and cooperation in the classroom and neighborhood. They become aware of history as they observe their own school and neighborhood change over time.

The primary purpose for having children engage in the study of community is to help them begin to understand how communities work and to recognize the needs and responsibilities people share when they live and work together. When we vote for an activity, take a trip to the store, divide the snack evenly between children, or pay the fare as we board the bus, we are helping children learn about community.

Who Am I in My Environment?

Where you live shapes your life. It determines what you see. It influences what you eat, the kind of housing you need, the clothing you wear, the transportation you use, your recreational and work opportunities, the ethnic and cultural groups you encounter, and even your attitudes and values.

Young children's immediate environment is their homes, community, and locale. Infants begin to explore the place around them as soon as they become mobile. By the time they attend preschool, they have had many direct experiences that contribute to their understanding of place, and they are ready to learn more. Every location is full of opportunities for investigation. Children will be interested in knowing what their place is like and what makes it special. They will begin to consider how it is the same or different from places they have visited, read about, or seen in films or on television. They can learn that their environment has certain characteristics that affect their lives.

They can also learn that people depend upon and affect places. Children need to understand how important it is to care for the environment, and in doing so they are introduced to the study of ecology. It is not too early for children to become aware of our dependence on the environment and to learn about issues affecting the environment and our role in caring for it.

Children are natural geographers when they explore and try to understand their environment. The attributes of different environments can be experienced through the senses. They revel in the textures, the smells, the sounds, the sights, and the tastes of a place. They are fascinated by weather and seasons. A globe or a map may draw children to talk about place names. They talk excitedly about places they have visited, what they saw, and what they did.

As they learn about these things, children are experiencing geography. Geographers look at places and maps and seek explanations for what they see. They look for patterns in the arrangement and distribution of cities, economics, politics, peoples, transportation, and other phenomena.

Many familiar activities provide a foundation for developing geographical concepts and skills. As you take trips into the world beyond the school walls and represent what you have seen through maps, photographs, and drawings, children are studying geography. We have seen young children studying geography by mapping the school with blocks or on paper, taking a trip to the harbor, creating

During the Trip. Use homemade or commercial clipboards as "tripboards" for sheets with questions or tasks linked to the topic. A tripboard is a way for children to record observations and organize information gathered. They are children's introduction to the scientist's practice of making field notes. Tripboards should match the developmental stage and abilities of children. Four-year-olds might draw a picture of flowers seen at a garden or fruit seen at the market. Children who can write might use a checklist to identify items at the store or tally the numbers and kinds of uniforms at the airport. Ask open questions. Pay attention to what children notice and write down what they are curious about. If possible, take pictures on the trip. If you go with a large group, divide up and provide all adults with a sheet of information and suggestions for questions they might ask children.

After the Trip. Follow-up activities help children learn. Tripboards can be used as references. Children can share tripboard entries. Prediction and inventory charts can be reviewed to validate what was true. Things that were not predicted can be added. Group stories based on tripboards emphasize the sequence of events: What did we do? What did we see? What do you know about now that you didn't know before we took our trip? Tripboard sheets can be used as pages for trip books.

Children can use blocks to recreate a place visited. Bring builders together to review tripboards and plan work based on information. Photograph or sketch structures and file them in portfolios. In dramatic play, children may assume roles based on people they met. Relevant props can be introduced. A brief discussion may serve as the initial point for dramatic play. Other follow-up projects can include writing, art, math, science, and food and cooking activities.

---

imaginary islands out of papier maché, examining relief maps, and looking at a globe to see where a child was going on a vacation (Figure 14.1).

The Environment

Social studies content can contribute to a vital and interesting classroom environment. The block and dramatic play areas are important places for children to act upon themes from the social studies. Writing and art areas in which children can record and report their experiences are important to social studies, as is a library well stocked with many carefully selected books that will enhance and extend social studies themes.

Children learn about social studies as we select what we bring into their environment. What do the books and photographs show? Do they show many kinds of people and places? Do they refute age and gender stereotypes? Social studies is part of your environment when it reflects cultural diversity. The dramatic play area can include multi-racial dolls, culturally diverse clothing, and props for a variety of ages and careers. The classroom can be decorated with fine art posters and photographs that

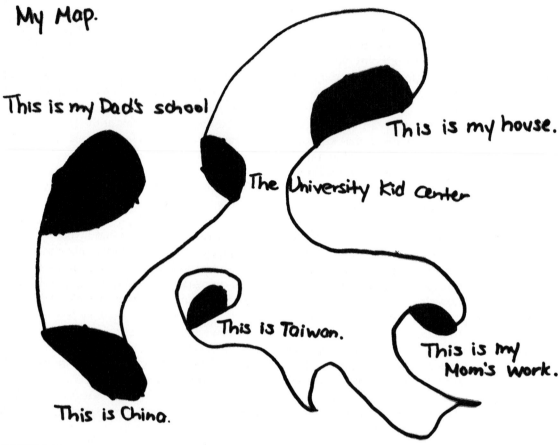

My Map.

This is my Dad's school

This is my house.

The University Kid Center

This is Taiwan.

This is my Mom's work.

This is China.

FIGURE 14.1
Victoria's map of the University Kid Center

reflect many cultures. You may have to seek out props for blocks and puzzles that show diversity of age, sex role, abilities, and race. Similarly materials that extend children's awareness of history, place, and community (such as old photos, firefighter props, and photographs of different environments) support social studies learning.

The world beyond the school is the classroom for social studies. It would be difficult, and a little silly, to teach about the community without ever venturing into it or to study geographic features without every going to look at them. As you help children learn about social studies you will want to make use of the environment surrounding your program; indeed, it will profoundly influence what social studies areas you will pursue. If you work in New York City you will have a different social studies curriculum than if you work in rural North Carolina or the Pacific Northwest. Whether you go on a trip to the shops located on your street or take a walk to the taro patch down the block, you can use the environment beyond the program walls to provide early experiences with economics, anthropology, geography, sociology, and history. At the same time you are helping children to develop understanding and appreciation of themselves, other people, and their environment.

Supporting Learning

It takes thoughtful planning based on knowledge of child development to weave social studies topics into meaningful learning experiences for young children. Basic strategies include direct experiences in the classroom and the world around it, follow up on experiences, and good questions. It is important to be awake to the social studies learning possibilities inherent in the children, families, program, and community.

Because social studies is such a broad area and can be approached in so many different ways, it is an excellent tool for organizing and integrating curriculum. Food preparation, visits from resource people, songs, dances, artifacts (from a family, culture, or place), books, and trips all contribute to concept development in the social sciences. Follow-up activities can occur in every area of the curriculum. Children gain deeper understanding when they recreate and re-experience concepts in blocks, dramatic play, artwork, graphs, child-authored books, songs, and games.

The things that we do, say, and reveal in our expectations make an impact. Children learn about power and rules by the way we treat them. They learn about acceptance and bias from us. You can help children understand sensitive social and political concepts by providing a model of a strong, competent, compassionate, active person regardless of your gender, age, race, or culture. Your own feelings about age, race, class, handicapping conditions, and sex role will communicate to children, and you will want to make sure that you give positive, affirming, anti-bias messages. You can make sure that books, puzzles, pictures, and other educational materials present a similarly non-biased view.

It is important to learn to talk thoughtfully and openly to children when social and political subjects come up and to think ahead about some of the things that you might do and say to help extend their understanding of things that worry and perplex them. A four-year-old in a group that one of us taught brought a newspaper photograph to school that showed a starving child in Cambodia. His concern led to a study of a geographic area and a political situation that we would never have chosen but that interested the group and that led to worthwhile, if sobering, learning.

Older children can use the tools of the social scientist. They can read and record information in a systematic and thoughtful way. You can involve them in planning and teamwork and create more elaborate, product-oriented activities. We once observed a group of second graders in Hawaii who were busy studying the harbor. Some children investigated and set up a supply store (the ship's chandler); others built models of the buildings that they had visited. Some investigated the loading procedures. Others mapped, wrote, and illustrated books about

---

Reflect and write about . . .

how social studies was taught in your schools

How was social studies taught in the schools of your childhood? What do you remember most vividly? Did these experiences influence what you have done as an adult? How do you use what you learned in your life today? What are the implications of these reflections for social studies experiences that you would like to provide for young children?

the harbor. These children used both the tools of the social scientist and the play of children to learn more about a subject that was interesting and meaningful to them.

FINAL THOUGHTS

Exploring how the world works and thinking about why things happen are the processes by which young children learn math, science, and social studies. They learn by doing, observing, and interacting. Through play they will construct and order knowledge. As an early childhood educator you will guide children on this voyage of discovery and help them to understand the world in which they live. As you do so, you support their natural curiosity, develop their love of learning, and help them to be the thinkers and problem-solvers of the future.

PROJECTS

Observe a Program: Use the environment checklist from Chapter Eight to observe an early childhood program. Report on the extent to which the program seems to support children's cognitive development. Suggest some ways to provide additional experiences from which children would benefit.

Design an Environment: Design an ideal early childhood environment for the support of discovery in math, science, and social studies. Describe what you included and why. Share your plan with an early childhood educator and a member of a young child's family and describe their response and suggestions.

Observe a Child: Observe a child for a morning and focus on how he or she is involved in math, science, and social studies. Report on:

- The ways and the circumstances in which the child discovers, inquires, and solves problems.
- How the environment supports the development of inquiry.
- How adults support this child's development of inquiry.
- What might enhance this child's learning.

446

Observe an Educator: Observe an educator for a morning and then interview her or him about how she or he helps young children learn math, science, and social studies. Report on:

- The activities and routines that you saw that contribute to children's learning in these areas.
- Any evidence you saw of planning for math, science, and social studies.
- The educator's goals for children in the development of inquiry.
- The ways in which the goals and what you actually observed match or don't match.

Plan for Inquiry: Write and implement a plan for math, science, or social studies using the activity planning format (Figure 10.7). Report on how children responded and on how you felt about what you did. What worked? What might you do differently next time? How might you expand on this experience for children?

Observe a Program: Observe an early childhood program's approach to math, science, and social studies. Report on the ways that it addresses these areas. Does the program meet children's needs and why? What implications does this have for your future work?

Compare Two Programs: Observe a second early chldhood program's approach to math, science, and social studies. Compare and contrast it with the first program.

Compare Two Ages: Observe two programs, one preschool and one for infants and toddlers or for primary school children. Report on how they are similar and different and how each enhances children's development of inquiry. Talk to the educators about how they make their curriculum choices in this area.

BIBLIOGRAPHY

Barclay, K. H., and W. C. Breheny. (1994). Letting The Children Take Over More of Their Own Learning: Collaborative Research in the Kindergarten Classroom. *Young Children* 49(6):33–39.

Barnat, V. (1993). Teaching Peace. *Young Children* 48(3):36–39.

Barratta-Lorton, M. (1972). *Workjobs.* Menlo Park, CA: Addison-Wesley.

Barratta-Lorton, M. (1976). *Math Their Way.* Menlo Park, CA: Addison-Wesley.

Barratta-Lorton, M. (1979). *Workjobs II.* Menlo Park, CA: Addison-Wesley.

Carlsson-Paige, N., and D. Levin. (1985). *Helping Young Children Understand Peace, War, and the Nuclear Threat.* Washington, DC: National Association for the Education of Young Children.

Charlesworth, R., and D. J. Radeloff. (1991). *Experiences in Math for Young Children.* 2nd ed. Albany, NY: Delmar.

Cliatt, M.J.P., and J.M. Shaw. (1992). *Helping Children Explore Science.* Englewood Cliffs, NJ: Merrill/Prentice Hall.

Cohen, R., and B. P. Tunick. (1993). *Snail Trails and Tadpole Tails: Nature Education Guide for Young Children.* St. Paul, MN: Redleaf Press.

Costa, A. (1974). *Basic Teaching Behaviors.* San Anselmo, CA: Search Models Unlimited.

Derman-Sparks, L., and A. B. C. Task Force. (1989). *Anti-Bias Curriculum: Tools for Empowering Young Children.* Washington, DC: National Association for the Education of Young Children.

DeVries, R., and L. Kohlberg. (1990). *Constructivist Early Education: Overview and Comparison with Other Programs.* Washington, DC: National Association for the Education of Young Children.

Dighe, J. (1993). Children and the Earth. *Young Children* 48(3):58–63.

Edwards, C. P. (1986). *Social and Moral Development in Young Children.* New York: Teachers College Press.

Elkind, D. (1974). *Children and Adolescents: Interpretive Essays on Jean Piaget.* 2nd ed. New York: Oxford University Press.

Feeney, S., and E. Moravcik. (1995). *Discovering Me and My World.* Circle Pines, MN: American Guidance Service.

Flavell, J. H. (1977). *Cognitive Development.* Englewood Cliffs, NJ: Prentice Hall.

Forman, G., and D. S. Kushchner. (1977). *The Child's Construction of Knowledge.* Monterey, CA: Brooks/Cole.

Greenberg, P. (1994). How and Why to Teach All Aspects of Preschool and Kindergarten Math—Part 2. *Young Children* 49(2):12–18.

Harcourt, L. (1988). *Explorations.* Menlo Park, CA: Addison-Wesley.

Harlan, J. (1992). *Science Experiences for the Early Childhood Years.* 5th ed. New York: MacMillan.

Healy, J. M. (1990). *Endangered Minds.* New York: Simon & Schuster.

Healy, J. M. (1992). *Is Your Bed Still There When You Close the Door and Other Playful Ponderings.* New York: Doubleday.

Hill, D. M. (1977). *Mud, Sand, and Water.* Washington, DC: National Association for the Education of Young Children.

Hirsch, E. (1984). *The Block Book.* Washington, DC: National Association for the Education of Young Children.

Holt, B. G. (1977). *Science with Young Children.* Washington, DC: National Association for the Education of Young Children.

Hopkins, S., and J. Winters. (1990). *Discover the World: Empowering Children to Value Themselves, Others and the Earth.* Philadelphia: New Society Publishers.

Judson, S., ed. (1984). *A Manual on Nonviolence and Children.* Philadelphia: New Society Publishers.

Kamii, C. (1982). *Number in Preschool and Kindergarten: Educational Implications of Piaget's Theory.* Washington, DC: National Association for the Education of Young Children.

Kamii, C., and R. DeVries. (1993). *Physical Knowledge in Preschool Education.* New York: Teachers College Press.

Kendall, F. E. (1983). *Diversity in the Classroom: A Multi-cultural Approach to the Education of Young Children*. New York: Teachers College Press.

Mitchell, A., and J. David, eds. (1992). *Explorations with Young Children*. Mt. Rainier, MD: Gryphon House.

Mitchell, L. S. (1934). *Young Geographers*. New York: John Day.

Neugebauer, B., ed. (1987) *Alike and Different: Exploring Our Humanity with Young Children*. Redmond, WA: Exchange Press.

Neugebauer, B., ed. (1989). *The Wonder of It: Exploring How the World Works*. Redmond, WA: Exchange Press.

Nuffield, M. P. (1967). *I Do and I Understand*. New York: Wiley.

Parry, A. (1993). Children Surviving in a Violent World—Choosing Non-Violence. *Young Children* 48(6):13–15.

Perry, G., and M. Rivkin. (1992). Teachers and Science. *Young Children* 47(4):9–16.

Rivkin, M. (1992). Science Is a Way of Life. *Young Children* 47(4):4–8.

Seefeldt, C. (1989). *Social Studies for the Preschool-Primary Child*. 3rd ed. Englewood Cliffs, NJ: Merrill/Prentice Hall.

Seefeldt, C., ed. (1992). *The Early Childhood Curriculum: A Review of Current Research*. New York: Teachers College Press.

Seefeldt, C. (1993). Social Studies: Learning for Freedom. *Young Children* 48(3):4–9.

Severeide, R., and E. Pizzini. (1984). The Role of Play in Science. *Science and Children* 21(8):58–61.

Sunal, C. (1990). *Early Childhood Social Studies*. Englewood Cliffs, NJ: Merrill/Prentice Hall.

Taylor, B. J. (1993). *Science Everywhere: Opportunities for Very Young Children*. Fort Worth, TX: Harcourt Brace Jovanovich.

VanScoy, I. J., and S. H. Fairchild. (1993). It's About Time! Helping Preschool and Primary Children Understand Time Concepts. *Young Children* 48(2):21–24.

Wasserman, S., and G. W. G. Ivany. (1988). *Teaching Elementary Science: Who's Afraid of Spiders?* New York: Harper & Row.

Wichert, S. (1989). *Keeping the Peace: Practicing Cooperation and Conflict Resolution with Preschoolers*. Philadelphia: New Society Publishers.

Wittmer, D. S., and A. Honig. (1994). Encouraging Positive Social Development in Young Children. *Young Children* 49(5):4–12.

PART V

Special Relationships

This final section acquaints you with additional skills you will need as an early childhood educator. Chapter Fifteen, Working with Children with Special Needs, will help you identify and work with children who require special attention. Chapter Sixteen, Working with Families, provides you with information that enables you to work cooperatively with families of young children.

Working with Children with Special Needs

Do what you can with what you have.   Theodore Roosevelt

In this chapter we discuss some things that early childhood educators can do to effectively include children with special needs in their classrooms. We describe some characteristics of children with special needs, and we discuss ways to work effectively with their families.

Everyone has unique needs. As we thought about the children we have known and taught, we realized that there are many ways to have special needs. An individualized approach to teaching is required for every child—the unusually active, the very quiet, the exceptionally intelligent, the child who learns with difficulty, and all of the others. A child from a different culture, a child who speaks another dialect or language, a child who learns like a three-year-old but has the feelings of a six-year-old, a child who wears glasses, a child from a single-parent family, a child with a lisp—all have special needs. In every early childhood program, there are as many special needs as there are children, and every child requires attention to his or her individual characteristics and needs.

Some children face greater challenges in their lives than others. Their needs may be harder to meet and their differences great enough that you may need to learn some new ways to work with them. Working effectively with these children may require extra effort on your part. Although some children may have a significant disability or delay in one or more aspects of growth and learning, others may be coping with a serious illness such as cancer or AIDS. Others may learn more at a more rapid rate than other young children; they, too, require individual attention to be appropriately stimulated and challenged.

Many terms have been used to describe these children—*handicapped, disabled, special-needs, exceptional,* and others. According to McCormick,

> An *exceptional child* is one who is different enough from the "standard" or "average" child to require special methods, materials, services and possibly equipment in order to attain desired learning objectives. Children may differ in the rate at which they learn (compared to age-peers) *or* they may learn in different ways. Some parents and professionals prefer using the term *children with special needs* to describe such children. (McCormick 1994, 95)

Three valuable guidelines to adopt in speaking of children with special needs are: to speak of the child first and his disability second (for example: a child with cerebral palsy, not a cerebral palsy child); to emphasis the child's abilities, not his disabilities; and to refer to a child as having a disability *only* when that information is relevant in a particular situation.

Early identification and intervention can provide needed help for a child when it will be most effective. As an early childhood educator, you get to know each child within the natural context of daily activities. Your knowledge of child development and your observational skills have prepared you to identify a child who seems different in one or more significant ways from other children in your group. For example, we know a teacher who observed that a child in her class often seemed to drift off in daydreams. She was not making progress comparable to that of the other children. When the problem was explored, it was determined that the child suffered from a form of epilepsy. The daydreaming episodes were actually petit mal seizures and her developmental lags were caused by this undiagnosed condition. Medical intervention was needed and was provided. To get children help in a timely fashion, early childhood educators, like this one, must observe children carefully and know the signs of physical, emotional, or mental conditions that can occur among young children. Early intervention can help avoid certain developmental repercussions that may be more difficult to remedy as the child gets older.

In your career, you will have many opportunities to work with children who have special challenges. For some, you are the first to identify them as having special needs, and you will seek diagnosis and assistance for them (as in the situation just described). You are also likely to encounter children who are identified with mild disabling conditions such as hearing impairments, speech impairments, visual impairments, asthma, epilepsy, or diabetes. And it is becoming increasingly common for children with more profound disabilities to be formally or informally included in regular classrooms.

Your training in early childhood education will have prepared you to view each child as

---

Reflect and write about . . .

your experiences with people with disabilities

Recall a relationship or an interaction that you have had as an adult with an individual with a disability. How did you feel? Did this change your ideas about disabled people? How?

unique—with different skills, interests, and needs—but you will need to supplement your general knowledge with additional knowledge of appropriate techniques for dealing with some special needs. Remember that your best source for information about the child will be his or her parents. Pediatricians, therapists, special education teachers, workshops, and classes are other sources of information to help you understand and work with the child.

IDENTIFYING A CHILD WITH SPECIAL NEEDS

Fifteen eager four-year-olds are eating morning snack. It is now the middle of the school year, and they have all learned how to cooperate to make snack a pleasant time. Except Jeremy. Jeremy cruises the edges of the room, stopping briefly to dump a puzzle from a shelf and run his hands through the pieces, only to be distracted by the morning's paintings drying nearby. As he passes a table of children, his attention is again deflected. He tries to squeeze his body onto a chair occupied by another child. The result is a struggle in which Jeremy quickly loses interest. This has disrupted snack for the other children, and Jeremy himself has been unable to participate appropriately in an important classroom activity.

Jeremy's behavior is usually like this. His actions consistently precipitate conflicts with children and adults. He seems unable to engage for any length of time in meaningful activity. As his teacher you might feel irritated and frustrated. You know from your training and experience that many young children are easily distractible at age four. Jeremy's case seems extreme. You suspect that Jeremy may need extra help to cope with the demands of the preschool classroom. You now need to find out what he needs and how you can help him.

For many early childhood educators, a situation similar to this one becomes their first experience in working with a child with special needs—a child whose condition has not been formally identified and who is not yet receiving any appropriate intervention. The behavior of a child like Jeremy may perplex you. Your feelings can cue you to a possible problem and the need for some extra help to best serve the child. Many developmental or psychological issues are first detected when a child enters an early childhood program. You have an opportunity to identify and help these children, who may benefit greatly from a careful evaluation and special services.

What steps do you take when you believe a child in your care has a condition that may require special help? Start by observing the child in some systematic way. Note all the ways the child is functioning appropriately and similarly to other children. Then pinpoint those ways in which his or her behavior and skills are significantly different. Make written anecdotal records, being careful to make objective statements about what you observe the child doing: When is the problem behavior manifested? In what contexts do you see it occurring? Is it age-appropriate behavior? Once you have a more objective view of the child's behavior, you can decide whether the second step—getting help—is necessary.

Share your observations and concerns with a co-worker or supervisor. The support they provide may help you to sort out and organize your thoughts and feelings. Colleagues can also offer useful insights from a more objective point of view. Ask them to make an independent observation of the child. Consider possible modifications of the environment and schedule that might have a positive effect. Sometimes adult expectations for children's behavior are "developmentally inappropriate." The resulting problems are ones that we have created for the children and ourselves.

When you have collected observational data and researched community resources, schedule a conference with the child's family.

Avoid approaching the family by saying "I want to talk with you about Jeremy," or "Jeremy has a problem." This invariably arouses their anxiety to such a degree that open communication becomes difficult, if not impossible. Instead, Ellen Galinsky (1988) suggests making a simple statement about the problem: "Jeremy has some difficulty in getting involved in play activities either alone or with other children. I'd like to talk with you about what we're trying at school and see what works for you at home. Can we get together some afternoon this week to discuss this?"

Start the meeting on a positive note. Parents appreciate hearing what you especially enjoy about their child, so begin with positive comments: Tell them what you see as their child's strengths and capabilities. Then share those observations that caused your concern; show parents the observations you have recorded. Work to build an alliance with the family by asking them if and when they have ever observed similar behavior and how they have handled it. Together you can explore various possibilities and ideas on how to find some answers to the questions you have raised.

Often parents have had concerns but have not known whether or where to turn for help. They may be relieved to learn that you are committed to supporting them as you attempt to find answers to your mutual questions. The information and insight you offer may prompt them to arrange a referral for evaluation of the child, or they may ask the school to arrange for the referral. However, some families may react defensively and reject the possibility that something could be "wrong" with their child. They may prefer to believe it is something the child will outgrow. If this occurs, you can explore other avenues for getting help and support while you continue working with the family. All families need reassurance that the need for extra help for their child does not necessarily mean they or their child will be rejected by you or the program.

Be persistent. As an early childhood educator, you will naturally feel responsible for getting help in meeting the child's needs. But it is not necessary to assume total responsibility. Enlist the support of your colleagues and program administrator. Ask for ideas for community resources that might be helpful to you in supporting the child and family. Both public and private agencies provide screening, evaluation, and consultation for children with special needs. Your own program may be able to provide such services. A good place to begin looking for help is your state or county department of health, human services, or education. If they do not provide the services you require, they can probably direct you to the appropriate agency. Private agencies such as the Association for Children and Adults With Learning Disabilities or children's hospitals may also be able to provide assistance.

Reflect and write about . . .

your own abilities and challenges

Think about your own abilities and challenges (the things that were hardest for you). How have they affected your life? How they did they influence your childhood experiences? What do you wish your teachers had known? What are the implications of these experiences for your work with young children?

INCLUDING CHILDREN WITH SPECIAL NEEDS IN EARLY CHILDHOOD PROGRAMS

Passage of federal legislation (P.L. 94–142) in 1975 marked the beginning of an alliance of families of children with special needs and professionals and other advocates in the field of special education. This law (now the Individuals with Disabilities Education Act, or IDEA) mandates a free and appropriate education, including special education and related services (for example, transportation and therapy) for all children (ages three to twenty-one) with disabilities. The law states that educational services are to be provided in the "least restrictive environment." It reflects a strong commitment to educating each child in the school and classroom that the child would attend if he or she did not have a disability.

Because the terms *mainstreaming, integration,* and *inclusion* have sometimes been used interchangeably, you may have the impression that they are synonyms—that they all refer to the practice of providing educational services for children with disabilities and other special needs in regular education programs. This is not quite accurate. *Mainstreaming* refers to placing children with disabilities in programs and classes with their peers who do not have disabilities. There is not necessarily any planning or support for the children and the staff in the setting. *Integration* also refers to placing children with disabilities in educational settings with their peers who do not have disabilities. However, with integration, there is typically some planning and support for the children and the staff. *Inclusion* is more complex. It differs from the traditional ways of providing integrated services. It is more than merely placing a child in a regular early childhood class or program. Inclusion involves making modifications (in the curriculum and the learning environment) to enhance and enrich the learning experiences of children with special needs in the

same way that you enhance and enrich the learning experiences of their typically developing peers.

These practices are guided by the assumption that since all children differ in abilities, interests, and needs, classrooms can be designed to provide learning experiences for every child. They are also based on the view that all children benefit by having children with a range of abilities together in the classroom. Children with special needs benefit from the modeling of normal peers and from expectations that they can do many of the things that their peers can do. The other children in a group benefit by learning that children who may appear different at first are like them in many ways and can be good playmates. It can also be a valuable lesson in caring and helping.

You may have a child with a disability placed in your classroom. If a child already in your classroom is identified as having special needs, he or she may remain there. If you know you will have a child with special needs in your classroom, the suggestions in In Practice may be helpful.

Preparing for Inclusion

Before the child with special needs enters your classroom, reflect on how you can create the best possible experience for this child and for the others in your group. Think about how you can help the group understand and accept a child with special needs. How can you best work with the child's family? How can you get special training that will help you to work effectively with this child? Who can help you learn special skills that might be required, such as using sign language or responding to a seizure? You may also want to explore the possibility of finding volunteer assistance or reducing your class size so that you can continue to provide every child with a quality program.

Ask yourself, "Who is this child as a person? What are his or her likes, dislikes, learning

---

IN PRACTICE

Recommendations for Including a Child with Special Needs

- Learn about a child by talking with his or her family members. They will be your best source of information about the child's strengths and needs.
- Consult with the child's doctor, therapists, or teachers who have worked with the child for additional information. Ask whether the child is taking medication and if there are side effects. Ask what special classes or forms of therapy the child participates in, and find out if there are precautions, limitations, or requirements you should know about.
- Maintain regular communication with the family and other specialists who are working with the child.
- Find out what services will be available to support your work with the child.
- Ask yourself questions like, "How can I make group time relevant to this child and also meet the needs of the other children?"
- Brainstorm with the experts and consultants on how you can best support the development of this child.
- Be flexible and open to learning new things about children and about yourself.

---

style, friends, and personal qualities, and what can I do to support his or her development?" This approach reminds you that children are more alike than different—a disability or special need is only one characteristic of a person. For example, Amanda wears a brace on her leg. When she sits on the floor to work a puzzle or stands at an easel to paint, your first response will be to her competence at working the puzzle or the beauty of her painting. When she is on the playground and cannot run or climb like the other children, you will help her find alternatives. Your focus needs to be on what she *can* do, not on what she cannot do.

You may find yourself encountering feelings about a child with special needs that you are not "supposed" to have. A friend of ours told us about Kevin, a child with a neurological impairment who drooled continuously. Our friend, an excellent preschool teacher, was sur-

prised to find herself feeling repulsed by Kevin's drooling. It brought up childhood memories of another youngster who had been teased and tormented by other children, including herself, as the neighborhood "dummy." Our friend took care to spend extra time with Kevin, made an effort to see him as a whole child, and eventually found that she not only forgot about her response to his drooling but also deeply treasured this child's sense of humor and his affection for her. She also worked hard to help the other children in her class accept Kevin—something you want to do for every child in your group.

If you were the teacher of Jeremy, the child we described at the beginning of this chapter, you might find yourself overwhelmed and exhausted. It might be difficult to keep from reacting negatively to such an unfocused, perpetually moving child. Yet it is important to do your best to remain positive and supportive, for we know that children with attention deficits often develop low self-esteem, become negative, do very badly in school, and may develop symptoms of emotional disturbance when they are in nonsupportive environments.

It is also important to remember that you must balance the needs of an individual child with those of the entire group. Occasionally a child with special needs may demand so much of your time that you find yourself in an ethical dilemma: The needs of the individual child are in conflict with the needs of the group. If the situation is actually harmful to the safety and welfare of the other children, it will be necessary to find help or to locate a more appropriate setting for the child. One preschool we know has made arrangements with the special education department of the state university to provide student volunteers to assist gifted and disabled children in their setting. Even if your school is not located near a college or university, you may be able to find volunteers through a public service agency or club.

Preparing the other children in your group for the inclusion of a child with special needs requires sensitivity on your part. A simple explanation of the disability with some examples to which they can relate a personal experience is probably the best method. You might say about a child with an expressive language problem, for example, *"Mark has trouble saying what he wants to say sometimes. Do you ever want to tell someone something and the words come out all mixed up?"*

As much as possible you will want to treat child with special needs just as you do any other child in the group. Making the child appear too different is not a good idea because other children may then become either excessively helpful and overprotective or may exclude the child, believing he or she is not capable of participating. You can help young children understand that no one can do everything and that every one of us has strengths and weaknesses. By demonstrating to children that all of us need the opportunity to try, you enable them to see that when we do things on our own, we have a better chance to acquire skills and competencies. Show the children in your class specific ways they can include a child with a disability in their play. For example, you might encourage them to help a child with little vision feel the shape of an elaborate block structure and then to give verbal guidance so that the child can place blocks in the structure.

Answer children's questions about disabilities as honestly and directly as you can. Help them understand any differences they observe. You could say, "Rose wears a hearing aid so that she can hear us when we talk to her." With the child's permission, other children may want to try the hearing aid. Or you may be able to ask a speech therapist to bring some hearing aids for children to try and to explain how they work.

Be ready to assure other children that a disability isn't "catching." Some children may initially laugh at or ridicule any child who is different. Remember that this response is fueled by their own embarrassment. It provides you with an opportunity to talk about the wide range of differences among people and the value of helpful and respectful relationships. Early childhood educators report time and again that the caring relationships developed among the children are an overwhelmingly positive outcome of inclusion. Your warm, accepting attitude will provide a powerful model for the development of these relationships.

Modifying the Program

When you work with a child who has an identified disability, begin by getting to know the child as an individual. Observe and find out the child's likes and dislikes, abilities, interests, and areas in which help is needed. It is not necessary to become an expert on the causes, symptoms, and nature of that particular disability. Although that knowledge may help you deal with your anxiety, it does not help you to know the child. No two children with the same disability are alike. There are, however, some sound strategies that will help you to work with a child with special needs in your program.

Play is the primary vehicle for learning for all young children. Sometimes teachers get so concerned with remedial tasks that they forget that *all* children need opportunities for play. Play is particularly important for children who have disabilities because it is through play that they experience those feelings of mastery, resourcefulness, and competence that are so crucial for development of a positive self-concept.

To facilitate play, provide children who have disabilities with support and guidance. This may include helping them cope with fear of unfamiliar experiences. Allow them additional time to develop comfort and competence in play situations and assist them in learning specific play skills they may not have developed. You may need to include more time for direct teaching of play skills and take a more

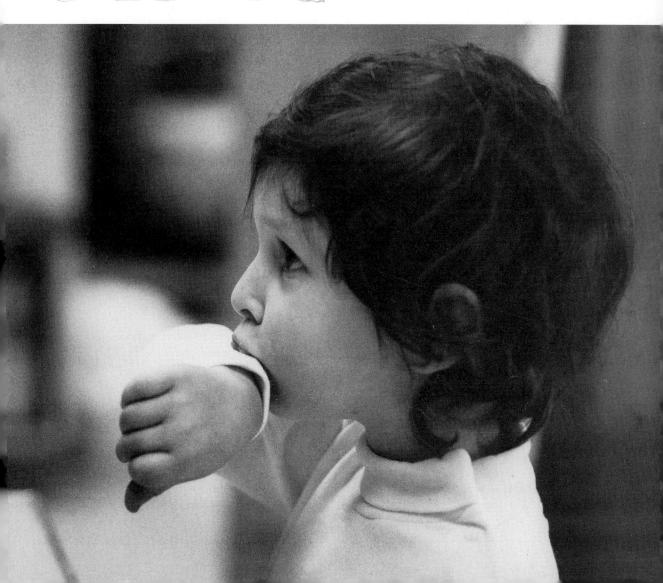

active role in helping them strengthen these newly developing skills.

Children with special needs, like all children, need opportunities to engage with a variety of both open-ended and specific-purpose materials. Clay, paint, and blocks stimulate exploration and creative play. More defined activities such as lotto, puzzles, and pegboards provide experiences in developing and strengthening specific skills and problem-solving strategies. Some materials can be easily adapted for use by children with disabilities. For example, yarn or masking tape wrapped around pencils and marking pens makes them easier to hold and use.

A daily routine that includes a variety of learning experiences is just as important to a child with special needs as it is to other children. Free play and teacher-directed times, child and teacher-chosen activities, large as well as small groups all provide valuable opportunities for learning.

If necessary, plan individual sessions with the child with special needs on a regular basis. The focused attention of an adult may help the child, and it allows you to concentrate on the child's particular interests and needs. You may need to enlist help from volunteers or support from your co-workers to allow you to schedule this individual time.

Planning

Your knowledge of what is developmentally appropriate for young children in general will guide your planning as you decide what materials and activities to use, how to introduce them, and what responses you will expect. For some children, especially those who are intellectually impaired, a task analysis approach in planning is a useful tool. This involves breaking down tasks or skills into their component parts and teaching them separately as a series of subskills, not unlike the way you slowly help a toddler learn to pull up his or her underpants.

You may find it helps to break down such tasks as putting on clothes and going to the bathroom for certain children who require practice with each subskill for a period of time before they can succeed with the overall activity. You can attend a special education class or workshop to learn about task analysis.

Observation supplemented by data from assessment instruments can help your planning. They enable you to identify a child's strengths and weaknesses and help you discover the best conditions and strategies for supporting learning. You can then understand where the child experiences difficulty and will be able to set objectives and design activities that will help you meet those needs. Co-workers or volunteers may be needed to free you to take the time necessary to do systematic observation.

Teaching Strategies

In many ways, the teaching strategies in early childhood education and care programs are effective in working with special needs. With *all* children it is effective to:

- Respond to their interests.
- Focus on what they are *intending* to communicate rather than their actual words.
- Arrange the learning environment (including materials and activities) to promote engagement and interactions with peers.
- Use open-ended and provocative questions to assist them in interacting successfully with people and materials.
- Use modeling and assist them to learn through observation and interaction with their peers.

We have found the following general strategies useful in our work with children with special needs. For highly distractible children, you can control the amount of stimulation by simplifying the task or presenting only one part at a time. Keep transitions short within and be-

Reflect and write about . . .

your experiences with children with special needs

Think about the ways that disabled children were a part of your early school experiences. How do you think your teachers felt about these children? How did you feel? What implications does this have for your teaching?

tween activities. Be sure that all procedures are planned and materials organized so that long lapses can be avoided. Include many opportunities for individual and small group activities. Large group activities may be over stimulating and require more waiting than some children can tolerate. Help these children to focus on the task at hand by using attention-getting words such as *look, listen,* or *watch me* and allow children to touch and manipulate materials.

For children with communication disabilities, be especially careful to pay attention to children's efforts at communication whenever and wherever they occur. If the child has difficulty with expressive language, listen closely to decipher communication. Ask to make sure you have understood what the child meant: "You have a bunny like that at your house?" If a child has difficulty understanding language, simplify your speech somewhat. Encourage children to talk about their feelings during times of stress, frustration, or excitement. And encourage talking among children. When a child shares with you or calls your attention to something, acknowledge this and sometimes redirect the communication to another child, "Could you tell Willie what you just told me?"

When helping children to develop concepts, focus on contrast by giving lots of positive and negative instances. For example, if you are helping children to develop the concept of a circle, present contrasting shapes so children can see "circle" versus "not circle," and present

many real-life examples such as a bracelet, saucer, hula hoop, and so on. Present examples of the concept throughout the day: Join hands to make a circle at group time, eat round crackers for snack, make circular vegetable prints during art. In general, teach much the same way you would with other children, but keep in mind that you may need to spend a longer period of time with some special-needs children.

CHARACTERISTICS OF CHILDREN WITH SPECIAL NEEDS

The Individuals with Disabilities Education Act (IDEA) defines over a dozen disability categories. Despite widespread criticism over several decades, the practice of grouping children by disability is still in use and is likely to continue until a better system for determining who is in need of and eligible for special services is established. We have organized this section of the chapter according to characteristics of disabilities to help you identify children who may need special assistance. We want to caution you not to discuss a child as belonging to a disability group. Recognize that the characteristics observed in children in one category are often very similar to those of children in some or all other categories. Children with a similar diagnosis often differ from each other as much as they differ from children in other categories. Refrain from falling into the trap of referring to any child by a label. Refer to children by their names.

Disabilities vary widely. The severity will determine to what degree special techniques, equipment, or materials will be needed to support the child's development. In general, children with mild and sometimes moderate disabilities can be fairly easily included in regular programs. Others may have challenges that will require considerable support to enable them to benefit from inclusion.

Four areas of functioning may be limited by disabling conditions: mobility, communication, information acquisition, and information processing. Children may have problems in more than one of these areas. In addition to knowledge about children with disabling conditions, you will also need special knowledge and skills to deal with children who are gifted, children who come from families experiencing unusual stresses, and children who have been physically, sexually, or psychologically abused or neglected.

How to Identify Different Kinds of Special Needs

An early childhood educator may be the first person in a child's life to recognize the possible existence of abuse, giftedness, a physical disability, sensory impairment, emotional problem, speech difficulty, or developmental delay. Major impairments are almost always detected by physicians or parents prior to the time children enter early childhood programs. Although you should be alert to physical and behavioral characteristics that suggest the need for evaluation, it is not your role to diagnose a disability. This chapter gives a very brief overview of the information you need in order to recognize the signs and symptoms of the various disabilities. It is not comprehensive. An excellent reference book is *Children with Special Needs in Early Childhood Settings* by Paasche, Gorrill, and Strom (1990). As the authors point out, a single

symptom such as poor coordination can have many causes.

Children with Physical Disabilities

Children with physical disabilities may be unable to control or easily move their bodies. They may have limitations because of an injury or a missing limb or have difficulty coordinating body movements. Problems associated with pregnancy and birth, hereditary and genetic factors, injury, or disease may cause a physical disability. Some children who are physically disabled may also have additional problems such as hearing loss or mental retardation (In Practice).

Encourage a child with a physical disability to participate as fully as possible in your program. See suggestions for designing the learning environment and supporting learning in Chapter Eleven, The Physical Development Curriculum. Some adaptations of your classroom environment may make this easier. Adjustments of table height or easel height, the relocation of certain supplies and toys to make them more accessible, and the rearrangement of furniture are some things to consider. Consult with the family and the physical therapist before you make changes. Ask about what adaptations can be made to standard equipment like tricycles to enable the child to engage in as many regular activities as possible. Let the child discover abilities and limitations by trying activities, and encourage independence through teaching self-help skills, like dressing or eating.

Consult with the family and therapist to learn about activities the child enjoys that can be used or adapted for use with the whole group. For example, body awareness activities will be helpful in improving all the children's appreciation for their bodies. Emphasize activities that give a child with a physical disability the opportunity to play as typically as possible with other children. Young children are often fascinated by special equipment, like walkers

---

IN PRACTICE

Some Characteristics of Children with Physical Impairments

Children who are mildly or moderately physically impaired may:

- Stumble and bump into things often.
- Have difficulty with large muscle activities such as crawling, climbing stairs, or riding a tricycle.
- Have difficulty with activities involving eye-hand coordination, such as stringing beads, building a tower of blocks, cutting, or drawing (also a sign of possible visual impairment).
- Have speech problems because of inability to control their breathing and the muscles needed in articulation.
- Have difficulty chewing or swallowing.
- Show a lack of stamina and display overall weakness.

---

or wheelchairs, used by a classmate. Check with the family—they may be willing for the children to satisfy their curiosity by trying out the equipment.

Children with Visual Impairments

During the early childhood years, all children are learning to coordinate, control, and focus their eye muscles. Visual impairments are often not diagnosed until a child enters an early childhood program. A child whose inability to see interferes with easy participation in daily activities is considered visually impaired. A child with partial sight may have a visual acuity problem that is correctable with glasses. Few children are completely unable to see. Many can see light and dark areas or broad shapes, but not details. Some have peripheral rather than frontal vision.

The development of children whose blindness occurred after birth more closely resembles that of other children, but the development of children who were blind at birth tends to be much slower. Because they lack visual stimulation, which encourages exploration of the environment, children with visual impairments often lag in physical development. Many large and small muscle activities are learned by imitation: Children watch and then copy the movement. But movement will be perceived as dangerous when the consequence might be getting hurt by bumping into something. Fear of movement may in turn affect social development as young children's social play is generally physically active and centered on toys. Not surprisingly, children with visual impairments may be advanced in speech and language and may excel at listening and memory activities (In Practice).

There are many ways to help a child with a visual impairment enjoy and benefit from your program. Provide good overall lighting and try to avoid having areas of glare or deep contrasts between light and shade. Keep the room arrangement and traffic patterns simple and uncluttered, and when a change is needed, have children participate in making it. To introduce an activity or game, use detailed description to accompany your actions. Keep the child close to you for group activities such as action songs, fingerplays, and stories. Provide the child with

---

IN PRACTICE

Some Characteristics of Children with Visual Impairments

Children with vision problems may:

- Rub their eyes excessively, squint, or frown.
- Shut or cover their eyes or tilt or thrust their head forward.
- Hold objects close to their eyes and show difficulty with tasks requiring close use of eyes.
- Stumble over objects.
- Be unable to identify distant things.
- Be irritable or blink frequently when doing close work.
- Have inflammation or other eye problems such as swelling or sties.

---

larger toys and materials to which you have added either different textures or sounds. Help the child learn to look in the direction of the person speaking. Remember that social cues such as facial expressions that express feelings may not be seen, so you will need to assist with verbal descriptions.

Children with Hearing Impairments

Children are considered hearing impaired when they have difficulty understanding and responding to speech or sounds (In Practice). The problem may be in perceiving the volume or clarity of sound. When children cannot hear,

---

IN PRACTICE

Some Characteristics of Children with Hearing Impairments

Children with hearing impairments may:

- Have trouble paying attention, especially in group activities.
- Not answer when called.
- Get confused about directions or not understand them at all.
- Frequently give the wrong answer to questions.
- Often say "what?" or look confused by questions, statements, or directions.
- Have undeveloped speech, substitute sounds, omit sounds, or have poor voice quality.
- Avoid people; prefer to play alone.
- Get tired early in the day.
- Turn one side of the head towards sounds, indicating a hearing loss in one ear.

eye contact and thus attract and hold attention. In a group activity, have the children sit in a circle, so all faces are visible. Address the child by name, speak clearly in a normal voice, and use simple phrasings but whole sentences. When a child seems not to understand, rephrase your sentence instead of repeating it. Use visual clues and gestures to aid understanding. Remember, though, that the child needs time to direct attention to an object or gesture and then look back at you. Encourage participation in activities like dramatic play and puppetry. If the child is receiving speech therapy, ask the therapist for ideas for games you can adapt for group. If the child uses a hearing aid, ask the family to teach you how it works and how to care for it—you can't tell just by looking whether the hearing aid is actually functioning!

Children with Speech-Language Disorders/Delays

Problems with speech and language occur quite often in young children. Some lack of fluency is part of normal speech development; so are errors in articulation. However, speech and language problems may be associated with one or more of a variety of factors: speaking another language, a hearing impairment, a cleft palate, autism, cerebral palsy, attention deficit disorder, an emotional problem, or a learning disability. Some of these are permanent; some may be temporary (In Practice).

Children with receptive language problems have difficulty understanding the meaning of words or the way words are put together. Children with auditory processing problems may be unable to tell the difference between speech sounds (auditory discrimination), may be unable to isolate the important sounds from a noisy background, may have trouble remembering what they hear, may confuse the correct order of a series of sounds, and may consequently have problems forming concepts. Children who lack the ability to use language effec-

even with the use of a hearing aid, they are said to be deaf. Children who are hard of hearing have a permanent but less severe hearing loss in which the use of a hearing aid is helpful. Damage to the outer or middle ear (conductive loss) and damage to the inner ear or the nerves that carry sound to the brain (sensori-neural loss) can occur before or after birth. Sometimes the loss is temporary, caused by a middle ear infection, but frequent, untreated infections of this nature can cause permanent hearing loss.

When children cannot hear a language model, they have difficulty learning to speak. Then spoken words may be unclear and difficult to understand. The rhythm and voice quality of their speech may sound unusual. Social interactions can be hindered when it is difficult for children to express feelings or needs or to have others understand them. Cognitive skills may be slower to develop if hearing loss has resulted in a language delay.

Whether a child's hearing loss is temporary or permanent, there are techniques that you can use to help. Place yourself facing the light source and at the child's eye level to establish

IN PRACTICE

Some Characteristics of Children with Speech or Language Disorders/Delays

Children with speech-language difficulties may:

- Not talk by age two.
- Not speak in two- or three-word sentences by age three.
- Be very difficult to understand after age three (still relying mostly on vowel sounds and omitting the beginnings and endings of words).
- Use poor sentence structure after age five, such as "Me school go."
- Stutter after age five.
- Have poor voice quality.
- Have difficulty hearing speech sounds.
- Have difficulty understanding what is said.
- Appear shy and embarrassed when speaking.
- Have trouble following directions, describing things, using correct parts of speech, or putting words into sentences, compared with other children.

tively (a problem with expressive language) have difficulty verbalizing ideas, selecting appropriate words, or using correct grammatical structures.

Children with speech problems have trouble being understood. There are many normal articulation errors in preschool children as, for example, substituting an *f* sound for *th* (*wif* for *with*). When these articulation difficulties persist beyond the age of five, or if a child's speech is characterized by unusual pitch, volume, or voice quality, an evaluation by a speech therapist is in order.

When a child you work with has a speech or language problem, you want to be careful not to interrupt, rush, or pressure him or her. Model correct language, using simple constructions and vocabulary, and expand the child's own comments. Provide many opportunities for the child to enjoy language use, build on learning activities like field trips, and incorporate songs, rhymes, and chants into daily routines.

Children with Cognitive Deficits

Although all children learn at different rates, some children have a significantly slower overall rate of learning and development. During the preschool years these children appear much younger than their chronological age and may have difficulty learning skills and developing concepts. They may be unable to remember things that they have already learned or be unable to use information to solve problems in new or unfamiliar situations. Children who have cognitive deficits may have trouble developing and using language, playing cooperatively, initiating activities or interactions, and learning to function independently (In Practice). Cognitive deficits, often called *retardation,* can occur before, during, or after birth.

Children with mild cognitive deficits may seem little different than the youngest children in an age group. Children with moderate deficits will have greater difficulties in self-help skills,

---

IN PRACTICE

Some Characteristics of Children with Cognitive Deficits

Children with mild to moderate cognitive deficits may:

- Be unable to follow directions that contain more than one or two steps.
- Have a short attention span for their age.
- Not be able to choose an activity independently.
- Have a tendency to imitate rather than create.
- Have poor eye-hand coordination.
- Be slow to learn simple games or classroom routines.
- Be very slow in learning language.

---

motor development, social skills, and language development. They may tend to behave like children about half their age. Children with severe impairment will have trouble functioning in most areas of development. Since there is no certain way to discover the cognitive competency of a young child, do not prejudge what a child can do and can't do. The best approach is positive: Encourage the child to try.

When you have a child in your group who has some degree of cognitive deficit, relate as you would to a slightly younger child. Give directions one step at a time, simplify and guide daily routines, and allow more time to make transitions. Use shorter sentences and simplified vocabulary. Spend time showing a new activity, and use a multi-sensory approach to teaching. Repetition of a demonstration may be needed until an activity is mastered. After that, provide many opportunities for a child to successfully practice the new skill. Encourage growing independence by emphasizing self-help skills.

Children with Learning Disabilities and Attention Deficit Disorder

The term *learning disabilities* is used to refer to a variety of problems exhibited by children with normal intelligence but below age-level academic functioning. Children with learning disabilities tend to be extremely uneven in their development. For example, a child may have good motor skills but have a considerable delay in language. In school-age children, these inconsistencies often lead to their being accused of not trying hard enough or of being lazy, uncontrollable, or stubborn. During the early childhood years, learning disabilities are difficult to identify. Your knowledge of the normal developmental range of behaviors and skills may help you to assess whether a child should be evaluated for a possible learning disability .

Other children will exhibit the inability to attend. They may show impulsive behavior beyond what seems developmentally appropriate and an inability to focus and stay on task. Sometimes these children have been called *hyper-kinetic* or *hyperactive,* or been said to have minimal brain dysfunction. These symptoms are now referred to as *attention deficit disorder (ADD).* This behavior occurs more frequently in boys and tends to appear by age three. Children with an attention deficit disorder are easily excitable, have trouble waiting for explanations or taking turns, and can seldom pause long

IN PRACTICE

Some Characteristics of Children with Attention Deficit Disorders

Children with attention deficit disorders may:

- Be impulsive, acting quickly without thinking about the consequences.
- Have a short attention span, unable to concentrate on one task or activity long enough to complete it, or switch from activity to activity without seeming to gain satisfaction.
- Have difficulty organizing and completing work and lack direction.
- Be distractible, have trouble paying attention to the task at hand, and be unable to redirect attention to original task once distracted.
- Be constantly in motion even when surroundings are quiet and be restless and fidgeting all the time.

---

enough to relax, watch, or listen. Many cannot tolerate physical restriction and may have trouble getting along with other children. Jeremy, the child in the example at the beginning of this chapter, may be suffering from this disorder. Be careful not to assume that every active young child has an attention deficit disorder. Children with this problem are identifiable because of the extremes of their behavior.

Attention deficit disorder is a behavioral description that can be the result of a variety of causes, including perinatal insult, childhood trauma, psychosocial stressors, or learning disabilities, or any combination of these. Not all children with learning disabilities will suffer from ADD. Some children with ADD will be hyperactive; others will not.

You may find it helps to provide a very clear structure for a child with ADD. Simplify the physical environment and reduce visual stimulation to assist the child to focus on a task. Define the child's work or play area and position yourself nearby so you can offer assistance or encouragement. Make picture charts showing the sequence of a daily routine, such as getting ready for nap. Warn the child of changes in schedule and state your expectations for behavior clearly. A child with an attention deficit disorder is usually quite disruptive in the classroom and needs a professional evaluation to determine the best course of action.

Children with Emotional Problems

Frequent and severe emotional difficulties can result from a number of different causes, including inadequate nurture, abuse and neglect, physical injury, or biochemical imbalance. Some stressful life events such as death, divorce, separations, moving, and community violence can provoke temporary signs of emotional distress. Emotional problems interfere with establishing meaningful relationships, with learning, and with the development of a positive sense of self.

In mild and moderate cases, children with emotional problems tend to be more aggressive, unhappy, anxious, or withdrawn than their peers. Children with severe problems are more extreme in their reactions and may require specialized care. Their behavior may be characterized by withdrawal, anxiety, or aggression. Unusual behaviors such as self-

mutilation, rocking, running with arms flapping, extreme fearfulness, withdrawal, or total loss of self-control may be displayed.

If you have a child in your group who seems to require an unusual amount of adult supervision and assistance, or one who is overlooked because he or she so rarely interacts with others, carefully document your observations and share your concerns with the family. A child may exhibit symptoms of emotional disturbance in response to highly stressful situations that will dissipate with time or as a learned behavior pattern requiring more aggressive long-term intervention. In any case, the child may benefit from treatment if it is available.

In today's society where there is lack of adequate of support for families and increased societal violence, especially in the inner cities, we are seeing more disturbed children with behavioral problems in early childhood programs. Help for these children and their families may be difficult to find, but there may be programs and services available if you are persistent in seeking help for the troubled child and family.

A child with emotional problems may be difficult for you to handle, not only because the child is so intense but also because there is so much disagreement among experts about the causes, classification, and treatment of these conditions. You will need someone to help you understand and work with such a child. If it is possible, have one or more mental health professionals available to your program for consultation.

Children Who Have Been Abused or Neglected

A child who is abused or neglected has another kind of special need that you should learn to identify and to which you need to respond. Child abuse is defined as intentional physical and/or emotional maltreatment of a child by an adult, usually a person responsible for the child's welfare. Adults with poor coping skills may maltreat children when confronted with too much stress in their lives. Commonly found stress factors include low income, inadequate housing, unemployment, absence of support systems, a disabled family member, and unwanted pregnancy. Family conflict, substance abuse, and mental health problems often exacerbate these situations. The abusing adult may

IN PRACTICE

Some Characteristics of Abused or Neglected Children

Children who have been abused and neglected may:

- Be overly compliant and passive or show extreme avoidance of confrontation with children and adults.
- Be extremely demanding, aggressive, and filled with rage.
- Be prematurely competent; for example, they may prepare meals, take the bus alone, or care for younger siblings when it is neither developmentally nor culturally appropriate to do so.
- Be extremely dependent.
- Be developmentally delayed or regressed with infantile behavior.

have been abused as a child and thus learned to use physical, sexual, or verbal violence as a means to control others and to release tensions and frustrations (In Practice).

When you see symptoms of emotional disturbance in a child and observe physical injuries such as burns, unusual bruises, or marks at different stages of healing, you need to look more closely. Observation of children's imaginative play may provide additional clues. Children often reveal intense feelings and concerns in their play themes. You may see a child acting out the violent adult, with another child or a doll as a passive or powerless victim. This kind of play might also be a child's way of trying to work through the many instances of violence and sexuality that are a large part of today's television fare.

In cases of neglect, a child's attendance may be inconsistent, or arrival and pickup may be late. The child may appear hungry, underweight, unwell, dirty, or inappropriately dressed. Some neglected children demonstrate unusual competence in caring for themselves and assume adult responsibilities. This type of behavior often indicates that a child has had to learn survival skills such as dressing and feed-

ing without assistance because a nurturing adult has not been available. Keep in mind that though we value independence in children, it is not developmentally appropriate for a three-year-old to prepare breakfast every morning or for a four-year-old to walk to school alone each day. Neglected children may have difficulty playing cooperatively with other children or handling changes in the daily routine.

A major signal for concern is when children show precocious sexual awareness in play or talk. This may be the outward evidence of sexual abuse, such as being made to observe adult sexual behavior or of being the unintended witness of sexual acts. Today this may also be related to inappropriate television viewing. You will want to be aware of the tone and pattern of adult-child interactions. Does the child seem frightened or intimidated when with a particular family member?

When family members withhold emotional support and positive attention or make strong verbal attacks, characterized by threats of physical harm, name-calling, or profanity directed at the child, you must consider the likelihood that the child is being subjected to emotional abuse.

Discipline and child abuse are part of a continuum. This makes it difficult sometimes to discern whether there is simply a difference in values and cultural norms or whether there is real abuse to the child. A director we know of a center in a community with a large Pacific island population had to carefully examine her criteria for what behaviors she would consider physically abusive to children in light of the fact that a physical response to children's misbehavior was almost universally accepted by that community. Early childhood educators may incorrectly identify children as abused or neglected when in reality what they are seeing is culturally sanctioned or the result of family poverty or lack of education. Although the consideration of cultural differences may enable us to accept a wider range of discipline strategies, we should never use cultural diversity as a way to excuse behaviors that cause harm to children.

Early childhood educators have a professional obligation and are mandated by law to report suspected cases of child abuse or neglect. It is your responsibility as a professional and an advocate for children to be aware of the indicators of abuse and neglect and to report suspected cases to the appropriate agency so that the child and family can receive the help they need as soon as possible. The program in which you work should have a policy of informing families of the program's reporting obligation as part of their orientation to the program. Staff should receive written procedures for how to report suspected cases. If your program does not have these policies and procedures, urge the administration to develop some immediately. Offer to help and get other staff members involved. Refer to the NAEYC Code of Ethical Conduct (Appendix 1) for ethical guidelines and seek the support of trained specialists. With so much public attention focused on reported cases of child neglect and abuse, especially sexual abuse, many communities have created special task forces or ex-

panded services to deal with the problem. Be sure you know what is available in your community. Remember that we can use our child protection laws not just as a deterrent to child abuse and neglect, but also as an occasion for educating families about how to interact with their children in constructive ways and about the risks to the child (and to them) of excessively harsh behaviors.

The child who has been abused has special needs, many of which the program setting can meet if there is thoughtful planning. To rebuild a healthy self-concept and the ability to trust adults, extra time and attention must be devoted to the child. One person in a team should be designated as the child's primary contact, responsible for being physically and

emotionally available to meet needs for positive attention, care, comfort, and positive discipline. The consistency of an adult's loving firmness can help the child realize that adults can be trustworthy, predictable in their reactions, and in control of themselves and the environment. The child's experience of daily activities and expectations should be carefully structured to promote feelings of mastery, security, and control. A caring adult can participate with the child in sensory activities, such as playdough and water play, first as a way to foster the nurturing relationship and then as a bridge to encourage normal interest in play activities and socialization with other children and adults.

Children with Special Gifts and Talents

Children who have unusual strengths, abilities, or talents are often called *gifted*. They are highly individual in their development and abilities. There is no single measure that can identify giftedness in children. They may have a single unusual strength or ability, such as a child who has a phenomenal ability to remember, read, or perform music at a very young age. They may also have both a "gift" and a disability, as did the son of a friend of ours who had unusual verbal and artistic ability *and* dyslexia (In Practice).

If you have a child in your program who has many of these characteristics, you should make observations and then talk to the family about what this may imply for the child's future. You can provide encouragement by providing many opportunities for the child to develop and extend his or her interests. These children need learning materials that are open-ended, require active involvement and self-direction, and stimulate thinking. Find out what the child really wants to know or do, and then find the materials that will support his or her desire to learn. You may have to consult with experts and find materials designed for chidren older than the one with whom you are working. The child who is gifted may have less need

IN PRACTICE

Some Characteristics of Gifted Children

Children who are gifted may:

- Exhibit intense curiosity, ask many questions, and conduct investigations into how things work.
- Develop passionate interest in a particular topic or a series of topics.
- Have advanced reasoning ability or demonstrate the capacity for abstract thinking and the use of symbol systems at an early age.
- Be highly independent in thought and behavior.
- Be unusually perceptive and aware of people and things in their environment.
- Have extraordinary memories.
- Show great persistence in self-chosen tasks; are motivated to pursue the interest and accomplish a goal at a self-determined high standard.
- Have advanced language ability with an unusually large and sophisticated vocabulary and the ability to use and appreciate humor.

Reflect and write about . . .

your experiences with people with disabilities

Explore your thoughts and feelings about working with special-needs children. Are you comfortable? Why or why not? What implications does this have for you as a teacher?

for structure than most other children and may work quite independently. Large blocks of time for exploration will give the child the opportunity to concentrate and to work in depth. You support his or her learning by providing the materials and the time and by being available as a resource. Variety and the introduction of new materials on a regular basis are important.

WORKING WITH FAMILIES

Working with families has always been an integral part of the field of early childhood education and care. Your relationship with the families of children with special needs will be in most ways like your relationship with all of the children in your care. The information presented in Chapter Sixteen, Working with Families, should give you general guidance.

There are some additional things that you may want to know and think about in working with the families of children with special needs, especially those whose children have an identified disability. First, keep in mind that the family of the special-needs child has some additional challenges: accepting the fact that their child has a disability, finding help for the child, providing special care, and interacting with professionals who are working with the child and family. These families, like all families, need your respect and support. Keep in mind that they have their own culture and a unique set of strengths, values, skills, expectations, and

service needs. They need acceptance, open communication, and to be treated as part of a team working on behalf of the child.

Support for the family should include regular communication and sharing of information about the child. Be sure that the family has access to you in several different ways. Conferences should feel "safe" to family members so that they can hear information about their child without feeling it is prejudiced or judgmental. The anecdotal records you keep on the child can serve as the basis for a dialogue between you and family members. Make a special effort to collect data on children with disabilities, as the more data you have, the easier it will be to see progress that you can share with the family. Having a sharing notebook for each child may make it easier for some family members who may be more comfortable with sharing a concern in writing than in speaking to you directly.

If the family has been in your program for a while before their child is identified as having a disability, you may need to increase the frequency of communication to ensure that the child and family get needed services. Make a special effort to keep the family involved in ordinary events as well. Even if they can't participate much while they are adjusting to this new dimension of their lives, later they will appreciate being kept informed.

Families need to be included in the community and given social support. Just as it is important to avoid making a child with special needs appear too different, so it is necessary to

Reflect and write about . . .

how you might feel as the parent of a child with special needs

If you were the parent of a child with a disability, what kind of educational program do you think you would want for your child? How do you think you would like your child to be treated? How would you like early childhood professionals to treat you?

help the family feel a welcome part of the ongoing life of the program. If the family is new to your program, be sure they meet other families at program activities or when they drop off or pick up their child. You might say, "Mrs. Brown, I'd like you to meet Mrs. Nishimoto. Her daughter Lisa was Nicole's partner on our field trip today." Don't hesitate to ask the family members of a child with a disability to help at a work day or provide field trip transportation just as you would with any other family.

The families of disabled children have a right and a responsibility to play a primary role in determining the nature and extent of services provided for them and their child. They should always be involved in decisions about and give their consent to any special services their child receives other than the usual program routine. You may be the bridge for the family to therapists or other professionals who will work with their child. Your role will be to ensure that communication is clear among home, school, and professional helpers.

Confidentiality is an important issue. How much is appropriate to reveal to others about a child's disability? Other families in your program may have questions you must be prepared to answer. Like children, they may need to be reassured that the disability itself or the child's behaviors are not "catching." They need to know that children rarely adopt any developmentally inappropriate behavior displayed by a child with a disability. It is important to keep private specific details about the disability or the family.

To a pointed question you might reply, "Amy needs extra help in some ways. If you'd like to know more about it, you might want to ask her parents." You can offer general reassurance, emphasizing the benefits of learning to accept differences and of being caring and respectful in relationships with all people. You can also encourage families to help the family of the child with a disability feel welcome. Your own attitude will provide a positive model.

FINAL THOUGHTS

Almost every chapter in this book contains information that will help you work with all kinds of children—children who differ physically, in the language spoken in their homes, in interests, and in their skills and abilities. That same information is valid for working with children with the kinds of special needs described in this chapter. You may find it helpful to seek assistance and support of the child's family, coworkers, program administrators, and health and mental health specialists. Working with a child who has special needs has the potential to be an unprecedented learning experience in your own development as an educator. You will learn about the child and family, and you will develop skills in collaboration as you help to coordinate the efforts of individuals working with the child. And you will learn more about our shared humanity within the wide spectrum of individual differences.

PROJECTS

Observe a Program: Observe an early childhood program that includes a special-needs child. Report on how the staff attempts to meet the child's needs. Describe your impressions of the staff's attitudes regarding this work. Reflect and then comment on the effect this has on all of the children in the program. What are the implications of this observation for you as an early childhood educator?

Interview a Teacher: Interview a teacher of a child who has been evaluated and placed in a regular early childhood classroom to find out what procedures were followed in identifying and planning for his or her educational experience. Describe this process and your feelings about it.

Observe a Child I: For at least an hour, observe and "put yourself in the shoes" of a child who you suspect has a disability. Try to experience the program as the child might. Describe what you think the child's experience may be. Based on this experience, suggest how the program might be structured to meet this child's needs.

Observe a Child II: Observe a disabled child in a regular preschool setting. Report on what you would do if you were going to have a conference with the child's parents. What would you tell them? What questions would you ask? How would you create a climate of safety and trust within the conference?

Research Resources: Find out what services your local departments of education and health and/or social services (and other agencies) offer to disabled children between birth and age eight. Write a pamphlet for teachers that explains this information. Include a brief description of the services, who is eligible, phone numbers, and names of contact persons.

BIBLIOGRAPHY

Allen, K. E. 1992. *The Exceptional Child: Mainstreaming in Early Childhood Education.* 2nd ed. Albany, NY: Delmar.

Atwater, J. B., J.J. Carta, I.S. Schwartz, and S.R. McConnell. 1994. Blending Developmentally Appropriate Practice and Early Childhood Special Education: Redefining Best Practice. In B. L. Mallory and R. S. New, *Diversity and Developmentally Appropriate Practices: Challenges for Early Childhood Education* (pp. 185–201). New York: Teachers College Press.

Bailey, D. B., and M. Wolery. 1992. *Teaching Infants and Preschoolers with Disabilities.* 2nd ed. Englewood Cliffs, NJ: Merrill/Prentice Hall.

Chandler, L. 1993. Steps in Preparing for Transition. *Teaching Exceptional Children* 25(4):52–55.

Featherstone, H. 1980. *A Difference in the Family: Life With a Disabled Child.* New York: Basic Books.

Galinsky, E. 1988. Parents and Teacher-Caregivers: Sources of Tension, Sources of Support. *Young Children* 43(3): 4.

Guralnick, M. 1990. Major Accomplishments and Future Directions in Early Childhood Mainstreaming. *Topics in Early Childhood Special Education* 10:1–18.

Murray, K. 1985. Reporting Child Abuse: What Are Teachers' Responsibilities? *Beginnings* 2(4): 35–37.

Kaplan-Sanoff, M., and E. F. Kletter. 1985. The Developmental Needs of Abused Children: Classroom Strategies. *Beginnings* 2(4): 15–19.

Koplow, L. 1985. Premature Competence in Young Children: A False Declaration of Independence. *Beginnings* 2(4): 8–11.

McCormick, L. 1994. Infants and Young Children with Special Needs. In N. Haring, L. McCormick, and T. Haring, eds., *Exceptional Children and Youth* (pp. 86–113). Englewood Cliffs, NJ: Merrill/Prentice Hall.

Meisels, S. J., and B. A. Wasik. 1990. Who Should Be Served? Identifying Children in Need of Early Intervention. In S. J. Meisels and J. P. Schonkoff, eds., *Handbook of Early Childhood Intervention*. New York: Cambridge University Press.

Noonan, M. J., and L. McCormick. 1993. *Early Intervention in Natural Environments: Methods and Procedures*. Pacific Grove, CA: Brooks/Cole.

Paasche, C., L. Gorrill, and B. Strom. 1990. *Children with Special Needs in Early Childhood Settings*. Menlo Park, CA: Addison-Wesley.

Peck, C. A., S.L. Odom, and D. Bricker. 1993. *Integrating Young Children with Disabilities into Community Programs: Ecological Perspectives on Research and Implementation*. Baltimore, MD: Paul H. Brookes.

Ranck, E. R. 1985. Protecting Children, Centers, Teachers, and Parents from Child Abuse: A Center Checklist. *Beginnings* 2(4): 42–43.

Souweine, J., S. Crimmins, 1981. *Mainstreaming: Ideas for Teaching Young Children*. Washington, DC: National Association for the Education of Young Children.

Surr, J. 1992. Early Childhood Programs and the Americans with Disabilities Act. *Young Children* 47(5): 18–21.

Wolery, M., P. S. Strain, and D. B. Bailey. 1992. Reaching Potentials of Children with Special Needs. Bredekamp and Rosegrantz, eds. *Reaching Potentials: Appropriate Curriculum and Assessment for Young Children*. Washington DC: National Association for the Education of Young Children.

Wolery, M., and J. S. Wilbers, eds. 1994. *Including Children with Special Needs in Early Childhood Programs*. Research Monographs, Vol. 6. Washington DC: National Association for the Education of Young Children.

CHAPTER SIXTEEN

Working with Families

Just keep in mind though it seems hard I know,
Most parents were children long ago—incredible.
H. Rome

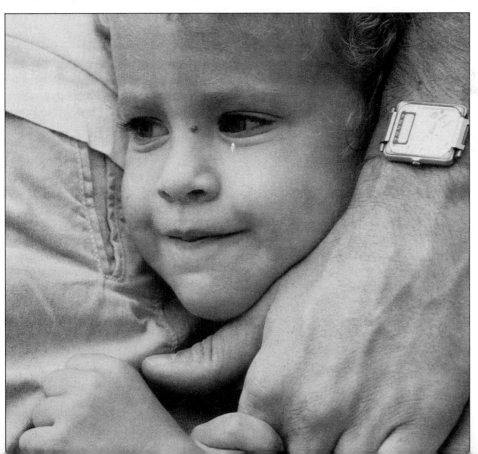

This chapter focuses on the importance of children's families, and of building relationships with them, in early childhood programs. We discuss the awareness, knowledge, and skills you need to work productively with families. These include appreciation for the challenges of raising children, skill in building relationships, ability to communicate information about child development and early childhood education, and knowledge of resources for families. We explore a variety of ways that programs can involve family members—information sharing, participation in the program, and education.

Children come to school wrapped in the values, attitudes, and behaviors of their families. Although your first challenge and primary role is often working directly with children, you need to see and support each child as a part of a unique family whose members are also important teachers. Families today take a variety of forms that sometimes include adults other than parents (step-parents, siblings, grandparents, and other relatives or friends) who may assume parental roles. To simplify the wording of this chapter, we speak of both *parents* and *families* and in so doing are speaking of the entire cast of adults who play an intimate and significant role in a child's life. When we speak of *parenting,* we are discussing the nurturing done by these important adults.

You probably chose to become an early childhood educator because of your interest in and allegiance to children and may not have recognized working with families as a part of your job. The needs of children cannot be adequately met, however, if you do not also take families into consideration. The relationships that you build with family members will bring about collaboration between home and school to enhance children's development. Contemporary research suggests that the most effective programs for young children are those that involve their families.

Interacting with family members can also be gratifying. Those who recognize the importance of their children's early years appreciate your effort and skill as few others can. Since parents know their children best, they will be the first to notice when your work has had a positive impact. As you enrich their children's lives and help them with the task of parenting, you can develop warm relationships that may even blossom into friendships. Learning that you have made a difference to a family is among the most rewarding experiences that a teacher can have.

Relating to children's families has its own unique challenges and demands. The awareness and sensitivity that you have developed in

---

Reflect and write about . . .

how your family was involved

Recall the ways your family participated in your educational experiences. How did the school encourage family participation? What impact did this have on your attitude toward school?

---

your work with children are also important as you work with adults. Adults need relationships in which they feel safe and respected just as children do. Families may differ in their needs, interests, awareness, knowledge, and skill, but there are similarities among them. Families are concerned with the welfare of their children. They want the best for them and want to be kept informed of the important events of their children's lives away from home. The basis for your relationships with families is your commitment to a joint venture of providing good experiences for their children.

You do not need to become intimate friends with children's families, nor do you need to be the ultimate authority on child rearing to be effective. You can offer yourself, a knowledgeable professional who cares about their children and who is able to relate to family members and support their child's growth.

Working with families may seem difficult at times because you have fewer skills in working with adults and because the results of this work are not always easy to observe. Unlike their young children, parents cannot always live in the moment. The attention that they have to give their child's teacher is limited by their concerns for other, possibly more critical, aspects of their lives. If you are a young teacher with no children of your own, you may feel that you are viewed as inexperienced or incapable. Working with adults may seem more problematic than working with children because adults may seem more likely to make negative judgments.

Just as you examined your attitudes about working with children, you will want to look at your values and attitudes regarding your relationship with families. You will encounter people with a variety of approaches to child-rearing that reflect differences in values, cultures, and lifestyles. Others will have different values about education, and you will want to be prepared to deal with these differences in constructive ways—without assuming the role of "expert" or assigning blame. It may be difficult to feel accepting of families whose goals for children are very different from yours. Because of your commitment to children, it may be hard to accept parents who appear uncaring or who seem to treat a young child in a harsh or inappropriate way. It may sometimes be difficult to decide which behavior simply reflects a difference in values or skill and those that are abuse where you have a legal and ethical obligation to intervene. You need to keep in mind that parenting *is* difficult, that there are few resources available, and that the great majority of families *are* doing the best they can given their circumstances.

WHAT YOU NEED TO KNOW TO WORK WITH FAMILIES

The knowledge and skills that you developed to work with children will serve you well as you work with families. There are additional knowledge and skills that you will need which relate specifically to this part of your work. You will need to:

- Understand what parenting is like.
- Understand how relationships are built.
- Know how to communicate information to adults.
- Know how to support families in stress.

What Parenting Is Like

The context of growing up now is quite different from what we remember in our childhoods, and this implies new responsibilities for those who care for young children. Today's world is extremely complex. Television pervades almost all of our lives, and instant replay of historical events makes the world seem much smaller than it once did. Violence is widespread, as is abuse against children.

Your work with families will be enhanced by your awareness of the many aspects of parenting—the joys as well as the difficulties. Being sympathetic and supportive is easier when you realize that parenting is not an easy task. It involves a total, day-in, day-out responsibility that is unrelenting and that cannot be ignored or avoided. The stresses can sometimes overshadow the pleasures. You can help parents renew their pleasure in their child's stage of development and enjoy the process of parenting.

It is also helpful to understand that people enter into childrearing with many kinds of expectations. The reality is almost certain to be different than the expectation. As parents develop, they seem to follow a relatively predictable sequence. Ellen Galinsky (1987) describes the early childhood years as the time when parents learn to be nurturers and define themselves as authority figures in the family.

The purpose of the family has enlarged from the performance of specific survival functions, such as providing food, shelter, clothing, and supervision to ensure children's physical well-being (Pickarts and Fargo 1971). It now includes the more abstract tasks of providing psychological security and skills in dealing with an increasingly complex and dangerous world. Society's view of family roles has changed over the last several decades. Today we are aware of the importance of the early years. Some families feel pressure to hurry their children into the activities that are supposed to ensure success—music, dance, and athletic lessons; early academics; and entrance into the "best" preschool to ensure access to the best primary school, high school, and even college.

Methods of child rearing have changed since today's parents were children. The extremes of strict discipline versus total permissiveness have given way to a number of different and sometimes contradictory approaches. The process of learning about these approaches and choosing those that are consistent with personal values is complex.

The very structure of the family has also been changing. The extended family is less common; families move frequently with an accompanying loss of community. Single parents and step-parents are commonplace, and you can expect that many of the children in your care will come from such families. Newly "blended" families that include the children of a parent's new marriage, grandparents, and other related and unrelated adults are also common. When a family changes, it is usually stressful even if the change is positive and wanted. There are many things that you can do to let families know that their structural diversity is accepted. One of the simplest and most important is to learn the names of all the important people in the child's life and include them when you share information.

Financial uncertainty is another factor that may be a part of a family's life. Both parents are often part of today's workforce. In 1993, nearly 60 percent of all children under the age of six had working mothers. Families in which two parents are working must deal with multiple roles and the resulting time and energy constraints. Moreover, there is a dramatic increase in one-parent families (most frequently mothers) who are operating under severe financial constraints. In 1992, nearly 22 percent of all children lived in poverty. One in four children below the age of six lived in poverty (Children's Defense Fund 1994). We are concerned today about the large numbers of homeless children and how to provide education and care programs for them.

Changes in the nature of child-rearing require new skills and responses that many adults are not prepared for. They may find it difficult to try to develop the skills they need and to find resources for acquiring them, especially if they are struggling to survive financially. They may be forced to rely on social agencies, including early childhood education and care programs, to perform many of the roles that were once the responsibility of the extended family. Your program can be a very good place for providing support to families. Your good relationships with families will help them to feel easier about turning to you for assistance and about sharing some of the responsibility for their child with you.

Building Relationships with Families

To work effectively with families, you need to focus on building good relationships with them. Although this need not be difficult or time-consuming, it does require thoughtfulness and attention. Good relationships with families do not develop simply because you have good intentions.

Relationships begin with the attitudes that you hold and express. All people are more trusting and open in an atmosphere of concern, respect, acceptance, and individual attention. The things that you do to build such an atmosphere for families in your program are usually small, easy to overlook, and as simple as common courtesy.

Good relationships begin when families feel welcome in your program. This can be accomplished if you know names, greet individuals daily, and have provisions for regular sharing of information. Since all relationships are based on sharing and trust, begin by learning about each other. Take time to find out what family members are interested in, what they do, and what they care about. Share information that will help them know something about you—remember, though, it is not appropriate to share *your* personal problems. Acknowledge events and transitions in the child's life at school and in the family's life at home. Recognize and share a family's joys and sorrows. Be scrupulous about maintaining confidentiality: Nothing destroys trust faster than idle gossip and broken confidences.

You will want to convey to families that you are committed to hearing their concerns (at an appropriate time) and that you will face

problems that these may present with them rather than avoiding issues or insisting on your own methods. Skills in active listening, giving I-messages, and avoiding roadblocks will help. You may sometimes feel that listening to families' concerns is extra work. Remember that the time that you spend may ultimately contribute to the relationship and to the child's well-being at home and in school.

Communicating Information to Adults

Your knowledge of child development influences your relationships with children and serves as a basis for the kind of program you plan for them. You need to be able to clearly communicate your understanding of this theory so families can understand why the program is a good one for their children.

Communicating specialized information means translating the sometimes puzzling professional terms that you use with your colleagues into words that have meaning to the uninitiated. Simply saying that you provide opportunities for motor development is not as valuable as letting a family know that creative movement, swinging, sliding, trike riding, and climbing help their child to develop skill, strength, and coordination in the arms legs and torso and that using pegboards, the easel, puzzles, and beads helps develop skills in manipulating with hands and fingers that will be essential in learning to write. Additionally, all of this may not be nearly as meaningful as letting them know that physical competence and the related confidence that it brings also contribute to social and academic success.

Both families and you have information that contributes to the child's well-being and that allows you to meet each other on equal ground. Families bring knowledge and experience of their child as a unique human being, and you bring your theoretical knowledge of children in general. Both types of information are vital if you are to create the best possible educational experience for each child.

You will be comfortable with what you are doing and better able to explain your program choices and rationale when your decisions are based on knowledge of children and curriculum and on clear value choices. As you explain what you do and why, it is important to separate and communicate your *preferences* in curriculum and child management from your *knowledge* about what constitutes appropriate, desirable practice in working with children. As they observe your approach to curriculum and classroom management and learn more about the rationale for what you do, they will learn more about development and will have a broader understanding of their choices. For example, you can tell families that you have chosen not to provide workbook experiences for young children because you know that they learn concepts through real experiences. You might then show a sorting activity where children make discriminations similar to a workbook task and share some ways that similar activities (such as sorting and putting away the silverware) might be provided at home.

Providing families with information that is meaningful to them is a skill that you will develop with time and experience. Share what you know and be willing to admit what you don't know but are willing to learn more about. Remember that you and the parents both have worthwhile ideas and that neither of you is infallible. You *are* the professional in these situations, however, and although you need to be respectful of families, you also need to act on your best professional judgment. If requests violate what you know to be best for children, you have an ethical responsibility to do what is right for children, but you will want to explain the reasons.

As an accessible professional with knowledge of a range of choices, you may find yourself being asked for advice or may feel a strong desire to offer it when you are not asked. We have found that it works better to offer such advice in a tentative fashion. To a parent who has difficulty coping with a whiny child at a late pick-up you might say, "All of the children seem to get cranky when they're hungry and it's close to supper. I have found that it helps when families bring a small, nutritious snack to give to them on the ride home."

How to Support Families in Stress

Even though you are not a counselor, you will need to have information and strategies for supporting families during times of stress. Some kinds of stress are relatively minor, the result of juggling the responsibilities of a busy life; others are more serious.

As an early childhood educator, you may be the first professional who identifies a problem that has an impact on a child. Problems may be as simple as a change in schedule that is causing a child to have difficulty staying awake in school or as serious as case of child abuse or neglect.

Family Changes

Families often need assistance when there is a change in family structure, such as a new baby, death, divorce, or remarriage. One of the simplest ways that you can help is by keeping a child's school life as stable as possible during the period of the change. You will want to have knowledge of programs such as children's guidance and divorce clinics, mental health services, family mediation organizations, and neighborhood resources to help parents find needed assistance for dealing with these transitions.

As a person who works closely with a family in today's society, it is almost inevitable that you will find yourself being asked to play a supportive role for one or both parents in divorce or child custody conflicts. Since these conflicts can be traumatic, policies and procedures need to be established prior to a problem occurring. A clear policy statement can help the parents to understand that your primary com-

Reflect and write about . . .

ways you know to support families

What do you see as your potential strengths and/or weaknesses in working
with families? What understandings and skills do you have that will help you in
your work with families?

mitment is to the child's welfare and that such problems are by no means unique or a sign of family failure. When a divorce or custody battle does take place, it can be tempting to express a preference for one or another parent. Keep in mind that you serve a child better by maintaining neutrality unless the child appears endangered. In cases where family members are in conflict, the NAEYC Code of Ethical Conduct states in section P-2.10, "We shall work openly, sharing our observations of the child, to help all parties involved make informed decisions. We shall refrain from becoming an advocate for one party" (see Appendix One).

Abuse and Neglect

One of the most difficult situations faced by an early childhood educator is addressing a case of suspected child abuse or neglect. Every program should have written policies that notify families of the program's obligation to report child abuse and neglect and of policies designed to protect children.

You have an ethical and in most states a legal obligation to report suspected cases of abuse or neglect of children (discussed in Chapter Fifteen, Working with Children with Special Needs), but you also need to continue to work with the family with sensitivity and respect. When you suspect that child abuse or neglect might be occurring, you need to confer with the family and attempt to develop mutually acceptable strategies, provide consultation and parent education as appropriate, and make

referrals to agencies that might help the family deal with potentially abusive behavior. If you are convinced that the child is being abused and you make a report to a child protective agency, you should inform the family that the referral has been made unless you believe that this might result in harm to the child.

Make every effort to maintain positive relationships with the family at this time: Focus on positive aspects of the child in discussion and make an effort to notice and comment on attempts to handle the child's behavior in a constructive way. Parents who are under the stress of an investigation of child abuse will need extra support from staff, not less. Let the family know that your goal is to support the family and help them cope better. Avoid adversarial comments that make the parent feel inadequate or incompetent. Neither child nor parent should be labeled as "abused" or "abuser" and confidentiality should be scrupulously kept.

INVOLVING FAMILIES IN EARLY CHILDHOOD PROGRAMS

Family involvement in early childhood programs can run the gamut from programs that act as an extended family and involve parents at all levels to those in which staff members talk to parents rarely and only when there is a problem. In ideal situations you and families work closely in a variety of ways. Family members can participate in classroom activities, plan or attend parent education programs, serve on policy-making groups, and contribute to the program through work on facilities, fund raising, and lobbying in the community on its behalf.

Family involvement begins when you provide information about the kinds of involvement available in your program. It is important to find out some things about the family members: what they want and need, their level of interest in the program, their time constraints, and the kinds of activities in which they might enjoy participating.

Sharing Information

You help families to understand and support your program by sharing information with them. It helps them to contribute and to be better equipped to work with their children at home in activities that support learning when they know what you are doing and why.

The first opportunity to share information with a family will occur when they visit your program to learn about it and to decide if it is right for them. Staff members aid families in their decision making by exchanging information with them. You will need to provide an understandable explanation of what is done in the program and why. You also will want to encourage families to tell you what their child is like and what kind of program they are seeking. During your discussion you can share, in an unbiased way, what you know about other program alternatives in your community. This is especially important if you suspect that what is desired by the family is different from what your program offers. Such an open sharing of information sets the stage for a truly collaborative effort between your program and home. It also increases the likelihood that the family will become committed to the program and find meaningful, fulfilling ways to become involved.

Once a family has chosen your program, there are other avenues for continuing and ex-

panding this new relationship. At the beginning of a year or when there are a number of new families, you may wish to have an orientation meeting. These meetings tend to work best when they combine information sharing with an opportunity for socializing. We have found it effective to begin a meeting at the end of a day when the families arrive to pick up their children. Provide for a shared meal and informal conversation, followed by introductions and sharing of information about the program. Participation will be facilitated if you can offer child care for older and younger children as well as those enrolled in the program.

The initial visit and a good orientation meeting are useful in setting the climate for future interactions and family involvement; however, they are only the beginning of an ongoing process of communication. The basis for your relationship with families is your intimate knowledge of and your commitment to their child. Because of previous experiences with schools and teachers, some people do not feel comfortable in their initial contacts with a formal program. In the beginning, you will need to take the lead and assume the bulk of the responsibility for building the relationship. You can accomplish this by frequent and positive sharing of information about the program's activities and your experiences with and observations of their child. Sharing the small joys and sorrows of the child's life creates a bond between you and the family.

Good daily communication with families requires flexible and creative planning, and it is important to use all the avenues that are available to you. Keeping in contact with busy working parents involves a special effort. Responsibility for greeting family members at early arrival or late departure may need to be assigned to one staff member because you may not get to talk during your normal work hours. A message center where each family has a mailbox or message pocket helps to make communication easier. A hand-printed summary of the day's experiences can be posted here. In some programs this is also where journals are kept. Staff and family members share information about the child through the journals, which they both read and write in frequently.

As you observe children you can keep both mental and written notes to share at the end of the day, in the journal or by phone call: "Christopher worked really hard in the block area today. He was very persistent and figured out how to make his tower as tall as the shelf. His face shone with delight when he finally was able to make his tower strong enough not to topple."

Families can be informed of the activities of the program by reading a week's plans posted near the sign-in area or sent home each week. Bulletin boards, notes, and newsletters offer opportunities to explain aspects of the program in greater detail, to solicit assistance from families, and to provide information about child development and other topics of interest. These techniques are most successful if they are very visible, attractive, short and to the point, and

easy to read. If reading them is built into some other routine, such as sign-in, they are more likely to get the attention of family members.

Another way to communicate to families that they are valued parts of the program is to create a family corner near the entrance to the building or room. This area might have a comfortable adult chair or couch, reading material, coffee or tea, pictures of the children at play, or even a slide/tape presentation about the program. Parents may enjoy talking to one another in this area or a child and parent might spend a quiet moment there together.

If some of the families in your program have special communication needs, if they are non-English speaking, or if literacy is a problem, then you will need to make a special effort to ensure that you communicate with them. Bilingual staff and family members might be designated as translators and others as readers for those who may have difficulty reading. Information can be presented graphically as well as in written form to enhance the communication. The guiding principle in reaching everyone is to present the same information in many different forms.

Addressing Families' Concerns

Because families are so deeply concerned about their children, it is inevitable that issues and questions will arise regarding the care and education that their children are receiving. In good relationships, moments of concern and questioning lead to open exchange of information and ideas and often to greater insight into values and goals.

Very predictably, families have concerns about their child's health and safety in the program, about the care of their child's possessions and clothing, and about the purpose of play and the child's academic progress. Despite a good relationship, addressing these concerns can be worrisome. It is essential that families feel heard, that their issues are addressed, and

that their efforts and judgment are respected. If you consistently display sensitivity in dealing with their concerns, it is more likely to be reciprocated. To be prepared, you need to be able to respond to questions and concerns in ways that keep the lines of communication open and without being defensive or devastated by being questioned or challenged.

Questions may arise from the nature and philosophy of the program. Young children's programs often are very different from other kinds of educational settings. The materials and experiences provided seem to bear little relationship to conventional learning. Families may wonder why their children play so much, why they're not learning "academic" skills, why they come home dirty, or why you let them do things that appear dangerous.

Concerns about play often reflect a lack of understanding of how young children learn. Family members may relax as you help them to understand that children learn in significantly different ways from adults and that the development of motor and perceptual skills form the base of later, more abstract learning. Since the

most recent formal educational experiences of most adults have usually been in lecture situations, they may have lost touch with the learning that goes on in active, hands-on experiences. Remind them of the things that they have learned by doing—cooking, driving a car, bathing a baby, using a computer—and that *doing* is an important way of learning, too. Explain the sequence of development in very concrete terms: "Children first have to learn to tell the difference between more obvious things like blue round beads and square purple ones before they can tell the difference between more subtle things like numbers and letters." This will help adults to see the purpose of the activities that you do with children.

When families do not agree with you about the curriculum, it is essential that you take their concerns seriously and not dismiss them. It is equally important that you speak from your own knowledge and experience of developmentally appropriate practice. We are educators because of our specialized expertise, and it is our responsibility to address families' concerns with sensitivity from the knowledge base of the field. For example, dialogue with a mother who has expressed a concern about a four and half year old learning to read might sound something like this:

Mother: You know, I think it is time that you start teaching Rebecca to read. She is always looking at books, and she can read the names of all the stores at the shopping center.

Teacher: You're right, Rebecca is expressing a strong interest in reading lately. I've noticed that she is spending time at the writing center and is incorporating letters into her paintings and drawings. She doesn't want me to write her name on her work anymore—she wants to do it by herself. I've been fascinated to watch this because it's just what I've been reading about how children develop literacy (that's the new term for reading readiness). What the specialists are saying is that children learn to read and write through their experiences with reading and writing in their day-to-day life.

Mother. What about teaching her letters and words? I bought a workbook at the drugstore last week, and Rebecca has been coloring all the pictures. I can't keep her away from it. Why aren't you teaching her anything like that at school?

Teacher: What I've been doing here at school is that I've introduced a word bank for each of the children. Here's Rebecca's file of "special words." She has all the names of her friends and family. I've also been introducing more print into the room. You know, back at the beginning of the year I put up some labels on different things in the classroom like here where I put *chair* on this chair. Since Rebecca and a few of the other children have been so interested we've been labeling other things together. Rebecca asked to put *Squeakers* on the mouse cage. She and Joni made this word book together right after that.

The messes inherent in the sensory development, art, and science curricula are also the topic of concern. Knowing the purpose of these activities may make them easier for families to appreciate. Discomfort may be eased if the activities are announced in advance, if children are sent to school play clothes, and if you provide smocks to protect clothing from damage.

Some adults may be astonished and alarmed by the physical challenges that children undertake in the early childhood education and care setting. They may never have allowed children to climb to the top of the jungle gym or to use functional saws, scissors, or cooking equipment. They may not understand why you do. Families often cannot provide independent or adventurous physical activities. They may not be aware of what young children can safely do with close supervision. People vary greatly in their judgment of what is or is not dangerous. Adults may judge an activity or

piece of equipment based on their own experience. We find it helpful to let family members know that we share their concerns and then go on to talk about the value of the activity and the safeguards that we take. You can let families and children know that you won't allow or encourage children to attempt activities that are clearly beyond their capacities, but that your situation safely provides opportunities for exploration that contribute to development.

Conducting Conferences

A conference provides you and family members with time to share information and perceptions. They provide for in-depth and personal exchange of information that is not possible in other ways. A central purpose of your conference is to form an alliance with the family to help the child grow and learn. During conferences, you may explore issues relating to the child at home and in the program. This is a time when you may learn about personal or family problems. You can then help family members express and clarify their feelings and values, provide information, and help them develop their skills and resources. Regular conferences support your work and build relationships. If conferences are held rarely or only in the event of a problem, they will be more stressful and less productive.

Planning will help you to spend conference time effectively. First you will need to plan for quiet, undisturbed space and sufficient time. Providing these ensures that the conference will be unpressured and productive. Scheduling ten conferences for twenty minutes each on one day is neither an effective nor pleasant way to plan for this important part of your role.

You can prepare for the conference by looking over your anecdotal records, assessments, samples of work, and other records on the child. You might write a summary or fill out a checklist to use as a conference guideline.

Family members may be apprehensive if they do not understand the purpose of the conference. You will want to begin by explaining that you and they are there to share information and get to know one another better. Assure them that you welcome their ideas and questions and that the conference is a joint process. As you share your perceptions of the child in school, try to describe what the child *does* rather than saying what he or she *is*: "Matthew usually watches the others use a new piece of equipment before he tries it. He seems to like to have a quiet space and a long period of time." Do not say, "Matthew is very shy." In positive conferences the child's areas of strength are discussed and other areas are looked at in terms of growth and direction.

When it is necessary to discuss a problem, assume that solutions can be found. You can use conference time to clarify the issues, agree on goals, develop a plan of action for home and in the program, and decide when you will meet again to evaluate what you have done.

It is natural and necessary for families to be intense, emotional, and partial to their child. Educators play a different role—they must be less intense and more objective. In approaching conferences, assume that family members have good intentions and that they will share honestly as you do. You may disagree with one another because of your different experiences in life and with the child, but you are ultimately on the same side—the child's.

Family Involvement in the Program

You play an important role in encouraging and supporting family participation in your program. Involved family members can work with the children, orient other families to classroom participation, provide input into program policy, and strengthen the relationship of the entire program to the community. When family members participate as volunteers it can enrich your program and enable you to do more.

They support children's experience when they work with individuals and small groups in the classroom and accompany you as you take children on trips outside of the program environment.

When family members volunteer in the classroom, everyone can benefit: the families, the staff, and the children.

When *family members* participate in the program, they:

- Have an opportunity to learn about new ways of guiding growth and development.
- Gain firsthand insight into the meaning of the curriculum that they may be able to apply at home.
- Gain a sense of competence and a feeling of being needed as they contribute to the program.

When family members participate in the program, *children:*

- Have a chance to see their family members in a different role.
- Become acquainted with adults who have other skills, feelings, and ways of relating than their own family members and teachers.
- Have more individualized attention available to them.
- Experience a richer curriculum.

When family members participate in the program, *teachers:*

- Have a chance to expand their program because of the improved ratio.
- Can learn from the knowledge and expertise parents bring and share.
- Have an opportunity to observe the relationship between the child and members of the family.
- Have a chance to develop a more meaningful relationship with individual family members.
- Have more opportunity to interact with individual children.

It takes a while for staff and families to get comfortable, so begin in easy stages. It is easy to invite family members to visit and observe their child in the classroom. With just a little additional planning and work, parents can be invited to come for special occasions such as a birthday or a special child-prepared luncheon. More thought and preparation are required when family members work with you and the children in the program. To ensure a successful first experience, have family members begin with a simple task such as reading a story to two or three children or assisting you as you set up activities. It is important to allow family members to participate in ways that feel comfortable and natural to them and to offer them support in developing skills. As they gain skill, they can take a more active part in the program by planning with you and possibly sharing unique abilities or special knowledge.

You may need to make an effort to ensure that men as well as women participate, since they may feel that the early childhood program is not their natural province and may not be certain that they have anything to contribute. In fact, most will be perfectly comfortable doing the activities just suggested. They may require a special invitation from you to feel assured that they are welcome.

An orientation to learn routines and procedures is imperative, both to help family members to feel prepared and to ensure that they understand program philosophy and policies so that quality is maintained. A satisfying classroom experience is enhanced when you can find time to cooperatively plan activities and meet at the end of the school day to discuss experiences and give each other feedback. Remember that when family members participate, you have the additional responsibility of supervising them.

A card file containing information about activities and jobs that need to be done is useful for letting family members know what kind of participation is needed and will be welcomed. Posting written statements in each area of the classroom describing the purpose of the activities and how adults can interact with children is another good technique for supporting participation.

Family members who lack the time or who are uncomfortable participating in the classroom may be involved in a variety of other ways. It is important to be especially aware of including options for single-parent families who may have greater stress and less time (but no less interest) than two-parent or extended families.

Some family members may volunteer to use their skills to create items for the classroom. Others may enjoy making educational materials at home. If people express an interest in this, help them get started by organizing a workshop on how to create learning games. Involve them in identifying what specific learning games would help round out the curriculum in their child's classroom. This workshop should include ideas for useful junk to save and materials to be purchased.

As families become involved and committed to the program, they may recognize its budgetary limitations and offer to help in finding additional resources. They may be willing to participate in fund-raising events or grant-writing projects. Others may be willing to join together with the staff to do renovation, repair, or clean-up projects. Many programs hold special workdays periodically at which families and staff spend a whole day cleaning or doing repairs on the facility. Workdays are better attended if families have had some say in what most needs doing and can choose their jobs based on skill and interest. To ensure a successful workday, the staff and families must identify the work to be accomplished, gather the required equipment and materials, arrange for child care and food, and make sure that the jobs can be done in the designated time. If participants can end the workday with a feeling of accomplishment, they are more likely to volunteer for another one.

Family members can also be involved in groups such as advisory and policy boards. This form of involvement can help your program more accurately reflect the interests and needs of the families you serve. Family members who participate in policy making feel that the program truly belongs to them and their children. They are willing to expend more of their energy and resources because of their greater commitment. The parents become valuable advocates.

As the staff member who works directly with children, you are the person most likely to know the special interests, concerns, and talents of the families. Family members, children, and the program benefit when you invite families to participate.

Family Education

Traditionally, many programs for young children and their families have included family education activities. Family education can help family members to understand the importance of their role in their child's development and education. As they come to know and trust you, some will seek advice about problematic areas in their relationship with their child. When you find commonly shared areas of concern, you can structure opportunities to provide them with appropriate information about child development, early childhood education, and child-rearing skills.

Family education can take many forms. You may act as a direct provider of education, or you may help families to find other resources. Informally, you may talk with them and model effective strategies for interacting with children in the course of your daily contacts. Such informal education can be very powerful. More formal methods such as newsletters, workshops, discussion groups, and child-rearing courses can also be provided. Programs we have worked in have offered many educational services to families including: a weekly newsletter with a "Help Your Child Learn at Home" feature; workshops on making and choosing toys, preparing children for kindergarten, language and reading, and nutrition; courses on parenting skills; and parent-coordinated support groups.

Family education can encompass many topics. The only limits are the imaginations of the families and staff. Obviously, many of the topics will be beyond the skills and expertise you gain in your preparation to become an early childhood educator.

However, you need only be aware of the special skills and interests of the families and community members who are and have been involved in your program, and you will likely have a vast store of resources for a family education program. Family members who understand the values and goals of the program will often be willing to share their special skills and knowledge and even invite their friends to contribute.

Like other aspects of the early childhood program, a family education program requires some careful planning. Probably the single most important step in planning is to survey the families to learn what they most wish to learn about. It is very disconcerting to invite an expert on child development to speak to a group and present your speaker with a nearly empty house. If you go to the trouble to uncover the reason for a low turnout for such an event, you may discover that the topic was a staff idea and the families would have come out to a meeting on another subject. It is also important to realize that the success of a meeting is not measured by the number of bodies in the room but by the impact on the individuals who did attend. Assessing the interests and needs of families can be accomplished in a variety of ways. Small groups can get together and brainstorm everything they would like to learn about children and family life. Even if the representation is small, the initial list of topics can be distributed to the rest of the families for additions, comment, and prioritization. After an initial list of topics has been generated, you can distribute the list in subsequent years with space for families to indicate

Reflect and write about . . .

family education you have seen

Think about a program that you have observed or worked in. What kinds of family participation did you observe? What appeared to be the attitudes of the school staff toward family involvement?

topics they would like to know more about and those in which they have special knowledge and skill that they would be willing to share with others. Do leave space for adding new topics.

When you have a list of topics relevant to the families currently enrolled in your program, a good idea of some likely presenters, or knowledge of other sources of the desired information (films, videos, printed materials), it is time to attend to the quality of presentation. Printed materials can be made available to families in the special area or room you provide for them in your facility. Films and videos can also be screened in a family lounge or area of the school if you have the appropriate equipment. Workshops, courses, or lectures, like all other family meetings, need to be scheduled at a convenient time for family members. If provisions for child care, a meal, and a comfortable location are offered, participation will be enhanced.

Finally, to ensure a well-received session, it is essential that someone from the program communicate to presenters about the skill and knowledge level of the families and check that the presentation will be lively and appropriate. The best learning experiences for adults almost always combine the presentation of information with the opportunity for active participation.

FINAL THOUGHTS

As an early childhood educator you will work with children and their families. In the field of early childhood education and care, we generally think we are to provide education and care for children. In fact, in caring for the children we are also caring for their families.

Contemporary families confront many challenges as they strive to nurture and support their children. Some do not have the resources required to meet the needs of their family members for food, shelter, and clothing. Others have the ability to meet the basic physical needs of their family and even to have many physical comforts. However, they must commit so much time to professional and social obligations that they have little time to enjoy each other's company.

As an early childhood educator you will play an important role in the lives of many families. You will be an important part of the network of people who will lend support to the families' efforts to function in a complex society while nurturing their children. Families and early childhood professionals share common goals—to educate and care for children in ways that support optimal development. Childhood needs protection from many of the stresses of contemporary life, and as an early childhood professional you will support families as they provide their children with the protection and nuturance they need if they are to develop and learn.

PROJECTS

Interview and Observe in a Program: Choose two early childhood programs. Interview the director or family involvement coordinator in each to discover the kinds of family involvement available, the program's philosophy regarding family involvement, and the ways the program communicates with families. Observe the school environment and note any efforts to communicate with families (for example, parent bulletin boards). Compare and contrast the programs and discuss what you learned from your exploration.

The Family Materials Comparison: Choose two early childhood programs. Collect a sample of the materials that each program gives to families: brochure, application, handbook, newsletter, policy statements, etc. Compare and evaluate the materials based on the ideas presented in this chapter and discuss how the programs appear to differ in their philosophy and attitudes toward families. What did you learn from this experience that may be helpful to you as a teacher?

Family Interviews: Interview one or two family members of children in early childhood programs. Ask them to talk about the day-to-day experience of parenting a young child. What do they expect from their child's program in terms of information and support? How well do they think the program is doing in providing these things? Report on what you learned and its implication for you as an early childhood educator.

Interview your Family: Interview your own parents/guardians. Ask them to recall what it was like to parent you as a young child and what kinds of support they got from programs and institutions such as the schools, recreation programs, and so on. Ask them to describe the ways they were involved in programs you were in as a child.

BIBLIOGRAPHY

Berger, E. H. 1991. *Parents as Partners in Education: The School and Home Working Together.* 3d ed. Englewood Cliffs, NJ: Merrill/Prentice Hall.

Bredekamp, S. 1987. *Developmentally Appropriate Practice in Early Childhood Programs Serving Children From Birth Through Age 8.* Expanded ed. Washington, DC: National Association for the Education of Young Children.

Children's Defense Fund. 1994. *The State of America's Children.* Washington DC: Author.

Elkind, D. 1981. *The Hurried Child: Growing Up Too Fast, Too Soon.* Menlo Park, CA: Addison-Wesley.

Feeney, S., and K. Kipnis. 1990. *Code of Ethical Conduct and Statement of Commitment* (brochure). Washington, DC: National Association for the Education of Young Children.

Galinsky, E. 1981. *Between Generations: The Six Stages of Parenting*. New York: Times Books.

Gonzalez-Mena, J. 1993. *The Child in the Family and the Community*. New York: Macmillan

Gordon, T. 1974. *Parent Effectiveness Training*. New York: David McKay.

Hetznecker, W., L. E. Arnold, and A. Phillips. 1980. Teachers, Principals, and Parents: Guidance by Educators. In L. E. Arnold, ed., *Helping Parents Help Their Children*. New York: Brunner/Mazel.

Honig, A. 1975. *Parent Involvement in Early Childhood Education*. Washington, DC: National Association for the Education of Young Children.

Katz, L. 1980. Mother and Teaching—Some Significant Distinctions. In L. Katz, ed., *Current Topics in Early Childhood Education, vol. 3*. Norwood, NJ: Ablex.

Lawrence, G., and M. Hunter. 1978. *Parent-Teacher Conferencing*. El Segunda, CA: Theory into Practice.

Lightfoot, S. L. 1978. *Worlds Apart: Relationships Between Families and Schools*. New York: Basic Books.

Power, D. R. 1989. *Families and Early Childhood Programs*. Washington, DC: Research Monographs of the National Association for the Education of Young Children.

Pickarts, E., and J. Fargo. 1971. *Parent Education: Toward Parental Competence*. New York: Appleton-Century-Crofts.

Rappoport, R., R. Strelitz, and Z. Strelitz. 1980. *Fathers, Mothers and Society: Perspectives on Parenting*. New York: Vintage Books.

Ricci, I. 1980. *Mom's House/Dad's House*. New York: Collier Books.

Simmons-Martin, A. 1975. Facilitating Parent-Child Interactions Through the Education of Parents. *Journal of Research and Development in Education* (Winter).

Stevens, J. H., and M. Matthews, eds. 1979. *Mother/Child, Father/Child Relationships*. Washington, DC: National Association for the Education of Young Children.

Stipek, D., et al. 1994. Making Parents Your Allies. *Young Children* 49(3):4–9.

Stone, J. G. 1987. *Teacher-Parent Relationships*. Washington, DC: National Association for the Education of Young Children

Stonehouse, A. 1994. *How Does It Feel? Child Care from a Parent's Perspective*. Canberra, Australia: Australian Early Childhood Association.

Taylor, K. 1981. *Parents and Children Learn Together*. 3rd ed. New York: Teachers College Press.

The NAEYC Code of Ethical Conduct

PREAMBLE

NAEYC recognizes that many daily decisions required of those who work with young children are of a moral and ethical nature. The NAEYC Code of Ethical Conduct offers guidelines for responsible behavior and sets forth a common basis for resolving the principal ethical dilemmas encountered in early childhood education. The primary focus is on daily practice with children and their families in programs for children from birth to eight years of age: preschools, child care centers, family day care homes, kindergartens, and primary classrooms. Many of the provisions also apply to specialists who do not work directly with children, including program administrators, parent educators, college professors, and child care licensing specialists.

Standards of ethical behavior in early childhood education are based on commitment to core values that are deeply rooted in the history of our field. We have committed ourselves to:

- Appreciating childhood as a unique and valuable stage of the human life cycle;
- Basing our work with children on knowledge of child development;
- Appreciating and supporting the close ties between the child and family;
- Recognizing that children are best understood in the context of family, culture and society;
- Respecting the dignity, worth and uniqueness of each individual (child, family member and colleague);
- Helping children and adults achieve their full potential in the context of relationships that are based on trust, respect and positive regard.

The Code sets forth a conception of our professional responsibilities in four sections,

Stephanie Feeney and Kenneth Kipnis. 1989. Code of Ethical Conduct and Statement of Commitment. *Young Children* 45(1):24–29.

each addressing an arena of professional relationships: 1) children, 2) families, 3) colleagues, and 4) community and society. Each section includes an introduction to the primary responsibilities of the early childhood practitioner in that arena, a set of ideals pointing in the direction of exemplary professional practice, and a set of principles defining practices that are required, prohibited and permitted.

The ideals reflect the aspirations of practitioners. The principles are intended to guide conduct and assist practitioners in resolving ethical dilemmas encountered in the field. There is not necessarily a corresponding principle for each ideal. Both ideals and principles are intended to direct practitioners to those questions which, when responsibly answered, will provide the basis for conscientious decision-making. While the Code provides specific direction for addressing some ethical dilemmas, many others will require the practitioner to combine the guidance of the Code with sound professional judgment.

The ideals and principles in this Code present a shared conception of professional responsibility that affirms our commitment to the core values of our field. They publicly acknowledge the responsibilities that we in the field have assumed and in so doing they support ethical behavior in our work. Practitioners who face ethical dilemmas are urged to seek guidance in the applicable parts of this Code and in the spirit that informs the whole.

SECTION I: ETHICAL RESPONSIBILITIES TO CHILDREN

Childhood is a unique and valuable stage in the life cycle. Our paramount responsibility is to provide safe, healthy, nurturing and responsive settings for children. We are committed to supporting children's development by cherishing individual differences, by helping them learn to live and work cooperatively, and by promoting their self-esteem.

Ideals:

I-1.1 To be familiar with the knowledge-base of early childhood education and to keep current through continuing education and in-service training.

I-1.2 To base program practices upon current knowledge in the field of child development and related disciplines and upon particular knowledge of each child.

I-1.3 To recognize and respect the uniqueness and the potential of each child.

I-1.4 To appreciate the special vulnerability of children.

I-1.5 To create and maintain safe and healthy settings that foster children's social, emotional, intellectual, and physical development and that respect their dignity and their contributions.

I-1.6 To support the right of children with special needs to participate, consistent with their ability, in regular early childhood programs.

Principles:

P-1.1 Above all, we shall not harm children. We shall not participate in practices that are disrespectful, degrading, dangerous, exploitative, intimidating, psychologically damaging or physically harmful to children. **This principle has precedence over all others in this Code.**

P-1.2 We shall not participate in practices that discriminate against children by denying benefits, giving special advantages or excluding them from programs or activities on the basis of their race, religion, sex, national origin, or the status, behavior or beliefs of their parents. (This principle does not apply to programs that have a lawful mandate to provide services to a particular population of children.)

P-1.3 We shall involve all of those with relevant knowledge (including staff and parents) in decisions concerning a child.

P-1.4 When, after appropriate efforts have been made with a child and the family, a child still does not appear to be benefiting from a program, we shall communicate our concern to the family in a positive way and offer them assistance in finding a more suitable setting.

P-1.5 We shall be familiar with the symptoms of child abuse and neglect and know community procedures for addressing them.

P-1.6 When we have evidence of child abuse or neglect we shall report the evidence to the appropriate community agency and follow up to insure that appropriate action has been taken. When possible, parents will be informed that the referral has been made.

P-1.7 When another person tells us of their suspicion that a child is being abused or neglected but we lack evidence, we shall assist that person in taking appropriate action to protect the child.

P-1.8 When a child protective agency fails to provide adequate protection for abused or neglected children, we acknowledge a collective ethical responsibility to work toward improvement of these services.

SECTION II: ETHICAL RESPONSIBILITIES TO FAMILIES

Families are of primary importance in children's development. (The term *family* may include others, besides parents, who are responsibly involved with the child.) Because the family and the early childhood educator have an interest in the child's welfare, we acknowledge a primary responsibility to bring about collaboration between the home and school in ways that enhance the child's development.

Ideals:

I-2.1 To develop relationships of mutual trust with the families we serve.

I-2.2 To acknowledge and build upon strengths and competencies as we support families in their task of nurturing children.

I-2.3 To respect the dignity of each family and its culture, customs and beliefs.

I-2.4 To respect families' child-rearing values and their right to make decisions for their children.

I-2.5 To interpret each child's progress to parents within the framework of a developmental perspective and to help families understand and appreciate the value of developmentally appropriate early childhood programs.

I-2.6 To help family members improve their understanding of their children and to enhance their skills as parents.

I-2.7 To participate in building support networks for families by providing them with opportunities to interact with program staff and families.

Principles:

P-2.1 We shall not deny family members access to their child's classroom or program setting.

P-2.2 We shall inform families of program philosophy, policies, personnel qualifications, and explain why we teach as we do.

P-2.3 We shall inform and, when appropriate, involve families in policy decisions.

P-2.4 We shall inform and, when appropriate, involve families in significant decisions affecting their child.

P-2.5 We shall inform the family of accidents involving their child, of risks such as exposures to contagious disease that may result in infection and of events that might result in psychological damage.

P-2.6 We shall not permit or participate in research which could in any way hinder the education or development of the children in our programs. Families shall be fully informed of any proposed research projects involving their children and shall have the opportunity to give or withhold consent.

P-2.7 We shall not engage in or support exploitation of families. We shall not use our relationship with a family for private advantage or personal gain, or enter into relationships with family members that might impair our effectiveness in working with children.

P-2.8 We shall develop written policies for the protection of confidentiality and the disclosure of children's records. The policy documents shall be made available to all program personnel and families. Disclosure of children's records beyond family members, program personnel and consultants having an obligation of confidentiality shall require familial consent (except in cases of abuse or neglect).

P-2.9 We shall maintain confidentiality and shall respect the family's right to privacy, refraining from disclosure of confidential information and intrusion into family life. However, when we are concerned about a child's welfare, it is permissible to reveal confidential information to agencies and individuals who may be able to act in the child's interest.

P-2.10 In cases where family members are in conflict we shall work openly, sharing our observations of the child, to help all parties involved make informed decisions. We shall refrain from becoming an advocate for one party.

P-2.11 We shall be familiar with and appropriately use community resources and professional services that support families. After a referral has been made, we shall follow up to ensure that services have been adequately provided.

SECTION III: ETHICAL RESPONSIBILITIES TO COLLEAGUES

In a caring, cooperative workplace human dignity is respected, professional satisfaction is promoted and positive relationships are modeled. Our primary responsibility in this arena is to establish and maintain settings and relationships which support productive work and meet professional needs.

A. Responsibilities to Co-Workers

Ideals:

I-3A.1 To establish and maintain relationships of trust and cooperation with co-workers.

I-3A.2 To share resources and information with co-workers.

I-3A.3 To support co-workers in meeting their professional needs and in their professional development.

I-3A.4 To accord co-workers due recognition for professional achievement.

Principles:

P-3A.1 When we have concern about the professional behavior of a co-worker, we shall first let that person know of our concern and attempt to resolve the matter collegially.

P-3A.2 We shall exercise care in expressing views regarding the personal attributes or professional conduct of co-workers. Statements should be based on firsthand knowledge and relevant to the interests of children and programs.

B. Responsibilities to Employers

Ideals:

I-3B.1 To assist the program in providing the highest quality of service.

I-3B.2 To maintain loyalty to the program and uphold its reputation.

Principles:

P-3B.1 When we do not agree with program policies, we shall first attempt to effect change through constructive action within the organization.

P-3B.2 We shall speak or act on behalf of an organization only when authorized. We shall take care to note when we are speaking for the organization and when we are expressing a personal judgment.

C. Responsibilities to Employees

Ideals:

I-3C.1 To promote policies and working conditions that foster competence, well-being and self-esteem in staff members.

I-3C.2 To create a climate of trust and candor that will enable staff to speak and act in the best interests of children, families, and the field of early childhood education.

I-3C.3 To strive to secure an adequate livelihood for those who work with or on behalf of young children.

Principles:

P-3C.1 In decisions concerning children and programs, we shall appropriately utilize the training, experience and expertise of staff members.

P-3C.2 We shall provide staff members with working conditions that permit them to carry out their responsibilities, timely and non-threatening evaluation procedures, written grievance procedures, constructive feedback, and opportunities for continuing professional development.

P-3C.3 We shall develop and maintain comprehensive written personnel policies that de-

fine program standards and, when applicable, that specify the extent to which employees are accountable for their conduct outside of the workplace. These policies shall be given to new staff members and shall be available for review by all staff members.

P-3C.4 Employees who do not meet program standards shall be informed of areas of concern and, when possible, assisted in improving their performance.

P-3C.5 Employees who are dismissed shall be informed of the reasons for their termination. When a dismissal is for cause, justification must be based on evidence of inadequate or inappropriate behavior which is accurately documented, current, and available for the employee to review.

P-3C.6 In making evaluation and recommendations, judgments shall be based on fact and relevant to the interests of children and programs.

P-3C.7 Hiring and promotion shall be based solely on a person's record of accomplishment and ability to carry out the responsibilities of the position.

P-3C.8 In hiring, promotion and provision of training, we shall not participate in any form of discrimination based on race, religion, sex, national origin, handicap, age, or sexual preference. We shall be familiar with laws and regulations that pertain to employment discrimination.

SECTION IV: ETHICAL RESPONSIBILITIES TO COMMUNITY AND SOCIETY

Early childhood programs operate within a context of an immediate community made up of families and other institutions concerned with children's welfare. Our responsibilities to the community are to provide programs that meet its needs and to cooperate with agencies and professions that share responsibility for children. Because the larger society has a measure of responsibility for the welfare and protection of children, and because of our specialized expertise in child development, we acknowledge an obligation to serve as a voice for children everywhere.

Ideals:

I-4.1 To provide the community with high quality, culturally sensitive programs and services.

I-4.2 To promote cooperation among agencies and professions concerned with the welfare of young children, their families and their teachers.

I-4.3 To work, through education, research and advocacy, toward an environmentally safe world in which all children are adequately fed, sheltered, and nurtured.

I-4.4 To work, through education, research and advocacy, toward a society in which all young children have access to quality programs.

I-4.5 To promote knowledge and understanding of young children and their needs. To work toward greater social acknowledgment of children's rights and greater social acceptance of responsibility for their well-being.

I-4.6 To support policies and laws that promote the well-being of children and families. To oppose those that impair their well-being. To cooperate with other individuals and groups in these efforts.

I-4.7 To further the professional development of the field of early childhood education and to strengthen its commitment to realizing its core values as reflected in this Code.

Principles:

P-4.1 We shall communicate openly and truthfully about the nature and extent of services that we provide.

P-4.2 We shall not accept or continue to work in positions for which we are personally unsuited or professionally unqualified. We shall not offer services that we do not have the competence, qualifications, or resources to provide.

P-4.3 We shall be objective and accurate in reporting the knowledge upon which we base our program practices.

P-4.4 We shall cooperate with other professionals who work with children and their families.

P-4.5 We shall not hire or recommend for employment any person who is unsuited for a position with respect to competence, qualifications or character.

P-4.6 We shall report the unethical or incompetent behavior of a colleague to a supervisor when informal resolution is not effective.

P-4.7 We shall be familiar with laws and regulations that serve to protect the children in our programs.

P-4.8 We shall not participate in practices which are in violation of laws and regulations that protect the children in our programs.

P-4.9 When we have evidence that an early childhood program is violating laws or regulations protecting children, we shall report it to persons responsible for the program. If compliance is not accomplished within a reasonable time we will report the violation to appropriate authorities who can be expected to remedy the situation.

P-4.10 When we have evidence that an agency or a professional charged with providing services to children, families or teachers is failing to meet its obligations, we acknowledge a collective ethical responsibility to report the problem to appropriate authorities or to the public.

P-4.11 When a program violates or requires its employees to violate this Code, it is permissible, after fair assessment of the evidence, to disclose the identity of that program.

The NAEYC Statement of Commitment

As an individual who works with young children, I commit myself to furthering the values of early childhood education as they are reflected in the NAEYC Code of Ethical Conduct.

To the best of my ability I will:

- Ensure that programs for young children are based on current knowledge of child development and early childhood education.
- Respect and support families in their task of nurturing children.

- Respect colleagues in early childhood education and support them in maintaining the NAEYC Code of Ethical Conduct.
- Serve as an advocate for children, their families and their teachers in community and society.
- Maintain high standards of professional conduct.
- Recognize how personal values, opinions and biases can affect professional judgment.
- Be open to new ideas and be willing to learn from the suggestions of others.
- Continue to learn, grow and contribute as a professional.
- Honor the ideals and principles of the NAEYC Code of Ethical Conduct.

The Statement of Commitment expresses those basic personal commitments that individuals must make in order to align themselves with the profession's responsibilities as set forth in the NAEYC Code of Ethical Conduct.

Ethical Cases

You can use the following ethical cases as a starting place for thinking about ethics. Reread the section on core values in Chapter One and the Code of Ethical Conduct in Appendix One and use them to think about what the good early childhood educator should do in the following situations.

ETHICAL CASE 1:
THE ABUSED CHILD

Mary Lou, a five-year-old in your school, is showing the classic signs of abuse: multiple bruises, frequent black eyes, and psychological withdrawal. Her mother, a high-strung woman, says Mary Lou falls a lot, but nobody at the center has noticed this. There were two times

Stephanie Feeney. (1987). Ethical Case Studies for NAEYC Reader Response, *Young Children*, 42(4), 24–25.

when Mary Lou's father seemed to be drunk when he picked her up. The law says you must report suspicions of abuse to the Children's Protective Office. But, in your experience, when the authorities get involved they are usually unable to remove the child from the home or improve the family's behavior. Sometimes the families simply disappear, or things become worse for the children.

ETHICAL CASE 2:
THE WORKING MOTHER

Timothy's mother has asked you not to allow her four-year-old son to nap in the afternoon. She says, "Whenever he naps he stays up until 10:00 at night. I have to get up at 5:00 in the morning to go to work. I am not getting enough sleep." Along with the rest of the children, Timothy takes a one-hour nap almost every day. He seems to need it in order to stay in good spirits in the afternoon.

ETHICAL CASE 3:
THE DIVORCED PARENTS

Martin is the recently divorced father and custodial parent of four-year-old Tracy. Carla, the girl's mother (and the noncustodial parent), visits her often at the school during the day. Tracy's father has changed since the divorce. He always has a stressed expression on his face and avoids contact with the staff. He neglects to sign Tracy out—a violation of school policy—and has twice caused minor damage with his car in the parking lot. Tracy is now absent two or three days a week and is usually late for school when she comes. Tracy's father became very angry at the staff and his daughter when Tracy's lunch box was misplaced. Some of the teachers are a bit afraid of him, calling him "the ticking bomb." Efforts to talk with him have been unsuccessful. Despite the absences, Tracy has seemed healthy and well-adjusted though in recent weeks she has difficulty completing school tasks.

Carla has heard rumors that her former husband is behaving strangely. She tells you she is unable to reach her daughter by telephone or pick her up at the times specified in the court agreement. She asks what is happening and if you have concerns about Martin.

ETHICAL CASE 4:
THE AGGRESSIVE CHILD

Eric is a large and extremely active four-year-old who often frightens and hurts other children. You have discussed the situation repeatedly with the director, who is sympathetic but unable to help. The parents listen but feel that the behavior is typical for boys his age. They won't get counseling. A preschool specialist from the Department of Mental Health has observed the child, but her recommendations have not helped either. Meanwhile, Eric terror-izes other children and parents are starting to complain. You are becoming stressed and tired and your patience is wearing thin. You and your co-teacher are spending so much time dealing with Eric that you are worried the other children are not getting the attention they need.

ETHICAL CASE 5:
THE "ACADEMIC" PRESCHOOL

Heather has been a teacher at a preschool for several years, seems happy there, and receives a good salary. She has just gone back to school to get her CDA credential; she has been assigned as your trainee. You have gone to observe her class and have seen three- and four-year-olds using workbooks for long periods of time each day. The daily program also includes repetitious drill on letters and numbers. Children are regularly being "taught" the alphabet and rote counting from one to a hundred. You also notice that most interactions are initiated by adults and that children have few opportunities to interact with materials.

You have mentioned to Heather that you do not think that the school's curriculum is appropriate for preschool children. She replies that she had a similar reaction when she began working there, but that the director and other teachers assured her that there was no problem with the curriculum. They told her that this is the way they have always taught and that parents are satisfied with it.

ETHICAL CASE 6:
THE STAFF-CHILD RATIO

When you began your job as teacher in a class of three-year-olds, you were not well informed about state regulations. You found your work extremely tiring and after some time you learned that regulations in your state require a staff-child ratio of no more than one to twelve for three-year-olds. You are teaching alone in a group that sometimes has as many as seventeen children in it. When the licensing worker comes to inspect, the director explains that the cook is part of the staff and works regularly in your classroom.

DISCUSSING ETHICAL CASES

A good way to begin to understand ethics and learn how to resolve ethical dilemmas is to practice discussing ethics with your colleagues using cases like these. Although there is no one way to discuss an ethical issue, the following strategies will help you:

- Discuss the case and identify the core values that seem to be in conflict.
- Restate the problem in terms of what the good early childhood educator owes to children, parents, colleagues, directors, and themselves.
- Brainstorm all possible solutions without evaluating them.
- Critically evaluate each solution and try to reach consensus about what the good early childhood educator would do. If you cannot reach consensus, acknowledge both majority and minority viewpoints.
- Use the NAEYC Code of Ethical Conduct to identify what sections of the code guide the early childhood professional.

Organizations and Journals

ORGANIZATIONS

ACEI
Association for Childhood Education International
11141 Georgia Ave., Suite 200
Wheaton, MD 20902

ACT
Action for Children's Television
46 Austin St.
Newtonville, MA 02160

ACYF
Administration for Children, Youth and Families
P.O. Box 1182
Washington, DC 20013

American Montessori Society
175 Fifth Ave.
New York, NY 10010

Children's Defense Fund
122 C St., NW
Washington, DC 20001

CEC
Council for Exceptional Children
1920 Association Dr.
Reston, VA 22091

CWLA
Child Welfare League of America, Inc.
440 First St., NW, Suite 310
Washington, DC 20001

DCDCA
Day Care and Child Development Council of America
1401 K St., NW
Washington, DC 20005

ERIC/ECE
Educational Resource Information Center on Early Childhood Education
805 W. Pennsylvania Ave.
Urbana, IL 61801

International Montessori Society
912 Thayer Ave.
Silver Spring, MD 20910

NAEYC
National Association for the Education of
Young Children
1834 Connecticut Ave., NW
Washington, DC 20009

National Association for Family Child Care
5900 Dudley St.
Arvada, CO 80004

OMEP
Organization Mondiale pour L'Education
Prescholaire and the U.S. National
Committee for Early Childhood
Education
81 Irving Place
New York, NY 10003

SECA
Southern Early Childhood Association
P.O. Box 5403
Brady Station
Little Rock, AR 72215

JOURNALS

Child Care Information Exchange
P.O. Box 2890
Redmond, WA 98073

Child Development
Society of Research in Child Development
University of Chicago Press
5801 Ellis Ave.
Chicago, IL 60637

Childhood Education
ACEI
11141 Georgia Ave., Suite 200
Wheaton, MD 20902

Children Today
Office of Human Development Services
Superintendent of Documents
U.S. Government Printing Office
Washington, DC 20402

Day Care and Early Education
Human Sciences Press
72 Fifth Ave.
New York, NY 10011

Dimensions
Southern Early Childhood Association
P.O. Box 5403, Brady Station
Little Rock, AR 72215

Early Childhood Research Quarterly
National Association for the Education of
Young Children
Ablex Publishing Company
355 Chestnut St.
Norwood, NJ 07648

Exceptional Children
Council for Exceptional Children
1920 Association Dr.
Reston, VA 22091

Interracial Books for Children Bulletin
1841 Broadway
New York, NY 10023

*Journal of Research in Childhood
Education*
Association for Childhood Education
International
11141 Georgia Ave., Suite 200
Wheaton, MD 20902

Young Children
National Association for the Education of
Young Children
1834 Connecticut Ave., NW
Washington, DC 20009

Name Index

Subject Index